ACADEMY of TELEVISION
ARTS & SCIENCES
FOUNDATION

TELEVISION, FILM, AND DIGITAL MEDIA PROGRAMS

556 OUTSTANDING PROGRAMS
AT TOP COLLEGES AND UNIVERSITIES
ACROSS THE NATION

First Edition

By the Staff of The Academy of Television Arts and Sciences Foundation
& the Staff of The Princeton Review

Random House, Inc.

New York

www.PrincetonReview.com

The Princeton Review, Inc.
2315 Broadway
New York, NY 10024
E-mail: bookeditor@review.com

ISBN   0-375-76520-4
ISBN-13   978-0-375-76520-9

Publisher: Robert Franek
Editor: Suzanne J. Podhurst
Production Manager: Scott Harris
Production Editor: Christine LaRubio
Copy Editor: Monica Gaydos
Data Collection Director: Ben Zelevansky

Manufactured in the United States of America

9 8 7 6 5 4 3 2 1

CONTENTS

ACKNOWLEDGMENTS

This book would not have been possible without the commitment and support of many people, including the members of the Academy of Television Arts and Sciences Foundation Board, whose ongoing support gives guidance to programs and initiatives like the guide; the Educational Programs & Services Committee members; and the Television Academy Foundation staff, whose perseverance and commitment to these programs help make them a reality.

Many thanks go to the board members: Steve Mosko, *Chairman*; Robert Levi, Vice-Chair; Nelson Davis, *Secretary*; Charles W. Fries, *Treasurer*; Thomas W. Sarnoff, *Chairman Emeritus*; Loreen Arbus, Dick Askin, Joel Berman, Donna Cassyd, Leo Chaloukian, Robert Cook, Suzanne de Passe, Richard H. Frank, Joseph Hurley, Donna Kanter, Margaret Loesch, Delbert Mann, Jerry Offsay, Mark Pedowitz, Dorothea Petrie, Jerry Petry, Hank Reiger, Richard Robertson, John Shaffner, Melville Shavelson, and Don Tillman.

We are also grateful to the advisory council: Chris Albrecht, Linda Hope, Leslie Moonves, Thomas S. Murphy, Sumner M. Redstone, Frank N. Stanton, Donald L. Taffner, R.E. "Ted" Turner, and Robert C. Wright.

Thanks to the Educational Programs & Services Committee: Dave Bell, Barry Bernson, Bruce Bilson, Dan Birman, Carroll Parrott Blue, Karen Lee Copeland, *Ivan Cury, Rich Eisbrouch, Tom Fick, Stephen Fisch, Michael Gallant, Dr. Jack Genero, Gary Goldberger, *Steve Gordon, *Chair*; A.P. Gonzalez, John Gregory, *Lynne Gross, *Ken Harwood, Deborah Hemela, Paul Lewis, Nanci Linke-Ellis, Marc. B. Lorber, Bernie Luskin, Nancy A. Meyer, Damon Romine, Kelsey Scott, Eric Stein, Victoria Sterling, Ron Taylor, and Victor M. Webb. (*Also served on the editorial board for the guide, as did Academy Governor Lori Schwartz.)

Finally, we are grateful to the Television Academy membership and to future Television Academy members.

Price Hicks
Director, Educational Programs & Services Department
Academy of Television Arts & Sciences Foundation
Coauthor, *Television, Film, and Digital Media Programs*

Nancy Meyer
Television Development Executive
Coauthor, *Television, Film, and Digital Media Programs*

The Princeton Review wishes to thank Suzanne Podhurst, the imaginative editor of this book; Ben Zelevansky, data collector extraordinaire; Christine LaRubio, Monica Gaydos, and Scott Harris, our stellar production team; and Rob Franek, the visionary for the entire operation. Thanks also to Andrew Baker, Lisa Marie Rovito, Katie Kurtz, Robin Raskin, and Harriet Brand. We are deeply grateful to our publishing team at Random House and in particular wish to thank Tom Russell, Nicole Benhabib, Shaina Malkin, Jeanne Krier, Candice Chaplin, Alison Skrabek, and Sophie Ye Chin. Finally, we are indebted to all of the school administrators who worked with us to make this resource possible.

FOREWORD

When I graduated from Hofstra University in the 1970s, television was defined by the broadcast networks, motion pictures were defined by the studios, and there was no definition for digital media. So many changes have taken place in the years since—changes in how we view television and film, in who provides the content, and in how programming is made, to name just a few. I've been an executive with HBO for 20 years, and another series of technological revolutions has taken place. Technology has been critical to all the changes in the media and entertainment, but the most crucial element in our industry has always been people.

My first job out of college was as a stand-up comedian and the manager of a comedy club. The people I met and the friendships and business associations that I established informed my later work as an agent and a talent consultant and led me to my job at HBO. Relationships are the most important resource in our business. Our present and future success is and will be based on all the people who work with us.

A constant topic of conversation in our business is future thinking. Sometimes the future is limited to a change in a production schedule or a week of programming, but most often the future is seen as a long-term strategy. How do we meet the challenges and opportunities of tomorrow? Who are the people who will reinvent the creative and technological revolution in ways that will surprise and excite future audiences? The answers will come from the next generation of professionals—the producers, costumers, writers, directors, technicians, executives—who are now students entering colleges and universities across the United States.

Just as choices in television and film have grown, television, film, and digital media studies and programs in colleges and universities have grown too. College applicants considering a future in the industry have hundreds of alternatives in programs and institutions and a breadth of future careers to investigate. A guide to help students make informed decisions is a necessity. Thankfully, the Television Academy Foundation has identified that need.

HBO has a long history with the Academy of Television Arts & Sciences. Our programs have won Emmys, and we've participated in education events sponsored by the Academy of Television Arts & Sciences Foundation. Given our relationship with the Television Academy and the need for a publication of this kind, I'm happy to provide the Foreword and Introduction to this guide. I can't think of a better partner in your college selection process than the Television Academy Foundation. Their programs are synonymous with excellence and a commitment to education.

—Chris Albrecht, Chairman and CEO, Home Box Office, Inc.

INTRODUCTION

Everybody has a story, and we hear these stories often in our line of work. "Scott" is a top broadcast network programming executive who created his own fall television schedule as an 11-year-old. "Carla" is a writer/producer for a top-rated dramatic television series who was a self-confessed *Star Trek* nerd in her adolescence. "John," a sports statistics geek who practiced color commentary for his favorite football team in his basement, is an expert in mobile satellite technology for news and sports events. Stories about how people entered the industry, whether by fulfilling a lifelong interest or by happenstance, are countless. They verify the unpredictable yet committed journeys of individuals who chose careers in the business of television, film, and digital media.

For more than 30 years, the Academy of Television Arts & Sciences Foundation has been involved with top-rated educational programs, including the College Television Awards and the Student Internship Program. That involvement has fostered relationships with thousands of students and faculty. These relationships have, in turn, given us some special insights into the concerns of students who are searching for the college, or universities that best suit their academic and future professional needs. The Academy of Television Arts & Sciences Foundation is uniquely qualified to create a guidebook because of its wide-ranging and ongoing contact with colleges and universities nationwide as well as its unparalleled access to industry experience and expertise.

ACT ONE: GETTING A HEAD START

SCENE ONE: WHY WE PRODUCED THIS GUIDE FOR YOU

Because programs and resources are numerous and varied, the Academy of Television Arts and Sciences Foundation partnered with The Princeton Review to produce this resource. This is the book for high school students, parents, counselors, and college students seeking to transfer to another institution or considering graduate studies. It offers a point of entry into a dynamic and multifaceted realm so that aspiring directors, producers, writers, actors, filmmakers, animators, cinematographers, and their peers may become the next generation of successful industry professionals.

SCENE TWO: PRACTICE, PRACTICE, PRACTICE

If you know that you aspire to work in the realm of television, film, and digital media, then start preparing right away. There's a lot you can do early on to get a head start. Read books, magazines, and articles about television, film, and digital media. Buy or borrow a camcorder, and start shooting.

Experiment with movie making. Not everything you create has to be Emmy®-worthy, but the exercise of putting together these projects will prove invaluable later on.

> ★ **Tip**
>
> *If you don't own a camcorder, see if you can borrow one from your local library or high school.*

Shooting short films or commercials offers an excellent opportunity to learn how to tell a visual story. If you can get access to a computer-driven editing program, use it to create a coming attraction or trailer for a television show or film. An exercise that we recommend is to create two trailers for the same movie that convey two vastly different plots. Think about how you can manipulate the same images and sounds—literally, the same footage—to generate a series of unique portraits.

> ★ **Tip**
>
> *If you can't access equipment through your local library or school, pay a visit to your local television network, and try to make an arrangement with someone there to use the station's equipment. People who are passionate about media studies tend to be enthusiastic about helping the next generation of industry professionals.*

ACT TWO: THE VALUE OF A COLLEGE EDUCATION

 ### SCENE ONE: THE SELECTION PROCESS

Achieving academic success is the first step you must take toward winning a place in an extremely demanding industry—and it starts with college and university selection. Programs of study that address the various aspects of this dynamic industry, cover the numerous technical requirements, and promote the acquisition of related skills often prove challenging. But the challenges do not come without benefits: Faculty members are often accomplished professionals in their fields, and they share their training and experience with students. Many courses are project-based and offer opportunities to collaborate with fellow students and sometimes industry professionals as well. The sum of your courses and campus life experiences will prepare you for the competitive world of television and film—and for your life.

I think it's very difficult to go wrong with a liberal arts education.
—*Rachel Axler, writer for* The Daily Show with Jon Stewart *and Williams College alumna*

 ### SCENE TWO: THE EXPERIENCE IN ITS ENTIRETY

Although the primary aim of this book is to help you identify the television, film, and digital media programs that best match your interests and aspirations, it would be silly (not to mention downright erroneous) to suggest that the vast majority of your valuable college experiences will occur within your specialized field of study. College is not merely about the major you have chosen or will choose; it is, rather, both an educational and a life experience. Although you will spend more time in your area of concentration than in other subjects, your education is a process that involves exposure to ideas and studies that broaden your mind and your perspective. The aggregate value of a college education is its ability to provide you with a sense of the big picture—the 60-inch plasma screen experience of other cultures, forms of communicating, and ways of thinking and seeing the world. (Grad school, if you choose to pursue it, provides a much more focused perspective.) College presents a time to enjoy your freedom, develop critical thinking skills, begin making informed intellectual and emotional decisions, and build friendships and a network of future colleagues. The process in its entirety will broaden and enrich you. For that reason, you will see that each school profile includes information about the college at large. Your program will not exist in a bubble—and neither should your research.

While all of the profile statistics (size of department and so forth) apply just to undergraduate programs, you'll notice that we've also included comprehensive lists that apply to both undergraduate and graduate programs of degrees and department facilities. If you're applying at the undergraduate level, you should know there are advantages and disadvantages to attending a school that offers graduate programs of study in your area. On the plus side, you're likely to have access to a greater breadth of resources and facilities, and you'll have a group of slightly older and more experienced peers whom you can ask for advice and guidance. You should also bear in mind, however, that departments serving both undergrad and grad students may direct a significant (potentially disproportionate) share of their faculty attention and resources toward the latter group.

ACT THREE: THE NO-LONGER-ELUSIVE SEARCH
FOR THE RIGHT COLLEGE

 ## Prologue: A word about education today

The group of students who are starting their education today is sometimes described as the *Net generation*, the first generation raised on computers and fully accustomed to the rapid changes in technology and the marketplace. As students head to campuses across the country, they bring their latest gizmos—the iPod, BlackBerry, and cell phone capable of downloading VOD—and they set the standard for what will become mainstream. These innovations are profoundly altering the worlds of television, film, and digital media. In response, the academic landscape continues to develop more complex fields of study and more career possibilities; for example, universities and private entities now invest heavily in campus-based digital institutes.

 ## Scene One: Some self-examination

[Enter, Stage Left—College] Students are drawn to television and film studies for many reasons. For some, programs in these areas provide an outlet for expression; for others, they offer the opportunity to cultivate a special skill or talent. Some students choose to explore their curiosity about the world through the media of television and film; from behind a lens, they may gain an interesting and unique perspective about the cultural forces that have shaped our age. Of course, not to be overlooked is the sheer excitement of engaging in the fascinating, challenging, and sometimes glamorous business of providing the world with its entertainment and news.

☆ *Tip:*

The media and entertainment industries have changed immensely in the past 25 years. Staying up-to-date and adapting to changes are key career survival skills.

Inspired by the graphics in *The Matrix*, cinematography in *Amélie*, plot twists in *Lost*, or humor of *The Simpsons*, many high school students may have an idea of what they hope to pursue but remain uncertain about how to take the next step—or even about what that next step may be. For most, college is the critical interim step between early dreams and entry into the professional world; and for some, graduate school promises to be another key step. Because landing a dream job without the necessary training and experience is so difficult, it's particularly important for students to seek and find the right fit in an educational program. Finding the best match can make the difference in gaining key professional—and life—experience. The connections that students make and the paths they forge are integral components of their potential future success.

SCENE TWO: FINDING THE RIGHT INSTITUTION

The college selection and admissions process can be occasionally confusing, sometimes stressful, and more often than not, daunting. Our advice: Start small. Ask yourself what you *really* like to do. That is, if you didn't need a paycheck, what would you do? If you're reading this book, your answer probably relates to television, film, and digital media studies. The next step for you, then, is to find a program that will allow you to do what you love—and ultimately, get paid for it.

To be nobody but yourself in a world which is doing its best, night and day, to make you everybody else means to fight the hardest battle which any human being can fight; and never stop fighting.

—*e.e. cummings*

Next ask yourself: How do you interact with others? What particular skills do you already have? Do you thrive in a highly structured work environment? Are you a self-starter? Do you like doing detail-oriented work? Do you enjoy the creative process? These are some of the questions that, when honestly answered, can help point you toward the right college and the right program. Institutions vary widely in their academic priorities, expectations, and demands on students. It's a good idea to feel that you are a solid fit with the ethos of the colleges to which you apply.

Get started by making a list of colleges that already appeal to you and your particular interests. It is tempting to limit your list of choices to just a few schools and overlook the many formidable programs and institutions that exist between the entertainment capitals of Los Angeles and New York. Northwestern University in Chicago and the University of Texas at Austin, for example, have stellar programs in theater and related fields. Competition for acceptance to the handful of "prestigious" (that is to say, big-name) schools is fearsome. Broaden your search to include the many excellent institutions across the country that offer outstanding programs in television, film, and digital media. Many of these schools have programs that allow students to spend time in Los Angeles or New York during the semester or during summer and winter breaks.

Consider also the availability of undergraduate internships. Some universities have long-established internship programs with media companies, television stations, and advertising agencies. A program that can help you create your own network of colleagues is always preferable. Beyond this, find out whether the schools you're considering have competitions for student production work. It's a good sign if a school encourages student participation, and such "calling card" endeavors not only look great on your resume, but also will help potential future employers (not to mention grad schools) distinguish you from the pack.

SCENE THREE: FINDING THE RIGHT PROGRAM

It's important not just to find the best institution at which to cultivate your craft, but also to identify the ideal curriculum and emphasis for your interests. In this book, you'll find listings of 556 unique programs at 215 colleges and universities across the nation. In many cases, the program listings provide just an introduction to the available offerings at a given school. If you like what you see in the school profile and descriptions of popular programs, then continue your research of the offerings at these schools! To begin narrowing down your search, ask yourself: Are you interested in the professional side of television, film, and digital media—that is, in learning the fundamentals of video and film production and current technology as well as gaining hands-on

Take your role as a prospective student seriously!

The following are some questions you should ask yourself as you search for good-match schools:

✓ How important is it to you to attend a so-called top school?

✓ Is class size a key issue for you? What kind of relationship do you want with your professors?

✓ Are you seeking a college or university with diverse student and faculty populations?

✓ Do you want to stay close to home or move far away?

✓ Is climate important to you? Honestly—if you cannot stand cold weather, that might eliminate a number of colleges from your consideration.

✓ Do you prefer an urban, a suburban, or a rural setting?

✓ How safe are the campuses you're considering? The Department of Education website (www.ed.gov) has important information about campus security and safety.

✓ What kind of college experience do you aspire to have—a highly social one, an especially studious one, or one with a healthy mix of social and academic life? Do you hope to spend most of your time with others in your major, or would you prefer a greater mix of majors among your friends and roommates?

✓ What can you and your family afford, and what kind of financial aid package would you receive from each of the schools you're considering?

practical training in independent and commercial filmmaking? Or, are you drawn to the artistic or scholarly side of these media—such topics as the social and cultural force of pop culture and film theory? When considering a particular school or program, you should ask, What will classes be like? If you aspire to be a cinematographer, then you'll want to make sure you log in plenty of for-credit filmmaking hours. If it's a professorship that you seek, you'll want to work within a curriculum that encourages you to spend hours in the library or in discussion groups, and you'll ultimately need to pursue a terminal degree, whether it's a PhD or an MFA. The difference between a practical and theory-based program could be as stark as a potential career in Hollywood versus a foray into grad school and an ultimate career in academia. Finding the program that meets all of your needs—from subjects of study to mentoring and beyond—is essential. When you read the thumbnails of prominent industry figures, you'll see that they often tout the special features of their undergraduate (and in some cases, graduate) programs, and many attribute their career successes at least in part to the solid educational foundations they received.

You should be aware of the various types of classes offered in your area, and you should be prepared to choose the ones that will best prepare you for your future career. For instance, history, criticism, and literature will be like other classes: They will involve lectures, group discussions, and projects. These programs will emphasize aesthetics, theory, cultural influences, and scholarship. Students of digital media and graphic design will clock in extra hours at university computer labs and on their personal computers. Production classes offer opportunities to hone skills in single-camera or multiple-camera television or film. Media and related departments often have relationships with or access to professional facilities, such as equipment houses, local television networks, PBS stations, or cable stations. Many of these facilities will be listed in the school profiles that follow. If you have questions about a specific piece of equipment, contact the program or department head.

It is important to note there is little uniformity among the names of programs or among the structures of programs, departments, and universities. (Given the creative nature of the field, that should come as no surprise!) The first major academic division you will encounter is between theory and practice. Theory includes studies in motion picture history and in criticism. Related fields may venture into women's studies, African American studies, genre studies, and beyond. Practical course work emphasizes hands-on training and production-minded technical development. Digital media programs also train students in computer programming, animation, graphics, gaming, and video/audio editing. Within the realm of digital media programs are interactive media studies, which focus on the bevy of new technologies making their way into the mainstream (think virtual environments in which real people can interact with a story you've created). The bottom line is that there are many domains—and even more possibilities for still unknown realms—into which your creative processes may venture.

In the course of your program research, you'll quickly find that the nomenclature varies significantly from one school to another. For instance, sometimes television or electronic journalism is found in a Telecommunications Department, sometimes in the Journalism Department, and sometimes in the School of Journalism. The profiles in this guide will direct you to the appropriate contacts at each school, and the

Appendix provides a partial list of the various departments in which you'll be able to undertake studies in television, film, and digital media. Throughout your program of study, you should have an ultimate goal—that is, a career—in mind. In Act Eight, we describe for you many of the careers you may opt to pursue, followed by the programs that are likely to give you the best preparations for each.

☆ Tip

If you admire the work of a particular director, documentarian, writer, actor, animator, or other artist, find out where he or she received training. A program or a professor at his or her alma mater may have been a source of inspiration, and the program and/or professor may still be there. The artist may still have a relationship with the institution, as well.

Though it goes without saying, we'll say it anyway: Be sure to check out the websites of the schools you're considering. That said, virtual tours are helpful, but whenever possible, supplement them with actual campus visits. While you're visiting, try to sit in on classes, see a college news program being taped, and seek out current and former students with whom you can have candid conversations. You should also check out the facilities for yourself. See how up-to-date and well-maintained they are. Ask about whether undergrads have access to them (and if so, how much and on what terms). Find out what course-related activities and opportunities are available—such as internships, student production projects, industry lectures, and workshops. While you're there, ask *everything*—after all, you're deciding how to direct your time, money, and potential future path.

ACT FOUR: THE COLLEGE APPLICATION PROCESS

 ## SCENE ONE: THE APPLICATION

Applying to college involves more than just filling out an application, gathering together some paperwork, and dropping it in the mailbox or clicking "Submit" on your online application. You'll need to determine how you want to position yourself before the admissions committee. You'll also need to decide whether you're going to apply early action, early decision, or regular decision.

Every step of the application process says something about you as an individual. You want to represent yourself as a worthy candidate for this school. Since admissions officers read hundreds of applications (all of them quickly), it's crucial to take time to prepare your application thoughtfully. Reading the directions, following instructions, and meeting deadlines will communicate that you're a viable candidate.

Applications that require essays and short answers are looking for ways to find out how well you can articulate your thoughts on a given subject. This provides a more personal look at you than do your test scores, course work, and grade point average, so spend significant time conceiving and writing your responses.

 ## SCENE TWO: THE INTERVIEW

At some colleges, all interviews are handled by the most junior members of the admissions staff. Schools do use interviews partly for evaluation, but mostly for personal contact and as a resource for students. The interview most likely won't make or break your chances, but admissions officers do factor it in, along with all your other credentials, when deciding whether or not you'll get the fat envelope. It's to your advantage to take it seriously and prepare. Think about why you are there, and don't ask questions that are answered in the brochures you've been sent. Reading those brochures will also help you come up with questions that you might not have thought of before.

If there is a popular conception of the school (that it's a party school, a jock school, or a school that has too many grad students teaching survey classes), don't ask about it. Your interviewer will have heard the same question 10 billion times. Save this question for your tour guide or for other students you meet while on campus. You don't want to seem off the wall by asking bizarre questions; but even more, you don't want to sound exactly like every other boring kid who was in there before you. Challenge yourself to come up with creative and interesting questions whose answers pique your curiosity.

Before the actual interview, practice. Sit down with a parent, teacher, or friend (one who can do this without cracking up), and have him or her ask you real, thought-provoking questions. Then answer them honestly and seriously. Allow your "interviewer" to critique you, and listen to what he or she has to say. This practice interview is a great way to become aware of little things that you might not have even realized you were doing wrong. It will also help you start thinking about your answers and give you a sense of how you'll feel during the real thing.

SCENE THREE: LETTERS OF RECOMMENDATION

If admissions officers are faced with a decision between you and a person with similar grades and test scores, they will have to look at more intangible factors, such as those represented in your essay, extracurricular activities, and recommendations. For that reason, letters should come only from people who know you well. The letter writer should know exactly what you're going to school for and write to support your goals. Give him or her enough information about the school(s) and the program(s) you'd like to pursue so that the letter can emphasize a good program fit. Perfunctory letters of recommendation from well-meaning friends are a waste of everyone's time.

You should start thinking about recommendations well before your junior year rolls around. Take the opportunity to get to know teachers when you can. By visiting teachers outside of the classroom, you will give them the opportunity to get to know you academically and socially. To impress admissions committees, make sure you pick a teacher who knows you well and will write a persuasive and enthusiastic endorsement of you and your stellar qualities. Don't be afraid to ask potential recommenders whether they feel comfortable writing such a recommendation for you. Finally, make sure you give your recommenders plenty of advance notice. Don't forget to write them thank-you notes, as well—they will have helped you get into college!

SCENE FOUR: PAYING FOR YOUR DEGREE

College is a very expensive proposition. It's always a sound idea to start planning for it as early as possible. In what follows, we'll outline for you some fundamental information about paying for your degree. You'll probably need to start by filling out the FAFSA (Free Application for Federal Student Aid) and potentially the CSS/Financial Aid PROFILE form as well. Depending on the particular requirements of the schools to which you're applying, you may need to fill out additional forms. Once you've applied for financial aid, the financial aid offices of the schools that have accepted you will get to work preparing packages for you.

> **Tip**
>
> *Even once you've received your financial aid package, you (or better yet, your parents) can still negotiate with your dream school's financial aid office.*

Any aid packages you receive will consist of three types of financial assistance: grants and scholarships (these are ideal because you don't have to pay them back!), federal work-study (you may use your federally-subsidized earnings to pay tuition or offset your living expenses), and student loans (these are low-interest and often subsidized, but you'll still need to pay them back eventually). The aid package is meant to address your family's need.

> **Tip**
>
> *Don't rule out applying to a private school just because it has a high sticker price. In quite a few cases, the amount of aid you receive is not set, but rather contingent upon the cost of the school you choose. You could end up paying the same amount of money to attend an Ivy as you would to attend a state school. Our advice: Choose the best-match schools for you, and then work with financial aid officers to make your package manageable.*

The need component of your package is equal to the total cost of college (tuition, room and board, fees) minus your EFC (expected family contribution). Note that financial aid offices have a lot of latitude to make (and often, subsequently to adjust) decisions. After looking at the EFC determined by the FAFSA calculations, they may decide that, for example, your EFC ought to be lower than the computations determined. At times, the package that a financial aid office puts together reflects the degree of its desire to make sure the student is in the incoming freshman class. Schools that can give non-need-based aid (merit scholarships, for example) often do, so it's to your advantage to earn good grades and score well on standardized tests.

What You Should Know about the FAFSA

✓ Filing electronically is much quicker (it's the difference between 4 to 6 weeks and 7 to 10 days!). The electronic form also makes sure you've filled out all of the information correctly. Visit www.fafsa.ed.gov.

✓ If you do file a paper financial aid form, make photocopies of everything you submit. You can obtain a paper copy from your high school guidance counselor.

✓ Incoming first-years often have earlier deadlines than returning students. Deadlines are the dates by which forms should be received.

✓ Be sure to check school- and state-specific deadlines. They may be (and often are) earlier than federal deadlines.

✓ You don't have to wait until your taxes are filed to complete the FAFSA—and you shouldn't! You can fill in your estimated income and then complete your taxes as soon as possible thereafter.

ACT FIVE: IS GRAD SCHOOL THE NEXT STEP?

 ## SCENE ONE: SOME MORE SELF-EXAMINATION

In brief, the determination of whether grad school is right for you depends on two primary factors: what your field is and what your career aspirations are.

Not all fields require that you have a terminal degree for you to land a high-level (and high-paying) position. Some of the more technical roles—editing, sound, cinematography, lighting, and even producing—often don't use an advanced degree as a measure of qualifications or success. In fact, for these, it's often to your advantage to spend your time getting on-the-job experience and climbing the ranks. If you are involved in directing, however, then you are likely to benefit from having an MFA. Your pursuit of the degree will afford you the opportunity to write and direct films, an experience that will set you on the path toward making a feature film in the future.

If you are considering pursuing an advanced degree in the industry, you should think about the kind of training you hope to receive, and ultimately, the kind of movies or television shows you hope to have a hand in creating. If you think you're well-suited to the indie scene, then you may be a good fit for Tisch at NYU; if it's a Hollywood career you fancy, then you may be better off at USC. Find out about which industry professionals came out of each of the schools you're considering, and ask members of the faculty, administration, and student body about each school's philosophy and approach to television or film. Also check out the famous alumni lists in the school profiles that follow, and note the schools that your heroes and heroines call their alma mater. As was the case for undergraduate programs in television, film, and digital media studies, you'll notice that the names of departments vary greatly, even when those departments cover the same or similar material. The Appendix has a partial list of many of the possible department names. You should, once again, look beyond the name, and research the emphases of the departments to which you're considering applying. (This is especially important at the graduate level!)

If you ever hope to teach your art at the college level, you will need an MFA (or other terminal degree, such as a PhD). Regardless of your craft or level of success in it, the credential to teach is one that—with very few exceptions—only a terminal degree can bring you. If indeed you do aspire to teach, you should also seek out a program, such as the one at Columbia, that will give you a solid foundation in academic and theoretical matters.

 ## SCENE TWO: EXPLORING WHAT OTHERS HAVE DONE

As you read through the profiles in this book, you'll notice that a few featured artists went on to pursue graduate studies in their fields, but most did not. Those who continued their studies often cited the desire to gain additional training and practical experience in their fields, to study and work with prominent industry professionals, and to form their own networks with creative and talented artists.

Know what to ask!

Once you've decided to apply to grad school in your field, find out the answers to the following questions:

✓ Are the faculty members known for being experts in your primary area of interest?

✓ How often do directors, actors, screenwriters, or other industry insiders visit the program? How connected is the program to the local or national film or television community?

✓ What are the research interests of the faculty and other graduate students?

✓ What are the thesis requirements? Is there an opportunity to submit a creative thesis if you choose to do so?

✓ Does the program fit with your postgraduate career goals?

ACT SIX: APPLYING TO GRAD SCHOOL

SCENE ONE: THE APPLICATION

Each school is likely to have its own set of requirements. The basic requirements for almost all graduate-level programs are as follows:

1. Bachelor's degree from an accredited college or university

2. Official transcripts from all colleges or universities attended (including undergraduate and, if applicable, graduate schools)

3. GRE General Test scores (minimum score requirements vary)

4. TOEFL score (for non-native English speakers; minimum score requirements vary)

5. Letters of recommendation (typically, two to three)

6. Letter of intent or statement of purpose

7. Writing sample (not always required)

8. Interview (not always required)

9. Application forms

10. Application fee (or fee waiver)

Some schools may require, in addition to the above, creative portfolios. The creative portfolio for the Kanbar Institute of Film and Television at Tisch, for example, requires one visual and three written submissions. The visual submission can consist of video, photographs, or slides; and the written submissions must include a story synopsis for a four-minute silent film, a dialogue scene between two people, and a concept for a feature-length script, narrative, or documentary. (Note: These are partial summaries of the requirements, current as of the publication date of this book; please check the school website for a complete and up-to-date listing of all requirements.)

This is all to say that you should start thinking about your grad school applications sooner rather than later. You'll need to allot time—either during your undergraduate years or at some point thereafter—to conceive of and then put together the various components of each application. Good ideas, while occasionally the products of *Eureka!* moments, are more often than not the results of thoughtful reflection; of drafts written, rewritten, and then discarded; and ultimately, of much-edited and deliberated-over text.

One advantage to attending an undergraduate institution with a strong focus on television, film, and digital media studies is that you will be surrounded by a cohort of like-minded and similarly-bound classmates, professors, and administrators. As a result, you're likely to have more opportunities to create portfolio-enhancing products. Seize those opportunities! If you go to a more liberal-arts-minded college, be sure to go to the necessary office hours, enter the relevant film contests, and do everything you can to make yourself a competitive candidate in the graduate school admissions process.

SCENE TWO: PAYING FOR YOUR DEGREE

Unlike undergraduate institutions, graduate schools in general (and master's programs in particular), do not always seek to meet all or even most of your need. Many, if not most, expect you to finance the entire degree yourself by taking out student loans that you'll repay for years to come. To do this, you'll need, once again, to complete the FAFSA. (See Act Four, Scene Four for more information about that.) Some schools offer full- or partial-tuition scholarships to a select group of students (those whom they'd really like to see in their student body, and ultimately, among their alumni); these are typically awarded on the basis of merit. Many schools also offer various student assistantships, that is, financial aid in exchange for the fulfillment of particular teaching, research, or administrative duties. The availability of funds varies greatly from one school to another; we recommend that you check with the schools to which you're applying for further information. You should also ask current (and if you can, former) students about how they're financing their educations. It will give you a sense of whether you'll really have time to teach, for example, and whether the differences in aid among students create tensions within the department.

There are also a number of scholarships available to degree candidates in the arts. The financial aid offices of the schools you're considering are likely to keep lists of these scholarships. You can also conduct scholarship searches on The Princeton Review's website, www.PrincetonReview.com.

☆ *Tip*

You should apply for as much outside aid as possible! Unlike scholarships for undergrads, those for grad students often directly offset the amount you'll have to pay.

ACT SEVEN: MOVING FROM THE STUDENT WORLD TO THE REAL WORLD*

*(WHATEVER THAT IS)

 ### SCENE ONE: GETTING STARTED

Earlier in the text, we listed many of the professional specialties in the industry, from the most imaginative of the creative arts to the nitty-gritty business components. People tend to gravitate toward the artistic positions, but not everyone should be a producer, director, writer, or performer. The industry is brimming with scores of careers to consider.

Talking about dreams is like talking about movies, since the cinema uses the language of dreams; years can pass in a second and you can hop from one place to another. It's a language made of image. And in the real cinema, every object and every light means something, as in a dream.

—*Federico Fellini*

Everyone has to start somewhere. For most college graduates, an entry-level position offers the best opportunity to launch a career as a hopeful industry professional. Short-term internships also provide a good introduction to the industry. Most internships are unpaid (or certainly underpaid), but many are available for college course credit. Many interns begin in development; they read, analyze, and write reports about books and scripts. If you perform well as an intern, you will be high on the list of applicants should a job within the company become available. In addition, you can use your employer as a reference for other jobs. He or she can also refer you to jobs and productions that arise.

> ### ☆ *Tip*
> *Keep in touch with former employers and internship supervisors! They may tell you about new opportunities, and the entertainment industry is one in which your network of contacts is especially important.*

One of the events in the Television Academy Foundation's yearly faculty seminar is the Developing Career Strategies panel. The faculty members on the panel provide many wonderful tips for starting a career in the industry, and we'd like to share their suggestions with you.

✓ *Start your research early—as in, before you graduate. Do research on internships and opportunities open to recent alumni. The Academy Foundation internships are available to full-time students and recent graduates. Do research on people you admire and companies for which you'd like to work. Get addresses, phone numbers, and e-mails of people for whom you could work at those companies. Try to make contact with them (in a courteous, but not pushy or off-putting, manner). If you are a student writer, producer, or director, then research student film festivals at which you may be able to exhibit your work.*

✓ Grow a network of industry contacts among alumni, guest speakers, professors, and the attendees of student competitions and film festivals.

✓ Familiarize yourself with trade publications such as Variety, Hollywood Reporter, and Broadcasting & Cable as well as resource publications such as the Hollywood Creative Directory and the Studio Directory.

✓ Be prepared for every meeting. If you get the opportunity to meet with an industry professional, know his or her credits and accomplishments. Research the history and current projects of the company or organization for which he or she works.

✓ Know how to sell yourself. Much of this industry is about buying and selling ideas, scripts, people for certain roles, and so forth. You have to be able to sell yourself and to market your abilities, education, and attitude.

✓ Have the right attitude. All six panelists agreed that the single most important attribute for entry into the industry is attitude. The right attitude consists of a combination of the willingness to listen, focus, commitment to whatever task you are assigned, and enthusiasm.

✓ Demonstrate stamina. The entertainment industry is very demanding. The hours are long (an average production day is 12 hours), and starting pay is low. The competition is fierce for even the lowliest of jobs, and you never *really* stop paying your dues. It helps to have an entrepreneurial spirit (the ability to seize opportunities and never tire of the challenges) and a freelance mentality (the ability to step into different environments and thrive, regardless of the instability).

SCENE TWO: HOLLYWOOD, OR WHATEVER

In the 90-year history of the motion picture industry and the 65-year history of television, Hollywood has been the recognized center of the entertainment industry. Today for many reasons the industry is less rooted in the geographic Hollywood of Los Angeles than it has been at any other time in its history. The corporate entities of media companies, broadcast news, and advertising are primarily in New York. Discovery has its main offices in Bethesda, Maryland. Scripps, the media entity that owns HG, DIY Network, and Food Network, has production offices in Nashville, Tennessee. TNT and CNN have their main offices in Atlanta, Georgia. You can build a professional life in industrial films, advertising, or local news anywhere in the country. Yet when students think of media, or of the film and television industry, they still picture the Hollywood sign in the Hollywood Hills above Los Angeles. This indeed demonstrates the power of an image and the mystique of the industry. It does not, however, mean that you are limited to a single geographic area if you are to succeed in this volatile, challenging, and incredibly exciting industry.

A note to actors: Although the industry is significantly more spread out now than it has ever been before, you're likely still to find the single greatest proportions of auditions in Los Angeles and New York City. You may, however, land a role that takes you to Chicago, Cleveland, Paris, or wherever.

ACT EIGHT: CAREERS IN TELEVISION AND FILM

SCENE ONE: WALKING THE LINE

You can find entertainment news on many of the 900 channels available in the digital cable or satellite spectrum, as part of broadcast news, or in syndication; but entertainment coverage skims the surface of an industry that is vast and complex, equal parts business and creativity. Hundreds of careers are available at media corporations, networks, studios, production companies, and all of their support companies and organizations. Another way of looking at the variety of available careers is by considering whether a given career is *above the line* or *below the line*. The phrases *above the line* and *below the line* are industry jargon for categorizing job titles and costs in production budgets. Above-the-line people are those involved in the creative process of a production (writers, producers, directors, and actors), whereas below the line people are those who provide skilled craft and technical services. A college and perhaps additional graduate program can help you find the right career to suit your personality, work ethic, and talents.

SCENE TWO: CAREERS AND THE MAJORS THAT LEAD TO THEM

In what follows, you'll find descriptions of many possible careers in the industry. Following each is a list of degree programs that are likely to give you the best preparation for that field. For more information about departmental nomenclature, please refer to the Appendix.

Animator: Animation opportunities flourish in areas such as broadcast design, game design, Web design, CD-ROM design, simulations, product design and visualization, and television/film effects. Related jobs include animation checker, animation computer programmer, animation modeler, animation sculptor, animation technical director, animation voice director, background artist/stylist, character designer, film-tape editor, ink and paint supervisor, and layout artist.
Suggested programs: animation, art, computer programming, digital media studies, drawing, film studies, new media, technology, visual and media arts.

Art director/production designer: If you find the prospect of designing and building sets for theater productions, music videos, or commercials; finding the ideal location for a student film; or creating the background for news anchors appealing, you might be interested in this field. In film and television, the art director/production designer is responsible for designing sets and adjusting practical locations to meet the needs of the script and the vision of the director and producer.
Suggested programs: Architecture, art, design, engineering, visual and media arts.

Artist representative: Professional artists' representatives, also known as agents or entertainment managers, have daily contact with their clients and with producers as well as development and production executives.
Suggested programs: Communications, film studies, mass media, new media, telecommunications, visual and media arts, visual and performing arts.

Audio technician: Sound people have to face the demands of this detail-oriented position, and there are new challenges with every single remote broadcast.

Suggested programs: Audio/visual studies, film studies, visual and media arts.

Auditor/estimator: A production auditor is the accountant for a production. Responsibilities include overseeing the budget, payroll for cast and crew members, petty cash, and vendor payments. The auditor makes sure bills are paid and everyone in the production is informed about the costs. An estimator is in charge of creating the budget and estimating the week-to-week costs of the production. A production auditor is a freelance position, while an estimator usually has more job security.

Suggested programs: Accounting, business, communications, visual and media arts, visual and performing arts.

Business and legal affairs representative: Behind the scenes, there is always someone with business and legal savvy who can close the many deals in discussion.

Suggested programs: Business, communications, entertainment law.

Camera operator: In live television, the show is in the cameraperson's hands, and the action happens only once! It is a career position that translates to studio, film, and documentary/reality production.

Suggested programs: Film studies, telecommunications, visual and media arts, visual and performing arts.

Casting director: Casting directors are integral to the success of features as well as drama, comedy, and reality series. They are charged with finding the right person for the right role, and every role is critical. Casting requires an understanding of actors and the craft of acting and a commitment to the perpetual search for talent, in addition to a general knowledge of television and film.

Suggested programs: Communications, film studies, media studies, theater, visual and media arts, visual and performing arts, telecommunications.

Cinematographer (director of photography/DP): The cinematographer makes camera and lighting choices to ensure that the visuals serve the story and accomplish the goals of the director and producer. Passion for photography and telling stories through pictures is a must, as is knowledge and understanding of camera and lighting equipment, since the cinematographer oversees the camera department. Because the cinematographer determines the visuals of the story, it's not unusual for motion picture directors to double as DPs. Doug Liman (*Swingers, The Bourne Identity*) and Steven Soderbergh (*Traffic, Ocean's Eleven*) are contemporary directors who perfected their visual storytelling as cinematographers.

Suggested programs: Art, photography, visual and media arts, visual and performing arts.

Comedy (sketch) writer: Writers in this field create comedy with character and situation, and the pace is fast. They typically do this in just a few minutes.

Suggested programs: Cinema and media culture, creative writing, communications, English, visual and media arts.

Composer (music): The composer writes the musical score for the television production or feature. The composer may also select source music—contemporary or otherwise—as part of the music score. A series or film sound track, the theme for a syndicated talk show, or the music preceding a news program can provide instant identification and emotional subtext for viewers.

Suggested programs: Film studies, music composition, music performance, music theory.

Continuity writer: Continuity writers compose commercial and promotional copy for local television and radio stations. Experience in this position can position the aspiring comedy writer, for example, for a successful transition into a broader market.

Suggested programs: Cinema and media culture, communications, English, film studies, journalism, mass marketing, visual and media arts.

Copywriter: Copywriters write advertising copy for print and broadcast media. Many advertising writers have used their marketing prowess to achieve success in other fields.

Suggested programs: Cinema and media culture, communications, creative writing, English, journalism, mass media.

Costume designer: If you like defining a character and telling a story through wardrobe selection and costume design, or you can trace history through the rise and fall of women's hemlines and the height of men's collars, then this is the job for you. A costume designer creates the outward appearance of a character through originally-designed costumes, a made-to-order wardrobe, or a rented or purchased wardrobe.

Suggested programs: Art, design, fashion design, visual and media arts.

Director: The director supervises the entire creative process and helps shape the performance or production into a cohesive creative vision.

Suggested programs: Audio/visual studies, English, film studies, media studies, music, theater, visual and media arts, visual and performing arts.

Distributor: Syndication and domestic/international distribution are critical divisions of any media corporation. Activities include sales, marketing, promotion, and program development.

Suggested programs: Broadcasting, business, communications, telecommunications, mass media.

Documentary/nonfiction writer: The documentary or nonfiction writer is close in spirit to a news writer or journalist. This type of writing is based on observation, research, and facts.

Suggested programs: Cinema and media culture, communications, English, film studies, journalism, mass marketing, visual and media arts.

Editor: The editor sees and assembles film, tape, or computer images/text, and determines how those pieces should fit together to tell a story. The news or ENG editor edits the tape of breaking stories from the field to make real-time deadlines. The editor on a prime time series has to edit and post an episode every seven to ten days. Reality television editors identify dramatic story points and compelling characters from hundreds of hours of tape. The motion picture editor works with the director to render the plot, sound effects, music, graphics, and visual effects into the feature film that the director envisions.

Suggested programs: Communications, computer programming, film studies, telecommunications, visual and media arts, visual and performing arts.

Engineer in charge (EIC): Individual responsible for the engineering component of production in local and national broadcasting. Technical skills and the ability to work well under pressure are key. Employment opportunities include positions in television news, sports, and variety.

Suggested programs: Broadcast, communications, radio, and television.

Feature development executive: Feature development executives must know and love movies, past and present, and they must be able to handle lots of reading. They must have sharp critical analysis skills so they may figure out (and capitalize on) what people will go to the movies to see. Producers and directors, production companies, and studios have development departments and positions, but the competition is fierce.
Suggested programs: Cinema and media culture, English, film studies, visual and media arts, visual and performing arts.

Feature writer: Feature writers start off writing spec scripts or pitching their stories to producers, directors, or film companies. Once established, some feature writers prefer assignments, while others prefer to develop their own material. As features are a director's medium, many writers become directors and producers to make sure their work gets produced.
Suggested programs: Cinema and media culture, communications, creative writing, English, film studies, visual and media arts, visual and performing arts.

Film buyer: It's a happy day in Park City when a Sundance film finds distribution. The film buyer puts his or her faith in the film against the vicissitudes of the marketplace.
Suggested programs: Business, film studies, media culture, visual and media arts.

Film critic: Do you love movies and enjoy bringing a hidden gem to the attention of friends? Do you want to see every movie that's out, from documentaries to thrillers to foreign films from Bulgaria? Film critics have deep knowledge of film and the arts—and the passion to share that knowledge, not to mention great films, with others. Film critics are print journalists and sometimes on-air personalities who must get through great volumes of work with speed and accuracy.
Suggested programs: Cinema and media culture, English, film studies, journalism, visual and media arts, visual and performing arts.

Industrial scriptwriter: This meta (of sorts) job is for the person who wants to create scripts and films that promote knowledge of the inner workings of the industry. (Robert Altman began his film career by making industrial films.)
Suggested programs: Cinema and media culture, creative writing, English, film studies, visual and media arts, visual and performing arts.

Lighting technician: This position requires a great eye and thorough knowledge of artificial and natural lighting.
Suggested programs: Audio/visual studies, film studies, visual and media arts.

Makeup artist: This person works closely with the costume designer to paint (literally and figuratively) the intended picture of the character to the audience.
Suggested programs: Art, design, fashion design, visual and media arts.

Network advertising and promotion executive: Network advertising and promotion staff and executives work with programming executives creating on-air promotion and high-profile spots. The promotion departments of local television stations publicize the station's image, programs, and activities. Graduates making the segue to network advertising and promotion must have strong writing and editing skills as well as knowledge of editing systems, including Avid.
Suggested programs: Business, communications, mass marketing, telecommunications.

News writer: News writers for electronic media follow news stories and write for local, regional, and national news programs. They must stay abreast of the latest releases and have a clear understanding of the global media marketplace.

Suggested programs: Cinema and media culture, communications, English, film studies, journalism, mass marketing, visual and media arts.

Producer: The producer's job description varies from motion pictures to television to news, but the necessity of solving problems and overcoming obstacles does not. Responsibilities can include developing material, selecting the directors and cast, financing the project, and of course, seeing through all the elements of production, post-production, marketing, and distribution. The positive side of producing is artistic and financial satisfaction. The negative side is the freelance lifestyle, financial instability, and fierce competition.

Suggested programs: Business, communications, English, film studies, mass media, telecommunications, visual and media arts, visual and performing arts.

Programming executive: The work of a programming executive entails selecting programs from suppliers (producers, production companies, studios) and creating a program schedule that appeals to large audiences. The programming executive relies on the network development executives to identify and develop successful material for future programming, and on current development executives to maintain programming at a high level. Strong verbal and writing skills and knowledge of the television marketplace are necessary.

Suggested programs: Business, communications, mass media, new media, telecommunications.

Promotional writer: Promotional writers compose on-air promotion and high-profile spots. They have to be intimately familiar with the product, intended audience, and market trends.

Suggested programs: Cinema and media culture, communications, film studies, journalism, mass marketing.

Public relations writer: PR writers prepare press releases and copy on behalf of their clients—and of course, figure out how to spin news stories to their clients' advantage. Note that in many news and sports organizations, Web content developers write online content that may also be used for PR purposes.

Suggested programs: Cinema and media culture, communications, film studies, journalism, mass marketing.

Publicist: Who's that person with the earpiece standing near the star on the red carpet? Chances are it's the celebrity's publicist. Relationship building is key, and the objective to get word of the client's name, brand, or product out to the public. Verbal and people skills as well as the ability to build a network of media contacts are crucial.

Suggested programs: Communications, English, film studies, mass media, telecommunications.

Script analyst: Want to read 30 or 40 scripts a week and then write synopses and critiques of each script, compare strengths and weaknesses with previously read scripts, and continuously monitor what you've read? If you hope to be a development executive or a writer, then you may want to begin your career as a script analyst. Many writers attribute their success to the years they've spent analyzing other writers' work. Script analysts build a working knowledge of marketable scripts and talented writers—this valuable information can help them step into development positions, as well. A good script analyst knows the marketplace and is able to judge a script in the context of television or features. It's also helpful to have some background in writing, theater, and comparative literature.

Suggested programs: Cinema and media culture, communications, English, film studies, mass media, telecommunications, visual and media arts, visual and performing arts.

Scenic designer: The scenic designer prepares the building plans of sets for the construction department, which does the actual building. This involves detail work and physical labor.

Suggested programs: Architecture, art, design, engineering, visual and media arts.

Set designer/decorator: A set designer drafts technical drawings to build or modify sets. A set decorator creates the décor (furniture and set props; all the individual elements that are placed on the set) and works with the Swing Gang—the crew members who pick up the items from the suppliers, work with transportation to get the items the set, and place the items on the set.

Suggested programs: Architecture, art, design, engineering, visual and media arts.

Special visual effects director: To be nominated for a Special Visual Effects Oscar, the images in a film must be entirely imaginary. The people who create special visual effects work in cell animation, scale modeling, claymation, digital compositing, and morphing and CGI.

Suggested programs: Animation, computer programming, digital media studies, film studies, interactive media design and production, visual and media arts.

Studio promotion and marketing executive: This is the motion picture/film equivalent of network advertising and promotion. Individuals in this field design every promotional product, from print ads and posters to toy figure giveaways at fast food chains.

Suggested programs: Business, communications, film studies, mass marketing.

Television critic: Television has its detractors, but television critics are often the champions of programs that audiences have not yet discovered. Television critics have a long memory of television's past and a broad understanding of pop culture. Television critics are print journalists and are often social commentators, as well.

Suggested programs: Communications, journalism, mass media, telecommunications, visual and media arts.

Television development executive: Before a movie is made or a television program appears on the air, the development executive reads and analyzes it; meets with writers, agents, and managers; hears pitches; and evaluates the specified material for possible development. The television development executive has a thorough knowledge of the broadcast and cable marketplace—which programs are in development, where, with whom, and at what stage of development. Each category of programming has its own development executives. The networks are considered the buyers, and everyone else is a seller.

Suggested programs: Communications, English, mass media, telecommunications.

Television series writer: Individuals in this field start out by writing spec scripts and doing freelance work. Ultimately, they join the staff of a series and work their way through the ranks to create their own shows. Although some crossover is possible, the industry tends to pigeonhole a writer into the genre in which he or she has had success. The writer/producer is the driving creative force in television and is respected as such.

Suggested programs: Communications, creative writing, English, film studies, mass media, telecommunications, visual and media arts.

If you look at the titles and credits of motion pictures and television, you will see dozens of names, and these credited titles are a small percentage of the many jobs that make up the industry. The Television Academy awards Emmys® to honor excellence in television programming and individual disciplines. The Academy of Motion Picture Arts awards Academy Awards® (Oscars®) to honor similar excellence in motion pictures. The Emmys® and the Academy Awards® provide an opportunity to acknowledge publicly those individuals who work behind the scenes and behind the camera—as well as those who appear in front of it, of course. (If you're interested in learning more about the daily technical work of the craft, check out the Television Academy Foundation's DVD set, *Journeys Below the Line,* which spotlights Fox Broadcasting's *24* and NBC's *ER.*)

EPILOGUE: SOME FINAL WORDS

Once you have the education you need to get a real-world job, you should put yourself out there, network, experiment, create, explore, and persevere. The college (and certainly the graduate) degree sends a strong signal to a future employer that you are prepared for and committed to the industry. The television, film, and digital media industry can be erratic and volatile. There is no blueprint for building your future, but we hope this book will guide you through the selection process. Remember: If Take One doesn't go as you'd hoped, there's always Take Two. Be prepared, patient, persistent, and enjoy your search!

THUMBNAILS OF INDUSTRY FIGURES*
*(THEY MADE IT, AND YOU CAN TOO!)

Writer

RACHEL AXLER

☆ Rachel Axler is a comedy writer and budding playwright.

☆ She attended Williams College, from which she received a bachelor's degree with a double major in English and theater. For graduate school, she attended the University of California at San Diego, from which she received an MFA in playwriting.

WHAT FACTORS GOVERNED YOUR CHOICE TO ATTEND WILLIAMS COLLEGE AND THEN UCSD?

Although I knew I wanted to go into the arts since I was about eight years old, for college, as with high school, I wound up prizing academic excellence and a liberal arts education over any sort of conservatory experience. And, you know what? Probably a good thing, too. Because if I'd limited my schooling to one artistic pursuit earlier than I did, I would have gone to school for acting, and I never would have gotten the chance to discover how much I suck at calculus.

In terms of graduate school, UCSD's an amazing place for anyone interested in theater. (The acting, directing, playwriting, design, and stage management programs are all top-notch, and integrated enough to function as a miniature production company.) I met and worked with extraordinarily talented people at UCSD and greatly value the time I spent there. I will say, although it wasn't quite asked of me: not sure how positive the experience is for undergraduate theater students at UCSD. At least during my years there, the graduate theater program was so strong that it overwhelmed the department's attentions and production capacities. The undergrads seemed to play supporting roles (assisting, etc.) at best, whereas at a college or university with no grad department, they might have had the opportunity to take on larger roles and responsibilities.

WHAT DO YOU CONSIDER THE MOST HELPFUL ADVICE FOR SELECTING THE RIGHT SCHOOL?

Honestly, I think it's very difficult to go wrong with a liberal arts education. It gives you a fundamental breadth of knowledge to draw on later, when you're doing whatever very specific thing you choose to do. So, I suppose my most helpful guidance would be to steer (most) people away from programs that are too focused, too early on.

Another helpful method is to rate schools by motto.

General rule of thumb: Latin motto = better school.

IN WHICH TELEVISION ACADEMY FOUNDATION PROGRAM DID YOU PARTICIPATE?

I was a Television Academy Foundation Scriptwriting Intern in 2004. In terms of the intern program: I'd recommend it, without reservation, to anyone who wants a foot in the door. It's an amazing program that succeeds at the most basic level—which is to say, it provides students with access to parts of the TV-creating world that they otherwise would never have been given. At least, not so readily. I was coming from the world of theater, with an outsider's inkling that I might want to write for TV some day, but no real, substantial basis for that idea. After spending two months in the writers' room at NBC's *American Dreams*—watching with admiration as scripts and characters were outlined, written, edited, re-written, torn up, rebuilt . . . all with the passion and integrity of great writers aiming to create great stories—I was hooked. I couldn't imagine that kind of job being out there and my not having it. Plus, they bought me lunch everyday. You can get used to that. My internship didn't directly earn me my current writing position. But if I hadn't seen what writing for television was like firsthand, and hadn't left with such a strong desire to do so, I might not have pursued my career as strongly as I did. OK, I might have. But I might not have.

WHAT IS YOUR CURRENT POSITION?

Currently employed in my dream job: Writer for *The Daily Show with Jon Stewart* on Comedy Central. Before that, I temped.

SOME RANDOM THOUGHTS/COMMENTS:

One other thing: I still regret not taking Neuroscience 101. What was I—afraid I'd ruin my GPA? I was a friggin' *theater* major. So, in terms of advice once you've chosen a school: I'd say, take Neuroscience 101. Then maybe send me your notes?

Writer and executive producer

BRANNON BRAGA

☆ Brannon Braga is a writer and executive producer. At the start of his career, he worked on *Star Trek: The Next Generation*. He was named the executive producer of *Star Trek: Voyager* and cocreated *Star Trek: Enterprise*. He also cowrote the features *Star Trek: Generations* and *Star Trek: First Contact* as well as *Mission Impossible II*.

☆ He attended Kent State University in Kent, Ohio, for two years; he then transferred to and ultimately graduated from the University of California—Santa Cruz.

WHAT FACTORS GOVERNED YOUR CHOICE OF KENT STATE AND THEN UC–SANTA CRUZ?

I chose Kent State because it was close to where I was living in Ohio and because it allowed me to get my general education requirements out of the way. I transferred to UC—Santa Cruz because it had a small but excellent film program where I could focus on my specific career interests. I was also captivated by the breathtaking natural environment of Santa Cruz itself, which was creatively stimulating.

WHAT DO YOU CONSIDER THE MOST HELPFUL ADVICE FOR SELECTING THE RIGHT SCHOOL?

It seems pretty obvious to me that you'd choose a university with a curriculum that would help cultivate your interests. Also, since you'll be living there for several years, you might consider the locale and culture. Will you enjoy being there day to day? Is it an environment that you'll find stimulating?

IN WHICH TELEVISION ACADEMY FOUNDATION PROGRAM DID YOU PARTICIPATE?

I received a Scriptwriting Internship with the Academy of Television Arts and Sciences Foundation in 1990.

WHAT IS YOUR CURRENT POSITION?

I currently have an overall development deal with Paramount Pictures, where I've been working for the past 15 years as a writer/producer for various *Star Trek* television shows. I most recently created a CBS sci-fi drama called *Threshold*.

Producer

MARTIN BRUESTLE

☆ Martin Bruestle's credits as a producer include *Northern Exposure*, *Cupid*, and *The Sopranos*, for which he won an Emmy® Award.

☆ He attended the University of Minnesota, College of Liberal Arts, in Minneapolis, Minnesota.

WHAT FACTORS GOVERNED YOUR CHOICE TO ATTEND THE UNIVERSITY OF MINNESOTA?

[Because I was] a resident of Minnesota, there were definite financial reasons for attending the University of Minnesota. Since I grew up in a very small community in northern Minnesota, moving to the Twin Cities was an exciting idea. Most importantly, I knew that the University of Minnesota was an excellent school. With more than 15 different colleges/schools within the campus, I knew that the diversity would provide a great environment.

WHAT DO YOU CONSIDER THE MOST HELPFUL ADVICE FOR SELECTING THE RIGHT SCHOOL?

Choosing a university is a very personal decision. It is okay to be selfish in this process, because one is deciding on the direction of his or her future. However, selecting a college or university will not determine the future. It is [just] a foundation for the future. I would recommend choosing a school that best fits your personal needs—financial, emotional, geographic; and most importantly, I believe that one should follow one's passions. If you are passionate about something, everything else will fall into place.

IN WHICH TELEVISION ACADEMY FOUNDATION PROGRAM DID YOU PARTICIPATE?

I was an intern, episodic, in the summer of 1987 on the series *thirtysomething*.

WHAT IS YOUR CURRENT POSITION?

I am currently a producer on [the HBO series] *The Sopranos*.

Writer

IAN BUSCH

☆ Ian Busch is a comedy writer who has written for *Malcolm in the Middle* and *Life with Bonnie*. Past credits include working as a production assistant for *My So-Called Life* and appearing as an actor in *Felicity*.

☆ He attended Marquette University in Milwaukee, Wisconsin.

WHAT FACTORS GOVERNED YOUR CHOICE TO ATTEND MARQUETTE?

That its liberal arts education had both philosophy and theology requirements . . . that there were many options (acting, writing, directing, producing) for me within the Broadcasting Department and the Theater Department . . . and that Marquette allowed its students onto its TV production equipment sooner than the other universities I was looking into.

WHAT DO YOU CONSIDER THE MOST HELPFUL ADVICE FOR SELECTING THE RIGHT SCHOOL?

Look for the school where you can "hit the ground running." So basically [consider]: (a) How accelerated is the freshman curriculum? and (b) How open are the extracurricular clubs and activities to allowing a high level of freshman participation?

IN WHICH TELEVISION ACADEMY FOUNDATION PROGRAM DID YOU PARTICIPATE?

Internship. Movies of the Week, in 1993.

WHAT IS YOUR CURRENT POSITION?

Freelance comedy writer. I'm currently writing a live-action pilot for the Cartoon Network.

Director/writer/producer

SHARI COOKSON

☆ Shari Cookson is a producer, writer, and director of documentaries. Her credits include *All Aboard! Rosie's Family Cruise*, which she produced and directed, *Living Dolls: The Making of a Child Beauty Queen*, which she wrote, produced, and directed, and *Skinheads USA: Soldiers of the Race War*, which she directed.

☆ She attended the University of Southern California's School of Journalism.

WHAT FACTORS GOVERNED YOUR CHOICE TO ATTEND USC?

USC has a strong journalism program. The faculty included many respected professionals working in the field. The school also offered me a scholarship.

WHAT DO YOU CONSIDER THE MOST HELPFUL ADVICE FOR SELECTING THE RIGHT SCHOOL?

A focused curriculum and a faculty with experience working in the field.

IN WHICH TELEVISION ACADEMY FOUNDATION PROGRAM DID YOU PARTICIPATE?

The College Television Awards (1982).

WHAT IS YOUR CURRENT POSITION?

President of Sceneworks, a small production company I run with my husband, Charlton McMillan. I am a director, writer, and producer. My last project was *All Aboard! Rosie's Family Cruise*, which I directed and produced for HBO.

VP

DEBRA CURTIS

☆ Debra Curtis's credits include serving as production executive for the TV series *Strong Medicine*. She was also the assistant executive in charge of production for the 1994 Billboard Music Awards.

☆ She attended Brandeis University in Waltham, Massachusetts.

WHAT FACTORS GOVERNED YOUR CHOICE TO ATTEND BRANDEIS UNIVERSITY?

I was looking for a liberal arts school where the professors were accessible and personal attention was a possibility.

WHAT DO YOU CONSIDER THE MOST HELPFUL ADVICE FOR SELECTING THE RIGHT SCHOOL?

The campus visit is key in making the final decision. Sit in on classes. Talk to students. Eat in the cafeteria.

IN WHICH TELEVISION ACADEMY FOUNDATION PROGRAM DID YOU PARTICIPATE?

I participated in the Internship Program, Broadcast Promotions, in 1991.

WHAT IS YOUR CURRENT POSITION?

I'm vice president, current programming, Sony Pictures Television.

Production designer

JACK FORRESTEL

☆ Jack Forrestel has worked as a television art director and is also a novelist. His credits include a 2003 Emmy nomination for Outstanding Achievement in Art Direction/Set Decoration/Scenic Design for a Drama Series for *The Bold and the Beautiful.*

☆ He attended The Philadelphia College of Art (now part of The University of the Arts) for his undergraduate studies and received a BFA in 1981. He attended Temple University School of Communications and Theatre for graduate school and earned his MFA in 1984.

WHAT FACTORS GOVERNED YOUR CHOICES TO ATTEND FIRST THE PHILADELPHIA COLLEGE OF ART AND THEN TEMPLE UNIVERSITY?

Both schools were located in Philadelphia (my hometown), and both offered curricula that I was interested in pursuing at the time.

My undergraduate experience was motivated by an interest in the pursuit of fine art as an expression. My graduate school time was spent trying to mold that experience into a practical field that would not only allow me to express myself artistically, but also provide me with a means of supporting myself in a viable profession.

WHAT DO YOU CONSIDER THE MOST HELPFUL ADVICE FOR SELECTING THE RIGHT SCHOOL?

Have a vague idea of what knowledge you would like to come away from the experience with. Find out as much about the faculty as possible. Most schools offer bios of the professors at their institutions. Visit the schools you're interested in attending, and see how their environments fit [with your interests]. As a prospective student, you may be able to sit in on a class or two. If you're unsure about some detail or protocol regarding a school, ask questions!

IN WHICH TELEVISION ACADEMY FOUNDATION PROGRAM DID YOU PARTICIPATE?

As a second-year grad student I interned through the Television Academy Foundation's summer internship program in Art Direction. I now cohost that program each summer with the help of some very talented film and television designers.

WHAT IS YOUR CURRENT POSITION?

I am currently the production designer of *The Bold and the Beautiful* on CBS.

Producer

ERICK GARCIA

☆ Erick Garcia's credits include producing the short films *Valette*, *Definite Maybe*, and *Shine on Me*.

☆ He attended the University of Southern California in Los Angeles.

WHAT FACTORS GOVERNED YOUR CHOICE TO ATTEND USC?

I was a part of two schools: the Marshall School of Business (the top entrepreneurial school in the United States, according to many publications) and the School of Cinema-Television (the top film school in the world, according to many publications). It's also one of the most culturally diverse universities in the United States.

WHAT DO YOU CONSIDER THE MOST HELPFUL ADVICE FOR SELECTING THE RIGHT SCHOOL?

[Students should consider the] resources and programs available based on their major or career interests.

IN WHICH TELEVISION ACADEMY FOUNDATION PROGRAM DID YOU PARTICIPATE?

[I participated in] the College Television Awards, 2002 Drama, and won second place for *Shine on Me* by Amaya Cervino. [Editor's note: The College Television Awards go to the producers of student films.]

WHAT IS YOUR CURRENT POSITION?

I am the producer/production manager for the National Association for Latino Independent Producers, the NALIP.org.

Comedy writer/
executive producer

NEIL GOLDMAN

☆   Neil Goldman is a comedy writer and executive producer. He has written for a number of television series, including *Family Guy* and *Scrubs*.

☆   He attended Yale University in New Haven, Connecticut.

WHAT FACTORS GOVERNED YOUR CHOICE TO ATTEND YALE?

I just decided I was going to go to the best school that accepted me. It boiled down to Yale and Duke, and Yale was only an hour away from home, so Yale it was.

WHAT DO YOU CONSIDER THE MOST HELPFUL ADVICE FOR SELECTING THE RIGHT SCHOOL?

Visiting the campus, getting a feel for the energy of the place, and being able to talk to current students—even sneaking into a few classes while you're there.

IN WHICH TELEVISION ACADEMY FOUNDATION PROGRAM DID YOU PARTICIPATE?

1993 Episodic Internship.

WHAT IS YOUR CURRENT POSITION?

I'm co-executive producer of *Scrubs*.

Writer/producer/director

DAVID GOYER

☆ David Goyer is a writer, producer, and director for television and film. His extensive credits include writing the *Blade* trilogy and *The Crow: City of Angels*; coproducing *Mission to Mars*; and directing the pilot of *Threshold*.

☆ He attended the University of Southern California in Los Angeles.

WHAT FACTORS GOVERNED YOUR CHOICE TO ATTEND USC?

At the time, USC [in its School of Cinema—Television] offered the only undergraduate screenwriting program in the country. Generally, it is also considered the top film school in the world.

WHAT DO YOU CONSIDER THE MOST HELPFUL ADVICE FOR SELECTING THE RIGHT SCHOOL?

If [you're considering] a film and television school, you would want to find out who the faculty members are and how well endowed [the school] is, [particularly] in terms of equipment (cameras and such).

IN WHICH TELEVISION ACADEMY FOUNDATION PROGRAM DID YOU PARTICIPATE?

I was in the Internship Program, Development, class of 1988.

WHAT IS YOUR CURRENT POSITION?

I am a working writer/director/producer for film and television. I wrote the 2005 feature *Batman Begins* (last summer). I also directed the pilot for the CBS series *Threshold* and wrote/executive produced the pilot for the new *Blade* series (June 2006). Currently, I am editing *The Invisible*, a feature film that I directed for Touchstone.

Network executive

PAUL LEWIS

☆ As a child, Paul Lewis knew what he wanted to be when he grew up: the president of a television network. Paul has been a television network executive at Fox Broadcasting and is currently at Nickelodeon.

☆ He attended the University of Florida in Gainesville.

WHAT FACTORS GOVERNED YOUR CHOICE TO ATTEND THE UNIVERSITY OF FLORIDA?

It was important for me to stay in the state so I could stay close to my family. The main reason I chose UF over other Florida schools was that UF has a PBS station on campus for students to work at and gain valuable hands-on experience [in the process].

WHAT DO YOU CONSIDER THE MOST HELPFUL ADVICE FOR SELECTING THE RIGHT SCHOOL?

Besides [considering] the curriculum offered, [you should ask:] What opportunities for hands-on experience exist at the university? Are there radio/television stations on campus?

IN WHICH TELEVISION ACADEMY FOUNDATION PROGRAM DID YOU PARTICIPATE?

The Internship Program, Children's Programming, in 1991.

WHAT IS YOUR CURRENT POSITION?

I'm director of development and production at Nickelodeon.

Executive producer/director/writer

RICO MARTINEZ

☆ Rico Martinez is a writer, producer, and director in television; he is also an independent filmmaker. His credits include producing and directing *Angels!* and working on a number of MTV projects.

☆ He attended the University of California in San Diego.

WHAT FACTORS GOVERNED YOUR CHOICE TO ATTEND UCSD?

Being totally honest, I didn't put too much thought into what college I went to. I got lucky—the school turned out to be perfect for me.

WHAT DO YOU CONSIDER THE MOST HELPFUL ADVICE FOR SELECTING THE RIGHT SCHOOL?

From the perspective of a writer, director, or producer, what would be important to me is whether the TV/film school was more art-based or commercially- and technically-based. For me, I wanted more of an art-based experience. I wanted to focus more on the creative than the technical [aspects of television and film studies]. Ultimately, I got the technical and commercial perspective by working in the industry after I graduated (and also thanks to my internship with the Television Academy Foundation, which helped me get my first job!), but those early days in school of being wildly creative and artistically rebellious were important to me, and I think they helped inform how I look at things now. I tend to do projects that are more out-of-the-box, and for that reason I think I made the right choice. But each person has to figure that out for him- or herself.

IN WHICH TELEVISION ACADEMY FOUNDATION PROGRAM DID YOU PARTICIPATE?

I was the Cinematography Intern in 1987. That was almost twenty years ago! Scary. I chose cinematography because I thought that to be a good director (which was my goal), the camera was the most important thing to know. It's the beginning of the image, and it's the soul and art of the story. I still use my cinematography experience constantly as both an executive producer and a director. I can speak the language of camera with the DP (director of photography) and let him or her know exactly what I want.

WHAT IS YOUR CURRENT POSITION?

I am an executive producer, director, and writer for a first-look, nonexclusive deal with MTV. Basically, it means they have to pay me to have the first shot at my ideas and the first shot at me executing their ideas, but ultimately I can say yes or no to any of it.

It's what's considered the sexiest deal you can get as a creator, since you are guaranteed pay while being able to pick and choose your projects, rather than having to pitch all over town and try to sell your shows. Some of my credits at MTV include: *Viva la Bam, Real World/Road Rules Gauntlet* and *Battle of the Sexes,* and *Damage Control.*

I also continue to develop independent film projects. I have a dark comedy that is close to getting financing, with Margaret Cho attached as a lead.

Entertainment journalist

DAMON ROMINE

☆ Damon Romine began his career as a television development executive. He segued into entertainment journalism, a field in which he has worked as a writer and editor at several magazines and authored a best-selling children's book. He is a member of the Television Academy Foundation's Educational Programs & Services Committee and is editor of the Foundation's academic/student newsletter *Debut*.

☆ He attended the University of Missouri in Columbia, and graduated in 1988 with BJ and BA degrees.

WHAT FACTORS GOVERNED YOUR CHOICE TO ATTEND THE UNIVERSITY OF MISSOURI?

The University of Missouri, Columbia has one of the nation's most prestigious schools of journalism. Not only was it the first school of journalism in the world, but it also continues to be ranked first among broadcast and advertising professionals as well as editors—[especially when they] are asked which school does the best job in preparing students for a job in journalism. The school runs on the principle that the best way to learn journalism is to practice it. Students publish the city's daily newspaper and operate the newsroom of the market's number one television station, NBC affiliate KOMU. When you graduate from the University of Missouri, you go on to find your second job because you've held your first journalism job while still in school.

WHAT DO YOU CONSIDER THE MOST HELPFUL ADVICE FOR SELECTING THE RIGHT SCHOOL?

I think picking the right college requires knowing as a senior in high school exactly what you want to be doing five years down the road after college. And really, how often can we say we know what we want to be doing five years from now? College is the time to try new things and learn about new career paths. I went to the University of Missouri because of the journalism program. Halfway through, I realized my real interest was in entertainment, television, and film. I tried to make the best of the situation by getting degrees both in journalism and in communications. The lesson is, if you change career directions, you should adapt while you're in school or look at a school that can better suit your needs.

IN WHICH TELEVISION ACADEMY FOUNDATION PROGRAM DID YOU PARTICIPATE?

1987 Academy Foundation Summer Intern: Daytime Programming (I was placed in the writers' office of *Days of Our Lives*). The Academy Foundation's internship brought me to Hollywood and broadened my career options.

WHAT IS YOUR CURRENT POSITION?

Entertainment Media Director for the Gay & Lesbian Alliance Against Defamation (GLAAD), the nation's lesbian, gay, bisexual, and transgender (LGBT) media advocacy group.

Business and legal affairs director

VICTORIA STERLING

☆ Victoria Sterling has worked in programming and development; she is currently involved in standards and practices.

☆ In 1985 she received her bachelor's degree in communications from Trinity University in San Antonio, Texas. The following year, she received a master's in communications management from the Annenberg School of Communication at the University of Southern California in Los Angeles, California.

WHAT FACTORS GOVERNED YOUR CHOICE TO ATTEND TRINITY AND THEN USC?

For undergraduate studies: the small size of the school, faculty/student ratio, ability to balance liberal arts curriculum with pre-professional major, large variety of courses offered in major, beauty of campus, location in/near a major city. For graduate school: proximity to the entertainment business and location in a major city (Los Angeles), variety of courses offered, excellent reputation of school and professors as well as the graduate programs, ability to take courses in subjects on the cutting edge of the communications field.

WHAT DO YOU CONSIDER THE MOST HELPFUL ADVICE FOR SELECTING THE RIGHT SCHOOL?

Primary factors include the student's interests, any known future career aspirations, what he or she is looking for in a communications program, and whether or not the school offers a balance of liberal arts and technical courses. Many schools emphasize technical opportunities in the classroom, but critical thinking and the ability to problem-solve are really key in landing any job in the industry, and those abilities often spring from studying courses in other areas, including liberal arts, science, history, and humanities. I would also advise that students select a variety of colleges to apply to and visit each one before making a decision. It's important to see and get a feel for each school, including the faculty and students, the campus, the department [of their intended major] and its resources, the living and dining facilities, and the life they would have at the school. Finances and financial aid are also a primary consideration, and I would emphasize [the importance of] going to a college that provides individual attention over [one that is] a big-name school where a student might pay a lot more, but not receive as much attention in his or her studies.

IN WHICH TELEVISION ACADEMY FOUNDATION PROGRAM DID YOU PARTICIPATE?

I was the Network Programming Management intern in 1987. I was placed in the Children's Programming department at ABC Entertainment and worked on several animated series, including *Winnie the Pooh* and *The Real Ghostbusters*.

WHAT IS YOUR CURRENT POSITION?

My current position is director, standards & practices, business and legal affairs, Fox Cable Networks, in Los Angeles, California. We cover cable networks including: FX, Fox Movie Channel, Fox Reality Channel, Fox Sports Network (FSN), FUEL Channel, SPEED Channel, Fox Soccer Channel, Fox College Sports, regional Fox Sports networks, and National Geographic. Previous cable and network television positions have been in programming & development for movies and miniseries at both ABC Entertainment and CBS Entertainment, and standards & practices for the Fox Family Channel.

Technology director

STEVE TOBACK

☆ Steve Toback's experience includes being the studio manager of EFX and directing studio technology at Walt Disney Television Animation and DisneyToon Studios.

☆ He attended the University of Miami in Coral Gables, Florida.

WHAT FACTORS GOVERNED YOUR CHOICE TO ATTEND THE UNIVERSITY OF MIAMI?

The University of Miami was one of the only music schools offering a degree in music engineering that combined a world-class music program with the opportunity to take classes in other disciplines, such as fully-accredited electrical engineering classes as well as classes in film/television production. It also allowed me to finish in 3.5 years so I could get my second minor in film.

WHAT DO YOU CONSIDER THE MOST HELPFUL ADVICE FOR SELECTING THE RIGHT SCHOOL?

Flexibility is key. Rather than attending a specific trade-type school, attending a university that offers programs in diverse disciplines offers a student the ability to experiment to see if something clicks. A diversified education will provide a depth of experiences whose benefits will be of great value—especially in a creative industry.

IN WHICH TELEVISION ACADEMY FOUNDATION PROGRAM DID YOU PARTICIPATE?

I had a 1987 internship in Production Sound.

WHAT IS YOUR CURRENT POSITION?

Director, Technology, DisneyToon Studios. I'm responsible for production, business, and postproduction technology as well as software and database development.

Producer

KEVIN WEHRENBERG

☆ Kevin Wehrenberg has worked as a producer for *Fear Factor*, *It's a Miracle*, and *Suburban Monogamy*.

☆ He attended the University of Wisconsin—Oshkosh.

WHAT FACTORS GOVERNED YOUR CHOICE TO ATTEND UW-OSHKOSH?

I choose my college because they had the best radio/TV/film program in the Midwest.

WHAT DO YOU CONSIDER THE MOST HELPFUL ADVICE FOR SELECTING THE RIGHT SCHOOL?

It is important to understand whether or not a large or small school is right for you. My choice to go to a midsize state college allowed me access to television and film equipment as a freshman; this would not have been possible at a large school.

IN WHICH TELEVISION ACADEMY FOUNDATION PROGRAM DID YOU PARTICIPATE?

I participated in the Internship Program, Production Management, in 1993.

WHAT IS YOUR CURRENT POSITION?

I am a producer for *Fear Factor*.

THE SCHOOLS

ACADEMY OF ART UNIVERSITY

79 New Montgomery Street, San Francisco, CA 94105
Phone: 800-544-ARTS **E-mail:** info@academyart.edu
Website: www.academyart.edu

Campus Life
Environment: Metropolis. **Calendar:** Semester.

Students and Faculty
(All Undergraduate Programs)
Enrollment: 8,400. **Student Body:** 50% female, 50% male, 60% out-of-state, 15% international. African American 4%, Asian 12%, Caucasian 42%, Hispanic 7%. Student/faculty ratio: 18:1. 135 full-time faculty, 11% hold PhDs. 80% faculty teach undergrads.

Admissions
(All Undergraduate Programs)
Average high school GPA: 2.83. Regular notification: Rolling.

Costs and Financial Aid
(All Undergraduate Programs)
Annual tuition $14,400. Room & board $12,000. Required fees $280. Average book expense $864. **Financial Aid Statistics:** % freshmen/undergrads who receive need-based scholarship or grant aid: 14/19. % freshmen/undergrads who receive need-based self-help aid: 29/35. Priority financial aid filing deadline: 7/10.

TV/Film/Digital Media Studies Programs
**Number of undergraduates
 in these programs:** 2,729
**Number of 2005 graduates from these
 programs:** 370
Degrees conferred to these majors: BFA.
Also available at Academy of Art University: MFA, Associate of Arts, certificate programs.
**Number of full-time faculty in these
 programs:** 29
**Number of part-time faculty in these
 programs:** 70
Equipment and facilities: The Academy of Art University has more than 50 Final Cut Pro editing stations, 8 Avid Xpress DV editing stations, 3 Avid Adrenaline nonlinear editing stations, 14 linear tape-to-tape, and a Bosch Telecine transfer facility. A 6 Kem flatbed editing facility for celluloid linear editing and screenwriting lab with 10 Final Draft computers are also available to students. Additionally, there are 5 cinematography/lighting teaching stages, an acting stage with multiple sets, a Green Screen studio, and a 150-seat theater. The department also provides a full array of Super 8 film cameras, 32 16 mm Bolex cameras, Arrisflex SR 16 mm sync sound cameras, Arrisflex III 35 mm camera, 2 Betacam SP DV cameras, Canon 1-chip video cameras, Panasonic SVHS video cameras, 24p DVX100a video cameras, one Hi Def camera, a 35 mm Panavision camera, and an extensive inventory of lighting and second grip equipment.

% of graduates currently employed in related field: 80% working in art and design.
Career development services: Career counseling, job listings, internship boards, industry events, and an annual spring show.
Notable alumni: Scott Postiglione, writer under Stephen Boccho for *NYPD Blue* and *Law & Order*. Ian Takahashi, DP on one feature film sold to distribution and starting DP on ssecod film; worked with John Toll, bigtime DP. Amy Wheeler, assistant production designer for *Sex and the City*. Rich Cascio, worked with Roger Corman on two pictures.

In Their Own Words
The School of Motion Pictures & Television fosters creativity and independence in filmmaking as an art. We also provide instruction in the commercial aspects of filmmaking as a business. Our approach is dedicated to practical, hands-on training within a collaborative framework. Our program offers state-of-the-art equipment and guidance by top industry professionals.

ADELPHI UNIVERSITY

Levermore Hall 114, One South Avenue, Garden City, NY 11530
Phone: 516-877-3050 **E-mail:** admissions@adelphi.edu
Website: www.adelphi.edu

Campus Life
Environment: Metropolis. **Calendar:** Semester.

Students and Faculty
(All Undergraduate Programs)
Enrollment: 4,718. **Student Body:** 72% female, 28% male, 8% out-of-state, 3% international (47 countries represented). African American 13%, Asian 5%, Caucasian 45%, Hispanic 8%. Student/faculty ratio: 11:1. 257 full-time faculty, 90% hold PhDs. 100% faculty teach undergrads.

Admissions
(All Undergraduate Programs)
Freshman Admissions Requirements: Test(s) required: SAT or ACT; ACT with Writing component. Average high school GPA: 3.2. 23% in top tenth, 58% in top quarter. SAT Math (25/75 percentile): 510/620. SAT Verbal (25/75 percentile): 490/600. Projected SAT Writing (25/75 percentile): 550/650. Regular notification: Rolling.

Costs and Financial Aid
(All Undergraduate Programs)
Annual tuition $18,620. Room & board $9,100. Required fees $1,100. Average book expense $1,000. **Financial Aid Statistics:** % freshmen/undergrads who receive any aid: 93/88. % freshmen/undergrads who receive need-based scholarship or grant aid: 77/78. % freshmen/undergrads who receive need-based self-help aid: 76/79. Priority financial aid filing deadline: 3/1. Financial aid notification on or about: 3/1.

TV/Film/Digital Media Studies Programs
Number of undergraduates in these programs: 166
Number of 2005 graduates from these programs: 54
Degrees conferred to these majors: BA.
Number of full-time faculty in these programs: 7

Number of part-time faculty in these programs: 11
Equipment and facilities: Mac workstations (with Final Cut Pro, Adobe Creative Suite, AfterEffects, and other relevant video production software), Steenbeck film editing flatbeds, animation stand, and Pro Tools.
Other awards of note: 2001 Academy Award nomination for one of our faculty members.

% of graduates who pursue further study within 5 years: 25
% of graduates currently employed in related field: 80
Career development services: Alumni-networking opportunities, career counseling, internship listings, job fairs, job listings. Alumni come to visit senior thesis classes to discuss career building.

In Their Own Words
We offer students much more access to equipment than do most other institutions. We have an internship program that most students take advantage of and often use as starting points to their first jobs. All of our faculty are very active in their areas of interest: three currently have book contracts; another is an active filmmaker whose work screens regularly in major film festivals.

POPULAR PROGRAMS

COMMUNICATIONS-MEDIA STUDIES
Department chair: Margaret Cassidy, PhD
Number of full-time faculty: 7
Number of part-time faculty: 4
Focus/emphasis: The study of theories of human communication and social science approaches to the study of media and society.

COMMUNICATIONS-JOURNALISM
Department chair: Margaret Cassidy, PhD
Number of full-time faculty: 7
Number of part-time faculty: 7
Focus/emphasis: The study of the role of journalism in American society, as well as the practice of print and electronic journalism.

COMMUNICATIONS-MOVING IMAGE ARTS

Department chair: Margaret Cassidy, PhD
Number of full-time faculty: 7
Number of part-time faculty: 3
Focus/emphasis: The creation of moving image media and the aesthetic analysis of such media.

ALLEGHENY COLLEGE

Admissions Office, Box 5, 520 North Main Street, Meadville, PA 16335
Phone: 814-332-4351 **E-mail:** admissions@allegheny.edu
Website: www.allegheny.edu

Campus Life

Environment: Town. **Calendar:** Semester.

Students and Faculty
(All Undergraduate Programs)

Enrollment: 2,016. **Student Body:** 53% female, 47% male, 36% out-of-state. African American 1%, Asian 3%, Caucasian 93%, Hispanic 1%. Student/faculty ratio: 14:1. 135 full-time faculty, 95% hold PhDs. 100% faculty teach undergrads.

Admissions
(All Undergraduate Programs)

Freshman Admissions Requirements: Test(s) required: SAT or ACT. Average high school GPA: 3.76. 45% in top tenth, 77% in top quarter. SAT Math (25/75 percentile): 570/660. SAT Verbal (25/75 percentile): 570/660. Projected SAT Writing (25/75 percentile): 620/690. *Academic units required:* 4 English, 3 math, 3 science, 2 foreign language, 3 social studies, 1 academic elective. Early decision application deadline: 11/15. Regular application deadline: 2/15. Regular notification: 4/1.

Costs and Financial Aid
(All Undergraduate Programs)

Annual tuition $28,000. Room & board $7,000. Required fees $300. Average book expense $900
Financial Aid Statistics: % freshmen/undergrads who receive any aid: 99/97. % freshmen/undergrads who receive need-based scholarship or grant aid: 70/68. % freshmen/undergrads who receive need-based self-help aid: 54/56. Priority financial aid filing deadline: 2/15. Financial aid notification on or about: 3/1.

TV/Film/Digital Media Studies Programs

Degrees conferred to these majors: BA.
Number of full-time faculty in these programs: 5
Number of part-time faculty in these programs: 2
Equipment and facilities: Television studio, digital nonlinear editing lab, computer art lab, portable digital cameras.
Career development services: Alumni networking opportunities, career counseling, internship listings, job fairs, job listings.
Famous alumni: Ben Burtt, Ted Shaker.
Notable alumni: Lloyd Segan, film producer, execuive producer, *The Dead Zone*; Jeff Verszyla, chief meteorologist, KDKA-TV Pittsburgh, PA; Scott Wludyga, sports director, Jet-TV, Erie, PA.

In Their Own Words
Students intern in television, film, and other media services around the country, including New York City, Los Angeles, Boston, and Pittsburgh.

ALMA COLLEGE

614 West Superior Street, Alma, MI 48801-1599
Phone: 989-463-7139 **E-mail:** admissions@alma.edu
Website: www.alma.edu

Campus Life

Environment: Village.

Students and Faculty
(All Undergraduate Programs)

Enrollment: 1,284. **Student Body:** 58% female, 42% male, 6% out-of-state. African American 2%, Caucasian 93%, Hispanic 2%. Student/faculty ratio: 13:1. 82 full-time faculty, 88% hold PhDs. 100% faculty teach undergrads.

Admissions
(All Undergraduate Programs)

Freshman Admissions Requirements: Test(s) required: SAT or ACT. Average high school GPA: 3.46. 32% in top tenth, 62% in top quarter. SAT Math (25/75 percentile): 510/650. SAT Verbal (25/75 percentile): 520/670. Projected SAT Writing (25/75 percentile): 580/700. *Academic units required:* 3 English, 3 math, 3 science, 3 social studies. Regular notification: Rolling.

Costs and Financial Aid
(All Undergraduate Programs)

Annual tuition $22,170. Room & board $7,774. Required fees $210. Average book expense $700. **Financial Aid Statistics:** % freshmen/undergrads who receive any aid: 99/99. % freshmen/undergrads who receive need-based scholarship or grant aid: 76/76. % freshmen/undergrads who receive need-based self-help aid: 60/62. Priority financial aid filing deadline: 3/1. Financial aid notification on or about: 3/1.

TV/Film/Digital Media Studies Programs

Degrees conferred to these majors: BA.
Number of full-time faculty in these programs: 8
Equipment and facilities: Alma College offers several computer labs, including the Digital Media Production Studio. The college also has an advanced workstation for digital media development.
Career development services: Career counseling, job fairs.

In Their Own Words

The focus at Alma is to provide hands-on digital media training individually and in small groups. The Creative Digital Project Group provides opportunities for students to work on specific digital media projects beyond the campus. Students intern with top media and design firms.

POPULAR PROGRAMS

NEW MEDIA STUDIES

Department chair: Micheal Vickery
Number of full-time faculty: 8
Focus/emphasis: New Media Studies is an interdisciplinary minor designed to expose students to the applications and effects of new communication media. This includes graphic design, Web page development, video production, and music and sound.

PROGRAMS OF EMPHASIS

Department chair: Ray Riley
Number of full-time faculty: 1
Focus/emphasis: Students craft individual academic programs that consist of existing courses across disciplines as well as practica and internships in their areas of interest. Recent "Programs of Emphasis" have been in music technology, new media, and interactive media.

Students Should Also Know

Alma's approach centers on flexibility and providing opportunities for individual study and pursuing areas of specialization. Alma also has state-of-the-art facilities for digital media production and sound and recording technologies.

AMERICAN FILM INSTITUTE–CONSERVATORY

2021 North Western Avenue, Los Angeles, CA 90027
Phone: 323-856-7628
Website: www.afi.com

Admissions
(All Undergraduate Programs)

Regular application deadline: 12/1. Regular notification: 4/15.

Costs and Financial Aid
(All Undergraduate Programs)

Annual tuition $29,975. Room & board $13,050. Required fees $2,100. Supplies $4,400.

TV/Film/Digital Media Studies Programs

Also available at American Film Institute-Conservatory: MFA and certificate programs.

Equipment and facilities: The large, central Warner Communications/Warner Bros. Building houses a soundstage, classrooms, screening rooms, production offices, and computer labs. The Louis B. Mayer Library houses a collection of unique and specialized reading, reference, and research materials. The Sony Digital Arts Center houses AFI's post-production facilities, embracing the entire spectrum of contemporary nonlinear digital editing, including the latest Avid Symphony editing systems networked by the Avid Unity media storage system.

Other awards of note: Alums/fellows have won numerous awards including Robert Richardson (C, 1979), who won the 2005 Academy Award for Best Cinematography for *The Aviator*; Jorge Gaggero (D, 2000), a Special Jury Prize (World Cinema) Dramatic Jury for *Live-in Maid* at the 2005 Sundance Film Festival. Four 2005 graduates swept the 27th Annual College Television Awards: Namarata Tandon, producer, Drama,1st Place for *Trojan Cow*; Chris Ranta, producer, Drama, 2nd Place for *Left at the Rio Grande*; Seth Kaplan, producer, Drama, 3rd Place for *Duncan Removed*; and Barbara Stepansky, director, Directing Award for *Trojan Cow*. Jesse Alexander (screenwriter, 1992) won the Golden Globe for Best Television Series, Drama, for *Lost*; Michael Cain (producer, 1988) won the Special Jury Prize at the 2006 Sundance Film Festival for his film, *TV Junkie*. Robert Elswit (cinematographer, 1977) won the 2005 Independent Spirit Award in Cinematography for *Good Night, and Good Luck*. Brian Burgoyne (cinematographer, 2005) won the American Society of Cinematographers 2005 Jordan Cronenweth Student Heritage Award for *The Red Veil*. Joo Wan Lee (editor, 2006) won the American Cinema Editors Award for Best Student Editing. Doug Ellin (director, 1992) won the 17th Annual Producer's Guild Award for Television Series: Comedy, for *Entourage*. Justin Bull (director, 2005) and Nicolas Emiliani (producer, 2007) won the Short Film Competition at the China-America Festival of Film and Culture Awards for their film, *Homefront*. Sheldon Collins (director, 2003) won a grant from Showtime's 2006 Black Filmmaker Showcase for *The Sunday Morning Stripper*.

Career development services: Showcase of thesis films and production design projects with invitations going to agents, managers, production companies, and other film and television professionals; distribution of thesis films; annual Script Log Book; professional internship programs.

Famous alumni: David Lynch, Janusz Kaminsky, Patty Jenkins, Mimi Leder, Carl Franklin, Edward Zwick, Marshall Herskovitz, Paul Schrader, Amy Heckerling, Susannah Grant.

In Their Own Words

Fellows across all disciplines attend the Harold Lloyd Master Seminar series, which brings world-renowned filmmakers to campus to share their work and experiences in an informal and accessible setting. Seminar guests include leading actors, cinematographers, directors, editors, producers, production designers, and screenwriters who impart not only practical advice on making movies, but also speak about their influences, early experiences, and dedication to their craft. Guests have included: Frank Darabont (The Shawshank Redemption), *Alexander Payne* (Sideways), *George Lucas* (Star Wars), *Michael Mann* (Collateral), *and Paul Haggis* (Crash).

POPULAR PROGRAMS

CINEMATOGRAPHY

Number of full-time faculty: 6

Focus/emphasis: Focusing on the art and craft of visual storytelling, fellows receive instruction from professional cinematographers while learning how to move an audience with their visual interpretation of the narrative. Classroom training, stage-lighting workshops, digital video, HD video, and 16 mm and 35 mm film exercises provide fellows with practical experience and training. Fellows graduate adept at making fast, informed, and inspired creative decisions. Three short narrative projects are at the core of the first year. With training in new media technology incorporated throughout the curriculum—from pre-visualization to advanced image manipulation and control—fellows develop their storytelling skills by photographing narrative projects on digital video. In the second year, fellows team to shoot 30-minute thesis productions, which may be photographed in a variety of formats. Completion of the cinematography thesis portfolio also includes the shooting of a short MOS 35 mm project.

DIRECTING

Number of full-time faculty: 7

Focus/emphasis: Great directors must be great storytellers. The directing program offers fellows a thorough understanding of the process of production from script to screen, focusing on narrative, visual language, and performance. Fellows learn to collaborate with screenwriters and producers, work with professional actors, and incorporate the visions of cinematographers, production designers, and editors into all their produced projects. First-year fellows direct three substantial narrative projects, offering them an invaluable opportunity to work with actors from the Screen Actors Guild in a supportive, collaborative environment. The curriculum also requires participation in a directing workshop, examining diverse directing styles, techniques, and strategies with specific attention to narrative point of view. Second-year directing fellows team with those in other disciplines to create a short narrative thesis production, guided by professional faculty. Directors also develop a feature film or television project to be included in their thesis portfolios.

EDITING

Number of full-time faculty: 9

Focus/emphasis: Based in a state-of-the-art postproduction facility that includes 15 Avid Symphony editing systems, networked by the Avid Unity media storage system and a DS Nitris system, first-year editors learn all aspects of digital-based postproduction, cutting six narrative projects and two introductory exercises. A team effort by all disciplines, each project teaches editing fellows to collaborate effectively while learning the editing process. First-year editors also learn aesthetics of sound design, as they create and mix sound with Pro Tools audio workstations. Second-year editing fellows cut at least two thesis projects, with each project taken through a complete postproduction process, replicating high-end, real-world practice.

PRODUCING

Number of full-time faculty: 8

Focus/emphasis: Developing in-depth knowledge of all aspects of creative and physical production, producing fellows graduate with an ability to think creatively and lead with confidence and authority. First-year fellows produce three narrative projects in collaboration with fellows from other disciplines. They participate with their teams in both creative and production meetings, during which their individual projects are discussed and developed. Producing fellows also attend weekly workshops and seminars where they learn about the producer's role and responsibilities in the filmmaking process. In the second year, producers team with fellows in other disciplines to produce a short narrative thesis production. Additionally, they are required to develop a feature film or television project as an integral component of their individual thesis portfolio. Producing fellows also engage in a series of workshops and seminars on all aspects of creative entrepreneurial producing.

PRODUCTION DESIGN

Number of full-time faculty: 7

Focus/emphasis: Attracting artists from architecture, interior design, theater arts, scenic design, and other related fields, the production design curriculum focuses on the creative process of visually and physically developing an environment that becomes an essential component of the storytelling process. Production designers must possess a keen understanding of the story in order to create a believable and realistic world on screen. First-year fellows collaborate on at least three produced narrative projects, learning to transform designs into reality on a soundstage or location, while adhering to restricted budgets. Fellows develop design skills through classes, workshops, and practical set construction, learning traditional drafting methods as well as computer-aided design. Digital design tools and techniques are integral to the curriculum. Second-year fellows design an entire thesis production while completing an independent design project for their portfolio. The curriculum also includes special workshops on set illustration, drafting, model building, budgeting, color theory, and the latest digital design. These courses help production design fellows learn to communicate their visions to their AFI production teams, as well as to future professional colleagues.

SCREENWRITING

Number of full-time faculty: 11

Focus/emphasis: Focusing on narrative storytelling in an environment designed to simulate the world of the professional screenwriter, screenwriting fellows find their unique voices while learning the essence of working as part of a creative team. The heart of the screenwriting program lies in the relationship between the fellow and the exemplary faculty who serve as teachers and mentors, guiding and supporting each writer's development in an intimate workshop setting. In the core screenwriting workshops, fellows grow as cinematic storytellers through critique and analysis of their work by faculty and peers. The first year begins with an immersion in the production process

in order for writers to learn how screenplays are visualized. Initially writing short screenplays—one of which will be the basis for a first-year production—screenwriting fellows collaborate with producing and directing fellows to see their work move from page to screen. By the end of the first year, fellows write a feature-length screenplay. Second-year fellows may develop material for television—including biopics, television movies, and spec scripts for sitcoms or one-hour dramas—in addition to writing theatrical films. They also have the opportunity to work closely with their peers from other disciplines, by either writing a script for second-year thesis projects or by participating with directing and producing fellows in developing thesis portfolio material.

ARIZONA STATE UNIVERSITY–TEMPE

Box 870112, Tempe, AZ 85287-0112
Phone: 480-965-7788 **E-mail:** ugrading@asu.edu
Website: www.asu.edu

Campus Life

Environment: City. **Calendar:** Semester.

Students and Faculty
(All Undergraduate Programs)

Enrollment: 39,649. **Student Body:** 51% female, 49% male, 24% out-of-state, 3% international (124 countries represented). African American 4%, Asian 5%, Caucasian 69%, Hispanic 13%, Native American 2%. Student/faculty ratio: 22:1. 1,878 full-time faculty, 84% hold PhDs. 70% faculty teach undergrads.

Admissions
(All Undergraduate Programs)

Freshman Admissions Requirements: Test(s) required: SAT or ACT. Average high school GPA: 3.3. 27% in top tenth, 53% in top quarter. SAT Math (25/75 percentile): 500/620. SAT Verbal (25/75 percentile): 490/610. Projected SAT Writing (25/75 percentile): 550/660. *Academic units required:* 4 English,

4 math, 3 science (3 science labs), 2 foreign language, 1 social studies, 1 history, 1 fine arts.

Costs and Financial Aid (All Undergraduate Programs)

Annual in-state tuition $4,311. Out-of-state tuition $13,918. Room & board $6,768. Required fees $95. Average book expense $948.

Financial Aid Statistics: % freshmen/undergrads who receive any aid: 71/65. % freshmen/undergrads who receive need-based scholarship or grant aid: 35/34. % freshmen/undergrads who receive need-based self-help aid: 20/31. Priority financial aid filing deadline: 3/1.

TV/Film/Digital Media Studies Programs

Degrees conferred to these majors: BA.

Also available at Arizona State University— Tempe: MA.

Equipment and facilities: The Cronkite School is committed to integrating the latest technology into its curriculum. The school maintains five dedicated computer laboratories for writing, editing, layout and design, and digital imaging. Students also have access to a modern television studio and control room, nonlinear audio and video editing facilities, and a broadcast journalism newsroom. The school maintains close ties with KAET-TV, one of America's most successful public television stations. Students have access to KASC Radio, the student radio station; Channel 2 Television, a cable outlet for students; The State Press; and the online Web Devil.

Career development services: Internship listings, job listings.

Notable alumni: Al Michaels, ABC Sports; James Loper, Academy of Television Arts and Sciences; Richard Lacher, NBC Entertainment; Linda Williams, KSAZ-TV and Fox 10 News; Michael Wong, KAET-TV.

In Their Own Words

Students at the Cronkite School have an opportunity to learn and apply broadcast skills at the campus radio station, produce their own television news program, and develop their print and online skills at the campus newspaper and website. In addition to the nearly 200 Arizona media professionals who visit campus each academic year to give guest lectures or participate in activities sponsored by Cronkite School student organizations, at least six media practitioners or executives from around the country spend time in the unit through the William Randolph Hearst Foundation Endowment for Visiting Professionals. The program, established through a $200,000 endowment awarded by the Hearst Foundation in 1991, enables the school to bring media professionals to ASU for short periods of time. The endowment, which has grown considerably through the years, has allowed the school to establish relationships with media outlets across the country. The visiting professionals interact extensively with students and faculty members. Visitors have included print journalists, broadcasters, photojournalists, online experts, and public relations practitioners.

POPULAR PROGRAMS

JOURNALISM (CRONKITE)

Focus/emphasis: The mission of the journalism concentration is to teach our students the writing, reporting, editing, and presentation skills necessary to succeed in modern print, broadcast, and online newsrooms, as well as to ground them in the historical, ethical, and legal traditions and requirements of the journalism profession. This concentration is designed to allow students who wish to become professional journalists to gain the basic skills necessary to report, write, edit, and present hard news and features for the major news media, whether for newspapers, magazines, radio, television, online outlets, or any combination of these. Although students may focus most of their course work on a particular medium, they will gain enough exposure to the varying style and presentation requirements of other media to be able to adapt to the rapidly changing demands of the converged-media newsrooms of tomorrow.

PUBLIC RELATIONS AND STRATEGIC MEDIA (CRONKITE)

Focus/emphasis: This concentration allows students to develop the organizational and communication skills necessary to represent for-profit, nonprofit, and political entities in a positive manner through electronic and print mediums. Courses in writing for the media, politics and the media, electronic publication design, and public relations campaigns are included in this concentration. Public relations is widely recognized as both a communication and management function in business, government, and nonprofit organizations. Its stated goal, according to the Public Relations Society of America, is to contribute to "mutual understanding among groups and institutions. It serves to bring private and public policies into harmony." The public relations practitioner plays an integral role both within an organization and between the organization and its external environment. Based on the journalism core course of newswriting, the strategic media and public relations emphasis focuses on developing skills across the wider range of public relations tools: news releases and media kits for both print and broadcast media, memos and letters, speeches, audiovisual presentation, internal and external publications, annual reports, and collateral materials as well as public relations programs and campaigns. The curriculum now reflects an emphasis on home page and site design via the World Wide Web, Internet search strategies, database retrieval, and applications and linkages. Both theory and practice are emphasized and integrated, along with pertinent topic areas including, but not limited to, advertising, marketing, organizational communication, and cross-cultural concerns. Public relations courses and the internship are complemented and enhanced by active student participation in an on-campus student organization sponsored through the Cronkite School— The Public Relations Student Society of America. This group is linked to the professional community and provides opportunities for majors to identify mentors, participate in professional development sessions, attend national conferences, gain professional experience, and compete for local and national scholarships.

MEDIA ANALYSIS AND CRITICISM (CRONKITE)

Focus/emphasis: This concentration enables students to examine critically and better appreciate the mass media's dynamic role and impact on both consumers and professionals in an emerging global society. Courses include issues in mass-mediated pop culture; visual communication; international communication; history of mass communication; race, gender, and the media; political communication; media and politics; American political film; sex, love, and romance in the mass media; emerging technologies; editorial interpretation; and mass media problems. This concentration is research- and theory-based. It focuses on deep examination and thorough consideration of media forms and content with a view toward applications on behalf of both the public and the profession. Students in this concentration will develop critical evaluation skills as well as an understanding of the societal, aesthetic, and ethical implications of mass media forms and content and the media technologies and systems that disseminate mass-mediated communication. This concentration prepares students for positions involving the critical and analytical assessment of the production and consumption of the form and content of mass-mediated communication. These positions include press critics, media ombudspersons, entertainment and arts writers and commentators, columnists and critics, editorial writers, media researchers and consultants, and media literacy advocates and educators, including media ethicists. In addition, this concentration offers a strong foundation for students who plan to pursue master's and doctoral degrees in journalism/mass communication or cultural/critical studies.

MEDIA MANAGEMENT (CRONKITE)

Focus/emphasis: The mission of the media management concentration is to allow students to develop an understanding of the role and structure of the mass communication industries in a global economy, as well as to develop the analytical, communication, and business skills needed to obtain an entry-level position in a track leading toward a media management position. This concentration is designed to allow students with interests in media management to obtain the entry-level skills often required for positions that later lead to management careers in the media. Specifically, the objectives are to provide training in the business areas of the media, including sales, promotion, programming and research in electronic media. Currently, organizations such as traditional radio and television stations, cable television systems and networks, and programming syndicators provide entry-level positions for students in this concentration. It is anticipated that the curriculum will evolve to include management training in all media.

MEDIA PRODUCTION (CRONKITE)

Focus/emphasis: Media Production (Cronkite School): The mission of the electronic media production concentration is to give undergraduate students proficiency in the areas of content design and creation within the information program genre, as well as to develop the skills necessary for the presentation of such journalistic and information content. Students take courses in multiple media applications, including audio and video production, writing, videography, multimedia design, Web design, public relations, documentation, and corporate/freelance combinations. Skills involve organization, writing, analog and digital technology, production design, and information processing. The concentration is devised to prepare students with creative interests in media production to obtain entry-level positions in both structured and freelance settings; for example, television stations, production houses, creative organizations such as public relations or advertising agencies, and government, independent, or corporate media facilities.

INTERCULTURAL COMMUNICATIONS AND CULTURAL STUDIES (HUGH DOWNS)

Focus/emphasis: Intercultural communication involves the study across cultural and intercultural contexts of verbal and nonverbal messages, the dynamics of human interaction, the challenges of intercultural transitions, and the intricacies of intercultural relationships. We explore how communication impacts and how it is influenced by factors such as identity, communication style, peace and conflict, historical memories, and religion. The focus is on both domestic and international contexts.

INTERPERSONAL COMMUNICATION (HUGH DOWNS)

Focus/emphasis: Interpersonal communication involves the study of verbal and nonverbal messages in dyadic interaction. We explore the various ways that communication functions in both social and personal relationships along a range of topics, including affection, competition, conflict, dating, emotion, health, and maintenance in such relational contexts as marriage, friendship, initial interaction, and family relationships.

ORGANIZATIONAL COMMUNICATION (HUGH DOWNS)

Focus/emphasis: We believe that organizations are primary sites of meaning-making, identity formation, knowledge production, security, health and wellness, and democracy in contemporary society. Because organizations are increasingly complex, our organizational communication area adopts a multiperspective dynamic approach to the study of organizational life.

PERFORMANCE STUDIES (HUGH DOWNS)

Focus/emphasis: Performance studies is concerned with communication embedded in aesthetic texts and contexts. Undergraduate courses provide students with a multitude of communication and critical performance experiences. These include performance of literary texts, voice improvement, interactive performance, performance ethnography, the study of oral traditions, communicative dimensions of self and others as performance (gender, race, sexuality, age), performance in social contexts, and performance theory. Undergraduate students may also participate in co-curricular performance activities at The Empty Space, join activities sponsored by The Interpreters Theater Club, participate in community outreach performance projects, and apply for the performance studies internship in The Hugh Downs School.

RHETORIC STUDIES AND PUBLIC COMMUNICATIONS (HUGH DOWNS)

Focus/emphasis: The graduate program in rhetoric and public communication at ASU focuses on understanding issues at the social level, including popular culture, social movements, and political communication.

THE ART INSTITUTES INTERNATIONAL–MINNESOTA

15 South Ninth Street, Minneapolis, MN 55402
Phone: 612-332-3361 **E-mail:** kozela@aii.edu
Website: www.aim.artinstitutes.edu

Campus Life
Environment: Metropolis. **Calendar:** Quarter.

Students and Faculty
(All Undergraduate Programs)
Enrollment: 1,594. **Student Body:** 54% female, 46% male, 6% out-of-state. African American 2%, Asian 2%, Caucasian 38%, Hispanic 1%. Student/faculty ratio: 20:1. 56 full-time faculty. 100% faculty teach undergrads.

Costs and Financial Aid
(All Undergraduate Programs)
Annual tuition $17,904. Room $6,864. Average book expense $1,125.

TV/Film/Digital Media Studies Programs
Number of undergraduates in these programs: 304
Number of 2005 graduates from these programs: 42
Degrees conferred to these majors: BS.
Number of full-time faculty in these programs: 10
Number of part-time faculty in these programs: 2
Equipment and facilities: Green screen studio, professional sound studio, software (Shake, Combustion, AfterEffects for compositing; MAYAfor 3-D elements), editing on Mac G5s that run Final Cut Pro, and professional camera and digital recording equipment.

% of graduates currently employed in related field: 65.4 (animation)/100 (visual effects).
Career development services: Alumni networking opportunities, career counseling, internship listings, job fairs, job listings.
Notable alumni: Kao Lee Thao received the HerShow award in 2001.

In Their Own Words
Blockhead Animation and Visual Effects Festivals; students have created a feature-length film, Terror Report; visual effects students assisted in the visual effects for Planetfall; guest lecturers in 2006 have included Shane Black, Cory Edwards, and Miles Teves. Visual effects students have gone to the annual VES conference in Los Angeles, CA, and our instructors are working animation and visual effects professionals.

POPULAR PROGRAMS

GRAPHIC DESIGN
Department chair: Erika Dodge
Focus/emphasis: The Graphic Design Program at The Art Institutes International Minnesota is the first step toward a career in commercial graphics. Initially, students develop an understanding of color, composition, design, typography, and drawing board skills. As they progress through the program, students are trained in creative problem-solving and learn to offer solutions that are effective in the business of graphic design. Emphasis is placed on learning the skills and techniques of computer graphics, electronic imaging, and production. Tools include scanners, digital cameras, and computer-based hardware and software. Advanced training includes the execution of assignments encountered by professionals in the field.

MEDIA ARTS AND ANIMATION

Department chair: Pete Patsiavos

Focus/emphasis: The Bachelor of Science in Media Arts and Animation refines and synthesizes the students' competencies in the field of computer animation. Students apply advanced techniques in drawing, characterization, animation in both 2-D and 3-D computerized environments, and interactive technologies.

PHOTOGRAPHY

Department chair: Shawn Boeckman

Focus/emphasis: In our Photography Program (BFA), you get focused with basic classes in photography, design, and layout. As you gain proficiency, you increase your skill level with coursework in studio and product photography, the "zone" system, color, and digital photographic imaging. You sharpen your camera skills using lenses, filters, and formats. Manipulate light to create drama then play with the color. You scout your locations and then get in the darkroom for some hands-on processing and printing.

VISUAL EFFECTS AND MOTION GRAPHICS

Department chair: Pete Patsiavos

Focus/emphasis: The Visual Effects and Motion Graphics Program at The Art Institutes International Minnesota offers students the opportunity to acquire skills in a new specialization that focuses on communication arts for film, television, and the Web. By combining graphic design, filmmaking, animation, and sound, graduates of this program will be qualified for entry-level positions creating attention-grabbing visuals that inform and entertain. An education in visual effects and motion graphics will teach students how to use digital compositing to create layered and textural landscapes that engage both the mind and the emotions. Students will learn how to build a seamless presentation that is both visually arresting and commercially effective, through the integration of live action footage, programming clips, graphic elements, and sound.

INTERACTIVE MEDIA DESIGN

Department chair: Shawn Boeckman

Focus/emphasis: By working in classrooms and computer labs, students of this program develop a strong foundation in drawing and design, digital image manipulation, interactive design, graphic design, and animation. In later quarters, students become involved in more complex course work, combining animation tools such as personal computers and touch-screen monitors, in addition to software applications to integrate text, sound, images, animation, and video to complete a project. As you may imagine, a dynamic field such as this requires a lot of ongoing practice and high-technical proficiency. This is true, but a strong foundation of core courses lays down the framework. Courses in drawing, design, color theory, and computer applications get you moving in the right direction. From there, you jump into digital imaging and illustration, sound design, information design, and writing for television and media.

ADVERTISING

Department chair: Brian Arnold

Focus/emphasis: Our Bachelor of Science degree in Advertising covers both creative and business professional know-how, beginning with an introduction to design, color theory, typography, and business and marketing practices. You'll also learn about the history of mass communication because you can't change the future if you don't understand the past. You'll build your skills as a communicator through the use of powerful words and visuals. Coupled with your education in business and marketing, you'll understand proper application and distribution of these ideas. Our program goes way beyond simply developing your already innate sense of creativity. You'll understand how to amplify it to its maximum potential.

AUSTIN COLLEGE

900 North Grand Avenue, Suite 6N, Sherman, TX 75090-4400
Phone: 903-813-3000 **E-mail:** admission@austincollege.edu
Website: www.austincollege.edu

Campus Life
Environment: Town. **Calendar:** 4-1-4.

Students and Faculty
(All Undergraduate Programs)
Enrollment: 1,291. **Student Body:** 55% female, 45% male, 9% out-of-state, 1% international (14 countries represented). African American 4%, Asian 12%, Caucasian 74%, Hispanic 9%. Student/faculty ratio: 13:1. 91 full-time faculty, 98% hold PhDs. 100% faculty teach undergrads.

Admissions
(All Undergraduate Programs)
Freshman Admissions Requirements: Test(s) required: SAT or ACT; ACT with Writing component. 44% in top tenth, 75% in top quarter. SAT Math (25/75 percentile): 580/670. SAT Verbal (25/75 percentile): 580/680. Projected SAT Writing (25/75 percentile): 630/710. *Academic units required:* 4 English, 3 math, 3 science (2 science labs), 2 foreign language, 2 social studies, 1 academic elective, 1 fine arts. Early decision application deadline: 12/1. Regular application deadline: 5/1. Regular notification: By 4/1 and on space-available basis thereafter.

Costs and Financial Aid
(All Undergraduate Programs)
Annual tuition $21,426. Room & board $7,741. Required fees $160. Average book expense $800. **Financial Aid Statistics:** % freshmen/undergrads who receive any aid: 97/96. % freshmen/undergrads who receive need-based scholarship or grant aid: 56/54. % freshmen/undergrads who receive need-based self-help aid: 42/42. Priority financial aid filing deadline: 4/1. Financial aid notification on or about: 3/1.

TV/Film/Digital Media Studies Programs
Number of undergraduates
  in these programs: Approx. 12–15 of total communication arts majors.

Number of 2005 graduates from these programs: 6
Degrees conferred to these majors: BA.
Number of full-time faculty in these programs: 2
Equipment and facilities: ENG/EFP; 2-Cam Color Studio; multiple nonlinear postproduction editing labs.

% of graduates who pursue further study within 5 years: approx 30%.
Career development services: Alumni networking opportunities; career counseling; central resource(s) for employers to browse headshots, writing samples, reels; internship listings; job fairs; job listings.
Famous alumni: Robert M. Johnson, CEO of the Robert M. Johnson Group, McLean, VA; producer of recent nationally distributed documentary *Paper Clips*.

In Their Own Words
Regularly secure summer internships for our students, typically in Texas, and part-time employment with local broadcast and cable television outlets in the community. Students have opportunities to enter individual projects in festivals at their initiative.

AZUSA PACIFIC UNIVERSITY

901 East Alosta Avenue, Azusa, CA 91702
Phone: 626-812-3016 **E-mail:** admissions@apu.edu
Website: www.apu.edu

Campus Life
Environment: Town. **Calendar:** Semester.

Students and Faculty
(All Undergraduate Programs)
Enrollment: 4,602. **Student Body:** 64% female, 36% male, 21% out-of-state, 2% international (68 countries represented). African American 3%, Asian 6%, Caucasian 72%, Hispanic 12%. Student/faculty ratio: 11:1. 333 full-time faculty, 70% hold PhDs. 100% faculty teach undergrads.

Admissions
(All Undergraduate Programs)

Freshman Admissions Requirements: Test(s) required: SAT or ACT. Average high school GPA: 3.67. 41% in top tenth, 74% in top quarter. SAT Math (25/75 percentile): 500/610. SAT Verbal (25/75 percentile): 510/610. Projected SAT Writing (25/75 percentile): 570/660. Regular application deadline: 6/1. Regular notification: Rolling; 2 weeks after students apply.

Costs and Financial Aid
(All Undergraduate Programs)

Annual tuition $21,550. Room & board $6,336. Required fees $660. Average book expense $1,242. **Financial Aid Statistics:** % freshmen/undergrads who receive need-based scholarship or grant aid: 62/58. % freshmen/undergrads who receive need-based self-help aid: 55/55. Priority financial aid filing deadline: 3/2. Financial aid filing deadline: 7/1. Financial aid notification on or about: 3/1.

TV/Film/Digital Media Studies Programs

Number of undergraduates in these programs: 110
Number of 2005 graduates from these programs: 16
Degrees conferred to these majors: BA.
Number of full-time faculty in these programs: 15
Number of part-time faculty in these programs: 1
Equipment and facilities: APU shoots on DV (Sony PD150 & Panasonic DVX100a). We have 10 Mac G5 edit bays with Final Cut Studio & Avid DV Pro software. We have a soundstage, studio cameras, control room, 16 mm Arri SRI, and lots of grip/lighting gear.

% of graduates currently employed in related field: 40%
Career development services: Alumni networking opportunities; assessment tests; career counseling; central resource(s) for employers to browse head-shots, writing samples, reels, etc.; graduate school resources; internship listings; job fairs; job listings; mock interviewing; resume writing.

Notable alumni: Erik Rosales (San Francisco reporter).

In Their Own Words

Located close to Hollywood, we have adjuncts from the industry. Our student films are recognized as top award winners in national and regional student film contests (Broadcast Educator's Festival & Paste Festival). Students intern at major studios as well as small boutiques. Alumni are working as associate producers (Entertainment Tonight), script supervisors (upcoming NBC telenova), post-supervisors (Crossing Jordan), and anchors (Eric Rosales, ABC 7 in San Francisco).

POPULAR PROGRAMS

LIBERAL STUDIES
Department chair: Nancy Brashear, PhD
Number of full-time faculty: 21
Number of part-time faculty: 9
Focus/emphasis: The liberal studies degree provides future teacher candidates planning to be elementary school teachers with possible opportunities to teach up to basic ninth-grade level subject(s) and to pass the California Subject Examination for Teachers: Multiple Subject (CSET). Because of the increasing need for college graduates with broad, diverse academic backgrounds, a liberal studies graduate is frequently in demand in business and communication fields, as well as education.

COMMUNICATION STUDIES
Department chair: William James Willis, PhD
Number of full-time faculty: 15
Number of part-time faculty: 1
Focus/emphasis: Students majoring in communication studies will be able to apply the basic concepts of communication theory and research to their life's work. They will be able to incorporate individual and group communication styles that relate to the achievement of their personal and professional goals. The program will also prepare students to utilize appropriate communication

skills for solving problems, making decisions, managing conflict, executing change strategies, and promoting the intellectual, spiritual, and emotional growth of those with whom they live and work. Students will learn to understand the moral and ethical implications of communicators' responsibilities in the construction of a social world.

MUSIC

Department chair: Rodney Cathey, DMA
Number of full-time faculty: 20
Number of part-time faculty: 6
Focus/emphasis: Theory, performance, experience, and practice permeate School of Music students' education. During their tenure, music undergraduates perform in annual recitals, attend 14 on-campus recitals or concerts per year, and participate in a performance-based exam (applied jury) before a panel of faculty. Students also gain practical experience through internships in recording studios, churches, schools, and ensembles. In keeping with its commitment to excellence, the School of Music continually refines and upgrades its programs. This pursuit in the classroom and in performance draws, sharpens, blends, and matures the talents of each student.

ENGLISH

Department chair: David Esselstrom, PhD
Number of full-time faculty: 17
Number of part-time faculty: 1
Focus/emphasis: English is a fundamental liberal art at a university such as Azusa Pacific. Four objectives demonstrate the centrality of English to the curriculum. The program certifies the writing skills of all students to be collegiate level and enhances those skills involving research, personal and creative expression, and expository and argumentative modes. It provides literature and film courses that contribute to the cultural experience of students and enriches their enjoyment of literature as an avenue to truth and social comment as well as self-expression. The program offers a balanced selection of courses in writing, film, and literature for students majoring in English so that their breadth of reading and literary analysis includes the best world literature and the development of critical skills currently practiced by the finest literary critics. The program satisfies professional needs, especially those of prospective teachers.

CINEMA AND BROADCAST ARTS

Department chair: William James Willis, PhD
Number of full-time faculty: 15
Number of part-time faculty: 1
Focus/emphasis: The cinema and broadcast arts major prepares students to integrate a Christian worldview into their study of the history, theory, and philosophy of narrative and communicative media (film, television, radio), guiding and assisting them as they develop, write, produce, and evaluate critical and creative efforts that prepare them for involvement in the entertainment and communication industries and other ministries.

MARKETING

Department chair: Julia Underwood, PhD
Number of full-time faculty: 18
Number of part-time faculty: 1
Focus/emphasis: The marketing major provides students with a strong general business foundation, plus marketing courses that address the primary functional concerns of marketing in industry and commerce. The program stresses academic preparation, skill building, marketing, problem solving, and internship experience. Students will also be familiar with e-commerce and the Web and information technology aspects of marketing, which are important in the marketplace.

BALL STATE UNIVERSITY

Office of Admissions, 2000 University Avenue, Muncie, IN 47306
Phone: 765-285-8300 **E-mail:** askus@bsu.edu
Website: www.bsu.edu

Campus Life
Environment: City. **Calendar:** Semester.

Students and Faculty
(All Undergraduate Programs)
Enrollment: 17,269. **Student Body:** 52% female, 48% male, 7% out-of-state. African American 7%, Caucasian 90%, Hispanic 2%. Student/faculty ratio: 17:1. 910 full-time faculty, 76% hold PhDs. 84% faculty teach undergrads.

Admissions
(All Undergraduate Programs)
Freshman Admissions Requirements: Test(s) required: SAT or ACT; ACT with Writing component. 14% in top tenth, 41% in top quarter. SAT Math (25/75 percentile): 470/570. SAT Verbal (25/75 percentile): 470/570. Projected SAT Writing (25/75 percentile): 540/620. *Academic units required:* 4 English, 3 math, 3 science (2 science labs), 3 social studies. Regular notification: On a rolling basis, with no specific date.**Costs and Financial Aid**
(All Undergraduate Programs)
Annual in-state tuition $6,030. Out-of-state tuition $15,790. Room & board $6,680. Required fees $428. Average book expense $880.
Financial Aid Statistics: % freshmen/undergrads who receive any aid: 58/55. % freshmen/undergrads who receive need-based scholarship or grant aid: 41/36. % freshmen/undergrads who receive need-based self-help aid: 44/44. Priority financial aid filing deadline: 3/10. Financial aid notification on or about: 4/1.

TV/Film/Digital Media Studies Programs
Number of undergraduates in these programs: Approximately 1,200
Number of 2005 graduates from these programs: 140
Degrees conferred to these majors: BA.

Also available at Ball State University: MA.
Number of full-time faculty in these programs: 21
Number of part-time faculty in these programs: 12
Equipment and facilities: 4 multimedia computer labs; 20 audio production suites; 5.1 surround sound editing; 40 Final Cut Pro editing stations; HD Sony 900 cameras in addition to 50 digital cameras; HD editing; field gear; animation software and lab; 5 TV studios, 2 licensed radio stations; 1 licensed (PBS) and 1 campus TV station; new media building under construction to open in 2007.
ATAS interns: 5
Other awards of note: Student Academy Award, 2005; Students Academy Award finalist, 2006; Television Broadcasting School of the Year, 2005, Indiana Association of School Broadcasters; 16 Regional Emmys from Cleveland Chapter 5 Addy Awards, 2006.

% of graduates who pursue further study within 5 years: 11
% of graduates currently employed in related field: 56
Career development services: Alumni networking opportunities, career counseling; central resource(s) for employers to browse headshots, writing samples, reels, etc.; etiquette dinners; internship listings; job fairs; job listings; practice interview clinics; preparation for graduate school.
Famous alumni: David Letterman.
Notable alumni: Sarah Parsons, Nielsen Media Research; Jim Tobolski, Arbitron; Midwest Sales Manager Bill Vincent, CMT new media content; Director Jay Williams, vice president Promotion, Walt Disney Studios; Phil Lengyel, vice president, Indianapolis Motor Speedway; Natalie Murray, vice president, Fox Television Sales; Kacy Andrews, founder, Philippine School of Film; Cebu Doug Jones, actor; Dean Hill, host, HGTV.

In Their Own Words
Ball State University was recently named the #1 wireless university by Intel; the broadcasting school was named in "The Top 8 Broadcasting

Schools" by Leonard Mogel in the book "This Business of Broadcasting" (2004). BSU hosts the Frog Baby Film Festival. The Telecommunications Department has won 16 Emmy Awards, many of which were in professional (not student) categories; this department graduated a Student Academy Award winner in 2005. With an emphasis on immersion and experiential learning, the College of Communication, Information, and Media has built a converged newsroom called NewsLink Indiana, which immerses students in the news, performing live, daily newscasts for TV while also creating content for online, radio, and print news.

POPULAR PROGRAMS

TCOM PRODUCTION
Department chair: Nancy Carlson
Number of full-time faculty: 5
Number of part-time faculty: 5
Focus/emphasis: Film school—in this program students produce digital films and create television programming.

CCIM DIGITAL MEDIA MINOR
Department chair: Roger Lavery
Number of full-time faculty: 1
Number of part-time faculty: 6
Focus/emphasis: Integrated, cross-disciplinary minor combining the digital elements of telecommunications, journalism, communication studies, music, and art.

TCOM FILM MINOR
Department chair: Wes Gehring
Number of full-time faculty: 1
Number of part-time faculty: 3
Focus/emphasis: Analysis and criticism of film.

TCOM NEWS
Department chair: Nancy Carlson
Number of full-time faculty: 5
Number of part-time faculty: 1
Focus/emphasis: Broadcast journalism school, including weather and sports, emphasizing immersive learning and converged media.

TCOM SALES/PROMOTION
Department chair: Nancy Carlson
Number of full-time faculty: 2
Number of part-time faculty: 3
Focus/emphasis: Business side of the industry.

MUSIC ENGINEERING TECHNOLOGY
Department chair: Robert Kvam
Number of full-time faculty: 2
Number of part-time faculty: 1
Focus/emphasis: Music recording and electronic composition.

ELECTRONIC ART AND ANIMATION
Department chair: John Fillwalk
Number of full-time faculty: 2
Number of part-time faculty: 1
Focus/emphasis: Digital art and 3-D animation.

TCOM MULTIMEDIA
Department chair: Nancy Carlson
Number of full-time faculty: 2
Number of part-time faculty: 2
Focus/emphasis: Computer-based content production (DVD, CD, Web design).

TCOM TELEVISION AND FILM STUDIES
Department chair: Nancy Carlson
Number of full-time faculty: 3
Focus/emphasis: A general, nonproduction degree for pre-graduate school studies.

DIGITAL STORYTELLING MA
Department chair: Jim Chesebro
Number of full-time faculty: 1
Number of part-time faculty: 6
Focus/emphasis: A 2-year master's program emphasizing content production.

Students Should Also Know
Independent of individual academic units, the Center for Media Design conducts media research for outside partners and distributes grants to integrated,

cross-displinary project teams. Students, faculty, and businesses work on projects through CMD—the group of project managers has received $40 million of grant money from the Lilly Endowment and other foundations and businesses in the past five years.

BARD COLLEGE

Office of Admissions, Annandale-on-Hudson, NY 12504
Phone: 845-758-7472 **E-mail:** admission@bard.edu

Campus Life
Environment: Rural. **Calendar:** Semester.

Students and Faculty
(All Undergraduate Programs)
Enrollment: 1,555. **Student Body:** 57% female, 43% male, 69% out-of-state, 8% international (46 countries represented). African American 2%, Asian 4%, Caucasian 73%, Hispanic 4%. Student/faculty ratio: 9:1. 130 full-time faculty, 79% hold PhDs. 100% faculty teach undergrads.

Admissions
(All Undergraduate Programs)
Average high school GPA: 3.5. 63% in top tenth, 85% in top quarter. SAT Math (25/75 percentile): 580/690. SAT Verbal (25/75 percentile): 640/720. Projected SAT Writing (25/75 percentile): 680/740. Regular application deadline: 1/15. Regular notification: 4/1.

Costs and Financial Aid
(All Undergraduate Programs)
Annual tuition $34,080. Room & board $9,850. Required fees $743. Average book expense $750. **Financial Aid Statistics:** % freshmen/undergrads who receive any aid: 69/68. % freshmen/undergrads who receive need-based scholarship or grant aid: 53/50. % freshmen/undergrads who receive need-based self-help aid: 38/43. Priority financial aid filing deadline: 2/1. Financial aid filing deadline: 2/15. Financial aid notification on or about: 4/1.

TV/Film/Digital Media Studies Programs
Number of undergraduates in these programs: Approximately 100
Number of 2005 graduates from these programs: 23
Degrees conferred to these majors: BA.
Also available at Bard College: MFA.
Number of full-time faculty in these programs: 7
Number of part-time faculty in these programs: 2
Equipment and facilities: Full range of 16 mm film equipment and digital video equipment, including editing for film (flatbeds) and nonlinear video editing.
Career development services: Alumni networking opportunities, career counseling, internship listings, job listings.

In Their Own Words
Excellent creative program that is well integrated into a wider liberal arts curriculum, supporting narrative, experimental, and documentary forms of film and video. Guests range from Donald Richie (film history) to Jim Jarmusch (narrative film) to Stan Brakhage (experimental).

POPULAR PROGRAMS

DIGITAL MEDIA AND FILM PRODUCTION
Department chair: Peter Hutton, Chair, Film and Electronic Arts
Number of full-time faculty: 1 (Peter Hutton, production)
Number of part-time faculty: 1 (Ed Halter, film history)
Focus/emphasis: Innovation, originality, and creative risk apply to everything we teach.

PRODUCTION, SCRIPTWRITING, FILM HISTORY, FILM/VIDEO
Number of full-time faculty: 5 (Peggy Ahwesh, Leah Gilliam, Jacqueline Goss, production; Jean Ma, John Pruitt, film history)
Number of part-time faculty: 2 (Marie Regan, Joan Tewksbury, scriptwriting)

Students Should Also Know

This is not a film school but a very strong film/video program integrated into the curriculum of an excellent liberal arts college.

BENNINGTON COLLEGE

Office of Admissions and Financial Aid, Bennington, VT 05201
Phone: 800-833-6845 **E-mail:** admissions@bennington.edu
Website: www.bennington.edu

Campus Life

Environment: Town. **Calendar:** 15-week fall and spring terms with a 7-week winter work term.

Students and Faculty
(All Undergraduate Programs)

Enrollment: 571. **Student Body:** 66% female, 34% male, 98% out-of-state, 3% international (8 countries represented). African American 2%, Asian 2%, Caucasian 85%, Hispanic 3%. Student/faculty ratio: 7:1. 66 full-time faculty, 74% hold PhDs. 100% faculty teach undergrads.

Admissions
(All Undergraduate Programs)

Freshman Admissions Requirements: Average high school GPA: 3.63. 30% in top tenth, 74% in top quarter. SAT Math (25/75 percentile): 540/640. SAT Verbal (25/75 percentile): 610/700. Projected SAT Writing (25/75 percentile): 660/720. Early decision application deadline: 11/15. Regular application deadline: 1/3. Regular notification: 4/1.

Costs and Financial Aid
(All Undergraduate Programs)

Financial Aid Statistics: % freshmen/undergrads who receive any aid: 73/78. % freshmen/undergrads who receive need-based scholarship or grant aid: 66/67. % freshmen/undergrads who receive need-based self-help aid: 64/67. Priority financial aid filing deadline: 3/1. Financial aid notification on or about: 3/30.

TV/Film/Digital Media Studies Programs

Degrees conferred to these majors: BA.
Career development services: Alumni mentors, alumni networking opportunities, assistance with resume and cover letter preparation, career counseling, housing listings, internship listings, job listings.

In Their Own Words

The principle of learning by practice underlies every major feature of a Bennington education: the mentor-apprentice model of teaching and learning; the requirement that students direct the course of their own education; the winter Field Work Term (an annual seven-week internship term), which gives students work experience and connects them to the greater community. Bennington is grounded in the conviction that as a college education develops students' professional capacities, it should also prepare them to be deeply thoughtful and actively engaged citizens of the world.

BERKLEE COLLEGE OF MUSIC

1140 Boylston Street, Boston, MA 02215-3693
Phone: 617-747-2222 **E-mail:** admissions@berklee.edu
Website: www.berklee.edu

Campus Life

Calendar: Semester.

Students and Faculty
(All Undergraduate Programs)

Enrollment: 3,799. **Student Body:** 82% out-of-state, 25% international (75 countries represented). African American 4%, Asian 3%, Caucasian 54%, Hispanic 4%. Student/faculty ratio: 12:1. 193 full-time faculty.

Admissions
(All Undergraduate Programs)

Academic units required: 4 English, 1 math, 1 science (1 science lab), 2 social studies, 6 academic electives,

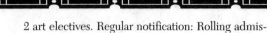

2 art electives. Regular notification: Rolling admissions.

Costs and Financial Aid (All Undergraduate Programs)

Annual tuition $20,350. Room & board $10,900. Required fees $2,640. Average book expense $500. Financial Aid Statistics:. Financial aid notification on or about: 4/3

TV/Film/Digital Media Studies Programs

Also available at Berklee College of Music: BM, professional diploma.

Equipment and facilities: Film scoring equipment, including 6 film-scoring labs, which offer students the opportunity for hands-on study in the areas of film music composition, editing, and sequencing and of computer applications incorporating digital audio. The technical resources available to film scoring majors include two labs equipped with 16 mm 6-plate flatbed Moviola editing machines; a complete 35 mm editing lab containing 2 upright 35 mm Moviolas and an editing bench with rewinds, synchronizers, sound readers, and splicers; two personal computers running Auricle film scoring software; three video-screening rooms with keyboards and video playback, where students develop their film music compositions and where individual student-faculty project screenings and evaluations are held; a dedicated digital audio editing lab featuring Digidesign Pro Tools hardware and software; and a dedicated video/scoring/sequencing lab that provides the opportunity to sequence music cues with video interlock, and the capability for synthesizer playback into live sessions on the department's scoring stage. The Film Scoring Department's self-contained scoring stage and audio-video control room allows students to conduct ensembles in the performance and recording of their music, as well as the postproduction synchronization of their music to video. The scoring stage is equipped with synchronization hardware and a large video projection system for conducting to picture. The control room is a fully equipped digital audio facility for the production of student scoring compositions. The Professional Writing MIDI Lab consists of 12 fully-configured student workstations, and a teaching station. A separate similarly equipped studio for live overdubbing mirrors the real-world, computer-based MIDI studio of the writing entrepreneur who must utilize rapidly developing technologies in a contemporary professional environment. The Music Production and Engineering Department oversees the college's recording studio complex, which consists of 10 lab facilities. The complex includes four 24-track control rooms, two 8-track mix-down control rooms, a digital audio/video postproduction editing suite, two 8-track teaching rooms, and one 24-track teaching room. Three of the control rooms are tied to the Berklee Performance Center for live recording, and all studios are connected via network for sharing of data and hardware equipment. Professional-level equipment from Digidesign, Lexicon, Otari, Solid State Logic, Sony, Studer, Yamaha, Summit Audio, Tubetech, Sonetec, Sonic Solutions, GML, and other manufacturers offers music production and engineering majors the hands-on training they require to prepare for careers in the music industry. Our consoles are SSL4000g+, Otari Concept 1, Sony, and Yamaha 02R.

Career development services: Internship listings, job listings.

Famous alumni: Aimee Mann, Branford Marsalis, Bruce Hornsby, Kevin Eubanks, Alan Silvestri, and Quincy Jones.

POPULAR PROGRAMS

FILM SCORING

Department chair: Donald F. Wilkins

Number of full-time faculty: 8

Focus/emphasis: Students majoring in film scoring will develop a foundation of creative musical skills, including composition, counterpoint, orchestration, conducting, and computer/synthesis skills, and will learn the technical basis and mechanics of preparing synchronous music for use with visual media. The students will also develop an interpretive sensitivity to the dramatic effectiveness of music as suggested or demanded by emotional and dramatic considerations. To demonstrate mastery of these skills and concepts, the students will complete portfolios that each include a finished score of a short film, fully produced and synchronized to videotape format; a similarly produced and synchronized main title theme for a television series; a professional resume and letter of application suitable for the purpose of career placement and advancement; and an audio cassette including a variety of musical examples composed and produced by the students and selected to function as a demo tape to accompany an application portfolio. The students will study acknowledged masterpieces of film scoring and, through this exposure, will develop an aesthetic vision and the ability to recognize and discuss quality work in film scoring. Interpersonal and other situational skills will be developed through the cooperation necessary to realize finished projects: working with performers, studio personnel, and technical assistants, and participating in other students' projects. Film scoring majors will develop sufficient skills and knowledge to function as composers, orchestrators, music supervisors, and music editors or technical production workers in the film and television industry, and will have sufficient knowledge of basic concepts to adapt with success to changing conditions that are typical of the entertainment industry.

MUSIC PRODUCTION AND ENGINEERING

Department chair: Robert J. Jaczko Jr.
Number of full-time faculty: 20
Focus/emphasis: Students majoring in music production and engineering (MP&E) will learn about the creation and production of recordings of music and will learn how to successfully complete recording projects that are typical of those found in contemporary professional recording and production environments. The student's mastery of the discipline will be shown through the completion of recording and production projects of professional quality. Through classroom emphasis on artistic and professional excellence and exposure

to resident and visiting professionals, students will develop informed and critical aesthetic visions. They will learn to define quality using both musical and technical criteria and to apply those criteria to their own work and to that of others. Students will learn to work effectively with others in the wide range of circumstances typically found in the recording and production professions through participation as engineers and producers on various projects, and by interacting effectively with musicians on these projects. The students will acquire sufficient knowledge of the principles and practices of engineering methodology and creative production techniques to permit them to adapt quickly and effectively to the rapidly changing technology and stylistic genres in the discipline over the years. The music production and engineering graduate will be prepared to enter the contemporary music production field as an effective professional in a number of roles. It should be noted that admission to the music production and engineering major is competitive and is based on musicianship, prior academic record, and aptitude. Students apply for acceptance to this major after their first or second semester at Berklee. Applicants indicating preference for this major will be sent detailed information by the Office of Admissions.

BLOOMFIELD COLLEGE

1 Park Place, Bloomfield, NJ 07003
Phone: 973-748-9000 **E-mail:** admission@bloomfield.edu
Website: www.bloomfield.edu

Campus Life
Environment: Town. **Calendar:** Semester.

Students and Faculty
(All Undergraduate Programs)
Enrollment: 2,212. **Student Body:** 69% female, 31% male, 3% out-of-state, 2% international (7 countries represented). African American 52%, Asian 4%, Caucasian 16%, Hispanic 18%. Student/faculty ratio

14:1. 62 full-time faculty, 77% hold PhDs. 100% faculty teach undergrads.

Admissions
(All Undergraduate Programs)
Freshman Admissions Requirements: Test(s) required: SAT or ACT. Average high school GPA: 2.74. 1% in top tenth, 11% in top quarter. SAT Math (25/75 percentile): 390/480. SAT Verbal (25/75 percentile): 380/470. Projected SAT Writing (25/75 percentile): 450/540. Regular application deadline: 7/1: Regular notification: Rolling.

Costs and Financial Aid
(All Undergraduate Programs)
Annual tuition $16,100. Room & board $8,100. Required fees $406. Average book expense $500. **Financial Aid Statistics:** % freshmen/undergrads who receive any aid: 95/82. % freshmen/undergrads who receive need-based scholarship or grant aid: 84/70. % freshmen/undergrads who receive need-based self help aid: 76/70. Priority financial aid filing deadline: 3/15. Financial aid filing deadline: 10/1. Financial aid notification on or about: 3/15.

TV/Film/Digital Media Studies Programs
Number of undergraduates in these programs: 113
Number of 2005 graduates from these programs: 11
Degrees conferred to these majors: BA, BS.
Number of full-time faculty in these programs: 6
Number of part-time faculty in these programs: 13
Equipment and facilities: Music synthesizers, musical recording equipment, recording studio, video cameras, still cameras, lighting, microphones, green screen studio.
Career development services: Alumni networking opportunities, career counseling, internship listings, job fairs, job listings, career assessments.

In Their Own Words
1) Totally integrated interdisciplinary program 2) International student exchanges 3) Mandatory internships and senior capstone projects 4) Project-oriented classes 5) State-of-the-art facilities.

POPULAR PROGRAMS

ANIMATION
Department chair: Lynn Oddo
Number of full-time faculty: 1
Number of part-time faculty: 1
Focus/emphasis: A degree in animation will give you marketable skills in 3-D modeling, web design, special effects, commercial advertising, game development, architecture, animated shorts, and feature-length films. You will also develop skills in creative writing, problem solving, and critical thinking while you master the technology of computer-generated art.

GRAPHICS—PRINT AND DIGITAL MEDIA
Department chair: Nancy Bacci
Number of full-time faculty: 1
Number of part-time faculty: 1
Focus/emphasis: Get hands-on experience with the latest digital hardware and software which will help you become a graphic artist in the fields of advertising, magazine and book publishing, merchandising, web design, or printing and packaging. You will graduate with a portfolio that showcases you as a well-rounded professional.

MUSIC TECHNOLOGY—RECORD PRODUCTION AND MUSIC SUPERVISION
Department chair: Chris White
Number of full-time faculty: 1
Number of part-time faculty: 1
Focus/emphasis: Our goal is to make you a better musician by providing you with a solid understanding of music theory and exposing you to the most current hardware and software developments in music technology. The music major functions in an atmosphere that encourages musical exploration without limits. The new track has two kinds of students in mind: The student who wants to be an audio engineer/sound designer or

the student who wants to be a record producer/artist developer.

DIGITAL VIDEO

Department chair: Hank Smith
Number of full-time faculty: 1
Number of part-time faculty: 2
Focus/emphasis: Join the digital video revolution and be ready for a career as a producer or an independent artist in web video, commercials, special effects, news and documentaries, or television studio; or as a producer or independent artist. There are many career opportunities available to professionals in this field, and new positions continue to be developed in this area. When you graduate with a degree in digital video, you'll be ready for the work that's ready for you.

GAME DEVELOPMENT—DESIGN AND PROGRAMMING

Department chair: John Towsen
Number of full-time faculty: 1
Number of part-time faculty: 2
Focus/emphasis: Game Development is the newest concentration in CAT. It is a booming industry, with revenues considerably higher than the film business. CAT'S years of experience teaching multimedia, video, animation, audio, and graphics puts us in a strong position to launch a major in this technologically demanding field. We offer a 13-course program in two interrelated tracks: Game Design and Game Programming. One appeals most to artists, the other to programmers. These tracks enable you to pursue careers in game programming; game design; level design; animation; and special effects production.

INTERACTION MULTIMEDIA AND THE WORLD WIDE WEB

Department chair: John Towsen
Number of full-time faculty: 1
Number of part-time faculty: 4
Focus/emphasis: Become a master of the virtual universe. You'll study audio, animation, interactive design and programming, and 2-D and 3-D modeling. You'll be ready for work in Web design, game development, interactive television, telecommunications, and more.

BOSTON COLLEGE

140 Commonwealth Avenue, Devlin Hall 208
Chestnut Hill, MA 02467-3809
Phone: 617-552-3100 **E-mail:** ugadmis@bc.edu

Campus Life

Environment: City. **Calendar:** Semester.

Students and Faculty (All Undergraduate Programs)

Enrollment: 9,019. **Student Body:** 52% female, 48% male, 71% out-of-state, 2% international (97 countries represented). African American 6%, Asian 9%, Caucasian 73%, Hispanic 8%. Student/faculty ratio: 13:1. 662 full-time faculty, 98% hold PhDs. 100% faculty teach undergrads.

Admissions (All Undergraduate Programs)

Freshman Admissions Requirements: Test(s) required: SAT and SAT Subject Tests or ACT; ACT with Writing component. 75% in top tenth, 95% in top quarter. SAT Math (25/75 percentile): 640/720. SAT Verbal (25/75 percentile): 610/700. Projected SAT Writing (25/75 percentile): 660/720. Regular application deadline: 1/1. Regular notification: 4/15.

Costs and Financial Aid (All Undergraduate Programs)

Annual tuition $30,950. Room & board $10,845. Required fees $832. Average book expense $650. **Financial Aid Statistics:** % freshmen/undergrads who receive any aid: 70/70. % freshmen/undergrads who receive need-based scholarship or grant aid: 39/36. % freshmen/undergrads who receive need-based self-help aid: 41/39. Priority financial aid filing deadline: 2/1. Financial aid notification on or about: 4/15.

TV/Film/Digital Media Studies Programs

Number of undergraduates in these programs: 57 film majors; 62 film minors.
Number of 2005 graduates from these programs: 11 film majors; 29 film minors.
Degrees conferred to these majors: BA.
Number of full-time faculty in these programs: 4

Number of part-time faculty in these programs: 8

Equipment and facilities: 3 media classrooms; 1 demonstration classroom with 25 seats; 5 editing rooms; 16 mm film camera set-up; 8 Super-8 cameras and accessories; 8 Canon GL 1/2 cameras; 2 Sony 100 DVX cameras, lights, etc.; 15 Final Cut Pro stations; 1 Adrenaline Editing Station; 4 Avid Express stations.

Other awards of note: Faculty films: 3 Regional Emmy nominations.

% of graduates who pursue further study within 5 years: 8–10

% of graduates currently employed in related field: 10

Career development services: Alumni networking opportunities, career counseling, internship listings, job fairs, job listings.

Notable alumni: Thomas Curran, director of *Adrift*; Thomas McCarthy, director of *The Station Agent*; Brian Sloane, director/producer Xanadu Productions; John J. Michalczyk, producer/director *Nazi Medicine* (PBS).

In Their Own Words

Internship possibilities: Museum, production houses, production companies, and faculty films shown on PBS and national and international festivals. Guest lecturers: Stan Brakage, Fred Wiseman.

POPULAR PROGRAMS

FILM MAJOR

Department chair: Co-directors: John J. Michalczyk and Richard A. Blake

Number of full-time faculty: 4

Number of part-time faculty: 8

Focus/emphasis: Twelve courses that focus on the introduction to film art, production, American film history, European film history, and independent projects (scripts, thesis, films).

FILM MINOR

Department chair: Co-directors: John J. Michalczyk and Richard A. Blake

Number of full-time faculty: 4

Number of part-time faculty: 8

Focus/emphasis: Six courses covering an introduction to film art, film history, and filmmaking, and electives in photo, film, video production and history, criticism, and film scriptwriting.

Students Should Also Know

The history, criticism, and production courses are based in a larger liberal arts curriculum that provides depth to the content of the film work.

BOSTON UNIVERSITY

121 Bay State Road, Boston, MA 02215
Phone: 617-353-2300 **E-mail:** admissions@bu.edu
Website: www.bu.edu

Campus Life

Environment: Metropolis. **Calendar:** Semester.

Students and Faculty
(All Undergraduate Programs)

Enrollment: 16,538. **Student Body:** 59% female, 41% male, 81% out-of-state, 6% international (104 countries represented). African American 3%, Asian 13%, Caucasian 57%, Hispanic 6%. Student/faculty ratio: 12:1. 1,454 full-time faculty, 85% hold PhDs. 75% faculty teach undergrads.

Admissions
(All Undergraduate Programs)

Freshman Admissions Requirements: Test(s) required: SAT and SAT Subject Tests or ACT; ACT with Writing component. Average high school GPA: 3.49. 58% in top tenth, 87% in top quarter. SAT Math (25/75 percentile): 600/690. SAT Verbal (25/75 percentile): 580/680. Projected SAT Writing (25/75 percentile): 630/710. *Academic units required:* 4 English, 3 math, 3 science (3 science labs), 2 foreign language, 3 social studies. Early decision application deadline: 11/1. Regular application deadline: 1/1. Regular notification: Late-March through mid-April.

Costs and Financial Aid
(All Undergraduate Programs)

Annual tuition $31,530. Room & board $10,080. Required fees $436. Average book expense $754.
Financial Aid Statistics: % freshmen/undergrads who receive any aid: 70/67. % freshmen/undergrads who receive need-based scholarship or grant aid: 47/42. % freshmen/undergrads who receive need-based self-help aid: 42/40. Financial aid filing deadline: 2/15. Financial aid notification on or about: 3/27.

TV/Film/Digital Media Studies Programs

Degrees conferred to these majors: BA, BS.
Also available at Boston University: MFA, MS.
Equipment and facilities: The Film Program is equipped with state-of-the-art production and post-production facilities, including 10 Arriflex SR cameras, Nagras, DATdecks, lighting and grip equipment, a sound studio, amultitrack mixing facility, 12 Steenbeck (flatbed) editing and 12 nonlinear digital editing workstations. The department's new Digital Media Lab is equipped with the latest Avid editing software, as well as Photoshop, Illustrator, and After Effects. This lab can accommodate material shot both at 24 frames per second (the standard for film and most high-definition video projects) and 30 frames per second (the standard for projects originating on conventional video). For research, students may use the Krasker Library, a collection of thousands of film and video titles, many of which are very rare. Mugar Library, the university's main library, also has extensive holdings of books, periodicals, and personal papers related to film, as well as screening stations for viewing videos held on reserve. Finally, the department's screening rooms include facilities for projection of 35 mm, 16 mm, DVD, laser disk, and various video formats. In the television area, we have two modern and recently upgraded broadcast studios: one news-specific studio with a news desk and TelePrompTers and one larger general production studio. Both studios include Mole-Richardson lighting fixtures, Sony 3-chip studio cameras, Echolab switching and distribution equipment, and Panasonic decks. We have a total of 18 postproduction and editing suites that include nine linear stations and nine digital stations. The digital stations use Apple G5 CPUs, running a mix of Avid Xpress Pro, Final Cut Pro 4, Adobe AfterEffects, and Adobe Photoshop. Each digital suite has a DVCAM/DVSP firewire deck for tape output as well as DVD recorders with Toast software for optical masters. Two graphic stations with industry-standard image manipulation tools and still-store and DV output complement the facility. Our location equipment includes 16 Sony small-form ENG cameras and 18 Sony P-150 DV cameras. Lowell field-lighting kits and Audio-Technica/Sennheiser audio gear are the standard field camera accompaniment. Our audio lab consists of four Pro Tools stations, each with the capability to output to either CD or MD. The Broadcast Journalism Program is equipped with two modern broadcast studios where student-anchors present newscasts, news magazines, and creative television programs. One studio is set up for news production, complete with digital editing suites. Participation in BUTV, our in-house television production company, is encouraged. BUTV produces a wide range of television shows that air on local cable networks. Students learn how to operate state-of-the-art studio cameras, TelePrompTers, audio boards, switchers, and playback decks. BU undergraduates and graduate students direct productions from two separate control booths and write and produce scripts using a "paperless" computerized newsroom. Students learn digital and linear video editing in 18 postproduction editing suites and two graphic stations containing the editing and graphic software used in the market place. BU students also learn how to produce news packages, documentaries, and programming using field equipment including 16 Sony ENG cameras and 18 digital cameras as well as lighting kits, and audio gear standard in field production. Most cameras are less than two years old.
Career development services: Career counseling, internship listings, job listings.
Notable alumni: Michael Williams, COM 1979, co-founder and principal, SCOUT Productions; Kevin Merida, COM 1979, associate editor, *The Washington Post.*

In Their Own Words

Boston University Cinematheque features live meetings with actors, filmmakers, and critics, and screenings of important, innovative films and videos sponsored by the Film and Television Department, BU College of Communication. The BU Cinematheque has been ongoing for a decade. Among the many guests who have been at BU are Paul Schrader, Thelma Schoonmaker, Gordon Willis, Tsai-Ming Ling, Sarah Polley, Betty Comden and Adolph Green, Tom Noonan, Mark Rappaport, Budd Schulberg, Todd Solondz, Dusan Makavejev, Whit Stillman, James Toback, Tom Tykwer, Frederick Wiseman, Ross McElwee. Just as important, the Cinematheque has been a showcase for young, upcoming filmmakers whose work is innovative and visionary, including BU graduates. BU also hosts The Redstone Film Festival. Attendees enjoy a variety of powerful and funny short films, written and directed by graduate and undergraduate filmmakers from the Department of Film and Television. Sponsored by Sumner Redstone, Chairman of Viacom, this is Boston University's annual unveiling of our top student films of the year. BU College of Communication students have held internships at the following organizations: HBO, MTV, NBC, ABC, CBS, Discovery, Nickelodeon, Turner Networks, Miramax, SCOUT Productions, WHDH-TV, WCVB-TV WBZ-TV, WGBH-TV, DiNovi Pictures, The Donners Company, Revolution Studios, Walt Disney Company, Boston Casting Company.

POPULAR PROGRAMS

BROADCAST JOURNALISM

Department chair: Robert Zelnick
Number of full-time faculty: 28
Focus/emphasis: The department provides all undergraduates with the opportunity to study journalism in its broadest aspects: its history and literature; its laws, regulations, and ethics; its traditional role as a motivator and critic of government in a dynamic, democratic society; and its total effect as a social and economic institution. In addition, students acquire professional skills training, including reporting, feature and editorial writing, editing, producing, news selection, photography, and media management. Boston, as the state capital and a recognized cultural, financial, media, educational, and scientific center, provides special opportunities for the training of journalists. The Department of Journalism offers programs with specializations in newspaper reporting and editing, magazine writing, photojournalism, multimedia and interactive publishing, and television and radio journalism. At the end of the sophomore year, in consultation with an advisor, journalism majors select liberal arts concentrations in one of three areas: social sciences, humanities, or sciences. Students take five courses in the selected area, three of which must be in the same department. For example, a student with an interest in reporting urban affairs may choose a specialization in social science, and during junior and senior year, may take courses in political science, history, and economics. The Broadcast Journalism sequence emphasizes original reporting in television and radio. The program is designed for students who seek careers in writing, researching, and production of television and radio news and documentary programming. Students are encouraged to participate in broadcast journalism internships at local radio or television stations during the summer months. Students are directed, wherever possible, to take on assignments for the university radio station, WBUR-FM; the campus radio station, WTBU; and Neighborhood Network News, Boston's cable television news program.

FILM

Department chair: Charles Merzbacher
Number of full-time faculty: 19
Focus/emphasis: The Film Program provides a comprehensive examination of film while ensuring that students receive a strong liberal arts education. The program focuses on three critical

areas: film studies, screenwriting, and film production. Students study the works of master filmmakers to learn from those who came before them. At the same time, students practice the art of storytelling through their screenwriting courses and apply what they have learned in their production courses. The faculty's goal is to enable each student to graduate with a short film capable of winning student film festivals, as well as a feature-length screenplay. The department is divided into two programs: film and television. Film and television have developed as individual media with their own histories of production techniques, artistic disciplines, content, and business operations. However, there is much sharing and mutual influence between these media. New technologies and increased concentration of media ownership already blur many of the traditional distinctions between media, and many career opportunities span both film and television. The Department of Film and Television responds to this situation by providing flexible programs of study. Although students are required to select an area of concentration in the second semester of the sophomore year—either the film or the television program—they also have options for tailoring a major that fits their interests and career goals. Students may vary the number of courses in hands-on production, critical studies, and management-related courses. The College of Communication provides facilities and equipment for instruction in studio and field production in both video and film. Students are responsible for videotape, film, and film processing expenses. Students are encouraged to participate in the extracurricular activities of the student-operated radio station, WTBU; the student television organization, BUTV; Neighborhood Network News; the student-run video organization, Television Production Hothouse; and the student chapters of various professional organizations.

TELEVISION

Department chair: Charles Merzbacher
Number of full-time faculty: 19
Focus/emphasis: The Television Program recognizes that the creative and intellectual center of all television production is to be found in the producer. The producer is not simply responsible for the budgeting and costing of a project. Often, the producer conceives, writes, and sometimes even directs it. The television producer has a creative role unique in the media, and it is around this role that the television course of study has been shaped. Students in the Television Program are encouraged to include courses from the Film Program, as well as courses from other departments of the college and of the university at large.

BOWLING GREEN STATE UNIVERSITY

110 McFall Center, Bowling Green, OH 43403
Phone: 419-372-2478 **E-mail:** admissions@bgnet.bgsu.edu
Website: www.bgsu.edu

Campus Life
Environment: Rural. **Calendar:** Semester.

Students and Faculty
(All Undergraduate Programs)
Enrollment: 15,846. **Student Body:** 55% female, 45% male, 8% out-of-state, 1% international. African American 8%, Caucasian 84%, Hispanic 3%. Student/faculty ratio 19:1. 851 full-time faculty, 77% hold PhDs. 88% faculty teach undergrads.

Admissions
(All Undergraduate Programs)
Freshman Admissions Requirements: Test(s) required: SAT and SAT Subject Tests or ACT. Average high school GPA: 3.23. 14% in top tenth, SAT Math (25/75 percentile): 460/570. SAT Verbal (25/75 percentile): 460/570. Projected SAT Writing (25/75 percentile): 530/620. *Academic units required:* 4 English, 3 math, 3 science (2 science lab), 2 foreign language, 3 social studies, 1 visual/performing arts. Regular application deadline: 7/15. Regular notification: rolling.

Costs and Financial Aid
(All Undergraduate Programs)

Annual in-state tuition $9,060. Out-of-state tuition $16,368.

Financial Aid Statistics: % freshmen/undergrads who receive need-based scholarship or grant aid: 27/26. % freshmen/undergrads who receive need-based self help aid: 47/48. Financial aid notification on or about: 4/15.

TV/Film/Digital Media Studies Programs

Degrees conferred to these majors: BA.

Also available at Bowling Green State University: MA.

Number of full-time faculty in these programs: 17

Number of part-time faculty in these programs: 7

Equipment and facilities: The program benefits from BGSU's long-standing leadership in the areas of performance studies, popular culture, and international cinemas. Its commitment to excellence is demonstrated by its significant collection of research materials in the Jerome Library and by its well-established, individually-curated International Film Series held each semester in the beautiful Gish Theater. The Gish Film Theater and Gallery, named to commemorate the achievements of Ohio natives Dorothy and Lillian Gish in the history of American film, was dedicated at Bowling Green State University on June 11, 1976. The naming of the theater coincided with the establishment of the film program. The Gish scholarship is awarded annually to an outstanding student in film. Students can participate in numerous film-related opportunities. Approximately five public film showings occur on campus weekly and students serve on the committees that select these films. Students also contribute film articles and reviews to the campus daily newspaper or assist in the preparation of *The Projector*.

In Their Own Words

The Department of Theater and Film Grant-In-Aid program provides financial support for gifted students participating in the areas of theater performance, Technical Theater, Forensics, and Film. Grant-in-Aid is a financial award given to an individual on a competitive basis in exchange for significant supervised participation in the department's production program. The amount of financial awards varies from year to year. Information and application forms are available online as well as in the Department Office, 338 South Hall. Applications must be completed and returned to the office in early February. Eva Marie Saint Scholarship: This is for entering first-year students only. This award was established to attract students to Bowling Green State University who possess exceptional talent in theater. The award is based upon the annual interest generated from the endowment and is governed by the following criteria: 1. The award shall be used to recruit outstanding students in theater. The award shall be made annually to an incoming new first-year student. 2. The award shall be nonrenewable and limited to one recipient per year. 3. Financial need may be a consideration, but the primary focus must be based on theatrical talent. 4. The selection shall be made by the Scholarship/Grant-in-aid committee in the Department of Theater and Film. 5. The award shall be coordinated with the Director of Student Financial Aid. 6. The administrator of the fund shall be the Chair of the Department of Theater and Film. 7. You must enroll in THFM 146 each semester. Application forms are available from the Department Office, 338 South Hall. Deadline for application and recommendations is in early February.

POPULAR PROGRAMS

FILM

Focus/emphasis: The film major gives students a foundation in film history, aesthetics, production, and methods of analysis that illuminate global and cultural perspectives. Students who select the specialization in film production gain experience in all aspects of production and are prepared to begin careers as writers, producers, and directors. BGSU graduates have been accepted into prestigious MFA film programs and highly competitive professional programs such as those sponsored by the Director's Guild of America. Students who choose the specialization in film studies develop expertise in electronic publishing and in analyzing the film industry and individual films. They are prepared to begin careers in journalism, festival organization, film acquisition and distribution, and, with professional training, entertainment law. Film studies students have been accepted into graduate film studies programs and have launched successful electronic publications on film, media, and culture. Both lower and upper division courses in film are designed to develop skills in critical thinking and media literacy, to increase understanding of cultural histories, and to sharpen awareness of the complex interactions between film practice and its socioeconomic contexts. As a consequence, the film major serves as a valuable program for students interested in graduate work in film or cultural studies as well as for students who want to work "above the line" in film and media production as writers, producers, and directors.

Students Should Also Know

Film majors are required to have a minor. Students meet with advisors in the Department of Theater and Film to select a minor. Minors useful for film majors include: Africana Studies, American Culture Studies, Art (BA program), Art History, Canadian Studies, Computer Science, Creative Writing, Electronic and Computer Technology, English, Entrepreneurship, Ethnic Studies, General Studies in Business, History, International Business, Interpersonal Communication, Journalism, Latino/Latina Studies, Marketing, Music, Political Science, Popular Culture, Telecommunications, Theater, Women's Studies, or any of the minors in foreign languages.

BRADLEY UNIVERSITY

1501 West Bradley Avenue, Peoria, IL 61625
Phone: 309-677-1000 **E-mail:** admissions@bradley.edu
Website: www.bradley.edu

Campus Life
Environment: City. **Calendar:** Semester.

Students and Faculty
(All Undergraduate Programs)
Enrollment: 5,343. **Student Body:** 55% female, 45% male, 11% out-of-state, 1% international (37 countries represented). African American 6%, Asian 3%, Caucasian 85%, Hispanic 2%. Student/faculty ratio: 14:1. 326 full-time faculty, 85% hold PhDs. 100% faculty teach undergrads.

Admissions
(All Undergraduate Programs)
Freshman Admissions Requirements: Test(s) required: SAT or ACT. 28% in top tenth, 59% in top quarter. SAT Math (25/75 percentile): 520/640. SAT Verbal (25/75 percentile): 500/630. Projected SAT Writing (25/75 percentile): 560/670. *Academic units required:* 4 English, 3 math, 2 science (2 science labs), 2 social studies. Regular application deadline: Rolling. Regular notification: Rolling.

Costs and Financial Aid
(All Undergraduate Programs)
Annual tuition $18,500. Room & board $6,450. Required fees $130. Average book expense $500. **Financial Aid Statistics:** % freshmen/undergrads who receive any aid: 97/93. % freshmen/undergrads who receive need-based scholarship or grant aid: 65/68. % freshmen/undergrads who receive need-based self-help aid: 51/55. Priority financial aid filing deadline: 3/1.

TV/Film/Digital Media Studies Programs
Number of undergraduates in these programs: 203
Number of 2005 graduates from these programs: 48
Degrees conferred to these majors: BA, BS.

Number of full-time faculty in these programs: 8

Number of part-time faculty in these programs: 7

Equipment and facilities: Bradley's Caterpillar Global Communications Center boasts seven high-end computer labs; fully digital audio and video Avid editing bays; all mediated classrooms with full Internet2 videoconferencing; a state-of-the-art videoconference center; a complete broadcast capable television studio with control rooms; a scene shop, a green room, and a dressing room (for the exclusive use of undergraduate majors); a new digital media production/performance studio; and two high-definition production systems. Students have 24/7 access to this building and its technology. Specific technology includes a 3-camera, 60 x 40 television studio complete with scene shop, lighting grid, di mmer board, TelePrompTer system, server-based playback and record, and all support equipment, as well as a full-time engineer to maintain the entire facility.

ATAS College TV Awards recipients: 1

ATAS Faculty Seminar participants: 1

Other awards of note: Dr. Robert Jacobs, Professor of Electronic Media (Video Production) has received numerous honors as a writer, producer, director, editor, and on-air talent. These award-winning productions were created in collaboration with Dr. Jacob's advanced undergraduate television production students at Bradley University: First place, Mixed Division, BEA International Video and Film Festival, January 2002, for *Bobbye Sings the Blues*, a one-hour documentary on blues singer Bobbye King; vice-president WT-TV (PBS), Peoria, Illinois, September 2001; *Postcards from Home*, weekly three-minute feature series for WEEK-TV, Channel 25, Peoria, IL, NBC Affiliate and number one station in market; seven nominations for regional Emmy Awards in category of Outstanding Editing, News, 1999–2005, Chicago/Midwest Chapter of the National Academy of Television Arts and Sciences; Emmy Award, 1999, for Outstanding Editing, National Academy of Television Arts and Sciences, Chicago/Midwest Chapter; first place and Best in

Festival, News Division, BEA International Video and Film Festival, April, 2003; first place, News Division, BEA International Video and Film Festival, 1997, 1998, 1999, 2001, and 2002; Bronze Telly Award, 2001; Crystal Award of Excellence, The Communicator Awards, 1996, 1998, 1999, 2000, 2001; first place, Mixed Division, Juried Faculty Production Competition, BEA, 1998, for *Peoria 911*, a half-hour program featuring the Peoria Emergency Communications System; Diploma of Excellence, Videofuego, International Video Competition, Badajos, Spain, 1998, for A New Medium: *The Verdehr Trio in Concert*, hosted by Peter Schickele, a 30-minute musical special, 1995; first place winner and Best in Show, BEA Juried Faculty Production Competition, 1996; Nominated for Emmy Awards by Chicago/Midwest Chapter of National Academy of Television Arts and Sciences in two categories: Outstanding Director^Edited and Outstanding Entertainment Program; judged by New York Chapter of NATAS. Dr. Paul Gullifor, professor of broadcasting, received the International Radio and Television Society Stephen H. Coltrin Communication Professor of the Year Award in 2002.

% of graduates currently employed in related field: 91

Career development services: Alumni networking opportunities; career counseling; central resource(s) for employers to browse headshots, writing samples, reels; internship listings; job fairs; job listings. Bradley conducts an annual videoconference with our entertainment industry alumni from Chicago and Los Angeles who provide career advice to our graduating seniors.

Famous alumni: Include David C. Horowitz, Emmy Award-winning broadcast journalist and consumer advocate through Fight Back radio, television, and online programs; Charley Steiner, sports anchor, color commentator, and voice of the New York Yankees and the Los Angeles Dodgers; Ralph Lawler, sports anchor, color commentator and voice of the Los Angeles Clippers; Neil Flynn, actor, star of NBC sitcom *Scrubs*, and co-star of the feature film *Mean Girls*; Dr. Lillian Glass, renowned entertainment and media communication expert; Jack Brickhouse, legendary Radio Hall of Fame Sportscaster; Chicago Dick Kay, award-winning reporter/commentator for NBC 5 in Chicago.

Notable alumni: Lisa Helfrich Jackson, Emmy Award-winning producer and co-executive producer of *Ellen*, *Everybody Loves Raymond*, and *The New Adventures of Old Christine*; Jonathan Buss, Emmy Award-winning writer, director, and producer of many television and film specials including *Everybody Loves Raymond*, *Rush Hour 2*, *Pirates of the Carribean*, *The Hulk*, *The Pink Panther*, and *Black Hawk Down*, among many others; Jim Tanker, prominent Emmy Award-winning Hollywood director of more than 100 major television national broadcasts including series television (*Will and Grace*, *West Wing*, *American Idol*, *Drew Carey*, *Whoopi on Broadway*), major award shows and events (Primetime Emmy Awards, Academy Awards, Kennedy Center Honors, People's Choice Awards, the Golden Globes, Grammy Awards, Daytime Emmy Awards, 2004 Democratic Convention), sports (Salt Lake City Winter Olympics Opening and Closing Ceremonies; XVII Winter Olympic Games; XXV, XXVI, and XXVII Summer Olympic Games), game shows, and many others; Tami Lane, Academy Award nominee for special effects makeup for the *Lord of the Rings* and Academy Award winner for *The Chronicles of Narnia: The Lion, the Witch, and the Wardrobe*, special effects makeup artist, KNB FX, Hollywood, WETA Digital Imaging Studio; Cheryl Corley, award-winning Chicago bureau reporter, National Public Radio.

In Their Own Words

Every year, Bradley offers four expedition courses in broadcasting, programming, management and marketing, sports communication, and production in film, television, and radio. The students travel with their professors on-site to Los Angeles and New York City for 2-week January and May interim courses in which they meet directly with executives, production artists, talent, agents, writers, and managers. Students in electronic media and multimedia have completed professional internships with leading media and entertainment production companies including Atlantic Video, Washington, DC; HBO, Los Angeles and New York; Warner Brothers, Los Angeles; CBS, Los Angeles and New York; and Disney, Los Angeles and Orlando, to name a few. The Electronic Media Program sponsors a wholly student-produced award-winning weekly 30-minute news magazine. To date, Bradley has developed more than 30 collaborations with more than 25 institutions. Among these projects are the following, with emphases on broadcasting, television, film, performance, and digital media, including screenwriting with California State University at Los Angeles: distributed theater production of Sophocles' Antigone with the University of Central Florida; distributed theater production of Samuel Beckett's Catastrophe with the University of Waterloo in Ontario, Canada. Advanced students in multimedia complete digital media design professional commissions. Assistant Professor Carlos Avila and 11 multimedia students competed in the National Film Challenge where they had 48 hours to make an 8-minute film using a specified prop, line, and character.

POPULAR PROGRAMS

ELECTRONIC MEDIA (2 DIFFERENT TRACKS)
Department chair: Ali Zohoori
Number of full-time faculty: 4
Number of part-time faculty: 3
Focus/emphasis: The program integrates the academic study of communication with a commitment to pre-professional education in electronic media. In addition to required liberal arts courses, students complete a 9-credit hour foundational communication curriculum as well as a 30-credit hour concentrated track of electronic media courses in production or operations & strategies. Students gain experience in radio and television production, directing, media sales and administration, research, and broadcast production through

course instruction and career-related "hands-on" projects. Through the use of Internet2, students participate in classes with leading entertainment industry professionals in Hollywood and New York City. The Slane College Hollywood Center Network offers internships, expedition courses, and job opportunities with our large number of Bradley alumnae.

MULTIMEDIA

Department chair: James Ferolo
Number of full-time faculty: 4
Number of part-time faculty: 4
Focus/emphasis: Multimedia is the use of multiple media to make CD-ROMS, DVDs, and Internet sites. Multimedia combines text, audio, video, illustration, photography, and animation with concepts and creativity to convert your ideas into virtual reality. Multimedia is nonlinear—our work escapes the limits of time order and spatial constraints and lets us create digital projects that have cutting-edge flexibility and design. Our focus is on creativity and conceptual problem solving, creating within a framework of new media theory. Multimedia students plan projects and do research. They work in the production environment and with the aesthetic conventions of each media type. We want to nurture your inherent media interest, combining it with the substance and aesthetic awareness required to make your art and communication design most effective. We provide a real-world perspective. Our students experience the entire industry process—from client proposals and project management through authoring and final production. We not only teach you aesthetic conventions, we teach you why the conventions hold true. Multimedia is constantly and rapidly changing. We equip our students for the lifelong pursuit of creative problem solving in new media communication, many areas of which are yet to be imagined.

Students Should Also Know

Outside of the classroom, Bradley electronic media students have a wealth of co-curricular and pre-professional learning experiences to choose from.

WRBU, The Edge, is Bradley's student-run radio station. Students are invited to participate in any of the various aspects that go along with running the station. *Midstate Magazine* is Bradley's student-produced television program. The half-hour show is produced weekly and highlights the news, arts, and special events happening in the Peoria community. *Midstate Magazine* gives students the opportunity to gain real-world production experience in a professional setting. Other leadership opportunities include American Advertising Federation, Bradley Media Society, Bradley Scout, Bradley Speech Team, Public Relations Student Society of America, Society of Professional Journalists, and the Peoria Ad Club. We encourage multimedia students to gain as much experience as possible with internships and commissioned work in our dynamic local media base. Our program's classroom experiences are modeled after real-world production environments that complete real-world projects for real-world clients. Students can work on faculty-directed projects, build portfolios, and sometimes even be paid by outside clients for the work they do.

BRIAR CLIFF UNIVERSITY

Admissions Office, PO Box 2100, Sioux City, IA 51104-0100
Phone: 712-279-5200 **E-mail:** admissions@briarcliff.edu
Website: www.briarcliff.edu

Campus Life
Environment: City. **Calendar:** Trimester.

Students and Faculty
(All Undergraduate Programs)
Enrollment: 1,081. **Student Body:** 61% female, 39% male, 33% out-of-state. African American 2%, Asian 2%, Caucasian 91%, Hispanic 4%. Student/faculty ratio: 13:1. 56 full-time faculty, 57% hold PhDs. 100% faculty teach undergrads.

Admissions
(All Undergraduate Programs)
Freshman Admissions Requirements: Test(s) required: SAT or ACT; SAT Subject Tests. Average

high school GPA: 3.23. 15% in top tenth, 36% in top quarter. SAT Math (25/75 percentile): 387/650. SAT Verbal (25/75 percentile): 420/560. Projected SAT Writing (25/75 percentile): 490/620. Regular notification: Must reply by 5/1 or within two weeks if notified.

Costs and Financial Aid (All Undergraduate Programs)

Annual tuition $16,560. Room & board $5,433. Required fees $465. Average book expense $825. **Financial Aid Statistics:** % freshmen/undergrads who receive any aid: 100/98. % freshmen/undergrads who receive need-based scholarship or grant aid: 74/81. % freshmen/undergrads who receive need-based self-help aid: 74/81. Priority financial aid filing deadline: 3/15.

TV/Film/Digital Media Studies Programs

Number of undergraduates in these programs: 45

Number of 2005 graduates from these programs: 7

Degrees conferred to these majors: BA.

Number of full-time faculty in these programs: 3

Number of part-time faculty in these programs: 2

Equipment and facilities: The university's radio station reaches a potential audience of 100,000 listeners/viewers in Iowa and South Dakota. A color video camera places a live, in-studio image over cable TV. The radio's music library houses approximately 4,000 CDs for access by its student announcers and is equipped with Simian, a digital audio automation system. A 3-camera television studio is also available. The acquisition format is by way of two Super-VHS professional cameras. Studio productions are mastered to 3/4"-U-matic videotape. Nonstudio production media is downloaded directly to the nonlinear, digital editor. The department maintains two 3/4"-video editors in addition to the nonlinear, digital editor. The Integrated Multimedia Center (IMC) is the central hub for all television/film/digital media courses and is connected to the university radio studio and staff offices.

The IMC is a fully digital production area. The facility has film, slide transparency, and photo-scanning capability; three digital nonlinear video- and audio-editing systems; CD-ROM production; and Web page design. The student newspaper, the *Cliff News @ Briar Cliff University*, is produced and placed on the Internet on a weekly basis. The lab includes Nikon D70 digital cameras and digital audio automation editing software for the radio studio. The facility serves as a digital darkroom where student print to one of three Epson 4000 color inkjet printers. Images can be scanned at one of the seven scanning stations that include film and flatbed scanners. Video production is accomplished on Final Cut Pro software. The lab is accessible 24 hours a day.

Other awards of note: The department chair, Michael Crowley, is in demand as a curriculum consultant for other institutions' media programs and exhibits his photographic work regionally. Other department faculty members have received teaching excellence awards, have won several regional and national awards for newswriting, and have had work selected for juried exhibitions. The department has received numerous grant awards under the U.S. Department of Education's Title III program.

% of graduates currently employed in related field: 92

Career development services: Alumni networking opportunities, career counseling, internship listings, job fairs, job listings, semester internships in Chicago, study abroad.

Notable alumni: Mike Wankum—nominated for 14 Emmy Awards, has won nine for Best Weathercaster-Individual Achievement from The National Academy of Television Arts & Sciences; won four consecutive AP Awards in weathercasting from the Massachusetts-Rhode Island Associated Press; and three first-place awards from the Massachusetts Broadcasters Association. Kelly Jo Weiner—director of operations for Ron Schara Enterprises, received an Emmy for her work on *Hunt of a Lifetime* and produces shows for NBC, ESPN2, and the Outdoor Channel.

In Their Own Words

The mission of the Department of Mass Media is to prepare competent, well-trained, and liberally educated men and women in the converging field of mass media. Students will gain knowledge through theory, practical, and applied learning that will provide the valuable education and experience needed for a career in this challenging field. The Department of Mass Media offers programs in which students seriously interested in the wide and varied careers in communication can become personally involved by working with and learning from people both inside and outside the profession. The faculty in the department are aware of the skills that those in the businesses of radio, television, print, public relations, photography, advertising, graphic design, and new media demand of incoming professionals in a converging industry.

POPULAR PROGRAMS

MASS COMMUNICATION

Department chair: Michael Crowley
Number of full-time faculty: 3
Number of part-time faculty: 1
Focus/emphasis: Students who complete the mass communication major at Briar Cliff University will obtain: 1) knowledge, information, and theoretical concepts and be able to interpret the role the media and how it has affected society from an historical perspective; demonstrate an understanding of the profession within the context of convergence; and have knowledge of theories and concepts prevalent in the field. 2) ethical, legal, and social responsibility and be familiar with important legal issues that face the field of mass communication; develop personal values based on ethical standards; recognize ethical dilemmas that face mass media professionals; and recognize the power of the media and its effects on society, 3) experience writing for the communication field and be able to demonstrate proficiency in the various writing styles appropriate for the communi-

cation professions; demonstrate the ability to write and edit articles for publication; and critically evaluate written and oral presentations for style and content, 4) visual communication skills and be able to interpret, create, and disseminate visual information, 5) electronic applications skills and be able to obtain and demonstrate the skill necessary to use technologies appropriate to the field; and be able to plan, create, and complete projects using electronic media, 6) applied learning and be able to apply the knowledge and skills appropriate in the communication field and demonstrate skills needed for an entry-level position in the profession, 7) research experience in mass communication and be able to understand, analyze, and evaluate research and demonstrate an understanding of research methods.

Students Should Also Know

Briar Cliff University students interested in Television, Film, and Digital Media will benefit from a faculty who understand, practice, and effectively teach the important skills and perspectives needed to work in these exciting and converging fields. Our programs emphasize hands-on learning and internship opportunities for students and provide the theoretical bases needed for successful participation in the professions. By the time you graduate, you will have the beginnings of an impressive resume, a media portfolio, and practical experience that will make you a highly competitive candidate for entry-level positions in a variety of media fields.

BRIGHAM YOUNG UNIVERSITY (UT)

A-153 ASB, Provo, UT 84602-1110
Phone: 801-422-2507 **E-mail:** admissions@byu.edu
Website: www.byu.edu

Campus Life
Environment: City. **Calendar:** Semester.

Students and Faculty
(All Undergraduate Programs)

Enrollment: 30,798. **Student Body:** 49% female, 51% male, 72% out-of-state, 2% international (121 countries represented). Asian 3%, Caucasian 63%, Hispanic 3%. Student/faculty ratio: 21:1. 1,321 full-time faculty.

Admissions
(All Undergraduate Programs)

Freshman Admissions Requirements: Test(s) required: ACT. Average high school GPA: 3.73. 49% in top tenth, 35% in top quarter. SAT Math (25/75 percentile): 570/670. SAT Verbal (25/75 percentile): 550/660. Projected SAT Writing (25/75 percentile): 610/690. *Academic units required:* 4 English, 3 math, 2 science (2 science labs), 2 foreign language, 2 history, 2 literature or writing. Regular application deadline: 2/15.

Costs and Financial Aid
(All Undergraduate Programs)

Annual tuition $3,410. Room & board $5,790. Average book expense $1,240.

Financial Aid Statistics: % freshmen/undergrads who receive any aid: 20/36. % freshmen/undergrads who receive need-based scholarship or grant aid: 13/29. % freshmen/undergrads who receive need-based self-help aid: 6/15. Priority financial aid filing deadline: 4/15. Financial aid notification on or about: 4/20.

TV/Film/Digital Media Studies Programs

Number of undergraduates in these programs: 180
Number of 2005 graduates from these programs: 44
Degrees conferred to these majors: BA, BFA.
Number of full-time faculty in these programs: 5
Number of part-time faculty in these programs: 1
Notable alumni: Jared Hess, Sundance Film Festival's *Napoleon Dynamite* and Slamdance Film Festival's *Peluca*; Greg Whitely, Sundance Film Festival's *New York Dolls*; Andrew Black, Slamdance Film Festival's *The Snell Show*; Brad Barber, Slamdance Film Festival's *Yardsale*; Tim Skousen, Slamdance Film Festival's *Sasquatch Dumpling Gang*.

POPULAR PROGRAMS

MEDIA ARTS STUDIES

Department Chair: Rodger Sorensen
Number of full-time faculty: 9
Number of part-time faculty: 15

The media arts studies BA program is part of the Theatre and Media Arts (TMA) department. Students in media arts studies complete core courses in the following areas: (1) Introduction to Film: Analytical studies for understanding and appreciating media forms and messages as well as basic history, theory, and aesthetics; (2) Collaboration, Research, and Visualization: Overview and practical applications of principles of collaboration, research, and visualization as essential elements of appreciation and production of theater and media; (3) Reading and Constructing Narratives: Analysis of basic narrative principles and conceptualization and writing of narratives for theater and media; (4) Basic Media Production: Introduction to the basics of film and video production, including both lecture and practical lab experiences with audio and video; (5) Media Arts History: Survey of social, aesthetic, business and technical dimensions of film and media from 1895 to the present; (6) History of Documentary and Nonfiction Film: Introduction to and contextualization of documentary film from its inception to the present; (7) Screenwriting: Intermediate conceptualization, screenwriting, and development for narrative or non-narrative projects; (8) Intermediate Production: Survey and application of the basics of narrative and nonfiction, including 16-mm film. Lecture, discussion, lab, and individual/group experiences and critiques; (9) Narrative Directing: Advanced narrative preproduction and production of short projects, including digital and 16-mm sound film in narrative form. Discussion, lab, and individual/group experiences and critiques; (10)

Media Arts Theory: Identification and analysis of contemporary film and media theories with applications to specific media texts.

ANIMATION
Department Chair: Kelly Loosli
Number of full-time faculty: 3
Focus/emphasis: The animation BFA program is interdisciplinary in nature and has one full-time faculty member from each media arts, visual arts, and engineering. Students in the animation program have a multitude and range of internship opportunities available to them, as the program offers many connections to the profession. Animation students have won a number of awards, including a Bronze Student Academy Award® in 2006 for the short computer-animated film "Turtles."

Students Should Also Know
The media arts studies major is designed to foster disciplined scholars and artists, committed to the gospel of Jesus Christ, whose skills and conduct model leadership, inspiration, and achievement. This degree is designed to produce graduates with practical skills, intellectual attributes, and spiritual awareness to assist themselves, their families, and others in "their quest for perfection and eternal life."

BUENA VISTA UNIVERSITY
610 West Fourth Street, Storm Lake, IA 50588-1798
Phone: 712-749-2235 E-mail: admissions@bvu.edu
Website: www.bvu.edu

Campus Life
Environment: Village. **Calendar:** 4-1-4.

Students and Faculty
(All Undergraduate Programs)
Enrollment: 1,198. **Student Body:** 52% female, 48% male, 22% out-of-state. African American 3%, Asian 2%, Caucasian 90%, Hispanic 2%. Student/faculty ratio: 13:1. 81 full-time faculty, 69% hold PhDs. 100% faculty teach undergrads.

Admissions
(All Undergraduate Programs)
Freshman Admissions Requirements: Test(s) required: SAT or ACT. Average high school GPA: 3.3. 16% in top tenth, 38% in top quarter. *Academic units required:* 4 English, 2 science, 2 social studies. Regular notification: Rolling.

Costs and Financial Aid
(All Undergraduate Programs)
Annual tuition $21,688. Room & board $6,054. Average book expense $750.
Financial Aid Statistics: % freshmen/undergrads who receive any aid: 99/98. % freshmen/undergrads who receive need-based scholarship or grant aid: 92/90. % freshmen/undergrads who receive need-based self-help aid: 84/79. Priority financial aid filing deadline: 6/1. Financial aid notification on or about: 2/20.

TV/Film/Digital Media Studies Programs
Number of undergraduates in these programs: 14
Number of 2005 graduates from these programs: 6
Degrees conferred to these majors: BA.
Number of full-time faculty in these programs: 1
Number of part-time faculty in these programs: 2

Equipment and facilities: Our production facility is equipped with two nonlinear Avid editing bays, a full-working studio, a fiber-optics field remote system, a streaming video port, and a live studio & field control room with an audio sound production studio.

% of graduates currently employed in related field: 90

Career development services: Alumni networking opportunities, career counseling, internship listings, job fairs, job listings.

In Their Own Words

All students are given access to professional digital media equipment that allows them to broadcast live sports, special events, short digital films, and weekly programs. The program has won top honors in the college division of the Iowa Motion Picture Association Awards in 2004 and 2005. The program supports a student-managed campus and television station, the University Cable Network. UCN broadcasts programming seven days a week on Cable Channel 3. We are about exploring television and media, giving students the opportunity to bridge theory with hands-on experience in a professional production atmosphere.

POPULAR PROGRAMS

TELEVISION/BROADCASTING; UNIVERSITY CABLE NETWORK

Department chair: Michael Whitlatch
Number of full-time faculty: 1
Number of part-time faculty: 1
Focus/emphasis: Emphasis on television broadcasting, production, and digital media. Journalism: *The Tack.*
Number of full-time faculty: 1
Number of part-time faculty: 1
Focus/emphasis: Emphasis on journalism, print and online. The paper serves as a primary information source for and voice of BVU students and provides important opportunities for students to obtain real-world experience working on a professional newspaper.

RADIO (KBVU RADIO)

Number of full-time faculty: 1
Focus/emphasis: Emphasis on radio broadcasting. KBVU is a student-run, 6,000-watt FM commercial radio station.

GRAPHIC DESIGN

Number of full-time faculty: 1
Focus/emphasis: The Graphic Design Program provides a broad professional and cultural base for students interested in careers in the area of visual communications.

MULTIMEDIA DESIGN

Focus/emphasis: The Multimedia Program provides a broad base in digital design, authoring, and Internet design.

BUTLER UNIVERSITY

4600 Sunset Avenue, Indianapolis, IN 46208
Phone: 317-940-8100 **E-mail:** admission@butler.edu
Website: www.butler.edu

Campus Life
Environment: Metropolis. **Calendar:** Semester.

Students and Faculty
(All Undergraduate Programs)
Enrollment: 4,384. **Student Body:** 61% female, 39% male, 40% out-of-state, 3% international (63 countries represented). African American 3%, Asian 2%, Caucasian 90%, Hispanic 2%. Student/faculty ratio: 14:1. 279 full-time faculty, 85% hold PhDs. 97% faculty teach undergrads.

Admissions
(All Undergraduate Programs)
Freshman Admissions Requirements: Test(s) required: SAT or ACT; ACT with Writing component. Average high school GPA: 3.56. 44% in top tenth,

74% in top quarter. SAT Math (25/75 percentile): 540/650. SAT Verbal (25/75 percentile): 530/630. Projected SAT Writing (25/75 percentile): 600/670. *Academic units required:* 4 English, 3 math, 3 science, 2 foreign language, 2 history, 2 academic electives. Regular notification: Rolling.

Costs and Financial Aid
(All Undergraduate Programs)
Annual tuition $24,710. Room & board $8,316. Required fees $244. Average book expense $800. **Financial Aid Statistics:** Priority financial aid filing deadline: 3/1. Financial aid notification on or about: 3/15.

TV/Film/Digital Media Studies Programs
Number of undergraduates in these programs: 152
Number of 2005 graduates from these programs: 40
Degrees conferred to these majors: BA.
Number of full-time faculty in these programs: 8
Number of part-time faculty in these programs: 3.5
Equipment and facilities: Field gear, remote truck, two TV studios, multitrack recording studio, audio for video room, streaming media capable, campus cable channel, nonlinear editing bays, computer classroom.
ATAS Faculty Seminar participants: 1
Other awards of note: Winner of numerous awards including Telly, Society of Professional Journalists, BEA Festival of Media Arts, Axiem, and MarCom awards.

% of graduates currently employed in related field: 90%.
Career development services: Alumni networking opportunities, career counseling, internship listings, job fairs, job listings.
Famous alumni: Correy McPherrin, Chicago; David Juday, ESPN Radio, Chicago; Brian Hammans, Golf Channel; Kevin Calabro, voice of Seattle Supersonics; Anqunette Jamison, news anchor, WXFT, Boston.

Notable alumni: David Melnick, writer, *Homicide: Life on the Street* and HBO's *The Wire*; Rob Dauber, producer; *Rosie O'Donnell Show, Ally & Jack, Martha Stewart*; Howard Schrott, CFO, The Liberty Media Group; Kristin Smith, senior attorney, Qwest Communications.

In Their Own Words
Major internship program; recent guest lecturers have included Ken Auletta, media critic of the New Yorker Magazine, *and Cindy Patrick, vice president for operations at CNN.*

CALIFORNIA COLLEGE OF THE ARTS
1111 Eighth Street, San Francisco, CA 94107
Phone: 415-703-9523 **E-mail:** enroll@cca.edu
Website: www.cca.edu

Campus Life
Environment: Metropolis. **Calendar:** Semester.

Students and Faculty
(All Undergraduate Programs)
Enrollment: 1,312. **Student Body:** 59% female, 41% male, 35% out-of-state, 7% international (26 countries represented). African American 2%, Asian 12%, Caucasian 57%, Hispanic 9%. Student/faculty ratio: 14:1. 41 full-time faculty. 409 part-time faculty. 84% faculty teach undergrads.

Admissions
(All Undergraduate Programs)
Average high school GPA: 3.13. 9% in top tenth, 36% in top quarter. Regular notification: Rolling.

Costs and Financial Aid
(All Undergraduate Programs)
Annual tuition $27,624. Room & board $8,935. Required fees $290. Average book expense $1,300. **Financial Aid Statistics:** % freshmen/undergrads who receive any aid: 75/75. % freshmen/undergrads who receive need-based scholarship or grant aid: 64/71. % freshmen/undergrads who receive need-based self-help aid: 60/68. Priority financial aid filing

deadline: 3/1. Financial aid notification on or about: 4/1.

TV/Film/Digital Media Studies Programs

Number of undergraduates in these programs: 38

Number of 2005 graduates from these programs: 8

Degrees conferred to these majors: BFA.

Number of full-time faculty in these programs: 3

Number of part-time faculty in these programs: 7

Equipment and facilities: Media arts supports digital video, Super-8, and 16 mm film production with state-of-the-art digital production tools and sound-editing stations, and a hybrid lab for interactive media.

ATAS College TV Awards recipients: 1

Other awards of note: Student awards: Noah Cunningham and Paul Trillo, finalists, Scion xPress Fest, 2006; Lisa Mishima, national finalist, Student Academy Awards, 2006; Noah Cunningham and Lisa Mishima, Official Selections, Resfest International Digital Film Festival, 2005; Bonnie Berry, Official Selection, Los Angeles International Short Film Festival, 2004; Gina Carducci, Official Selection, Venice Biennale Film Festival, 2003; Lindsay Daniels, national finalist, Student Academy Awards, 2003.

Career development services: Alumni networking opportunities; career counseling; central resource(s) for employers to browse headshots, writing samples, reels; internship listings; job fairs; job listings.

Famous alumni: Wayne Wang, director, whose work (17 films to date) includes *Chan is Missing*, *The Joy Luck Club*, and *Maid in Manhattan*.

Notable alumni: Joplin Wu, a successful cinematographer; Etienne Kallos, producer and director of award-winning documentary *Living in Conflict*; Elizabeth Block, a writer and film artist, whose short films have been screened throughout the United States and Canada; Anthony Discenza, whose solo and collaborative work has been shown at many national and international venues including the New York Video Festival, the Museum of Modern Art in New York, and the 2000 Whitney Biennial; Ritu Sarin, director of documentary *Dreaming Lhasa*.

In Their Own Words

CCA offers students access to a faculty of practicing artists who are recognized and innovative in their fields. Members of the faculty include Jeanne Finley, whose award-winning films have been screened at festivals in the United States and abroad; Kota Ezawa, an internationally exhibiting artist whose works incorporate digital animation; and Academy Award-winning documentary filmmaker Rob Epstein. Our dynamic visiting faculty program recently brought media artists Michele O'Marah, Euan Macdonald, and film festival favorite Caveh Zahedi to work with our students. Students also have the opportunity to work with Jim Kenney, the principal of InterStitch Films, a motion graphics and design film studio. CCA students have shown work in film festivals and have interned in Bay Area film studios, such as Tippett Studio, Pixar, and Citizen Studio.

CALIFORNIA INSTITUTE OF THE ARTS

24700 McBean Parkway, Valencia, CA 91355
Phone: 661-255-1050 **E-mail:** admiss@calarts.edu
Website: www.calarts.edu

Campus Life

Environment: City. **Calendar:** Semester.

Students and Faculty (All Undergraduate Programs)

Enrollment: 821. **Student Body:** 44% female, 56% male, 53% out-of-state, 8% international. African American 7%, Asian 10%, Caucasian 61%, Hispanic 12%, Native American 1%. Student/faculty ratio: 7:1. 150 full-time faculty. 100% faculty teach undergrads.

Admissions
(All Undergraduate Programs)
25% in top tenth. Regular notification: Rolling.

Costs and Financial Aid
(All Undergraduate Programs)
Annual tuition $29,300. Room & board $8,130. Required fees $515. Average book expense $2,085. **Financial Aid Statistics:** % freshmen/undergrads who receive need-based scholarship or grant aid: 58/68. % freshmen/undergrads who receive need-based self-help aid: 52/62. Priority financial aid filing deadline: 3/1. Financial aid filing deadline: 3/1. Financial aid notification on or about: 4/1.

TV/Film/Digital Media Studies Programs
Number of undergraduates in these programs: 461

Number of 2005 graduates from these programs: 89

Degrees conferred to these majors: BFA.

Also available at California Institute of the Arts: MFA.

Number of full-time faculty in these programs: 106

Number of part-time faculty in these programs: 46

Equipment and facilities: Field equipment, sound-stages, and production studios—permanent set, black-and-white studio, film-directing studio, video studio, videographics lab and telecine animation studios, postproduction facilities for film and linear video editing, dubbing computer labs for 2-D animation computer labs, 3-D computer animation lab, digital imaging/compositing lab, multimedia lab, sound facilities—basic sound room, recording studio/video mixing, film-mixing theater, Pro Tools workstations, transfer room, sync flatbed telecine theater, Channel 8 closed-circuit television.

% of graduates currently employed in related field: 87

Famous alumni: Brad Bird (1976), character animation, wrote the screen story for and directed *The Iron Giant*, which was among the best-reviewed animated features of 1999. It won the Annie Award for Outstanding Achievement and was named best animated film of the year by the Los Angeles Film Critics Association. After joining Pixar Animation Studios, Bird wrote and directed the feature *The Incredibles* (2004 Academy Award, Animated Feature, for Sound Editing). Tim Burton (1979), character animation, has directed the movies *Pee-Wee's Big Adventure*, *Beetlejuice*, *Batman*, *Edward Scissorhands*, *Batman Returns*, and *Ed Wood*, among others. One of his more recent features was a new version of the classic *Willy Wonka and the Chocolate Factory* entitled *Charlie and the Chocolate Factory*, which was released in 2005. Pete Docter (BFA, 1990), character animation, is one of the key figures at Pixar Animation Studios. He codirected the Disney/Pixar hit *Monsters, Inc.*, which was nominated for the Best Animated Feature Award at the 2002 Academy Awards. Docter also worked on the original story and provided additional voices for the film. Previously, he had won an Annie Award for cowriting *Toy Story 2* and received an Academy Award nomination for cowriting *Toy Story*. Ralph Eggleston (1986), character animation, has worked at Pixar Animation Studios since 1992. His film *For the Birds* won the Academy Award for Best Animated Short in 2002. He also holds an Annie Award for his production design work on *Toy Story*. Eggleston has been named by *Animation Magazine* as one of the most creative people in animation. Steve Hillenburg (MFA, 1992), experimental animation, is the creator of the hit animated series *SpongeBob SquarePants* on Nickelodeon. In 2002, the show became the highest-rated kids' show on cable television. *The SpongeBob SquarePants Movie* was released in the fall of 2004. Glen Keane (1974), experimental animation, has been the supervising animator for memorable characters such as Tarzan, Pocahontas, Aladdin, the Beast in *Beauty and the Beast*, Ariel in *The Little Mermaid*, and Marahute in *The Rescuers Down Under*. He won an Annie Award for his character animation work on *Beauty and the Beast* and received an Annie nomination for *Tarzan*. In 2004, he received the Friz Award for Lifetime Achievement. John Lasseter (BFA, 1979), character animation, is executive vice president of creative development at Pixar Animation Studios—described by the *Los Angeles Times* as "the most reliable creative force in Hollywood." Lasseter has directed *Toy Story*, *A Bug's Life*, and *Toy Story 2* and executive-produced *Monsters, Inc.* and *Finding Nemo*. He has won Academy Awards for *Toy Story* (special achievement) and *The Tin Soldier* (Best Animated Short). His original screenplay for *Toy Story* was also nominated for an Academy Award. James Mangold (BFA, 1985), film and video, directed the acclaimed *Girl, Interrupted*. His other movies include *Identity*, *Kate and Leopold*, *Copland and Heavy*, for which he was named best director at the 1995 Sundance Film Festival. He worked on the feature *Walk the Line*, a biopic about Johnny Cash. Craig McCracken (1992), character animation, is the creator of *The Powerpuff Girls*, an Emmy-nominated series on the Cartoon Network. The show originated as *The Whoopass Girls*—a work McCracken made at CalArts. Jen Sachs (MFA, 2001), experimental animation, was named as one of the "25 New Faces of Independent Film" by the magazine *Filmmaker*. She has made waves on the festival circuit with the award-winning *Velvet Tigress*, an animated documentary about the infamous 1931 trial of "Trunk Murderess" Winnie Ruth Judd.

In Their Own Words

With an emphasis on independent vision, CalArts' School of Film/Video offers courses of study that strongly emphasize independent artistic and intellectual vision. The school's faculty is comprised of innovators and leaders in each specialty—filmmakers, animators, and video and multimedia fine artists who have distinguished themselves at the highest levels. All faculty members are practicing professionals. The school offers a low student-faculty ratio, small classes, and individualized instruction. All students work closely with their own mentors, faculty members who serve as each student's artistic and academic advisor. The School of Film/Video constantly updates and expands a

wide array of equipment resources. These include 16 mm, Betacam, and DV cameras; soundstages, sets, and production studios; 16 mm, 35 mm, Avid, Final Cut Pro, and nonlinear digital editing systems; sound-mixing and -editing facilities; 2-D and 3-D computer animation systems; and a variety of multimedia applications and tools. During the academic year, equipment and facilities are generally available for student use around the clock. CalArts' Bijou Theater is a dedicated screening facility used for presenting student work. In addition to the year-end Bijou Festival, the school organizes several other showcases and special screenings, both on campus and at venues throughout the Los Angeles area—including the Roy and Edna Disney/CalArts Theater—to present selected student films, videos, and animated works. Producers and other film and television professionals regularly attend these events. With flexible programs designed by artists for artists, CalArts gives its students a greater voice in shaping their pursuits than comparable institutions. The school's programs are highly challenging but also flexible enough to accommodate the individual creative interests of each student. The School of Film/Video invites a wide variety of leading film- and videomakers, installation artists, animators, screenwriters, producers, critics, and curators to lecture, discuss their work, and meet with students. These visiting artists add their experience and vision to the expertise of the school's resident faculty. CalArts encourages cross-pollination in the arts. In addition to extensive cross-stylistic collaborations within the School of Film/Video, students are encouraged to seek out interdisciplinary projects with visual and performing artists across all of CalArts. Many School of Film/Video students gain valuable experience by teaching CAP workshops and classes at community art centers and public schools throughout Los Angeles County.

POPULAR PROGRAMS

CHARACTER ANIMATION

Focus/emphasis: Character animation (BFA only) is designed for students who seek an understanding of the art of acting animation. It provides comprehensive technical training and helps each student develop as a full-fledged animation artist. To best instruct, guide, and mentor students, the program features a faculty of experienced professionals who work at the forefront of both traditional and independent animation. The first year of the program's intensive four-year curriculum is devoted to courses in life drawing, color and design, storytelling, and character animation. The second year takes this work to a higher level by incorporating elements such as dialogue, sound effects, and music. In the third year, students typically move to the advanced level in their coursework, which can include story classes geared toward the short form (such as commercials and short films), 3-D computer animation classes, and specialized work in background painting, special effects, "inbetweening," and cleanup. In the fourth and final year, students move up to the highest level of the core classes and can customize their curriculum according to their own specific areas of interest. During the course of their studies, students develop a professional-caliber portfolio. In addition to its course requirements, the program calls on students to attend lectures, demonstrations, and screenings as part of an extensive visiting artist series, which features noted animators, filmmakers, actors, and comedians.

FILM DIRECTING

Focus/emphasis: The Film Directing Program (MFA only) is a three-year graduate course of study that concentrates on narrative film directing and includes writing, acting, and directing for theater. While one of the program's chief objectives is to encourage directing students to explore new and innovative approaches to dramatic storytelling, its curriculum is built on the enduring traditions of drama that stretch from Sophocles and Aristotle to Shakespeare and Chekhov; from Griffith and Murnau to Ford, Hitchcock, Godard, Peckinpah, and von Trier. Directing students investigate these traditions in acting studios, which are vital to each student's development. For this reason, all students in this program are expected to perform publicly. Although the curriculum includes a number of technical courses, its main focus is the staging of well-acted dramatic action for the camera. Acting studios and writing workshops are the forums in which students share and examine their own experiences, hone their powers of observation, work closely with actors, and develop methods for shaping stories—both invented and adapted—that convey emotional truths and life-worn textures. The first year of the Film Directing Program covers acting, writing, storytelling, dramatic structure, theater directing, film and video production, editing, film grammar, and film history. During the second semester, students complete short projects in film or video and perform on stage in a weekly scene class. At the end of the first year, each student proposes a required thesis project: a film, a theater production, or a writing project. The second-year curriculum adds thesis development, dramatic writing, cinematography, scene study, and film directing to ongoing work in acting, directing, and film studies. Each student is assigned a variety of classes and exercises related to his or her declared thesis. In addition, every student directs a five-minute dramatic film or video, which must include full postproduction techniques. Students also take directing assignments in theater and may direct one or more one-act plays. All students are expected to support one another and may be assigned to a colleague's project as crew. Prior to the end of the second year, all directing students must submit their thesis scripts for approval by the thesis committee. Once these are approved, the third year in residence is devoted primarily to thesis production. In addition, each student's mentor may require the student to take on additional course work in any semester.

CALIFORNIA STATE UNIVERSITY– DOMINGUEZ HILLS

100 East Victoria Street, Carson, CA 90747
Phone: 310-243-3600 **E-mail:** lwise@csudh.edu
Website: www.csudh.edu

Campus Life
Environment: City. **Calendar:** Semester.

Students and Faculty
(All Undergraduate Programs)
Enrollment: 8,698. **Student Body:** 69% female, 31% male, 1% out-of-state, 2% international. African American 27%, Asian 9%, Caucasian 13%, Hispanic 36%. Student/faculty ratio: 22:1. 252 full-time faculty, 76% hold PhDs.

Admissions
(All Undergraduate Programs)
Freshman Admissions Requirements: Test(s) required: ACT with Writing component. Average high school GPA: 3.04. SAT Math (25/75 percentile): 370/480. SAT Verbal (25/75 percentile): 360/470. Projected SAT Writing (25/75 percentile): 430/540. *Academic units required:* 4 English, 3 math, 2 science (2 science labs), 2 foreign language, 2 social studies, 1 history, 1 academic elective, 1 visual/performing arts. Regular application deadline: 6/1. Regular notification: Rolling.

Costs and Financial Aid
(All Undergraduate Programs)
Annual in-state tuition $1,815. Out-of-state tuition $7,380. Room & board $5,801. Required fees $300. Average book expense $630.
Financial Aid Statistics: % freshmen/undergrads who receive need-based scholarship or grant aid: 66/64. % freshmen/undergrads who receive need-based self-help aid: 21/35. Priority financial aid filing deadline: 3/2. Financial aid filing deadline: 4/15. Financial aid notification on or about: 4/19.

TV/Film/Digital Media Studies Programs
Number of undergraduates in these programs: 125
Number of 2005 graduates from these programs: 100
Degrees conferred to these majors: BA.
Number of full-time faculty in these programs: 5
Number of part-time faculty in these programs: 3
Equipment and facilities: HDV high-definition engineering/efp cameras, Avid editing systems, Adobe Premiere, AfterEffects editing systems, mini-DV, Betacam SP aquisition gear, SAN storage, fully refurbished and soundproofed 1,500 square-foot TV studio, Grass Valley switcher, Mackie soundboard, CG, still store.
Other awards of note: Faculty have won many national awards, including Tellys, Aegis, Communicators, and Videographers.

% of graduates currently employed in related field: 80
Career development services: Alumni networking opportunities, career counseling, internship listings, job fairs, job listings.
Notable alumni: Lela Rochon, actress, film and television credits as listed on IMDB.com, including *Any Given Sunday*, *Ruby Bridges*, *Gang Related*, *The Outer Limits*, *Waiting to Exhale*, *The Fresh Prince of Bel-Air*, *21 Jump Street*; Louil Silas, Jr., record executive; please see the university and alumni association Web pages for more.

In Their Own Words
Extensive internship program; graduates placed in many A-list area studios, cable companies, production houses, corporate production departments, agencies, and TV stations. Students have won Emmys® and regional and statewide awards.

POPULAR PROGRAMS

ELECTRONIC MEDIA PRODUCTION
Department chair: James Sudalnik

DIGITAL MEDIA ARTS, TV ARTS
Department chair: Rod Butler

THEATER ARTS
Department chair: William Deluca

DIVISION OF PERFORMING, VISUAL, AND ART DEPARTMENT
Department chair: Bernard Baker

Students Should Also Know
Students receive a top-notch education at very reasonable rates. For further information about the specific programs, please see the university's website: www.csudh.com.

CALIFORNIA STATE UNIVERSITY– FULLERTON

800 North State College Boulevard, Fullerton, CA 92834-6900
Phone: 714-773-2370 **E-mail:** admissions@fullerton.edu
Website: www.fullerton.edu

Campus Life
Environment: Metropolis. **Calendar:** Semester.

Students and Faculty
(All Undergraduate Programs)
Enrollment: 25,261. **Student Body:** 60% female, 40% male, 1% out-of-state, 4% international (78 countries represented). African American 3%, Asian 24%, Caucasian 34%, Hispanic 24%. Student/faculty ratio: 21:1. 754 full-time faculty, 84% hold PhDs.

Admissions
(All Undergraduate Programs)
Freshman Admissions Requirements: Test(s) required: SAT. Average high school GPA: 3.2. 15% in top tenth, 45% in top quarter. SAT Math (25/75 percentile): 440/560. SAT Verbal (25/75 percentile):

420/530. Projected SAT Writing (25/75 percentile): 490/590. *Academic units required:* 2 science (2 science labs), 2 history, 1 academic elective, 1 visual/performing arts. Regular application deadline: 4/15. Regular notification: Rolling.

Costs and Financial Aid
(All Undergraduate Programs)
Out-of-state tuition $5,904. Room & board $3,953. Required fees $1,881. Average book expense $1,080. **Financial Aid Statistics:** % freshmen/undergrads who receive need-based scholarship or grant aid: 30/29. % freshmen/undergrads who receive need-based self-help aid: 15/21. Priority financial aid filing deadline: 3/2. Financial aid notification on or about: 3/1.

TV/Film/Digital Media Studies Programs
Degrees conferred to these majors: BA.
Equipment and facilities: For audio production, digital recording equipment and editing software are available. For video production, the department features digital video (DV) camera equipment and a 20-station nonlinear editing lab. For film production, students shoot with 16 mm cameras and edit digitally. The department also maintains a fully-outfitted, 3-camera television studio and control room. 12 Mac G4s, dual 500MHz with 80 GB internal HDs, 17" dual monitors; 8 Mac G4s, dual 800 MHz, 15" dual screen panels with 75 GB internal HDs and 70 GB swappable external Firewire HDs; 8 DSR-11 DV decks; 6 DSR-30 DV decks; 1 DSR-20 DV deck; 20 9' NTSC external monitors; 20 external speaker systems with headphone jacks; Mac OSX 10.3; F.C.P. 4.5 HD; QuickTime Pro 6; AfterEffects 5.5; LiveType; SoundTrack; iDVD; iPhoto; CinemaTools 1-JVC combo DV/VHS decks; 1-monitor; 1-Sennheiser boom mic; 1 Mac G4, dual 500MHz with 80 GB internal HDs; 17" dual monitors; 70 GB swappable external Firewire HDs; 1 DSR-20 DV deck; 15' JVC NTSC external monitors; external speaker systems with subwoofer and headphone jacks; 1 Mackie audio mixer.
Career development services: Career counseling, internship listings, job fairs, job listings.

In Their Own Words

Titan Communications is the home to Cal State–Fullerton's digital media center, which provides students with a living-learning classroom and an opportunity to work and learn about television and radio broadcast management in a professional, hands-on environment. We strive to provide students with an environment that supports academic achievement with opportunities to work on television and radio programs and learn the broad-ranging skills needed today to succeed in a broadcast career. Since it began in 1998, Titan Communications has grown from an office, control room, and a small television set to a full-scale television studio, a control room, audio and editing labs equipped with MACs and PCs, a sound booth, and the Titan Internet Radio station. Titan Communications is home to productions such as Conversations with President Gordon and Special Guests, On the Edge, *College of Communications classrooms, and the Titan Internet Radio.*

POPULAR PROGRAMS

RADIO/TV/FILM

Department chair: Ed Fink
Number of full-time faculty: 10
Number of part-time faculty: 11
Focus/emphasis: The Bachelor of Arts in Radio/TV/Film offers a comprehensive and active learning environment that prepares students for meaningful and rewarding careers in radio, television, and film. Students also receive the preparation they need to pursue graduate study in the broader areas of media and communication. At Cal State—Fullerton, the Department of Radio/TV/Film has developed a program that emphasizes current theory, practice, research and hands-on creative activities. Students are challenged to expand their knowledge through intellectual inquiry and receive a solid foundation that allows them to develop skills they will use throughout their careers—both as critical, life-long learners and as content creators in a media-savvy society. Because Cal State—Fullerton is located near the center of one of the largest concentrations of mass media in the world, the bachelor's degree program also places an emphasis on contributing ethically, intellectually, and economically to the media industry. A student who earns the bachelor's degree in radio/TV/film knows the foundational history of the film and electronic media industry and how that history shapes the industry's present and future; understands the structure and function of film and electronic media in society; can apply fundamental production concepts to aural and visual productions; can apply fundamental story concepts to script analysis and writing; can contribute ethically to the media industry; consumes film and electronic media critically; has the opportunity to create at least one quality project or portfolio piece prior to graduation, such as a script, production, or thesis; and experiences a meaningful internship, resulting in exposure to the real workings of the radio, television, and/or film industry.

ENTERTAINMENT STUDIES

Department chair: Wendell Crow
Number of full-time faculty: 27
Number of part-time faculty: 50
Focus/emphasis: Courses in this concentration introduce students to theory, trends, and practices emerging in entertainment and tourism. The concentration is designed to prepare students for career opportunities in entertainment communication and management in a growing range of sectors including business, industries, agencies, and nonprofit organizations. This major is part of an interdisciplinary program between the colleges of communications, business, and the arts. Each college offers an entertainment curriculum in their particular interests by allowing students to take courses from all three colleges. Please also visit the Center for Entertainment and Tourism's website for more information on these programs.

JOURNALISM

Focus/emphasis: Journalism: The principal objective of the journalism concentration is to provide the skills and practice necessary for careers in the electronic media. Specifically, the concentration objectives are (1) to provide experience in writing various types of news stories and to develop skills in reporting and news-gathering techniques, (2) to develop critical acumen necessary to check news stories for accuracy and correctness, (3) to develop skills in graphics or photography that complement the journalistic writing skills, (4) to provide actual on-the-job experience by enabling students to work on the campus newspaper and at internships, and (5) to add breadth and depth to the professional's specialized skills through collaborative courses. The concentration includes three emphases: print journalism, broadcast journalism, and visual journalism.

ADVERTISING

Focus/emphasis: The objective of the advertising concentration is to prepare students for entry-level positions in one or more of the four basic advertising activities: creative (copy, layout design), media planning and buying, research, and management. Students are provided with knowledge and skills needed to work with an advertiser, advertising agency, the print and broadcast media, or support-service industry.

PHOTOCOMMUNICATIONS

Focus/emphasis: The photocommunications concentration provides a comprehensive study of the aesthetics, theories, and practices of contemporary photography for professional careers in magazine and newspaper photojournalism and advertising/commercial photography.

CALIFORNIA STATE UNIVERSITY–LONG BEACH

1250 Bellflower Boulevard, Long Beach, CA 90840
Phone: 562-985-5471 **E-mail:** eslb@csulb.edu
Website: www.csulb.edu

Campus Life
Environment: Metropolis. **Calendar:** Semester.

Students and Faculty
(All Undergraduate Programs)
Enrollment: 28,514. **Student Body:** 60% female, 40% male, 1% out-of-state, 5% international. African American 6%, Asian 22%, Caucasian 32%, Hispanic 25%. Student/faculty ratio: 20:1. 966 full-time faculty, 88% hold PhDs. 100% faculty teach undergrads.

Admissions
(All Undergraduate Programs)
Freshman Admissions Requirements: Test(s) required: SAT or ACT. Average high school GPA: 3.34. 82% in top quarter. SAT Math (25/75 percentile): 470/580. SAT Verbal (25/75 percentile): 450/560. Projected SAT Writing (25/75 percentile): 520/620. Regular application deadline: 11/30. Regular notification: Rolling.

Costs and Financial Aid
(All Undergraduate Programs)
Out-of-state tuition $10,170. Room & board $6,648. Required fees $2,864. Average book expense $1,314. **Financial Aid Statistics:** % freshmen/undergrads who receive need-based scholarship or grant aid: 39/42. % freshmen/undergrads who receive need-based self-help aid: 27/39. Priority financial aid filing deadline: 3/2. Financial aid notification on or about: 4/1.

TV/Film/Digital Media Studies Programs
Number of undergraduates in these programs: 299
Number of 2005 graduates from these programs: 96
Degrees conferred to these majors: BA.
Number of full-time faculty in these programs: 10
Number of part-time faculty in these programs: 11
Equipment and facilities: Soundstage, ENG/EFp equipment, animation stands, radio board for production, digital studio.
ATAS interns: 2
Other awards of note: Brian Fischer (2004) won four of the top five awards at the 2005 CSU Media Arts Festival with his film *L'Histoire de Billy Matter*. His short, *Fellini's Donut*, made with a

Kodak grant, was featured at the Kodak Theatre in October of 2004 and was shown at the Tribeca and Beverly Hills film festivals in 2005. Eight of our student films have been accepted into the Newport Film Festival, taking place in May, and SONY featured our student films in a special showing at Sundance. Our students are also on the cutting edge of new short films for the Internet. Ifilm, the leading distributor of such works, has had two of our students' films in the top ten, nationally, in terms of "hits." At this year's CSU Media Arts Festival, FEA students placed very well once again. Cynthia Aguirre won the Kodak Cinematography Award for *Fragments*. Geri Logan placed second in the music video category for "Holy Ghost Fire." Cynthia Aguirre placed second in the narrative category for *Fragments*, and Nausheen Dadabhoy placed third for *Twelfth Man*. Ryan Silveira placed second in the experimental category for *Bee Goldin*. This is yet another wonderful achievement for our students.

% of graduates who pursue further study within 5 years: 5

% of graduates currently employed in related field: 75

Career development services: Alumni networking opportunities; career counseling; central resource(s) for employers to browse headshots, writing samples, reels; internship listings; job fairs; job listings.

Famous alumni: Guy Bee, David Twohy, Steven Spielberg, John Dykstra, Mark Stephen Johnson.

Notable alumni: Stu Rosen won ten Emmys for children's programming.

In Their Own Words

We offer two options and a minor to upper-division students with a 3.0 GPA or better. The first option is in production, from which we have produced students who have had their films selected for showing at the Tribeca and Newport Beach Film Festivals. The second option is in media studies. The minor is in media studies. In the fall, we will launch our MFA in Dramatic Writing by accepting six graduate students into the select program. Reider Jonsson, My Life as a Dog, *will conduct a seminar for them.*

POPULAR PROGRAMS

FILM AND ELECTRONIC MEDIA

Department chair: Dr. Craig Smith
Number of full-time faculty: 10
Number of part-time faculty: 11
Focus/emphasis: Film and Electronic Arts (BA only) is an innovative academic program that emphasizes both professional education and liberal arts, both theory and practice. Focusing on the integration of media and the arts in our information society, as well as on the impact of technology on our culture and the media themselves, the curriculum is designed to provide technical skills while developing a sound foundation in the arts and the humanities. The faculty includes a diversity of expertise and interests that cross traditional media lines, resulting in ongoing discussion and experimentation while integrating the traditional film, audio, and video production modes. Theory and aesthetics are taught as an integral part of the development of production skills. Part-time lecturers include a variety of highly qualified Los Angeles-area media professionals.

FILM AND VIDEO PRODUCTION

Department chair: Dr. Craig Smith
Number of full-time faculty: 10
Number of part-time faculty: 11

CALIFORNIA STATE UNIVERSITY– NORTHRIDGE

PO Box 1286, Northridge, CA 91328-1286
Phone: 818-677-3700 **E-mail:** lorraine.newlon@csun.edu
Website: www.csun.edu

Campus Life
Environment: Metropolis. **Calendar:** Semester.

Students and Faculty
(All Undergraduate Programs)
Enrollment: 20,955. **Student Body:** African American 9%, Asian 15%, Caucasian 33%, Hispanic 24%.

Admissions
(All Undergraduate Programs)

Freshman Admissions Requirements: Test(s) required: SAT or ACT. Average high school GPA: 3.1. 33% in top quarter. *Academic units required:* 4 English, 3 math, 1 science (2 science lab), 2 foreign language, 2 history, 1 academic elective, 1 visual/performing arts. Regular notification: Rolling.

Costs and Financial Aid
(All Undergraduate Programs)

Annual in-state tuition $1,506. Out-of-state tuition $7,874. Room & board $5,801. Average book expense $648.

TV/Film/Digital Media Studies Programs

Degrees conferred to these majors: BA.

Also available at California State University— Northridge: MA.

Number of full-time faculty in these programs: 16

Equipment and facilities: Cinematheque, a motion picture theater, often part of a university or private archive, showing experimental or historically important films. The only venue of its kind in the San Fernando Valley, the CSUN Cinematheque is an innovative year-round film screening program housed in the Alan and Elaine Armer Theater, a state-of-the-art 130-seat motion picture theater on the CSUN campus. Programs include thematically designed retrospectives of classic films, as well as aesthetically significant contemporary releases—in conjunction with the appearance of featured guest artists for lectures and panel discussions. Conceptual presentations are devoted to many areas of the film world: Important directors, writers, actors, cinematographers; essential genre works; seminal documentaries; major literary, philosophical, and narrative themes and traditions; defining technical and artistic models and styles.

In Their Own Words

Our full-time faculty is a healthy mix of academics and professionals, responsible over the years for having written, directed, or produced approximately 5,000 feature motion pictures, television shows, stage plays, or industrial films. *Faculty members have functioned in every capacity from screenwriter to executive producer to network vice president, and have received most of the industry's major honors: the Emmy, Peabody, Cindy, Golden Mike, and Voice of America awards, among others. The college's proximity and close ties to the area's entertainment industry have allowed the department use of a variety of industry locations and facilities, and make it possible for us to offer student internships undreamed of outside of Southern California. Our annual showing of senior student films, held at the Academy of Television Arts and Sciences or the Academy of Motion Picture Arts and Sciences, continues to attract accolades from leading film professionals. The hosts of these programs have been Academy Award-winning directors and producers, including Robert Wise and William Friedkin. Several of our courses are regularly taught on the lot at CBS Studio City, and the department's annual banquet has been held on the Seinfeld Street at the studio. Our internship program is acknowledged to be among the finest in the country. We have placed students in some of the best radio, television, and film companies on the West Coast. CTVA students have earned an excellent reputation in the media world and are in much demand. To quote an internship host: "Our average is excellent." A high percentage of our internship students find paying positions with their host companies. Many others find related work soon after graduation based on recommendations or contacts made as a result of their internships.*

POPULAR PROGRAMS

CINEMA AND TV ARTS (ELECTRONIC MEDIA MANAGEMENT)

Department chair: Robert Gustafson

Focus/emphasis: Operational and management aspects of independent, studio, and network electronic media—including business structures, personnel, budgets, advertising, sales, research, and regulation of the media industries. A minor is also offered in this option.

CINEMA AND TELEVISION ARTS (FILM PRODUCTION)

Department chair: Nate Thomas

Focus/emphasis: Conceptualization, production, directing, editing, and distribution of film projects for both entertainment and informational purposes.

CINEMA AND TV ARTS (MEDIA THEORY AND CRITICISM)

Department chair: John Schultheiss

Focus/emphasis: History, theory, and critical analysis of the culture of film and electronic media—providing a background for all professional training, with specific preparation for careers in teaching or research. Screenwriting Option: Research, structure, and writing for dramatic and nondramatic scripts for film, radio, television, and multimedia.

CINEMA AND TELEVISION ARTS (MULTIMEDIA)

Department chair: Mary C. Schaffer

Focus/emphasis: preproduction; production; distribution of digital material for film, television, and the World Wide Web. Students acquire effective computer skills to design websites; create streaming audio and video; design and create DVDs and CD-ROMS; develop games in the interactive media environment.

CINEMA AND TV ARTS (RADIO AND TV PRODUCTION)

Department chair: Thelma Vickroy

Focus/emphasis: preproduction, production, and postproduction techniques for all electronic media formats—encompassing directing and all other creative aspects of studio and field production.

CINEMA AND TELEVISION ARTS (SCREENWRITING)

Department chair: Jon Stahl

Focus/emphasis: Research, structure, and writing for dramatic and nondramatic scripts for film, radio, television, and multimedia.

Students Should Also Know

The mission of the Department of Cinema and Television Arts (formerly Radio-Television-Film) is to instill in students the knowledge, expertise, and creative skills that will help them to achieve their goals in the fields of radio, television, film, or multimedia, and to promote the critical, analytical, and conceptual thinking that will enrich their academic and professional careers. The Cinema and Television Arts major provides students with academic and professional training for careers in the entertainment industries and educational/corporate media fields. The major prepares students for creative and management careers in commercial or educational radio, television, film, and multimedia positions, as well as related scholarly areas. The program is strongly committed to a balance between theoretical and practical education. The Department of Cinema and Television Arts has been evaluated by a distinguished panel of outside educators who were "overwhelmed by the potential of [the] Department of Cinema and Television Arts at California State University—Northridge to expand its current academic influence beyond the boundaries of Southern California to verily reach around the globe with its educational impact." The school anticipates the move into a new building, complete with state-of-the-art studios, classrooms, postproduction facilities, and 130-seat screening room, will be a large step towards reaching future potential. The CTVA Department is affiliated with the University Film and Video Association, the Society for Cinema Studies, the Broadcast Education Association, and the National Association of Broadcasters.

CALVIN COLLEGE

3201 Burton Street S.E., Grand Rapids, MI 49546
Phone: 616-526-6106 **E-mail:** admissions@calvin.edu
Website: www.calvin.edu

Campus Life

Environment: Metropolis. **Calendar:** 4-1-4.

Students and Faculty
(All Undergraduate Programs)
Enrollment: 4,040. **Student Body:** 54% female, 46% male, 41% out-of-state, 7% international (60 countries represented). African American 1%, Asian 3%, Caucasian 85%, Hispanic 1%. Student/faculty ratio: 12:1. 309 full-time faculty, 82% hold PhDs. 100% faculty teach undergrads.

Admissions
(All Undergraduate Programs)
Freshman Admissions Requirements: Test(s) required: SAT or ACT; SAT and SAT Subject Tests. Average high school GPA: 3.57. 26% in top tenth, 54% in top quarter. SAT Math (25/75 percentile): 550/670. SAT Verbal (25/75 percentile): 540/663. *Academic units required:* 3 English, 3 math, 2 science, 2 social studies, 3 academic electives. Regular application deadline: 8/15. Regular notification: Rolling.

Costs and Financial Aid
(All Undergraduate Programs)
Annual tuition $18,925. Room & board $6,585. Required fees $225. Average book expense $730. **Financial Aid Statistics:** % freshmen/undergrads who receive any aid: 95/93. % freshmen/undergrads who receive need-based scholarship or grant aid: 62/61. % freshmen/undergrads who receive need-based self-help aid: 52/51. Priority financial aid filing deadline: 2/15. Financial aid notification on or about: 3/15.

TV/Film/Digital Media Studies Programs
Number of undergraduates in these programs: 125
Number of 2005 graduates from these programs: 25
Degrees conferred to these majors: BA.
Number of full-time faculty in these programs: 6
Number of part-time faculty in these programs: 4
Equipment and facilities: Full-time engineer, fully interconnected screening facility/video theater with HD capability that seats 150, television studio, three 16 x 9 studio cameras, SDI switcher with 3-D special effects, three HDV field cameras, audio studio, 48-channel digital audio board, six audio-editing suites, 10 video-editing suites, and software suites—Avid, AfterEffects, and Sequoia.
Career development services: Alumni networking opportunities; career counseling; central resource(s) for employers to browse headshots, writing samples, reels; internship listings; job fairs; job listings. We have an internal internship program in the department, and we network actively with alums, posting job openings through e-mails to majors.
Notable alumni: Wayne Vriesman, WGNTV, Chicago; Steve Vriesman, Channel 4, Denver; Joel Veenstra, development, Alcon Entertainment; Jeff Veen, author of *The Art and Science of Web Design*; Rob Prince, documentary filmmaker and assistant professor at the University of Alaska—Fairbanks.

In Their Own Words
Internships with broadcast stations, video production facilities, advertising agencies, film production facilties. Hosted National Press Photographers Association and the West Michigan Film and Video Association conferences. Los Angeles screenwriter Rik Swartzwelder teaches for us. Mira Nair (director of Monsoon Wedding) lectured for us. David McFadzen (producer for Home Improvement) lectured for us. Ken Wales, producer of the Christy television series lectured for us. Steve Vriesman (chief news editor for Channel 4 in Denver) teaches for us. Polar Express writer Chris Van Allsburg lectured in conjunction with the opening of the film.

POPULAR PROGRAMS

MEDIA STUDIES
Department chair: Helen Sterk
Number of full-time faculty: 4
Number of part-time faculty: 4
Focus/emphasis: Currently, media studies focuses on preparing students to analyze, evaluate, and make media products for film and television. Next year, we will have a media production major and a media studies major, splitting the two emphases.

FILM STUDIES

Number of full-time faculty: 2

Focus/emphasis: Film studies prepares students to know the history, art, and criticism of American and non-American film.

CARNEGIE MELLON UNIVERSITY

5000 Forbes Avenue, Pittsburgh, PA 15213
Phone: 412-268-2082 **E-mail:** undergraduate-admissions@andrew.cmu.edu
Website: www.cmu.edu

Campus Life

Environment: Metropolis. **Calendar:** Semester.

Students and Faculty
(All Undergraduate Programs)

Enrollment: 5,389. **Student Body:** 39% female, 61% male, 76% out-of-state, 12% international (93 countries represented). African American 5%, Asian 23%, Caucasian 42%, Hispanic 5%. Student/faculty ratio: 10:1. 806 full-time faculty, 98% hold PhDs.

Admissions
(All Undergraduate Programs)

Freshman Admissions Requirements: Test(s) required: SAT or ACT. Average high school GPA: 3.6. 72% in top tenth, 95% in top quarter. SAT Math (25/75 percentile): 680/770. SAT Verbal (25/75 percentile): 610/710. Projected SAT Writing (25/75 percentile): 660/730. *Academic units required:* 4 English, 4 math, 3 science (3 science labs), 2 foreign language, 3 academic electives. Early decision application deadline: 11/15. Regular application deadline: 1/1. Regular notification: 4/15.

Costs and Financial Aid
(All Undergraduate Programs)

Annual tuition $31,650. Room & board $8,606. Required fees $394. Average book expense $925. **Financial Aid Statistics:** % freshmen/undergrads who receive any aid: 70/66. % freshmen/undergrads who receive need-based scholarship or grant aid: 52/48. % freshmen/undergrads who receive need-based self-help aid: 51/49. Priority financial aid filing deadline: 2/15. Financial aid filing deadline: 5/1. Financial aid notification on or about: 3/15.

TV/Film/Digital Media Studies Programs

Degrees conferred to these majors: BFA, BSA, BHA.

Also available at Carnegie Mellon University: MFA.

Equipment and facilities: The 2,400-square-foot 3-D lab comprises a machine room, an assembly room, a spray room, and a materials room. Industrial design students work on class projects here after taking a proficiency workshop during their sophomore year. The 3-D lab is open 82 hours per week. Metal-, plastic-, and wood-forming equipment are available, and a wide variety of model-making materials are sold at cost. The John Reese Memorial Electronic Studio is reserved for design students who want to do 3-D modeling, image processing, illustration, animation, and other creative digital work. It is open 110 hours per week with support staff always available. The Reese Cluster equipment includes 15 2.0-GHz Power Mac G5s with 20" LCD displays; 15 3.4 GHz Pentium 4s with 17" LCD displays; A/V capture and editing equipment; industry-standard software such as Macromedia Studio MX, Adobe Creative Suite, AfterEffects, Audition, Premiere, Encore, Peak, Final Cut Pro, iLife and iWork, and Solidworks; and a wide selection of cross-platform OpenType(TM) fonts. The Robert Smillie Digital Imaging Lab supports advanced teaching, research, and production with imaging technologies. The lab features eight Power Mac G5s, a 60-inch continuous-feed HP color printer, two smaller Epson printers, and assorted peripheral devices including high-resolution scanners. We have a shooting studio for photographing 3-D models and other subjects and a copy stand for photographing flat work. Darkrooms are available for developing, enlarging, and printing photographic images in black and white or color. These facilities are useful for documenting student projects as well as for producing original works. Among the numerous public computer clusters across the university, the Multimedia Studio provides the most comprehensive range of hardware and software for producing electronic and time-based artwork. The Multimedia Studio houses both Mac and Windows clusters, as well as rooms dedicated to video and audio recording and editing. During the semester, the Mac and Windows clusters are open 24 hours, and students can borrow an "after-hours card" to access the video-editing cluster, which normally closes when the cluster is not staffed. The Multimedia Studio also houses an equipment lending collection consisting of digital video cameras, tripods, microphones, digital and analog audio-recording equipment, and various other audiovisual equipment. Equipment in this collection is available to all members of the university community through a check-out system in which users apply for an equipment access card that enables them to borrow the equipment free of charge. Loans are granted on a 24-hour basis, and late fees are assessed for overdue items. In addition to the equipment available in the Multimedia Studio collection, the School of Art also maintains a supplemental collection of equipment including video cameras, tripods, lighting kits, and video projectors, which are available exclusively to art students enrolled in electronic media courses and to art faculty, staff, and graduate students.

Career development services: Internship listings, job listings.

Famous alumni: John Wells, Rob Marshall.

Notable alumni: Stephanie Palmer, executive, senior story editor, MGM; Chris Goutman, director, *As the World Turns*; George Romero, writer/director, *Night of the Living Dead*; Bob Finkel, director/producer, *The Bob Newhart Show* and *Barney Miller*; Paula Wagner, producer, Cruise-Wagner Productions, and executive producer, *Mission Impossible* & *Mission Impossible 2*.

In Their Own Words

Lecturers have included Bob Dickinson, a prominent Los Angeles television lighting designer, who lights many awards and other television shows; Eddie Castro, a costume designer in Los Angeles for film and TV; Rick Parks, a TV and screenwriter (Ever After, Anna and the King, Sweet Home Alabama).

POPULAR PROGRAMS

DESIGN

Department chair: Dan Boyarski
Number of full-time faculty: 28
Number of part-time faculty: 10
Focus/emphasis: CMU believes learning by doing, in a human-centered design process, and in the value design brings to a range of human problems. CMU is training professionals who will leave a cross-disciplinary, collaborative university environment prepared to provide innovative solutions for real-world problems. The School of Design offers undergraduate, master's, and doctoral degrees, as well as a minor for undergraduates and a summer program for high school students. Students have access to excellent facilities, as well as opportunities to study abroad.

ART

Number of full-time faculty: 22
Focus/emphasis: The curriculum is at the heart of the School of Art. Innovative and progressive, the School of Art embraces new and established technologies in both physical and virtual realms. It is comfortable with the mix of the manual, the machine, the mind, and the Mac (or PC), and yet officials note that they're don't ever want to become too comfortable. Edging into new territories, imaginary or real, is part of what they're about. One of the curricular edges is the blend of concept and media studios. Concept studios focus on generating and developing ideas in courses devoted to broad themes, such as the self and the human being, time and space, and systems and processes before proceeding to the unique community affiliation and senior-year projects. Media studios focus on the materials, techniques, and processes of art ranging from charcoal to cast aluminum to constructions in cyberspace. The curriculum as a whole integrates form and content, technique, and concept. The first two years provide a broad and balanced exposure to the complete range of media that CMU has to offer and a variety of creative processes and conceptual

approaches. Juniors and seniors may specialize in one of three areas of concentration: Electronic and time-based art (including animation, video, robotic art, and other digital and interactive media); painting, drawing, and printmaking (with courses ranging from figure drawing to 2-dimensional projections in space, artists' books to mixed media); or sculpture, installation, and site work (with special topics courses such as environmental sculpture, sound installation, and media such as metals, foundry, clay, and wood). Many students cross over concentrations as well as mixing their media in a flexible program that suits and stimulates individual interests. An interdisciplinary approach permeates all aspects of the programs. Whether it's drawing inspiration from Dante's *Divine Comedy* in Concept Studio I or designing sets for a Bartok opera in an advanced painting course or supporting a double major in art and human computer interaction, CMU relishes and promotes the inescapable and stimulating intersections between art and other disciplines. BFA students blend their professional training with academic courses. At least one in four courses are nonstudio academic courses, building a broader education that better informs a creative life.

DRAMA—DIRECTING

Number of full-time faculty: 4

Focus/emphasis: Directing a play is like conducting a symphony and requires achieving a harmonious balance between all the dramatic elements to create a cohesive, singular experience. The CMU School of Drama offers undergraduate and graduate directors the opportunity to study the rich heritage of their field while honing their creative skills in classrooms, workshops, and full studio productions. Whether directing for the stage or camera, directors must have a thorough grounding in all aspects of drama: its history, theory, and techniques. The undergraduate directing program provides a detailed exploration of the techniques of directing for the stage and for the camera. The curriculum is designed for those serious about the art of directing and intending to pursue a career in theater, film, or television.

Directing students receive broad-based training in a number of vital fields: acting, theater history, criticism, playwriting, and theater management. Advanced studies include classroom scene work, short films, multicamera projects, and other theatrical productions.

DRAMA—DESIGN

Number of full-time faculty: 7

Focus/emphasis: For undergraduate students, CMU's School of Drama offers a strong grounding in all aspects of design. For four years, students engage in a challenging curriculum with comprehensive studies in lighting, costume, and scenic design. The undergraduate program promotes design history, creative technique, problem-solving skills, and the art of collaboration in theatrical productions. Whether your focus is costume, lighting, or scenic design, the CMU School of Drama offers you a challenging, exciting opportunity to study, practice, and shape your craft.

DRAMA—PRODUCTION TECHNOLOGY AND MANAGEMENT

Number of full-time faculty: 5

Focus/emphasis: The undergraduate PTM program consists of a well-rounded curriculum that exposes students to all areas of technology and management. Students also get valuable hands-on experience by working on multiple School of Drama productions. All undergraduate students begin with the development of visual and written communication skills. The first four semesters immerse the student in a range of collaborative and individual studies: scenery, costume, and lighting design fundamentals; dramatic structure and interpretation; manual and computer-based drafting; perspective and figure drawing; fundamentals of directing; production management and preparation; history of art; and history of architecture and decor. The last four semesters focus in the student's analytical skills within their chosen area of concentration: technical management or production management. Technical managers are offered classes in material applications, metal-working processes, structural design, scenic crafts, scenic construction design and detailing, machinery design, rigging techniques, power system and electronic design fundamentals, introduction to sound design, automation system technology, technical management, and production management. Technical managers may take a single semester internship at an approved regional or commercial producing organization in lieu of one semester of study. Student-selected elective courses, outside the School of Drama, provide balance and breadth to the professional undergraduate education offered in the PTM program of study. Production managers are offered classes in stage management, production planning and scheduling, theater management, introduction to accounting, cash budgeting, producing for television and film, camera lab, computer applications, technical management, organizational behavior, principles of economics, business communications, and production management workshop. Production managers may take a single semester internship at an approved regional or commercial producing organization in lieu of one semester of study. Student-selected elective courses, outside the School of Drama, provide balance and breadth to the professional undergraduate education offered in the PTM program of study.

CASTLETON STATE COLLEGE

Office of Admissions, Castleton, VT 05735
Phone: 802-468-1213 **E-mail:** info@castleton.edu
Website: www.castleton.edu

Campus Life
Environment: Rural. **Calendar:** Semester.

Students and Faculty
(All Undergraduate Programs)
Enrollment: 1,840. **Student Body:** 58% female, 42% male, 34% out-of-state. Caucasian 90%. Student/faculty ratio: 14:1. 89 full-time faculty, 93% hold PhDs. 100% faculty teach undergrads.

Admissions
(All Undergraduate Programs)
Freshman Admissions Requirements: Test(s) required: SAT or ACT; ACT with Writing component. Average high school GPA: 2.8. 5% in top tenth, 20% in top quarter. SAT Math (25/75 percentile): 460/540. SAT Verbal (25/75 percentile): 430/550. Projected SAT Writing (25/75 percentile): 500/610. *Academic units required:* 4 English, 3 math, 2 science (2 science labs), 3 social studies. Regular notification: Rolling.

Costs and Financial Aid
(All Undergraduate Programs)
Annual in-state tuition $6,312. Out-of-state tuition $13,632. Room & board $6,674. Required fees $320. Average book expense $800.
Financial Aid Statistics: Priority financial aid filing deadline: 2/15. Financial aid notification on or about: 2/15.

TV/Film/Digital Media Studies Programs
Number of undergraduates in these programs: 125
Number of 2005 graduates from these programs: 35
Degrees conferred to these majors: BS.
Number of full-time faculty in these programs: 5
Number of part-time faculty in these programs: 8
Equipment and facilities: Television studio, Final Cut edit bays, photojournalism computers, portable video production equipment.

% of graduates who pursue further study within 5 years: 5
% of graduates currently employed in related field: 75
Career development services: Alumni networking opportunities, career counseling, job fairs.

In Their Own Words
Our small size allows individual attention to students. Our alumni compare their educations favorably to industry colleagues from larger universities. Alums have gone on to work in all areas of film and video including major positions

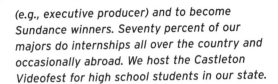

(e.g., executive producer) and to become Sundance winners. Seventy percent of our majors do internships all over the country and occasionally abroad. We host the Castleton Videofest for high school students in our state.

POPULAR PROGRAMS

MASS MEDIA
Focus/emphasis: Analysis and production of mass media products.

PUBLIC RELATIONS

DIGITAL MEDIA
Focus/emphasis: Integration of digital media and Internet delivery.

JOURNALISM

CENTENARY COLLEGE

400 Jefferson Street, Hackettstown, NJ 07840
Phone: 800-236-8679 **E-mail:** admissions@centenarycollege.edu
Website: www.centenarycollege.edu

Campus Life
Environment: Town. **Calendar:** Semester.

Students and Faculty (All Undergraduate Programs)
Enrollment: 2,469. **Student Body:** 64% female, 36% male, 12% out-of-state. Student/faculty ratio: 17:1. 58 full-time faculty, 71% hold PhDs. 100% faculty teach undergrads.

Admissions (All Undergraduate Programs)
Freshman Admissions Requirements: Test(s) required: SAT or ACT. Average high school GPA: 2.6. 3% in top tenth, 18% in top quarter. SAT Math (25/75 percentile): 400/500. SAT Verbal (25/75 percentile): 410/510. Projected SAT Writing (25/75 percentile): 480/570. *Academic units required:* 4 English, 3 math, 2 science (2 science labs), 2 history, 3 academic electives. Regular notification: Rolling.

Costs and Financial Aid (All Undergraduate Programs)
Annual tuition $21,230. Room & board $9,100. Required fees $900. Average book expense $666. **Financial Aid Statistics:** Priority financial aid filing deadline: 6/1. Financial aid notification on or about: 3/1.

TV/Film/Digital Media Studies Programs
Number of undergraduates in these programs: 66
Degrees conferred to these majors: BA, BFA.
Number of full-time faculty in these programs: 5
Career development services: Alumni networking opportunities, career counseling, internship listings, job fairs, job listings.

POPULAR PROGRAMS

GRAPHIC DESIGN AND MULTIMEDIA ARTS
Department chair: Carl Wallnau
Number of full-time faculty: 5

ART AND DESIGN
Department chair: Carl Wallnau
Number of full-time faculty: 5

CENTRAL MICHIGAN UNIVERSITY

105 Warriner Hall, Mount Pleasant, MI 48859
Phone: 989-774-3076 **E-mail:** cmuadmit@cmich.edu
Website: www.cmich.edu

Campus Life
Environment: Town. **Calendar:** Semester.

Students and Faculty (All Undergraduate Programs)
Enrollment: 19,715. **Student Body:** 57% female, 43% male, 2% out-of-state. African American 6%, Asian 1%, Caucasian 83%, Hispanic 2%. Student/faculty ratio: 22:1. 704 full-time faculty, 82% hold PhDs. 95% faculty teach undergrads.

Admissions
(All Undergraduate Programs)

Freshman Admissions Requirements: Test(s) required: ACT. Average high school GPA: 3.29. 15% in top tenth, 38% in top quarter. SAT Math (25/75 percentile): 450/580. SAT Verbal (25/75 percentile): 450/570. Projected SAT Writing (25/75 percentile): 520/620. Regular notification: Rolling.

Costs and Financial Aid
(All Undergraduate Programs)

Annual in-state tuition $5,868. Out-of-state tuition $13,632. Room & board $6,376. Average book expense $750.

Financial Aid Statistics: % freshmen/undergrads who receive any aid: 52/48. % freshmen/undergrads who receive need-based scholarship or grant aid: 48/40. % freshmen/undergrads who receive need-based self-help aid: 43/46. Priority financial aid filing deadline: 3/21. Financial aid notification on or about: 4/1.

TV/Film/Digital Media Studies Programs

Number of undergraduates in these programs: 371

Number of 2005 graduates from these programs: 79

Degrees conferred to these majors: BA, BS, BFA.

Also available at Central Michigan University: MA, BS in education, BAA.

Number of full-time faculty in these programs: 14

Number of part-time faculty in these programs: 3

Equipment and facilities: Anspach Studio: three Ikegami HC090 cameras, three Vinten pneumatic studio camera pedestals, Ross RVS-216A video switchers, Strand MX lighting board, AVS Manuscript Elite Character Generator, Mackie 1642VLZ PRO Audio Board, Sony mini-disc player, Clear-Com headset/intercom communications system, 360 instant replay audio machine, two QTV M-12 TelePrompTer, Panasonic 27" Proline stereo color video monitor. Moore 119 Edit Facilities: six Apple G-5 workstations, gigabit network with Apple X-Serve (2.1 Terabyte RAID), two DVC-Pro AJD-250 Digital Video Cassette Recorders, two DV Panasonic AG-DV2500 Digital Video Cassette Recorders, software (Avid DV Xpress, Apple Final Cut Pro HD, Adobe Photoshop CS, AfterEffects 6.5, Macintosh Studio MX 2004 with Flash Professional), DVC-Pro/SVHS/DV Dubbing Station. MHTV Control Room: Fiberoptic feed from Rose Arena for sports and university events, Ash Val slow-motion controller, Ross RVS-316 video switcher, Sony DFS-300 DME switcher, Soundcraft Delta Audio Board, Fostex D-5 digital audio recorder, Denon CD/Cassette recorder, Leitch 3101 CU Still Store System, Chyron Maxine character generator, two 360-instant replay audio machines, Elmo Eu-500AF visualizer, five Panasonic DVC-Pro digital video cassette recorders, Thomson Grass Valley M-122A, Leightronix Network-Management video-system controller, Clear-Com headset/intercom communications system, Accuweather integrated weather system, non-linear editing station (Apple Final Cut HD, DVD Studio Pro, Adobe Photoshop, AfterEffects, Sorenson Squeeze). Field equipment: 10 Panasonic VHS camcorders with Bogen tripods, four Canon GL-2 Mini-DV digital video camcorders, six Panasonic AJ-D200P DVC-Pro digital video camcorders, 12 Gitzo fluid head tripods, two Panasonic AG-EZ1UP digital video camcorders, six Panasonic GY-DV500 Mini-DV digital video camcorders, two Panasonic GY-DV5000 Mini-DV digital video camcorders with Focus Firestore FS-3 DV storage, four professional light kits (containing Cool Lux Hollywood soft-light, Desisti Fresnel, Pepper Spot, Mini Cool, Lowel and Mini Cool Dimmers, Matthews "C" Strands, "Lite Disc", assorted gels and materials), Losmandy Spider Dolly, Matthews Baby Jib, two Apple Powerbooks with Firewire drives with FCP-HD for field editing, remote multicamera studio unit (contains Panasonic WJ-MX digital video switcher, six 5" Ikegami B/W Monitors, two 9" Panasonic color monitors, 166 XL compressor limiter/gate, FP42 Shure Audio Mixer, Portacom headset/communications system, Formac Studio DV/TV Digital I/O, Analog I/O, Panasonic

AJD-650 video cassette recorder). Moore 187 WMHW-FM Master Control Room: ENCO digital delivery system with touch-screen monitor, PR&E Airwave 12 console, Sony mini-disc, Electrovoice RE 20 microphones and booms. Moore 184 Multitrack Production Control Room & Moore 182 Studio A: Mackie 24 x 8 x 2 analog console, Tascam DA-88 8-track recorder, Yamaha REV-5 digital reverb unit, dbx160 compressors, ADA D1280 digital delay unit, Symtrex paprmetric equalizer, Gatex 4-channel gate/expander units, Yamaha 02R 24x16x2 digital console, Alessi ADAT 8-track recorders, minidisk recorder/player, Tascam DA40 Tascam DAT recorder/player, Macintosh G4 with Pro Tools HD/2 TDM digital audio workstation, RE20 dynamic cardioid microphone, Sennheiser 421 dynamic cadioid microphone, Beyerdynamic M-88 dynamic cadioid microphones, Shure SM-58 dynamic cardioid microphones, Countryman Type 85 direct boxes, 8-track patchbay, AKG headphones, JBL 4104 speakers, Tannoy speakers.

ATAS Faculty Seminar participants: 2

Other awards of note: MHTV has won the Michigan Association of Broadcasters designation of College Television Station of the Year in each of the last five years (2002–2006).

% of graduates who pursue further study within 5 years: 15

% of graduates currently employed in related field: 55

Career development services: Alumni networking opportunities; career counseling; central resource(s) for employers to browse headshots, writing samples, reels; internship listings; job fairs; job listings.

Famous alumni: Cara Carriveau, air personality, 97.9, The Loop, Chicago.

Notable alumni: Brett Holey, director, *NBC Nightly News*; Gary Lico, CEO, CableReady cable syndication company; Mike Feltz, director, National Account Development, Yahoo!; Jeff Dengate, Web content developer, NBA Communications; Paul Boscarino, station manager, Clear Channel Radio of Grand Rapids; Eduardo Fernandez, vice president & general manager, Telemundo TV-44, Chicago; Mimi Levich, editor and executive producer, Voice of American English Programs Division; Tim Jackson, senior director, Emerging Media, PanAmSat.

In Their Own Words

BCA has been designated as one of only 11 programs nationwide whose students are eligible to receive scholarships and paid internships from the John Bayliss Broadcast Foundation. Supported by the major radio programs, Bayliss recognitions are the most prestigious scholastic awards given in the radio industry. The foundation has selected only the top collegiate radio programs to receive its support, and BCA is one of these. In summer 2005, Bayliss gave out 12 $5,000 scholarships. BCA was the only program whose students received more than one of the awards. BCA has been designated as a CNN Student News Bureau by that cable network, and the department's news unit head was selected as a trainer for the heads of similar operations on other campuses. BCA faculty have authored four textbooks now in use throughout our discipline. One of these works is in a seventh edition, and two are in their second editions. BCA students are consistently winning top honors in the Communicator Awards for their video news stories and other productions. In these competitions, they are up against media professionals, not just other students. A BCA faculty member is the only university professor to be inducted into the Michigan Association of Broadcasters Hall of Fame. BCA is one of only nine Midwest programs selected as eligible to receive student scholarships from the Ronald and Trishamiller Memorial Broadcast Journalism Scholarship Fund. A BCA faculty member won the Broadcast Education Association's 2001 Distinguished Education Service Award, the highest honor given out by our discipline's major academic organization. Since 1992, the Broadcast Education Association's national scholarship program has been administered by a BCA faculty member. Since 1991, the association's annual Faculty Salary Survey has been conducted by BCA. BCA has just been selected to host the regional convention of the National Broadcasting Society in November 2006. NBS is the principal student organization in the discipline. BCA has attracted two nationally prominent professionals to serve as unpaid adjunct professors. One of them is Dr. Larry Patrick, CEO of Patrick Communications, one of the country's largest media brokerage firms. He also owns the radio group Legend Communications. In addition, he is currently serving as CEO of the PAX television network. The second one is Edward Christian, who is CEO of Saga Communications, which owns of over 100 radio and television stations and three state radio networks. Saga is consistently rated as one of the 200 best-run small businesses in the country. Though both have been pursued by major doctoral-granting programs in our field, Mr. Christian has accepted adjunct appointment only with BCA. Dr. Patrick has accepted adjunct appointments only from BCA and Georgetown Law School.

POPULAR PROGRAMS

BROADCAST AND CINEMATIC ARTS

Department chair: Dr. Peter B. Orlik
Number of full-time faculty: 14
Number of part-time faculty: 3
Focus/emphasis: (BAA) No group requirements beyond university program and competency courses. Students may select virtually any minor.

BROADCAST AND CINEMATIC ARTS

Focus/emphasis: For students with a fine arts background (BFA). Enlarged BCA major. Instead of a minor, a 25-hour fine arts concentration that can be assembled from art, English (creative writing), dance, or music and theater. Student must present fine arts portfolio to department chair to ascertain eligibility.

BROADCAST AND CINEMATIC ARTS

Focus/emphasis: (BA) Earn a BCA major as well as speech-teaching certification. Enlarged major includes speech communication and dramatic arts, interpersonal and public communication, and theater and interpretation course work. Teachable minor required as is the professional education sequence.

BROADCAST AND CINEMATIC ARTS

Focus/emphasis: (BS) Foreign language required. Minor optional. Block requirements in humanities, natural sciences, and social sciences.

(BROADCAST & CINEMATIC ARTS)

Focus/emphasis: Minor optional. Block requirements in humanities, natural sciences, and social sciences.
Focus/emphasis: Science minor required. Block requirements in humanities, natural sciences, and social sciences.

CENTRAL WYOMING COLLEGE

2660 Peck Avenue, Riverton, WY 82501
Phone: 307-855-2000 **E-mail:** admit@cwc.edu

Campus Life
Environment: Village. **Calendar:** Semester.

Students and Faculty
(All Undergraduate Programs)
Enrollment: 1,027. **Student Body:** 65% female, 35% male, 4% out-of-state, 1% international (10 countries represented). Caucasian 76%, Hispanic 4%, Native American 15%. Student/faculty ratio: 14:1. 41 full-time faculty, 10% hold PhDs. 100% faculty teach undergrads.

Costs and Financial Aid
(All Undergraduate Programs)
Annual in-state tuition $1,416. Out-of-state tuition $4,272. Room & board $3,060. Required fees $504. Average book expense $800.

Financial Aid Statistics: % undergrads who receive any aid: 55. % freshmen/undergrads who receive need-based scholarship or grant aid: 37/47. % freshmen/undergrads who receive need-based self-help aid: 21/31. Priority financial aid filing deadline: 4/15. Financial aid notification on or about: 5/1.

TV/Film/Digital Media Studies Programs

Number of undergraduates in these programs: 26

Number of 2005 graduates from these programs: 6

Degrees conferred to these majors: BA, BFA.

Also available at Central Wyoming College: AAS, AA.

Number of full-time faculty in these programs: 3

Number of part-time faculty in these programs: 2

Equipment and facilities: CWC has a student-run radio station on campus and specialized video-editing production equipment. It also has three different-sized theater stages (960 seats, 160 seats, and a studio) to give students a range of experiences in different spaces. The school also has a machine shop in which students get experience hanging lights, building stages, and creating scenery.

Other awards of note: CWC has won some Telly awards and have been recognized by the Rocky Mountain Theatre Association to perform two selected shows in their festival.

Career development services: Career counseling, internship listings, job fairs, job listings, job referral, help in developing job search skills, and summer theater placement.

Notable alumni: Devin Sanchez, actress in Off-Broadway plays in New York; Jonas Dickson, actor in Off-Broadway plays in New York; Emmett Buhmann, technical director and lighting designer; Terry Cortez, producer in Chicago at a local sports cable TV station; Amanda Watkins, producer/director of an NBC affiliate in San Jose; Ernest Whiteman, producer; Rom Bowers, producer; Ricky Tollman, writer; Ellen Bredehoft, costume shop manager for NYU.

In Their Own Words

We have a partnership with Wyoming Public Television (WPTV), and in fact, they are housed entirely on our campus, so students get exceptional experience and access to a studio and TV equipment. We offer internship opportunities, scholarships, and work experience with pay for students working in our programs.

POPULAR PROGRAMS

ELECTRONIC MEDIA

Department chair: Charlotte Donelson

Number of full-time faculty: 1

Number of part-time faculty: 1

Focus/emphasis: This program is designed to provide training for students who wish to acquire entry-level skills for a career in radio/TV broadcasting and/or other media production and operations, such as working on an educational distance delivery network.

THEATER

Department chair: Mark Nordeen

Number of full-time faculty: 1

Focus/emphasis: This program offers students opportunities to explore various aspects of acting within the context of a liberal education. The department stresses that it is not a professional training school; it does, however, provide experiences in many areas of production and prepares students for supplemental-level undergraduate, professional, or apprenticeship training.

GRAPHIC DESIGN

Department chair: Charlotte Donelson

Number of part-time faculty: 1

Focus/emphasis: The graphic design option is targeted to those individuals who have a desire to obtain proficiency in graphic design as it relates to both the web and print media. Participants will use cutting-edge Web page and graphic design tools and theory to create digital media and graphic layouts for both Web and print applications.

TECHNICAL THEATER

Department chair: Mark Nordeen
Number of full-time faculty: 1
Focus/emphasis: This program offers students opportunities to explore various aspects of technical theater within the context of a liberal education. The department stresses that it is not a professional training school; it does however, provide experiences in many areas of production and prepares students for upper-level undergraduate, professional, or apprenticeship training.

CHAPMAN UNIVERSITY

One University Drive, Orange, CA 92866
Phone: 714-997-6711 **E-mail:** admit@chapman.edu
Website: www.chapman.edu

Campus Life
Environment: Metropolis. **Calendar:** 4-1-4.

Students and Faculty
(All Undergraduate Programs)
Enrollment: 3,839. **Student Body:** 59% female, 41% male, 20% out-of-state, 2% international (37 countries represented). African American 2%, Asian 8%, Caucasian 67%, Hispanic 11%. Student/faculty ratio: 14:1. 264 full-time faculty, 89% hold PhDs. 100% faculty teach undergrads.

Admissions
(All Undergraduate Programs)
Freshman Admissions Requirements: Test(s) required: SAT or ACT; ACT with Writing component. Average high school GPA: 3.66. SAT Math (25/75 percentile): 551/662. SAT Verbal (25/75 percentile): 543/656. *Academic units required:* 2 English, 2 math, 2 science (1 science lab), 2 foreign language, 3 social studies. Regular application deadline: 1/31. Regular notification: Rolling.

Costs and Financial Aid
(All Undergraduate Programs)
Annual tuition $29,900. Room & board $10,500. Required fees $848. Average book expense $1,100.

Financial Aid Statistics: % undergrads who receive any aid: 79. % freshmen/undergrads who receive need-based scholarship or grant aid: 63/61. % freshmen/undergrads who receive need-based self-help aid: 51/52. Priority financial aid filing deadline: 3/2. Financial aid notification on or about: 3/15.

TV/Film/Digital Media Studies Programs
Degrees conferred to these majors: BA.
Also available at Chapman University: MFA.
Equipment and facilities: Lights, cameras, and all the hardware you'll need to bring your dreams to life. Students have full use of the following industry standard production and location equipment: six Arri SR 16 mm sync sound cameras; six Super16 mm sync sound cameras; five 24p cameras; 12 ArriS nonsync cameras; DAT packages with four mics each and additional wireless lav mics; more than 120 camera packages for intro classes; additional sync and nonsync cameras for class exercises; professional dolly grip equipment, including three Fisher dollies; lighting equipment for location shooting, including Kino Flo, HMIs, and tungsten lighting kits; more than 40 Avid digital editing systems with networked and removable storage of more than five terabytes; more than 20 digital audio Pro Tools workstations; four dedicated compositing workstations, as well as a render farm and compositing software on more than 20 computers; a green screen stage; a scene shop with all the tools necessary to design and build sets; a warehouse/stage with 300 amp service power distribution; scene dock for a selection of flats and set pieces; props; and costume storage.
Other awards of note: Coca Cola Refreshing Filmmakers Award—three Chapman students were awarded finalist spots; one Chapman student was the grand-prize winner.

In Their Own Words
Guests lecturers have included Richard Donner, William Friedkin, Alexander Payne, Eric Roth, and Babaloo Mandel.

POPULAR PROGRAMS

FILM AND TV PRODUCTION

Department chair: Ken O'Donnell
Number of full-time faculty: 32
Focus/emphasis: Students may elect to specialize in writing/directing, postproduction, cinematography, producing, sound, or new media. The film production degree provides professional education in a liberal arts environment, a combination that prepares students to create as film artists who understand the social, cultural, and historic context of film language while developing their skills in one or more areas of production. FTV 130, Introduction to Visual Storytelling, is a gateway class to the program. Students must enroll in it the first semester at Chapman that they enroll in any film and television production classes and may not enroll in most other courses until they have successfully passed FTV 130 with a grade of B- or better. If students receive grades lower than B-, then they must repeat the courses, and additional courses that may be taken concurrently are restricted to 100- and 200-level courses until the successful completion of FTV 130 with a grade of B- or better.

FILM STUDIES

Focus/emphasis: The film studies degree offers students the opportunity to explore film history, theory, and criticism in depth along with a hands-on introduction to production. This combination of theoretical study with production experience gives students a unique understanding of how film creates meaning. Film studies students may choose to focus their analysis of film through a specialization in film history or American film.

SCREENWRITING

Focus/emphasis: The study of screenwriting is an intensive program aimed at helping screenwriters develop their individual creative voices as they explore the intricacies of story structure, character development, writing believable dialogue, and understanding film language and genres. Students will learn to write in a variety of forms, including the short film, the feature film, and episodes (television and mini series).

CITY UNIVERSITY OF NEW YORK– BROOKLYN COLLEGE

2900 Bedford Avenue, Brooklyn, NY 11210-2889
Phone: 718-951-5001 **E-mail:** adminqry@brooklyn.cuny.edu
Website: www.brooklyn.cuny.edu

Campus Life

Environment: Metropolis. **Calendar:** Semester.

Students and Faculty
(All Undergraduate Programs)

Enrollment: 11,068. **Student Body:** 60% female, 40% male, 2% out-of-state, 7% international (82 countries represented). African American 28%, Asian 11%, Caucasian 41%, Hispanic 12%. Student/faculty ratio: 15:1. 517 full-time faculty, 90% hold PhDs. 80% faculty teach undergrads.

Admissions
(All Undergraduate Programs)

Freshman Admissions Requirements: Test(s) required: SAT, ACT. Average high school GPA: 2.8. 14% in top tenth, 42% in top quarter. SAT Math (25/75 percentile): 490/590. SAT Verbal (25/75 percentile): 450/570. Projected SAT Writing (25/75 percentile): 520/620. Regular notification: Rolling.

Costs and Financial Aid
(All Undergraduate Programs)

Annual in-state tuition $4,000. Out-of-state tuition $10,800. Required fees $375. Average book expense $800.
Financial Aid Statistics: % freshmen/undergrads who receive any aid: 78/78. % freshmen/undergrads who receive need-based scholarship or grant aid: 73/68. % freshmen/undergrads who receive need-based self-help aid: 69/72. Priority financial aid filing deadline: 4/1. Financial aid notification on or about: 5/1.

TV/Film/Digital Media Studies Programs

Number of undergraduates in these programs: 535

Number of 2005 graduates from these programs: 117

Degrees conferred to these majors: BA, BS.

Also available at CUNY—Brooklyn College: MFA, MA, certificates.

Number of full-time faculty in these programs: 23

Number of part-time faculty in these programs: 17

Equipment and facilities: Equipment and facilities that will enhance student's learning experience: Computer labs for nonlinear editing and postproduction effects; 6.5 computer with digital component stations; a flatbed room for traditional hands-on film editing; audio sound room; mini-DVD cameras, projectors, and screens; DVD duplicators; and microphones.

ATAS interns: 2

Other awards of note: Films screened in competition at various festivals, including the Sundance Film Festival and Mill Valley Film Festival. Other awards include Broadcasting Education Association awards, Al Tanger scholarships, Himan Brown Radio awards, and Spielman scholarships.

% of graduates who pursue further study within 5 years: 22 in film, 25 in TV and radio.

% of graduates currently employed in related field: 50 in film, 85 in TV and radio

Career development services: Alumni networking opportunities; career counseling; central resource(s) for employers to browse headshots, writing samples, reels; internship listings; job fairs; job listings; list services for alumni, department majors, and job seekers.

Famous alumni: Bill Chase, HBO; Scott Herman, CBS radio; Skeery Jones, Z100; Steve Ridgeway, *Jay Leno Show*.

Notable alumni: Oren Moverman, writer of the screenplay for the acclaimed independent film *Jesus' Son*; Terry Lawler, executive director of New York Women in Film and Television; Cliff Charles, a cinematographer with nearly 20 film credits,

recently profiled in *American Cinematographer* magazine; Chul Heo, San Francisco faculty member; Saul Spicer, CUNY-TV.

In Their Own Words

Graduates are employed in the media and film industries throughout the world. Student work and films have been entered into various festivals in North and South America, Europe, and Asia, including the National Academy of Television Arts and Sciences, Broadcast Education Association, and the Asian American/Asian Research Institute. The Department of TV and Radio offers five courses with internship opportunities, and internships are also available for students who want them. Nationally famous guest speakers include Scott Herman, radio; William Chase, HBO; Agnieska Holland, director/writer in residence in fall of 2006; Skeery Jones, Z100; Amy Goodman, NPR and public television. Elizabeth Weis, a professor in the film department, is the executive director of the National Society of Film Critics.

POPULAR PROGRAMS

BROADCAST JOURNALISM

Department chair: George Rodman

Focus/emphasis: Broadcast journalism focuses on news writing, production, and critical thinking in all areas of news.

FILM MARKETING

Department chair: Dan Gurskis

Focus/emphasis: Film marketing is a unique program that offers concentrated study in the marketing, promotion, and distribution of film and media.

FILM PRODUCTION

Department chair: Dan Gurskis

Number of full-time faculty: 11

Number of part-time faculty: 7

Focus/emphasis: Film production majors receive technical training in directing, producing, screenwriting, editing, cinematography, and sound design, as well as practical film industry-related study.

FILM SCREENWRITING
Department chair: Dan Gurskis
Focus/emphasis: The screenwriting concentration is the only undergraduate, liberal arts-based screenwriting program in the country.

FILM STUDIES
Department chair: Dan Gurskis
Focus/emphasis: Film studies explores American and international cinemas, a variety of film genres, the history of film, and film theory.

TELEVISION AND RADIO
Department chair: George Rodman
Number of full-time faculty: 12
Number of part-time faculty: 10
Focus/emphasis: Television and radio is a multi-faceted program with the main emphasis on writing for the media, television and radio production, and critical analysis.

Students Should Also Know
The unique draw of Brooklyn College's media and film programs is its renowned faculty and the network of successful alumni working in the industry that the programs have produced.

CITY UNIVERSITY OF NEW YORK– CITY COLLEGE
Convent Avenue at 138th Street, New York, NY 10031-9198
Phone: 212-650-6977 **E-mail:** admissions@ccny.cuny.edu
Website: www.ccny.cuny.edu

Campus Life
Environment: Metropolis. **Calendar:** Semester.

Students and Faculty
(All Undergraduate Programs)
Enrollment: 9,107. **Student Body:** 49% female, 51% male, 12% out-of-state. Student/faculty ratio:
11:1. 534 full-time faculty. 100% faculty teach under-grads.

Admissions
(All Undergraduate Programs)
Freshman Admissions Requirements: Test(s) required: SAT or ACT. Average high school GPA: 2.76. SAT Math (25/75 percentile): 460/610. SAT Verbal (25/75 percentile): 420/560. Projected SAT Writing (25/75 percentile): 490/620. *Academic units required:* 4 English, 2 math, 2 science (2 science labs), 2 foreign language, 4 social studies, 1 fine or performing arts. Regular notification: Rolling.

Costs and Financial Aid
(All Undergraduate Programs)
Annual in-state tuition $4,000. Out-of-state tuition $8,640. Required fees $289. Average book expense $832.
Financial Aid Statistics: % freshmen/undergrads who receive any aid: 70/68. % undergrads who receive need-based scholarship or grant aid: 61. % undergrads who receive need-based self-help aid: 27. Priority financial aid filing deadline: 4/1. Financial aid notification on or about: 5/15.

TV/Film/Digital Media Studies Programs
Number of undergraduates in these programs: 100
Number of 2005 graduates from these programs: 50
Degrees conferred to these majors: BFA.
Also available at CUNY—City College: MFA.
Number of full-time faculty in these programs: 7
Number of part-time faculty in these programs: 6
Equipment and facilities: The department houses Avid digital nonlinear suites, Final Cut Pro nonlinear suites, and Pro Tools audio-post suites. Cameras include Bolex, Arri-SB, Arriflex SRII for 16 mm and mini-DV, DVCam, 24P, and HD digital video. The program utilizes its own fully-equipped soundstage.

% of graduates who pursue further study within 5 years: 20

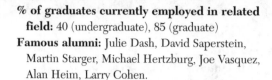

% of graduates currently employed in related field: 40 (undergraduate), 85 (graduate)
Famous alumni: Julie Dash, David Saperstein, Martin Starger, Michael Hertzburg, Joe Vasquez, Alan Heim, Larry Cohen.

In Their Own Words

The undergraduate Film and Video Program provides a broad range of fundamental production skills in the areas of fiction and documentary media production. Courses in screenwriting, production, and editing prepare students to produce their own projects in both 16 mm film and digital video. In addition to production courses, students are also required to take courses in history, theory, and aesthetics of film to reinforce and contextualize the production skills they learn. Students graduating from this program are well prepared for entry-level positions in the film and video industry or to apply to a graduate program in media production. The Department of Media and Communication Arts also offers a graduate program leading to an MFA in Media Arts Production. This intensive two-year program prepares students to navigate and prosper in the quickly expanding field of media arts, including film and digital video production with an emphasis on strong, original storytelling in documentary and fiction. This is the only graduate-level program of its kind in the region offered at an affordable and accessible public institution. The City College campus is located in New York City, the hub of international media arts production.

CITY UNIVERSITY OF NEW YORK– THE COLLEGE OF STATEN ISLAND

2800 Victory Boulevard, Building 2A Room 102,
Staten Island, NY 10314
Phone: 718-982-2010 **E-mail:** admissions@mail.csi.cuny.edu
Website: www.csi.cuny.edu

Campus Life
Environment: Metropolis. **Calendar:** Semester.

Students and Faculty
(All Undergraduate Programs)
Enrollment: 10,920. **Student Body:** 61% female, 39% male, 1% out-of-state, 4.7% international (114 countries represented). African American 11.3%, Asian 9.1%, Caucasian 67.6%, Hispanic 11.8%, Native American 0.2%. Student/faculty ratio: 18:1. 330 full-time faculty, 87% hold PhDs. 86% faculty teach undergrads.

Admissions
(All Undergraduate Programs)
Average high school GPA: 3.02. SAT Math (25/75 percentile): 485/565. SAT Verbal (25/75 percentile): 460/560. Projected SAT Writing (25/75 percentile): 530/620. *Academic units required:* 4 English, 3 math, 2 science, 2 foreign language, 4 social studies, 1 social science. Regular notification: Rolling.

Costs and Financial Aid
(All Undergraduate Programs)
Annual in-state tuition $4,000. Out-of-state tuition $8,640. Required fees $328.
Financial Aid Statistics: % freshmen/undergrads who receive need-based scholarship or grant aid: 53/50. % freshmen/undergrads who receive need-based self-help aid: 16/22. Financial aid notification on or about: 5/5.

TV/Film/Digital Media Studies Programs
Number of undergraduates in these programs: 246
Number of 2005 graduates from these programs: 49
Degrees conferred to these majors: BS.
Also available at CUNY—College of Staten Island: MA.

Number of full-time faculty in these programs: 12

Number of part-time faculty in these programs: 16

Equipment and facilities: Television studio, digital update to be implemented in the summer. Mac lab for digital video production, featuring Final Cut Pro and other software.

Career development services: Alumni networking opportunities, career counseling, internship listings, job listings.

In Their Own Words

Students have interned at MTV–New York, MTV–Los Angeles, All My Children (ABC), Nickelodeon, Silvercup Studios, Law and Order (NBC), independent film productions, Museum of Modern Art, press office of Senator Hillary Clinton, and prestigious ad firms.

POPULAR PROGRAMS

CINEMA STUDIES

Department chair: Cindy Wong (acting)
Number of full-time faculty: 5
Number of part-time faculty: 5
Focus/emphasis: Students learn theories and practices of film and television.

COMMUNICATION, PUBLICATION DESIGN

Department chair: Cindy Wong (acting)
Number of full-time faculty: 2
Number of part-time faculty: 3
Focus/emphasis: Students learn the theory and history of communication, with an emphasis on desktop digital production.

Students Should Also Know

The school also offers bachelor's degrees in communications in areas of media studies, corporate communication, and journalism.

CITY UNIVERSITY OF NEW YORK– HUNTER COLLEGE

695 Park Avenue, New York, NY 10021
Phone: 212-772-4490 **E-mail:** admissions@hunter.cuny.edu
Website: www.hunter.cuny.edu

Campus Life

Environment: Metropolis. **Calendar:** Semester.

Students and Faculty
(All Undergraduate Programs)

Enrollment: 14,357. **Student Body:** 69% female, 31% male, 4% out-of-state, 7% international (150 countries represented). African American 15%, Asian 17%, Caucasian 40%, Hispanic 20%. Student/faculty ratio: 14:1. 633 full-time faculty, 87% hold PhDs. 96% faculty teach undergrads.

Admissions
(All Undergraduate Programs)

Freshman Admissions Requirements: Test(s) required: SAT or ACT. Average high school GPA: 2.9. 21% in top tenth, 48% in top quarter. SAT Math (25/75 percentile): 500/590. SAT Verbal (25/75 percentile): 480/580. Projected SAT Writing (25/75 percentile): 540/630. *Academic units required:* 2 English, 2 math, 1 science (1 science lab). Regular application deadline: 3/15. Regular notification: Rolling.

Costs and Financial Aid
(All Undergraduate Programs)

Annual in-state tuition $4,000. Room $3,250. Required fees $349. Average book expense $832. **Financial Aid Statistics:** % freshmen/undergrads who receive any aid: 91/94. % freshmen/undergrads who receive need-based scholarship or grant aid: 64/56. % freshmen/undergrads who receive need-based self-help aid: 15/27. Priority financial aid filing deadline: 5/1. Financial aid notification on or about: 5/15.

TV/Film/Digital Media Studies Programs

Number of undergraduates in these programs: 675

Number of 2005 graduates from these programs: 232

Degrees conferred to these majors: BA.

Number of full-time faculty in these programs: 22

Number of part-time faculty in these programs: 57

Equipment and facilities: Digital media lab, video-editing lab, television studio, interactive media lab, journalism lab.

Career development services: Alumni networking opportunities, career counseling, internship listings, job fairs, job listings.

In Their Own Words

Journalist Wayne Barrett was named Newfield Visiting Professor. Madonna taught a Hunter College film class; Hunter film professors Tami Gold and Kelly Anderson have been nominated for Emmys.

POPULAR PROGRAMS

MEDIA STUDIES

Department chair: Roman James

Number of full-time faculty: 20

Number of part-time faculty: 37

Focus/emphasis: The program deals with subjects such as the history and aesthetics of film, video, and television; genre studies; the production and distribution of print and broadcast news; the representation of race, class, and gender in various media; domestic and international policy and regulatory issues in print, broadcasting, telecommunications, and new media; Hollywood's past and present configurations; and the intricate relationships between the mass media, popular culture, and society.

FILM

Department chair: Roman James

Number of full-time faculty: 9

Number of part-time faculty: 10

Focus/emphasis: The major combines theoretical perspectives and practical production experience to provide students with a thorough understanding of the cinema and of their creative potential as filmmakers. The major is composed of required and elective courses in film and video production and film studies. Students are introduced to the aesthetics of filmmaking, the historical background of the film industry, alternative filmic practices, current critical theories, and various national and multicultural perspectives on cinema. Production courses include screenwriting, screen directing, film producing, sound, editing, and cinematography.

FILM PRODUCTION

Department chair: Roman James

Number of full-time faculty: 2

Number of part-time faculty: 5

Focus/emphasis: The program constitutes a vital element of both the film and media studies majors. The production curriculum is designed to offer students in-depth understanding of applied aesthetics, creative concepts, and technical proficiency through a diverse range of rigorous practicum courses in film, video, television studio, newswriting, screenwriting, graphics, layout, and new digital media. Production offerings encourage students to produce original work in dramatic narrative, documentary, and experimental forms, permitting them to cultivate a creative voice that can find expression across the range of contemporary media technologies.

CITY UNIVERSITY OF NEW YORK– QUEENS COLLEGE

65-30 Kissena Boulevard, Flushing, NY 11367
Phone: 718-997-5600 **E-mail:** admissions@qc.edu
Website: www.qc.cuny.edu

Campus Life

Environment: Metropolis. **Calendar:** Semester.

Students and Faculty
(All Undergraduate Programs)

Enrollment: 12,320. **Student Body:** 61% female, 39% male, 1% out-of-state, 8% international (140 countries represented). African American 9%, Asian 18%, Caucasian 48%, Hispanic 17%. Student/faculty ratio: 16:1. 577 full-time faculty, 85% hold PhDs. 90% faculty teach undergrads.

Admissions
(All Undergraduate Programs)

Freshman Admissions Requirements: Test(s) required: SAT or ACT. Average high school GPA: 3.2. SAT Math (25/75 percentile): 490/580. SAT Verbal (25/75 percentile): 440/550. Projected SAT Writing (25/75 percentile): 510/610. *Academic units required:* 4 English, 3 math, 2 science (2 science labs), 3 foreign language, 4 social studies. Regular notification: Rolling.

Costs and Financial Aid
(All Undergraduate Programs)

Annual in-state tuition $4,000. Out-of-state tuition $10,800. Required fees $377.

Financial Aid Statistics: % freshmen/undergrads who receive any aid: 76/44. % freshmen/undergrads who receive need-based scholarship or grant aid: 23/27. % freshmen/undergrads who receive need-based self-help aid: 12/14. Priority financial aid filing deadline: 2/1. Financial aid notification on or about: 3/1.

TV/Film/Digital Media Studies Programs

Number of undergraduates in these programs: 373 (media studies), 22 (film studies)

Number of 2005 graduates from these programs: 119 (media studies), 1 (film studies)

Degrees conferred to these majors: BA.

Number of full-time faculty in these programs: 12

Number of part-time faculty in these programs: 9

Equipment and facilities: Apple postproduction and audio design: Final Cut Pro HD, LiveType, DVD Studio Pro, Pro Tools, AfterEffects. Midsized 3-camera TV studio, control room, CG, TelePrompTer, Grass Valley switcher. Sony mini-DV and DV camera, Lowell light kits, Bolex 16 mm film cameras, and Steenbeck editing tables. Xsan server.

Other awards of note: NATAS (NY) Foundation Scholarship.

% of graduates who pursue further study within 5 years: 25

% of graduates currently employed in related field: 45

Career development services: Alumni networking opportunities, career counseling, internship listings, job fairs, job listings. The Media Studies department promotes alumni mentoring through job placement and guest lecturers.

Famous alumni: Jerry Seinfeld

Notable alumni: Dr. Alan Wurtzel, president of research and development at NBC; Laurie Younger, president of Buena Vista Worldwide—TV distribution; Garry Hart, former president of Paramount Network TV; Dan Greenblatt, former executive vice president of Warner Bros.—TV distribution; Carmon Johnston, senior vice president and director of creative services; Dennis Elsas, *WFUV City Folks* host, on-air DJ radio personality; Jeff Gomez, president and CEO, Starlight Runner Entertainment; Dante Amato, Hearst Entertainment, International Broadcast Materials; Eric Dorfschneider, producer of CBS Sports; Dr. Paul Allen, vice president of network operations, NGTV; Robert Batscha (deceased), president Museum of Television & Radio; Gerry Red Wilson (deceased), comedian, TV actor.

In Their Own Words

Our mission is to enable students to explore aesthetic possibilities of media technologies by creating narrative and nonfiction works in film, video, and computational forms. This highly competitive program culminates in two honors programs. The honors internship program participates with 500 employers in the New York media industry, including major networks, cable, and independent film companies. Our NATAS Honors Seminar enrolls ten highly qualified juniors and seniors in a month-long program each semester where students meet with senior executives and members of the Board of the National Academy of Television Arts and Sciences (NY Chapter).

CLARK ATLANTA UNIVERSITY

223 James P. Brawley Drive at Fair Street, Atlanta, GA 30314
Phone: 404-880-8000 **E-mail:** admissions@panthernet.cau.edu

Campus Life
Environment: Metropolis. **Calendar:** Semester.

Students and Faculty
(All Undergraduate Programs)
Enrollment: 3,667. **Student Body:** 70% female, 30% male, 56% out-of-state. African American 69%. Student/faculty ratio: 16:1. 290 full-time faculty, 84% hold PhDs.

Admissions
(All Undergraduate Programs)
Freshman Admissions Requirements: Test(s) required: SAT or ACT. Average high school GPA: 3.1. SAT Math (25/75 percentile): 360/580. SAT Verbal (25/75 percentile): 330/593. *Academic units required:* 4 English. Early decision application deadline: 3/1. Regular application deadline: 6/1. Regular notification: Rolling.

Costs and Financial Aid
(All Undergraduate Programs)
Annual tuition $14,522. Room & board $10,978. Required fees $550. Average book expense $1,000. **Financial Aid Statistics:** % freshmen/undergrads who receive need-based scholarship or grant aid: 75/76. % freshmen/undergrads who receive need-based self-help aid: 34/29. Priority financial aid filing deadline: 3/1. Financial aid filing deadline: 4/1. Financial aid notification on or about: 2/27.

TV/Film/Digital Media Studies Programs
Equipment and facilities: Digital Teleproductions Laboratory (multimedia lab)—ensures the provision of state-of-the-art training facilities to media students and serves to strengthen the communications arts curricula.

In Their Own Words
Students gain a wealth of studio and field production experience through membership in Drop Frame Productions—the official student television production organization of the Mass Media Arts Department. Drop Frame Productions is aired on CAU-TV; 4 Reel Productions is a student-based organization that focuses on the development and creation of film projects (including public service announcements, shorts, and features); WCLK-FM is a 24-hour, daily NPR member station licensed by Clark Atlanta University presenting jazz, blues, gospel, Latin, and reggae, and offering students opportunities to receive hands-on training in radio production; CAU-TV is an educational access television station that provides a variety of informative programming thereby serving the Atlanta community as an educational and community resource. While providing programming that informs and educates, CAU-TV serves as a hands-on training laboratory for broadcast majors in the Atlanta University Center and an outlet for student video, film, and multimedia productions; Internships here are academically monitored learning experiences in professional media organizations. Internship partners have included CNN, Atlanta Constitution, WSB-TV, Ketchem Public Relations, La Face Records, and many other media/music outlets; The African Film Festival celebrates excellence in the richness and diversity of African World Cinema, showcasing stories about the multifaceted, global experience of African and African-descended people told through the eyes of Screen Griots; WSTU serves as a radio outlet for student broadcasters and presents a hands-on training opportunity to apply communication concepts and practices; Mass Media Arts Club is open to all stu-

dents interested in the field of communications. In addition to keeping members abreast of internships/job opportunities and scheduling regular seminars with speakers who are working in the field, the group spearheads workshops on various aspects of communications, such as how to prepare resumes and how to operate computer software. It also holds a leadership seminar every year; CAU-TV's Student News Center is a student-produced program that brings you news and information from campuses across the city and also features stories making national and international headlines.

POPULAR PROGRAMS

MASS MEDIA

Department chair: Anita Fleming-Rife
Number of full-time faculty: 13
Focus/emphasis: One of two units in the Division of Communication Arts, provides students with rigorous academic and professional training that is complemented with a strong liberal arts education. The department recognizes that the fundamental prerequisites to success depend on students' abilities to compete in an employment climate that is competitive, dynamic, and global. To this end, while the department encourages effective communication skills, both oral and written, it also facilitates the development of sophisticated abilities in the gathering, analysis, and dissemination of information. The result is that students are able to create award-winning productions based on the highest academic and professional standards. At the same time, they are prepared for the most competitive graduate programs in the discipline. Concentrations within Mass Media Arts include journalism; public relations; and radio, television, and film. The Department of Mass Media Arts reviews trends in the media industries and recognizes that students need to have a competitive edge in the use and understanding of media technology. To accomplish this, training laboratories provide students with the opportunity to enhance their abilities in their academic course work and assist in practical, hands-on experiences.

DEPARTMENT OF SPEECH COMMUNICATION AND THEATER ART

Department chair: Carol Mitchell-Leon
Number of full-time faculty: 5
Focus/emphasis: The curriculum is designed to educate and train students in the strategic use of verbal, nonverbal, and written communication. Both speech communication and theater majors are provided quality instruction in theoretical and practical concepts to aid in the understanding of the communication process. Majors in speech communication take courses to prepare them for careers in areas such as corporate communication, communication education, government, and politics. Theater arts majors are prepared for careers in theatrical directing, theater and film performance, technical theater production, play and scriptwriting, and theater management. Departmental courses prepare all students, regardless of major, for graduate and professional studies as specialists in oral and written communication and provide them with a foundation to manage communications. Students from other programs may elect to minor in either speech communication or theater arts. As communication skills are directly related to personal and professional success, all students who enter Clark Atlanta University receive instruction in the fundamentals of speech as a general education requirement. Students who seek careers in other areas, such as business, education, politics, and law, find speech communication courses of critical importance.

CLARK UNIVERSITY
950 Main Street, Worcester, MA 01610-1477
Phone: 508-793-7431 **E-mail:** admissions@clarku.edu

Campus Life
Environment: City. **Calendar:** Semester.

Students and Faculty
(All Undergraduate Programs)
Enrollment: 2,142. **Student Body:** 60% female, 40% male, 61% out-of-state, 7% international (58 countries represented). African American 2%, Asian 4%, Caucasian 65%, Hispanic 2%. Student/faculty ratio: 10:1. 167 full-time faculty, 98% hold PhDs. 100% faculty teach undergrads.

Admissions
(All Undergraduate Programs)
Freshman Admissions Requirements: Test(s) required: SAT or ACT. Average high school GPA: 3.44. 34% in top tenth, 70% in top quarter. SAT Math (25/75 percentile): 540/650. SAT Verbal (25/75 percentile): 560/660. Projected SAT Writing (25/75 percentile): 620/690. Early decision application deadline: 11/15. Regular application deadline: 1/15. Regular notification: 4/1.

Costs and Financial Aid
(All Undergraduate Programs)
Annual tuition $31,200. Room & board $5,900. Required fees $265. Average book expense $800. **Financial Aid Statistics:** % freshmen/undergrads who receive any aid: 78/77. % freshmen/undergrads who receive need-based scholarship or grant aid: 54/54. % freshmen/undergrads who receive need-based self-help aid: 45/45. Priority financial aid filing deadline: 2/1. Financial aid filing deadline: 2/1. Financial aid notification on or about: 3/31.

TV/Film/Digital Media Studies Programs
Number of undergraduates in these programs: 112 (31 in screen studies and 81 in communication and culture)
Number of 2005 graduates from these programs: 41 (7 in screen studies and 34 in communication and culture)
Degrees conferred to these majors: BA.
Number of full-time faculty in these programs: 15
Number of part-time faculty in these programs: 3
Career development services: Alumni networking opportunities, career counseling, internship listings, job fairs, job listings.

In Their Own Words
For more information on the screen studies major, please visit www.clarku.edu/academiccatalog/program.cfm?id=27&m=1. For more information on the Communication and Culture Major, please visit www.clarku.edu/academiccatalog/program.cfm?id=6&m=1.

POPULAR PROGRAMS

COMMUNICATION AND CULTURE STUDIES
Department chair: Matthew Malsky
Number of full-time faculty: 13
Focus/emphasis: The major is designed to engage students in focused inquiry into the cultural foundations of communication in its various forms. As a liberal arts major, the program of study emphasizes the development of a conceptual framework for understanding the role of communication in both transmitting and creating culture through practices of verbal and nonverbal communication. Through an interdisciplinary approach involving faculty from different fields of expertise in the humanities and social sciences, students study media, discourse, and global influences and developments in communication. The curriculum covers historical and current topics, and the range of communicative forms considered includes visual and graphic images, everyday discourse, literary works, journalistic writing, music, and material productions. Although not a production-oriented or preprofessional major, students have opportunities for practicum and internship learning.

SCREEN STUDIES
Department chair: Tim Shary
Number of full-time faculty: 4
Focus/emphasis: Clark offers one of the few undergraduate programs in the nation that specializes in screen studies, which deals with arts and artifacts of the moving two-dimensional image, usually combined with sound. It is concerned, in other words, with the study of film, television, video, and evolving forms of digital visual media. The program offers both a major and a minor and stresses the importance of a liberal arts

background, for the screen arts touch on and are affected by all sectors of contemporary culture and society. Screen studies provides a core of basic and advanced knowledge of the screen arts and media while encouraging students to explore diverse connections and influences, ranging from the visual arts, drama, literature, and aesthetics to sociology, psychology, history, and economics.

COGSWELL POLYTECHNICAL COLLEGE

1175 Bordeaux Drive, Sunnyvale, CA 94089-1299
Phone: 408-541-0100 **E-mail:** admin@cogswell.edu
Website: www.cpgswell.edu

Campus Life
Environment: Village. **Calendar:** Semester.

Students and Faculty
(All Undergraduate Programs)
Enrollment: 282. **Student Body:** 12% female, 88% male, 15% out-of-state. African American 1%, Asian 9%, Caucasian 59%, Hispanic 7%. Student/faculty ratio: 8:1. 14 full-time faculty, 25% hold PhDs. 100% faculty teach undergrads.

Admissions
(All Undergraduate Programs)
Academic units required: 3 English, 3 math, 1 science. Regular notification: Within 1 month.

Costs and Financial Aid
(All Undergraduate Programs)
Annual tuition $14,984. Required fees $40. Average book expense $1,242.
Financial Aid Statistics: % freshmen/undergrads who receive any aid: 65/65. Priority financial aid filing deadline: 3/2. Financial aid notification on or about: 4/30.

TV/Film/Digital Media Studies Programs
Number of undergraduates in these programs: 160

Number of 2005 graduates from these programs: 21
Degrees conferred to these majors: BA, BS.
Number of full-time faculty in these programs: 8
Number of part-time faculty in these programs: 15
Equipment and facilities: Fully operational movie soundstage with fully equipped store of resources, including cameras, c-stands, lights, lighting kits, etc. The soundstage has a blue-screen cyclorama and a fully enclosed isolation booth for audio recording.
Career development services: Internship listings, job listings.
Notable alumni: Kirby Atkins, *Jimmy Neutron* (DNA Productions); Eric Bermender, *Harry Potter & the Goblet of Fire*, *The Island*, *The Mummy Returns*, and *Mission to Mars* (ILM); Colin Hodges, *Shrek*, *Fantastic Four*, *Garfield* (Stan Winston Studios); Marc Miller, *Open Season* (Sony Pictures); Alan Orcutt, animated short films and several have been viewed at various festivals (independent); Mike Rosenthal, director and cinematographer for commercials; Steve Sorenson, *The Madagascar Penguins in a Christmas Caper*, *Shrek*, *Shrek 2* (PDI); Chad Stubblefield, Disney animator; Angela Traeger, *Butterflies*, *The Hulk*, *Peter Pan* (ILM & Lucas Ranch); Tosh Xiong, *Full Circle—The Epic Return to Trinity* documentary (independent); Paul Yan, animated short films (independent).

In Their Own Words
Craig Baldwin, internationally known filmmaker, has given guest presentations, as has award-winning producer Michelle Turnure-Salleo. Students have traveled to Sundance Film Festival to promote work, and others have had work chosen at various Bay Area Festivals.

POPULAR PROGRAMS

DIGITAL ART AND ANIMATION
Focus/emphasis: For more information on this program, please visit www.cogswell.edu/digitalArts1.html

DIGITAL AUDIO TECHNOLOGY

Focus/emphasis: For more information on this program, please visit www.cogswell.edu/audio.html

DIGITAL MOTION PICTURE

Focus/emphasis: For more information on this program, please visit www.cogswell.edu/motion.html

---

COLLEGE MISERICORDIA

301 Lake Street, Dallas, PA 18612
Phone: 570-674-6264 **E-mail:** admiss@misericordia.edu
Website: www.misericordia.edu

Campus Life
Environment: Town. **Calendar:** Semester.

Students and Faculty
(All Undergraduate Programs)
Enrollment: 1,966. **Student Body:** 74% female, 26% male, 17% out-of-state. African American 2%, Caucasian 96%, Hispanic 2%. Student/faculty ratio: 12:1. 90 full-time faculty, 80% hold PhDs. 90% faculty teach undergrads.

Admissions
(All Undergraduate Programs)
Freshman Admissions Requirements: Test(s) required: SAT or ACT. Average high school GPA: 3.11. 11% in top tenth, 40% in top quarter. SAT Math (25/75 percentile): 450/550. SAT Verbal (25/75 percentile): 450/540. Projected SAT Writing (25/75 percentile): 520/600. *Academic units required:* 4 English, 4 math, 4 science, 4 social studies. Regular notification: Rolling.

Costs and Financial Aid
(All Undergraduate Programs)
Annual tuition $19,800. Room & board $8,640. Required fees $1,030. Average book expense $800. **Financial Aid Statistics:** % freshmen/undergrads who receive any aid: 100/98. % freshmen/undergrads who receive need-based scholarship or grant aid:

80/80. % freshmen/undergrads who receive need-based self-help aid: 65/68. Priority financial aid filing deadline: 3/1. Financial aid filing deadline: 5/1. Financial aid notification on or about: 3/15.

TV/Film/Digital Media Studies Programs
Number of undergraduates in these programs: 30
Number of 2005 graduates from these programs: 2
Degrees conferred to these majors: BA.
Number of full-time faculty in these programs: 3
Number of part-time faculty in these programs: 2
Equipment and facilities: All-digital equipment and facilities, including ENG/EFP camcorders, studio cameras and control room, and nonlinear video- and audio-editing suites.

% of graduates currently employed in related field: 80

In Their Own Words
Now five years old, the communications program continues to grow and will be graduating six seniors this year. All faculty have professional backgrounds in addition to their educational experience. Industry pros visit regularly from the nearby major markets.

POPULAR PROGRAMS

COMMUNICATIONS WITH MEDIA PRODUCTION
Department chair: Richard Crew, PhD
Number of full-time faculty: 1.5
Number of part-time faculty: 1
Focus/emphasis: Video and audio studio and field production.

COMMUNICATIONS WITH JOURNALISM
Department chair: Richard Crew, PhD
Number of full-time faculty: 1.5
Number of part-time faculty: 1
Focus/emphasis: Writing, newsgathering, and public relations principles.

Students Should Also Know

Minors are available in marketing, theater, English, political science, and history.

THE COLLEGE OF NEW JERSEY

PO Box 7718, Ewing, NJ 08628-0718
Phone: 609-771-2131 **E-mail:** admiss@vm.tcnj.edu
Website: www.tcnj.edu

Campus Life

Environment: Village. **Calendar:** Semester.

Students and Faculty
(All Undergraduate Programs)

Enrollment: 5,836. **Student Body:** 58% female, 42% male, 5% out-of-state. African American 6%, Asian 5%, Caucasian 77%, Hispanic 7%. Student/faculty ratio: 12:1. 341 full-time faculty, 86% hold PhDs. 95% faculty teach undergrads.

Admissions
(All Undergraduate Programs)

Freshman Admissions Requirements: Test(s) required: SAT or ACT. 68% in top tenth, 94% in top quarter. SAT Math (25/75 percentile): 600/700. SAT Verbal (25/75 percentile): 570/670. Projected SAT Writing (25/75 percentile): 620/700. *Academic units required:* 4 English, 3 math, 3 science (2 science labs), 2 foreign language, 2 social studies. Early decision application deadline: 11/15. Regular application deadline: 2/15. Regular notification: Rolling.

Costs and Financial Aid
(All Undergraduate Programs)

Annual in-state tuition $7,051. Out-of-state tuition $12,314. Room & board $8,458. Required fees $2,806. Average book expense $736.
Financial Aid Statistics: % freshmen/undergrads who receive need-based scholarship or grant aid: 17/15. % freshmen/undergrads who receive need-based self-help aid: 23/27. Priority financial aid filing deadline: 3/1. Financial aid filing deadline: 10/1. Financial aid notification on or about: 7/15

TV/Film/Digital Media Studies Programs

Number of undergraduates in these programs: 261
Number of 2005 graduates from these programs: 89
Degrees conferred to these majors: BA.
Equipment and facilities: The Department of Communication Studies is located in the 83,000-square-foot Kendall Hall, one of the original Georgian buildings on the central quadrangle of the campus. Built in 1930 and extensively renovated in 1992, the building houses the campus radio station, a modern television studio, numerous editing suites, an audio classroom, faculty offices, classrooms, the distance learning center, and audio/video equipment center. In addition, it contains a full complement of theatrical space, including the 875-seat Kendall Main theater, a 150-seat black box theater, and a scene shop.
Career development services: Alumni networking opportunities, career counseling, internship listings, job fairs, job listings.

COLORADO STATE UNIVERSITY

Spruce Hall, Fort Collins, CO 80523-8020
Phone: 970-491-6909 **E-mail:** admissions@colostate.edu
Website: www.colostate.edu

Campus Life

Environment: City. **Calendar:** Semester.

Students and Faculty
(All Undergraduate Programs)

Enrollment: 20,584. **Student Body:** 52% female, 48% male, 18% out-of-state. African American 2%, Asian 3%, Caucasian 83%, Hispanic 6%, Native American 1%. Student/faculty ratio: 18:1. 851 full-time faculty, 99% hold PhDs. 97% faculty teach undergrads.

Admissions
(All Undergraduate Programs)

Freshman Admissions Requirements: Test(s) required: SAT or ACT. Average high school GPA: 3.5. 17% in top tenth, 46% in top quarter. SAT Math

(25/75 percentile): 510/620. SAT Verbal (25/75 percentile): 500/610. Projected SAT Writing (25/75 percentile): 560/660. *Academic units required:* 4 English, 3 math, 2 science, 2 foreign language, 3 social studies. Regular application deadline: 7/1. Regular notification: Within 1–2 weeks of completed application.

Costs and Financial Aid (All Undergraduate Programs)

Annual in-state tuition $3,381. Out-of-state tuition $14,343. Room & board $6,316. Required fees $1,181. Average book expense $900.

Financial Aid Statistics: % freshmen/undergrads who receive any aid: 64/63. % freshmen/undergrads who receive need-based scholarship or grant aid: 27/27. % freshmen/undergrads who receive need-based self-help aid: 25/33. Priority financial aid filing deadline: 3/1. Financial aid notification on or about: 3/1.

TV/Film/Digital Media Studies Programs

Number of undergraduates in these programs: 73

Number of 2005 graduates from these programs: 36

Degrees conferred to these majors: BA.

Number of full-time faculty in these programs: 5

Number of part-time faculty in these programs: 2

Equipment and facilities: Our program utilizes digital video cameras and nonlinear computerized video-editing workstations with Avid and Final Cut Pro software. We have eight dedicated video-editing suites and three full-sized computer labs for training. In addition, a companion department, Student Media, has three edit suites and a full-service production studio.

Other awards of note: Too many to list, from organizations such as the Broadcast Education Association, the Society of Professional Journalists, College Media Advisors, and College Broadcasters, Inc.

% of graduates who pursue further study within 5 years: Only a fraction

% of graduates currently employed in related field: 50

Career development services: Alumni networking opportunities, career counseling, internship listings, job fairs, job listings.

In Their Own Words

Colorado State University students focus on the production of information-based programming and have earned more than 250 regional and national awards for news, sports, entertainment, and documentary programs since 1990. Students in our program intern primarily in Denver for television stations, independent production companies, and cable facilities. CSU graduates are working in television stations and production facilities across the country and internationally.

POPULAR PROGRAMS

TELEVISION NEWS AND VIDEO COMMUNICATION

Department chair: Garrett O'Keefe

Number of full-time faculty: 5

Number of part-time faculty: 2

Focus/emphasis: Students focus on learning how to put together information-based programming from shooting video to writing copy to production.

COMPUTER-MEDIATED COMMUNICATION

Department chair: Garrett O'Keefe

Number of full-time faculty: 5

Number of part-time faculty: 2

Focus/emphasis: Students in this area focus on learning to produce information-based media for the Internet and other new communication technologies.

COLUMBIA COLLEGE CHICAGO (IL)

600 South Michigan Avenue, Chicago, IL 60605-1996
Phone: 312-344-7130 **E-mail:** admissions@colum.edu
Website: www.colum.edu

Campus Life

Environment: Metropolis. **Calendar:** Semester.

Students and Faculty
(All Undergraduate Programs)

Enrollment: 10,039. **Student Body:** 51% female, 49% male, 22% out-of-state, 1% international (61 countries represented). African American 12%, Asian 3%, Caucasian 57%, Hispanic 8%. Student/faculty ratio: 11:1. 299 full-time faculty. 100% faculty teach undergrads.

Admissions
(All Undergraduate Programs)

Average high school GPA: 2.86. 7% in top tenth, 23% in top quarter. Regular notification: Rolling.

Costs and Financial Aid
(All Undergraduate Programs)

Annual tuition $15,588. Room & board $11,080. Required fees $820. Average book expense $1,300. **Financial Aid Statistics:** % freshmen/undergrads who receive any aid: 63/62. Priority financial aid filing deadline: 8/1.

TV/Film/Digital Media Studies Programs

Number of undergraduates in these programs: 2,641
Number of 2005 graduates from these programs: 479
Degrees conferred to these majors: BA.
Also available at Columbia College Chicago (IL): MA.
Number of full-time faculty in these programs: 59
Number of part-time faculty in these programs: 229
Equipment and facilities: The Theater and Film Annex at 1415 South Wabash Avenue houses the Directing Center for the Film and Video Department. It consists of two stages and an equip-ment/prop storage room. The large stage (114) is 2,800 square feet (roughly 40' x 70'), and has a 14'-high pipe grid for hanging lights, two 900-amp power supplies on each end of the stage, and enough flats, lights, and grip equipment to support student shoots. There is one dolly for the stage with a pump-action jib arm and 16' of straight track. This space is used primarily for Directing II and Directing for the Camera classes, as well as being available to independent projects as a shooting stage. The smaller stage (115) is 1,000 square feet (roughly 20' x 50'), has black walls, a 14'-high pipe grid, and its own 900-amp power supply. This class-room is used primarily for Directing I and Acting Techniques for the Filmmaker classes, but it is also available for smaller shooting projects. The equip-ment/prop storage room is accessible to both stages, with enough furniture and props to support several simultaneous class projects. The college also has a television studio. Equipment available to students includes two Oxberry Filmmaker 16 mm animation stands, one Oxberry Master Series 16/35 mm com-puter controlled stand, one Acme double-pole man-ual animation stand, 36 traditional individual draw-ing stations with Acme disks, 10 networked Windows 2000 workstations running Softimage soft-ware, 10 networked NT workstations running Alias software, 10 networked NT workstations running Lightwave software, 10 networked Windows 2000 workstations running USAnimation software, two animation controls, and four Lunchbox Sync with Visualizer video pencil test systems. Complete sound, film, and video analog and digital editing facilities are equipped with G3 & G4 Macs, a screenplay library, a MacIntosh computer lab, and classroom space for beginning, intermediate, and advanced screenwriting courses. Producing facilities include classrooms, a student production office, and a 90-seat screening room. postproduction audio facilities are located on the seventh floor of the Ludington Building and include a Foley studio, facilities for ADR, DAW labs, and two state-of-the-art mixing theaters. Cameras are just some of the resources available to cinematography students at Columbia. In addition to intermediate and advanced camera facilities, a well-equipped lighting

stage serves as a hands-on classroom for beginning, intermediate, and advanced lighting and cinematography classes. Specialized screening rooms host analysis classes while a wide selection of portable lighting equipment kits are available for location shooting. The postproduction Center of the Film and Video Department is located on the sixth floor of the Ludington Building and features a state-of-the-art teaching and editing environment. Audio and video files can be stored on a central server, allowing advanced students access to their projects from individual edit stations or classrooms. The center houses a Bosch telecine, which does double duty as a teaching tool and a workhorse for transferring several hundred-thousand feet of student film each year.

Career development services: Alumni networking opportunities; career counseling; central resource(s) for employers to browse headshots, writing samples, reels; internship listings; job fairs; job listings.

In Their Own Words

The Film/Video Department offers nearly 200 specialized undergraduate and graduate courses that embody the most comprehensive curriculum of any film school in the country. In small classes that provide a nurturing and challenging atmosphere, students get the personalized attention needed to hone their skills. Entering students quickly get immersed in the filmmaking process. In the first class, students learn the fundamentals of the medium while working on script ideas, and, at the beginning of the second semester, each makes a film. After completing the departmental core courses, students either design a unique course of study tailored to their career goals or select a major area of concentration. Taught in distinctive learning centers, areas of concentration include animation (traditional and digital), audio, cinema studies, cinematography, directing, documentary, editing, producing, and screenwriting. Some students choose to prepare for a working life in one of the specialized disciplines; others opt to graduate as an independent filmmaker with all-round experience. We value the making of individual films or videos that develop students' creative potential and reflect their technical abilities. These films become the all-important sample reel needed to begin a professional career. Of course, making movies costs money. Once films have been finished, exhibition and distribution become crucial. Our annual student film festival The Big Screen has become one of the most anticipated film events in Chicago. This juried competition of student-produced films and videos celebrates the creative diversity and incredible talent in the department, while also offering cash awards and trophies for Best of the Fest, Audience Award, Best Script, and Best Treatment. The department also provides local exposure through its Wednesday night screenings. In addition, Chicago provides exhibition venues such as the Chicago Underground Film Festival and Chicago International Film Festival. Finally, the Film Department helps students submit their work to national and international film festivals. Taken for credit, industry internships provide professional production or postproduction training. This important career preparation helps many students land exciting jobs locally and nationally. The Film/Video Department maintains connections in several cities, including New York and Los Angeles. For example, an active West Coast Alumni Association and our own office on the CBS television lot in Hollywood cements the Los Angeles relationship. In addition, we currently offer a semester in Los Angeles program. For those interested in a Hollywood career, this excellent introduction includes meetings and classes with an extensive array of working professionals eager to share their knowledge and offer students practical guidance. Our methodology, philosophy, and curriculum have evolved over 30 years as we have grown into an internationally renowned center of teaching excellence. We boast a vibrant location, low tuition rates, sophisticated technical facilities, a comprehensive curriculum, and a faculty of working professionals, film scholars, and independent filmmakers. But, ultimately,

successful graduates and the production of artistic, entertaining films testify to our unsurpassed knowledge and dedication to instruct, support, and inspire all who enter our program.

POPULAR PROGRAMS

FILM/VIDEO—GENERAL
Department chair: Bruce Sheridan
Number of full-time faculty: 36
Number of part-time faculty: 138

FILM/VIDEO—DIRECTING
Department chair: Bruce Sheridan
Number of full-time faculty: 36
Number of part-time faculty: 138

FILM/VIDEO—CINEMATOGRAPHY
Department chair: Bruce Sheridan
Number of full-time faculty: 36
Number of part-time faculty: 138

FILM/VIDEO—EDITING
Department chair: Bruce Sheridan
Number of full-time faculty: 36
Number of part-time faculty: 138

FILM/VIDEO—ANIMATION
Department chair: Bruce Sheridan
Number of full-time faculty: 36
Number of part-time faculty: 138

TELEVISION
Department chair: Michael Neiderman
Number of full-time faculty: 14
Number of part-time faculty: 48

INTERACTIVE MULTIMEDIA
Department chair: Annette Barbier
Number of full-time faculty: 10
Number of part-time faculty: 42

DIGITAL MEDIA TECHNOLOGY
Department chair: Annette Barbier
Number of full-time faculty: 10
Number of part-time faculty: 42

GAME DESIGN
Department chair: Annette Barbier
Number of full-time faculty: 10
Number of part-time faculty: 42

COLUMBIA COLLEGE–HOLLYWOOD
18618 Oxnard Street, Tarzana, CA 91356
Phone: 818-345-8414 **E-mail:** admissions@columbiacollege.edu
Website: www.columbiacollege.edu

Campus Life
Environment: Metropolis. **Calendar:** Quarter.

Students and Faculty
(All Undergraduate Programs)
Enrollment: 150. **Student Body:** 31% female, 69% male, 10% international (24 countries represented). African American 9%, Asian 5%, Caucasian 60%, Hispanic 14%. Student/faculty ratio 6:1. 100% faculty teach undergrads.

Admissions
(All Undergraduate Programs)
Freshman Admissions Requirements: Average high school GPA: 3.3. Regular notification: As accepted.

Costs and Financial Aid
(All Undergraduate Programs)
Annual tuition $11,400. Required fees $225. Average book expense $400.
Financial Aid Statistics: % freshmen/undergrads who receive any aid: 78/75. % freshmen/undergrads who receive need-based scholarship or grant aid: 48/50.

TV/Film/Digital Media Studies Programs
Number of undergraduates in these programs: 210
Number of 2005 graduates from these programs: 32
Degrees conferred to these majors: BA.
Also available at Columbia College—Hollywood: AA.

Number of full-time faculty in these programs: 2

Number of part-time faculty in these programs: 34

Equipment and facilities: Shooting stage; projection theater; casting room; insert stage with make-up room and wardrobe area; film editing facilities; videotape and digital editing facilities; sound recording and Foley room; dubbing rooms (two video, one film). The 5,000-square-foot library houses over 4,000 volumes, periodicals, videocassettes, DVDs, and scripts. A computer lab with movie budgeting and scriptwriting software is open during campus hours. Camera Systems: Arriflex SRI and SRII, Bolex 16, Eclair 16 NPR, CP16 Digital Cameras: Canon XL2, XL1(S); Panasonic DVX100A with 4 x 4 matte box and follow focus; Sony VX2000; various mini DV cameras; professional SVHS camcorders and VHS camcorders. Lighting Equipment: 1K, 2K, and 5K lights, fresnels, 1K open face and soft lights; two & three riser stands. Grip Equipment: Fisher Dolly with track; c-stands; sandbags; apple boxes; flags & other grip items. Sound Equipment: Nagra 4.2 TC sound recorder; Smart Slate; Fostex DAT; Sony MiniDisc; shotgun and handheld microphones; XLR connectors; boom poles and Mackie mixers. Editing Systems: 16 mm moviolas and 16 mm and 35 mm flatbeds, AVID, Final Cut Pro, Pro Tools, AfterEffects, and Photoshop suites.

Other awards of note: Sundance Film Festival, AFFMA Festival.

% of graduates who pursue further study within 5 years: 20

% of graduates currently employed in related field: 85

Career development services: Alumni networking opportunities; career counseling; central resource(s) for employers to browse headshots, writing samples, reels, etc.; internship listings; job listings.

Famous alumni: Robert Schwentke, Jamie Farr, Timothy Bui, Robert Ferretti.

Notable alumni: Tom Anderson, optical film specialist; Rusty Gellar, SOC Steadicam operator; Ryan Sheridan, digital camera specialist; Kevin Schwab, visual effects specialist.

In Their Own Words

Unlike other film schools in the area that are part of a larger university, Columbia College–Hollywood specializes solely in film and television production. This is the key to a unique educational experience that is more like a conservatory than a college. CCH is about hands-on learning. At Columbia College–Hollywood, we believe that the best film- or videomaker is one who understands all aspects of the process: What is involved in writing a script, the kinds of choices a cinematographer confronts, how actors reveal subtext, how sound and music can enliven and transform a scene, the way images are assembled in an editing room. The best way to understand these things is by experiencing them firsthand. Our three-tier core curriculum ensures that all our students will have exposure to the essential crafts of moviemaking and television.

POPULAR PROGRAMS

CINEMA/TELEVISION PRODUCTION

Department chair: Alan Gansberg

Number of full-time faculty: 1

Number of part-time faculty: 12

Focus/emphasis: The combined Cinema/Television program is designed to provide the student with knowledge of the technical, managerial, and creative aspects of both television and cinema production. The program objective is to guide the student through several levels of proficiency in different aspects of television and filmmaking, culminating with the Production Workshop series of classes that enables students to make their own films.

CINEMA STUDIES

Department chair: Charles Rose

Number of full-time faculty: 1

Number of part-time faculty: 8

Focus/emphasis: The program is designed to provide the student with knowledge of the technical, managerial, and creative aspects of filmmaking. The program guides the student through several levels of proficiency in different aspects of film-making, culminating with the Production Workshop series of classes.

TELEVISION/ VIDEO PRODUCTION
Department chair: Rick Mitz
Number of part-time faculty: 10
Focus/emphasis: The program is designed to provide the student with knowledge of the technical, managerial, and creative aspects of the television/video industry. Through practical hands-on training, the student will gain experience in the workings of commercial, cable, and educational television.

Students Should Also Know
The goal is to graduate students with portfolios that demonstrate their mastery of film, television, and video techniques and that will lead to their getting work as producers; directors; camera operators; assistant camera operators; technical directors; or production assistants. Note: Assistant positions are typically entry-level positions; however, some students have gone on to direct, produce, and shoot films and video productions right out of Columbia.

COLUMBIA UNIVERSITY–
COLUMBIA COLLEGE
212 Hamilton Hall MC 2807, 1130 Amsterdam Avenue,
New York, NY 10027
Phone: 212-854-2521
Website: www.columbia.edu

Campus Life
Environment: Metropolis. **Calendar:** Semester.

Students and Faculty
(All Undergraduate Programs)
Enrollment: 4,115. **Student Body:** 50% female, 50% male, 74% out-of-state, 6% international (54 countries represented). African American 9%, Asian 12%, Caucasian 51%, Hispanic 8%. Student/faculty ratio: 6:1. 704 full-time faculty. 100% faculty teach undergrads.

Admissions
(All Undergraduate Programs)
Freshman Admissions Requirements: Test(s) required: SAT and SAT Subject Tests or ACT; ACT with Writing component. Average high school GPA: 3.78. 85% in top tenth, 98% in top quarter. SAT Math (25/75 percentile): 660/760. SAT Verbal (25/75 percentile): 660/760. Projected SAT Writing (25/75 percentile): 690/760. Early decision application deadline: 11/1. Regular application deadline: 1/2. Regular notification: 4/4.

Costs and Financial Aid
(All Undergraduate Programs)
Annual tuition $31,924. Room & board $9,338. Required fees $1,322. Average book expense $1,000. **Financial Aid Statistics:** % freshmen/undergrads who receive any aid: 42/41. % freshmen/undergrads who receive need-based scholarship or grant aid: 40/40. % freshmen/undergrads who receive need-based self-help aid: 40/42. Financial aid filing deadline: 2/10. Financial aid notification on or about: 4/1.

TV/Film/Digital Media Studies Programs
Number of undergraduates in these programs: Approximately 80 undergraduate film studies majors.
Number of 2005 graduates from these programs: 40
Degrees conferred to these majors: BA.
Number of full-time faculty in these programs: 4
Number of part-time faculty in these programs: 12

% of graduates who pursue further study within 5 years: 25
% of graduates currently employed in related field: 40
Notable alumni: Dan Harris, writer-director of *Imaginary Heroes* (starring Sigourney Weaver and Jeff Daniels), screenwriter of *X-Men II*; Henry Alex Rubin, Oscar-nominated director of *Murderball*; Rahmin Bahrani, director of *Man Push Cart*, selected for 2006 Sundance Film Festival.

In Their Own Words

The renowned full-time faculty includes James Schamus, producer (Brokeback Mountain) and screenwriter (The Ice Storm); Richard Pena, director of the New York Film Festival; film critic Andrew Sarris; and Director of Undergraduate Film Studies Annette Insdorf, author of books on Truffaut, Kieslowski, and Holocaust Cinema. Undergrad film majors get to attend the MFA Program's Guest Speaker series, whose recent guests include Wim Wenders, Daniel Day-Lewis, Mira Nair, and Mike Leigh. They also have access to numerous internships with film companies and to Columbia graduate students who give them experience working on short films.

POPULAR PROGRAMS

FILM STUDIES

Department chair: Annette Insdorf

Focus/emphasis: The major in film studies is scholarly, international in scope, and writing-intensive. Students usually declare the major toward the end of the second year. Film studies majors take workshops in screenwriting and filmmaking, but the program is rooted in film history, theory, and criticism. The educational goal is to provide film majors with a solid grounding in cinema history and theory; its relation to other forms of art; its synthesis of visual storytelling, technology, economics, and sociopolitical context, as well as the means to begin writing a script and making a short film.

CONNECTICUT COLLEGE

270 Mohegan Avenue, New London, CT 06320
Phone: 860-439-2200 **E-mail:** admission@conncoll.edu
Website: www.conncoll.edu

Campus Life

Environment: Town. **Calendar:** Semester.

Students and Faculty
(All Undergraduate Programs)

Enrollment: 1,898. **Student Body:** 61% female, 39% male, 80% out-of-state, 4% international (41 countries represented). African American 4%, Asian 5%, Caucasian 73%, Hispanic 5%. Student/faculty ratio: 10:1. 162 full-time faculty, 91% hold PhDs. 100% faculty teach undergrads.

Admissions
(All Undergraduate Programs)

54% in top tenth, 83% in top quarter. SAT Math (25/75 percentile): 620/700. SAT Verbal (25/75 percentile): 630/700. Projected SAT Writing (25/75 percentile): 670/720. Early decision application deadline: 11/15. Regular application deadline: 1/1. Regular notification: 3/31.

Costs and Financial Aid
(All Undergraduate Programs)

Comprehensive fee: $44,240.

Financial Aid Statistics: % freshmen who receive any aid: 41. % freshmen/undergrads who receive need-based scholarship or grant aid: 35/39. % freshmen/undergrads who receive need-based self-help aid: 34/38. Priority financial aid filing deadline: 11/15. Financial aid filing deadline: 2/1.

TV/Film/Digital Media Studies Programs

Number of undergraduates in these programs: 27

Number of 2005 graduates from these programs: 18

Degrees conferred to these majors: BA.

Also available at Connecticut College: Certificate.

Number of full-time faculty in these programs: 43

Number of part-time faculty in these programs: 4

Equipment and facilities: Digital visual media equipment hardware: Graphics workstations, virtual reality peripherals; head mounted displays, position trackers, gloves. Haptics devices software: Animation software (Maya), 3-D-modeling software (Autodesk 3-DS), Web authoring software, 3-D virtual environment-modeling software (Virtools), video- and audio-editing software, programming environments, digital music media equipment. The CEDS Lab boasts seven modern workstations, all running OS 10.3.3 (Panther). Three machines use 1.6Ghz G5 processors, while the other four are dual 1.25Ghz G4 machines. All machines run Pro Tools 6.3 and Max/MSP through either a Digidesign 001 or 002, as well as other software explained below. All workstations are connected to at least one synthesizer, an 88-key MIDI keyboard, a 16-channel digital mixing board, and a pair of high-quality studio monitors (loudspeakers). CD-duplicating and printing equipment is available. All machines are networked to the college network. The synthesizer that we teach on is the Roland XV-5050, a powerful, fully programmable, multitimbral synth. We have many other synthesizers, samplers, and effects processors available, as well as a variety of microphones appropriate for recording a wide variety of sources. Pro Tools is the industry standard in multi-track recording and editing. Our Digidesign hardware is high quality, offering crystal clear sound on eight inputs and eight outputs. Max/MSP is a graphical programming environment for audio projects. It works with both audio data and MIDI, allowing for it to be used to build and implement a wide variety of ideas, projects, and tools, ranging from digitally constructing a dynamic range compressor, to creating an entirely new and customizable digital instrument. Max/MSP is much easier to learn and work with than a lower level programming language such as C++ or even Java. Much more about Max/MSP is available from Cycling 74. Sibelius is a musical notation program, allowing a high level of customization over musical scores and interfaces with Pro Tools via MIDI import and export. Connecticut College Recording Studio is home to the brand new Pro Tools |HD 32-channel recording setup. It is connected to Fortune Hall, Evans Hall (link), and The CEDS Lab with multi-channel recording capability. The studio is equipped with an isolation booth for recording vocals and several high-quality microphones. The Connecticut College Recording Studio offers recording and mixing services to the college community and to the public. From time to time, jobs as recording assistants are available for qualified and interested students.

Other awards of note: Christof Putzel (2001) produced the short documentary *Left Behind*, which exposes the devastating effects of AIDS through the eyes and voices of Kenya's children and has garnered the Gold Medal Student Academy Award, the Student Emmy, the Silver Chris Plaque for Best Student Film at the Columbus International Film and Video Festival, and the most Outstanding Documentary at the 2002 Angelus Awards and HBO/Best Student Film Award.

% of graduates who pursue further study within 5 years: 30

% of graduates currently employed in related field: 50

Career development services: Alumni networking opportunities, career counseling, internship listings, job fairs, job listings. We also have a funded internship program in which students can receive up to $3,000 toward a summer internship.

Famous alumni: Scott Lowell, Wallis Nicita.

Notable alumni: Judy Irving (1968) is the executive director of Pelican Media in San Francisco. Pelican Media's objective is to produce films with environmental themes. Most recently, Emmy and Sundance award-winning Irving directed the documentary *The Wild Parrots of Telegraph Hill*, which portrays the remarkable relationship between a homeless street musician and a flock of wild red-and-green parrots. Edna Roth (1970) is the founder of Edna Roth and Associates. She helps individuals develop better presentation skills, executive presence, and one-on-one communication abilities. She has worked as a dialect coach in theater and film, assisiting Danny Aiello, Jeff and Lloyd Bridges, Richard Dreyfuss, and Holly Hunter. Kevin Wade (1976) is a writer at Back East Pictures. Wade's writing credits on films include the screenplay for *Maid in Manhattan*, *Meet Joe Black*, and *Mr. Baseball*. In addition, he has written *Junior*, *True Colors*, and *Working Girl* as well as the play *Key Exchange*. He has also acted in the films *Imposters* and *The Scenic Route*. Nina Sadowsky (1979), a dance major at Connecticut College, has been the president of Meg Ryan's production company Prufrock Productions since 1995 and is an independent filmmaker. Karen Church (1990), vice president of casting and talent at CBS, oversees casting for CBS comedies such as *Everybody Loves Raymond* and *King of Queens*. Her other projects include casting *Joan of Arc* with Leelee Sobieski and Peter O'Toole and *Fail Safe* with George Clooney, Richard Dreyfuss, and Harvey Keitel. Tim Sutton (1992), who owns his own production company, Wellsweep Films, Inc., specializes in both music video production and media-based educational program development. Vincent Farrell (1996), the founder of Iron Films, a New York-based production company, has produced several films, including the 2004 documentary *Until the Violence Stops*, which was shown at the Sundance Film Festival and aired on Lifetime; *Popcorn Shrimp*, which was directed by Christopher Walken and aired on Showtime; and *The Third Date*, which starred Sandra Bernhard and Sarah Clarke. Sean Fine (1996), the founder of Fine Productions, collaborated with his wife on *True Dads*, a two-hour documentary hosted by Bruce Willis that explored fatherhood in America. An Emmy Award-winning filmmaker and cinematographer, Fine has made documentaries for National Geographic, Discovery, *ABC News' Nightline* and Spike Television. Lee Eisenberg (1999), a writer for film and television in Los Angeles, has sold story ideas to *Curb your Enthusiasm* and Fox. Prior to that, Lee wrote the series finale to the HBO series *The Mind of the Married Man*, sold a freelance episode to the CBS series *Jag*, and wrote and produced the short film *Flush*, which premiered at the U.S. Comedy Arts Festival in Aspen. Jenny Marchick (1999) is a story editor for Mandeville Films/TV. Her credits include movies *Bringing Down the House*, *Raising Helen*, *The Last Shot*, and the current television series *Monk*. Her most recent movie projects include *Beauty Shop 2* with Queen Latifah and *The Shaggy Dog* with Tim Allen.

In Their Own Words

All students at Connecticut College are eligible to receive up to $3,000 toward an internship of their choosing through the Career Enhancing Life Skills (CELS) program. Through CELS, students can work with career counselors to secure an internship in television, film, and media studies. Students can also pursue an interdisciplinary program in digital media and the arts by pursuing a certificate program in the Center for Arts and Technology (CAT). Through interdisciplinary collaborations and individual work, students and faculty in CAT not only promote proficiency in working with technology, but also deepen the understanding of the meaning and role of technology within the larger context of the liberal arts. Students explore issues in arts and technology through individual studies, course work, internships, research assistantships, an associates program, and a certificate program that incorporates an intensive research project. The Film Studies major enables students to draw upon the interdisciplinary variety that characterizes the study of moving images—combining theory, criticism, history, and practice in developing the ability to think in filmic terms, and to gain an understanding of how film functions both as an art and a social force. The structure of the major allows a student to build a concentration within the major—on production, analysis, international cinemas, etc. Recent graduates from the program, more than half of whom are working in the film/television industry in some capacity, have won many prestigious awards, including the Academy of Motion Pictures Award for Best Student Documentary, among others.

POPULAR PROGRAMS

CREATIVE WRITING
Department chair: Janet Gezari
Number of full-time faculty: 12

Focus/emphasis: The program enables students majoring in English to concentrate in fiction, poetry, and nonfiction prose. Several faculty members within the department also offer courses that use film and have significant media components.

AMMERMAN CENTER FOR ARTS AND TECHNOLOGY CERTIFICATE

Department chair: Bridget Baird
Number of full-time faculty: 29
Focus/emphasis: The program enables students to explore the intersection of arts and technology and incorporates a self-designed integrative senior project, independent studies, course work, internships, and research opportunities. A select group of students applying in their freshman or sophomore year is admitted each year to the center's certificate program. The certificate is completed in addition to the student's major.

MUSIC AND TECHNOLOGY

Department chair: Art Kreiger
Number of full-time faculty: 6
Focus/emphasis: This major thoroughly prepares students for compositional work in a modern studio. It combines the majority of required classes for the music major with two classes in electroacoustic music and four more in related fields. Advanced composition classes can also be taken in electronic music. This approach ensures that students master fundamental aspects of music and musicianship, while focusing their creative energies on working effectively in the electronic medium.

THEATER

Department chair: Linda Herr
Number of full-time faculty: 5
Focus/emphasis: The major emphasizes acting and directing but encourages students to study and work on all elements of theater, including acting, direction, design, technical theater, playwriting, dramaturgy, and dramatic literature.

FILM STUDIES

Department chair: David Tetzlaff
Number of full-time faculty: 2
Focus/emphasis: At Connecticut College, Film Studies is considered a vital area of intellectual inquiry, valuable to a wide range of students, not merely vocational training for would-be media professionals. The goal of this program is to cultivate a true moving picture literacy, to educate students in the language of film and its uses. The college views Film Studies as an inherently interdisciplinary endeavor and encourages students to combine their interests in film with other areas of inquiry available at the college. In keeping with this philosophy, faculty offering Film Studies courses generally combine a knowledge of film with expertise in at least one other field. The school's method is to integrate theory with practice, combining film scholarship with creative work in film production. Students in our program engage in critical and historical analyses of the moving image in many forms, including not only the classic Hollywood cinema, but also other national cinemas, documentary, avant garde and experimental film, and television. Production classes are also an important part of our curriculum. However, these are designed not as mere technical training, but as courses in applied semiotics, active learning experiences in how the stylistic devices of film are used in the construction of meaning. As such, the production curriculum is designed to give each student a maximum of opportunities to act as the author of a creative project. In comparison to large film schools, where students are formed into large production crews and devote a great deal of time to perfecting craft in the service of someone else's creative vision, here students work individually or in pairs, and focus on the conceptual aspects of writing and directing.

CORNELL UNIVERSITY

Undergraduate Admissions, 410 Thurston Avenue, Ithaca, NY 14850
Phone: 607-255-5241 **E-mail:** admissions@cornell.edu
Website: www.cornell.edu

Campus Life

Environment: Town. **Calendar:** Semester.

Students and Faculty
(All Undergraduate Programs)

Enrollment: 13,515. **Student Body:** 50% female, 50% male, 61% out-of-state, 8% international (110 countries represented). African American 5%, Asian 16%, Caucasian 57%, Hispanic 5%. Student/faculty ratio 9:1. 1675 full-time faculty, 92% hold PhDs. 100% faculty teach undergrads.

Admissions
(All Undergraduate Programs)

Freshman Admissions Requirements: Test(s) required: SAT or ACT; SAT and SAT Subject Tests; ACT with Writing component. 80% in top tenth, 96% in top quarter. SAT Math (25/75 percentile): 660/760. SAT Verbal (25/75 percentile): 630/720. Projected SAT Writing (25/75 percentile): 670/740. *Academic units required:* 4 English, 3 math. Early decision application deadline: 11/1. Regular application deadline: 1/1. Regular notification: 4/1.

Costs and Financial Aid
(All Undergraduate Programs)

Annual tuition $31,300. Room & board $10,250. Required fees $167. Average book expense $680. **Financial Aid Statistics:** % freshmen/undergrads who receive any aid: 49/47. % freshmen/undergrads who receive need-based scholarship or grant aid: 46/44. % freshmen/undergrads who receive need-based self-help aid: 43/44. Financial aid filing deadline: 2/11. Financial aid notification on or about: 4/1.

TV/Film/Digital Media Studies Programs

Degrees conferred to these majors: BA.
Also available at Cornell University: MFA.

In Their Own Words

Film Exhibition: Cornell Cinema, Pentangle, Student Films, and Guest Filmmakers. Students are exposed to an immense sampling of films through Cornell Cinema, a unique program of the department. Cornell Cinema has been cited by The Village Voice *as one of the nation's top campus film exhibition programs, offering Cornell and the surrounding communities a wide range of literally hundreds of screenings and services typically found only in large metropolitan areas. The Pentangle Film Series screens a wide array of film classics annually, and Cornell Cinema sponsors guest filmmakers for campus visits, who often conduct workshops. Screenings of works made by students in the department's film and video production courses are wildly popular events each semester. Among the many student activities at Cornell are two filmmaking clubs: The long-standing IFMAC–Independent Filmmakers at Cornell and the newly-founded DV Club. Both clubs' members receive funding for equipment and projects from the Student Activities Finance Commission (SAFC), and both organize screenings of members' work. Study Abroad Students proficient in French may choose to spend the junior year at the Paris Center for Film and Critical Studies, of which Cornell is an active consortium member. Full Cornell credit is given for this work, which complements the film courses available on campus. The Cornell film major offers several avenues of study, which further emphasizes the department's goal of an individualized education. Cornell Cinema has been cited as one of the best campus film exhibition programs in the country, screening close to 400 different films/videos each year, seven nights a week in the beautiful Willard Straight Theatre. Each monthly calendar includes an array of classic Hollywood and foreign films, independent titles, documentaries, experimental work, recent international cinema, silent films with live musical accompaniment, cult classics, and recent Hollywood and arthouse hits, in addition to* guest appearances by visiting film and video-makers. Cornell Cinema began in 1970 as a university film society, but has evolved into a media arts center with a national reputation. Cornell Cinema's primary purpose is to expose Ithaca and regional audiences to alternative forms of cinema (such as documentary, classic, and experimental films) as well as alternative voices not usually heard through the mass media. Its secondary purpose is to provide affordable, second-run commercial entertainment for the Cornell community. In fulfillment of its educational goals, Cornell Cinema encourages audiences to reflect critically on commercial and other media by supplementing its over 750 annual screenings with the facilities of a media arts center. These include a media study library with extensive reference materials, publications, a film collection, and frequent guest artists and critics offering workshops and presentations. Cornell Cinema is a program of the Department of Theater, Film, and Dance and is cosponsored by the Office of the Dean of Students.

POPULAR PROGRAMS

FILM

Department chair: Don Fredericksen
Number of full-time faculty: 6
Focus/emphasis: Our program balances film studies and film production within a liberal arts major. We currently have 35 film majors, but many more students take our courses. Some choose the Film Major, some double-major in film and another discipline, and some create their own independent major. A considerable resource in film education at Cornell is the extraordinary film exhibition program of Cornell Cinema. Many courses in film or related media studies are offered outside the department, which also may be counted toward the major. Film Studies: Like other concentrations in the department, Cornell's film program is structured in a focused but flexible manner. A proliferation of film classes in this department—

as well as in the areas of Africana studies, anthropology, Asian studies, comparative literature, English, German studies, history, psychology, romance studies, and women's studies—makes the film program an interdisciplinary field, allowing for specialization according to students' interests. The Department of Theater, Film, and Dance offers numerous classes about the history and theory of various periods and genres of film, as well as an intense sequence of film and video-making. The course of study introduces the student to the vast field of professional film, while examining the many uses of the medium—theatrical or documentary filmmaking, film as an avenue for personal expression, and film within the larger context of visual and cultural studies—to name only a few. Film Production: We offer beginning-level courses in 16 mm filmmaking and digital video production, which emphasize creativity, developing original ideas, and practicing essential techniques of the craft. Students may choose to work in any genre of filmmaking: experimental, narrative, documentary, animation, etc. At the intermediate level of filmmaking, students learn sync-sound techniques for their original productions in narrative or documentary; increase their skills in video and audio editing and mixing on Final Cut Pro, Pro Tools, and optionally on Avid systems. In the advanced class, students develop a single project for the semester. All classes have public screenings of final projects at the end of each semester at Cornell Cinema, and the advanced class in the Schwartz Center for Performing Arts. In addition we offer a screenwriting course, a summer animation class, and several courses in theater which are highly recommended for film production students such as: Directing I and II, playwriting courses, and an acting sequence. The film program also participates in an interdisciplinary Media Studio course where students collaborate, explore, and intermix electronic and digital media to produce new forms of art work. Other departments and disciplines involved have included electronic music, architecture, digital art, theater, dance and computer science.

Students Should Also Know

The film program at Cornell University embraces the study and practice of film within artistic, theoretical, and cultural contexts. Students who major in film take a balanced selection of film studies and production courses. The film production program offers classes in 16 mm filmmaking and video production, as well as state-of-the-art film editing equipment. The department offers advanced study in filmmaking to students who qualify on the basis of outstanding achievement in film studies and film production courses. An abundance of film classes in the department—as well as in the areas of Africana studies, anthropology, Asian studies, comparative literature, English, German studies, history, psychology, romance studies, and women's studies—makes the film program an interdisciplinary field, allowing for specialization to students' interests.

DEPAUL UNIVERSITY

1 East Jackson Boulevard, Chicago, IL 60604-2287
Phone: 312-362-8300 **E-mail:** admitdpu@depaul.edu
Website: www.depaul.edu

Campus Life

Environment: Metropolis. **Calendar:** Quarter.

Students and Faculty
(All Undergraduate Programs)

Enrollment: 14,277. **Student Body:** 57% female, 43% male, 15% out-of-state, 1% international (85 countries represented). African American 8%, Asian 8%, Caucasian 49%, Hispanic 11%. Student/faculty ratio: 17:1. 834 full-time faculty, 80% hold PhDs. 99% faculty teach undergrads.

Admissions
(All Undergraduate Programs)

Freshman Admissions Requirements: Test(s) required: SAT or ACT. Average high school GPA: 3.4. 19% in top tenth, 43% in top quarter. SAT Math (25/75 percentile): 510/620. SAT Verbal (25/75 percentile): 530/630. Projected SAT Writing (25/75 percentile): 590/670. *Academic units required:* 4 English, 2 math, 2 science (2 science labs), 2 social studies, 4 academic electives. Regular notification: Rolling.

Costs and Financial Aid
(All Undergraduate Programs)

Annual tuition $20,900. Room & board $8,865. Required fees $70. Average book expense $1,000. **Financial Aid Statistics:** % freshmen/undergrads who receive any aid: 65/63. % freshmen/undergrads who receive need-based scholarship or grant aid: 46/49. % freshmen/undergrads who receive need-based self-help aid: 51/53. Priority financial aid filing deadline: 5/1. Financial aid filing deadline: 5/1. Financial aid notification on or about: 2/15.

TV/Film/Digital Media Studies Programs

Number of undergraduates in these programs: 300

Number of 2005 graduates from these programs: 25

Degrees conferred to these majors: BA, BS.

Number of full-time faculty in these programs: 10

Number of part-time faculty in these programs: 10

Equipment and facilities: We have eight HD cameras, 15 24p cameras, 10 XL-2s, 30 3ccd mini-DV cameras, light kits, portable greenscreen kits, a steady cam, a crane, and more.

Other awards of note: We have an Oscar winner on our faculty.

% of graduates currently employed in related field: 25

Career development services: Alumni networking opportunities; career counseling; central resource(s) for employers to browse headshots, writing samples, reels; internship listings; job fairs; job listings.

DESALES UNIVERSITY

2755 Station Avenue, Center Valley, PA 18034-9568
Phone: 610-282-4443 **E-mail:** admiss@desales.edu
Website: www.desales.edu

Campus Life
Environment: Town. **Calendar:** Semester.

Students and Faculty
(All Undergraduate Programs)
Enrollment: 2,489. **Student Body:** 58% female, 42% male, 18% out-of-state. Caucasian 40%, Hispanic 1%. Student/faculty ratio: 17:1. 92 full-time faculty, 72% hold PhDs. 90% faculty teach undergrads.

Admissions
(All Undergraduate Programs)
Freshman Admissions Requirements: Test(s) required: SAT or ACT. Average high school GPA: 3.25. 20% in top tenth, 48% in top quarter. SAT Math (25/75 percentile): 490/590. SAT Verbal (25/75 percentile): 490/590. Projected SAT Writing (25/75 percentile): 550/640. *Academic units required:* 4 English, 3 math, 2 science (2 science labs), 2 foreign language, 3 social studies. Regular application deadline: 8/1. Regular notification: Rolling.

Costs and Financial Aid
(All Undergraduate Programs)
Annual tuition $20,000. Room & board $7,880. Required fees $700. Average book expense $900. **Financial Aid Statistics:** Priority financial aid filing deadline: 2/1. Financial aid filing deadline: 5/1. Financial aid notification on or about: 2/15.

TV/Film/Digital Media Studies Programs
Number of undergraduates in these programs: 109
Number of 2005 graduates from these programs: 28
Degrees conferred to these majors: BA.
Number of full-time faculty in these programs: 3
Number of part-time faculty in these programs: 3

Equipment and facilities: 30' x 40' 3-camera production studio, 15 digital editing suites (Avid and Final Cut Pro), three Pro Tools suites, one MAYAsuite, six 24p mini-DV cameras, 25 additional mini-DV cameras, remote lighting packages, glide cam, jib arm, and two camera dollies.
Career development services: Alumni networking opportunities, business etiquette functions, career counseling, graduate school application assistance, internship listings, job fairs, job listings, mock interviews, resume/cover letter assistance.

In Their Own Words
The TV/Film Program at DeSales is young and growing. We combine practical and theoretical instruction with community service initiatives, vocational outreach, commitment to the study of ethics in media, and special program activities for women students in the major. A hallmark of the program is the practice of getting students involved in hands-on production experience beginning in their first semester.

POPULAR PROGRAMS

TV/FILM
Department chair: Scott Paul
Number of full-time faculty: 3
Number of part-time faculty: 3
Focus/emphasis: It is our mission in the TV/Film program at DeSales University to provide young men and women opportunities to discover and develop their aptitudes and talents in the field of communication arts. It is our philosophy that film and television professionals are among the most potent influencers of the global community and that a real responsibility rests with the creators and marketers of electronic media. Our program of study, therefore, is conceived as a multilayered experience-blending technical and creative instruction with ethical and professional standards. This type of experience goes far beyond course work and requires a particular brand of academic culture—a culture that has breadth and diversity of perspective. The Lehigh Valley is a deep reservoir of talent and potential for growth

in communication industries. A critical dimension of our emerging culture requires significant involvement with the professional community. Work-study, internships, visiting artist workshops, career symposia, professional mentoring, and alumni networking are among our new initiatives.

Students Should Also Know

Chuck Gloman, a member of the DeSales TV/Film faculty, reviews the newest AV gear before it hits the market. This allows our students the unique opportunity to get hands-on experience with the latest technology before anyone else in the industry. This past year our studets worked with the new Panasonic DXL-100B, the JVC GY-HD 100, and the Canon XLH1 and XDCAM HD (high-definition) cameras. Each semester brings a new wonder of media technology into our labs and classrooms.

DRAKE UNIVERSITY

2507 University Avenue, Des Moines, IA 50311-4505
Phone: 515-271-3181 **E-mail:** admission@drake.edu
Website: www.choose.drake.edu

Campus Life

Environment: Metropolis. **Calendar:** Semester.

Students and Faculty
(All Undergraduate Programs)

Enrollment: 3,015. **Student Body:** 57% female, 43% male, 61% out-of-state, 5% international (56 countries represented). African American 4%, Asian 4%, Caucasian 83%, Hispanic 2%. Student/faculty ratio: 15:1. 246 full-time faculty, 96% hold PhDs. 100% faculty teach undergrads.

Admissions
(All Undergraduate Programs)

Freshman Admissions Requirements: Test(s) required: SAT or ACT. Average high school GPA: 3.66. 37% in top tenth, 73% in top quarter. SAT Math (25/75 percentile): 510/650. SAT Verbal (25/75 percentile): 520/660. Projected SAT Writing (25/75 percentile): 580/690. Regular notification: Rolling.

Costs and Financial Aid
(All Undergraduate Programs)

Annual tuition $22,270. Room & board $6,500. Required fees $412. Average book expense $700.
Financial Aid Statistics: % freshmen/undergrads who receive any aid: 98/85. % freshmen/undergrads who receive need-based scholarship or grant aid: 65/62. % freshmen/undergrads who receive need-based self-help aid: 54/54. Priority financial aid filing deadline: 3/1. Financial aid notification on or about: 3/1.

TV/Film/Digital Media Studies Programs

Number of undergraduates in these programs: 115
Number of 2005 graduates from these programs: 22
Degrees conferred to these majors: BA.
Number of full-time faculty in these programs: 4
Equipment and facilities: Video server-based video editing, DVCam capture, Final Cut Pro HD editing, DVD Studio Pro, and Dreamweaver and Flash production, multicamera TV studio, video streaming, and podcasting video.
Other awards of note: Hearst Award, College Emmy.

% of graduates currently employed in related field: 88
Career development services: Alumni networking opportunities, career counseling, internship listings, job fairs, job listings.

In Their Own Words

Students do the largest student-produced sports production in the country. Internships in news, corporate, promotion, and website multimedia with international corporations.

POPULAR PROGRAMS

ELECTRONIC MEDIA—TELEVISION AND RADIO
Department chair: John Lytle
Number of full-time faculty: 4
Focus/emphasis: Practical approach to radio and TV production starting with studio production, advancing to location shooting and editing, and finishing with a capstone class heavily weighted with multimedia.

NEWS—INTERNET
Department chair: Kathleen Richardson
Number of full-time faculty: 3
Number of part-time faculty: 3
Focus/emphasis: Lots of news writing and Internet production, including but not limited to Web page design, image manipulation, and multimedia embedding.

DREXEL UNIVERSITY

3141 Chestnut Street, Philadelphia, PA 19104
Phone: 215-895-2400 **E-mail:** enroll@drexel.edu
Website: www.drexel.edu

Campus Life
Environment: Metropolis. **Calendar:** Varies

Students and Faculty
(All Undergraduate Programs)
Enrollment: 11,936. **Student Body:** 41% female, 59% male, 44% out-of-state, 6% international (100 countries represented). African American 9%, Asian 12%, Caucasian 63%, Hispanic 3%. 723 full-time faculty. 100% faculty teach undergrads.

Admissions
(All Undergraduate Programs)
Freshman Admissions Requirements: Test(s) required: SAT or ACT. Average high school GPA: 3.47. 30% in top tenth, 60% in top quarter. SAT Math (25/75 percentile): 550/660. SAT Verbal (25/75 percentile): 530/630. Projected SAT Writing (25/75 percentile): 590/670. *Academic units required:* 3 math, 1 science (1 science lab). Regular application deadline: 3/1. Regular notification: Rolling.

Costs and Financial Aid
(All Undergraduate Programs)
Annual tuition $32,000. Room & board $11,010. Required fees $1,380. Average book expense $1,575. **Financial Aid Statistics:** % freshmen/undergrads who receive any aid: 90/83. % freshmen/undergrads who receive need-based scholarship or grant aid: 26/26. % freshmen/undergrads who receive need-based self-help aid: 58/54. Priority financial aid filing deadline: 3/1. Financial aid notification on or about: 3/15.

TV/Film/Digital Media Studies Programs
Number of undergraduates in these programs: 384
Number of 2005 graduates from these programs: 63
Degrees conferred to these majors: BA, BS.
Also available at Drexel University: MS, Certificate in Digital Media, MS/MBA in TV Management.
Number of full-time faculty in these programs: 19
Number of part-time faculty in these programs: 17
Equipment and facilities: Film and video program has Steadicam and is acquiring HDTV.

% of graduates who pursue further study within 5 years: 5
% of graduates currently employed in related field: 50
Career development services: Alumni networking opportunities, career counseling, internship listings, job fairs, job listings. We place students in our arts programs in six-month cooperative education positions where they work hands-on with professionals in their fields.
Notable alumni: Tina DiFeliciantonio, documentary filmmaker.

In Their Own Words

Program students have won ATAS National Internships. A digital media faculty member and student had their 3-D modeling work cited and used in a public TV documentary about Benjamin Franklin.

POPULAR PROGRAMS

FILM AND VIDEO

Department chair: Karin Kelly

Number of full-time faculty: 7

Number of part-time faculty: 5

Focus/emphasis: The program prepares poised artists to secure these opportunities and leverage their skills and talent to realize their vision. Professors in the Film and Video Department are working filmmakers and writers who provide hands-on learning in film and video production. Students begin producing digital films in their freshman year and continue to produce right through to their final senior projects. In addition to video and 16 mm film, interdepartmental courses expand minds and cultivate the voices of the newest generation of filmmakers. A highly competitive program, only 50 freshmen are accepted annually. This allows for smaller classes that foster student-faculty interaction and mentoring, as well as ample access to equipment. The unique Drexel co-op program enhances the learning experience by providing students with professional employment experience.

DIGITAL MEDIA

Department chair: Blaise Tobia

Number of full-time faculty: 7

Number of part-time faculty: 8

Focus/emphasis: The program at Drexel embraces the latest digital technologies that surround our everyday lives: visual effects in blockbuster movies; MP3 content; motion graphics and interfaces on websites and DVDs, to name just a few. Integrating traditional design techniques and cutting-edge new technologies, the Digital Media program is designed to educate creative innovators and visual problem solvers in areas of theory and practice. After receiving a foundation in basic design, art history, and liberal arts in the freshman year, students may choose from a broad range of subjects in subsequent years including graphic design, digital still imaging, film and video, computer programming, and human-computer interaction. Concurrently, professional studio workshops in 3-D modeling, animation, multimedia interactivity, and visual effects provide hands-on instruction and practical application of concepts. The popular program offers a four-year bachelor's of science degree, a two-year master's of science degree, and an accelerated five-year bachelor's of science/master's of science degree option.

SCREENWRITING AND PLAYWRITING

Department chair: Ian Abrams

Number of full-time faculty: 2

Number of part-time faculty: 4

Focus/emphasis: The Westphal College Screenwriting and Playwriting Program is designed to guide and prepare students in their pursuit of a writing career for the stage or the screen. In their courses, students first acquire the essential skills of dramatic storytelling, then apply this knowledge to the creation of scripts that conform to professional standards. In addition, Drexel's pioneering co-op program affords hands-on experience in the field. Perhaps the most important skill screenwriting and playwriting students acquire at Drexel is the life-long process of accumulating a writer's capital—the tools of the mind with which they'll see and hear the world, spin from reality and imagination, and compellingly tell these stories.

TELEVISION MANAGEMENT

Department chair: Howard Homonoff

Number of full-time faculty: 3

Focus/emphasis: The program (MS/MBA) prepares students to break into one of today's most exciting industries or further advance an existing television career. A partnership between Drexel's

Antoinette Westphal College of Media Arts and Design and LeBow College of Business provides a unique integrated education in business and television production. The two-year, full-time professional degree program combines classroom study and independent research with hands-on experience working in the Drexel University cable station, DUTV. Using the station as their laboratory, students participate in the day-to-day operations of the station, whose programming reaches 300,000 homes in the Philadelphia area, and apply skills in strategic planning, sales and marketing, budget management, and production. As part of the MBA course of study, students may take advantage of the new Leonard Pearlstein Business Learning Center, featuring state-of-the-art classrooms, conference rooms, and technology upgrades.

Students Should Also Know

The favorable student-to-faculty ratio allows for close supervision and opportunities to engage with the faculty. All faculty are also working professionals in their field. Students have easy access to state-of-the-art, industry standard equipment.

DUQUESNE UNIVERSITY

600 Forbes Avenue, Pittsburgh, PA 15282
Phone: 412-396-6222 **E-mail:** admissions@duq.edu
Website: www.duq.edu

Campus Life

Environment: Metropolis. **Calendar:** Semester.

Students and Faculty
(All Undergraduate Programs)

Enrollment: 5,606. **Student Body:** 59% female, 41% male, 18% out-of-state, 2% international (79 countries represented). African American 4%, Asian 2%, Caucasian 81%, Hispanic 1%. Student/faculty ratio: 15:1. 429 full-time faculty, 88% hold PhDs. 95% faculty teach undergrads.

Admissions
(All Undergraduate Programs)

Freshman Admissions Requirements: Test(s) required: SAT or ACT; ACT with Writing component. Average high school GPA: 3.6. 28% in top tenth, 58% in top quarter. SAT Math (25/75 percentile): 510/620. SAT Verbal (25/75 percentile): 510/610. Projected SAT Writing (25/75 percentile): 570/660. *Academic units required:* 4 English, 2 math, 2 science, 2 foreign language, 2 social studies, 4 academic electives. Early decision application deadline: 11/1. Regular application deadline: 7/1. Regular notification: Rolling.

Costs and Financial Aid
(All Undergraduate Programs)

Annual tuition $19,721. Room & board $8,054. Required fees $1,759. Average book expense $600. **Financial Aid Statistics:** % freshmen/undergrads who receive any aid: 93/85. % freshmen/undergrads who receive need-based scholarship or grant aid: 65/56. % freshmen/undergrads who receive need-based self-help aid: 62/56. Financial aid filing deadline: 5/1. Financial aid notification on or about: 3/1.

TV/Film/Digital Media Studies Programs

Number of undergraduates in these programs: 63 (undergraduate), 54 (graduate).

Number of 2005 graduates from these programs: 29 (undergraduate), 33 (graduate)

Degrees conferred to these majors: BA.

Also available at Duquesne University: MS.

Number of full-time faculty in these programs: 10

Number of part-time faculty in these programs: 8

Equipment and facilities: The journalism and media arts labs contain 50 state-of-the-art PCs complete with DVD burners, 19-inch monitors, and high-end video cards. Each workstation is equipped with Firewire and network access that enables students to log on the department server as well as access all of the software needed for assignments. The lab is also equipped for wireless access and permits students to connect to the network via a wireless card from their notebook computers. There are several Macintosh platform-based machines, including a dedicated Media 100 digital-editing station. Classroom instruction is facilitated by a projection system with touch-screen capability, allowing instructors and students to conduct classroom demonstrations on an interactive "whiteboard" that is wired to a desktop PC. Projection of video sources, including DVD and VHS tape, are also possible. The lab is equipped with a camera and a video switcher that permits the instuctor to broadcast the class sessions to distant learners via the Internet. Also in the lab is an established bluescreen area complete with lighting equipment for recording video.

% of graduates who pursue further study within 5 years: 5

% of graduates currently employed in related field: 50

Career development services: Alumni networking opportunities; career counseling; central resource(s) for employers to browse headshots, writing samples, reels; internship listings; job fairs; job listings.

Notable alumni: John Clayton, ESPN, NFL Analyst, Renton, WA; Frederick Young, Hearst-Argyle Television, senior vice president, News NYC, NY.

In Their Own Words

Students in the journalism and media arts undergraduate degree program learn media theory and the practical skills that enable them to become successful media practitioners. Our students go on to work for newspapers, magazines, television, and radio stations; for-profit and nonprofit public relations and advertising agencies and organizations; and a wide array of Web and multimedia design and development industries in the public and private sectors. Students can choose a major in print or broadcast journalism, media management and development, public relations and advertising, multimedia development, or Web design. The Department of Journalism and Media Arts features dedicated teachers who aspire to educate, inspire, and mentor students. Some are scholars

who publish research in the areas of multimedia theory and design, media ethics, media history, media economics and electronic media. Full- and part-time faculty members continue to practice their professional craft to ensure that they are up-to-date with ever-evolving media paradigms, industries, practices, and technologies.

POPULAR PROGRAMS

MULTIMEDIA DEVELOPMENT

Department chair: Dr. John Shepherd

Focus/emphasis: The major focuses on new media, the organization and display of information, and the development of interactive applications. Students are free to pursue their creative, artistic talents or their desire to aspire to the more technical component of multimedia development.

BROADCAST JOURNALISM

Department chair: Dr. John Shepherd

Focus/emphasis: The program prepares students to be effective and conscientious civic communicators in the fields of print, broadcast, and online journalism. Hands-on professional courses, taught by scholars who possess substantial experience in the news media, are connected to a strong liberal arts curriculum that emphasizes critical thinking and media responsibility. Duquesne University trains its journalism majors to be critical thinkers and fluent communicators, and therefore, much more than mere careerists with a set of work skills.

MEDIA PRODUCTION AND MANAGEMENT

Department chair: Dr. John Shepherd

Focus/emphasis: The multiple goals of the major include preparing students to become media managers, content producers, and fully literate consumers and practioners in an increasing complex and global media environment. These goals will be met by providing a thorough grounding in each of the three major component areas of media studies: audiences, institutions, and messages. The media production and management major is a coherent blend of media studies (history, theory, and industry study) and media practice (including experiences with both on-campus and major market media outlets).

EAST TENNESSEE STATE UNIVERSITY

ETSU Box 70731, Johnson City, TN 37614-0731
Phone: 423-439-4213 **E-mail:** go2etsu@etsu.edu
Website: www.etsu.edu

Campus Life
Environment: Town. **Calendar:** Semester.

Students and Faculty
(All Undergraduate Programs)
Enrollment: 9,486. **Student Body:** 58% female, 42% male, 8% out-of-state, 1% international (61 countries represented). African American 4%, Asian 1%, Caucasian 90%, Hispanic 1%. Student/faculty ratio 17:1. 480 full-time faculty, 70% hold PhDs.

Admissions
(All Undergraduate Programs)
Freshman Admissions Requirements: Test(s) required: SAT or ACT. Average high school GPA: 3.25. 18% in top tenth, 38% in top quarter. SAT Math (25/75 percentile): 450/570. SAT Verbal (25/75 percentile): 450/590. Projected SAT Writing (25/75 percentile): 520/640. *Academic units required:* 4 English, 3 math, 2 science (1 science lab), 2 foreign language, 1 social studies, 1 history, 1 visual/performing arts. Regular notification: As application and credentials arrive.

Costs and Financial Aid
(All Undergraduate Programs)
Annual in-state tuition $3,678. Out-of-state tuition $12,990. Room & board $4,822. Required fees $809. Average book expense $942.
Financial Aid Statistics: % freshmen/undergrads who receive need-based scholarship or grant aid: 50/36. % freshmen/undergrads who receive need-based self-help aid: 31/34. Priority financial aid filing deadline: 4/1. Financial aid notification on or about: 4/15.

TV/Film/Digital Media Studies Programs
Number of undergraduates in these programs: 330
Number of 2005 graduates from these programs: 65
Degrees conferred to these majors: BA, BS.
Also available at East Tennessee State University: MA.
Number of full-time faculty in these programs: 11
Number of part-time faculty in these programs: 8
Equipment and facilities: 24/7 radio station, completely computerized; full functioning television production studio and seven digital editing stations and 10 analog editing stations; new lab with dedicated 17 station dual processor, dual monitor PC computer labs optimized for animation, video, 3-D modeling, and interactive media production; Green screen stage, 19 digital video cameras (standard mini cams and professional HD), digital still cameras, light kits, tripods, graphics tablets, light boxes and animation stands, external drives, portable green screens, etc. for student check out. Library of DVD and CD training resources, publications, and books for student use in the labs. Extended open lab hours in the Digital Media Center with two Macintosh labs for editing. Galleries to display student work.
Other awards of note: Student Video documentary, *Terra Firma*, accepted in the New York Film and Video Festival. KAFI: Cartoon Challenge: Student team from from ETSU Digital Media program chosen as one of five teams to compete in the Kalamazoo Animation Festival International Cartoon Challenge. Digital Media Demo Reel of Student work won Telly Award in 2005 and a Gold ADDY Award.

% of graduates who pursue further study within 5 years: 15

% of graduates currently employed in related field: 60

Career development services: Alumni networking opportunities, career counseling, internship listings, job fairs, job listings. Portfolio Development Course. In addition to developing and producing both print and electronic (demo reel or web) portfolios, it includes teaching students how to do an effective targeted job search, as well as developing team and presentation skills. Digital media online forum and a posting board at the digital media center lists all jobs that come to our attention. Area employers are starting to send us info as jobs become available.

Famous alumni: Kenny Chesney.

Notable alumni: Many of our students are working for large game development companies such as Sony Interactive, Electronic Arts, etc. and several have spun off their own companies that are very successful on the West Coast. Jack Dempsey is the General Manager of the local CBS affiliate.

In Their Own Words

We produce two regular television programs for area PBS stations and a regular sports show for ESPN. We host the Blue Plum Animation Festival, a student-driven enterprise. At least three nationally recognized speakers per year in the Digital Media Internships available with many regional companies. Summer (one-week) Digital Media Camp for high school students. Undergrads and grad students in Digital Media program work as mentors in the program. Very Active Student SIGGRAPH Chapter, one of 23 chapters worldwide. "Real world" professional learning projects frequently incorporated into class work to give students experience with clients and professional expectations. ETSU's Digital Media EDGE Club took first prize and was awarded $2,500 in a regional competition on Social Venture Showcase and Symposium hosted by the Appalachian IDEAS Network for the Blue Plum Animation Festival entrepreneurial project. Class Project Building the Future television spot Wins Silver Addy Award for special effects and was shown on the nationally tele-vised coaches' show featured on Fox College Sports TV. Annual SIGGRAPH S.P.A.C.E. Poster competition: three to four winners per year for the past three years. Assigned as a class project in sophomore Raster-based imaging classes.

POPULAR PROGRAMS

TELEVISION PRODUCTION
Department chair: Charles Roberts
Number of full-time faculty: 4
Number of part-time faculty: 3
Focus/emphasis: Preparing students for careers in television broadcast production.

TELEVISION PERFORMANCE
Department chair: Charles Roberts
Number of full-time faculty: 4
Number of part-time faculty: 2
Focus/emphasis: Preparing students for careers in television and video presentation both in creative roles and reality roles.

TELEVISION NEWS
Department chair: Charles Roberts
Number of full-time faculty: 4
Number of part-time faculty: 2
Focus/emphasis: Preparing students for careers in television broadcast news as reporters and on-air personalities.

DIGITAL ANIMATION
Department chair: Keith Johnson
Number of full-time faculty: 7
Number of part-time faculty: 5
Focus/emphasis: Preparing students for careers in animation in any media/software with strong skills in one of several specialty areas (3-D animation, 2-D animation, motion graphics.)

DIGITAL INTERACTION
Department chair: Keith Johnson
Number of full-time faculty: 7
Number of part-time faculty: 5

Focus/emphasis: Preparing students for careers in designing and developing media/software with an emphasis on usability, interactive design, problem-solving, production processes, animation, and interactive programming.

DIGITAL VISUALIZATION
Department chair: Keith Johnson
Number of full-time faculty: 7
Number of part-time faculty: 5
Focus/emphasis: Preparing students for careers in creating 3-D digital models that solve visual problems and provide solutions for both the physical and virtual worlds.

TELEVISION MANAGEMENT
Department chair: Charles Roberts
Number of full-time faculty: 4
Number of part-time faculty: 1
Focus/emphasis: Preparing students for careers in television broadcast management.

RADIO PRODUCTION
Department chair: Charles Roberts
Number of full-time faculty: 1
Focus/emphasis: Preparing students for careers in radio production.

RADIO PERFORMANCE
Department chair: Charles Roberts
Number of full-time faculty: 1
Focus/emphasis: Preparing students for careers in radio presentation.

EMERSON COLLEGE
120 Boylston Street, Boston, MA 02116-4624
Phone: 617-824-8600 **E-mail:** admission@emerson.edu
Website: www.emerson.edu

Campus Life
Environment: Metropolis. **Calendar:** Semester.

Students and Faculty
(All Undergraduate Programs)
Enrollment: 3,165. **Student Body:** 56% female, 44% male, 63% out-of-state, 3% international (31 countries represented). African American 2%, Asian 4%, Caucasian 77%, Hispanic 5%. Student/faculty ratio: 14:1. 143 full-time faculty, 74% hold PhDs. 97% faculty teach undergrads.

Admissions
(All Undergraduate Programs)
Freshman Admissions Requirements: Test(s) required: SAT or ACT; ACT with Writing component. Average high school GPA: 3.57. 36% in top tenth, 83% in top quarter. SAT Math (25/75 percentile): 560/650. SAT Verbal (25/75 percentile): 590/670. Projected SAT Writing (25/75 percentile): 640/700. *Academic units required:* 4 English, 3 math, 3 science, 3 foreign language, 3 social studies. Regular application deadline: 1/5. Regular notification: 4/1.

Costs and Financial Aid
(All Undergraduate Programs)
Annual tuition $25,248. Room & board $10,870. Required fees $586. Average book expense $720. **Financial Aid Statistics:** % freshmen/undergrads who receive any aid: 76/66. % freshmen/undergrads who receive need-based scholarship or grant aid: 46/41. % freshmen/undergrads who receive need-based self-help aid: 53/51. Priority financial aid filing deadline: 3/1. Financial aid notification on or about: 4/1.

TV/Film/Digital Media Studies Programs
Number of undergraduates in these programs: 1,274
Number of 2005 graduates from these programs: 276
Degrees conferred to these majors: BA, BFA.
Also available at Emerson College: MFA.
Number of full-time faculty in these programs: 33
Number of part-time faculty in these programs: 68
Equipment and facilities: Emerson has extensive film facilities, a film equipment center, television

studios, audio production/postproduction facilities, and digital editing and production labs.

The digital film labs are equipped with Avid Media Composer Adrenaline, Avid Xpress with Mojo boards, and a dailies-screening facility. Individual film suites include Meridien based Avid Xpress, Final Cut Pro, Steenbeck flatbed editors, Magnasync dubbers, Oxberry Animation/Title Stand, J-K Optical Printers. The Mix-to-Pix studios include Digidesign Pro Tools, Mackie 32 x 8 mixing consoles, 16 mm interlocked projectors and Magnasync professional film sound recorders, Foley pits, and several analog and digital peripherals including DAT recorders and digital 8-track.

The college's Film Equipment Center has an inventory of 16 mm Bolex cameras; cinema products; lights; light meters; tripods; grips; Arriflex cameras with peripheral support gear; Panasonic DVC Pro; mini-DV; Sony PD150 and PDX10 cameras; and Beyer and Audio Technica shotgun mics (with boom poles). The center also supplies 35 mm and medium-format still photo cameras and supports the operation of a photo/dark room lab.

Emerson's television studios and control rooms were designed by Sony and include House Time, controlled by GPS received from the Naval Observatory atomic clock. Studios include a 40' x 28' sound-treated space containing a Sony 9000 switching system and routing network, Sony DXC 35W and DXC 50W solid-state cameras with Vinton ProPed pedestals, Vinton Vision Pan/Tilt heads, and TelePrompTer systems. A second, 40' x 43' studio is comparable to network-affiliated television stations and production houses. It contains a 14' grid, ETC dual processor Obsession II computer-lighting system, and UltraMatte green chroma key system and curved infinity wall, Sony digital video recorders, Chryon Duet character generation, and Aprisa graphic still and motion storage systems, Genelec studio audio monitors, and a Yamaha audio mixer with a DigiCart audio storage system.

The audio production/postproduction facilities on campus comprise three classroom studios and eight production suites that support advanced film/video/new media sound. The equipment includes Pro Tools HD systems, advanced sound-processing plug-ins, 5.1 mixing, a Yamaha digital console, Kurzweil K2600, single or dual Tascam DA-78s, video monitoring, Mackie 32 x 8 analog consoles, a full array of multimedia applications, advanced multitracking/mixing, patch bay, and MIDI music production software/hardware including Reason, Live, and Max/Jitter. The audio production suites also include Pro Tools Digi systems, Genelec studio monitors, DAT, seamless integration with Avid and Final Cut Pro via Digitranslator, and DV Toolkit for advanced time-code-based digital image postproduction.

Emerson's digital production and editing labs feature both Macs and PCs with respective versions of Adobe (Photoshop, AfterEffects, Illustrator, InDesign, Acrobat) and Macromedia (Director, Dreamweaver, Fireworks, Flash) software. Additional workstations with Final Cut Pro 4.5 and Avid Pro and Mojo boards augmented by Photoshop and AfterEffects production bundles can handle longer length projects or advanced complex new media requiring extensive memory and high-end video finishing (a Dolby sound room with digital mixing board and a Pro Tools 192 system allowing Dolby mixes up to 64 tracks is available).

% of graduates currently employed in related field: 89

Career development services: Alumni networking opportunities, career counseling, internship listings, job fairs, job listings. Emerson has an extensive career resource library with trade publications, career exploration books and resources, industry directories, handouts, and more. There are: career-related educational programs, panels, and events; self-assessment instruments/interpretation; mock interviews; and services for undergraduates, graduate students, and alumni.

Famous alumni: Henry Winkler, Jay Leno, Norman Lear, Jay Bienstock, Andy Wachowski, Max Mutchnick, Kevin Bright, Vin DiBona, Denis Leary.

Notable alumni: More than a dozen Emerson alumni have been nominated for Emmy Awards in each of the last three years, including Jay Bienstock (*Survivor*), Steve Welch (*Malcolm in the Middle*), Lori Eskowitz-Carter (*Will & Grace*), Kate Boutilier (*Rugrats: All Growed Up*), Kevin Bright (*Friends*), Chrisi Karvonides Dushenko (*American Dreams*), and Lewis Gould (*Law & Order*). A number of other alumni hold successful professional positions, including Doug Herzog, president, USA Networks; Andrea Giannetti, senior vice president, Columbia Pictures; J.J. Johnson, visual effects director, Century III; Al Jaffe, vice president, ESPN; Michael Rosen, supervising producer, VH-1; Patricia Murphy, 2006 Edward R. Murrow award winner, NPR; Flora Johnstone, documentary and series development, MTV; Judy Tygard, senior producer, *CBS News' 48 Mystery*; Linda Corridina, executive producer, *Martha Stewart Living*; Jeff Arch, 2005 Humanitas Prize finalist, CBS' *Saving Milly*; and William Ludel, director, *General Hospital*.

In Their Own Words

Emerson's Department of Visual & Media Arts is committed to providing students with a challenging and artistic environment, made up of state-of-the-art facilities and equipment and fueled by an accomplished and dedicated faculty. The department's curriculum ensures that students acquire a depth of knowledge and expertise in their selected areas, as well as a breadth of understanding that allows them to work across the media in a variety of genres. With more than two dozen advanced film, video, and audio projects per year, as well as active co-curricular student organizations, Emerson students have a wealth of opportunity to practice their art. The college offers an optional summer film program in Prague and an extensive network of internships in film, television, audio production/postproduction, and digital media, including exclusive placements at the college's Los Angeles Center (a residential study and internship program in the heart of the entertainment capital).

POPULAR PROGRAMS

FILM PRODUCTION
Department chair: Michael Selig
Number of full-time faculty: 8
Number of part-time faculty: 16
Focus/emphasis: Film production is designed to explore in-depth the use of film as a media product format. Students are required to develop a broad technical, theoretical, and artistic familiarity with film as a creative endeavor.

STUDIO TELEVISION/VIDEO PRODUCTION
Department chair: Michael Selig
Number of full-time faculty: 6
Number of part-time faculty: 12
Focus/emphasis: TV/Video explores the production of multicamera video in the studio for the creation of television programming, including situation comedies, soap operas, and public affairs programming. Exploration of new multicamera genres are encouraged. Studies also include television and nonbroadcast producing and the use of studios and soundstages for single-camera production.

AUDIO PRODUCTION/RADIO (SOUND DESIGN)
Department chair: Michael Selig
Number of full-time faculty: 4
Number of part-time faculty: 8
Focus/emphasis: Audio production/radio (sound design, audio production/postproduction/radio) is an intensive program of study in the theory and practice of all phases of producing creative and professional soundtracks for film, video, and all new media forms of expression. The specialty emphasizes concept development; sound principles and audio production; field recording; ADR and Foley techniques; surround sound design; and mastering to DVD.

NEW MEDIA (ANIMATION, MOTION GRAPHICS)
Department chair: Michael Selig
Number of full-time faculty: 4
Number of part-time faculty: 8

Focus/emphasis: New media (animation, motion graphics, interactive media) focuses on computer animation, visual effects, motion graphics, film animation, and compositing techniques. Students take a broad range of courses and will produce original work in digital 2-D animation, 3-D modeling, and frame-by-frame film animation. Students will also perform web design.

MEDIA STUDIES

Department chair: Michael Selig
Number of full-time faculty: 7
Number of part-time faculty: 15
Focus/emphasis: A program for serious media arts students who want to start their careers with as broad a background as possible. The integrated curriculum of media history, criticism, theory, and production is also a good choice for graduate-level course work in media studies, business, or entertainment law. The college's production equipment and facilities are available to help students develop an expertise within a general media framework.

SCREENWRITING

Department chair: Michael Selig
Number of full-time faculty: 4
Number of part-time faculty: 8
Focus/emphasis: The screenwriting specialty fosters learning through writing, critique, and rewriting. Students will be encouraged to be innovative and individualistic in their style and expression. They will also have the opportunity to write feature-length scripts, situation comedies, one-hour prime time dramas, and short scripts suitable for film, television, video, or new media.

EMORY UNIVERSITY

Boisfeuillet Jones Center, Atlanta, GA 30322
Phone: 404-727-6036 **E-mail:** admiss@emory.edu
Website: www.emory.edu

Campus Life
Environment: Metropolis. **Calendar:** Semester.

Students and Faculty
(All Undergraduate Programs)
Enrollment: 6,378. **Student Body:** 58% female, 42% male, 69% out-of-state, 4% international (50 countries represented). African American 9%, Asian 16%, Caucasian 59%, Hispanic 3%. Student/faculty ratio: 7:1. 1,236 full-time faculty, 100% hold PhDs. 90% faculty teach undergrads.

Admissions
(All Undergraduate Programs)
Freshman Admissions Requirements: Test(s) required: SAT or ACT; ACT with Writing component. Average high school GPA: 3.8. 90% in top tenth, 98% in top quarter. SAT Math (25/75 percentile): 660/740. SAT Verbal (25/75 percentile): 640/730. Projected SAT Writing (25/75 percentile): 680/740. *Academic units required:* 4 English, 3 math, 2 science (2 science labs), 2 foreign language, 2 social studies, 2 history, 2 academic electives. Early decision application deadline: 11/1. Regular application deadline: 1/15. Regular notification: 4/1.

Costs and Financial Aid
(All Undergraduate Programs)
Annual tuition $30,400. Room & board $9,752. Required fees $394. Average book expense $1,000. **Financial Aid Statistics:** % freshmen/undergrads who receive any aid: 60/59. % freshmen/undergrads who receive need-based scholarship or grant aid: 35/35. % freshmen/undergrads who receive need-based self-help aid: 29/32. Priority financial aid filing deadline: 2/15. Financial aid filing deadline: 4/1. Financial aid notification on or about: 4/15.

TV/Film/Digital Media Studies Programs

Number of undergraduates in these programs: 51

Number of 2005 graduates from these programs: 12

Degrees conferred to these majors: BA.

Also available at Emory University: MA.

Number of full-time faculty in these programs: 4

Number of part-time faculty in these programs: 5

Equipment and facilities: Film studies courses are taught in multimedia-equipped classrooms of White Hall, which provides facilities for 70 mm, 35 mm, and 16 mm projection, as well as superior sound systems for lecture, discussion, and screening sessions. Seminars are taught in the Rich Building, which is comparably equipped. The Heilbrun Music and Media Library, located on the fourth floor of the Robert W. Woodruff Library, holds more than 100 16 mm feature films and has several thousand narrative, documentary, experimental, and other titles on DVD, laserdisc, and videotape. The Heilbrun also provides extensive viewing facilities, including a state-of-the-art, acoustically treated room with a large screen television for analyzing such materials. In addition to its comprehensive book holdings, the Woodruff Library has extensive runs of foreign and American journals of criticism and history and basic research materials.

% of graduates who pursue further study within 5 years: 70

% of graduates currently employed in related field: 90

Career development services: Alumni networking opportunities; career counseling; central resource(s) for employers to browse headshots, writing samples, reels; internship listings; job fairs; job listings.

In Their Own Words

The film studies faculty at Emory University offers a master's program and a PhD certificate in the methodologies of film theory, history, and criticism. The program trains its students to be astute and discriminating critics and analysts of film art; it strengthens their critical thinking through an awareness of the philosophical and aesthetic debates in film theory. It provides students with a thorough knowledge of the cinema's history as a dynamic form of cultural expression. With this background, our master's alumni are well qualified for continuing work toward the PhD as well as for administrative and/or teaching careers. Our PhD alumni are well qualified for careers in teaching and scholarly research. Created in 1986, film studies at Emory features four full-time faculty members who are widely published and who teach a broad range of courses with a strong commitment to individualized, quality education. The curriculum is comparable to that of the best small programs at private liberal arts universities across the country and offers an opportunity for graduate film study unique to the Southeast. Financial aid in the form of tuition waivers is available to master's candidates who study on campus.

POPULAR PROGRAMS

DEPARTMENT OF FILM STUDIES

Department chair: David A. Cook

Number of full-time faculty: 4

Number of part-time faculty: 6

Students Should Also Know

We do not offer film, televison, and radio production courses and do not have production facilities. For more information, visit www.filmstudies.emory.edu.

THE EVERGREEN STATE COLLEGE

2700 Evergreen Parkway NW, Office of Admissions, Olympia, WA 98505
Phone: 360-867-6170 **E-mail:** admissions@evergreen.edu
Website: www.evergreen.edu

Campus Life

Environment: Town. **Calendar:** Quarter.

Students and Faculty
(All Undergraduate Programs)

Enrollment: 3,962. **Student Body:** 55% female, 45% male, 22% out-of-state, (13 countries represented). African American 5%, Asian 5%, Caucasian 69%, Hispanic 4%, Native American 4%. Student/faculty ratio: 21:1. 158 full-time faculty, 86% hold PhDs. 100% faculty teach undergrads.

Admissions
(All Undergraduate Programs)

Freshman Admissions Requirements: Test(s) required: SAT or ACT. Average high school GPA: 3.07. 8% in top tenth, 24% in top quarter. SAT Math (25/75 percentile): 480/600. SAT Verbal (25/75 percentile): 530/650. Projected SAT Writing (25/75 percentile): 590/690. *Academic units required:* 4 English, 3 math, 2 science (1 science lab), 2 foreign language, 3 social studies, 1 academic elective, 1 fine, visual, or performing arts elective or other college prep elective from the areas above. Regular notification: Rolling.

Costs and Financial Aid
(All Undergraduate Programs)

Annual in-state tuition $4,128. Out-of-state tuition $14,538. Room & board $6,924. Required fees $209. Average book expense $894.

Financial Aid Statistics: % freshmen/undergrads who receive any aid: 47/67. % freshmen/undergrads who receive need-based scholarship or grant aid: 24/44. % freshmen/undergrads who receive need-based self-help aid: 30/48. Priority financial aid filing deadline: 3/15. Financial aid notification on or about: 4/15.

TV/Film/Digital Media Studies Programs

Number of undergraduates in these programs: 275
Number of 2005 graduates from these programs: 55
Degrees conferred to these majors: BA.
Number of full-time faculty in these programs: 6
Number of part-time faculty in these programs: 7

Equipment and facilities: Multimedia lab with 14 stations; nonlinear and linear edit suites; animation labs (2-D; 3-D), design lab; full 16 mm production facility; Oxberry animation stand, DVCAM digital video production, professional lighting instruments, 16-track sound studio, electronic music labs.

% of graduates who pursue further study within 5 years: 32
% of graduates currently employed in related field: 71
Career development services: Alumni networking opportunities, career counseling, internship listings, job fairs, job listings.
Famous alumni: Craig Bartlett, Matt Groening, Linda Weinman.
Notable alumni: Rhyena Halpern, PBS producer; Peter Speek, former owner of Warren Miller Films; Michael Solinger, postproduction management/sound, major Hollywood films; Pamela Kurie, assistant director, major Hollywood films; Lisa Farnham, producer and owner of regional production company.

In Their Own Words

Extensive regional internship program; all undergraduate curriculum emphasizes experiential learning; visiting artist series (annually); focused in-depth full-time study in media arts combined with many inventive interdisciplinary programs that combine media study/production with many disciplines (including natural sciences, community studies, cultural studies, environmental studies, and more).

POPULAR PROGRAMS

MEDIAWORKS

Department chair: Ann Fischel
Number of full-time faculty: 2
Focus/emphasis: Evergreen's unique perspective on liberal arts education provides the context for our approach to teaching media. Media production is fundamentally interdisciplinary. Our programs have historically focused on nonfiction,

alternative, and experimental media. More recently we have begun to incorporate animation and narrative production into our curriculum. This program is designed to provide students with background in some aspects of film and video history and theory, as well as training in 16 mm and digital filmmaking. Focus is on the nonfiction image, including documentary, experimental film, installation, video art, autobiography, and mixed media.

STUDENT ORIGINATED STUDIES: MEDIA

Department chair: Ruth Hayes
Number of full-time faculty: 2
Focus/emphasis: This is a program for advanced media students interested in developing learning communities with other media students. Student studies will be pursued in small groups that share common reading, research interests, and/or production goals. Credit will be awarded in areas of student work—e.g., media studies, film production, video production, audio production, digital film production, multimedia performance, animation, installation, and film history and theory.

FAIRFIELD UNIVERSITY

1073 North Benson Road, Fairfield, CT 06824-5195
Phone: 203-254-4100 **E-mail:** admis@mail.fairfield.edu
Website: www.fairfield.edu

Campus Life
Environment: Town. **Calendar:** Semester.

Students and Faculty
(All Undergraduate Programs)
Enrollment: 3,688. **Student Body:** 57% female, 43% male, 74% out-of-state, (41 countries represented). African American 2%, Asian 3%, Caucasian 82%, Hispanic 4%. Student/faculty ratio: 13:1. 226 full-time faculty, 93% hold PhDs. 100% faculty teach undergrads.

Admissions
(All Undergraduate Programs)
Freshman Admissions Requirements: Test(s) required: SAT or ACT. Average high school GPA: 3.35. 31% in top tenth, 69% in top quarter. SAT Math (25/75 percentile): 560/640. SAT Verbal (25/75 percentile): 550/630. Projected SAT Writing (25/75 percentile): 610/670. *Academic units required:* 4 English, 3 math, 3 science (3 science labs), 2 foreign language, 3 social studies. Regular application deadline: 1/15. Regular notification: 4/1.

Costs and Financial Aid
(All Undergraduate Programs)
Annual tuition $31,450. Room & board $9,600. Required fees $505. Average book expense $500. **Financial Aid Statistics:** % freshmen/undergrads who receive any aid: 69/65. % freshmen/undergrads who receive need-based scholarship or grant aid: 48/42. % freshmen/undergrads who receive need-based self-help aid: 43/40. Priority financial aid filing deadline: 2/15. Financial aid filing deadline: 2/15. Financial aid notification on or about: 4/1.

TV/Film/Digital Media Studies Programs
Number of undergraduates in these programs: 60
Number of 2005 graduates from these programs: 10
Degrees conferred to these majors: BA.
Number of full-time faculty in these programs: 3
Number of part-time faculty in these programs: 10
Equipment and facilities: one 32-foot mobile satellite uplink HDTV truck; two fully-equipped sound and television/film studios with control rooms; one sound studio with sound booth for voiceovers, sound mixes, and music production, with Apple Logic Pro 7 and Pro Tools software; 14 Avid and Final Cut Pro editing suites; four media intensive screening rooms/classrooms/seminar rooms; one multimedia software lab with entire Adobe Suite products, Avid, Final Cut Pro, Storyboard Artist, Gorilla Production software package, Dreamweaver and Flash for web page design, Final Draft for

screenwriters, and other media software packages; a large inventory of Arriflex lighting kits, audio equipment, dollies and tracks, steadicams, Arriflex film cameras, and other video cameras including Sony HDR FX1 Cameras, DVC Pro 25 and 50, and PDX 10s Canon GL1 and GL2.

ATAS College TV Awards recipients: 1

Other awards of note: Our staff and faculty have won numerous awards of distinction and excellence from The New York Festivals, the Telly Awards, the Communicator Awards, Videographer Awards, and the Aurora Awards festivals.

% of graduates who pursue further study within 5 years: 30

% of graduates currently employed in related field: 50

Career development services: Alumni networking opportunities, career counseling, internship listings, job fairs, job listings.

Notable alumni: We have many alumni working on television shows in Los Angeles and New York, including: producers of *Survivor* and *The Apprentice*; producers and production personnel in FOX News, ABC, and NBC News; production personnel on the MSG network, ESPN, and WWE, the *Daily Show*, and MTV Networks; and as production and postproduction personnel in numerous feature film and documentary projects.

In Their Own Words

Our program is relatively new and small (but growing)—with exciting new initiatives, including acquisition of our new 32-foot mobile satellite uplink truck. Students in our program are offered the opportunity as freshmen to immediately get their hands all over our equipment and studio facilities—with lots of close support and encouragement from a faculty and staff that is eager to help them develop their creative talents. Our program is housed within an award-winning on-campus production house and offers students the advantage of being instructed by onsite professional directors, writers, producers, cinematographers, and audio and lighting specialists and editors. Students join a real commu-nity of creative artists at Fairfield, with facilities and equipment equal to or better than larger programs. We are also close to New York and draw on the incredible opportunities there for internships and professional employment for our current students and graduates. All of this within a program of liberal arts study, which we believe is necessary for creative artists to find their voice or truth—the content of their media work.

POPULAR PROGRAMS

NEW MEDIA

Department chair: James Mayzik
Number of full-time faculty: 3
Number of part-time faculty: 10
Focus/emphasis: Our film track surveys the origins and development of motion picture art; analyzes periods, genres, and styles of filmmaking; and offers hands-on experience in film production technique. In production courses, students are introduced to the collaborative, creative process of filmmaking, with an emphasis on storytelling through a broad spectrum of aesthetic approaches.

NEW MEDIA

Department chair: James Mayzik
Number of full-time faculty: 3
Number of part-time faculty: 10
Focus/emphasis: Our television track surveys the technological and stylistic history of the medium; the particular visual and audio language of television texts; the genres, narrative, and generic conventions of television; and offers hands-on production experience designed to teach skills in studio and remote television production.

NEW MEDIA RADIO

Department chair: James Mayzik
Number of full-time faculty: 3
Number of part-time faculty: 10

Focus/emphasis: Our radio track surveys the programmatic and technological development of the medium; sound development and recording techniques; and broadcast management and production.

FLORIDA STATE UNIVERSITY

2500 University Center, Tallahassee, FL 32306-2400
Phone: 850-644-6200 **E-mail:** admissions@admin.fsu.edu
Website: www.fsu.edu

Campus Life
Environment: City. **Calendar:** Semester.

Students and Faculty
(All Undergraduate Programs)
Enrollment: 30,206. **Student Body:** 57% female, 43% male, 13% out-of-state, (136 countries represented). African American 12%, Asian 3%, Caucasian 73%, Hispanic 11%. Student/faculty ratio: 22:1. 1,265 full-time faculty, 92% hold PhDs. 100% faculty teach undergrads.

Admissions
(All Undergraduate Programs)
Freshman Admissions Requirements: Test(s) required: SAT or ACT; ACT with Writing component. Average high school GPA: 3.59. 26% in top tenth, 61% in top quarter. SAT Math (25/75 percentile): 540/630. SAT Verbal (25/75 percentile): 530/620. Projected SAT Writing (25/75 percentile): 590/660. *Academic units required:* 4 English, 3 math, 3 science (2 science labs), 2 foreign language, 1 social studies, 2 history, 3 academic electives. Regular application deadline: 3/1. Regular notification: 4/1.

Costs and Financial Aid
(All Undergraduate Programs)
Annual tuition $3,696.
Financial Aid Statistics: % freshmen/undergrads who receive any aid: 35/32. % freshmen/undergrads who receive need-based scholarship or grant aid: 23/21. % freshmen/undergrads who receive need-based self-help aid: 22/24. Priority financial aid filing deadline: 2/15. Financial aid notification on or about: 3/15.

TV/Film/Digital Media Studies Programs
Degrees conferred to these majors: BFA.
Also available at Florida State University: MFA.
Equipment and facilities: FSU is the only university in America that owns and makes available to its students Super-16 and 35 mm production equipment, including grip and camera trucks. Students work in dedicated production offices, shoot on professional soundstages, view their work in screening theaters tuned to industry specifications, and edit their work in nonlinear digital postproduction facilities.
Other awards of note: FSU Film School was recognized by the Directors Guild of America (DGA) for its distinguished contributions to American culture through film and television. Students have won many awards from a variety of festivals including Student Academy Awards for Todd Schulman (writer/director of *The Plunge*) and Dana Buning (writer/director of *Zeke*).
Career development services: Alumni networking opportunities, job listings, mentorships.
Notable alumni: Ron Friedman, screenwriter, *Brother Bear*; Melissa Carter, screenwriter, *Little Black Book*; Jonathan King, president of production, Lawrence Mark Productions, *I Robot*; Greg Marcks, director, *11:14*.

In Their Own Words
FSU has entered many film festivals in the past including: Academy of Motion Picture Arts and Sciences, Amnesty International Film Festival, Berlin International Film Festival (Berlinale), Cine Golden Eagle Film and Video Competition, Chicago International Film Festival, New York Film Festival, Slamdance International Film Festival, Sundance Film Festival, SxSW Film Festival (among many others).

POPULAR PROGRAMS

FILM
Number of full-time faculty: 1. The Florida State University Film School provides professional training to a limited number of the very brightest students in the world. Only 30 men and women are selected each year to attend its programs,

significantly fewer than any other major film school in America. Small enrollments allow the faculty of professional filmmakers to maintain the high caliber of education necessary for graduates to succeed in an extremely competitive industry. The Film School provides a one-on-one setting for the majority of instruction. Its curriculum focuses on the art, craft, and business of story-telling. The faculty of filmmakers is a blend of senior industry members that include Stuart Robertson, Richard Portman, Rexford Metz, and Chip Chalmers, and young accomplished professionals such as Valerie Scoon, Reb Braddock, Tim Long, and Vicky Meyer, all of whom have a record of excellent teaching in addition to their impressive industry credits. Faculty members work with students in a studio facility that consists of production offices, soundstages, screening theaters, digital production, and postproduction equipment, Super-16 and 35 mm cameras, and grip and camera trucks. FSU is the only film school in the country that pays for the production costs of all of its students' films, thereby creating a level playing field for students to focus on art, craft, and imagination, instead of fundraising. To ensure that this high caliber of education is available to the most talented student regardless of financial means, the university offers generous scholarships and assistantships as well as tuition costs that are among the lowest in the country.

FORT LEWIS COLLEGE

1000 Rim Drive, Durango, CO 81301
Phone: 970-247-7184 **E-mail:** admisson@fortlewis.edu
Website: www.fortlewis.edu

Campus Life
Environment: Village. **Calendar:** Semester.

Students and Faculty
(All Undergraduate Programs)
Enrollment: 3,829. **Student Body:** 48% female, 52% male, 29% out-of-state (13 countries represented). Caucasian 66%, Hispanic 6%, Native American 19%. Student/faculty ratio: 18:1. 177 full-time faculty, 78% hold PhDs. 100% faculty teach undergrads.

Admissions
(All Undergraduate Programs)
Freshman Admissions Requirements: Test(s) required: SAT or ACT. Average high school GPA: 3.0. 4% in top tenth, 20% in top quarter. SAT Math (25/75 percentile): 450/550. SAT Verbal (25/75 percentile): 458/560. Regular application deadline: 8/1. Regular notification: Rolling.

Costs and Financial Aid
(All Undergraduate Programs)
Annual in-state tuition $4,862. Out-of-state tuition $12,870. Room & board $6,160. Required fees $830. Average book expense $850.
Financial Aid Statistics: % freshmen/undergrads who receive any aid: 64/64. % freshmen/undergrads who receive need-based scholarship or grant aid: 25/31. % freshmen/undergrads who receive need-based self-help aid: 36/43. Priority financial aid filing deadline: 2/15. Financial aid notification on or about: 4/1.

TV/Film/Digital Media Studies Programs
Number of undergraduates in these programs: 90
Number of 2005 graduates from these programs: 36
Degrees conferred to these majors: BA.
Number of full-time faculty in these programs: 13
Number of part-time faculty in these programs: 1
Equipment and facilities: We have 16 PCs with Sony Vegas 6.0 video-editing software, 16 Sony DVD Architect 3.0 DVD-burning software, five Sony TRV 25 mini-DV cameras, three Panasonic DVC80 mini-DV cameras, one Sony HC1 HiDef camera.
ATAS Faculty Seminar participants: 1
Career development services: Career counseling, internship listings, job fairs, job listings, job search assistance (resume, cover letters, interview skills), vocational assessments.

Famous alumni: Chris Schauble
Notable alumni: Valerie Wigglesworth

In Their Own Words

These are headlines from local newspapers over the last couple of years dealing with our film program (links to full articles can be found on www.kurtlancaster.com): "Piece on Katrina steals the show at FLC film festival," "Making the disaster film: Student filmmakers document Hurricane Katrina aftermath," "Festival features several FLC student films," "In search of the cowboy mystique: Film festival screens locally produced 'Cowboy Way,'" "From desk to the big screen: Abbey Theatre to screen the work of student filmmakers," "Shorts, documentaries fill FLC Student Film Festival." Students write, shoot, and direct a short-fiction film and documentary in their first class. The advanced class shot a feature narrative last year using a student-written script. All student projects are screened at the local art house theater, Abbey Theatre, at the end of every semester. One of our professors has screened the following film at film festivals: Kurt Lancaster: The Kitchen—official selections of Boston Underground Film Festival (2003), Northampton Independent Film Festival (2003), and the Durango Film Festival (2004); documentary, Huckleberry August—an official selection of the Utah Film and Video Festival (2004), and the documentary, Folding Paper Cranes: the poet of an atomic veteran, Leonard Bird—an official selection of the Durango Film Festival (2005). He is currently completing the documentaries, Dreams from a Red Planet: the next giant leap for humanity—an official selection of the Durango Independent Film Festival (2006), and Skins: immersion into the poetry of Elizabeth Ingraham. He is a member of the International Documentary Association, the Academy of Television Arts & Sciences, and the Digital Film Society.

POPULAR PROGRAMS

BUSINESS ADMINISTRATION
Department chair: Thomas C. Harrington
Number of full-time faculty: 17
Number of part-time faculty: 6
Focus/emphasis: Provides a general understanding of the principles of modern business and organizational practices and the opportunity to apply academic learning in preparation for a business career in a dynamic global environment.

PSYCHOLOGY
Department chair: Ziarat Hossain
Number of full-time faculty: 11
Number of part-time faculty: 7
Focus/emphasis: To meet the needs of many students, all of whom have an interest in the scientific study of behavior and its causes, which is the most general definition of modern psychology.

TEACHER EDUCATION
Department chair: David Hayes
Number of full-time faculty: 14
Number of part-time faculty: 6
Focus/emphasis: Designed to enable students to qualify for a Colorado teaching license.

ART
Department chair: Michael Freeman
Number of full-time faculty: 7
Number of part-time faculty: 9
Focus/emphasis: Designed to increase the student's awareness and understanding of art and its relationship to society within a broad liberal arts background.

BIOLOGY
Department chair: Sherell Kluss Byrd
Number of full-time faculty: 13
Number of part-time faculty: 2
Focus/emphasis: Designed to provide exposure to all major conceptual areas of biology.

EXERCISE SCIENCE
Department chair: Paul W. Petersen
Number of full-time faculty: 10

Number of part-time faculty: 8

Focus/emphasis: To meet the needs of our graduates to function more efficiently as professionals in our discipline and to compete more favorably in today's job market by providing students with a variety of opportunities to develop a scientific knowledge base, engage in practical experiences, and learn, develop, and master social and leadership skills.

ACCOUNTING

Department chair: Paul McGurr

Number of full-time faculty: 5

Number of part-time faculty: 2

Focus/emphasis: Prepares students to embark immediately on a career as a public, industrial, or governmental accountant and provides a foundation in accounting and business administration that will enable them to pursue graduate study.

BUSINESS ADMINISTRATION—MARKETING

Department chair: Bill Dodds

Number of full-time faculty: 4

Number of part-time faculty: 1

Focus/emphasis: Emphasizes the performance of business activities designed to plan, price, promote, and distribute goods and services to satisfy consumer needs and wants.

ENGLISH—COMMUNICATION

Department chair: Gordon P. Cheesewright

Number of full-time faculty: 13

Number of part-time faculty: 1

Focus/emphasis: Provides an emphasis on mass media theory and practice; preparation for graduate school or industry.

POLITICAL SCIENCE

Department chair: Dugald Owen

Number of full-time faculty: 5

Number of part-time faculty: 1

Focus/emphasis: Concerned with the relationship between the governed and the government, the nature of the political process, and the role of the citizen in a democratic society.

GANNON UNIVERSITY

University Square, Erie, PA 16541

Phone: 814-871-7240 **E-mail:** admissions@gannon.edu

Website: www.gannon.edu

Campus Life

Environment: City. **Calendar:** Semester.

Students and Faculty
(All Undergraduate Programs)

Enrollment: 2,394. **Student Body:** 60% female, 40% male, 22% out-of-state, 1% international (19 countries represented). African American 5%, Asian 1%, Caucasian 90%. Student/faculty ratio: 11:1. 180 full-time faculty, 68% hold PhDs. 95% faculty teach undergrads.

Admissions
(All Undergraduate Programs)

Freshman Admissions Requirements: Test(s) required: SAT or ACT. Average high school GPA: 3.26. 21% in top tenth, 48% in top quarter. SAT Math (25/75 percentile): 470/580. SAT Verbal (25/75 percentile): 470/570. Projected SAT Writing (25/75 percentile): 540/620. *Academic units required:* 4 English, 12 combination of remaining academic units based on planned major. Regular notification: Rolling.

Costs and Financial Aid
(All Undergraduate Programs)

Annual tuition $18,220. Room & board $7,410. Required fees $470. Average book expense $750. **Financial Aid Statistics:** % freshmen/undergrads who receive any aid: 90/90. % freshmen/undergrads who receive need-based scholarship or grant aid: 85/83. % freshmen/undergrads who receive need-based self-help aid: 85/72. Priority financial aid filing deadline: 3/15. Financial aid notification on or about: 11/1.

TV/Film/Digital Media Studies Programs

Number of undergraduates in these programs: 90

Number of 2005 graduates from these programs: 22

Degrees conferred to these majors: BA.

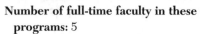

Number of full-time faculty in these
  programs: 5
Number of part-time faculty in these
  programs: 2
Equipment and facilities: Digital TV studio with
  three cameras, three sets, four digital editing suites,
  field production, digital audio, digital graphics.

% of graduates currently employed in related
  field: 78
Career development services: Alumni networking
  opportunities, career counseling, internship listings,
  job fairs, job listings.

In Their Own Words

*Gannon University's communications core
competencies are writing, performance, production, team-building, and adaptability. Our highly
motivated students have access to full digital
production equipment on campus. In addition,
the university owns a 3,000-watt student operated FM radio station–WERG. Gannon is surrounded by regional media outlets. Local broadcast, cable, and Web distribution services are
within walking distance of our downtown campus.*

POPULAR PROGRAMS

COMMUNICATION ARTS

Department chair: AJ Miceli, Department Chair
Focus/emphasis: The program is designed for
  motivated students who want thorough preparation in communication arts, specifically the electronic media.

Students Should Also Know

At Gannon University, you will learn from accomplished professionals who are also great teachers.

GEORGETOWN COLLEGE

400 East College Street, Georgetown, KY 40324
Phone: 502-863-8009 **E-mail:** admissions@georgetowncollege.edu
Website: www.georgetowncollege.edu

Campus Life
Environment: Village. Calendar: Semester.

Students and Faculty
(All Undergraduate Programs)
Enrollment: 1,364. Student Body: 55% female,
45% male, 15% out-of-state. African American 4%,
Caucasian 91%. Student/faculty ratio: 11:1. 101 full-
time faculty, 88% hold PhDs. 100% faculty teach
undergrads.

Admissions
(All Undergraduate Programs)
Freshman Admissions Requirements: Test(s)
required: SAT or ACT. Average high school GPA: 3.5.
31% in top tenth, 58% in top quarter. SAT Math
(25/75 percentile): 470/590. SAT Verbal (25/75 percentile): 480/590. Projected SAT Writing (25/75 percentile): 540/640. Regular application deadline: 8/1.
Regular notification: Rolling.

Costs and Financial Aid
(All Undergraduate Programs)
Annual tuition $20,700. Room & board $6,070.
Average book expense $1,050.
Financial Aid Statistics: % freshmen/undergrads
who receive any aid: 98/98. % freshmen/undergrads
who receive need-based scholarship or grant aid:
64/66. % freshmen/undergrads who receive need-
based self-help aid: 41/44. Priority financial aid filing
deadline: 2/15. Financial aid notification on or about:
3/1.

TV/Film/Digital Media Studies Programs
Degrees conferred to these majors: BA.
Number of full-time faculty in these
  programs: 3
Number of part-time faculty in these
  programs: 1

Career development services: Career counseling; central resource(s) for employers to browse head-shots, writing samples, reels; internship listings; job fairs; job listings.

Notable alumni: Theresa Boscheinen, stage manager, Mad Cow Theater, Orlando, FL; Joy Burns, actress; Evelyn Francis, theater director/teacher; Jonathan Fredrick, actor; James Hamblin, actor; Warren Hammack, actor/director, former artistic/producing director, Horse Cave Theater; Barry Lewis, director, Lake Worth, FL; Adam Luckey, actor, Lexington, KY; Billy Miller, talent agent; Joe Montgomery, actor; Bill Nave, playwright; Kristi Robison, drama teacher, Houston, TX; Ed Smith, theater professor, Georgetown College; Harry Thompson, executive vice president, director, producer, Maverick Productions; Barb Washburn, theater development officer; Matt Wallace, actor; Angie Wilson, drama specialist.

POPULAR PROGRAMS

THEATER AND PERFORMANCE STUDIES
Department chair: George McGee
Number of full-time faculty: 3
Number of part-time faculty: 1
Focus/emphasis: Students pursuing a major or minor engage in a two-step process of investigating both the act of aesthetic performance and the fact of performance in American and global culture. Because theater and drama synthesize all the arts and humanities, majors and minors will study the art of stage and screen acting, scenic design and stagecraft, directing for the screen and stage, the history of dramatic representation from Greece to the silver screen, as well as other courses in the department.

GEORGIA STATE UNIVERSITY
PO Box 4009, Atlanta, GA 30302-4009
Phone: 404-651-2365 E-mail: admissions@gsu.edu
Website: www.gsu.edu/index.htm

Campus Life
Environment: Metropolis. Calendar: Semester.

Students and Faculty
(All Undergraduate Programs)
Enrollment: 18,480. Student Body: 61% female, 39% male, 4% out-of-state, 3% international (167 countries represented). African American 31%, Asian 10%, Caucasian 37%, Hispanic 3%. Student/faculty ratio: 20:1. 1,054 full-time faculty, 85% hold PhDs.

Admissions
(All Undergraduate Programs)
Freshman Admissions Requirements: Test(s) required: SAT or ACT; ACT with Writing component. Average high school GPA: 3.3. SAT Math (25/75 percentile): 500/590. SAT Verbal (25/75 percentile): 490/590. Projected SAT Writing (25/75 percentile): 550/640. *Academic units required:* 4 English, 4 math, 3 science (2 science labs), 2 foreign language, 2 social studies, 1 history. Regular application deadline: 3/1. Regular notification: Rolling.

Costs and Financial Aid
(All Undergraduate Programs)
Annual in-state tuition $3,638. Out-of-state tuition $14,552. Room & board $6,980. Required fees $413. Average book expense $1,000.

Financial Aid Statistics: % freshmen/undergrads who receive need-based scholarship or grant aid: 34/44. % freshmen/undergrads who receive need-based self-help aid: 33/36. Priority financial aid filing deadline: 4/1. Financial aid filing deadline: 11/1. Financial aid notification on or about: 3/30.

TV/Film/Digital Media Studies Programs
Number of undergraduates
  in these programs: 450
Number of 2005 graduates from these
  programs: 74

Degrees conferred to these majors: BA.
Number of full-time faculty in these programs: 12
Number of part-time faculty in these programs: 1
Equipment and facilities: Cineon film scanner/recorder/digital effects system, central equipment room, two digital edit suites, two multi-seat computer labs for digital effect/editing/postproduction, film cameras, lighting, grip equipment, HD production, postproduction equipment, 38-seat audience response theater.
Career development services: Alumni networking opportunities, career counseling, career/interest testing, career library, employer recruitment on campus, individual job placement, internship listings, job bank, job fairs, job listings.

In Their Own Words

Our digital arts and entertainment lab is well positioned to contribute to Georgia's growth by creating jobs, and supplying business research data with mobile interactive devices. We offer university/industry collaboration and training on emerging digital effects technology. Partner with public and private corporations. Create high-end creative products and a skilled workforce and attract new business. Produce new media content through DAEL's "Producer in Residence" program. Incubate media arts related companies through Georgia Entertainment Business Development. Brought a new division of Kodak to Georgia. Supported Georgia House Bill 539 for aggressive tax incentives for producers. Hosted Future Entertainment Forum. Create media projects, Internet gaming, and museum exhibits through partnerships with GPB, Klaus Entertainment, and Pulseworks. Ongoing creation of historic documentation and preservation of Georgia with Balzar Documentary, Bremen Jewish Heritage Museum, and Carter Center. Students create over forty locally and nationally recognized media projects a year. Providing sponsored master classes with industry veterans and professional organizations (SMPTE, NAB, AICP, NATAS). Supported media projects on nationally broadcast programs on CNN, 60 Minutes, and Frontline. Culminated in establishing a Venture Fellow position relocating Robert Townsend. Incubating six media companies in DAEL's GEBD. FrameFlow LLC awarded a contract for digital effects for Sony Pictures Entertainment film, Adam Sandler's Click.

POPULAR PROGRAMS

BACHELOR OF ART IN FILM AND VIDEO
Department chair: Carol K. Winkler
Number of full-time faculty: 12
Number of part-time faculty: 1
Focus/emphasis: To provide the student with the knowledge and skills necessary to understand and apply this complex discipline in both an intellectual and artisitic way. This is reflected in the program structure, which includes critical studies (history, theory, industry, and criticism), production (film, video, digital), and writing. Students will cover all of these areas but may specialize in one or two in their work. Internships are available in the Atlanta metro area and beyond.

GOUCHER COLLEGE
1021 Dulaney Valley Road, Baltimore, MD 21204-2794
Phone: 410-337-6100 **E-mail:** admissions@goucher.edu
Website: www.goucher.edu

Campus Life
Environment: City. **Calendar:** Semester.

Students and Faculty
(All Undergraduate Programs)
Enrollment: 1,325. **Student Body:** 66% female, 34% male, 69% out-of-state. African American 4%, Asian 3%, Caucasian 67%, Hispanic 3%. Student/faculty ratio: 9:1. 113 full-time faculty, 90% hold PhDs. 100% faculty teach undergrads.

Admissions
(All Undergraduate Programs)
Freshman Admissions Requirements: Test(s) required: SAT or ACT; ACT with Writing component. Average high school GPA: 3.14. 26% in top tenth, 63% in top quarter. SAT Math (25/75 percentile): 540/640. SAT Verbal (25/75 percentile): 560/670. Projected SAT Writing (25/75 percentile): 620/700. *Academic units required:* 4 English, 3 math, 2 science, 2 foreign language, 3 social studies, 2 academic electives. Regular application deadline: 2/1. Regular notification: 4/1.

Costs and Financial Aid
(All Undergraduate Programs)
Annual tuition $28,900. Room & board $10,025. Required fees $425. Average book expense $825.
Financial Aid Statistics: % freshmen/undergrads who receive any aid: 57/60. % freshmen/undergrads who receive need-based scholarship or grant aid: 54/56. % freshmen/undergrads who receive need-based self-help aid: 51/53. Priority financial aid filing deadline: 2/15. Financial aid filing deadline: 2/15. Financial aid notification on or about: 4/1.

TV/Film/Digital Media Studies Programs
Number of undergraduates in these programs: 76
Number of 2005 graduates from these programs: 31
Degrees conferred to these majors: BA.
Number of full-time faculty in these programs: 3
Number of part-time faculty in these programs: 9
Equipment and facilities: Avid Express 2.0 editors (3); final cut 5.0 (5); Panasonic DVC Pro (3); Canon XL1 mini-DV (1); Panasonic portable digital switcher; Grass Valley 100 studio switcher; Compix 3500 CG; Yamaha Studio Production Audio Board; Infinity Audio board for webcasting; Sony 3000 cameras (3); 3-camera studio facility; complete audio facilities for webcasting and campus cable; complete facility for television campus cablecasting; digital arts studio.

% of graduates who pursue further study within 5 years: 33
Career development services: Alumni networking opportunities; career counseling; central resource(s) for employers to browse headshots, writing samples, reels; internship listings; job fairs; job listings.
Famous alumni: Toby Werthheim

In Their Own Words
We have, for a small, private liberal arts college, a comprehensive communication and media studies program that offers a wide variety of both theoretical and skills-oriented classwork. David Zurawik, nationally known syndicated TV critic, teaches half-time in our program. All of our students complete at least one internship (many do two) as required for the major. Our students are sought after and perform splendidly in their internships. Often students are offered jobs directly via their internship experience.

POPULAR PROGRAMS

COMMUNICATION AND MEDIA STUDIES
Department chair: Shirley Peroutka
Number of full-time faculty: 3
Number of part-time faculty: 9

Students Should Also Know
Our program nicely balances critical studies with applied knowledge: the best of both worlds.

GREENVILLE COLLEGE
315 East College Avenue, Greenville, IL 62246-0159
Phone: 618-664-7100 **E-mail:** admissions@greenville.edu
Website: www.greenville.edu

Campus Life
Environment: Village. **Calendar:** 4-1-4.

Students and Faculty
(All Undergraduate Programs)
Enrollment: 1,197. **Student Body:** 54% female, 46% male, 30% out-of-state, 1% international (12 countries represented). African American 8%, Caucasian 83%, Hispanic 2%. Student/faculty ratio: 15:1. 59 full-time faculty, 63% hold PhDs. 100% faculty teach undergrads.

Admissions
(All Undergraduate Programs)
Freshman Admissions Requirements: Test(s) required: SAT and SAT Subject Tests or ACT. Average high school GPA: 3.28. 16% in top tenth, 37% in top quarter. SAT Math (25/75 percentile): 430/555. SAT Verbal (25/75 percentile): 450/590. Projected SAT Writing (25/75 percentile): 520/640. Regular application deadline: 8/1. Regular notification: Rolling.

Costs and Financial Aid
(All Undergraduate Programs)
Annual tuition $17,812. Room & board $6,136. Required fees $120. Average book expense $800. **Financial Aid Statistics:** % freshmen/undergrads who receive any aid: 94/92. % freshmen/undergrads who receive need-based scholarship or grant aid: 84/85. % freshmen/undergrads who receive need-based self-help aid: 77/78. Financial aid notification on or about: 3/15.

TV/Film/Digital Media Studies Programs
Number of undergraduates in these programs: 43
Number of 2005 graduates from these programs: 15
Degrees conferred to these majors: BS.
Number of full-time faculty in these programs: 2
Career development services: Alumni networking opportunities, career counseling, internship listings, job fairs, job listings.

POPULAR PROGRAMS

DIGITAL MEDIA
Department chair: Ivan Filby
Focus/emphasis: The major prepares students to become content creators in a world that is constantly being shaped by technology. This preparation includes the cultivation of analytic and critical thinking skills as well as the ability to work and communicate with others on complex interdisciplinary projects integrating digital music and art, Web-based digital communications, and computer programming skills.

MEDIA PROMOTIONS
Department chair: Veronica Ross
Focus/emphasis: The major prepares students to enter the evolving world of media and music business that is being shaped by technology. This preparation includes the cultivation of analytical and critical thinking skills, as well as the ability to work and communicate with individuals, and within teams, on complex projects.

HAMPSHIRE COLLEGE
Admissions Office, 893 West Street, Amherst, MA 01002
Phone: 413-559-5471 **E-mail:** admissions@hampshire.edu
Website: www.hampshire.edu

Campus Life
Environment: Town. **Calendar:** 4-1-4.

Students and Faculty
(All Undergraduate Programs)
Enrollment: 1,362. **Student Body:** 59% female, 41% male, 82% out-of-state, 3% international (28 countries represented). African American 3%, Asian 4%, Caucasian 75%, Hispanic 4%. Student/faculty ratio: 12:1. 94 full-time faculty, 87% hold PhDs. 100% faculty teach undergrads.

Admissions
(All Undergraduate Programs)
Average high school GPA: 3.42. 28% in top tenth, 63% in top quarter. SAT Math (25/75 percentile): 560/660. SAT Verbal (25/75 percentile): 600/710. Projected SAT Writing (25/75 percentile): 650/730. Early decision application deadline: 11/15. Regular application deadline: 1/15. Regular notification: 4/1.

Costs and Financial Aid
(All Undergraduate Programs)
Annual tuition $31,939. Room & board $8,519. Required fees $580. Average book expense $500. **Financial Aid Statistics:** % freshmen/undergrads who receive any aid: 70/66. % freshmen/undergrads who receive need-based scholarship or grant aid: 52/55. % freshmen/undergrads who receive need-based self-help aid: 51/54. Financial aid filing deadline: 2/1. Financial aid notification on or about: 4/1.

TV/Film/Digital Media Studies Programs
Number of undergraduates in these programs: 70
Number of 2005 graduates from these programs: 41
Degrees conferred to these majors: BA.
Number of full-time faculty in these programs: 9
Number of part-time faculty in these programs: 4
Equipment and facilities: Visual artists at Hampshire explore film, video, and photography in a way that separates Hampshire's program from those at many other undergraduate institutions. In Hampshire's program, students learn primarily through independent experimentation with all forms of media. This individualized process of creation, along with access to excellent technical facilities and resources, ensures that Hampshire students develop their fullest artistic visions and the tools to produce them. Unlike many programs, the emphasis at Hampshire is on project-based learning with an increased focus on content so that students in these programs are given the necessary foundation in technique and production while being encouraged to examine compelling and current ideas that inform artistic expression. In addition to course offerings, the film, video, and photography program offers a series of lectures and internships meant to expose students to a wide variety of visual artists and their work. Through their interactions with successful artists from around the world students are further motivated to pursue careers in the arts and are inspired to pursue their own passions with the confidence that a life in the arts is a valuable and fulfilling one.

Career development services: Alumni networking opportunities; career counseling; central resource(s) for employers to browse headshots, writing samples, reels; internship listings; job fairs; job listings.
Famous alumni: Ken Burns.
Notable alumni: Alex Rivera's (F91) first film (and Division III project), *Papapapa*, was described by the *New York Times* as "a fresh and witty video...a personally ambitious example of how guerilla Filmmaking can thrive." *Papapapa* is an experimental documentary in which Alex used video, animation, and comedy to address the issues that matter most to him: assimilation, immigration, and the Latino community. The film follows the converging journeys of a man and a potato as they travel northward from Latin America and the transformation that they undergo as they assimilate into American culture. *Papapapa* has been screened at such prestigious institutions as The Museum of Modern Art, The Guggenheim Museum, Lincoln Center, on PBS, and other national venues. Alex received the International Documentary Association's 2003 Jacqueline Donnet Emerging Documentary Filmmaker Award.

Students Should Also Know
Hampshire offers many courses in film/photo/video, including computer animation courses. These are not formally divided into distinct programs.

HARVARD COLLEGE

Byerly Hall, Eight Garden Street, Cambridge, MA 02138
Phone: 617-495-1551 **E-mail:** college@fas.harvard.edu
Website: www.fas.harvard.edu

Campus Life
Environment: Metropolis. **Calendar:** Semester.

Students and Faculty
(All Undergraduate Programs)
Enrollment: 6,649. **Student Body:** 47% female, 53% male, 84% out-of-state, 7% international. African American 8%, Asian 18%, Caucasian 42%, Hispanic 8%. Student/faculty ratio: 8:1. 775 full-time faculty, 100% hold PhDs. 100% faculty teach undergrads.

Admissions
(All Undergraduate Programs)
Freshman Admissions Requirements: Test(s) required: SAT or ACT. 90% in top tenth, 98% in top quarter. SAT Math (25/75 percentile): 700/790. SAT Verbal (25/75 percentile): 700/800. Projected SAT Writing (25/75 percentile): 720/780. Regular application deadline: 1/1. Regular notification: 4/1.

Costs and Financial Aid
(All Undergraduate Programs)
Annual tuition $26,066. Room & board $8,868. Required fees $2,994. Average book expense $2,522. **Financial Aid Statistics:** % freshmen/undergrads who receive need-based scholarship or grant aid: 47/48. % freshmen/undergrads who receive need-based self-help aid: 34/41. Priority financial aid filing deadline: 2/1. Financial aid notification on or about: 4/1.

In Their Own Words
The Carpenter Center Lectures have included lectures by artists such as Sally Potter, Yvonne Rainer, and Willem de Rooij. Cinematic, *the student-run magazine, offers in-depth, scholarly film reviews, as well as analyses of trends and innovations shaping the industry. It is written by both students and faculty members and is published annually. The Film Study Center sustains endeavors, from the ethnographic to the experimental, that explore and expand the expressive potential of audiovisual media, especially through nonaction. To this end, it provides annual fellowships to students, faculty, and a small number of outstanding visiting imagemakers. The Harvard Film Archive (HFA) maintains a collection of 9,000 films and thousands of documents to support VES and film studies at Harvard. Finally, the HFA has an active conservation center in Watertown, MA. The purpose of the HFA is to further artistic and academic appreciation of cinema and moving image media by creating a setting where audiences have the opportunity to interact with filmmakers and artists. In 2004–2005, the HFA brought dozens of renowned filmmakers to campus for premieres and retrospectives, from Tsai Ming-liang and Hara Kazuo to Sally Potter and Dominique Cabrera to Todd Solondz and Melvin Van Peebles. A major series of Korean films brought Im Kwon-taek, Kim Dong-won, Kim Hong-jun, and E J-yong. Harvard teachers Ross McElwee, Julie Mallozzi, and Gina Kim screened work. The HFA also hosted archivists Andrew Lampert (anthology), Rick Prelinger, and Mark Toscano (academy).*

POPULAR PROGRAMS

VISUAL AND ENVIRONMENTAL STUDIES (VES)
Number of full-time faculty: 33
Focus/emphasis: Students who desire strong and rigorous training in film and visual studies may wish to concentrate in film studies within VES. Ordinarily, applicants have taken a half course in the department (preferably in film studies) and have a GPA of B or better. VES requires 14 half-courses. Film studies blends theoretical, analytic, and historical coverage in a way that is both focused and flexible. The interdisciplinary requirement means that students with particular interests in, for example, film and science, Japanese cinema, or contemporary digital culture, are more readily able to take essential background courses into a plan of study. Introductory courses

include three half-courses including Art of Film, Histories of Cinema I: Moving Pictures from the 1890s to the 1930s, and Histories of Cinema II: Sound, Space, and Image to 1960. Advanced courses include six (or seven) half-courses directly related to film and visual studies. Offerings under this heading will include both film studies classes offered in VES by regular and visiting faculty as well as pertinent film studies classes offered in departments outside of VES. At least two of these half-courses must be advanced film studies seminars. Interdisciplinary courses include two (or three) half-courses in other departments that provide pertinent interdisciplinary perspectives to film studies but are not courses whose main emphasis is film related. These choices are subject to the approval of the director of undergraduate studies on application to the department. Students who choose not to write a thesis will instead take two additional advanced film studies courses (these choices are subject to the approval of the director of undergraduate studies).

HOFSTRA UNIVERSITY

Admissions Center, Bernon Hall, Hempstead, NY 11549
Phone: 516-463-6700 **E-mail:** admitme@hofstra.edu
Website: www.hofstra.edu

Campus Life
Environment: City. **Calendar:** 4-1-4.

Students and Faculty
(All Undergraduate Programs)
Enrollment: 8,701. **Student Body:** 53% female, 47% male, 30% out-of-state, 2% international (65 countries represented). African American 9%, Asian 5%, Caucasian 61%, Hispanic 8%. Student/faculty ratio: 14:1. 527 full-time faculty, 91% hold PhDs. 85% faculty teach undergrads.

Admissions
(All Undergraduate Programs)
Freshman Admissions Requirements: Test(s) required: ACT with Writing component. Average high school GPA: 3.23. 24% in top tenth, 47% in top quarter. SAT Math (25/75 percentile): 540/620. SAT Verbal (25/75 percentile): 520/620. Projected SAT Writing (25/75 percentile): 580/660. *Academic units required:* 4 English, 3 math, 3 science (1 science lab), 2 foreign language, 3 social studies. Regular notification: Rolling.

Costs and Financial Aid
(All Undergraduate Programs)
Annual tuition $20,500. Room & board $9,500. Required fees $1,030. Average book expense $1,000. **Financial Aid Statistics:** % freshmen/undergrads who receive any aid: 89/81. % freshmen/undergrads who receive need-based scholarship or grant aid: 55/53. % freshmen/undergrads who receive need-based self-help aid: 48/51. Priority financial aid filing deadline: 2/15. Financial aid notification on or about: 3/15.

TV/Film/Digital Media Studies Programs
Number of undergraduates in these programs: 1,080
Number of 2005 graduates from these programs: 294
Degrees conferred to these majors: BA, BS.
Also available at Hofstra University: MA.
Number of full-time faculty in these programs: 26
Number of part-time faculty in these programs: 23
Equipment and facilities: 16 mm Bolex cameras; Arri SR Sync Sound cameras; Avid editing facilities; two fully-equipped TV studios; Pro Tools sound-editing stations; audio studios; fully digital campus radio station; journalism computer lab; news room.
Other awards of note: Dr. Sybil DelGaudio, 1 Emmy Award; Dr. Dennis Mazzocco, 16 Emmy Awards; Dr. Lisa Merrill, National Endowment of the Humanities Senior Scholar Award; Dr. Lisa Merrill, National Communication Association, Lilla Heston Prize.

% of graduates who pursue further study within 5 years: 19

% of graduates currently employed in related field: 90

Career development services: Alumni networking opportunities, career counseling, career library, career week, internship listings, job fairs, job listings, mock interviews, senior boot camp.

Famous alumni: Christopher Albrecht (1974, BA, drama), chairman and CEO, HBO; Francis Ford Coppola (1960, BA, drama), producer, writer, owner of American Zoetrope; Madeline Kahn (deceased, 1964, BA, speech arts), actor; Lainie Kazan (1960, BA, theater arts), actor, president of Bena Productions, Inc.; Philip Rosenthal (1981, BFA, theater arts), creator and executive producer of *Everybody Loves Raymond*; Susan Sullivan (1964, BA, drama), actor.

Notable alumni: Heather Cohen (1998, BA, audio/radio), associate program director of WOR 710AM New York; Melissa Cohen (aka Missy Cohen, 1990, BA, communication arts), film editor for sound and music, credits include *Silence of the Lambs*, *The Producers*, *Cinderella Man*, *Chicago*; John Discepolo, (1994, BA, communication arts), sports anchor, WNYW FOX 5; Scott Ross (1974, BA, communication arts), president, founder, & CEO of Digital Domain; Jeffrey Schaetzel (1983, BA, communication arts), executive producer for *ESPN's Sports Center*.

In Their Own Words

Proximity to New York City affords enormous opportunity for internships. Student work has been shown at domestic and international festivals. Faculty have won numerous awards, including Emmys, National Endowment for Humanities fellowships, and festival honors.

POPULAR PROGRAMS

FILM STUDIES AND PRODUCTION

Department chair: Nancy Kaplan
Number of full-time faculty: 7
Number of part-time faculty: 4
Focus/emphasis: The program educates students in both the theory and practice of film, the techniques of developing ideas, writing scripts, and all other aspects of filmmaking that will help them achieve their creative potential.

PUBLIC RELATIONS

Department chair: Barbara Kelly
Number of full-time faculty: 3
Number of part-time faculty: 1
Focus/emphasis: The program is designed to equip students with the knowledge, attitudes, and skills expected of professionals in the field of public relations. The degree curriculum is founded in the liberal arts and incorporates a broad-working knowledge of issues that include economics, political science, and business with an emphasis on understanding the ways in which to create effective public relations messages.

BROADCAST JOURNALISM

Department chair: Barbara Kelly
Number of full-time faculty: 2
Number of part-time faculty: 1
Focus/emphasis: The program teaches critical thinking, research, and effective oral and written expression, emphasizing the ethics, laws, and history of the profession. The program prepares students for careers as reporters and on-camera presenters of news as well as writers, producers, and directors of news for the broadcast media.

PRINT JOURNALISM

Department chair: Barbara Kelly
Number of full-time faculty: 4
Number of part-time faculty: 9
Focus/emphasis: The program teaches critical thinking, research, and effective oral and written expression, emphasizing the ethics, laws, and history of journalism. The program seeks to educate individuals for careers as responsible media professionals in newspapers, magazines, and emerging forms of media.

VIDEO/TELEVISION

Department chair: Nancy Kaplan
Number of full-time faculty: 6
Number of part-time faculty: 4

Focus/emphasis: In the program, students are trained using the latest technology in all areas of studio, field, and postproduction. This practical training is enhanced by a strong liberal arts curriculum. In addition, the studio and editing facilities are among the best in the Northeast. When not occupied by classes, the facilities are often used for professional projects, as well as for broadcast and nonbroadcast productions.

VIDEO/TELEVISION/FILM

Department chair: Nancy Kaplan

Focus/emphasis: The program adds a strong complement to film course work. This degree prepares students for a multitude of television, video, and film career paths with an emphasis on directing, editing, production management, and technically-oriented creative positions.

AUDIO/RADIO

Department chair: Nancy Kaplan

Focus/emphasis: The program prepares students for careers in radio broadcasting, writing, producing, and programming. In addition, the program is affiliated with WRHU-FM/88.7, Hofstra's FCC-licensed radio station.

SPEECH COMMUNICATION, RHETORIC, AND PERFORMANCE STUDY

Department chair: Nancy Kaplan

Number of full-time faculty: 9

Number of part-time faculty: 16

Focus/emphasis: The program is an examination of communication theory as an interpersonal or group experience, in the context of performance or intercultural communication. Study in the field of speech communication facilitates critical thinking, decision making, and the effective presentation of ideas.

MASS MEDIA STUDIES

Department chair: Barbara Kelly

Number of full-time faculty: 2

Number of part-time faculty: 3

Focus/emphasis: The program provides students with historical, analytical, and critical skills necessary to pursue a media-related career or to conduct scholarly research in the field. This major provides excellent preparation for law school and other types of graduate education.

VIDEO/TELEVISION/BUSINESS

Department chair: Ruth Prigoxy

Focus/emphasis: The program adds 21 credits of business courses from Hofstra's Zarb School of Business. This degree prepares students for a multitude of television and video career paths with an emphasis on production management and organizational leadership.

HOLLINS UNIVERSITY

PO Box 9707, Roanoke, VA 24020-1707
Phone: 540-362-6401 **E-mail:** huadm@hollins.edu
Website: www.hollins.edu

Campus Life

Environment: City. **Calendar:** 4-1-4.

Students and Faculty
(All Undergraduate Programs)

Enrollment: 818. **Student Body:** 48% out-of-state, 2% international (11 countries represented). African American 8%, Asian 1%, Caucasian 86%, Hispanic 2%. Student/faculty ratio: 10:1. 68 full-time faculty, 99% hold PhDs. 100% faculty teach undergrads.

Admissions
(All Undergraduate Programs)

Freshman Admissions Requirements: Test(s) required: SAT or ACT. Average high school GPA: 3.5. 19% in top tenth, 55% in top quarter. SAT Math (25/75 percentile): 490/590. SAT Verbal (25/75 percentile): 530/640. Projected SAT Writing (25/75 percentile): 590/680. *Academic units required:* 4 English, 3 math, 3 science, 3 foreign language, 3 social studies. Early decision application deadline: 11/15. Regular notification: Rolling.

Costs and Financial Aid
(All Undergraduate Programs)
Annual tuition $23,800. Room & board $8,160. Required fees $475. Average book expense $800. **Financial Aid Statistics:** % freshmen/undergrads who receive any aid: 97/93. % freshmen/undergrads who receive need-based scholarship or grant aid: 71/61. % freshmen/undergrads who receive need-based self-help aid: 55/56. Priority financial aid filing deadline: 2/15. Financial aid notification on or about: 3/15.

TV/Film/Digital Media Studies Programs
**Number of undergraduates
in these programs:** 11
**Number of 2005 graduates from these
programs:** 12
Degrees conferred to these majors: BA.
Also available at Hollins University: MFA, MA
(Screenwriting and Film Studies).
**Number of full-time faculty in these
programs:** 1
**Number of part-time faculty in these
programs:** 5
Career development services: Career counseling.

POPULAR PROGRAMS

FILM, SCREENWRITING, AND PHOTOGRAPHY
Department chair: Klaus Phillips
Number of full-time faculty: 1
Number of part-time faculty: 5
Focus/emphasis: The major balances instruction in applied photography, filmmaking, and video-making with courses in the history, aesthetics, and cultural significance of these art forms. Hollins is the only university in the region to offer a 16 mm film production program.

HOPE COLLEGE
69 East Tenth, PO Box 9000, Holland, MI 49422-9000
Phone: 616-395-7850 **E-mail:** admissions@hope.edu
Website: www.hope.edu

Campus Life
Environment: Town. **Calendar:** Semester.

Students and Faculty
(All Undergraduate Programs)
Enrollment: 3,070. **Student Body:** 61% female, 39% male, 26% out-of-state, 1% international (32 countries represented). African American 2%, Asian 2%, Caucasian 92%, Hispanic 2%. Student/faculty ratio: 13:1. 215 full-time faculty, 78% hold PhDs. 100% faculty teach undergrads.

Admissions
(All Undergraduate Programs)
Freshman Admissions Requirements: Test(s) required: SAT or ACT. Average high school GPA: 3.74. 34% in top tenth, 61% in top quarter. SAT Math (25/75 percentile): 560/680. SAT Verbal (25/75 percentile): 550/680. Projected SAT Writing (25/75 percentile): 610/710. *Academic units required:* 4 English, 2 math, 1 science (1 science lab), 2 foreign language, 2 social studies, 5 academic electives. Regular notification: Rolling.

Costs and Financial Aid
(All Undergraduate Programs)
Annual tuition $21,420. Room & board $6,668. Required fees $120. Average book expense $640. **Financial Aid Statistics:** % freshmen/undergrads who receive any aid: 84/87. % freshmen/undergrads who receive need-based scholarship or grant aid: 47/50. % freshmen/undergrads who receive need-based self-help aid: 43/46. Priority financial aid filing deadline: 3/1. Financial aid notification on or about: 3/20.

TV/Film/Digital Media Studies Programs
Degrees conferred to these majors: BA.
**Number of full-time faculty in these
programs:** 6

Number of part-time faculty in these programs: 5

Equipment and facilities: Hope College has just opened the Martha Milller Center for Global Communications. The state-of-the-art facility is equipped with the latest production and postproduction hardware and software. At the students' disposal are multiple Panasonic mini-DV and Panasonic HD cameras, Sony DVCAM cameras, and Ikegami studio cameras. There are currently 15 edit bays equipped with the latest Apple G5 computers loaded with Final Cut Pro, Pro Tools, and Adobe AfterEffects. The 38' x 43' foot television studio is equipped with three new Ikegami cameras with TelePrompTers, Mackie 24-channel audio board, and Echolab Nova digital switcher with DVE.

Career development services: Alumni networking opportunities, career counseling, internship listings, job fairs, job listings.

In Their Own Words

At Hope College, communication students are immediately immersed in the production environment. Unlike some programs that only allow upperclassmen to use equipment, Hope's communication program gives freshmen through seniors the opportunity to gain valuable hands-on experience with the latest technology. Hope also provides students the option of various internships, including local news stations, advertising agencies, and semester internship programs in Chicago, Philadelphia, and New York. Interns have been placed with NBC Today Show, New York; ABC, Chicago; Banyon Productions in Philadelphia; NFL Films.

HOWARD UNIVERSITY

2400 Sixth Street, NW, Washington, DC 20059
Phone: 202-806-2700 **E-mail:** admission@howard.edu
Website: www.howard.edu

Campus Life
Environment: Metropolis. **Calendar:** Semester.

Students and Faculty
(All Undergraduate Programs)
Enrollment: 7,164. **Student Body:** 67% female, 33% male, 77% out-of-state, 8% international (107 countries represented). African American 85%. Student/faculty ratio: 8:1. 1,069 full-time faculty, 86% hold PhDs. 64% faculty teach undergrads.

Admissions
(All Undergraduate Programs)
Freshman Admissions Requirements: Test(s) required: SAT or ACT. Average high school GPA: 3.2. 21% in top tenth, 54% in top quarter. SAT Math (25/75 percentile): 450/690. SAT Verbal (25/75 percentile): 460/680. Projected SAT Writing (25/75 percentile): 390/780. *Academic units required:* 4 English, 2 math, 2 science, 2 foreign language, 2 social studies, 2 history. Regular application deadline: 2/15. Regular notification: Rolling.

Costs and Financial Aid
(All Undergraduate Programs)
Annual tuition $11,490. Room & board $6,186. Required fees $805. Average book expense $1,020. **Financial Aid Statistics:** % freshmen/undergrads who receive any aid: 67/63. % freshmen/undergrads who receive need-based scholarship or grant aid: 34/34. % freshmen/undergrads who receive need-based self-help aid: 33/26. Priority financial aid filing deadline: 2/15. Financial aid filing deadline: 8/15. Financial aid notification on or about: 4/1.

TV/Film/Digital Media Studies Programs
Degrees conferred to these majors: BA.
Also available at Howard University: MFA, MA.
Number of full-time faculty in these programs: 57
Equipment and facilities: Television production students work with state-of-the-art digital video,

audio, and editing technology to create dramatic and documentary features of the highest quality. The Department of Radio, Television, and Film maintains a television studio, digital editing suites, audio production studios, an Internet streaming media studio, and a scriptwriting lab.

In Their Own Words

Audio production students serve as interns for some of the nation's top media companies, including Washington, DC-based radio stations: WKYS-FM, WPFW-FM, or Howard University's professional station, WHUR-FM; national and international networks/services: National Public Radio; Voice of America, or XM Satellite Radio-record studios/record companies: Atlantic Records or Horizon Studios. Film production students serve as interns for a wide range of media organizations based in the nation's capital. Such companies include the National Geographic Society, American Film Institute, Discovery Channel, Howard University's PBS television station (WHUT-TV, Channel 32), and all of the major broadcasting and cable corporations.

POPULAR PROGRAMS

AUDIO PRODUCTION

Department chair: Sonja Williams

Focus/emphasis: Students in this sequence are exposed to a wide range of "sound" career options and production techniques including radio production and promotion, sound for television and film, and multitrack recording/mixing. Audio production classes include radio production, advanced radio production, broadcast performance (announcing), audio for visual media, WHBC/WHUR lab, and radio practicum (internship). In addition, students have access to the latest digital equipment and new audio technologies. Students work as managers and staff members of the Department of Radio, Television, and Film's student operated station, WHBC-AM. Students also operate the department's Internet-only, all-talk radio station, www.glasshouseradio.com.

FILM PRODUCTION

Department chair: Sonja Williams

Focus/emphasis: The film production sequence introduces the student to the rudimentary aspects of organizing and structuring audio and visual material in cinematic formats. Sequence course offerings include scriptwriting, basic television and film production, cinematography, film directing, Third World cinema, documentary film criticism, and African Americans in film. The film production curriculum enables student to demystify the filmmaking process and encourage the social use of the medium; to write, direct, edit, and exhibit short films on celluloid; and to develop critical thinking to analyze the powerful aesthetic, psychological, and socio-political influences of the film medium. Each semester, some of the best creative works by student filmmakers are critiqued by fellow students and RTVF faculty during the department's end-of-the-semester screening. Also, nonstudents can experience the cinematic magic of film production majors through screenings at the American Film Institute's (AFI) Silver Theater in the Washington, DC area and throughout the United States and the Caribbean via RTVF's "Black Visions/Silver Screen" tours. In addition, the department sponsors its annual Paul Robeson Awards during the spring semester of each year. This awards competition and ceremony recognizes the best RTVF undergraduate and graduate student audio, video, and film productions. The awards were named in honor of the creative and socially-conscious legacy of celebrated African American actor, singer, and activist Paul Robeson. Film production majors hail from around the globe.

TELECOMMUNICATIONS MANAGEMENT

Department chair: Sonja Williams

Focus/emphasis: The sequence trains students to serve as innovative leaders in mass communications research and management and communications policy development or financial analysis. Also, telecommunications management majors study the impact of communications technology and advancement on cultures around the globe.

TELEVISION PRODUCTION

Department chair: Sonja Williams

Focus/emphasis: Our esteemed faculty provides a nurturing learning environment with opportunities for students to create their own productions. Also, students work on professional productions by faculty, outside producers, and producers at WHUT-TV. Through our Time Warner lecture series and Paul Robeson Awards program, our students attend workshops with highly accomplished industry professionals who also offer unique internship opportunities and professional critiques of student works. Courses are available in television production, directing, writing, and sound. Additionally, RTVF classes explore the historical, social, and cultural contributions of African American and other peoples of color from around the world to the powerful medium known as television.

INDIANA UNIVERSITY AT BLOOMINGTON

300 North Jordan Avenue, Bloomington, IN 47405-1106
Phone: 812-855-0661 **E-mail:** iuadmit@indiana.edu
Website: www.indiana.edu

Campus Life

Environment: Town. **Calendar:** Semester.

Students and Faculty
(All Undergraduate Programs)

Enrollment: 29,120. **Student Body:** 52% female, 48% male, 30% out-of-state, 4% international (150 countries represented). African American 5%, Asian 3%, Caucasian 85%, Hispanic 2%. Student/faculty ratio 18:1. 1,589 full-time faculty, 79% hold PhDs. 50% faculty teach undergrads.

Admissions
(All Undergraduate Programs)

Freshman Admissions Requirements: Test(s) required: SAT or ACT; ACT with Writing component. Average high school GPA: 3.4. 25% in top tenth, 57% in top quarter. SAT Math (25/75 percentile): 500/620.

SAT Verbal (25/75 percentile): 490/610. Projected SAT Writing (25/75 percentile): 550/660. *Academic units required:* 4 English, 3 math, 1 science (1 science lab), 2 social studies, 4 academic electives.

Costs and Financial Aid
(All Undergraduate Programs)

Annual in-state tuition $6,291. Out-of-state tuition $18,687. Room & board $6,240. Required fees $821. Average book expense $740.

Financial Aid Statistics: % freshmen/undergrads who receive any aid: 65/62. % freshmen/undergrads who receive need-based scholarship or grant aid: 19/20. % freshmen/undergrads who receive need-based self-help aid: 32/32. Priority financial aid filing deadline: 3/1. Financial aid filing deadline: 3/1. Financial aid notification on or about: 4/1.

TV/Film/Digital Media Studies Programs

Degrees conferred to these majors: BA, BFA.
Also available at Indiana University at Bloomington: MFA.
Career development services: Career counseling services; job placement assistance; a comprehensive Career Resource Library; 2-credit, 8-week courses on career exploration and job search strategies for liberal arts majors; and a variety of themed career fairs.

In Their Own Words

Honors in CMCL: Outstanding students in the Department can opt to undertake research or creative projects in order to earn distinction in the field. Students work closely with departmental faculty in directed readings or research and participate in courses reserved for honors students. Please see the Director of Undergraduate Studies for more information. Lambda Pi Eta: Lambda Pi Eta is the National Communication Honor Society, affiliated with the National Communication Association. Participating in LPE provides students in the department with the opportunity to become more actively involved with faculty, alumni, and with other students. Double Major: The flexible degree requirements of the Department allow CMCL majors to double major in a wide variety of disciplines.

Contact one of our Undergraduate Advisors for more information on expanding your studies with or beyond communication and culture. *Overseas Study:* Indiana University offers more than 60 study abroad programs, many of which have no foreign language requirement. Study abroad is an excellent way to round out your undergraduate curriculum in CMCL. *Internships:* The range of options available to CMCL majors wishing to gain professional experience while studying at IU is unusually rich. Students have held internships in a diverse group of organizations and corporations, including motion picture production companies, investment banking firms, marketing ventures, film festivals, museums, and television and radio stations–to name just a few! With contacts in the Bloomington area, across Indiana, and throughout the country, our majors can choose from innumerable internship opportunities.

POPULAR PROGRAMS

FILM STUDIES

Department chair: Gregory Waller

Focus/emphasis: Indiana University has a long and distinguished history in film studies, pioneering the development of film courses for the humanities in the 1960s and creating one of the first film studies programs. Today, the program is fully integrated into the Department of Communication and Culture. Providing a solid foundation in the history, theory, and criticism of film, television, and new media, the film and media curriculum examines the aesthetics of media forms and their authors; the industrial practices, narrative strategies, genres, and historical contexts that organize cultural production and reception within and across media; and the links among media, identity, ideology, and power that influence public cultures around the globe. Additionally, advanced students have the opportunity to gain invaluable production experience in both film and video.

IONA COLLEGE

715 North Avenue, New Rochelle, NY 10801
Phone: 914-633-2502 **E-mail:** icad@iona.edu
Website: www.iona.edu

Campus Life

Environment: Metropolis. **Calendar:** Semester.

Students and Faculty
(All Undergraduate Programs)

Enrollment: 3,327. **Student Body:** 54% female, 46% male, 19% out-of-state, 2% international (42 countries represented). African American 7%, Asian 2%, Caucasian 68%, Hispanic 11%. Student/faculty ratio: 15:1. 176 full-time faculty, 91% hold PhDs. 100% faculty teach undergrads.

Admissions
(All Undergraduate Programs)

Freshman Admissions Requirements: Test(s) required: SAT or ACT. Average high school GPA: 3.4. 29% in top tenth, 51% in top quarter. SAT Math (25/75 percentile): 520/610. SAT Verbal (25/75 percentile): 510/610. Projected SAT Writing (25/75 percentile): 570/660. *Academic units required:* 4 English, 3 math, 2 science (2 science labs), 2 foreign language, 1 social studies, 1 history, 1 academic elective. Regular application deadline: 2/15. Regular notification: 3/20.

Costs and Financial Aid
(All Undergraduate Programs)

Annual tuition $20,110. Room & board $9,898. Required fees $870. Average book expense $700. **Financial Aid Statistics:** % freshmen/undergrads who receive any aid: 97/87. % freshmen/undergrads who receive need-based scholarship or grant aid: 26/27. % freshmen/undergrads who receive need-based self-help aid: 61/57. Priority financial aid filing deadline: 2/15. Financial aid filing deadline: 2/15.

TV/Film/Digital Media Studies Programs

Number of undergraduates in these programs: 35
Number of 2005 graduates from these programs: 30
Degrees conferred to these majors: BA.

Number of full-time faculty in these
programs: 9

Number of part-time faculty in these
programs: 12

Equipment and facilities: Iona College provides
students in the video production field with mini-DV
camcorders to shoot their ENG projects. The mini-
DV format allows for a clear digital picture for the
students. We provide the students with a Canon
XL1 3CCD camcorder and a Pansonic AGDVC 30
3CCD camcorder. These cameras provide the student with a sharp digital image for their projects. In
addition, we also provide five Sony 1CCD camcorders and one Canon 1CCD camcorder. The students can then edit their work in the postproduction room. We have five MAC computers that the
students can use as editing bays. Three of these are
iMacs, and two are MAC Power PCs. The computers use Final Cut Pro 4 to edit their work and
export back to mini-DV, VHS, or DVD for the students to display their work.

Other awards of note: The National Academy of
Television Arts & Sciences, New York Chapter
Scholarship.

Career development services: Alumni networking
opportunities; career counseling; central resource(s)
for employers to browse headshots, writing samples,
reels; departmental job-related activities such as
portfolio supervision, job listings, and placement;
internship listings; job fairs.

Notable alumni: Producers for *ABC Sports*, *WB11
Morning News*, FOX News, Emmy Award-winning
screenwriter.

In Their Own Words

*Students are placed for internships in major
media outlets in New York City including MTV,
Live with Regis and Kelly, and ESPN. Major television executives conducted a workshop and
panel discussion. Speakers have included the
vice president for CBS News and the senior vice
president for CBS network.*

POPULAR PROGRAMS

TV AND VIDEO

Department chair: Orly Shachar
Number of full-time faculty: 9
Number of part-time faculty: 12
Focus/emphasis: The program features hands-on
studio, remote video production courses, and a
Web enhancement multimedia component.

IOWA STATE UNIVERSITY

100 Alumni Hall, Ames, IA 50011-2011
Phone: 515-294-5836 **E-mail:** admissions@iastate.edu
Website: www.iastate.edu

Campus Life

Environment: Town. **Calendar:** Semester.

Students and Faculty
(All Undergraduate Programs)

Enrollment: 20,364. **Student Body:** 43% female,
57% male, 20% out-of-state, 3% international (111
countries represented). African American 3%, Asian
3%, Caucasian 84%, Hispanic 2%. Student/faculty
ratio: 15:1. 1,419 full-time faculty, 91% hold PhDs.
70% faculty teach undergrads.

Admissions
(All Undergraduate Programs)

Freshman Admissions Requirements: Test(s)
required: SAT or ACT. Average high school GPA:
3.49. 24% in top tenth, 52% in top quarter. SAT Math
(25/75 percentile): 550/690. SAT Verbal (25/75 percentile): 530/660. Projected SAT Writing (25/75 percentile): 590/690. *Academic units required:* 4 English,
3 math, 3 science (2 science labs), 2 foreign language,
2 social studies. Regular application deadline: 8/1.
Regular notification: Rolling.

Costs and Financial Aid
(All Undergraduate Programs)

Annual in-state tuition $5,086. Out-of-state tuition
$15,580. Room & board $6,445. Required fees $774.
Average book expense $892.

Financial Aid Statistics: % freshmen/undergrads who receive any aid: 86/78. % freshmen/undergrads who receive need-based scholarship or grant aid: 56/56. % freshmen/undergrads who receive need-based self-help aid: 44/48. Priority financial aid filing deadline: 3/1. Financial aid notification on or about: 4/1.

TV/Film/Digital Media Studies Programs

Number of undergraduates in these programs: 110
Degrees conferred to these majors: BS.
Also available at Iowa State University: MS.
Number of full-time faculty in these programs: 5
Number of part-time faculty in these programs: 1
Equipment and facilities: We have two major studios, an audio lab, a multimedia lab, and a professional set donated by our NBC Des Moines affiliate.

% of graduates currently employed in related field: 85
Career development services: Alumni networking opportunities, career counseling, internship listings, job fairs.
Famous alumni: Jerry Bowen, CBS; Sean McLaughlin, MSNBC, *NBC Weekend Today Show*; Kevin and Mollie Cooney, KCCI; Terry Anderson, AP; Jack Shelley, WHO.

In Their Own Words
Our pride and joy is Jack Shelley, an icon in broadcast journalism, who covered WWII and is still active in our program. We have an apprenticeship program with network affiliates, an outsourcing program with Meredith Corporation, and an endowed fund of some $1 million that allows us to have state-of-the-art equipment.

POPULAR PROGRAMS

REPORTING, PRODUCTION, FILM, ONLINE, WEB DESIGN

Students Should Also Know
We teach broadcasters and online journalists the basics. We're known for "hardhat journalism." We provide you with state-of-the-art equipment, but focus more on reporting and production than on presentation. That assures success. We're accredited; all skills classes include no more than 18 students.

ITHACA COLLEGE
100 Job Hall, Ithaca, NY 14850-7020
Phone: 607-274-3124 **E-mail:** admission@ithaca.edu
Website: www.ithaca.edu

Campus Life
Environment: Town. **Calendar:** Semester.

Students and Faculty
(All Undergraduate Programs)
Enrollment: 5,997. **Student Body:** 55% female, 45% male, 53% out-of-state, 3% international (70 countries represented). African American 3%, Asian 3%, Caucasian 86%, Hispanic 3%. Student/faculty ratio: 12:1. 442 full-time faculty, 92% hold PhDs. 99% faculty teach undergrads.

Admissions
(All Undergraduate Programs)
Freshman Admissions Requirements: Test(s) required: SAT or ACT; ACT with Writing component. 29% in top tenth, 64% in top quarter. SAT Math (25/75 percentile): 550/640. SAT Verbal (25/75 percentile): 540/640. Projected SAT Writing (25/75 percentile): 600/680. *Academic units required:* 4 English, 3 math, 3 science, 2 foreign language, 3 social studies, 1 academic elective. Early decision application deadline: 11/1. Regular application deadline: 2/1. Regular notification: Rolling.

Costs and Financial Aid
(All Undergraduate Programs)
Annual tuition $25,194. Room & board $9,950. Average book expense $968.
Financial Aid Statistics: % freshmen/undergrads who receive any aid: 86/85. % freshmen/undergrads

who receive need-based scholarship or grant aid: 65/65. % freshmen/undergrads who receive need-based self-help aid: 68/63. Priority financial aid filing deadline: 2/1. Financial aid notification on or about: 2/15.

TV/Film/Digital Media Studies Programs

Degrees conferred to these majors: BA, BS, BFA.

Equipment and facilities: We provide everything from color and black-and-white darkrooms, digital editing suites, and a digital still-imaging lab to Aaton and Bolex cameras, digital and analog tape recorders, and three film and video studios.

Career development services: Alumni networking opportunities, internship listings, job listings.

Notable alumni: Michael Nathanson, former president of MGM Studios (until it was sold to Sony); Bill D'Elia, director/producer of *Ally McBeal*, *Chicago Hope*, *Boston Legal*; Cliff Plumer, chief technology officer for Lucasfilm and Industrial Light and Magic; Mike Royce, senior writer, *Everybody Loves Raymond*; David Lebow, EVP & GM, AOL Media Networks; Chris Regan, senior writer for the *Jon Stewart Show*; Jill Agostino, special projects editor for *The New York Times*; Jay Linden, executive vice president of NBC's Strategic Partnership Group; Erica Reynolds, senior editor, *Ebony* magazine.

In Their Own Words

Internships include BBC (London); MTV, CBS, ABC, NBC, Fox (all in NYC); Los Angeles studios where Scrubs and Malcolm in the Middle are produced, Capitol Records, Grey Global Group, Ithaca College James B. Pendleton Center in Los Angeles. You'll also find that a semester abroad at the Ithaca College London Center will give you not only the benefit of courses in British film and television, but also the opportunity to work for the London Radio Service, the British Film Institute, the BBC, and others. For the Jessica Savitch Distinguished Lecturer Series, speakers have included Ann Curry, news anchor, NBC's Today Show, and MSNBC; Emmy Award-winning reporter Cokie Roberts, ABC News pro-

gram anchor. For the Parks Distinguished Visitor, speakers have included Ken Burns, renowned documentary filmmaker; P. J. O'Rourke, best-selling author; and leading political satirist Skip Landen; the Professional-in-Residence Program focuses on bringing successful alumni of our communications program to campus for a three-day residency. During this time, they visit or lecture in classes, teach master classes, provide a public lecture, and participate in various social functions involving students, faculty, and staff. Past visitors include Sharon Otterman, Jay Linden, Bill D'Elia, Arthur Moore, Judith Girard, Bill Froelich, Steve Rathe, and Daniel Reeves.

POPULAR PROGRAMS

CINEMA AND PHOTOGRAPHY

Department chair: Steven Skopik

Number of full-time faculty: 12

Focus/emphasis: From your first semester, you'll be deeply involved in planning, shooting, and editing film and still photography projects. At the same time, you'll be learning the theory and history behind your work. Your introductory courses will teach you to evaluate your work with a deeper understanding of what gives an image impact and meaning. You'll venture forth from film production classes with a whole new appreciation for the amount of planning and work that goes into a movie long before the cameras start rolling. By your sophomore year, you'll select a concentration in still photography, cinema production, or screenwriting. If you choose still photography, you'll embark on an intensive course load that will include classes in color photography, digital photography, contemporary photographic issues, and American visual culture. If you're interested in cinema production, you'll take such courses as film theory, screenwriting, and directing. In addition to cinema studies, our new interdisciplinary screenwriting concentration features courses in theater, literature, and writing from the School of Humanities and Sciences.

TELEVISION AND RADIO

Department chair: Wenmouth Williams

Number of full-time faculty: 19

Focus/emphasis: Welcome to the Department of Television-Radio, which offers 2 majors: Television-radio, and integrated marketing communications. Now in its second year, integrated marketing communications combines business and communications courses to prepare students for the ever-changing world of advertising, public relations, and marketing. We have formed an industry advisory committee of professionals in these fields to help us keep abreast of future trends. IMC seniors can also participate in the award-winning Ad Lab, which teaches the essentials of planning an advertising campaign, including media strategy, positioning, and ad design. The television and radio major gives students a well-rounded look at the various communications industries in core courses ranging from writing to the study of the First Amendment and new media. Students then concentrate in audio production, video production, or scriptwriting. From their very first semester at Ithaca, communications students have the opportunity to get real-life, hands-on experiences within their concentration or areas of interest at one of the many student media outlets. Whether they're part of the team at the television or radio stations or writing for the newspaper or magazines, communications students gain experience, learn to deal with on-the-job challenges, and build their portfolios. The road to success in communications is built around the ability to be a critical thinker and an excellent writer with a solid grounding in the liberal arts. Establishing personal networks with media professionals adds to the likelihood of success after graduation. For this reason, many of our students participate in our internship program, which offers a wide range of opportunities. Our students have worked at such diverse placements as all four major American television networks, Capitol Records, Comedy Central, DDB Worldwide, and NPR.

FILM, PHOTOGRAPHY, AND VISUAL ARTS

Department chair: Steven Skopik

Focus/emphasis: The film, photography, and visual arts program differs from the BS program in cinema and photography by adding course work in the other fine arts. Rather than focusing on one specific medium, you'll be encouraged to explore the whole spectrum of visual culture. Beginning in your freshman year, you'll take many of the same classes in photography and film production as cinema and photography majors (bring your own 35 mm SLR camera and light meter), and you'll spend as much time in the darkroom or at an editing station as they do. But you'll also venture into the television studios for video production classes and trek over to the art studio for lessons in drawing. You will receive a thorough grounding in required courses in theory, history, and criticism. To round out your educational experience, you will choose from elective courses in theater, music, and writing. But the real emphasis is on producing images—photographs, paintings, films, videos, and drawings. The goal is to provide you with the skills and background you need to develop and express your artistic vision.

JAMES MADISON UNIVERSITY

Sonner Hall, MSC 0101, Harrisonburg, VA 22807
Phone: 540-568-5681 **E-mail:** admissions@jmu.edu
Website: www.jmu.edu

Campus Life

Environment: Town. **Calendar:** Semester.

Students and Faculty
(All Undergraduate Programs)

Enrollment: 15,287. **Student Body:** 61% female, 39% male, 30% out-of-state. African American 3%, Asian 5%, Caucasian 84%, Hispanic 2%. Student/faculty ratio: 17:1. 795 full-time faculty, 77% hold PhDs. 100% faculty teach undergrads.

Admissions
(All Undergraduate Programs)
Freshman Admissions Requirements: Test(s) required: SAT or ACT. Average high school GPA: 3.67. 28% in top tenth, 74% in top quarter. SAT Math (25/75 percentile): 540/630. SAT Verbal (25/75 percentile): 530/620. Projected SAT Writing (25/75 percentile): 590/660. *Academic units required:* 4 English, 4 math, 3 science (3 science labs), 3 foreign language, 1 social studies, 2 history. Regular application deadline: 1/15. Regular notification: 4/1.

Costs and Financial Aid
(All Undergraduate Programs)
Annual in-state tuition $6,290. Out-of-state tuition $16,236. Room & board $6,756. Average book expense $820.

Financial Aid Statistics: % freshmen/undergrads who receive any aid: 32/30. % freshmen/undergrads who receive need-based scholarship or grant aid: 16/12. % freshmen/undergrads who receive need-based self-help aid: 29/24. Priority financial aid filing deadline: 3/1. Financial aid notification on or about: 4/1.

TV/Film/Digital Media Studies Programs
Number of undergraduates in these programs: 210

Number of 2005 graduates from these programs: 55

Degrees conferred to these majors: BA, BS.

Number of full-time faculty in these programs: 6

Equipment and facilities: ENG/EFP HD equipment and HD Studio.

ATAS Faculty Seminar participants: 1

Other awards of note: In 2005, students received video awards for National BEA awards. In 2002, 2003, and 2004, faculty received video awards from BEA.

Career development services: Alumni networking opportunities, career counseling, internship listings, job fairs, job listings. The career service is run by the university and not by the department. The department keeps up with alumni. On-campus interviewing, JMU online alumni community, and MonsterTRAK for employers to post jobs.

Notable alumni: Don Rhymer, screenplay writer; Barbara Hall, TV producer; Phoef Sutton, TV writer; Herb Ankrom, ABC family producer for *Extreme Home Makeover*.

In Their Own Words
Students can obtain practicum and internship experience through the local PBS TV station; generally, students obtain summer internships through Discovery, Nickelodeon, and various NBC, CBS, ABC, and CNN affiliates in Washington, DC.

JOHN BROWN UNIVERSITY
2000 West University Street, Siloam Springs, AR 72761
Phone: 877-528-4636 **E-mail:** jbuinfo@jbu.edu
Website: www.jbu.edu

Campus Life
Environment: Village. **Calendar:** Semester.

Students and Faculty
(All Undergraduate Programs)
Enrollment: 1,608. **Student Body:** 51% female, 49% male, 72% out-of-state, 6% international (41 countries represented). African American 3%, Caucasian 84%, Hispanic 3%, Native American 2%. Student/faculty ratio: 12:1. 83 full-time faculty, 73% hold PhDs. 90% faculty teach undergrads.

Admissions
(All Undergraduate Programs)
Freshman Admissions Requirements: Test(s) required: SAT or ACT. Average high school GPA: 3.6. 29% in top tenth, 59% in top quarter. SAT Math (25/75 percentile): 510/640. SAT Verbal (25/75 percentile): 540/660. Projected SAT Writing (25/75 percentile): 600/690. Regular notification: Rolling.

Costs and Financial Aid
(All Undergraduate Programs)
Annual tuition $15,412. Room & board $5,956. Required fees $746. Average book expense $600.
Financial Aid Statistics: % freshmen/undergrads who receive any aid: 90/87. % freshmen/undergrads

who receive need-based scholarship or grant aid: 63/48. % freshmen/undergrads who receive need-based self-help aid: 62/57. Priority financial aid filing deadline: 3/1. Financial aid notification on or about: 3/1.

TV/Film/Digital Media Studies Programs

Number of undergraduates in these programs: 99

Number of 2005 graduates from these programs: 25

Degrees conferred to these majors: BS.

Number of full-time faculty in these programs: 5

Equipment and facilities: two PC labs, Mac lab, DM software (digital imaging and cinema, authoring of DVD, animation), TV studio, control room, DM lab, three "senior suites" that have Macs and PCs.

Career development services: Alumni networking opportunities, career counseling, job fairs, job listings.

In Their Own Words

Our goal is to graduate industry-ready professionals prepared for a career in digital media arts. One aspect that serves this purpose is our emphasis on foreign study and mission opportunities. Areas in which graduates find employment include Web design and publishing, disc and DVD authoring, television production, filmmaking, photography and image editing, illustration, 2-D and 3-D animation, advertising, and design work.

POPULAR PROGRAMS

DIGITAL MEDIA

Department chair: Neal Holland

Number of full-time faculty: 3

Focus/emphasis: JBU's Digital Media Program is one of the first of its kind. The major has the highest enrollment out of more than 50 majors. The cutting-edge education encourages innovation while maintaining strong artistic and academic discipline. Students receive a foundation in traditional illustration techniques, graphic design fundamentals, and practical mass media skills. Faculty with real-world experience, both past and present, work to prepare students for the convergence of technology, art, and electronic media. The faculty also stress the development of conceptual thought, aesthetics, and technical know-how. Students are consistently encouraged toward the integration and expression of their artistic creativity within the Christian faith.

JUNIATA COLLEGE

1700 Moore Street, Huntingdon, PA 16652
Phone: 814-641-3420 **E-mail:** admissions@juniata.edu
Website: www.juniata.edu

Campus Life

Environment: Village. **Calendar:** Semester.

Students and Faculty
(All Undergraduate Programs)

Enrollment: 1,379. **Student Body:** 53% female, 47% male, 28% out-of-state, 3% international (31 countries represented). African American 2%, Asian 2%, Caucasian 91%, Hispanic 1%. Student/faculty ratio: 13:1. 94 full-time faculty, 91% hold PhDs. 100% faculty teach undergrads.

Admissions
(All Undergraduate Programs)

Average high school GPA: 3.82. 43% in top tenth, 79% in top quarter. SAT Math (25/75 percentile): 550/640. SAT Verbal (25/75 percentile): 530/630. Projected SAT Writing (25/75 percentile): 590/670. *Academic units required:* 4 English, 3 math, 3 science (2 science labs), 2 foreign language, 1 social studies, 3 history. Early decision application deadline: 11/1. Regular application deadline: 3/1. Regular notification: Rolling.

Costs and Financial Aid
(All Undergraduate Programs)

Annual tuition $26,900. Room & board $7,680.

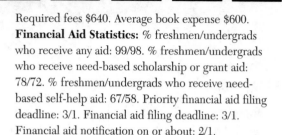

Required fees $640. Average book expense $600.
Financial Aid Statistics: % freshmen/undergrads who receive any aid: 99/98. % freshmen/undergrads who receive need-based scholarship or grant aid: 78/72. % freshmen/undergrads who receive need-based self-help aid: 67/58. Priority financial aid filing deadline: 3/1. Financial aid filing deadline: 3/1. Financial aid notification on or about: 2/1.

TV/Film/Digital Media Studies Programs

**Number of undergraduates
in these programs:** 4
Degrees conferred to these majors: BA, BS.
**Number of full-time faculty in these
programs:** 1
**Number of part-time faculty in these
programs:** 2
Equipment and facilities: High-definition video, video studio, audio studio.
Career development services: Alumni networking opportunities; career counseling; central resource(s) for employers to browse headshots, writing samples, reels; internship listings; job fairs; job listings.

In Their Own Words

Internships with local and regional broadcast television stations, close partnership with The Gravity Project—a professional theater company—producing interpretative, feature-length video, many experiential opportunities for students creating independent documentary productions and Web-delivered marketing productions. Juniata digital media students have also recently worked on feature films (including The New World), History Channel productions, and other professional documentaries.

POPULAR PROGRAMS

DIGITAL MEDIA

Department chair: Dr. Loren Rhodes
Number of full-time faculty: 1
Number of part-time faculty: 2
Focus/emphasis: The program is a new interdisciplinary major combining areas in IT, communica-
tion, arts, and theater arts that prepares students for work in media production.

KEAN UNIVERSITY

1000 Morris Avenue, PO Box 411, Union, NJ 07083-0411
Phone: 908-737-7100 **E-mail:** admitme@kean.edu
Website: www.kean.edu

Campus Life
Environment: City. **Calendar:** Semester.

Students and Faculty
(All Undergraduate Programs)
Enrollment: 9,612. **Student Body:** 63% female, 37% male, 2% out-of-state, 2% international (68 countries represented). African American 21%, Asian 6%, Caucasian 47%, Hispanic 20%. Student/faculty ratio: 15:1. 382 full-time faculty, 87% hold PhDs. 100% faculty teach undergrads.

Admissions
(All Undergraduate Programs)
Freshman Admissions Requirements: Test(s) required: SAT or ACT. Average high school GPA: 2.88. 7% in top tenth, 22% in top quarter. SAT Math (25/75 percentile): 430/530. SAT Verbal (25/75 percentile): 430/510. Projected SAT Writing (25/75 percentile): 500/570. *Academic units required:* 4 English, 3 math, 2 science (2 science labs), 2 history, 5 academic electives. Regular application deadline: 5/31. Regular notification: Rolling.

Costs and Financial Aid
(All Undergraduate Programs)
Annual in-state tuition $4,897. Out-of-state tuition $7,530. Required fees $2,608.
Financial Aid Statistics: % freshmen/undergrads who receive any aid: 79/69. % freshmen/undergrads who receive need-based scholarship or grant aid: 57/52. % freshmen/undergrads who receive need-based self-help aid: 57/51. Priority financial aid filing deadline: 3/15. Financial aid notification on or about: 3/15.

TV/Film/Digital Media Studies Programs

Number of undergraduates in these programs: 200

Number of 2005 graduates from these programs: 40

Degrees conferred to these majors: BA, BFA.

Number of full-time faculty in these programs: 5

Number of part-time faculty in these programs: 5

Equipment and facilities: ENG/EFP equipment, television studio, 20-station MAC G5 studio with Final Cut Studio Suite software, WKNJ-FM 90.3, 20-station PC lab with Adobe Premiere Pro software suite, Purple Violet Film Festival, master classes with visiting professionals, special topic courses taught by returning professionals from such locations as HBO, CBS News, Fox Sports, King World, CNBC, CNN, and the YES Network.

Other awards of note: Honolulu International Film Festival, NAPTE Faculty fellowship, IRTS Faculty fellowship; faculty and students have presented research or creative works at UFVA, BEA, NCA, NAB, and at international conferences in China and India.

Career development services: Career counseling, internship listings, job fairs, job listings.

Notable alumni: Though the program began in 2006, new graduates currently work at Sirius, MTV, BET, CBS, ABC, *Vibe*, *The Source*, *The Maury Povich Show*, and in the music industry, as well as other locations.

In Their Own Words

Internships in NYC and NJ for major credit. Locations include MTV, CBS, Telemundo, WFAN, Howard Stern, NBC, ABC, CNBC, WB-11, News 9, NJ 12, NY1, K-Rock, Z-100, Univision, Comcast, Sony Music, Sirius, and many other locations. CNN anchor Anderson Cooper was last year's graduation speaker.

POPULAR PROGRAMS

BROADCASTING

Department chair: Cathleen Londino, PhD
Number of full-time faculty: 5
Number of part-time faculty: 5

FILM

Department chair: Cathleen Londino, PhD
Number of full-time faculty: 5
Number of part-time faculty: 5

MULTICULTURAL PROGRAMMING AND MANAGEMENT

Department chair: Cathleen Londino, PhD
Number of full-time faculty: 5
Number of part-time faculty: 5

INTERNATIONAL BROADCAST JOURNALISM

Department chair: Cathleen Londino, PhD
Number of full-time faculty: 5
Number of part-time faculty: 5

KEENE STATE COLLEGE

229 Main Street, Keene, NH 03435-2604
Phone: 603-358-2276 **E-mail:** admissions@keene.edu
Website: www.keene.edu

Campus Life

Environment: Town. **Calendar:** Semester.

Students and Faculty
(All Undergraduate Programs)

Enrollment: 4,370. **Student Body:** 57% female, 43% male, 46% out-of-state (9 countries represented). Caucasian 94%. Student/faculty ratio: 17:1. 187 full-time faculty. 100% faculty teach undergrads.

Admissions
(All Undergraduate Programs)

Freshman Admissions Requirements: Test(s) required: SAT or ACT. Average high school GPA: 2.94. 4% in top tenth, 21% in top quarter. SAT Math (25/75 percentile): 450/550. SAT Verbal (25/75 percentile): 450/550. Projected SAT Writing (25/75 percentile): 520/610. *Academic units required:* 4 English,

3 math, 3 science, 2 social studies, 2 academic electives. Regular application deadline: 4/1. Regular notification: Rolling.

Costs and Financial Aid
(All Undergraduate Programs)
Annual in-state tuition $5,780. Out-of-state tuition $13,050. Room & board $7,027. Required fees $2,038. Average book expense $600.

Financial Aid Statistics: % freshmen/undergrads who receive any aid: 56/53. % freshmen/undergrads who receive need-based scholarship or grant aid: 40/35. % freshmen/undergrads who receive need-based self-help aid: 50/49. Financial aid filing deadline: 3/1.

TV/Film/Digital Media Studies Programs
Number of undergraduates in these programs: 50

Number of 2005 graduates from these programs: 13

Degrees conferred to these majors: BA.

Number of full-time faculty in these programs: 9

Number of part-time faculty in these programs: 1

Equipment and facilities: 25 Avid Platforms, DV and 16 mm capability

% of graduates who pursue further study within 5 years: 20

% of graduates currently employed in related field: 50

Career development services: Alumni networking opportunities; career counseling; central resource(s) for employers to browse headshots, writing samples, reels; internship listings; job fairs; job listings.

Notable alumni: Jennifer Dunnington, sound editor; Craig Morrison, producer, editor; David Meishner, Avid consultant; David D'Arville, film producer; Steve McMillan, set designer; Natali Pope, set dresser.

In Their Own Words
The film studies major balances theoretical and applied course work. The film production and critical studies options offer opportunities to prepare students for employment in a variety of fields. Graduates most often go on to further study or careers in the analysis and/or the production of film and television. Graduates also are prepared to go on to careers in the business world in areas such as personnel, counseling, public relations, and sales. Graduates from Keene State's Film Studies have been hired by Avid as instructors, others have been hired by radio station WMUR, the New Hampshire Film Corporation, Ken Burns' production studio, ESPN, HBO, and the Library of Congress. Graduates have worked on the sets of Ally McBeal, The Lord of the Rings, The Majestic, In The Bedroom, and The Aviator.

POPULAR PROGRAMS

FILM STUDIES
Department chair: Dr. Lawrence Benaquist
Number of full-time faculty: 9
Number of part-time faculty: 1
Focus/emphasis: The film studies major offers two program options: film production and critical studies.

KENTUCKY STATE UNIVERSITY
400 East Main Street, 3rd Floor, Frankfort, KY 40601
Phone: 502-597-6813 **E-mail:** james.burrell@kysu.edu
Website: www.kysu.edu

Campus Life
Environment: Village. **Calendar:** Semester.

Students and Faculty
(All Undergraduate Programs)
Enrollment: 1,912. **Student Body:** 59% female, 41% male, 42% out-of-state. African American 67%, Caucasian 28%. Student/faculty ratio: 15:1. 158 full-time faculty. 98% faculty teach undergrads.

Admissions
(All Undergraduate Programs)
Freshman Admissions Requirements: Test(s) required: SAT and SAT Subject Tests or ACT. Average high school GPA: 2.6. SAT Math (25/75 percentile): 360/480. SAT Verbal (25/75 percentile): 370/450. Projected SAT Writing (25/75 percentile): 440/520. *Academic units required:* 4 English, 3 math, 3 science, 2 foreign language, 3 social studies, 1 history, 7 academic electives. Regular notification: Rolling.

Costs and Financial Aid
(All Undergraduate Programs)
Annual in-state tuition $3,550. Out-of-state tuition $9,992. Room & board $5,621. Required fees $918. Average book expense $250.
Financial Aid Statistics: Priority financial aid filing deadline: 4/15. Financial aid filing deadline: 5/31. Financial aid notification on or about: 4/3.

TV/Film/Digital Media Studies Programs
Number of undergraduates in these programs: 19
Number of 2005 graduates from these programs: 5
Degrees conferred to these majors: BS.
Also available at Kentucky State University: Associate.
Number of full-time faculty in these programs: 2
Equipment and facilities: Full digital media lab.

% of graduates who pursue further study within 5 years: 25
% of graduates currently employed in related field: 100
Career development services: Alumni networking opportunities, career counseling, instructor relationship with private sector, internship listings, job fairs, job listings.
Notable alumni: Several students are involved with enhancing production with digital technology within their organization or place of business.

In Their Own Words
100 percent job placement for more than 20 years.

POPULAR PROGRAMS

COMPUTER GRAPHICS AND MULTIMEDIA
Department chair: Ashok Kumar, PhD
Number of full-time faculty: 2
Focus/emphasis: Industrial technology offers occupational and technical programs that lead to associate applied science degrees in computer graphics and multimedia production technology or computer electronics technology. These programs are designed to address the technical needs of students who seek employment for or a change in industrial employment, the in-service needs of technicians who seek to improve their technical knowledge and skills to keep pace with changing technology in the industry, and the needs of those who desire personal enrichment or orientation by taking courses in these areas. The goals of the program are to reinforce student interest and enhance achievement in academic and technical skills; integrate curriculum at both the secondary and postsecondary levels in a sequence of courses leading to an associate degree in a technical field; establish articulation among secondary/ postsecondary institutions, colleges, and universities; prepare and assist students for entry into the workforce; and upgrade vocational/technical courses to meet current and future needs.

ELECTRONIC TECHNOLOGY
Department chair: Ashok Kumar, PhD

KEYSTONE COLLEGE
One College Green, La Plume, PA 18440
Phone: 570-945-8111 **E-mail:** admissions@keystone.edu
Website: www.keystone.edu

Campus Life
Environment: Rural. **Calendar:** Semester.

Students and Faculty
(All Undergraduate Programs)
Enrollment: 1,632. **Student Body:** 61% female, 39% male, 12% out-of-state. African American 3%,

Caucasian 72%, Hispanic 1%. 62 full-time faculty, 23% hold PhDs.

Admissions
(All Undergraduate Programs)
Freshman Admissions Requirements: Test(s) required: SAT or ACT. SAT Math (25/75 percentile): 400/500. SAT Verbal (25/75 percentile): 400/500. Projected SAT Writing (25/75 percentile): 470/560. *Academic units required:* 4 English, 2 math, 2 science (1 science lab), 2 social studies, 3 history. Regular application deadline: 7/1. Regular notification: Rolling.

Costs and Financial Aid
(All Undergraduate Programs)
Annual tuition $14,946. Room & board $8,110. Required fees $920. Average book expense $1,200. **Financial Aid Statistics:** % freshmen/undergrads who receive any aid: 86/87. % freshmen/undergrads who receive need-based scholarship or grant aid: 82/78. % freshmen/undergrads who receive need-based self-help aid: 76/73. Priority financial aid filing deadline: 4/26. Financial aid filing deadline: 5/1. Financial aid notification on or about: 3/1.

TV/Film/Digital Media Studies Programs
Equipment and facilities: Students have access to ENG/EFP equipment, media lab, graphic arts studio, and FM radio station (WKCV).

Other awards of note: Julia Peterson has received several international awards for video production, including Telly, CINDY, CCAIT, and Communicator Awards. She is also a judge for the New York festivals.

Career development services: Career counseling, internship listings, job fairs, job listings.

Students Should Also Know
Keystone is currently developing a digital media specialization for students earning bachelor's degrees.

LASALLE UNIVERSITY
1900 West Olney Avenue, Philadelphia, PA 19141-1199
Phone: 215-951-1500 **E-mail:** admiss@lasalle.edu
Website: www.lasalle.edu

Campus Life
Environment: Metropolis. **Calendar:** Semester.

Students and Faculty
(All Undergraduate Programs)
Enrollment: 4,044. **Student Body:** 57% female, 43% male, 30% out-of-state, 1% international (13 countries represented). African American 11%, Asian 2%, Caucasian 75%, Hispanic 6%. Student/faculty ratio: 17:1. 197 full-time faculty, 81% hold PhDs. 100% faculty teach undergrads.

Admissions
(All Undergraduate Programs)
Freshman Admissions Requirements: Test(s) required: SAT; SAT and SAT Subject Tests. Average high school GPA: 3.1. 25% in top tenth, 55% in top quarter. SAT Math (25/75 percentile): 490/590. SAT Verbal (25/75 percentile): 490/600. Projected SAT Writing (25/75 percentile): 550/650. *Academic units required:* 4 English, 3 math, 1 science (1 science lab), 2 foreign language, 1 history, 5 academic electives. Regular application deadline: 4/1. Regular notification: Rolling.

Costs and Financial Aid
(All Undergraduate Programs)
Annual tuition $21,270. Room & board $7,810. Required fees $150. Average book expense $500. **Financial Aid Statistics:** % freshmen/undergrads who receive need-based scholarship or grant aid: 78/74. % freshmen/undergrads who receive need-based self-help aid: 60/59. Priority financial aid filing deadline: 2/15. Financial aid notification on or about: 11/15.

TV/Film/Digital Media Studies Programs
Number of undergraduates in these programs: 400
Number of 2005 graduates from these programs: 100

Degrees conferred to these majors: BA.
Number of full-time faculty in these programs: 12
Number of part-time faculty in these programs: 6
Equipment and facilities: Cable access channel that reaches Philadelphia homes; linear and nonlinear editing suites; mini-DV camcorders.
Career development services: Alumni networking opportunities, career counseling, internship listings, job fairs, job listings.
Notable alumni: John Ogden, traffic reporter for NBC-10 TV, Philadelphia, PA; Kathy Reynolds, news reporter for WZZM-TV, Grand Rapids, MI; Erin Flynn, producer for WLVT-TV, Bethlehem, PA.

In Their Own Words
Twelve students were chosen by NBC to intern with them at the 2006 Winter Olympics in Torino, Italy. La Salle 56, the university's cable TV channel, allows students to gain hands-on experience starting freshman year.

POPULAR PROGRAMS

COMMUNICATION
Department chair: Lynne Texter, PhD

LEE UNIVERSITY
PO Box 3450, Cleveland, TN 37320-3450
Phone: 423-614-8500 **E-mail:** admissions@leeuniversity.edu
Website: www.leeuniversity.edu

Campus Life
Environment: Town. **Calendar:** Semester.

Students and Faculty
(All Undergraduate Programs)
Enrollment: 3,573. **Student Body:** 58% female, 42% male, 62% out-of-state, 5% international (53 countries represented). African American 4%, Caucasian 81%, Hispanic 3%. Student/faculty ratio: 18:1. 148 full-time faculty, 75% hold PhDs. 100% faculty teach undergrads.

Admissions
(All Undergraduate Programs)
Freshman Admissions Requirements: Test(s) required: SAT or ACT. Average high school GPA: 3.34. 19% in top tenth, 43% in top quarter. SAT Math (25/75 percentile): 450/600. SAT Verbal (25/75 percentile): 480/610. Projected SAT Writing (25/75 percentile): 540/660. *Academic units required:* 4 English, 3 math, 2 science, 1 foreign language, 2 social studies, 1 history. Regular application deadline: 9/1. Regular notification: Rolling.

Costs and Financial Aid
(All Undergraduate Programs)
Annual tuition $9,400. Room & board $5,170. Required fees $210. Average book expense $800.
Financial Aid Statistics: % freshmen/undergrads who receive any aid: 40/70. % freshmen/undergrads who receive need-based scholarship or grant aid: 30/45. % freshmen/undergrads who receive need-based self-help aid: 23/44. Priority financial aid filing deadline: 3/15. Financial aid notification on or about: 2/1

TV/Film/Digital Media Studies Programs
Number of undergraduates in these programs: 113
Number of 2005 graduates from these programs: 11
Degrees conferred to these majors: BA, BS.
Number of full-time faculty in these programs: 3
Number of part-time faculty in these programs: 1
Equipment and facilities: Television studio, broadcast audio lab, student publication lab

% of graduates currently employed in related field: 60
Career development services: Alumni networking opportunities; career assessment, career counseling; central resource(s) for employers to browse head-

shots, writing samples, reels; education fair; internship listings; job fairs; job listings; job search inventory; majors fair; resume counseling; strength finder's (self-assessment).

Notable alumni: Jessica Morris (2003), news anchor for Channel 9 TV station, Chattanooga, TN. Amy Norton (2003), news anchor for a television station in West Virginia.

In Their Own Words

Lee's Communication/Telecommunication Department requires a very well-rounded, intensive internship program that allows students to receive hands-on experience in their discipline.

POPULAR PROGRAMS

TELECOMMUNICATIONS
Department chair: Dr. Michael Laney
Number of full-time faculty: 3
Number of part-time faculty: 1
Focus/emphasis: The BA and BS in telecommunications is designed to train students in professional or academic work in the area of mass communication, including television, radio, video and audio production, and Web content.

LOYOLA MARYMOUNT UNIVERSITY

1 LMU Drive, Suite 100, Los Angeles, CA 90045
Phone: 310-338-2750 **E-mail:** admissions@lmu.edu
Website: www.lmu.edu

Campus Life
Environment: Metropolis. **Calendar:** Semester.

Students and Faculty
(All Undergraduate Programs)
Enrollment: 5,590. **Student Body:** 59% female, 41% male, 23% out-of-state, 1% international (50 countries represented). African American 7%, Asian 13%, Caucasian 56%, Hispanic 19%. Student/faculty ratio: 13:1. 419 full-time faculty, 87% hold PhDs. 100% faculty teach undergrads.

Admissions
(All Undergraduate Programs)
Freshman Admissions Requirements: Test(s) required: SAT or ACT. Average high school GPA: 3.6. 30% in top tenth, 66% in top quarter. SAT Math (25/75 percentile): 540/640. SAT Verbal (25/75 percentile): 530/630. Projected SAT Writing (25/75 percentile): 590/670. Regular notification: Rolling.

Costs and Financial Aid
(All Undergraduate Programs)
Annual tuition $27,710. Room & board $8,709. Required fees $430. Average book expense $820. **Financial Aid Statistics:** % freshmen/undergrads who receive need-based scholarship or grant aid: 46/47. % freshmen/undergrads who receive need-based self-help aid: 42/44. Priority financial aid filing deadline: 2/15. Financial aid filing deadline: 4/1. Financial aid notification on or about: 5/1

TV/Film/Digital Media Studies Programs
Degrees conferred to these majors: BA.
Also available at Loyola Marymount University: MFA.
Equipment and facilities: The SPOT is our fully developed and student-run student production office team. The SPOT looks and operates like a real-world production office and helps our students with everything they need to complete a production. Here students can access phones, faxes, high-speed network connections, and meeting rooms. They will find a complete production handbook, as well as casting and location files and shooting permits. A complete computer lab with the latest version of EP Movie Magic Scheduling and Budgeting software is available to help them put together professional projects. The screenwriting lab has Macintosh and PC computers with the latest version of Final Draft installed. Our film program uses Arriflex SR II Super 16 mm, and 16 mm cameras. Each camera is fitted with a "studio package," and Sony PD150 and DSR390 digital video cameras are used for field production. Our film soundstage is equipped with a professional "green bed," including overhead state-of-the-art lighting grids, and, at over 5,000 square feet, it is large enough to accommodate several sets at once—many of which can be built in

our complete scene shop. And for your shoots, we offer new, professional dressing rooms, with fully equipped makeup and hair stations for the comfort of our actors. Our television stage is equipped with Sony DVX50 digital video cameras mounted on Cartoni studio pedestals and an Echolab digital production switcher. The lighting grid is controlled from a Strand console. Nagra Stereo and Fostex FR2 digital recorders are used for location and field recording. Both stages and the Grip & Electric Department are equipped with Mole-Richardson lighting instruments, JL Fisher dollies and accessories, and Matthews grip equipment. Our Animation Program uses traditional animation cameras, as well as the most comprehensive, up-to-the-minute computer hardware and software, including Adobe, Maya, Shake, Toonz, and 3-D Studio Max in the labs, running on both Mac and PC platforms. To complete their projects, students have 24/7 access to editing, ADR, Foley, Sound FX, music-recording, and music-mixing suites where Apple Final Cut Pro HD is used for editing pictures and postproduction audio and sound design are edited with Pro Tools software. And finally, we screen our creations in our beautiful Mayer Theatre, LMU's primary screening facility, which is equipped with both 16 mm and 35 mm film projectors as well as an American high-definition digital light projector—with all three formats accompanied by exceptional Dolby Digital Surround Sound.

Other awards of note: Awards earned by students include: 2004 DGA Annual Student Film Award— Best African American Film and screened at Cannes Emerging Filmmakers Showcase: *The Last Chair* by Leona Whitney Beatty; 2004 HBO Comedy Arts Festival selection: *Paul Is Dead* by John Carlson; 2005 inductee, Fox Diversity Writing Program: Jen LeeLoy; 2005 inductee, Warner Brothers Writing Workshop Drama: Nancy B. Jack.

Career development services: Alumni networking opportunities; assistance in developing professional portfolios, including DVDs, reels, scripts, and other key materials; career advisement and active connection to key internships, career counseling, connection to agents, managers, guilds, and associations, including DGA, WGA, PGA, SAG, Film and TV Academy, IATSE, and SIGGRAPH; connection to

key SFTV alumni; internship listings; pairing students with highly regarded and celebrated industry mentors. The school also helps students maximize their opportunities, including making full use of the film festival circuit for highest possible profile exposure and reward; helping students create a working career roadmap over the course of their undergrad and graduate years; offering industry networking opportunities in all five of our programs: film and television, animation, screenwriting, and recording arts; creating real-experience outreach to the film and television industries by way of internships, mentorships, a special lecture series, workshops, and festival field trips; strategizing screenplay and teleplay competitions for maximum benefit, producing the LMU SFTV "Film Outside the Frame" annual student film festival; establishing a global reach for SFTV students in both documentary and narrative filmmaking; managing the Transition After Graduation Program (TAG); and offering film-finishing funds, targeted access to key industry leaders; and full support for selected top students as they transition into the entertainment and emerging media industries.

Famous alumni: Brian Helgeland

Notable alumni: David Mirkin, Emmy Award-winning producer, *The Simpsons*; Winifred Hervey, writer, *The Cosby Show*, *The Golden Girls*, *The Fresh Prince of Bel-Air*, *In the House*, *The Steve Harvey Show*; Effie Brown, producer and winner of the Sundance Film Festival Dramatic Audience Award, *Real Women Have Curves*, *In The Cut*; Jason Constantine, vice president, acquisitions, Lions Gate Films.

In Their Own Words

We have a Monday Night Special Event Series in which industry luminaries (many Academy Award winners) present their most recent work and their perspectives on the creative process and the industry. Guests have included Alexander Payne, Martin Landau, Stacy Peralta, William Friedkin, Caleb Daschanel, Frank Darabont, and Julie Richardson. Workshops have included a costume and production design workshop with award-winning designers Jane Ruhm

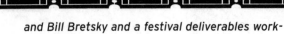

and Bill Bretsky and a festival deliverables work-shop and panel.

POPULAR PROGRAMS

ANIMATION
Department chair: Barbara Kelly
Number of full-time faculty: 27
Number of part-time faculty: 40
Focus/emphasis: The program represents a broadband approach to animation education within a liberal arts framework. There is course work in both traditional and digital animation, plus studies in experimental, interactive storytelling and alternative forms of the medium in small classroom settings. Animation is viewed as an art/communication form that has only two limitations: one's imagination and exhaustion. Each student sets their own direction. Therefore, films range from conceptual to cartoon, from object animation to computer, from entertainment to experimental, and from traditional animation to new animation. In four years at LMU, animation majors move from a traditionally based foundation in animation production techniques during the freshman year to the theory and practice of digital filmmaking and computer animation during the sophomore year. The third year is devoted to the study of multimedia and alternative forms of animation. During the senior year, students write, animate, and direct a thesis film/project for their portfolio.

FILM AND TELEVISION PRODUCTION
Department chair: Barbara Kelly
Focus/emphasis: Digital technologies have created new ways of working that transcend the traditional distinctions between film and television. They receive expert hands-on training in screenwriting, direction, cinematography, sound recording and design, and editing. Students learn the practical aspects of mounting a production: budgeting, location scouting, casting, set design and construction, postproduction, and the importance of safety in all aspects of what they do. Complete premier state-of-the-art equipment and technology are available 24/7, all in service of the story. Beginning with their work on a series of short and intermediate films, students forge the fundamental skills of visual storytelling. Each student's experience culminates with a senior project in which advanced students write, cast, direct, and edit their own thesis films. These projects may be entirely from the imagination, or they may document the real world. These finished works are produced and owned by the students, and many are distributed and celebrated far beyond the confines of our campus, through the exciting world of festivals, theatrical, television, and other channels of local, national, and international exhibition.

RECORDING ARTS
Department chair: Barbara Kelly
Focus/emphasis: The program is within the School of Film and Television for a good reason: we give equal emphasis to film/television sound and music engineering/production. Given the enormous influence of these media, it is vital that these studies are given perspective by courses in LMU's liberal arts core curriculum. Recording arts students are also required to take one music class that deals with the fundamentals of music theory. In upper-division courses, students study the science of sound behavior, reproduction, and modification. They learn audio techniques that apply to both film/television sound and music recording. The SFTV soundstages, studios, and audio workstations are the laboratories where students put their knowledge and creativity to work and build a portfolio. Each recording arts student gains experience with film and television sound production and produces an advanced multitrack music recording as a senior project. Because the music portion of the Recording Arts Program emphasizes the working relationship between the engineer/producer and the music artist, recording arts students do not perform and record their own music, but must seek out talented musicians and produce the best possible version of the work of others.

SCREENWRITING

Department chair: Barbara Kelly

Focus/emphasis: Students begin with a solid foundation in the liberal arts, taking classes in the university core that range from college writing, literature, and history to mathematics, philosophy, theology, and the social sciences, to deepen and broaden their capacity to communicate their world perspective to audiences. Once students begin their screenwriting major, they are encouraged to delve deep into their imaginations and their personal lives to come up with stories that will entertain, amuse, uplift, and even challenge audiences. To actualize these stories, students are introduced to the basic elements of screenwriting, learning about character, dialogue, plotting, visual writing, and classic and alternative structures. In intermediate and advanced courses, students write and rewrite feature-length screenplays, study genres, take classes in sitcom and dramatic television writing, and learn how to adapt stories to suit different media.

LYNCHBURG COLLEGE

1501 Lakeside Drive, Lynchburg, VA 24501
Phone: 434-544-8300 **E-mail:** admissions@lynchburg.edu
Website: www.lynchburg.edu

Campus Life

Environment: City. **Calendar:** Semester.

Students and Faculty
(All Undergraduate Programs)

Enrollment: 2,428. **Student Body:** 61% female, 39% male, 36% out-of-state. African American 8%, Asian 2%, Caucasian 76%, Hispanic 3%. Student/faculty ratio: 13:1. 148 full-time faculty, 76% hold PhDs. 100% faculty teach undergrads.

Admissions
(All Undergraduate Programs)

Freshman Admissions Requirements: Test(s) required: SAT or ACT. Average high school GPA: 3.06. 13% in top tenth, 39% in top quarter. SAT Math (25/75 percentile): 460/560. SAT Verbal (25/75 percentile): 470/560. Projected SAT Writing (25/75 percentile): 540/620. *Academic units required:* 4 English, 3 math, 3 science (2 science labs), 2 foreign language, 2 social studies, 2 history. Early decision application deadline: 11/15. Regular notification: Rolling.

Costs and Financial Aid
(All Undergraduate Programs)

Annual tuition $23,700. Room & board $6,400. Required fees $545. Average book expense $600. **Financial Aid Statistics:** % freshmen/undergrads who receive any aid: 97/95. % freshmen/undergrads who receive need-based scholarship or grant aid: 63/63. % freshmen/undergrads who receive need-based self-help aid: 57/58. Priority financial aid filing deadline: 3/1. Financial aid notification on or about: 3/5.

TV/Film/Digital Media Studies Programs

Number of undergraduates in these programs: 9
Degrees conferred to these majors: BA.
Number of full-time faculty in these programs: 1
Number of part-time faculty in these programs: 3
Equipment and facilities: Television studio, Adobe Premiere nonlinear editing stations, broadcast quality digital camcorders, CNN NewSource and DBS NewsPath affiliate feeds available for student use.
Other awards of note: College Emmy.
Career development services: Career counseling, internship listings, job fairs, job listings.
Notable alumni: Visit www.lynchburg.edu/academic/commstud/alumni.htm for a listing of notable alumni.

In Their Own Words

Students run Eye on LC, a cable video news-magazine. Students also do training videos, corporate and nonprofit organization videos, and other projects. Several students have obtained internships for George Michael Sports Machine.

LYNN UNIVERSITY

3601 North Military Trail, Boca Raton, FL 33431-5598
Phone: 561-237-7000 **E-mail:** admission@lynn.edu
Website: www.lynn.edu

Campus Life
Environment: City. **Calendar:** Semester.

Students and Faculty
(All Undergraduate Programs)
Enrollment: 2,761. **Student Body:** 51% female, 49% male, 56% out-of-state, 14% international (82 countries represented). African American 6%, Caucasian 50%, Hispanic 7%. Student/faculty ratio: 17:1. 93 full-time faculty, 62% hold PhDs. 92% faculty teach undergrads.

Admissions
(All Undergraduate Programs)
Freshman Admissions Requirements: Test(s) required: SAT or ACT. Average high school GPA: 2.59. 8% in top tenth, 33% in top quarter. SAT Math (25/75 percentile): 400/520. SAT Verbal (25/75 percentile): 410/510. Projected SAT Writing (25/75 percentile): 480/570. *Academic units required:* 4 English, 4 math, 4 science, 2 social studies, 2 history. Regular notification: Rolling.

Costs and Financial Aid
(All Undergraduate Programs)
Annual tuition $26,200. Room & board $9,650. Required fees $1,000. Average book expense $800. **Financial Aid Statistics:** % freshmen/undergrads who receive any aid: 71/72. % freshmen/undergrads who receive need-based scholarship or grant aid: 32/41. % freshmen/undergrads who receive need-based self-help aid: 29/36. Priority financial aid filing deadline: 3/1. Financial aid notification on or about: 2/1.

TV/Film/Digital Media Studies Programs
Number of undergraduates in these programs: 250
Number of 2005 graduates from these programs: 47
Degrees conferred to these majors: BA.

Also available at Lynn University: MS, BSD (Bachelor of Science in Design).
Number of full-time faculty in these programs: 19
Number of part-time faculty in these programs: 13
Equipment and facilities: Main Studio and Control Room—SDI video equipment, including three stages, five cameras with TelePrompTers, 24-input video switcher, monitor bank, CG, 96-channel digital audio, IFB. Field equipment—standard and high-definition video cameras. Editing facilities—four editing labs with 52 editing stations using Final Cut Pro and Avid, along with MAYAanimation.

% of graduates currently employed in related field: 70
Career development services: Career counseling, internship listings, job fairs, job listings.
Notable alumni: Lisa Gangel (2004), sports anchor/reporter, KING-TV, Seattle, WA; Jason Davis (2003), bureau chief, WJHG, Panama City, FL; Sheena Foster (2004), assignment editor, WPTV, West Palm Beach, FL; Michelle Jacobacci (2004), associate news producer, WPBS, West Palm Beach, FL.

In Their Own Words
Lynn University's College of International Communication provides students with the knowledge, skills, and experience necessary to build successful communications careers in the global media marketplace. The program includes state-of-the-art radio/television/film production studios and equipment, as well as a professionally oriented teaching faculty. The scholar-in-residence and guest lecture programs feature national media practitioners such as George F. Will, Judy Woodruff, Sidney Kraus, Robert Novak, Wolf Blitzer, and Anderson Cooper.

POPULAR PROGRAMS

BROADCASTING
Number of full-time faculty: 4
Number of part-time faculty: 2

FILM STUDIES
Number of full-time faculty: 4
Number of part-time faculty: 2

JOURNALISM
Number of full-time faculty: 3
Number of part-time faculty: 2

ADVERTISING AND PUBLIC RELATIONS
Number of full-time faculty: 3
Number of part-time faculty: 2

GRAPHIC DESIGN
Number of full-time faculty: 1
Number of part-time faculty: 2

PHOTOGRAPHY
Number of full-time faculty: 1
Number of part-time faculty: 2

DRAMA
Number of full-time faculty: 1

INTERNATIONAL COMMUNICATION
Number of full-time faculty: 2

COMPUTER ANIMATION
Number of part-time faculty: 1

MARIST COLLEGE
3399 North Road, Poughkeepsie, NY 12601-1387
Phone: 845-575-3226 **E-mail:** admissions@marist.edu
Website: www.marist.edu

Campus Life
Environment: Town. **Calendar:** Semester.

Students and Faculty
(All Undergraduate Programs)
Enrollment: 4,851. **Student Body:** 57% female, 43% male, 40% out-of-state. African American 3%, Asian 2%, Caucasian 78%, Hispanic 6%. Student/faculty ratio: 15:1. 201 full-time faculty, 83% hold PhDs. 98% faculty teach undergrads.

Admissions
(All Undergraduate Programs)
Freshman Admissions Requirements: Test(s) required: SAT or ACT; ACT with Writing component. Average high school GPA: 3.4. 29% in top tenth, 70% in top quarter. SAT Math (25/75 percentile): 550/640. SAT Verbal (25/75 percentile): 540/620. Projected SAT Writing (25/75 percentile): 600/660. *Academic units required:* 4 English, 3 math, 3 science (2 science labs), 2 foreign language, 2 social studies, 1 history, 2 academic electives. Early decision application deadline: 11/15. Regular application deadline: 2/15. Regular notification: 3/15.

Costs and Financial Aid
(All Undergraduate Programs)
Annual tuition $20,712. Room & board $9,364. Required fees $620.
Financial Aid Statistics: % freshmen/undergrads who receive any aid: 90/86. % freshmen/undergrads who receive need-based scholarship or grant aid: 61/58. % freshmen/undergrads who receive need-based self-help aid: 46/50. Priority financial aid filing deadline: 2/15. Financial aid filing deadline: 5/1. Financial aid notification on or about: 3/15.

TV/Film/Digital Media Studies Programs
Number of undergraduates in these programs: 324
Number of 2005 graduates from these programs: 100
Degrees conferred to these majors: BA, BS.
Number of full-time faculty in these programs: 10
Number of part-time faculty in these programs: 6
Equipment and facilities: Nonlinear editing stations; two 3-camera TV broadcast studios; two audio labs; 10-field production rigs; two digital multimedia labs; satellite downlink.

% of graduates who pursue further study within 5 years: 15
% of graduates currently employed in related field: 60
Career development services: Alumni networking opportunities, career counseling, internship listings,

job fairs, job listings, online interview and resume resources, preparation and advising for graduate school.

Famous alumni: J.W. Stewart, Brandon Tierney, Ian O'Connor.

Notable alumni: Michael J. McCarthy (1982), partner, Sports Capital Partners; Bernadette Grey (1984), editor in chief, Scholastic Inc.; Robert LaForty, production manager, *The Early Show*, CBS News; James Baumann, vice president, media, The Advertising Council Inc.; Christopher S. Mullen (1986), associate director, *The Young and the Restless*; Paul Murnane, news anchor, WCBS NEWSRADIO 880; Andrew Boris (1994) morning show host/music director, WRRV-FM; Rex Dickson (1995), game designer, Electronic Arts; Gregory Bibb (1996), president, Hantz Group Sports and Entertainment, LLC; Jonathan Reiss (2000), associate producer, History Channel en Español, A&E Television Networks.

In Their Own Words

The Communication Internship Program operates year-round and offers students the chance to work with dozens of major media companies in New York City. Each year more than 200 Marist students intern with television networks, film companies, syndicated radio shows, major magazines, public relations firms, and advertising agencies, as well as major New York sports teams. The program is highly flexible; many students do two or more internships, blending field experience with course work. Also, the School of Communication supports an International Internship Program that allows students to do internships as part of their study abroad plans in England, Ireland, and Australia. Non-Marist students can take advantage of the college's extensive contacts through the innovative New York Media Experience Program, which brings competitive students to New York City for a full-time semester of internship and study during fall and spring. The Communication Program recently added a specialization in video gaming to its interactive media concentration.

POPULAR PROGRAMS

RADIO, TELEVISION, FILM

Department chair: Sue Lawrence, PhD
Number of full-time faculty: 7
Number of part-time faculty: 2
Focus/emphasis: Through courses and internships, the program combines a strong liberal arts background with a professional focus. Inherent in the program's courses and internships is the integration of communication theories and the liberal arts tradition.

DIGITAL MEDIA

Department chair: Richard Lewis, MFA
Number of full-time faculty: 3
Number of part-time faculty: 4
Focus/emphasis: The program is designed to allow students the opportunity to explore, in depth, the field of digital media under the guidance of recognized working artists, designers, and educators. It combines courses in digital media with a balanced curriculum of studio art, art history, and liberal arts courses. Students will gain broad-based training in a wide range of new media, along with an understanding of the concepts, historical background, and heritage in the traditional media.

GAMING/INTERACTIVE MEDIA

Department chair: Sue Lawrence, PhD
Number of full-time faculty: 2
Focus/emphasis: The concentration emphasizes the analysis, critique, design, and production of multimedia communication. Drawing on the School of Communication and Arts' wide array of expertise in art, communication theory, graphics design, and media production, this concentration prepares students to create content for the digital and Internet technologies that will shape the commerce and culture of the 21st century.

MARQUETTE UNIVERSITY

PO Box 1881, Milwaukee, WI 53201-1881
Phone: 414-288-7302 **E-mail:** admissions@Marquette.edu
Website: www.marquette.edu

Campus Life
Environment: Metropolis. **Calendar:** Semester.

Students and Faculty
(All Undergraduate Programs)
Enrollment: 7,709. **Student Body:** 55% female, 45% male, 52% out-of-state, 2% international (80 countries represented). African American 5%, Asian 4%, Caucasian 85%, Hispanic 4%. Student/faculty ratio: 15:1. 592 full-time faculty, 88% hold PhDs. 77% faculty teach undergrads.

Admissions
(All Undergraduate Programs)
Freshman Admissions Requirements: Test(s) required: SAT or ACT; ACT with Writing component. 34% in top tenth, 65% in top quarter. SAT Math (25/75 percentile): 540/660. SAT Verbal (25/75 percentile): 540/650. Projected SAT Writing (25/75 percentile): 600/690. *Academic units required:* 4 English, 2 math, 2 science (2 science labs), 2 foreign language, 2 social studies, 2 academic electives. Regular notification: 1/31.

Costs and Financial Aid
(All Undergraduate Programs)
Annual tuition $22,950. Room & board $7,720. Required fees $396. Average book expense $900. **Financial Aid Statistics:** % freshmen/undergrads who receive any aid: 88/85. % freshmen/undergrads who receive need-based scholarship or grant aid: 54/52. % freshmen/undergrads who receive need-based self-help aid: 50/49. Financial aid notification on or about: 3/20.

TV/Film/Digital Media Studies Programs
Number of undergraduates in these programs: 184
Number of 2005 graduates from these programs: 44
Degrees conferred to these majors: BA.

Equipment and facilities: Marquette's broadcast facilities includes two TV studios, nine video-editing suites, three audio studios, computer graphics platforms, and advanced interactive digital equipment.
Career development services: Alumni networking opportunities, career counseling, internship listings, job fairs, job listings.

In Their Own Words
In your first year, you'll work in our production facilities and computer labs to produce radio, TV, and Internet programming—something freshmen at other universities rarely get to do. Real-world experience, crucial to professional placement after graduation, is yours through internships in Milwaukee and other major media markets like New York, Chicago, Los Angeles, and Atlanta. Students have worked with radio and television stations throughout the country, as well as programs like ABC World News Tonight, Entertainment Tonight, Late Show with David Letterman, All My Children, The Young and the Restless, and 20/20.

MARYLAND INSTITUTE COLLEGE OF ART

1300 Mount Royal Avenue, Baltimore, MD 21217
Phone: 410-225-2222 **E-mail:** admissions@mica.edu
Website: www.mica.edu

Campus Life
Environment: Metropolis. **Calendar:** Semester.

Students and Faculty
(All Undergraduate Programs)
Enrollment: 1,492. **Student Body:** 62% female, 38% male, 80% out-of-state, 5% international (48 countries represented). African American 4%, Asian 8%, Caucasian 68%, Hispanic 5%. Student/faculty ratio: 10:1. 118 full-time faculty, 86% hold PhDs. 95% faculty teach undergrads.

Admissions
(All Undergraduate Programs)

Average high school GPA: 3.51. 29% in top tenth, 62% in top quarter. SAT Math (25/75 percentile): 510/620. SAT Verbal (25/75 percentile): 540/650. Projected SAT Writing (25/75 percentile): 600/690. *Academic units required:* 4 English, 2 math, 2 science (1 science lab), 4 social studies, 3 history, 6 academic electives, 2 studio art, 2 academic electives. Early decision application deadline: 11/15. Regular application deadline: 2/15. Regular notification: 3/15.

Costs and Financial Aid
(All Undergraduate Programs)

Annual tuition $26,140. Room & board $7,530. Required fees $780. Average book expense $1,400. **Financial Aid Statistics:** % freshmen/undergrads who receive any aid: 81/74. % freshmen/undergrads who receive need-based scholarship or grant aid: 59/62. % freshmen/undergrads who receive need-based self-help aid: 52/55. Financial aid filing deadline: 3/1. Financial aid notification on or about: 4/15.

TV/Film/Digital Media Studies Programs

Number of undergraduates in these programs: 118
Number of 2005 graduates from these programs: 8
Degrees conferred to these majors: BA.
Number of full-time faculty in these programs: 8
Number of part-time faculty in these programs: 14
Equipment and facilities: A television studio, two Steinbecks, 27 digital video-editing stations, two sound recording studios.

% of graduates who pursue further study within 5 years: 23
% of graduates currently employed in related field: 60
Career development services: Alumni networking opportunities, career counseling, internship listings, job listings.
Notable alumni: Armando Salas, commercial cinematographer.

In Their Own Words

Internships at NPR, MTV, Discovery Channel, and with nationally known artists and filmmakers. Film series with filmmakers D.A. Pennebaker, Barry Levinson, Bruce Sinofsky, and Christine Vachon.

POPULAR PROGRAMS

EXPERIMENTAL ANIMATION

Department chair: Jamy Sheridan
Number of full-time faculty: 3
Number of part-time faculty: 1
Focus/emphasis: MICA approaches experimental animation as an art form, empowering students to create eloquent and original contemporary artworks through an understanding not only of the technology for production, but also the historical sources and contemporary social and artistic context for their work.

VIDEO

Department chair: Patrick Wright
Number of full-time faculty: 2
Number of part-time faculty: 9
Focus/emphasis: MICA's major in video allows students to address the particular technical and conceptual concerns of work in video and film with courses that explore the full range of opportunities for creating original artwork featuring the moving image. Major course work combines a strong foundation of technical practice with an understanding of the history of film and video and fosters the conceptual and intellectual sophistication necessary to develop a personal body of work. As a major in video at MICA, you will gain the skills to produce, examine, and critique moving images of all kinds and will develop strong problem-solving and production coordination skills.

INTERACTIVE MEDIA

Department chair: Esther Schooler
Number of full-time faculty: 3
Number of part-time faculty: 4

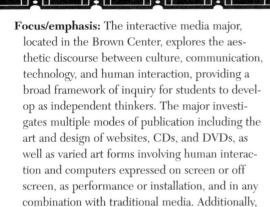

Focus/emphasis: The interactive media major, located in the Brown Center, explores the aesthetic discourse between culture, communication, technology, and human interaction, providing a broad framework of inquiry for students to develop as independent thinkers. The major investigates multiple modes of publication including the art and design of websites, CDs, and DVDs, as well as varied art forms involving human interaction and computers expressed on screen or off screen, as performance or installation, and in any combination with traditional media. Additionally, students will have the opportunity to create artwork that engages the audience online and offline through remote systems, micro-controllers, and programming.

MIDDLE TENNESSEE STATE UNIVERSITY

Office of Admissions, Murfreesboro, TN 37132
Phone: 800-433-6878 **E-mail:** admissions@mtsu.edu
Website: www.mtsu.edu

Campus Life
Environment: Village. **Calendar:** Semester.

Students and Faculty
(All Undergraduate Programs)
Student Body: 5% out-of-state. 90% faculty teach undergrads.

Admissions
(All Undergraduate Programs)
Average high school GPA: 2.96. 17% in top tenth, 51% in top quarter. Regular application deadline: 7/1. Regular notification: Rolling.

Costs and Financial Aid
(All Undergraduate Programs)
Annual in-state tuition $1,906. Out-of-state tuition $6,732. Room & board $3,030. Required fees $154. Average book expense $600.

TV/Film/Digital Media Studies Programs
Number of undergraduates in these programs: There are more than 775 electronic media communications majors.
Degrees conferred to these majors: BS.
Also available at Middle Tennessee State University: MFA, MS.
Number of full-time faculty in these programs: 65
Number of part-time faculty in these programs: 19
Equipment and facilities: Students get hands-on experience in television and radio studios; linear and nonlinear video-editing facilities; a mobile production lab; audio production labs; electronic newsrooms; and a 100,000-watt NPR-affiliated FM and a FCC licensed student radio station. A cable channel can be viewed by regular subscribers to Murfreesboro's cable TV system.
Other awards of note: MTSU students were honored at the 17th Annual Southeast Regional Emmy Awards. Matthew Pessoni, Scott Pessoni, Jason Bailey, and Rachel Pickel won the student production award for their piece called *Investigative Explorer.*
Career development services: Internship listings, internships.
Notable alumni: Ken Strickland, White House producer, NBC; Steve Dickert, vice president, Tennessee Titans Radio Network; Holly Thompson, anchor, WSMV-TV.

In Their Own Words
MTTV (Middle Tennessee Television) is a student-operated station that provides original student programming and a local newscast. Students are able to produce, write, direct, edit, or be talent on one of several student programs. The station is located in a fully equipped studio with three cameras, a video switcher, an audio board, and digital video effects. The International Television Association (organization dedicated to video production) student chapter holds monthly meetings bringing in speakers or holding workshops about production and job opportunities in the broadcast and

nonbroadcast industry. *The students are encouraged to work on special projects with professional ITVA members, increasing the opportunities for networking.*

POPULAR PROGRAMS

ELECTRONIC MEDIA COMMUNICATION
Department chair: Robert Spires
Number of full-time faculty: 19
Focus/emphasis: We are one of three departments in the accredited College of Mass Communication. The program is more than 775 majors strong and growing. We are studying and teaching digital media communication, television and radio production, electronic media journalism and management, digital animation, digital imaging, and photography. While we are heavy users of technology, we base our curriculum on mass communication principles. We use state-of-the-art technology to practice the creation of content based on those principles.

MEDIA DESIGN
Department chair: Dr. Carol J. Pardun
Number of full-time faculty: 3
Focus/emphasis: Media design is the major for students who enjoy creating, have a keen, inquisitive nature, and like working with words, tools, and concepts that enhance communication. A concentration in the School of Journalism at Middle Tennessee State University, media design is a fast-evolving component of the information revolution. At MTSU, media design involves all the elements of visual communication, from traditional typography to digital design for newspapers, magazines, and the Web. The sequence's main emphasis is publication design, including print and interactive media that deliver information, opinion, and entertainment through newspapers, magazines, books, newsletters, brochures, and the World Wide Web. Students learn creative skills using current technology in finalizing their visual presentations. The project-centered approach of the program requires students to use state-of-the-art computers extensively, with emphasis on developing creative solutions to practical design problems. Students use the latest Macintosh computer systems to arrange type and illustrations into successful design packages. The computer labs are wired to the Internet for research and design resources. Each lab contains the latest versions of all the major design applications, such as Macromedia Freehand, QuarkXPress, Adobe Photoshop, Adobe GoLive, and Adobe Illustrator.

MIDDLEBURY COLLEGE
The Emma Willard House, Middlebury, VT 05753-6002
Phone: 802-443-3000 **E-mail:** admissions@middlebury.edu
Website: www.middlebury.edu

Campus Life
Environment: Village. **Calendar:** 4-1-4.

Students and Faculty
(All Undergraduate Programs)
Enrollment: 2,415. **Student Body:** 51% female, 49% male, 92% out-of-state, 9% international (66 countries represented). African American 3%, Asian 7%, Caucasian 69%, Hispanic 5%. Student/faculty ratio: 9:1. 254 full-time faculty, 94% hold PhDs. 100% faculty teach undergrads.

Admissions
(All Undergraduate Programs)
Freshman Admissions Requirements: Test(s) required: SAT and SAT Subject Tests or ACT. Average high school GPA: 4. 84% in top tenth, 96% in top quarter. SAT Math (25/75 percentile): 650/730. SAT Verbal (25/75 percentile): 630/745. Early decision application deadline: 11/15. Regular application deadline: 1/1. Regular notification: 4/1.

Costs and Financial Aid
(All Undergraduate Programs)
Comprehensive fee $42,120. Average book expense $750.

Financial Aid Statistics: % freshmen/undergrads who receive any aid: 41/41. % freshmen/undergrads who receive need-based scholarship or grant aid: 45/43. % freshmen/undergrads who receive need-based self-help aid: 45/43. Priority financial aid filing deadline: 11/15. Financial aid filing deadline: 1/1. Financial aid notification on or about: 4/1.

TV/Film/Digital Media Studies Programs

Number of undergraduates in these programs: 32

Number of 2005 graduates from these programs: 13

Degrees conferred to these majors: BA.

Number of full-time faculty in these programs: 8

Equipment and facilities: The program offers student access to a sophisticated array of video production technology, including seven Final Cut Pro digital editing stations dedicated to students enrolled in FMMC production classes; 16 basic digital camera packages dedicated to our introductory production course, "Sight and Sound I;" and eight prosumer and professional camera packages for students working in advanced classes or on independent projects. Our equipment room is also equipped with light kits, microphones, camera-mounting hardware, including a car mount and a mini-steadicam. Students in the department are in the process of creating a student-run production entity that will produce its first project in Fall 2006. We are anticipating the construction of a new building that will house the program soon. The new facility will include a room dedicated to new media production, a production stage, and additional editing facilities.

Career development services: Alumni networking opportunities, career counseling, internship listings, job listings.

Notable alumni: Jim Bruce (1996), film editor, *Refugee All Stars* (winner, American Film Institute Film Festival 2005, Grand Jury Prize, Best Documentary); James Burke (1984), executive producer/director, Entitled Entertainment, *13 Conversations About One Thing* (starring Matthew McConaughey, John Turturro, Amy Irving, and Alan Arkin), *Levity* (starring Billy Bob Thornton, Morgan Freeman, Holly Hunter, and Kirsten Dunst), *Aurora Borealis* (starring Joshua Jackson, Donald Sutherland, Juliette Lewis, and Louise Fletcher), and *Borderline* (winner of awards at the Charleston World/Festival and the Houston Film Festival) and part of producer team on the top award-winning Broadway production of Eugene O'Neill's *Long Day's Journey Into Night* (starring Venessa Redgrave, Brian Dennehy, and Phillip Seymour Hoffman); David Collard (1994), writer, *Family Guy*, *Annapolis*, *Out of Time*; John Morrissey (1972), producer, The Truman-Morrissey Co., *Havoc*, *11:14*, *The Badge*, *What's the Worst That Could Happen*, *American History X*, *Booty Call*, *Dr. Jekyll and Ms. Hyde*, *The Tie That Binds*, *Deep Down*, *Sensation*, *9 1/2 Ninjas*; Bee Ottinger (1970), video editor, music videos (artists include Jennifer Lopez, Tracy Chapman, Christina Agullierra, Janet Jackson, Michael Jackson, The Bangles); commercials (for clients such as Chrysler, Reebok, Calvin Klein, Nissan, Toyota); Rob Perez (1995), freelance writer, feature film screenwriter, *40 Days and 40 Nights*; Shawn Ryan (1988), playwright/screenwriter, creator, and executive producer, *The Shield*, *The Unit*, *Power Money Fame Sex (A User's Guide)*, *Decoy*, *Angel*, *Nash Bridges*, and *Life with Louis*; Damien Saccani (1996), executive producer, producer, and line producer, *The Turning*, *The Express*, *Oldboy*, *The Tale of Despereaux*, *Catch That Kid*, *Out of Time*, *Alice*, *The Killer's Game*, *Annapolis*; Rick Shaine (1969), film editor and owner, *Lipstick*, *Enigma*, *Pitch Black*, *Enough*, *Always Outnumbered*, *Theodore Rex*, *Extreme Measures*, *Blink*, *Safe Passage*, *Blind Side*.

In Their Own Words

The program sponsors internships in NYC, LA, and elsewhere during the January term and also in the summer. Our extensive alumni contacts in media help place our students. Also available is a semester abroad program with the University of Southern California or New York University. This enables students at our small liberal arts college to have a semester at a major university's film program. Lastly, our courses in video production, screenwriting, and other production courses are conducted in small workshop settings with 12 students or less.

MONMOUTH COLLEGE (IL)

700 East Broadway, Monmouth, IL 61462
Phone: 309-457-2131 **E-mail:** admit@monm.edu
Website: www.monm.edu

Campus Life
Environment: Village. **Calendar:** Semester.

Students and Faculty
(All Undergraduate Programs)
Enrollment: 1,325. **Student Body:** 53% female, 47% male, 8% out-of-state, 1% international (15 countries represented). African American 3%, Caucasian 91%, Hispanic 3%. Student/faculty ratio: 13:1. 87 full-time faculty, 76% hold PhDs. 100% faculty teach undergrads.

Admissions
(All Undergraduate Programs)
Freshman Admissions Requirements: Test(s) required: SAT or ACT; SAT and SAT Subject Tests or ACT. Average high school GPA: 3.28. 12% in top tenth, 37% in top quarter. SAT Math (25/75 percentile): 560/580. SAT Verbal (25/75 percentile): 550/560. Projected SAT Writing (25/75 percentile): 610/620. *Academic units required:* 4 English, 3 math, 2 science (1 science lab), 1 social studies, 2 history. Regular notification: Rolling.

Costs and Financial Aid
(All Undergraduate Programs)
Annual tuition $21,100. Room & board $6,150. Average book expense $650.
Financial Aid Statistics: % freshmen/undergrads who receive any aid: 98/98. % freshmen/undergrads who receive need-based scholarship or grant aid: 76/81. % freshmen/undergrads who receive need-based self-help aid: 58/58. Priority financial aid filing deadline: 3/1. Financial aid notification on or about: 2/15.

TV/Film/Digital Media Studies Programs
Number of undergraduates in these programs: Approximately 50
Number of 2005 graduates from these programs: 8
Degrees conferred to these majors: BA.

Number of full-time faculty in these programs: 7
Number of part-time faculty in these programs: 3
Equipment and facilities: Television studio (newly all digital), 20-station computer-based editing lab, student-operated/-managed radio and TV (cable) programming in nicely equipped studios.

% of graduates who pursue further study within 5 years: 35
% of graduates currently employed in related field: 80
Career development services: Alumni networking opportunities; career counseling; central resource(s) for employers to browse headshots, writing samples, reels; internship listings; job fairs; job listings. Each major develops an electronic, Web-based portfolio highlighting their work and abilities.
Famous alumni: Helen Wagner.
Notable alumni: Dwight Tierney, head of Viacom Europe, Bonnie Shaddock, independent television producer.

In Their Own Words
Joe Angotti, former head of NBC News and executive producer of the NBC Nightly News with Tom Brokaw is on our faculty, as are several faculty from top university media programs (e.g. Iowa, Ohio University). All students do professional internships in their prefered career area, and there are lots of opportunities for undergraduates to begin hands-on experience in radio, TV, or filmmaking from their first semester on, with opportunites to rise to leadership positions with on-campus media.

POPULAR PROGRAMS

COMMUNICATION AND MEDIA
Department chair: Dr. Lee McGaan
Number of full-time faculty: 5
Number of part-time faculty: 2
Focus/emphasis: This program prepares students for careers that require excellent message development skills, especially in media contexts.

PUBLIC RELATIONS

Department chair: Dr. Lee McGaan
Number of full-time faculty: 6
Focus/emphasis: This program prepares students for careers that involve persuasion and image creation in public relations, marketing, advertising, and related fields.

THEATER

Department chair: Dr. Lee McGaan
Number of full-time faculty: 3
Number of part-time faculty: 1
Focus/emphasis: This program provides students wth a general background in performance and production skills suitable for live theater and film.

MONTANA STATE UNIVERSITY–BOZEMAN

New Student Services, PO Box 172190, Bozeman, MT 59717-2190
Phone: 406-994-2452 **E-mail:** admissions@montana.edu
Website: www.montana.edu

Campus Life

Environment: Town. **Calendar:** Semester.

Students and Faculty
(All Undergraduate Programs)

Enrollment: 10,771. **Student Body:** 47% female, 53% male, 30% out-of-state, 1% international (59 countries represented). Asian 1%, Caucasian 90%, Hispanic 1%, Native American 2%. Student/faculty ratio 16:1. 553 full-time faculty. 95% faculty teach undergrads.

Admissions
(All Undergraduate Programs)

Freshman Admissions Requirements: Test(s) required: SAT or ACT. Average high school GPA: 3.31. 17% in top tenth, 41% in top quarter. SAT Math (25/75 percentile): 500/630. SAT Verbal (25/75 percentile): 490/610. Projected SAT Writing (25/75 percentile): 550/660. *Academic units required:* 4 English, 3 math, 2 science (2 science lab), 3 social studies. Two years chosen from the following: foreign language, computer science, visual/performing arts, or approved vocational education units.

Costs and Financial Aid
(All Undergraduate Programs)

Annual in-state tuition $5,221. Out-of-state tuition $14,945. Room & board $6,156. Average book expense $980.

Financial Aid Statistics: % freshmen/undergrads who receive any aid: 53/53. % freshmen/undergrads who receive need-based scholarship or grant aid: 42/40. % freshmen/undergrads who receive need-based self-help aid: 43/46. Priority financial aid filing deadline: 3/1. Financial aid notification on or about: 4/1.

TV/Film/Digital Media Studies Programs

Number of undergraduates in these programs: 547
Number of 2005 graduates from these programs: 90
Degrees conferred to these majors: BA.
Also available at Montana State University—Bozeman: MFA.
Number of full-time faculty in these programs: 17
Number of part-time faculty in these programs: 6
Equipment and facilities: Includes two large soundstages, complete film and video equipment facilities, lighting studios, darkrooms, a 55 theater, and edit bays for film and sound editing.
Career development services: Alumni networking opportunities, career counseling, internship listings, job fairs, job listings.
Famous alumni: Craig Kilborn, host of *Late Late Show with Craig Kilborn*. Faculty: Bill Pullman, actor and producer.
Notable alumni: Faculty: Stephanie Campbell: http://mta.montana.edu/docs/people/campbell.html. Bill Neff: http://mta.montana.edu/docs/people/neff.html.

In Their Own Words
Please visit the following URL:
http://mta.montana.edu/docs/events.html.

POPULAR PROGRAMS

The Department of Media and Theater Arts offers students two emphases: Motion Picture/Video/Theater and Photography. Each is described in what follows:

MOTION PICTURE/VIDEO/THEATER

Department chair: Joel Jahnke
Number of full-time faculty: 5
Number of part-time faculty: 1
Focus/emphasis: The curriculum begins with first-year foundation courses emphasizing an understanding and analysis of motion pictures and theater and introduces students to the actual production process. Motion picture/video/theater requires that students meet specific requirements (see MPVT gate requirements below) and complete a series of eight skills classes related to film and theater production. In the third year, students who qualify by attaining a minimum average GPA in their MTA requirements in the first two years build on these basics in production process workshops that are required of all students in fiction, nonfiction, and stage. Additional course work in advanced film studies as well as professional practices courses and internship options compliment the upper-division requirements. The individual student's capstone senior project is approved by the entire faculty and developed in consultation with a team of faculty advisors assigned to the project through a workshop process.

PHOTOGRAPHY

Department chair: Joel Jahnke
Number of full-time faculty: 3
Focus/emphasis: The curriculum provides both artistic and applied approaches to the medium. This comprehensive four-year program includes course work in traditional silver-based and alternative processes and a growing emphasis on digital technologies.

SCIENCE AND NATURAL HISTORY FILMMAKING

Department chair: Joel Jahnke
Number of full-time faculty: 1

Number of part-time faculty: 2
Focus/emphasis: The graduate program is the first program of its type in the world and remains the largest and the most well-known. Students in the program have had their work broadcast in many major venues such as The Discovery Channel, National Geographic, The Science Channel, CNN, *Sixty Minutes II*, Larry King Live, *CBS Evening News*, and *NBC Nightly News*. They have produced films for the National Park Service, the National Science Foundation, the Department of Agriculture, NOAA, NASA, and such nonprofit organizations as the Wildlife Conservation Society, the Sierra Club, the Audubon Society, and the Nature Conservancy. Students' work has appeared in major museums, schools, and cultural venues too numerous to count. Our students literally travel the world with explorers and scientists to make films from the Pribilof Islands to Easter Island, the Galapagos, Australia, Japan, Mongolia, Africa, Chile, and under the sea. Students in the program continue to win an impressive array of major awards for their work, including a student Emmy, Tellies, and the best of show in major film festivals. Our mission is to provide new generations of filmmakers with a formal education and experience in science, engineering, or technology who have the knowledge to create accurate and interesting programs that advance the public understanding of science. Students in the program come from a wide variety of backgrounds, including the physical sciences, the social sciences, engineering, technology, medicine, and law. Applicants are not expected to have formal film or video experience (although any experience, amateur or professional, may help your application). Applicants to the program must have either a degree in science, engineering, or technology or, for candidates with degrees from other disciplines, at least a declared minor in science, engineering, or technology. The applications committee will consider applications for individuals without a declared minor provided the candidate can adequately demonstrate having completed the equivalent of one. (A minor is defined as a minimum of 30 hours of study in a concentrated area.)

MOUNT HOLYOKE COLLEGE

Office of Admissions, Newhall Center, South Hadley, MA 01075
Phone: 413-538-2023 **E-mail:** admission@mtholyoke.edu
Website: www.mtholyoke.edu

Campus Life
Environment: Village. **Calendar:** Semester.

Students and Faculty
(All Undergraduate Programs)
Enrollment: 2,064. **Student Body:** 75% out-of-state, 14% international (69 countries represented). African American 4%, Asian 12%, Caucasian 52%, Hispanic 5%. Student/faculty ratio: 10:1. 207 full-time faculty, 94% hold PhDs. 100% faculty teach undergrads.

Admissions
(All Undergraduate Programs)
Average high school GPA: 3.59. 51% in top tenth, 80% in top quarter. SAT Math (25/75 percentile): 610/690. SAT Verbal (25/75 percentile): 620/710. Projected SAT Writing (25/75 percentile): 660/730. Early decision application deadline: 11/15. Regular application deadline: 1/15. Regular notification: 4/1.

Costs and Financial Aid
(All Undergraduate Programs)
Annual tuition $32,430. Room & board $9,550. Required fees $168. Average book expense $750. **Financial Aid Statistics:** % freshmen/undergrads who receive any aid: 57/63. % freshmen/undergrads who receive need-based scholarship or grant aid: 56/60. % freshmen/undergrads who receive need-based self-help aid: 54/61. Priority financial aid filing deadline: 1/15. Financial aid filing deadline: 2/1. Financial aid notification on or about: 3/25.

TV/Film/Digital Media Studies Programs
Degrees conferred to these majors: BA.
Number of full-time faculty in these programs: 22
Equipment and facilities: For more information, visit www.mtholyoke.edu/acad/film/.
Career development services: Alumni networking opportunities; career counseling; central resource(s) for employers to browse headshots, writing samples, reels; internship listings; job fairs; job listings, on-campus recruiting, workshops, five college consortium recruiting.

In Their Own Words
Film studies at Mount Holyoke introduces students to the academic study of film from a variety of critical and disciplinary perspectives. Courses combine cultural, historical, formal, and theoretical analyses of films from a range of world cinematic traditions. In addition, some possibilities for the study of film/video production are available to students at the college and at the other five college institutions.

MUHLENBERG COLLEGE

2400 West Chew Street, Allentown, PA 18104-5596
Phone: 484-664-3200 **E-mail:** admission@muhlenberg.edu
Website: www.muhlenberg.edu

Campus Life
Environment: City. **Calendar:** Semester.

Students and Faculty
(All Undergraduate Programs)
Enrollment: 2,396. **Student Body:** 58% female, 42% male, 74% out-of-state. African American 2%, Asian 2%, Caucasian 91%, Hispanic 3%. Student/faculty ratio: 12:1. 152 full-time faculty, 86% hold PhDs. 100% faculty teach undergrads.

Admissions
(All Undergraduate Programs)
Freshman Admissions Requirements: Test(s) required: ACT with Writing component. Average high school GPA: 3.44. 42% in top tenth, 82% in top quarter. SAT Math (25/75 percentile): 570/670. SAT Verbal (25/75 percentile): 560/660. Projected SAT Writing (25/75 percentile): 620/690. *Academic units required:* 4 English, 3 math, 2 science (2 science labs), 2 foreign language, 2 history, 1 academic elective. Early decision application deadline: 2/1. Regular application deadline: 2/15. Regular notification: 3/15.

Costs and Financial Aid
(All Undergraduate Programs)
Annual tuition $30,260. Room & board $12,050.
Financial Aid Statistics: % freshmen/undergrads who receive any aid: 75/78. % freshmen/undergrads who receive need-based scholarship or grant aid: 46/41. % freshmen/undergrads who receive need-based self-help aid: 30/30. Priority financial aid filing deadline: 2/15. Financial aid filing deadline: 2/15. Financial aid notification on or about: 4/1.

TV/Film/Digital Media Studies Programs
Number of undergraduates in these programs: 200
Number of 2005 graduates from these programs: 65
Degrees conferred to these majors: BA.
Number of full-time faculty in these programs: 9
Number of part-time faculty in these programs: 3
Equipment and facilities: Digital television studio equipment; digital postproduction equipment.

% of graduates who pursue further study within 5 years: 20
% of graduates currently employed in related field: 80
Career development services: Alumni networking opportunities; career counseling; central resource(s) for employers to browse headshots, writing samples, reels; internship listings; job fairs; job listings; preparation of job application materials, such as cover letters and CVs.

In Their Own Words
Students placed in broadcast industry from David Letterman Show to Montel Williams to junior management and numerous production assistant positions in New York and Los Angeles.

POPULAR PROGRAMS

MEDIA AND COMMUNICATION
Department chair: David Tafler
Number of full-time faculty: 8
Number of part-time faculty: 3
Focus/emphasis: Analysis of media and society, knowledge of media industries, to explore media production as a form of creative expression.

FILM STUDIES
Number of full-time faculty: 1
Number of part-time faculty: 6
Focus/emphasis: Interdisciplinary study of technical and expressive components of the cinematic medium, including the study of all genres and national cinemas.

MURRAY STATE UNIVERSITY
113 Sparks Hall, Murray, KY 42071-0009
Phone: 270-809-3741 **E-mail:** Admissions@murraystate.edu
Website: www.murraystate.edu

Campus Life
Environment: Village. **Calendar:** Semester.

Students and Faculty
(All Undergraduate Programs)
Enrollment: 7,937. **Student Body:** 57% female, 43% male, 28% out-of-state, 2% international (56 countries represented). African American 6%, Caucasian 90%. Student/faculty ratio: 17:1. 386 full-time faculty, 78% hold PhDs. 100% faculty teach undergrads.

Admissions
(All Undergraduate Programs)
Freshman Admissions Requirements: Test(s) required: ACT. Average high school GPA: 3.55. 28% in top tenth, 65% in top quarter. *Academic units required:* 4 English, 3 math, 3 science (1 science lab), 2 foreign language, 3 social studies, 5 academic electives, 2 art appreciation, 1/2 physical education, 1/2 health. Regular application deadline: 8/3. Regular notification: Rolling.

Costs and Financial Aid
(All Undergraduate Programs)

Annual in-state tuition $3,792. Out-of-state tuition $5,464. Room & board $4,472. Required fees $636. Average book expense $700.

Financial Aid Statistics: % freshmen/undergrads who receive any aid: 95/90. % freshmen/undergrads who receive need-based scholarship or grant aid: 34/30. % freshmen/undergrads who receive need-based self-help aid: 30/43. Priority financial aid filing deadline: 4/1. Financial aid notification on or about: 4/15.

TV/Film/Digital Media Studies Programs

Number of undergraduates in these programs: 134

Number of 2005 graduates from these programs: 15

Degrees conferred to these majors: BA, BS.

Number of full-time faculty in these programs: 2

Number of part-time faculty in these programs: 1

Equipment and facilities: Television studio, master control, ENG equipment for field and studio production, cable access outlet that carries public television programming and student programs/productions, G5 iMacs with Final Cut Pro software.

Other awards of note: Best audio production award and grand prize winner, 2005 Professional Production Competition, National Broadcasting Society, for *Christmas in the Fifties* by Professor Bob Lochte.

% of graduates who pursue further study within 5 years: 3

% of graduates currently employed in related field: 40

Career development services: Alumni networking opportunities; career counseling; central resource(s) for employers to browse headshots, writing samples, reels; electronic posting of resumes; internship listings; job fairs; job listings, networking with employers and contacts, resume workshops.

Notable alumni: Mandy Murphy, anchor/reporter, Fox 2 News, KTVI, St. Louis, has won ten Emmys and two Edward R. Murrow Awards; Brad Holbrook, co-anchor *Business Week Weekend*, has received Emmy awards and has more than two decades' experience in several major markets; Jackie Hays, anchor/reporter for WAVE-TV, Louisville, KY, has received Emmy awards and other honors, and won awards in Philadelphia; Pamela Graham, co-anchor and reporter, Channel 7, Greenville-Spartanburg, SC, was awarded the Best Anchor Award by National Federation of Press Women for five consecutive years and has received awards from AP, SCBA, and NATAS; Heather Higdon, anchor/reporter with LEX 18 in Lexington, KY; Vicki Dortch, anchor, News Channel 32, WLKY, Louisville, KY; Cindy Klose, anchor, KWCH, Wichita, KS, has also anchored and reported for CNN in Atlanta and in Champaign, IL.

In Their Own Words

Electronic media is one of four degree programs in the ACEJMC-accredited Department of Journalism & Mass Communications; internships and cooperative education experiences are strongly suggested; students have ready access to hands-on experience from freshman year forward and opportunities with the National Broadcasting Society student organization and Alpha Epsilon Rho, the honor society.

POPULAR PROGRAMS

ELECTRONIC MEDIA

Department chair: Dr. Debbie Owens, degree program head

Number of full-time faculty: 2

Number of part-time faculty: 1

Focus/emphasis: The program takes a broad approach to the various functions of electronic media. Students take courses in basic audio and video production, digital media production, scriptwriting, studio production, radio-television operations, television field production, and television program development, plus a media theory course and mass communications law.

Students Should Also Know

A variety of elective courses are offered that allow students to tailor the program to their specific

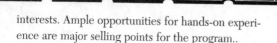

interests. Ample opportunities for hands-on experience are major selling points for the program..

NEW YORK INSTITUTE OF TECHNOLOGY

PO Box 8000, Northern Boulevard, Old Westbury, NY 11568
Phone: 516-686-7520 **E-mail:** admissions@nyit.edu
Website: www.nyit.edu

Campus Life
Environment: Village. **Calendar:** Semester.

Students and Faculty
(All Undergraduate Programs)
Enrollment: 5,141. **Student Body:** 38% female, 62% male, 10% out-of-state, 7% international. African American 11%, Asian 10%, Caucasian 33%, Hispanic 10%. Student/faculty ratio: 16:1. 218 full-time faculty, 89% hold PhDs. 90% faculty teach undergrads.

Admissions
(All Undergraduate Programs)
Freshman Admissions Requirements: Test(s) required: SAT or ACT. Average high school GPA: 3.1. SAT Math (25/75 percentile): 510/630. SAT Verbal (25/75 percentile): 470/580. Projected SAT Writing (25/75 percentile): 540/630. *Academic units required:* 4 English, 2 math, 1 science (1 science lab), 2 social studies, 7 academic electives. Regular notification: Rolling.

Costs and Financial Aid
(All Undergraduate Programs)
Annual tuition $16,926. Room & board $7,780. Required fees $300. Average book expense $1,200. **Financial Aid Statistics:** % freshmen/undergrads who receive need-based scholarship or grant aid: 56/79. % freshmen/undergrads who receive need-based self-help aid: 75/84. Priority financial aid filing deadline: 3/1. Financial aid notification on or about: 3/15.

TV/Film/Digital Media Studies Programs
Number of undergraduates in these programs: 400
Number of 2005 graduates from these programs: 100
Degrees conferred to these majors: BFA.
Also available at New York Institute of Technology: MA.
Number of full-time faculty in these programs: 19
Number of part-time faculty in these programs: 33

NEW YORK UNIVERSITY

22 Washington Square North, New York, NY 10011
Phone: 212-998-4500 **E-mail:** admissions@nyu.edu
Website: www.nyu.edu

Campus Life
Environment: Metropolis. **Calendar:** Semester.

Students and Faculty
(All Undergraduate Programs)
Enrollment: 20,150. **Student Body:** 61% female, 39% male, 58% out-of-state, 4% international (143 countries represented). African American 5%, Asian 17%, Caucasian 49%, Hispanic 8%. Student/faculty ratio: 11:1. 1,952 full-time faculty, 90% hold PhDs.

Admissions
(All Undergraduate Programs)
Freshman Admissions Requirements: Test(s) required: SAT and SAT Subject Tests or ACT; ACT with Writing component. Average high school GPA: 3.63. 68% in top tenth, 95% in top quarter. SAT Math (25/75 percentile): 620/710. SAT Verbal (25/75 percentile): 620/710. Projected SAT Writing (25/75 percentile): 660/730. *Academic units required:* 4 English, 3 math, 3 science (2 science labs), 2 foreign language, 4 history. Early decision application deadline: 11/1. Regular application deadline: 1/15. Regular notification: 4/1.

Costs and Financial Aid (All Undergraduate Programs)

Annual tuition $34,780. Room & board $11,480. Required fees $1,300. Average book expense $700. **Financial Aid Statistics:** % freshmen/undergrads who receive any aid: 60/61. % freshmen/undergrads who receive need-based scholarship or grant aid: 50/51. % freshmen/undergrads who receive need-based self-help aid: 51/49. Priority financial aid filing deadline: 2/15. Financial aid filing deadline: 2/15. Financial aid notification on or about: 4/1.

TV/Film/Digital Media Studies Programs

Number of undergraduates in these programs: 576

Number of 2005 graduates from these programs: 386

Degrees conferred to these majors: BA, BFA.

Also available at New York University: MFA, MA, MPS, PhD.

Number of full-time faculty in these programs: 101

Number of part-time faculty in these programs: 102

Equipment and facilities: Our students learn and work in one of the most modern and complete physical plants of any school of performing and media arts in the nation. Tisch School of the Arts' newly-designed facilities and state-of-the-art equipment are located in the Warner Communications Center, the William S. and Frances B. Todman Center for Film and Television, and the Iris and B. Gerald Cantor Film Center, creating one of the largest filmmaking facilities on the Eastern seaboard. Film and television students create, edit, and produce their work in a complex that houses two soundstages, 70 editing rooms, 25 film and video screening rooms, and sound-mixing studios. The newly renovated 8,000-square-foot Production Center supports every aspect of the well over 4,500 student projects shot every year, with technical seminars, industry-professional equipment, film stock and supplies, equipment repair services, and additional support for planning and development of student films. It is one of the largest facilities of its kind in the New York area. Film, video, and sound editing, audio mixing, film-to-tape transfers, and interformat duplication are provided in the postproduction area. Students are given curricular allotments and are trained on, and given access to, all the tools they need to complete their projects at a professional level. These tools include Steenbeck flatbed editing, Betacam SP cuts-only, a state-of-the-art sound mixing studio, Pro Tools, Final Cut Pro and Avid Media Composer, Xpress, Xpress-DV, and Symphony. Live-to-tape television productions are an everyday occurrence in our television studios. Each of our two fully equipped studios houses three Sony 3CCD cameras, an Echolab video switcher, a Mackie 24-track sound mixing board, a Colortran digital lighting console, a character generator, and a full complement of ancillary equipment. The animation studios, which support both traditional and computer animation, house Oxberry and Bolex stands, digital video lunchbox computer systems, and 3-D animation teaching and project labs. The Todman Center for Film and Television is a full-service production facility that includes casting, rehearsal, and shooting rooms, as well as a 2,500-square-foot film and television soundstage with a 50' x 30' hard cyclorama, surrounding drapes in two colors, and a roll-up chroma-key drop. The teaching soundstage has a full lighting grid and dimmer system as well as movable and permanent sets. It is equipped with cameras and film stock, grip and lighting equipment, props, and a house set. The library staff provides students with access to audition/rehearsal rooms, screening rooms, and an extensive collection of screenplays. Additionally, the library serves the classroom needs of our film and video faculty in both the undergraduate and graduate levels, supporting with classroom assistance, projection, and check-in and check-out of DVDs, laser discs, videos, films, screenplays, laptops, and computer software.

ATAS interns: 1

Career development services: Alumni networking opportunities; career counseling; central resource(s) for employers to browse headshots, writing samples, reels; internship listings; job fairs; job listings. The

Tisch Office of Career Development, located in the Office of Student Affairs, is an active and useful resource for Tisch students and recent alumni. The office offers a range of services, such as individual career counseling specific to the arts, resume-writing assistance, consultations, interview coaching, The Screenplay Bank, The Headshot Book for graduating Undergraduate Drama Students and the exclusive Tisch Office of Career Development Alumni List Serve. The List Serve offers current entry-level job opportunities, full-time, part-time, freelance positions and announcements, and networking opportunities for Tisch alumni interested in the New York and Los Angeles scenes in particular. The office also houses a reference library containing information ranging from fellowship sources to directories of theaters, film, commercial and postproduction companies, talent agencies, and many other professional organizations. The Tisch Office of Career Development conducts a series of discipline-specific professional workshops and special topic discussions. The Annual NY Job Fair for Tisch seniors and recent alumni attracts the likes of MTV, Court TV, Innovative Artists, The William Morris Agency, Ogilvy & Mather, New Line Cinema, ABC, CBS News, Grey Worldwide, *Blue's Clues*, The Public Theater, Curious Pictures, Comedy Central, BAM, DreamWorks, and many others.

Famous alumni: Chris Columbus, Oliver Stone, Brett Ratner, M. Night Shyamalan, Nancy Savoca, Jane Rosenthal, Karyn Kusama.

Notable alumni: Kisha Imani Cameron, producer, *Bamboozled, Sometime in April*; Liza Chasen, producer, *Bridget Jones's Diary, Nanny McPhee, About a Boy, Pride & Prejudice*; Ryan Fleck, film director, *Half Nelson*; Morgan Spurlock, director, *Supersize Me*; Phil Morrison, director, *Junebug*.

In Their Own Words

Each spring, the Kanbar Institute of Film and Television proudly presents the First Run Festival to showcase over 150 intermediate and advanced projects in film, video, and animation. This annual week-long festival begins with the Craft Awards Ceremony and Wasserman Semi-Finalists Announcement and culminates with the Wasserman Awards Ceremony featuring the Charles and Lucille King Family Foundation Awards. New features are screened three nights a week through our Director's Series. It is followed by a discussion hosted by the department's industry liaison and a guest filmmaker. Alumni guests include Martin Scorsese, Oliver Stone, Joel Coen, James Cox (Wonderland), master-writer Richard LaGravenese, Pete Sollett (Raising Victor Vargas), John Hamburg (Along Came Polly), world-famous cinematographer Darius Khondji, producer Martin Bregman (Scarface), Lindsay Crystal (My Uncle Burns), Nanette Burstein (Film School), as well as non-alumni George Lucas, Sir Ridley Scott, Keith Gordon (The Singing Detective), and Luke Greenfield (The Girl Next Door). While many directors come and screen their latest feature films, other guests include producers, actors, cinematographers, and anyone else connected with film. The weekly Contact Series invites a guest from the film/television/video industry to have an informal lunch with students to learn more about what the guest does in the industry. Past guests include David A. Isaacs, CEO, Zilo Networks; Bryan Singer, director of Usual Suspects, X-Men, X-Men 2, and the upcoming Superman Returns; and producer Mary Jane Skalski. The Media Internship Program runs each semester, allowing students registered in the class to earn academic credit for their experiences and expose our students to the most exciting work being done in the field, as they work side by side with established professionals. There is an array of study abroad opportunities. Students can study filmmaking, directing, and dramatic writing in Florence or screenwriting, cinema, and filmmaking in Paris. Some programs are taught in collaboration with local institutions, such as filmmaking in Prague with FAMU, one of the most prestigious European film schools. The academic year program in London includes television production with the British Broadcasting Corporation (BBC) and screenwriting with the Writers' Guild of Great Britain. In Dublin, courses in film and documentary production, cinema studies, and screenwriting are offered in collaboration with the Irish Film Centre. The Tisch School has made great strides in developing an extensive array of exit strategies for graduating students. Exit strategies include Tisch Alumni Def Filmmaker Award, created by the Simmons Lathan Media Group (SLMG), which provides production funding up to $300,000 for a feature film and up to $150,000 for a documentary project; SLMG will also secure distribution for the winning project/s in home video, television, and pay television outlets. The Public Theater and Tisch have a new operating partnership that will open the door to ongoing cooperation between the two institutions.

POPULAR PROGRAMS

DEPARTMENT OF DRAMA, UNDERGRADUATE

Department chair: Kevin Kuhlke
Number of full-time faculty: 39
Number of part-time faculty: 68
Focus/emphasis: The Department of Drama, Undergraduate combines rigorous conservatory training with comprehensive academic theater studies and liberal arts, while taking full advantage of the incomparable cultural resources of New York City. The department offers training in an array of theater disciplines and techniques, using the resources of world-renowned studios, including the Stella Adler Conservatory (acting), Collaborative Arts Project 21 (musical theater), the Experimental Theater Wing (acting and the creation of new work), the Atlantic Theater Company's Acting School (acting), the Meisner Extension (acting), the Playwrights Horizons Theater School (acting and directing), the Lee Strasberg Theater Institute (acting), and the Technical Production Track (production and pre-design studies).

UNDERGRADUATE DIVISION, KANBAR INSTITUTE OF FILM & TELEVISION

Department chair: Lamar Sanders
Number of full-time faculty: 59
Number of part-time faculty: 54
Focus/emphasis: The mission of the Undergraduate Division, Kanbar Institute of Film and Television is to educate our students in the art, craft, and technology of film, video, animation, and sound production. We nurture individual talent and skills while encouraging students to become creative and thoughtful practitioners in the world of media. Through a variety of theoretical and applied courses, students acquire the technical skills of the craft and learn how moving images and words may express the human condition. At the same time, students gain a solid foundation in storytelling, using a variety of technologies and media. This practical and theoretical training is combined with courses in the liberal arts that provide our students with the well-rounded intellectual background necessary for participation in the profession.

DEPARTMENT OF DANCE

Department chair: Linda Tarnay
Number of full-time faculty: 9
Number of part-time faculty: 15
Focus/emphasis: The Department of Dance offers comprehensive and concentrated training for students who are committed to entering the professional dance world as dancers or choreographers. The program provides a full range of technical training, and, for those interested in choreography, a solid base for creative work. In addition, students also train with guest teachers and choreographers drawn from New York City's national and international dance communities.

CLIVE DAVIS DEPARTMENT OF RECORDED MUSIC

Department chair: Jim Anderson
Number of full-time faculty: 3
Number of part-time faculty: 5
Focus/emphasis: The Clive Davis Department of Recorded Music offers a course of study that is designed to educate students in all aspects of contemporary recorded music, with a special focus on

the arts of producing records, identifying and cultivating musical talent, and developing creative material within the complex range of recorded music technologies. The program recognizes the creative record producer as an artist in his or her own right and musical recording itself as a creative medium. It allows students the unique opportunity of studying the cultural impact of recorded music and the history of a number of musical genres, including, but not limited to, rock, hip hop, R & B, and pop.

DEPARTMENT OF PHOTOGRAPHY AND IMAGING
Department chair: Lorie Novack
Number of full-time faculty: 10
Number of part-time faculty: 10
Focus/emphasis: The Department of Photography and Imaging is centered on the making and understanding of images. The curriculum is based on two principal areas: creative practice and cultural studies. A comprehensive understanding of the tradition of visual art directly supports students as they develop their personal creative identities. Courses in the liberal arts complement the students' education. The focus is on the progress of the individual. This diverse department embraces multiple perspectives, and our students work in virtually all modes of photo-based image making, using both analog and digital technologies.

RITA AND BURTON GOLDBERG DEPARTMENT OF DRAMATIC WRITING
Department chair: Richard Wesley
Number of full-time faculty: 15
Number of part-time faculty: 20
Focus/emphasis: The Rita and Burton Goldberg Department of Dramatic Writing offers a highly focused academic and professional writing program for students, committed to the rigorous training of writers for theater, film, and television. Our primary goal is to educate and train writers by encouraging them to develop their own voices and visions through an integrated curriculum of courses: a stepped series of writing workshops, a set of challenging theoretical and analytical cours-

es in text analysis, and production and professional training courses. The mission is to encourage dramatic writers to find truth and to have the courage to illuminate it through their stories.

DEPARTMENT OF CINEMA STUDIES
Department chair: Chris Straayer
Number of full-time faculty: 14
Number of part-time faculty: 15
Focus/emphasis: The Department of Cinema Studies offers a liberal arts program featuring a comprehensive curriculum of courses in the history, theory, criticism, and aesthetics of motion pictures. Students study cinema as an international art form in courses on film style, film genres, and cinema auteurs, and they are encouraged to reflect on the ways in which cinema, as a mass medium, shapes our understanding of gender, sexuality, race, and nation. The department is committed to the study of the moving image in all its manifestations, including broadcast television, video art, and new technologies.

Students Should Also Know
Courses in the liberal arts and sciences are an integral part of your education at Tisch. Combined with experiential professional training, your liberal arts courses will give you an overview of the relationship between the arts and other disciplines and provide a rich academic and societal context for your creative endeavors. You may choose from hundreds of courses throughout the university and at Tisch that will challenge your intellect and stimulate your imagination.

NORTH CAROLINA SCHOOL OF THE ARTS
1533 South Main Street, PO Box 12189,
Winston-Salem, NC 27127-2188
Phone: 336-770-3290 **E-mail:** admissions@ncarts.edu
Website: www.ncarts.edu

Campus Life
Environment: Metropolis. **Calendar:** Trimester.

Students and Faculty
(All Undergraduate Programs)
Enrollment: 721. **Student Body:** 41% female, 59% male, 52% out-of-state, 1% international. African American 10%, Asian 3%, Caucasian 83%, Hispanic 2%. Student/faculty ratio: 8:1. 135 full-time faculty. 100% faculty teach undergrads.

Admissions
(All Undergraduate Programs)
Freshman Admissions Requirements: Test(s) required: SAT or ACT. Average high school GPA: 3.48. 16% in top tenth, 45% in top quarter. SAT Math (25/75 percentile): 500/620. SAT Verbal (25/75 percentile): 540/640. Projected SAT Writing (25/75 percentile): 600/680. *Academic units required:* 4 English, 3 math, 3 science (1 science lab), 2 social studies, 1 history, 4 academic electives. Regular application deadline: 3/1. Regular notification: 4/1.

Costs and Financial Aid
(All Undergraduate Programs)
Annual in-state tuition $2,195. Out-of-state tuition $12,795. Room & board $5,115. Required fees $1,255. Average book expense $865.

Financial Aid Statistics: % freshmen/undergrads who receive need-based scholarship or grant aid: 57/43. % freshmen/undergrads who receive need-based self-help aid: 58/43. Priority financial aid filing deadline: 3/1. Financial aid notification on or about: 4/15.

TV/Film/Digital Media Studies Programs
Equipment and facilities: The School of Filmmaking opened a state-of-the-art training and exhibition complex in 1997, The Studio Village, that embraces a variety of filmmaking functions in a totally integrated and dynamic setting. The 62,036-square-foot Studio Village houses various production, postproduction, and exhibition activities and serves as a "back lot environment" where exterior scenes with a variety of looks can be filmed. The village includes several key buildings that are fashioned in a range of architectural styles and facades from Main Street, USA, to the Chicago El. One of the key objectives of the complex was to build facil-

ities that have a range of scale from the large block soundstage buildings to smaller structures, such as a brick classroom building. Electrical and other utility outlets are staged throughout the Studio Village so that filmmakers can easily support their equipment without running long lines of cable. The entire inner compound is designed so that exterior filming can take place undisturbed, with access to the facilities available around the perimeter of the filming area. The Production Complex includes three soundstages varying in size from 8,000 square feet to 4,000 square feet to 2,500 square feet, which provide professional production environments for film and video projects. The main stage boasts a 36-feet-to-the-grid workspace, and a brand new overhead lighting grid. The School of Filmmaking possesses a rental house's worth of professional film and video camera, lighting, production, and postproduction equipment for use by students—the same as equipment currently used in the industry. Over the course of their studies, students become trained and certified on the equipment used by the school. Highlights of the production equipment include 16 mm Arriflex SRIII camera packages; Panasonic, JVC, and Sony digital video camera packages; three complete stage grip and electric packages; location sound packages including NAGRA analogue; audio tape recorders and DAT recorders; Mini Panther and Super Panther dollies; two 14' production box trucks; four crew vans; two 4 x 4 pickup trucks; two 65-KW diesel trailer-mounted generators. postproduction equipment includes 24 Final Cut Pro HD editing stations, four Final Cut Pro/Aurora Igniter Systems, 1.75 Terabyte Apple Xserve RAID, an ADR/Foley Stage with Pro Tools and Gallery ADR Studio, seven Pro Tools digital audio workstations, Pro Tools Control 24 mixing board, Mackie HUI for audio predubs, four Avid Xpress DV stations, and two DEVA II hard disk recorders. The electronic music lab (Fall 2004) contains five Steenbeck 6-plate flat-bed editing tables. Also The Power Mac G5 lab features 16 Final Cut Pro HD workstations. Each system is based on a dual 2 GHz Power Mac G5 with a 17" Apple Studio Display. Students can edit projects shot on Panasonic 24p, DVC Pro, and mini-DV.

Projects are stored on a 1.75 Terabyte Apple Xserve RAID. Completed projects are burned to DVD using DVD Studio Pro and iDVD. There is also a film scoring stage, the ACE Exhibition Complex, the Moving Image Archives, and a student production office.

Other awards of note: Students have won numerous awards and shown at numerous festivals including Asheville Film Festival, Real to Reel Film Festival, Munich International Festival of Film, Cine Golden Eagle Awards, Eastman Kodak "Emerging Filmmaker Showcase" at the 2000 Cannes Film Festival, and Southern Exposure Film Festival. We have produced regional winners at Student Academy Awards and a Showtime's Black Filmmaker Showcase winner. Students' work has aired on Bravo and the Independent Film Channel, among others.

Notable alumni: David Gordon Green, director, *George Washington*; Rebecca Green, story editor, Lions Gate Entertainment; Will Files, assistant sound designer, *Shrek* and *A Walk to Remember*; Randolph Benson, director, *Man and Dog*.

In Their Own Words

The faculty of the School of Filmmaking consists entirely of working professionals—directors, writers, producers, editors, cinematographers, and production designers—who have established successful careers and continue to work in the film and television industries to stay current with practices and technology. The work of the faculty has won or has been nominated for the film industry's most prestigious awards including Academy, Emmy, Cannes Film Festival, Writers Guild of America, Cable ACE awards, and numerous others. The films of the faculty have been screened at major film festivals including Cannes International Film Festival, Berlin International Film Festival, Toronto Film Festival, Venice Film Festival, Deauville Festival, and many others. Guest artists have included Arthur Penn, director; Spike Lee, director; Robert Wise, director; Elmer Bernstein, composer; Kathy Bates, actress/director; Saul Zaentz, producer; Jack Valenti, chairman of Motion Picture Association of America.

POPULAR PROGRAMS

CINEMATOGRAPHY
Department chair: Barbara Kelly
Number of full-time faculty: 4
Focus/emphasis: In hands-on workshops and labs, students first learn the basics of film and digital video photography, including composition, cameras, lenses, film stock, lighting, and related areas. As students specialize in cinematography, they are taught rigging, pre-lighting, grip, and gaffer skills, and professional camera department skills and training on the Arriflex SR3 camera. They also learn film testing and working with the laboratory, digital imaging, and documentary camera technique. Students also become familiar with the work of cinematography masters on film.

DIRECTING
Department chair: Barbara Kelly
Number of full-time faculty: 4
Focus/emphasis: Students are taught the art of visual storytelling and directing the camera and actor. They progress from simple first-year exercises that stress the fundamentals of cinema language to their first directorial effort, a five-minute digital video production. Two more video productions are directed in the second year, with an increased emphasis on interpreting the screenplay through camera and performance. Students specializing in directing will become well versed in preparing the director's script, directing comedy and drama, and honing their collaborative skills with the various artists who work to realize the director's vision.

EDITING AND SOUND
Department chair: Barbara Kelly
Number of full-time faculty: 4
Focus/emphasis: From their arrival at the School of Filmmaking, students are introduced to the critical role editing and sound play in the creative process of making movies. Audio recording and sound design instruction are offered using both digital and analog equipment. More specialized instruction is offered in Final Cut Pro and Avid nonlinear digital editing systems, along with 16

mm film editing on the Steenbeck, sound synching, matchback to 16 mm film prints, and music and sound effects editing. Students use Pro Tools equipment to sound edit dialogue, ADR, music, and sound effects. The School of Filmmaking has its own Foley sound effects recording stage. Fourth-year students do a final dialogue, music, and sound effects mix on the Film Scoring Stage using Pro Tools technology. Full orchestral scores may also be recorded using musicians from the NCSA Symphony Orchestra; these and other original scores are written by graduate students in the School of Music's Film Music Composition program.

PRODUCING

Department chair: Barbara Kelly
Number of full-time faculty: 3
Focus/emphasis: Both creative and physical (or line) producing are emphasized in this program of instruction. Scheduling and budgeting both short films and feature films are taught using the latest software programs, in addition to how a producer options, develops, and sells material to the independent or studio marketplace. An overview of the Hollywood studio system and television markets is offered, as well as classes on marketing, distribution, and after-markets. Student productions are used as examples of how to manage a production, while extensive preparation can be done on a feature film budget, schedule, and breakdown.

PRODUCTION DESIGN

Department chair: Barbara Kelly
Number of full-time faculty: 3
Focus/emphasis: Students are exposed to the wealth of diversity in film production design, from set design and decoration to the creation of props and mechanical effects. Students study art history, color and design, drawing, film drafting, the history of decor, film graphics, and scene painting. Specific skills are taught to help the student work as an art director and production designer, including collaboration with the director and cinematographer, budgeting the art department, and main-taining an artistic overview of the design process on a motion picture or TV series.

SCREENWRITING

Department chair: Barbara Kelly
Number of full-time faculty: 4
Focus/emphasis: Instruction begins with basic immersion in storytelling and explorations into character, conflict, setting, dialogue, emotional tone, stage directions, and professional format. More advanced classes explore three-act structure, the value of rewriting, and genre writing—from classic genres such as the Western and detective thriller to contemporary independent film material. Extensive workshopping is done both on screenplays for school productions, particularly in the first and second years, and feature-length screenplays, two of which must be written in years three and four.

NORTH CAROLINA STATE UNIVERSITY

Box 7103, Raleigh, NC 27695
Phone: 919-515-2434 **E-mail:** undergrad_admissions@ncsu.edu
Website: www.hcsu.edu

Campus Life
Environment: Metropolis. **Calendar:** Semester.

Students and Faculty
(All Undergraduate Programs)
Enrollment: 20,546. **Student Body:** 42% female, 58% male, 7% out-of-state, 1% international (96 countries represented). African American 10%, Asian 5%, Caucasian 80%, Hispanic 2%. Student/faculty ratio: 16:1. 1,671 full-time faculty, 91% hold PhDs. 100% faculty teach undergrads.

Admissions
(All Undergraduate Programs)
Freshman Admissions Requirements: Test(s) required: SAT or ACT; ACT with Writing component. Average high school GPA: 4.07. 36% in top tenth,

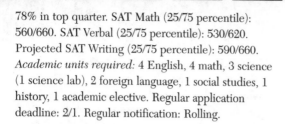

78% in top quarter. SAT Math (25/75 percentile): 560/660. SAT Verbal (25/75 percentile): 530/620. Projected SAT Writing (25/75 percentile): 590/660. *Academic units required:* 4 English, 4 math, 3 science (1 science lab), 2 foreign language, 1 social studies, 1 history, 1 academic elective. Regular application deadline: 2/1. Regular notification: Rolling.

Costs and Financial Aid
(All Undergraduate Programs)
Annual in-state tuition $3,530. Out-of-state tuition $15,728. Room & board $7,040. Required fees $1,254. Average book expense $900.

Financial Aid Statistics: % freshmen/undergrads who receive any aid: 61/60. % freshmen/undergrads who receive need-based scholarship or grant aid: 38/37. % freshmen/undergrads who receive need-based self-help aid: 30/30. Priority financial aid filing deadline: 3/1. Financial aid notification on or about: 3/1.

TV/Film/Digital Media Studies Programs
Number of undergraduates in these programs: 45
Number of 2005 graduates from these programs: 10
Degrees conferred to these majors: BA.
Number of full-time faculty in these programs: 6
Number of part-time faculty in these programs: 2

% of graduates who pursue further study within 5 years: 15
% of graduates currently employed in related field: 60

POPULAR PROGRAMS

COMMUNICATION
Department chair: Craig Allen Smith
Number of full-time faculty: 30
Focus/emphasis: Communication, including speech, communication disorders, and mass communication.

FILM STUDIES
Department chair: Maria Pramaggiore
Number of full-time faculty: 6
Focus/emphasis: Film history, analysis, theory, and production. See also www.ncsu.edu/chass/film.

COMMUNICATION, RHETORIC, AND DIGITAL MEDIA (PHD ONLY)
Program director: Carolyn R. Miller
Number of full-time faculty: 25
Focus/emphasis: For further information, please visit www.ncsu.edu/crdm.

NORTHERN ARIZONA UNIVERSITY
PO Box 4084, Flagstaff, AZ 86011-4084
Phone: 928-523-5511 **E-mail:** undergraduate.admissions@nau.edu
Website: www.nau.edu

Campus Life
Environment: Town. **Calendar:** Semester.

Students and Faculty
(All Undergraduate Programs)
Enrollment: 13,116. **Student Body:** 60% female, 40% male, 17% out-of-state, 2% international. African American 2%, Asian 2%, Caucasian 73%, Hispanic 12%, Native American 7%. Student/faculty ratio: 16:1. 723 full-time faculty, 78% hold PhDs. 90% faculty teach undergrads.

Admissions
(All Undergraduate Programs)
Average high school GPA: 3.4. SAT Math (25/75 percentile): 460/540. SAT Verbal (25/75 percentile): 460/540. Projected SAT Writing (25/75 percentile): 530/600. *Academic units required:* 4 English, 4 math, 3 science (1 science lab), 2 foreign language, 1 social studies, 1 history, 1 fine arts. Regular notification: Rolling.

Costs and Financial Aid
(All Undergraduate Programs)
Annual in-state tuition $4,223. Out-of-state tuition $12,853. Room & board $5,960. Required fees $170. Average book expense $800.

Financial Aid Statistics: % freshmen/undergrads who receive any aid: 62/62. % freshmen/undergrads who receive need-based scholarship or grant aid: 28/36. % freshmen/undergrads who receive need-based self-help aid: 33/42. Priority financial aid filing deadline: 2/14. Financial aid notification on or about: 2/14.

TV/Film/Digital Media Studies Programs

Degrees conferred to these majors: BA, BS, BFA.
Equipment and facilities: NAU supports the program with modern postproduction and audio facilities in addition to student-run (NAULive!) television and radio stations (KJACK).
Career development services: Internship listings.

POPULAR PROGRAMS

ELECTRONIC MEDIA

Department chair: Barbara Kelly
Number of full-time faculty: 2
Focus/emphasis: Our program involves study in the use of electronic media in the academic field of communication. The program encompasses the preparation, production, transmission, regulation, and management of electronic media messages. Many of the skills emphasized in the program are applicable to other related areas including: film, computer-based multimedia, corporate video production, media sales, public information, and media management.

VISUAL COMMUNICATION

Department chair: Barbara Kelly
Number of full-time faculty: 3
Focus/emphasis: Computer imaging is a creative process that utilizes art and technology to communicate ideas and images. By controlling color, computer images, type, animation, and photography, the designer/artist produces images to inspire and persuade the viewer. They collaborate with graphic designers, marketing researchers, photographers, animators, and printers to complete visually compelling projects. Graphic design is a creative process that utilizes art and technology to communicate ideas. By controlling color, type,

symbols, computer images, and photography, the designer combines aesthetic judgement with project management skills to develop overall communication strategies for clients. They collaborate with marketing researchers and public relations specialists to develop design alternatives. Graphic designers work with illustrators, computer artists, photographers, and printers to create compelling designs to effectively communicate the client's message. Students are encouraged to join professional organizations, such as the American Institute of Graphic Arts (AIGA), SIGGRAPH, and local user's groups, and to subscribe to professional publications such as *Print* and *Communication Arts* magazines and to read other current literature on design.

NORTHERN MICHIGAN UNIVERSITY

1401 Presque Isle Avenue, Marquette, MI 49855
Phone: 906-227-2650 **E-mail:** admiss@nmu.edu
Website: www.nmu.edu

Campus Life
Environment: Village. **Calendar:** Semester.

Students and Faculty
(All Undergraduate Programs)
Enrollment: 9,500. **Student Body:** 53% female, 47% male, 19% out-of-state. African American 2%, Caucasian 90%, Native American 2%. Student/faculty ratio: 23:1. 305 full-time faculty, 65% hold PhDs. 98% faculty teach undergrads.

Admissions
(All Undergraduate Programs)
Freshman Admissions Requirements: Test(s) required: SAT or ACT. Average high school GPA: 3.3.

Costs and Financial Aid
(All Undergraduate Programs)
Annual in-state tuition $5,858. Out-of-state tuition $9,602. Room & board $6,482. Average book expense $700.
Financial Aid Statistics: % freshmen/undergrads who receive any aid: 90/83. % freshmen/undergrads

who receive need-based scholarship or grant aid: 48/46. % freshmen/undergrads who receive need-based self-help aid: 51/54. Priority financial aid filing deadline: 3/1. Financial aid notification on or about: 4/1.

TV/Film/Digital Media Studies Programs

Number of undergraduates in these programs: 245
Number of 2005 graduates from these programs: 35
Degrees conferred to these majors: BA, BS, BFA.
Number of full-time faculty in these programs: 7
Number of part-time faculty in these programs: 4
Equipment and facilities: three Mac G5 labs, sound studio, green screen room, 30 video cameras, still video cameras. Close working relationship with WNMU-TV 13 (PBS).
Other awards of note: Student participation in RES fest; Michigan Association of Broadcasters Awards for audio and video production for 14 consecutive years.

% of graduates who pursue further study within 5 years: 20
% of graduates currently employed in related field: 75
Career development services: Career counseling, job fairs, job listings.
Notable alumni: Michael Fornwald, commecial director, selected for Museum of Modern Art collection.

In Their Own Words

New facility houses screening rooms with state-of-the-art projection facilities, and school sets up internships with studios and production houses. Student-produced programming airs on both the university's PBS and on cable access channels.

POPULAR PROGRAMS

DIGITAL CINEMA
Department chair: Michael Cinelli
Number of full-time faculty: 3
Number of part-time faculty: 1
Focus/emphasis: Studio production in digital cinema with emphasis on historical and social influences. Covers multiple genres including animated, narrative, documentary, and experimental cinema.

ELECTRONIC IMAGING
Department chair: Michael Cinelli
Number of full-time faculty: 2
Focus/emphasis: Studio production of multiple apsects of computer art including animation, Web design, imagery manipulation, and interactive media

ELECTRONIC JOURNALISM
Department chair: Donald Rybacki
Number of full-time faculty: 4
Number of part-time faculty: 3
Focus/emphasis: Students are taught how to research, write, shoot, edit, and produce news stories for electronic media. Course work is integrated with live student-produced newscasts that provide experience both in front of and behind the camera.

MEDIA PRODUCTION AND NEW TECHNOLOGY
Department chair: Donald Rybacki
Number of full-time faculty: 4
Number of part-time faculty: 3
Focus/emphasis: Students receive preparation for a variety of audio and video production careers ranging from the music recording industry to corporate video. Students use professionally-equipped studios to learn new concepts and ultimately to create award-winning content.

Students Should Also Know
Cross-over instruction (majoring in one of these programs and minoring in another) broadens a student's experience and provides an eclectic professional portfolio.

Northwestern University

PO Box 3060, 1801 Hinman Avenue, Evanston, IL 60204-3060
Phone: 847-491-7271 **E-mail:** ug-admission@northwestern.edu
Website: www.northwestern.edu

Campus Life
Environment: Town. **Calendar:** Quarter.

Students and Faculty
(All Undergraduate Programs)
Enrollment: 7,902. **Student Body:** 53% female, 47% male, 65% out-of-state, 5% international (95 countries represented). African American 5%, Asian 17%, Caucasian 61%, Hispanic 6%. Student/faculty ratio 7:1. 938 full-time faculty, 100% hold PhDs. 100% faculty teach undergrads.

Admissions
(All Undergraduate Programs)
Freshman Admissions Requirements: Test(s) required: SAT or ACT; ACT with Writing component. 82% in top tenth, 96% in top quarter. SAT Math (25/75 percentile): 670/760. SAT Verbal (25/75 percentile): 650/740. Projected SAT Writing (25/75 percentile): 690/750. Early decision application deadline: 11/1. Regular application deadline: 1/1. Regular notification: 4/15.

Costs and Financial Aid
(All Undergraduate Programs)
Annual tuition $33,408. Room & board $10,266. Required fees $151. Average book expense $1,488. **Financial Aid Statistics:** % freshmen/undergrads who receive any aid: 60/60. % freshmen/undergrads who receive need-based scholarship or grant aid: 44/42. % freshmen/undergrads who receive need-based self help aid: 41/40. Financial aid filing deadline: 2/1. Financial aid notification on or about: 4/15.

TV/Film/Digital Media Studies Programs
Number of undergraduates in these programs: 248
Number of 2005 graduates from these programs: 82
Degrees conferred to these majors: BA, BS.
Also available at Northwestern University: MFA, MA, PhD.

Number of full-time faculty in these programs: 13 full-time tenure/tenure track faculty; 4 full-time lecturers.
Number of part-time faculty in these programs: 7–8 part-time or visiting faculty.
Equipment and facilities: Nikon digital still cameras; DVCPro, DV25p, 16 mm film, and HD cameras; AVID and Final Cut Pro editing suites; compositing and computer animation lab; ProTools sound editing suites; two sound stages.
Other awards of note: Numerous Emmys and the George Peabody Award have been won by our alums.
Career development services: Alumni networking opportunities, career counseling, internship listings, job fairs, job listings.
Famous alumni: Zach Braff, Dina Bair, Alexis Alexanian, Professor Lawrence Lichty, Jon Gordon, David Tolchinsky, to name a few.
Notable alumni: Barry Weiss, Senior Vice President for Animation Production, Sony Image Works; Eric Bernt, writer, *Romeo Must Die*.

In Their Own Words
Active internship program that places students in media companies in Chicago, New York, and Los Angeles (year-round). Annual student film festival. Numerous symposiums and conferences with scholars, media makers, and screenwriters from international contexts. Students administer production groups that fund student projects outside of the classroom context in narrative, documentary, experimental, animation, music video, and TV comedy. Award-winning radio station WNUR. Guest lecturers on a monthly basis.

Nyack College

One South Boulevard, Nyack, NY 10960-3698
Phone: 845-358-1710 **E-mail:** enroll@nyack.edu
Website: www.nyackcollege.edu

Campus Life
Environment: Village. **Calendar:** Semester.

Students and Faculty
(All Undergraduate Programs)
Enrollment: 1,964. **Student Body:** 59% female, 41% male, 36% out-of-state, 4% international (46 countries represented). African American 30%, Asian 6%, Caucasian 35%, Hispanic 22%. Student/faculty ratio: 17:1. 83 full-time faculty, 63% hold PhDs. 86% faculty teach undergrads.

Admissions
(All Undergraduate Programs)
Average high school GPA: 2.78. 9% in top tenth, 23% in top quarter. SAT Math (25/75 percentile): 410/550. SAT Verbal (25/75 percentile): 430/560. Projected SAT Writing (25/75 percentile): 500/620.

Costs and Financial Aid
(All Undergraduate Programs)
Annual tuition $12,990. Required fees $800. **Financial Aid Statistics:** % freshmen/undergrads who receive need-based scholarship or grant aid: 76/82. % freshmen/undergrads who receive need-based self-help aid: 65/74. Priority financial aid filing deadline: 3/1. Financial aid notification on or about: 3/1.

TV/Film/Digital Media Studies Programs
Number of undergraduates in these programs: 82
Number of 2005 graduates from these programs: 31
Degrees conferred to these majors: BS.
Number of full-time faculty in these programs: 2
Number of part-time faculty in these programs: 5
Equipment and facilities: Final Cut Pro editing suites, AfterEffects compositing suites, Panasonic DVX-100A (3CCD) digital cameras.

% of graduates who pursue further study within 5 years: 15
% of graduates currently employed in related field: 60
Career development services: Career counseling, internship listings, job fairs, job listings. Internship placement in the entertainment industry is available.

Students have obtained internships at ABC, NBC, CBS, A&E, E!, The New York Mets, Disney, Universal Music Group, House of Blues, and Miramax Films. Student work has won awards at both the local and national level. Aside from NYC film festivals, students have won nationally-acclaimed awards, such as Tellys.

POPULAR PROGRAMS
FILM
Department chair: John K. Bucher, Jr.
Number of full-time faculty: 2
Number of part-time faculty: 5

TELEVISION
Department chair: John K. Bucher, Jr.
Number of full-time faculty: 2
Number of part-time faculty: 5

RADIO
Department chair: John K. Bucher, Jr.
Number of full-time faculty: 2
Number of part-time faculty: 5

DIGITAL MEDIA
Department chair: John K. Bucher, Jr.
Number of full-time faculty: 2
Number of part-time faculty: 5

MUSIC BUSINESS
Department chair: John K. Bucher, Jr.
Number of full-time faculty: 2
Number of part-time faculty: 5

OBERLIN COLLEGE
101 North Professor Street, Oberlin College, Oberlin, OH 44074
Phone: 440-775-8411 **E-mail:** college.admissions@oberlin.edu
Website: www.oberlin.edu

Campus Life
Environment: Rural. **Calendar:** 4-1-4.

Students and Faculty
(All Undergraduate Programs)
Enrollment: 2,831. **Student Body:** 55% female, 45% male, 90% out-of-state, 6% international. African American 5%, Asian 8%, Caucasian 76%, Hispanic 5%. Student/faculty ratio: 10:1. 288 full-time faculty, 97% hold PhDs. 100% faculty teach undergrads.

Admissions
(All Undergraduate Programs)
Freshman Admissions Requirements: Test(s) required: SAT or ACT; ACT with Writing component. Average high school GPA: 3.6. 65% in top tenth, 90% in top quarter. SAT Math (25/75 percentile): 620/710. SAT Verbal (25/75 percentile): 650/750. Projected SAT Writing (25/75 percentile): 690/750. *Academic units required:* 4 English, 4 math, 3 science, 3 foreign language, 3 social studies. Early decision application deadline: 11/15. Regular application deadline: 1/15. Regular notification: 4/1.

Costs and Financial Aid
(All Undergraduate Programs)
Annual tuition $32,524. Room & board $8,180. Required fees $200. Average book expense $734. **Financial Aid Statistics:** % freshmen/undergrads who receive any aid: 61/60. % freshmen/undergrads who receive need-based scholarship or grant aid: 43/50. % freshmen/undergrads who receive need-based self-help aid: 49/52. Priority financial aid filing deadline: 2/15. Financial aid filing deadline: 2/15. Financial aid notification on or about: 4/1.

TV/Film/Digital Media Studies Programs
Number of undergraduates in these programs: 60
Number of 2005 graduates from these programs: 25
Degrees conferred to these majors: BA.
Number of full-time faculty in these programs: 6
Number of part-time faculty in these programs: 1
Equipment and facilities: Media lab, student-directed film co-op.

Career development services: Alumni networking opportunities, career counseling, internship listings, job listings.

In Their Own Words
Oberlin offers a unique dual emphasis on cinema/film studies and liberal arts. The cinema studies major has a consortial arrangement with the film program at NYU's Tisch School of the Arts, and students may choose to study for a semester in the Tisch program.

OHIO NORTHERN UNIVERSITY
525 South Main Street, Ada, OH 45810
Phone: 419-772-2260 **E-mail:** admissions-ug@onu.edu
Website: www.onu.edu

Campus Life
Environment: Village. **Calendar:** Quarter.

Students and Faculty
(All Undergraduate Programs)
Enrollment: 2,541. **Student Body:** 46% female, 54% male, 13% out-of-state. African American 2%, Asian 1%, Caucasian 96%. Student/faculty ratio: 14:1. 205 full-time faculty, 82% hold PhDs. 100% faculty teach undergrads.

Admissions
(All Undergraduate Programs)
Freshman Admissions Requirements: Test(s) required: SAT or ACT. Average high school GPA: 3.55. 38% in top tenth, 66% in top quarter. SAT Math (25/75 percentile): 530/650. SAT Verbal (25/75 percentile): 530/630. Projected SAT Writing (25/75 percentile): 590/670. *Academic units required:* 4 English, 2 math, 2 science (2 science labs), 2 social studies, 2 history, 4 academic electives. Regular application deadline: 8/15. Regular notification: Rolling.

Costs and Financial Aid
(All Undergraduate Programs)
Annual tuition $28,050. Room & board $7,080. Required fees $210. Average book expense $1,200.

Financial Aid Statistics: % freshmen/undergrads who receive any aid: 86/83. % freshmen/undergrads who receive need-based scholarship or grant aid: 86/83. % freshmen/undergrads who receive need-based self-help aid: 86/83. Priority financial aid filing deadline: 4/15. Financial aid filing deadline: 6/1. Financial aid notification on or about: 2/15.

TV/Film/Digital Media Studies Programs

Number of undergraduates in these programs: 25
Number of 2005 graduates from these programs: 5
Degrees conferred to these majors: BS.
Number of full-time faculty in these programs: 1
Equipment and facilities: TV studio; edit suite; master control room; three linear edit systems; three Avid editing stations; Avid and Final Cut Pro editing training; 10 cameras (S-VHS and mini-DV); 3,000-watt commercial frequency radio station with digital editing.

% of graduates who pursue further study within 5 years: 15
% of graduates currently employed in related field: 50
Career development services: Alumni networking opportunities, career counseling, internship listings, job fairs, job listings, program website that provides links to all graduates of the program. Visit www.onu.edu/a+s/comm_arts/bem.html for more information.

In Their Own Words

The broadcasting and electronic media major is a professionally-guided liberal arts program within the Communication Arts Department of Ohio Northern University. Classes are small, with a focus on hands-on training beginning in the freshman year. Internships and practicum classes are required.

POPULAR PROGRAMS

BROADCASTING AND ELECTRONIC MEDIA
Department chair: G. Richard Gainey
Number of full-time faculty: 1

OHIO STATE UNIVERSITY–COLUMBUS

110 Enarson Hall, 154 West 12th Avenue, Columbus, OH 43210
Phone: 614-292-3980
E-mail: Freshmen and Transfer - askabuckeye@osu.edu
Website: www.osu.edu

Campus Life
Environment: Metropolis. **Calendar:** Quarter.

Students and Faculty
(All Undergraduate Programs)
Enrollment: 36,029. **Student Body:** 47% female, 53% male, 10% out-of-state, 3% international (85 countries represented). African American 8%, Asian 5%, Caucasian 79%, Hispanic 3%. Student/faculty ratio 13:1. 872 full-time faculty, 99% hold PhDs.

Admissions
(All Undergraduate Programs)
Freshman Admissions Requirements: Test(s) required: SAT or ACT; ACT with Writing component. 39% in top tenth, 76% in top quarter. SAT Math (25/75 percentile): 550/660. SAT Verbal (25/75 percentile): 530/640. Projected SAT Writing (25/75 percentile): 590/680. *Academic units required:* 4 English, 3 math, 2 science (2 science lab), 2 foreign language, 2 social studies, 1 academic elective, 1 visual and performing arts. Regular application deadline: 2/1. Regular notification: Rolling.

Costs and Financial Aid
(All Undergraduate Programs)
Annual in-state tuition $7,827. Out-of-state tuition $19,050. Room & board $7,275. Required fees $153. Average book expense $1,080.
Financial Aid Statistics: % freshmen/undergrads who receive any aid: 54/49. % freshmen/undergrads

who receive need-based scholarship or grant aid: 52/46. % freshmen/undergrads who receive need-based self-help aid: 46/48. Priority financial aid filing deadline: 3/1. Financial aid notification on or about: 4/5.

TV/Film/Digital Media Studies Programs
Degrees conferred to these majors: BA.
Also available at Ohio State University—
Columbus: Minor in Film Studies

POPULAR PROGRAMS

FILM STUDIES
Department Chair: John Davidson
Focus/emphasis: Incorporating other fields such as art, history, languages, popular culture, and communications, film studies offers the student extensive possibilities for experience and knowledge. Film studies majors learn to analyze, synthesize, and discern important information—they learn to read and write effectively and look at the world with a critical eye, but most importantly, they develop a critical and audiovisual literacy. In a culture that increasingly relies on visual information, a comprehension of how meaning grows out of the moving image becomes essential to various areas of society. Many graduates of film studies find positions with film companies, film archives, or festivals, or they work as art managers, critics, journalists, independent artists, and teachers at a variety of levels including P-12, academia, or nontraditional. Traditionally, graduates in Film Studies have pursued higher education in Film Studies, and majors have been competitive in graduate school acceptance and in job searches nationally in these areas. Students will also be prepared for the kinds of positions in government, nonprofit organizations, and industry that are open to other students majoring in the humanities.

OHIO UNIVERSITY–ATHENS
120 Chubb Hall, Athens, OH 45701
Phone: 740-593-4100 **E-mail:** admissions@ohio.edu
Website: www.ohio.edu

Campus Life
Environment: Rural. **Calendar:** Quarter.

Students and Faculty
(All Undergraduate Programs)
Enrollment: 17,207. **Student Body:** 52% female, 48% male, 13% out-of-state, 1% international (104 countries represented). African American 4%, Caucasian 93%, Hispanic 1%. Student/faculty ratio: 19:1. 869 full-time faculty, 89% hold PhDs. 100% faculty teach undergrads.

Admissions
(All Undergraduate Programs)
Freshman Admissions Requirements: Test(s) required: SAT or ACT; ACT with Writing component. Average high school GPA: 3.3. 16% in top tenth, 42% in top quarter. SAT Math (25/75 percentile): 490/600. SAT Verbal (25/75 percentile): 490/600. Projected SAT Writing (25/75 percentile): 550/650. *Academic units required:* 4 English, 3 math, 3 science, 2 foreign language, 3 social studies, 1 visual or performing arts. Regular application deadline: 2/1. Regular notification: Rolling.

Costs and Financial Aid
(All Undergraduate Programs)
Annual in-state tuition $7,848. Out-of-state tuition $16,923. Room & board $7,686. Average book expense $840.
Financial Aid Statistics: % freshmen/undergrads who receive any aid: 71/59. % freshmen/undergrads who receive need-based scholarship or grant aid: 22/19. % freshmen/undergrads who receive need-based self-help aid: 44/42. Priority financial aid filing deadline: 3/15. Financial aid filing deadline: 3/15. Financial aid notification on or about: 4/1.

TV/Film/Digital Media Studies Programs
**Number of undergraduates
in these programs:** 625

Number of 2005 graduates from these programs: 118

Degrees conferred to these majors: BA.

Also available at Ohio University—Athens: MA, PhD.

Number of full-time faculty in these programs: 21

Number of part-time faculty in these programs: 2

Equipment and facilities: Full compliment of production and postproduction equipment and technology. postproduction suites include 23 MACs. Games Research and Immersive Design Lab for students in digital media includes special effects, games, and animation sequence. Two TV studios; state-of-the-art multitrack recording studio.

Other awards of note: MTV—Best Studio Video, national winner; five regional Emmys by students.

% of graduates who pursue further study within 5 years: 21

% of graduates currently employed in related field: 78

Career development services: Alumni networking opportunities, internship listings, job fairs, job listings.

Famous alumni: Matt Lauer, David Collins, Brian Unger.

Notable alumni: Joel Berman, president, Paramount Television; Randall Winston, producer, *Scrubs*, Larry Patrick, president, Pax TV; Melvin Harris, Sony Pictures.

In Their Own Words

Students in the School of Telecommunications complete internships across the United States, including a dedicated internship with the Today Show *each quarter. They participate in an annual 48-Hour Shoot Out competition; numerous nationally-known guest lecturers from the film, television, recording, games, and radio industries have visited.*

POPULAR PROGRAMS

VIDEO PRODUCTION

Department chair: Frederick Lewis

Number of full-time faculty: 4

Number of part-time faculty: 2

Focus/emphasis: Designed to provide skills in video production with special emphasis on the creative responsibilities of producing and directing.

AUDIO PRODUCTION

Department chair: Jeff Redefer

Number of full-time faculty: 2

Focus/emphasis: Designed to provide skills in various areas of audio production, including commercial production, music recording, audio for multimedia, and sound for picture.

MEDIA MANAGEMENT

Department chair: Greg Newton

Number of full-time faculty: 3

Focus/emphasis: Designed for those who aspire to work in mid- to upper-level leadership positions in the media industries.

MEDIA STUDIES

Department chair: Norma Pecora

Number of full-time faculty: 8

Focus/emphasis: Designed to build critical thinking and analytical skills through understanding the social, cultural, and political impacts of media.

DIGITAL MEDIA: SPECIAL EFFECTS, GAMES, AND ANIMATION

Department chair: Roger Good

Number of full-time faculty: 4

Focus/emphasis: New program designed to provide students with skills in video game production and development, computer animation, and digital effects for video, film, and multimedia. Emphasis is placed on the processes of design and production and the responsibilities and opportunities of working within a creative team.

Students Should Also Know

As a whole, the School of Telecommunications provides strong preparation for professional success in the creative industries. Students focus in depth within areas of interest while gaining a well-rounded orientation to media as a creative business.

OLD DOMINION UNIVERSITY

108 Rollins Hall, 5115 Hampton Boulevard, Norfolk, VA 23529-0050
Phone: 757-683-3685 **E-mail:** admit@odu.edu
Website: www.odu.edu

Campus Life
Environment: City. **Calendar:** Semester.

Students and Faculty
(All Undergraduate Programs)
Enrollment: 14,605. **Student Body:** 59% female, 41% male, 8% out-of-state, 2% international (111 countries represented). African American 23%, Asian 6%, Caucasian 61%, Hispanic 3%. Student/faculty ratio: 18:1. 620 full-time faculty, 80% hold PhDs. 68% faculty teach undergrads.

Admissions
(All Undergraduate Programs)
Freshman Admissions Requirements: Test(s) required: SAT or ACT; ACT with Writing component. Average high school GPA: 3.25. 15% in top tenth, 44% in top quarter. SAT Math (25/75 percentile): 480/580. SAT Verbal (25/75 percentile): 480/580. Projected SAT Writing (25/75 percentile): 540/630. *Academic units required:* 4 English, 3 math, 3 science (2 science labs), 3 foreign language, 3 history, 1 academic elective. Regular application deadline: 3/15. Regular notification: Rolling.

Costs and Financial Aid
(All Undergraduate Programs)
Annual in-state tuition $5,430. Out-of-state tuition $15,210. Room & board $6,292. Required fees $184. Average book expense $900.
Financial Aid Statistics: % freshmen/undergrads who receive any aid: 68/72. % freshmen/undergrads who receive need-based scholarship or grant aid: 31/29. % freshmen/undergrads who receive need-based self-help aid: 32/35. Priority financial aid filing deadline: 2/15. Financial aid filing deadline: 3/15. Financial aid notification on or about: 2/1.

TV/Film/Digital Media Studies Programs
Number of undergraduates in these programs: 250
Number of 2005 graduates from these programs: 80
Degrees conferred to these majors: BA, BS.
Number of full-time faculty in these programs: 10
Number of part-time faculty in these programs: 5
Equipment and facilities: ENG/EFP equipment.

% of graduates who pursue further study within 5 years: 10
% of graduates currently employed in related field: 50
Career development services: Alumni networking opportunities, career counseling, internship listings, job fairs.

In Their Own Words
The university sets up internships, hosts the annual ODU Film and Video Festival, and has many visiting lecturers and professionals every year.

ORAL ROBERTS UNIVERSITY

7777 South Lewis Avenue, Tulsa, OK 74171
Phone: 918-495-6518 **E-mail:** admissions@oru.edu
Website: www.oru.edu

Campus Life
Environment: Metropolis. **Calendar:** Semester.

Students and Faculty
(All Undergraduate Programs)
Enrollment: 3,945. **Student Body:** 58% female, 42% male, 73% out-of-state, 15% international.

African American 20%, Asian 2%, Caucasian 58%, Hispanic 4%, Native American 1%. Student/faculty ratio: 14:1. 198 full-time faculty, 57% hold PhDs. 83% faculty teach undergrads.

Admissions
(All Undergraduate Programs)

Freshman Admissions Requirements: Test(s) required: SAT or ACT. Average high school GPA: 3.36. 27% in top tenth, 53% in top quarter. SAT Math (25/75 percentile): 465/590. SAT Verbal (25/75 percentile): 490/610. Projected SAT Writing (25/75 percentile): 550/660. *Academic units required:* 4 English, 2 math, 1 science (1 science lab), 2 foreign language, 2 social studies. Regular notification: Rolling.

Costs and Financial Aid
(All Undergraduate Programs)

Annual tuition $16,170. Room & board $7,060. Required fees $500. Average book expense $1,560. **Financial Aid Statistics:** % freshmen/undergrads who receive need-based scholarship or grant aid: 69/69. % freshmen/undergrads who receive need-based self-help aid: 64/64. Priority financial aid filing deadline: 3/1.

TV/Film/Digital Media Studies Programs

Number of undergraduates in these programs: 66

Number of 2005 graduates from these programs: 18

Degrees conferred to these majors: BS.

Number of full-time faculty in these programs: 3

Number of part-time faculty in these programs: 6

Equipment and facilities: Each student has a computer with Avid video editing, Adobe Photoshop, and AfterEffects. Software training includes Macromedia/Adobe Director, Apple Pro Suite (DVD Studio Pro, Final Cut, Motion, Compressor), Pro Tools, Flash, Illustrator, and Avid certified training. The school also has digital cameras, a Foley room, ADR, 24 48-channel audio consoles, and a broadcast facility (live shows to satellite with five cameras, three TV studios, multiple video edit suites, and a weekly campus television newscast).

Other awards of note: Several Tellys, a CINDY Award, and a Visual Communicator Award.

% of graduates who pursue further study within 5 years: 20

% of graduates currently employed in related field: 70

Career development services: Alumni networking opportunities, career counseling, internship listings, job fairs, job listings. Juniors attend weekly professional seminars; seniors work on real-world projects.

Notable alumni: Jonathan Martin, creator, *Pahoppahoey* series; Cory Edwards, Blue Yonder Films, *Hoodwicked*; Nick Barre, vice president, artist development, EMI; Phil Cooke, Phil Cooke Pictures; Mark Steele, Steele House Productions; Heidi Mehltretter, Snipe Hunt Films; Jay Shennum, two national Emmy Awards for technical achievement; Brian Poole, storyboards, Industrial Light & Magic; David Morris, Industrial Light & Magic; Rod Spence, editor, *Survivor*; Eric Welch, producer/director, Broken Poets Production; Tom Dooley, vice president, production, Winnercomm, creators of ESPN programming.

In Their Own Words

Students participate in internships in news, sports, corporations, education, entertainment, and interactive media.

POPULAR PROGRAMS

COMMUNICATION ARTS

Department chair: Laura Holland

Number of full-time faculty: 16

Number of part-time faculty: 6

Focus/emphasis: Courses in the Communication Arts Department are for students desiring (1) a general cultural background in the various aspects of communication, (2) a basis for pursuit of graduate work in any of the communication arts, (3) foundational preparation for a career in the mass media, (4) certification for teaching speech/drama in the secondary schools, and (5) ancillary preparation for communication-related careers such as the ministry, law, politics, public relations, sales management, and various areas of human resources development. The Communication Arts Department offers five majors: drama; drama/television/film performance; organizational/ interpersonal communication; communication arts education—speech/drama/debate education; and mass media communication. The mass media communication major offers four areas of concentration: journalism, broadcast journalism, public relations/advertising, and multimedia production, which includes video/audio production, single/multiple camera production, postproduction, facility design, interactive design for Web and disk (DVD/CD), and 3-D modeling and animation.

MUSIC

Department chair: J. Randall Guthrie
Number of full-time faculty: 14
Number of part-time faculty: 22
Focus/emphasis: The Music Department offers three degree programs: the bachelor of arts (music arts major), the bachelor of music (music composition, music performance, and sacred music majors), and the bachelor of music education. Technology-related concentrations are available in both the music arts major and the music composition major. These programs include all of the significant areas of music study, such as music theory, sight singing and ear training, history and literature of music, music teaching methods, and all fields of applied music and performance, including guitar. Minors are available in musical theater, worship leadership, and music technology; there is also a music minor. Courses are designed to facilitate development of music skills for use in the major areas of musical endeavors, including music teaching, music ministry, composition/arrangement, music technology, conducting, and performance. While the department does not offer a degree in jazz studies, there is experience available in jazz band, jazz combo, and vocal jazz for interested students.

ENGLISH

Department chair: William Epperson
Number of full-time faculty: 11
Focus/emphasis: One of the surest marks of an educated person is the ability to handle the English language with grace and precision. The English Department aspires to improve the students' use of the English language and to acquaint them with the world's great literature. The student graduating as an English major has the foundation for teaching, journalism, public relations, and advertising, as well as the background for responsible positions in government service and graduate work in law, library science, medicine, and religion. The English Department offers two majors (English literature and writing) and three minors (English, writing, and prepro-fessional English). The writing major may emphasize either literary or technical forms, preparing students for careers demanding a wide variety of writing and editing tasks. The literary writing courses focus on literary genres such as the short story, poetry, and scriptwriting. The technical courses are designed for students seeking careers in the publishing industry or business world. The English literature major includes 30 hours of course work in English and is a good choice for students planning graduate work in law, library science, or a variety of other graduate programs.

THE PENNSYLVANIA STATE UNIVERSITY—UNIVERSITY PARK

201 Shields Building, Box 3000, University Park, PA 16802-3000
Phone: 814-865-5471 **E-mail:** admissions@psu.edu
Website: www.psu.edu

Campus Life
Environment: Town. **Calendar:** Semester.

Students and Faculty
(All Undergraduate Programs)
Enrollment: 33,958. **Student Body:** 47% female, 53% male, 23% out-of-state, 2% international (120 countries represented). African American 4%, Asian

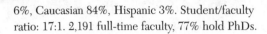

6%, Caucasian 84%, Hispanic 3%. Student/faculty ratio: 17:1. 2,191 full-time faculty, 77% hold PhDs.

Admissions
(All Undergraduate Programs)
Freshman Admissions Requirements: Test(s) required: SAT or ACT. Average high school GPA: 3.56. 41% in top tenth, 80% in top quarter. SAT Math (25/75 percentile): 560/660. SAT Verbal (25/75 percentile): 530/630. Projected SAT Writing (25/75 percentile): 590/670. *Academic units required:* 4 English, 3 math, 3 science, 2 foreign language, 3 social studies. Regular notification: Rolling.

Costs and Financial Aid
(All Undergraduate Programs)
Annual in-state tuition $11,024. Out-of-state tuition $21,260. Room & board $6,530. Required fees $484. Average book expense $992.
Financial Aid Statistics: % freshmen/undergrads who receive need-based scholarship or grant aid: 27/30. % freshmen/undergrads who receive need-based self-help aid: 40/43. Priority financial aid filing deadline: 2/15. Financial aid notification on or about: 2/15.

TV/Film/Digital Media Studies Programs
Number of undergraduates in these programs: 3,400
Number of 2005 graduates from these programs: 700
Degrees conferred to these majors: BA.
Also available at Penn State University Park: MA, PhD.
Number of full-time faculty in these programs: 60
Number of part-time faculty in these programs: 30
Equipment and facilities: TV studio, newsroom, Internet radio station, sound recording and audio production studios, Avid, Pro Tools, Final Cut Pro, digital and analog editing labs.
Other awards of note: Hearst Awards, AAF Awards, Dow Jones editing program.
Career development services: Alumni networking opportunities; career counseling; central resource(s)

for employers to browse headshots, writing samples, reels; internship listings; job fairs; job listings.
Famous alumni: Carmen Finestra, Donald Bellisario, Charles Bierbauer.

In Their Own Words
The university places 500 students in internships per year.

POPULAR PROGRAMS

JOURNALISM
Department chair: Ford Risley
Number of full-time faculty: 15

ADVERTISING & PUBLIC RELATIONS
Department chair: Robert Baukus
Number of full-time faculty: 11

TELECOMMUNICATIONS
Department chair: Matt Jackson
Number of full-time faculty: 10

FILM AND VIDEO
Department chair: Dorn Hetzel
Number of full-time faculty: 7
Focus/emphasis: Creative and production aspects of filmmaking.

SPORTS JOURNALISM
Department chair: Ford Risley
Number of full-time faculty: 2

MEDIA STUDIES
Department chair: John Nichols
Number of full-time faculty: 20

Students Should Also Know
Penn State has the largest communications program in the United States.

PRINCETON UNIVERSITY

PO Box 430, Admission Office, Princeton, NJ 08544-0430
Phone: 609-258-3060
Website: www.princeton.edu

Campus Life

Environment: Village. **Calendar:** Semester.

Students and Faculty
(All Undergraduate Programs)

Enrollment: 4,719. **Student Body:** 46% female, 54% male, 85% out-of-state, 9% international. African American 9%, Asian 13%, Caucasian 62%, Hispanic 7%. Student/faculty ratio: 5:1. 809 full-time faculty, 94% hold PhDs. 56% faculty teach undergrads.

Admissions
(All Undergraduate Programs)

Freshman Admissions Requirements: Test(s) required: SAT and SAT Subject Tests or ACT. Average high school GPA: 3.84. 94% in top tenth, 99% in top quarter. SAT Math (25/75 percentile): 690/790. SAT Verbal (25/75 percentile): 690/770. Projected SAT Writing (25/75 percentile): 720/770. Early decision application deadline: 11/1. Regular application deadline: 1/1. Regular notification: 4/14.

Costs and Financial Aid
(All Undergraduate Programs)

Annual tuition $33,000. Room & board $9,200. Average book expense $3,212.

Financial Aid Statistics: % freshmen/undergrads who receive any aid: 54/51. % freshmen/undergrads who receive need-based scholarship or grant aid: 52/50. % freshmen/undergrads who receive need-based self-help aid: 52/50. Priority financial aid filing deadline: 2/1. Financial aid notification on or about: 4/1.

TV/Film/Digital Media Studies Programs

Also available at Princeton University: Concentration in visual art, certificate.

In Their Own Words

Many lecturers have visted Princeton, including Christine Vachon, producer, founder, and partner, Killer Films. Princeton hosted the Magic and the American Avant-Garde Cinema, a conference featuring speakers Karen Beckman, Robert Kelly, Tom Gunning, Renata Jackson, Rani Singh, William Breeze, and David Levi Strauss.

POPULAR PROGRAMS

VISUAL ARTS

Number of full-time faculty: 17

Focus/emphasis: Princeton University's program in visual arts has a faculty of working artists of established reputation and outstanding teaching ability who offer studio courses in ceramics, digital photography, drawing, painting, photography, printmaking, sculpture, and video. They give seminars and lectures in contemporary artistic practice and the history and theory of film as well. Whether students are interested in a program of study leading to a special major in studio arts or a certificate program, or desire to take just one or two courses, the visual arts program provides them with excellent physical facilities and an atmosphere of serious intellectual inquiry. Princeton believes that a strong liberal arts education provides an essential foundation for the aspiring artist and is the best platform for understanding the place of the arts in modern society. Even a cursory glance at the dominant journals devoted to art, photography, and cinema indicates that the visual artists of today are engaged in a dialogue with art history, information theory, and literary criticism, and in debates about group identity and politics. As a result, the artist needs to be broadly familiar with the cultural history of the late-nineteenth and twentieth centuries and be aware of the multiplicity of issues that have excited artists of these periods; all of these things come together to form the ongoing traditions leading up to the present.

PURDUE UNIVERSITY—WEST LAFAYETTE

1080 Schleman Hall, West Lafayette, IN 47907
Phone: 765-494-1776 **E-mail:** admissions@purdue.edu
Website: www.purdue.edu

Campus Life
Environment: Town. **Calendar:** Semester.

Students and Faculty
(All Undergraduate Programs)
Enrollment: 30,545. **Student Body:** 41% female, 59% male, 29% out-of-state, 6% international (126 countries represented). African American 4%, Asian 5%, Caucasian 82%, Hispanic 3%. Student/faculty ratio: 14:1. 1,960 full-time faculty, 98% hold PhDs.

Admissions
(All Undergraduate Programs)
Freshman Admissions Requirements: Test(s) required: SAT or ACT; ACT with Writing component. Average high school GPA: 3.4. 27% in top tenth, 58% in top quarter. SAT Math (25/75 percentile): 530/650. SAT Verbal (25/75 percentile): 500/610. Projected SAT Writing (25/75 percentile): 560/660. *Academic units required:* 4 English, 3 math, 2 science (2 science labs), 2 foreign language. Regular notification: Rolling.

Costs and Financial Aid
(All Undergraduate Programs)
Annual in-state tuition $6,458. Out-of-state tuition $19,824. Room & board $6,830. Average book expense $980.
Financial Aid Statistics: % freshmen/undergrads who receive any aid: 80/76. % freshmen/undergrads who receive need-based scholarship or grant aid: 15/13. % freshmen/undergrads who receive need-based self-help aid: 36/36. Priority financial aid filing deadline: 3/1. Financial aid notification on or about: 4/15.

TV/Film/Digital Media Studies Programs
Number of undergraduates in these programs: 111

Number of 2005 graduates from these programs: 21
Degrees conferred to these majors: BA.
Also available at Purdue University—West Lafayette: MA, PhD.
Number of full-time faculty in these programs: 32
Career development services: Career counseling, internship listings, job fairs.
Famous alumni: Brian Lamb

POPULAR PROGRAMS

MEDIA, TECHNOLOGY, AND SOCIETY
Department chair: Dr. Howard Sypher
Focus/emphasis: The program is designed to aid the student in developing a systematic approach to understanding the processes and consequences of media and technology for a global society, including new and emerging information and communication technologies (ICTs). Current research being done in MTS at Purdue includes the impact of new technologies on media and society, cognitive and emotional reactions to media, children and video games, and health promotion in the media.

FILM AND VIDEO STUDIES
Department chair: Benjamin Lawton
Focus/emphasis: The interdisciplinary major is a professionally-oriented program based on a strong liberal arts foundation. It draws on faculty and courses from the Departments of Foreign Languages and Literatures, English, Communication, Visual and Performing Arts, and Computer Graphics Technology. The program is grounded in film and communication theory and history; it is implemented through a select number of production courses in new and evolving media. The goal of the program is to help prepare students to meet the new challenges they will encounter as citizens and workers in the information age. The program is designed to help students learn how to think, how to analyze, and how to integrate and apply the theories that form the basis of the film and video discipline.

QUINNIPIAC UNIVERSITY

275 Mount Carmel Avenue, Hamden, CT 06518
Phone: 203-582-8600 **E-mail:** admissions@quinnipiac.edu
Website: www.quinnipiac.edu

Campus Life

Environment: Town. **Calendar:** Semester.

Students and Faculty
(All Undergraduate Programs)

Enrollment: 5,542. **Student Body:** 61% female, 39% male, 70% out-of-state, 1% international (20 countries represented). African American 2%, Asian 2%, Caucasian 79%, Hispanic 4%. Student/faculty ratio: 15:1. 281 full-time faculty, 79% hold PhDs. 88% faculty teach undergrads.

Admissions
(All Undergraduate Programs)

Freshman Admissions Requirements: Test(s) required: SAT or ACT. Average high school GPA: 3.4. 21% in top tenth, 55% in top quarter. SAT Math (25/75 percentile): 540/610. SAT Verbal (25/75 percentile): 520/590. Projected SAT Writing (25/75 percentile): 580/640. *Academic units required:* 4 English, 3 math, 3 science (2 science labs), 2 social studies, 3 academic electives, 4 science and math in PT, OT, or PA. Regular notification: Rolling.

Costs and Financial Aid
(All Undergraduate Programs)

Annual tuition $25,240. Room & board $10,700. Required fees $1,040. Average book expense $800. **Financial Aid Statistics:** % freshmen/undergrads who receive any aid: 70/68. % freshmen/undergrads who receive need-based scholarship or grant aid: 58/55. % freshmen/undergrads who receive need-based self-help aid: 51/50. Priority financial aid filing deadline: 3/1. Financial aid notification on or about: 2/15.

TV/Film/Digital Media Studies Programs

Number of undergraduates in these programs: 300
Number of 2005 graduates from these programs: 75
Degrees conferred to these majors: BA.

Also available at Quinnipiac University: MS.
Number of full-time faculty in these programs: 6
Number of part-time faculty in these programs: 12
Equipment and facilities: The Ed McMahon Mass Communications Center is one of the best-designed and equipped academic media production facilities in the country. The school is among the very first universities in the nation to offer high-definition (1080i) production capabilities; the television studio features three Sony HDC-910 digital high-definition cameras, each with prompter; a Sony MVS-8000A HD/SD production switcher; GVG Profile video server; Sony HDCAM VTR; Sony digital audio console; ETC lighting console; Mole-Richardson studio lighting; DVCAM, Digital S, and Beta SP VTRs. Students shoot DV and edit with Final Cut Pro, AfterEffects, Photoshop, and other industry-standard applications; upper-level courses use 3-chip professional-level field cameras. The equipment room provides all manner of field gear for high-level audio and video work. two audio-recording studios feature Pro Tools, digital synthesizers, digital cart machines, DAT recorders, and mixing consoles. We maintain three computer labs featuring a host of professional applications such as Illustrator, Dreamweaver, Photoshop, Flash, Fireworks, Freehand, and AP wire service; color laser printers, flatbed scanners, DVD burners, and other peripherals.

Other awards of note: Our faculty and student awards have included a Judge's Commendation from the Rhode Island Film Festival, an Award of Excellence and Best of Festival awards from the Broadcast Education Association, and Emmy nominations.

Career development services: Alumni networking opportunities, career counseling, internship listings, job fairs, job listings. Our Dean's Office includes a veteran broadcaster who provides supplemental career counseling and guidance.

Notable alumni: Lester Ayala, oversees radio and TV advertising, Cronin & Company, Glastonbury, CT; Yana Gould, producer, *Martha Stewart Media and Videofashion!, E! Entertainment.*

In Their Own Words

We offer a number of opportunities for international study. Students have recently produced documentaries in South Africa and Ireland, and we offer a summer program in Nice, France in narrative production. Our internship program is very robust, with more than 900 field placement opportunities nationwide.

POPULAR PROGRAMS

PUBLIC RELATIONS

Department chair: Dr. Sharon Kleinman
Number of full-time faculty: 3
Number of part-time faculty: 7
Focus/emphasis: The major prepares entry-level public relations and corporate communications practitioners for careers in agency, corporate, government, and nonprofit communications. The program emphasizes research, writing, speaking, campaigns, and service learning. The School of Communications Public Relations Program is grounded in media history and theory as a prelude to professional practice or as preparation for graduate or professional school.

MEDIA PRODUCTION

Department chair: Margarita Diaz
Number of full-time faculty: 6
Number of part-time faculty: 7
Focus/emphasis: The central purpose of the media production concentration is to introduce students to various forms of media practice and help them become technically proficient, aesthetically grounded, and expressively mature. They are thoroughly immersed in the creative and technical aspects of digital production and gain experience in television studio practice, single-camera-style production, digital audio, editing, and interactive technologies and practice.

JOURNALISM

Department chair: Margarita Diaz
Number of full-time faculty: 8

Number of part-time faculty: 8
Focus/emphasis: The degree prepares students for careers in news and other fields that involve communicating information in an accurate, unbiased, clear, and timely fashion. Special emphasis is placed on the time-tested journalistic values of honesty and fairness. The curriculum includes both skills courses and courses on the relationship between communications and society.

MEDIA STUDIES

Department chair: Dr. Sharon Kleinman
Number of full-time faculty: 6
Number of part-time faculty: 12
Focus/emphasis: Our program is the most general and flexible of the majors offered by the School of Communications at Quinnipiac University. The program addresses both the communication issues of our society and the work of media practitioners. Students gain an understanding of how media influences, affects, and reflects society as well as analytical skills and professional techniques for dealing with today's rapidly evolving media landscape. The program is grounded in media history and theory and helps students gain a big-picture understanding of the professional, cultural, and societal aspects of modern media.

Students Should Also Know

Quinnipiac University is founded on three core values: high-quality academic programs, a student-oriented environment, and the fostering of a sense of community among all the members of the Quinnipiac family.

RADFORD UNIVERSITY

PO Box 6903, RU Station, Radford, VA 24142-6903
Phone: 540-831-5371 **E-mail:** ruadmiss@radford.edu
Website: www.radford.edu

Campus Life

Environment: Village. **Calendar:** Semester.

Students and Faculty
(All Undergraduate Programs)
Enrollment: 8,419. **Student Body:** 58% female, 42% male, 8% out-of-state. African American 6%, Asian 2%, Caucasian 88%, Hispanic 3%. Student/faculty ratio: 20:1. 377 full-time faculty, 83% hold PhDs. 93% faculty teach undergrads.

Admissions
(All Undergraduate Programs)
Freshman Admissions Requirements: Test(s) required: SAT or ACT. Average high school GPA: 3.07. 4% in top tenth, 22% in top quarter. SAT Math (25/75 percentile): 450/550. SAT Verbal (25/75 percentile): 460/550. Projected SAT Writing (25/75 percentile): 530/610. Regular application deadline: 2/1.

Costs and Financial Aid
(All Undergraduate Programs)
Annual in-state tuition $5,746. Out-of-state tuition $13,494. Room & board $6,218. Average book expense $800.

Financial Aid Statistics: % freshmen/undergrads who receive any aid: 63/71. % freshmen/undergrads who receive need-based scholarship or grant aid: 29/5. % freshmen/undergrads who receive need-based self-help aid: 33/35. Financial aid filing deadline: 3/1. Financial aid notification on or about: 4/15.

TV/Film/Digital Media Studies Programs
Number of undergraduates in these programs: 457
Number of 2005 graduates from these programs: 92
Degrees conferred to these majors: BA, BS.
Number of full-time faculty in these programs: 8
Number of part-time faculty in these programs: 4
Equipment and facilities: Television studio, extensive use of ENG equipment packages, comprehensive Apple labs with latest media software packages, three postproduction workstations with Media 100, Avid software.
Career development services: Alumni networking opportunities; career assessments and interpretations by a nationally-recognized authority in this field; career counseling; central resource(s) for employers to browse headshots, writing samples, reels; internship listings; job fairs; job listings.

In Their Own Words
Internships worldwide including those that place students in Web design, journalism, advertising, and production technology. Frequent visits by nationally-recognized speakers.

POPULAR PROGRAMS

DIGITAL MEDIA STUDIES
Department chair: Clayland Waite
Number of full-time faculty: 8
Number of part-time faculty: 4
Focus/emphasis: Utilizes a liberal arts theoretical framework to prepare students for a broad spectrum of media professions. Arms students with the necessary approach and skills to allow them to be adaptable and flexible to ever-changing economic, technical, and communicative environments with a media professions context.

REGENT UNIVERSITY
1000 Regent University Drive, Central Enrollment Management
Virginia Beach, VA 23464
Phone: 800-373-5504 **E-mail:** admissions@regent.edu
Website: www.regent.edu

Campus Life
Calendar: Semester.

Costs and Financial Aid
(All Undergraduate Programs)
Annual tuition $11,850. Required fees $175.

TV/Film/Digital Media Studies Programs
Degrees conferred to these majors: BA.
Also available at Regent University: MFA, MA.
Equipment and facilities: Cameras: Arriflex SR3 Super/Regular 16 mm, Arriflex SR2, Arriflex S, Arriflex BL, AATON, CP-16, Sony DSR PD150

DVCAM Camcorder, Sony DSR 570WSL DVCAM Camcorder, Sony TRV-900, Sony PDX 10, JVC DV 500. Lighting: eight Arri Combination light kits (with two 650-watt, and two 300-watt instruments each), Arri 1K Kit, Arri 575 HMI Arri 1K kit (three instruments), Arri 650-watt kit (four instruments), Lowel Omni-Light kits, Redhead kits (three instruments each), Mole Cart: Tweenie II, Mole Juniors kit, Mole Babys kit, Mole 2K zip soft light, Junior Mole instruments, Pepper kits (six instruments), Desisti 1200w HMIs, Chinaballs. Sound: Nagra IVS-TC recorder, Nagra IV-L recorder, Field DAT recorder, PSC AlphaMix Sound Mixer; Sennheiser 416 Shotgun, Sennheiser 816 Shotgun, Sennheiser ME67K6 Shotgun, Sony ECM-77B Lavalier, Sony ECM-50ps Lavalier, and Lectrosonic UCR100 wireless mike receivers, Lectrosonic UM100 wireless mike transmitters, Electrovoice 635A microphones, Sony MDR7506 headphones, sound boom poles, Sennheiser Pistol Grip and Zepplin, Rycote Pistol Grips and Zepplins, Rycote Zepplin Windsocks. Grip/Electric: Ford Truck with 18' box, Taco Cart, Applebox sets, C-stands with arms, Highboy stands, Lowboy stands, Ianiro lighting stands, Junior Mole stands, Baby Mole stands, eight ladder, 4 x 4 frames with silks, flags, single, and double, 6 x 6 frame with silk, flag, single, and double, 12 x 12 overhead set with silk, flag, single, and double, traffic cones, three straight, three curved-track sections for series, nine fisher dollies, sandbags, assorted stingers.

POPULAR PROGRAMS

DIRECTING

Department chair: Lorene M. Wales
Number of full-time faculty: 9
Focus/emphasis: The Department of Cinema—Television Arts is dedicated to graduating trained professionals in film and TV whose skills qualify them to become leaders in the media. It starts with incredible, well-told stories. At Regent, it continues through a program based on a foundation of theory and the practices of preproduction, directing actors, cinematography, creative editing, and audio postproduction.

RENSSELAER POLYTECHNIC INSTITUTE

110 Eighth Street, Troy, NY 12180-3590
Phone: 518-276-6216 **E-mail:** admissions@rpi.edu
Website: www.rpi.edu

Campus Life
Environment: City. **Calendar:** Semester.

Students and Faculty
(All Undergraduate Programs)
Enrollment: 4,921. **Student Body:** 24% female, 76% male, 52% out-of-state, 3% international (67 countries represented). African American 4%, Asian 11%, Caucasian 72%, Hispanic 5%. Student/faculty ratio: 14:1. 400 full-time faculty, 98% hold PhDs. 100% faculty teach undergrads.

Admissions
(All Undergraduate Programs)
Freshman Admissions Requirements: Test(s) required: SAT or ACT; ACT with Writing component. 61% in top tenth, 95% in top quarter. SAT Math (25/75 percentile): 640/730. SAT Verbal (25/75 percentile): 580/690. Projected SAT Writing (25/75 percentile): 630/720. *Academic units required:* 4 English, 4 math, 3 science, 2 social studies. Early decision application deadline: 11/15. Regular application deadline: 1/1. Regular notification: 3/20.

Costs and Financial Aid
(All Undergraduate Programs)
Annual tuition $31,000. Room & board $9,915. Required fees $900. Average book expense $1,770. **Financial Aid Statistics:** % freshmen/undergrads who receive any aid: 94/91. % freshmen/undergrads who receive need-based scholarship or grant aid: 75/70. % freshmen/undergrads who receive need-based self-help aid: 44/44. Priority financial aid filing deadline: 2/15. Financial aid notification on or about: 3/25.

TV/Film/Digital Media Studies Programs
Number of undergraduates in these programs: 223

Number of 2005 graduates from these programs: 60

Degrees conferred to these majors: BS.

Number of full-time faculty in these programs: 40

Number of part-time faculty in these programs: 17

Equipment and facilities: Laboratories and studios in the Arts and in the Language, Literature, and Communication Departments are equipped with the latest computing and collaborative communication equipment. The Visualization and Simulation Technology (VAST) Lab has cutting-edge graphics, animation, and video equipment for student classes and projects. Graphic design and hypermedia courses are taught in the Intel NT Lab. iEAR Studios (Integrated Electronic Arts at Rensselaer) are outfitted for producing professional-quality sound and broadcast-quality video. The Social and Behavioral Research Laboratory (SBRL), a collaborative effort between the Department of Language, Literature, and Communication; the Department of Cognitive Sciences; and the Department of Science and Technology Studies, provides an opportunity for students to participate on faculty research teams studying human-computer interaction, computer-mediated communication, and computer game design.

Other awards of note: Faculty and students in the Arts Department have received a variety of prestigious awards, including the Rockefeller Award, the Guggenheim Fellowship, and an Emmy. Faculty and students in the Language, Literature, and Communication Department have been named Associate Fellow of the Society for Technical Communication and have received the Creative Achievement Award for the International Visual Literacy Association, the Ad Club Scholarship, the Eastern Communication Association (ECA) Everett Lee Hunt Award for Outstanding Scholarship, and the Russell Nye Award for the best article published in the Journal of Popular Culture.

Career development services: Career counseling, internship listings, job fairs, job listings. The LL&C Department offers course credit for specific professional experiences through the Communication Internship, which can be used toward fulfilling culminating experience requirements.

Notable alumni: Jacob Slutsky, 3-D animator/compositor, broadcast design, UV Phactory; Ray Lutzky, director of marketing communications for CAMPUSPEAK, Inc., a national speakers bureau for college students based in Denver, CO; Mike Delprete, president, Agora Studios/Agora Games. In addition to those listed above, we have graduates working at the following places: Blue Sky Animation Studios, commercial animator/s, render wrangler/compositing support for *Chat the Planet*, an MTV show; assistant editor, Liquid Design; commercial 3-D animators & compositors; MusicBlitz, marketing services coordinator; Media Logic, Web designer, multimedia programmer, Internet marketing specialist.

In Their Own Words

The BS in Electronic Media, Arts, and Communication (EMAC) at Rensselaer is one of the first undergraduate programs of its kind in the United States. EMAC is jointly offered by the Arts Department, and the Department of Language, Literature, and Communication at Rensselaer Polytechnic Institute. The EMAC program integrates creative and critical thought with expertise in advanced electronic multimedia. The interdisciplinary approach of arts and communication produces entrepreneurs and critical thinkers who will use technology in innovative ways in commercial, academic, and artistic spheres.

POPULAR PROGRAMS

ELECTRONIC MEDIA, ARTS, AND COMMUNICATION

Department chair: Kathy High

Focus/emphasis: The BS in Electronic Media, Arts, and Communication (EMAC) curriculum provides theoretical frameworks for understanding and shaping the impact of these technologies on today's society as well as the professional skills to work with a wide range of electronic media.

COMMUNICATION

Department chair: Cheryl Geisler

Focus/emphasis: The Language, Literature, and Communication (LL&C) curriculum provides an interdisciplinary approach to the study of communication in today's information society. The BS in Communication provides both a theoretical foundation in basic communication principles and a hands-on education in applying those principles to communicating in a world driven by technology and new media. The BS in Communication with a concentration in graphic design provides a curriculum for undergraduate students who seek professional careers in graphic design. This concentration will prepare students for professional practice and graduate study in creative problem solving for print and electronic media. Students completing this sequence will know how to apply theory to the creation of conventional and unconventional communication objects (that includes but is not limited to advertising campaigns, editorial layouts, corporate communications including annual reports and corporate standards, event announcements, advocacy campaigns, and Web pages) that convey information to a target audience.

ELECTRONIC ARTS

Focus/emphasis: The BS degree in Electronic Arts provides students with an opportunity to pursue an arts degree with a particular emphasis on the use of technology and an interdisciplinary approach to electronic arts, including computer music, interactivity, video, computer imaging, animation, web, and multimedia installation and performance. The degree is designed for students who aspire to be artists and who are also strong in math, science, and technology. The program prepares students for careers as working artists and performers who use technology to make works of art and music. It also prepares students for graduate studies in the electronic arts. The program integrates an intensive curriculum of studio and theory courses in electronic and traditional arts and music with Rensselaer's rigorous core requirements in math and science. As an art pro-gram situated within the context of a technological university, we offer a unique creative environment in which to develop and realize cutting edge electronic art. Practical experiences in performing and exhibiting are also built into the curriculum, which takes advantage of the Arts Department's iEAR Presents! Performance Series and collaborations with the Arts Center of the Capital Region located in Troy.

RHODE ISLAND SCHOOL OF DESIGN

2 College Street, Providence, RI 02903
Phone: 401-454-6300 **E-mail:** admissions@risd.edu
Website: www.risd.edu

Campus Life
Environment: City. **Calendar:** 4-1-4.

Students and Faculty
(All Undergraduate Programs)
Enrollment: 1,882. **Student Body:** 66% female, 34% male, 12% international (44 countries represented). African American 2%, Asian 14%, Caucasian 51%, Hispanic 5%. Student/faculty ratio: 11:1. 146 full-time faculty. 100% faculty teach undergrads.

Admissions
(All Undergraduate Programs)
Freshman Admissions Requirements: Test(s) required: SAT or ACT. Average high school GPA: 3.3. 28% in top tenth, 54% in top quarter. SAT Math (25/75 percentile): 550/670. SAT Verbal (25/75 percentile): 530/660. Projected SAT Writing (25/75 percentile): 590/690. Regular application deadline: 2/15. Regular notification: 4/1.

Costs and Financial Aid
(All Undergraduate Programs)
Annual tuition $27,510. Room & board $7,709. Required fees $465. Average book expense $2,200. **Financial Aid Statistics:** % freshmen/undergrads who receive need-based scholarship or grant aid: 27/44. % freshmen/undergrads who receive need-based self-help aid: 42/48. Priority financial aid filing

deadline: 2/15. Financial aid filing deadline: 2/15. Financial aid notification on or about: 4/1.

TV/Film/Digital Media Studies Programs

Number of undergraduates in these programs: 123

Degrees conferred to these majors: BFA.

Also available at Rhode Island School of Design: MFA.

Equipment and facilities: The Film/Animation/Video Department is equipped to accommodate students working in all relevant disciplines. Facilities include shooting and lighting studios for film, video, 16 mm, 35 mm, and puppet animation; digital editing and sound-mixing rooms; film-to-tape transfer equipment; screening rooms; and a 600-seat auditorium with film and video projection. Various types of film and video cameras are available for student use. State of- the-art computer resources include CGI and Macintosh workstations with a full professional range of production and editing software.

Career development services: Job listings.

Famous alumni: Martha Coolidge, Gus Van Sant, Seth MacFarlane.

POPULAR PROGRAMS

FILM/ANIMATION/VIDEO

Department chair: Peter O'Neill

Number of full-time faculty: 6

Number of part-time faculty: 25

Focus/emphasis: The curriculum emphasizes the form, content, and structure of images moving in time. The program teaches you the technical skills necessary to produce artistic and professional photographic, electronic, and animated moving images. Students will learn to work in narrative, experimental, and documentary live action forms as well as animation. Some students may also choose to produce work that encompasses film and video within installations and performance art. In your sophomore year, you will attend production classes in all three departmental disciplines: film, animation, and video. As a junior, however, your focus becomes more concentrated on either live action or animation. In their senior year, students design and complete degree projects that are based in either film, animation, video, computer animation, or combined media.

RINGLING SCHOOL OF ART AND DESIGN

2700 North Tamiami Trail, Sarasota, FL 34234-5895
Phone: 941-351-5100 **E-mail:** admissions@ringling.edu
Website: www.ringling.edu

Campus Life

Environment: City. **Calendar:** Semester.

Students and Faculty (All Undergraduate Programs)

Enrollment: 1,088. **Student Body:** 49% female, 51% male, 45% out-of-state, 5% international (29 countries represented). African American 3%, Asian 4%, Caucasian 77%, Hispanic 11%, Native American 1%. Student/faculty ratio: 13:1. 60 full-time faculty, 70% hold PhDs. 100% faculty teach undergrads.

Admissions (All Undergraduate Programs)

Average high school GPA: 3.05. SAT Math (25/75 percentile): 450/580. SAT Verbal (25/75 percentile): 480/600. Projected SAT Writing (25/75 percentile): 540/650. Regular notification: Rolling.

Costs and Financial Aid (All Undergraduate Programs)

Annual tuition $23,700.

Financial Aid Statistics: % freshmen/undergrads who receive any aid: 72/79. % freshmen/undergrads who receive need-based scholarship or grant aid: 53/55. % freshmen/undergrads who receive need-based self-help aid: 60/63. Priority financial aid filing deadline: 3/1. Financial aid notification on or about: 4/1.

TV/Film/Digital Media Studies Programs

Degrees conferred to these majors: BFA.

Equipment and facilities: The Department of Computer Animation is dedicated to using the most current technology to provide students with as many advantages as possible in their work. This, coupled with Ringling's relationships with leading software and hardware development companies such as Pixar, Alias, Sony, Hewlett Packard, and IBM, ensures that students will work with the latest advances in software technology as well as emerging hardware developments. In the Department of Graphic & Interactive Communication, students will learn on the equipment and software used in the profession. In addition to Apple computers with 23" flatscreen monitors, students will have access to digital cameras [still and video] and video-editing stations. Print services include inkjet, laser, and large format.

Other awards of note: Ringling School won 17 Addy Awards in the local 2006 Advertising Federation Competition.

Career development services: Job listings, recruiting.

Notable alumni: Jeff Fowler (2002), computer animation, nominated for an Academy Award for Best Animated Short Film for his short, *Gopher Broke*.

POPULAR PROGRAMS

COMPUTER ANIMATION

Department chair: Jim McCampbell
Number of full-time faculty: 10
Focus/emphasis: In Ringling School of Art and Design's deep and specialized four-year computer animation degree program, you will develop skills in modeling, lighting, motion, and sound—while learning how to tell a story. At the same time, you will gain command of the technical skills required in today's highly competitive animation industry. Firms from all over the world look to Ringling School for the best and brightest computer animation artists because our students possess the proper balance of technical skills and aesthetic development. They have the ability to create as well as produce. Artist, animator, actor, storyteller, modeler, lighting director, set designer, costumer, sound designer, and film director—you will use all of these skills and more. At Ringling School, you will take courses that focus on both the conceptual and the technical, as you learn to master communication through movement and bring your ideas to life.

GRAPHIC & INTERACTIVE COMMUNICATION

Number of full-time faculty: 17
Focus/emphasis: Typography, images, the very latest in computer hardware and software—at Ringling School of Art and Design, the tools are all here, along with a problem waiting to be solved. Whether you are working in paint, ink and collage, digital video, or animation, it is up to you as the problem solver to organize, interpret, and magnify the images to best communicate your message. In Ringling School's Graphic & Interactive Communication Department, you will learn communication theory and principles, balancing that knowledge with an understanding of society and culture. The result is a graphic designer who can produce a broad range of visual images for print, electronic, and 3-D media in today's communication-oriented culture.

PHOTOGRAPHY & DIGITAL IMAGING

Department chair: Thomas Carabasi
Number of full-time faculty: 3
Focus/emphasis: From exposure to ideas to ideas on exposure—at Ringling School of Art and Design, discover the power of your own photographic voice along with the tools of your trade. From the creative, controlled environment of a studio shoot to the experiential side of going on location, you will explore photography from every angle. From traditional darkroom techniques to the endless possibilities stemming from the creative manipulation of images using the newest computer software, you will have at Ringling School the artistic freedom to explore many of the options available to today's professional photographer. As a

Photography & Digital Imaging major at Ringling School, you will not only master the techniques of this evolving medium, but you will also begin to understand its profound affect on our culture and our world.

ROBERT MORRIS UNIVERSITY

6001 University Boulevard, Moon Township, PA 15108-1189
Phone: 412-262-8206 **E-mail:** enrollmentoffice@rmu.edu
Website: www.rmu.edu

Campus Life
Environment: Metropolis. **Calendar:** Semester.

Students and Faculty
(All Undergraduate Programs)
Enrollment: 3,877. **Student Body:** 46% female, 54% male, 10% out-of-state, 2% international (27 countries represented). African American 8%, Caucasian 86%. Student/faculty ratio: 16:1. 157 full-time faculty, 82% hold PhDs. 100% faculty teach undergrads.

Admissions
(All Undergraduate Programs)
Freshman Admissions Requirements: Test(s) required: SAT or ACT. Average high school GPA: 3.16. 8% in top tenth, 27% in top quarter. SAT Math (25/75 percentile): 460/570. SAT Verbal (25/75 percentile): 450/540. Projected SAT Writing (25/75 percentile): 520/600. *Academic units required:* 4 English, 3 math, 2 science, 4 social studies, 3 academic electives. Regular application deadline: 7/1. Regular notification: Rolling.

Costs and Financial Aid
(All Undergraduate Programs)
Annual tuition $17,920. Average book expense $1,000.
Financial Aid Statistics: % freshmen/undergrads who receive any aid: 78/74. % freshmen/undergrads who receive need-based scholarship or grant aid: 76/68. % freshmen/undergrads who receive need-based self-help aid: 71/69. Financial aid notification on or about: 3/15.

TV/Film/Digital Media Studies Programs
Number of undergraduates in these programs: 76
Number of 2005 graduates from these programs: 9
Degrees conferred to these majors: BA, BFA.
Number of full-time faculty in these programs: 5
Number of part-time faculty in these programs: 4
Equipment and facilities: We have a very large television studio, equipped with state-of-the-art cameras, a broadcast control room with a digital switcher and DVCPRO recorders, various sets, and a small scene shop. For editing and motion graphics, we have 30 Final Cut stations with Creative Suite and AfterEffects software in classroom and lab configurations. We also have three Avid editing stations. Our newsroom is equipped with four DVCPRO tape-editing systems; news scripts and news producing are executed on iNews project management software. In addition, we have a five-camera portable package for taping sports, theater, and other events. We are a head-end for Comcast Channel 98 with 20,000 subscribers. Field production includes four DVCPRO packages, and four mini-DV packages. The Center for Documentary Production and Study houses another mini-DV field package and Final Cut editing station. Our black-and-white darkroom facilities include two developing rooms and 10 enlarging stations.
ATAS Faculty Seminar participants: 1
Other awards of note: The International Association of Business Communicators Golden Triangle Award for documentary, *America Talks*; two Videographer Awards, Award of Distinction for the Povertyneck Hillbillies music video and Award of Excellence for the documentary *The Baluh Boys*; two Communicator Awards, Award of Distinction for the 2004 Enrollment Video and Award of Excellence for the documentary *The Baluh Boys*; three regional awards from the Society of Professional Journalists (2004), one in sports reporting and two in news reporting; four regional awards from the Society of Professional Journalists (2005), two Awards of Distinction for news and public service announcements, a Crystal Award of Excellence

for the video *Fallen Heroes*, and one Honorable Mention for the Povertyneck Hillbillies' music video; a Telly Award for the documentary *The Baluh Boys*; Avid Education selection for an Avid promotional video; Aegis Award for the Povertyneck Hillbillies' music video.

% of graduates who pursue further study within 5 years: 50

% of graduates currently employed in related field: 75

Career development services: Alumni networking opportunities, career counseling, internship listings, job fairs, job listings. Creativity at Work is a half-day career conference for students in communications, English, and media arts. This annual conference features approximately 20 professionals working in creative fields such as advertising, design and multimedia, TV/video production, public relations, and journalism. Students attend panels to learn about career options and receive job/internship search advice. A networking segment is also featured to allow students an opportunity to talk individually with the speakers. The practice interview program provides students an opportunity to sharpen their interviewing skills. Practice interview sessions include a videotaped practice interview, personal feedback from a career consultant and a resume review. Students also have the opportunity to participate in a practice interview with employer volunteers on selected interview schedules offered throughout the year. The Career Library contains over 200 books, videos, and other resources relevant to researching careers and searching for jobs. CareerSearch is a powerful Internet database available for employer research. The database includes over two million employers nationwide and can be searched by industry, location, and keyword. It provides contact information and company/organization descriptions for potential internship or full-time positions. A wide variety of industries are included such as advertising and public relations, broadcast media organizations, performing arts, publications, and publishers. The Career Center operates on a school-specific model, with career consultants assigned to meet with students and alumni in spe-

cific academic schools or departments. Students and alumni may meet with their career consultant to discuss all aspects of career planning and job searching. The Career Center also offers two career decision-making assessments: the Strong Interest Inventory and the MBTI Career Report. Job fairs: The Career Center sponsors an annual job fair called the Career Expo. This event provides students and alumni the opportunity to meet with over 150 employers to obtain career information and discuss internships and full-time jobs. Job listings: hundreds of employers contact the Career Center each year seeking candidates for a variety of professional positions. Employers may post positions with the Career Center through MonsterTRAK, an online job posting database. Employers may opt to receive resumes through an online resume collection or set up an on-campus interview schedule. The Career Center also posts internship positions for employers through MonsterTRAK. In addition, the Career Center works in cooperation with academic departments to promote the Academic Internship Program. Over 400 students participate annually in this academic employment learning experience. The Career Center coordinates the program by assisting students through the application and internship search process. Alumni networking opportunities: Career Contact & Alumni Network provides students access to an online database of volunteer alumni mentors and networking contacts. The networking database is part of MonsterTRAK and is maintained by the Career Center. In addition, the Career Center works in cooperation with the Office of Alumni Relations & Special Events to sponsor several alumni networking events throughout the year.

In Their Own Words

Our program is unique because we emphasize field and documentary production plus live studio and taped television production. The centrally located Academic Media Center houses all the facilities and equipment. The program is hands-on, emphasizing practical experience in addition to classroom learning. Students produce their own television programs and a nightly newscast,

and shoot and direct video coverage of our football and basketball games. Under direction of
the Center for Documentary Production and
Study, students travel on international documentary exchanges. Exchanges in Germany,
Turkey, and Chile are ongoing and will be
expanded. Students work on a variety of documentaries under the direction of the Center for
Documentary Production and Study, two of
which aired on local PBS stations and one of
which was highlighted nationally on CBS.
Internships are an important part of the curriculum. Students intern at all the major television
stations, many production companies, and with
major sports teams, such as the Pittsburgh
Steelers. Nationally and internationally known
filmmakers visit regularly, including Louis
Massiah, documentary filmmaker from
Philadelphia, and Hollywood film editor Pasquale
Buba, producers of the feature film The Bread
My Sweet; Adrienne Wehr and Melissa Martin;
Hollywood producer Suzanne De Lorentis; docu-
mentary cinematographer Joe Seamans; docu-
mentary scholars Betsy McLane and Michael
Rabiger; international filmmakers Nurdan Arca,
Paul Cronin, and Elinor Kowarsky.

ROGER WILLIAMS UNIVERSITY

1 Old Ferry Road, Bristol, RI 02809-0000
Phone: 401-254-3500 **E-mail:** admit@rwu.edu
Website: www.rwu.edu

Campus Life
Environment: Town. **Calendar:** Semester.

Students and Faculty
(All Undergraduate Programs)
Enrollment: 4,358. **Student Body:** 49% female,
51% male, 87% out-of-state, 2% international (39
countries represented). African American 1%, Asian
2%, Caucasian 79%, Hispanic 2%. Student/faculty
ratio: 16:1. 178 full-time faculty, 80% hold PhDs.
100% faculty teach undergrads.

Admissions
(All Undergraduate Programs)
Freshman Admissions Requirements: Test(s)
required: SAT or ACT. Average high school GPA:
3.07. 11% in top tenth, 35% in top quarter. SAT Math
(25/75 percentile): 500/600. SAT Verbal (25/75 percentile): 490/580. Projected SAT Writing (25/75 percentile): 550/630. *Academic units required:* 4 English,
3 math, 2 science (2 science labs), 2 social studies, 2
history, 2 academic electives. Early decision application deadline: 12/1. Regular notification: Rolling.

Costs and Financial Aid
(All Undergraduate Programs)
Annual tuition $22,932. Room & board $10,693.
Required fees $1,134. Average book expense $700.
Financial Aid Statistics: % freshmen/undergrads
who receive any aid: 80/71. % freshmen/undergrads
who receive need-based scholarship or grant aid:
43/28. % freshmen/undergrads who receive need-
based self-help aid: 50/36. Priority financial aid filing
deadline: 1/1. Financial aid filing deadline: 2/1.
Financial aid notification on or about: 3/20.

TV/Film/Digital Media Studies Programs
**Number of undergraduates
in these programs:** 31
**Number of 2005 graduates from these
programs:** 10
Degrees conferred to these majors: BA.
**Number of full-time faculty in these
programs:** 4
Career development services: Alumni networking
opportunities, career counseling, internship listings,
job fairs, job listings.

In Their Own Words
An important element in the overall design of
the theater major is the semester-long London
Theater program. Students spend the fall
semester of their junior year in London under
the direction of the Roger Williams theater faculty and a group of English Theater professionals. They see over 40 plays, concerts, dance
events, and exhibitions; study the practical
workings of various professional theaters; and
meet with a range of working theater practitioners.

POPULAR PROGRAMS

THEATER
Number of full-time faculty: 4

Focus/emphasis: The theater program includes a major, a minor, and a core concentration. Beyond their more general studies, many students pursue specialization tracks through a series of courses and production experiences in the areas of performance or design. The sequence of courses in theater is designed to provide an understanding of each of these areas. As its particular focus and in keeping with the mission of Roger Williams University, the Theater Department offers a liberal arts theater degree with a strong emphasis on practical learning and professional skills.

ROWAN UNIVERSITY

201 Mullica Hill Road, Glassboro, NJ 08028
Phone: 856-256-4200 **E-mail:** admissions@rowan.edu
Website: www.rowan.edu

Campus Life
Environment: Town. **Calendar:** Semester.

Students and Faculty
(All Undergraduate Programs)
Enrollment: 8,065. **Student Body:** 54% female, 46% male, 2% out-of-state. African American 9%, Asian 3%, Caucasian 80%, Hispanic 7%. Student/faculty ratio: 14:1. 436 full-time faculty, 14% hold PhDs. 95% faculty teach undergrads.

Admissions
(All Undergraduate Programs)
Freshman Admissions Requirements: Test(s) required: SAT or ACT. Average high school GPA: 3.0. 10% in top tenth, 55% in top quarter. SAT Math (25/75 percentile): 510/620. SAT Verbal (25/75 percentile): 510/600. Projected SAT Writing (25/75 percentile): 570/650. *Academic units required:* 4 English, 3 math, 2 science (2 science labs), 2 social studies, 5 academic electives. Regular application deadline: 3/15. Regular notification: Rolling.

Costs and Financial Aid
(All Undergraduate Programs)
Annual in-state tuition $6,294. Out-of-state tuition $12,588. Room & board $8,242. Required fees $2,313. Average book expense $800.

Financial Aid Statistics: % freshmen/undergrads who receive any aid: 82/83. % freshmen/undergrads who receive need-based scholarship or grant aid: 53/48. % freshmen/undergrads who receive need-based self-help aid: 46/52. Priority financial aid filing deadline: 3/15. Financial aid filing deadline: 3/15. Financial aid notification on or about: 3/15.

TV/Film/Digital Media Studies Programs
Number of undergraduates in these programs: 371

Number of 2005 graduates from these programs: 95

Degrees conferred to these majors: BA.

Number of full-time faculty in these programs: 9

Number of part-time faculty in these programs: 6

Equipment and facilities: New $400,000 TV studio with permanent news and talk show sets. DVCPro and Panasonic DVX100 video cameras, Bolex and Arri film cameras, Sony digital audio recorders, editing on Avid and Adobe suite (includes Premiere Pro), 30 multimedia editing/postproduction/multimedia computer stations, many ENG light kits and sound systems, full film-field production accessories.

% of graduates who pursue further study within 5 years: 50

% of graduates currently employed in related field: 60

Career development services: Alumni networking opportunities, career counseling, internship listings, job fairs, job listings; Rowan RTF faculty have a database of over 400 RTF graduates. These graduates often provide internship opportunities and/or hire RTF graduates.

Famous alumni: Robert Heyges, Karen Thomas, Robin Rieger, Renae Ellison, Lisa Moser.

Notable alumni: Producers for *America's Most Wanted* (Cindy Smith, Mike Kaplan, and Gavin

Portnoy); Fox Family Network (Terry Coyle); *Ellen DeGeneres Show* (Melissa Costello); *What Not to Wear* (Rasheed Daniel); MSNBC/CNBC (Carolyn Scharf, Cassie Farnan, and Jennifer Shippert); major league baseball (Jason Weber); Oxygen Network (Kate Dagress); 15 RTF grads at ESPN; 40 grads at NFL Films; 15 grads at Comcast—Philadelphia; 30 grads at TV stations in Philadelphia; vice president Warner Brothers (Susal Kroll); vice president Morgan Creek Films (Joe Martino).

In Their Own Words

Rowan's radio/TV/film program is 30 years old. We have approximately 400 grads working at all levels of the radio/television/film/media world. Student documentaries have won four CINE Golden Eagles; a regional Emmy; first-place awards from CBI (College Broadcasters Inc.), NBS (National Broadcasters Society student competition), New Jersey Young Film and Video Makers Competition; Mark of Excellence Award from the Society of Professional Journalists; Gracie Award from the American Women in Radio and Television; many Crystal Awards of Excellence from the Communicator Awards; first-place awards from the Atlantic City, Birmingham, and Black Maria Film Festivals; POV-WHYY-Philadelphia and WYBE-Philadelphia airings of student documentaries; and two Dore Schary awards. Ken Burns, Gary Winnick, Abel Ferrara, and Hanif Karieshi are four film and television stars that have appeared in the Talking Pictures *guest media artists series sponsored by The Radio/Television/Film Department. Rowan RTF students intern throughout the New York City, New Jersey, and Philadelphia areas, as well as Hollywood and throughout the United States and the world.*

POPULAR PROGRAMS

RADIO/TV/FILM
Department chair: Ned Eckhardt
Number of full-time faculty: 9
Number of part-time faculty: 6

Focus/emphasis: The department offers students courses in radio, television, and film production, as well as courses in the history, business, and aesthetics of the media. Students can select one of two tracks within the program: The traditional production emphasis, which is based in the department's state-of-the-art digital production facilities, and a new nonproduction track in radio/TV/film studies. This track prepares the student for media studies in graduate school and/or careers in education and literary criticism. Students who complete both of these programs possess a broad-based liberal arts background and a strong preparation for either the media production industry or advanced media studies.

PUBLIC RELATIONS/ADVERTISING
Department chair: Susanne Fitzgerald
Number of full-time faculty: 7

JOURNALSIM
Department chair: Carl Houseman
Number of full-time faculty: 5

COMMUNICATIONS STUDIES
Department chair: Cindy Corrison
Number of full-time faculty: 11

WRITING ARTS
Department chair: Janice Rowan
Number of full-time faculty: 18

RUST COLLEGE

150 Rust Avenue, Holly Springs, MS 38635
Phone: 662-252-8000 **E-mail:** jbmcdonald@rustcollege.edu
Website: www.rustcollege.edu

Campus Life
Environment: Rural. **Calendar:** Semester.

Students and Faculty (All Undergraduate Programs)
Enrollment: 971. **Student Body:** 66% female, 34% male, 31% out-of-state. Student/faculty ratio: 20:1. 43 full-time faculty. 100% faculty teach undergrads.

Admissions
(All Undergraduate Programs)
Average high school GPA: 2.69. 15% in top tenth, 30% in top quarter. *Academic units required:* 4 English, 3 math, 3 science, 3 social studies, 6 academic electives. Regular notification: Rolling.

Costs and Financial Aid
(All Undergraduate Programs)
Annual tuition $6,000. Room & board $2,600. Average book expense $500.

Financial Aid Statistics: % freshmen/undergrads who receive need-based scholarship or grant aid: 95/76. % freshmen/undergrads who receive need-based self-help aid: 83/69. Priority financial aid filing deadline: 5/1. Financial aid notification on or about: 6/1.

TV/Film/Digital Media Studies Programs
Number of undergraduates in these programs: 55

Number of 2005 graduates from these programs: 15

Degrees conferred to these majors: BA.

Number of full-time faculty in these programs: 3

Equipment and facilities: Training facility resources include state-of-the-art campus-owned broadcast studios (cable access television channel and NPR affiliated public radio), digital video editing suites (Final Cut Pro and Avid), multimedia production, and online streaming capabilities.

ATAS Faculty Seminar participants: 1

% of graduates who pursue further study within 5 years: 25

% of graduates currently employed in related field: 75

Career development services: Alumni networking opportunities; career counseling; central resource(s) for employers to browse headshots, writing samples, reels; internship listings; job fairs; job listings.

Famous alumni: Zondra Hughes, Pam Chatman, Kelvin Buck, Clinton LeSueur, Lisa Dandridge, Patricia Willis, Sonya Walls.

In Their Own Words
Our broadcast journalism program is designed to give students advanced educational and technical training that prepare them for a competitive advantage in the job market, as well as potential graduate school attendance. Our program emphasizes experiential learning (hands-on) for students, and students have opportunity to train on equipment similar to those used by top broadcasting stations in the industry. Our competent academic and professional staff will guide you through theoretical and practical aspects of the program until you become proficient in your area of specialization, radio or television.

POPULAR PROGRAMS

BROADCAST JOURNALISM (TELEVISION AND RADIO)
Department chair: Dr. Debayo Moyo

Number of full-time faculty: 3

Focus/emphasis: Emphasis on experiential learning approach that enables students to acquire the skills and knowledge for a successful career in broadcasting.

SACRED HEART UNIVERSITY
5151 Park Avenue, Fairfield, CT 06825
Phone: 203-371-7880 **E-mail:** enroll@sacredheart.edu
Website: www.sacredheart.edu

Campus Life
Environment: Town. **Calendar:** Semester.

Students and Faculty
(All Undergraduate Programs)
Enrollment: 4,045. **Student Body:** 61% female, 39% male, 56% out-of-state. African American 5%, Asian 1%, Caucasian 86%, Hispanic 6%. Student/faculty ratio: 13:1. 186 full-time faculty, 78% hold PhDs. 96% faculty teach undergrads.

Admissions
(All Undergraduate Programs)

Freshman Admissions Requirements: Test(s) required: SAT or ACT; ACT with Writing component. Average high school GPA: 3.3. 8% in top tenth, 37% in top quarter. SAT Math (25/75 percentile): 500/580. SAT Verbal (25/75 percentile): 490/570. Projected SAT Writing (25/75 percentile): 550/620. *Academic units required:* 4 English, 3 math, 3 science (1 science lab), 2 foreign language, 3 social studies, 3 history, 3 academic electives. Early decision application deadline: 10/1. Regular notification: Rolling.

Costs and Financial Aid
(All Undergraduate Programs)

Annual tuition $23,750. Room & board $9,654. **Financial Aid Statistics:** % freshmen/undergrads who receive any aid: 84/80. % freshmen/undergrads who receive need-based scholarship or grant aid: 69/66. % freshmen/undergrads who receive need-based self-help aid: 60/58. Priority financial aid filing deadline: 2/15. Financial aid notification on or about: 3/1.

TV/Film/Digital Media Studies Programs

Number of undergraduates in these programs: 126
Number of 2005 graduates from these programs: 48
Degrees conferred to these majors: BA, BS.
Number of full-time faculty in these programs: 7
Number of part-time faculty in these programs: 7
Equipment and facilities: Extensive and up-to-date digital production equipment that is accessible to all our majors from their very first production class and features: JVC GY-DV5000U studio camcorders, Panasonic PVGS300 3 CCD DV camcorders, Canon EOS Digital Rebel digital cameras; light packages from Lowell and others; sound equipment from Sennheiser and others; Apple iBook laptops for all of our majors that include access to Adobe and Macromedia software; Apple Powermac G5 dual-processor workstations featuring Final Cut Studio software (Final Cut Pro, DVD Studio Pro, Soundtrack Pro, Motion); Adobe Creative Suite software (Photoshop, InDesign, Illustrator); Macromedia Studio software (Flash, Dreamweaver); Adobe AfterEffects software; additional television studio; DVD authoring stations; digital editing and effects lab; broadcast-quality studio and field cameras; TelePrompTers; ENG/EFP equipment; wireless campus; professional digital still cameras and printers; Open Student Television Network (OSTN) Web-casting agreement; campus radio station; campus TV channel; NPR affiliate, WSHU, broadcasted from the Sacred Heart University campus.

% of graduates who pursue further study within 5 years: 25
% of graduates currently employed in related field: 80
Career development services: Alumni networking opportunities; career counseling; central resource(s) for employers to browse headshots, writing samples, reels; internship listings; job fairs; job listings.
Famous alumni: Kevin Nealon, John Ratzenberger.

In Their Own Words

Nationally-recognized and award-winning faculty. Internships completed at major media outlets in NY area, including 95.9 Fox Radio, ABC News, Ascom Hasler Mailing Systems, Bee Harris Productions, Clear Channel Communications, Cox Radio, CBS, NBC, Comedy Central, Connecticut Post, Complete Graphix Inc., Constitution Capital Corporation, Cox Radio Star 99, CNN En Español, DataViz, Inc., Digital Photo IMA, DreamWorks Pictures, Extra!, Fairfield County Magazine, Fairfield Minuteman, Flying Pictures, Fox, Fox Sports World, GE Scholars Programs, Harrington Talents, HBO, HBO Sports, HWH Public Relations, Inside Edition, J Winthrop Lighthouse, KC101 Radio, Lamar Outdoor Advertising, Late Show with David Letterman, Lifetime, Live with Regis and Kathy Lee, Major Indoor Soccer League, Mediamania Summer Camp, MTV Productions, MTV News, MTV Total Request Live, Muse Entertainment, Niche Media, Nightline, Noggin,

Octagon Marketing, Outdoor Life Network, Pop Warner Football Camps, Raytheon, Rogers & Cowan Advertising Agency, Roxy Night Club, Ryan Partnership, Sally Jesse Raphael, Satellite Music Group, SHU athletics, SHU men's basketball, SHU women's hockey, SHU men's football, Soundkeeper Inc., TriBeca Films, Waterbury Republican American Newspaper, WEZN, WHDH-TV 7 NBC, WNEW, WPLJ, WNYW Fox 5, WSHU National Public Radio, WTNH-TV Channel 8, Univision, Youth Marketing, Zamar Outdoor Advertising, major NPR affiliate WSHU on campus. Student newspaper, student magazine, student-run campus radio station, student-run campus TV channel. Regular speakers and guest lecturers from all sectors of the media industry. Open Student Television Network (OSTN) Webcasting agreement. Students and faculty host and facilitate media literacy summer camps and after-school programs for at-risk youth.

POPULAR PROGRAMS

MEDIA STUDIES

Department chair: James Castonguay, PhD
Number of full-time faculty: 7
Number of part-time faculty: 6
Focus/emphasis: An innovative program offering a major that combines the study of communications theory and technology with the liberal arts. The program is designed with the understanding that the successful student must be technologically competent and must understand the historical, social, and philosophical aspects of media. Course work in the history, theory, and production of media is complemented by internships both within the university and at institutions related to the media/communications industries, such as radio and television stations, magazines, newspapers, advertising agencies, and public relations firms. A student majoring in communications or media studies examines the theories behind contemporary communications in newspapers, magazines, photography, film, radio, and television. Media workshops aimed at developing basic competence

in media production are considered an integral part of the program. The Media Studies Department also encourages students to pursue related interests in art, business, theater, speech, literature, computer science, writing, psychology, anthropology, and sociology.

COMMUNICATION AND TECHNOLOGY STUDIES

Department chair: James Castonguay, PhD
Number of full-time faculty: 7
Number of part-time faculty: 6
Focus/emphasis: An interdisciplinary program offered by the College of Arts and Sciences is housed in the Media Studies and Digital Culture Department. The program is directed to students who wish to become leaders in creating the communication environment of the future, to those interested in the broader implications of communication technology, in understanding the theory as well as the practice, and in adapting to a changing world. This is a program for those who understand that communication and technology are the unifying forces in the world, that cyberspace represents the marriage of humanism and technology, and that the liberal arts and technology are not mutually exclusive terms. Approaching the subject from the sociological, psychological, and philosophical perspectives will prepare students for leadership in a variety of professions and careers.

Students Should Also Know

The Department of Media Studies and Digital Culture combines social and cultural analysis of the media and communication technologies with media production, including video, film, print journalism, television, radio, photography, and digital multimedia. The curriculum is interdisciplinary by nature and international in scope, blending theory and practice, the historical and the contemporary, and the mainstream with the alternative. Our goal is to produce responsible media scholars, consumers, and communication professionals who are able to: 1) analyze the social effect, moral substance, and aesthetic value of the media and communication technologies, and 2) acquire the social and artistic skills involved in the conception, shaping, and execution of their own media/communication projects and career paths. By facilitating critical and creative thinking, our goal is to graduate a student who understands the ethical implications of producing mass-mediated messages and appreciates the profound social responsibility she or he has as a communication professional, while also gaining the necessary skills to put his or her ideas and ideals into action.

SAINT JOSEPH'S COLLEGE (IN)

PO Box 890, Rensselaer, IN 47978
Phone: 219-866-6170 **E-mail:** admissions@saintjoe.edu
Website: www.saintjoe.edu

Campus Life
Environment: Rural. **Calendar:** Semester.

Students and Faculty
(All Undergraduate Programs)
Enrollment: 991. **Student Body:** 62% female, 38% male, 28% out-of-state. African American 6%, Caucasian 88%, Hispanic 4%. Student/faculty ratio: 15:1. 56 full-time faculty, 79% hold PhDs. 100% faculty teach undergrads.

Admissions
(All Undergraduate Programs)
Freshman Admissions Requirements: Test(s) required: SAT or ACT. Average high school GPA: 3.14. 13% in top tenth, 40% in top quarter. SAT Math (25/75 percentile): 450/550. SAT Verbal (25/75 percentile): 430/550. Projected SAT Writing (25/75 percentile): 500/610. Regular notification: Rolling.

Costs and Financial Aid
(All Undergraduate Programs)
Annual tuition $19,960. Room & board $6,480. Required fees $160. Average book expense $700. **Financial Aid Statistics:** % freshmen/undergrads who receive any aid: 97/97. % freshmen/undergrads who receive need-based scholarship or grant aid: 80/76. % freshmen/undergrads who receive need-based self-help aid: 58/56. Priority financial aid filing deadline: 3/1. Financial aid notification on or about: 3/1.

TV/Film/Digital Media Studies Programs
Number of undergraduates in these programs: 38
Number of 2005 graduates from these programs: 10
Degrees conferred to these majors: BA, BS.
Number of full-time faculty in these programs: 2
Equipment and facilities: Vegas 6.0 digital audio and video nonlinear edit suites; Panasonic camcorders; CD recorders; Media 100 nonlinear editors; 3-camera television studio and control room; three audio production suites; FM radio station.
Other awards of note: ATAS Foundation Faculty seminar participant in 1997; DGA Workshop for Educators, 1985 and 1996.

% of graduates who pursue further study within 5 years: 25
% of graduates currently employed in related field: 30
Career development services: Alumni networking opportunities; career counseling; central resource(s) for employers to browse headshots, writing samples, reels; internship listings; job fairs; job listings.

In Their Own Words
Very hands-on; good interaction with professionals in markets in Chicago, Indianapolis, and elsewhere.

POPULAR PROGRAMS

MASS COMMUNICATION
Department chair: Fred Berger
Number of full-time faculty: 1
Focus/emphasis: Mass Media Production.

SAN FRANCISCO STATE UNIVERSITY

1600 Holloway Avenue, San Francisco, CA 94132
Phone: 415-338-6486 **E-mail:** ugadmit@sfsu.edu
Website: www.sfsu.edu

Campus Life
Environment: Metropolis. **Calendar:** Semester.

Students and Faculty
(All Undergraduate Programs)
Enrollment: 23,074. **Student Body:** 59% female, 41% male, 1% out-of-state, 5% international (149 countries represented). African American 6%, Asian 31%, Caucasian 29%, Hispanic 14%. Student/faculty ratio: 20:1. 865 full-time faculty, 77% hold PhDs. 74% faculty teach undergrads.

Admissions
(All Undergraduate Programs)
Average high school GPA: 3.18. SAT Math (25/75 percentile): 450/570. SAT Verbal (25/75 percentile): 440/560. Projected SAT Writing (25/75 percentile): 510/620. *Academic units required:* 4 English, 3 math, 2 science (2 science labs), 2 foreign language, 1 social studies, 1 history, 1 visual and performing arts. Regular application deadline: 11/30. Regular notification: Rolling.

Costs and Financial Aid
(All Undergraduate Programs)
Annual in-state tuition $2,724. Out-of-state tuition $12,894. Room & board $9,124. Required fees $646. Average book expense $1,400.
Financial Aid Statistics: % freshmen/undergrads who receive any aid: 62/46. % freshmen/undergrads who receive need-based scholarship or grant aid: 44/34. % freshmen/undergrads who receive need-based self-help aid: 60/45. Priority financial aid filing deadline: 3/2. Financial aid notification on or about: 1/1.

TV/Film/Digital Media Studies Programs
Degrees conferred to these majors: BA.
Also available at San Francisco State University: MFA, MA.

Equipment and facilities: The Three Space Lab is devoted to learning and production with 3-D computer graphics applications for animation, product design, and virtual worlds. State-of-the art sound-recording and mixing stages with an isolated machine room, separate Foley stage, automated mix consoles, and 24-track hard-disc recorders. Digital cinema postproduction facilities with industry-standard software for digital video editing, Web design, and DVD authoring as well as three Avid suites. Extensive audio and video production facilities, including three color television studios (the largest measures 4,700 square feet), videotape-editing laboratories equipped with off line and broadcast quality online editing systems, a digital postproduction "new media" laboratory for computer-based audio and video editing, an audio recording studio, a radio station, and audio practice laboratories. The department's instructional laboratories include some of the most extensive audio and video production facilities in Northern California. These facilities are dedicated exclusively to the support of the instructional programs in broadcast and electronic communication arts and afford students exceptional opportunities for hands-on media production experience.

Other awards of note: Christopher Boyes was presented the Oscar for Achievement in Sound Mixing, and Ethan Van der Ryn won the Oscar for Achievement in Sound Editing at the 78th Annual Academy Awards. Both won for their work on *King Kong*. After submitting only a rough-cut version of her film *Eyes of a Child* to the annual University Film and Video Association Conference held in Chicago in August 2005, San Francisco State cinema major Delphine Suter won an $8,000 scholarship. In 2000, *Entertainment Weekly* named the department one of the nation's top film schools.

Career development services: Internship listings, job listings.

Notable alumni: Academy Award winners Steven Zaillian (Best Screenplay, *Schindler's List*, 1994), Christopher Boyes (Best Sound, *Titanic*, 1998; *Pearl Harbor*, 2001; *Lord of the Rings: The Return of the King*, 2004), and Steve Okazaki (Best Short Documentary, *Days of Waiting*, 1991).

In Their Own Words

Developing exceptional talent takes exceptional teachers, mentors, and practitioners. The College of Creative Arts is home to such luminaries as art historian Whitney Chadwick; Pulitzer Prize-winning composer Wayne Peterson; award-winning composers Ronald Caltabiano and Richard Festinger; Dunham dance scholar Albirda Rose; artists Lewis DeSoto, David Kuraoka, and Mario Laplante; film scholars Bill Nichols and Joseph McBride; seminal media textbook author Stuart Hyde; and documentarian John Hewitt, among others. The working professionals who share expertise and wisdom with our students include artists-in-residence Branford Marsalis and the Alexander String Quartet; associate lighting director Joan Arhelger (designed more than 30 San Francisco Opera productions); former Magic Theater artistic director Larry Eilenberg; industrial designer, airport security systems, Martin Linder; and KRON-TV's weekend morning news co-anchor Marty Gonzalez.

POPULAR PROGRAMS

BROADCAST AND COMMUNICATION ARTS

Department chair: Phil Kipper
Number of full-time faculty: 35
Number of part-time faculty: 13
Focus/emphasis: The Broadcast and Electronic Communication Arts (BECA) Department offers course work leading to the Bachelor's of Arts in Radio and Television. The curriculum is designed to provide extensive educational experience for those who intend to use the modern media of electronic communication to serve the artistic, cultural, educational, informational, and social needs of society. The program involves both theory and practice, and students are expected to work successfully in both types of courses and activities. Graduates of the program are prepared for work in the broadcast and entertainment industries, in cable and online media, in video

and audio production, and other areas related to electronic communication. Many graduates go on to graduate-level study in the field of mass media. The BA program includes a core drawn from classes in the history and structure of electronic media in the United States, media aesthetics, media research, audio and video production, media ethics and regulation, mass communication theory and criticism, and writing and performance for the electronic media. In addition, students may elect to pursue one of the nine areas of emphasis within the department: audio production and recording, broadcast journalism, business aspects of the electronic media, educational and instructional media, mass communication theory and criticism, interactive media, radio production and programming, television/video production, and writing for the electronic media; or they can design an individualized area of emphasis in consultation with a department adviser.

CINEMA

Department chair: Stephen Ujlaki
Number of full-time faculty: 19
Focus/emphasis: The Cinema Department was founded amid the political activism and artistic experimentation of the 1960s. Today, as then, the Cinema Department is committed to a curriculum that recognizes cinema to be an independent, powerful, and unique medium in the world. Cinema programs combine theory and practice; students are encouraged to engage in scholarship and to pursue production in all forms of cinematic expression. In the 1990s, a new facility was constructed; it features a 2,500-square-foot shooting stage. It has greatly enlarged the department's postproduction studios and labs and is beginning the transition from analogue to digital processes. A new screening room, the Coppola Theatre (FA 101), equipped for both 16 mm and 35 mm projection and featuring a Dolby sound system, was named for former Dean of Creative Arts August Coppola, whose efforts were primarily responsible for funding the new building. Digital upgrades to sound and editing labs have further modernized

the department's production facilities. Undergraduate cinema majors can earn a Bachelor's of Arts in Cinema, a general program in theory and practice that also offers a distinct emphasis in animation; graduate students work toward a Master's of Arts in Cinema Studies or a Master's of Fine Arts in Cinema. SFSU cinema alumni have distinguished themselves as Oscar nominees and winners, high-profile animators, software designers, and faculty members teaching on campuses worldwide.

DESIGN AND INDUSTRY

Department chair: Ricardo Gomes
Number of full-time faculty: 11
Focus/emphasis: Students in the BAIA program develop an individualized course of study with the help of an advisor, choosing a technical emphasis in digital media, visual communication, product design, or industrial technology.

SANTA CLARA UNIVERSITY

500 El Camino Real, Santa Clara, CA 95053
Phone: 408-554-4700 **E-mail:** ugadmissions@scu.edu
Website: www.scu.edu

Campus Life
Environment: City. **Calendar:** Quarter.

Students and Faculty
(All Undergraduate Programs)
Enrollment: 4,552. **Student Body:** 56% female, 44% male, 33% out-of-state, 3% international (34 countries represented). African American 3%, Asian 18%, Caucasian 57%, Hispanic 13%. Student/faculty ratio 12:1. 447 full-time faculty, 91% hold PhDs. 82% faculty teach undergrads.

Admissions
(All Undergraduate Programs)
Freshman Admissions Requirements: Test(s) required: SAT or ACT. Average high school GPA: 3.6. 40% in top tenth, 72% in top quarter. SAT Math (25/75 percentile): 570/670. SAT Verbal (25/75 per-

centile): 550/650. Projected SAT Writing (25/75 percentile): 610/690. *Academic units required:* 4 English, 4 math, 3 science (2 science lab), 3 foreign language, 1 social studies, 1 history, 2 academic electives. Regular application deadline: 1/15. Regular notification: 4/1.

Costs and Financial Aid
(All Undergraduate Programs)
Annual tuition $28,899. Room & board $10,032. Average book expense $1,242.
Financial Aid Statistics: % freshmen/undergrads who receive any aid: 83/69. % freshmen/undergrads who receive need-based scholarship or grant aid: 33/38. % freshmen/undergrads who receive need-based self-help aid: 25/29. Priority financial aid filing deadline: 2/1.

TV/Film/Digital Media Studies Programs
Degrees conferred to these majors: BA
Equipment and facilities: Television Studio: Santa Clara University has a complete digital video and analog audio television studio located in the Arts and Sciences Building. The Communication Department's 2,200-square foot wide-screen format broadcast quality digital video production studio features a curved hard cyclorama, fully loaded lighting grid, three studio configured digital triax cameras with TelePrompTers, and a large screen video projection system. Control Rooms: Digital signals from studio cameras are switched through an Echo Lab digital switcher. Digital video effects (DVE), character generation, and still store capabilities are included in the video control space. Sources are monitored via a large wall of video monitors. The control room is adjacent to the studio, audio control, and master control. The audio control room boasts a 24-input Wheatstone analog mixing console, numerous outboard digital signal processing and recording devices (including DigiCart, Instant Replay, DAT, and CD). The control room also features Digidesign ProTools. Video Editing Suites: The television facility features eight professional nonlinear video editing suites. Our students are introduced to nonlinear editing in three Avid Xpress Pro edit bays. These bays also are equipped with

Apple Final Cut Pro, Apple DVD Studio Pro and Digidesign ProTools LE software. Five additional suites feature Avid Adrenaline nonlinear editing systems. These suites, used by the more advanced classes, have audio mixers, routing switchers, and external media storage. These bays are also equipped with Apple Final Cut Pro, Apple DVD Studio Pro, and Digidesign ProTools LE software. Instructional capabilities in the edit bays are enhanced with overhead observation cameras and sliding glass doors between most edit bays. In addition to these eight private editing suites, eight more editing seats are available in our Mac Video Lab. All 16 computers are tied to an Avid LANShare EX video server. Communication students enrolled in video production classes have 24-hour access to the editing facilities and can reserve them for four-hour blocks. Other communication students who have demonstrated proficiency with the equipment may make arrangements with faculty to schedule the equipment for projects. The edit suites also are used for the professional training courses the department offers in association with Avid and Apple. Additionally, the edit bays are available for rental. Mac Video Lab: Located on the first floor of the Arts and Sciences Building, Room 138, the Mac Video Lab was designed for the use of students in the course Comm 30, Visual Communication. The lab is also used for the professional training courses the department offers in affiliation with Avid and Apple. Each of the eight Apple Mac G5 computers is equipped with Apple's ILife production suite, Adobe Photoshop Elements, Avid Xpress Pro and Apple Final Cut Pro. Every machine is connected to an Avid LANShare EX video server. Communication students enrolled in video production classes have 24-hour access to the editing facilities and can reserve them for four-hour blocks. Other communication students who have demonstrated proficiency with the equipment may make arrangements with faculty to schedule the equipment for projects.

Career development services: Internship listings.

Notable alumni: Joe Tone is now a reporter with the *Cleveland Scene*, an alternative newsweekly in Cleveland, Ohio. Teri Okita (1989) is a correspondent for CBS Newspath, the affiliate news service of CBS News, and works in Los Angeles. She was a weekend evening anchor and reporter for WUSA-TV in Washington from 1996 to 2000. Before that she worked at KGMD-TV in Honolulu and at KECI-TV in Missoula. Michael Whalen (1989) has joined the Santa Clara Communication Department as an assistant professor in the video area. Osei Appiah (1990) received a PhD in 1997 in Communication from Stanford University and is now an assistant professor in the Greenlee School of Journalism at Iowa State University. Janine Gill (1997) is working as a television reporter at the NBC affiliate in Chico, CA. Among the journalism graduates, Melissa Segura works as a writer-reporter for *Sports Illustrated*; Jennifer Kanne is a reporter for the *Orange County Register*; Joe Tone works for the *Stockton Record*; and Nikki Collins for CBS in Illinois. Kara Lindquist (2003) works for Blueprint Entertainment in Los Angeles as Assistant to the Executive Producer. Becki Fowler (2003) is at A&R Partners, San Mateo, as an account associate for Palm's (Palm Handhelds) Enterprise Team, assisting with the customer reference program, analyst relations, and research for conferences. Other graduates have chosen public relations careers: Drew Millam works at Sony Playstation; Jenee Cline at Electronic Arts; Helen Allrich at Eastwick Communications; and Lauren Russell and Nicole Resz at Google.

In Their Own Words

Faculty specialties range from interpersonal communication, group dynamics, persuasion, and cultural/media studies to documentary film-making; from international communication and journalism history to video production; from news reporting and writing to the political economy of the media; from health communication, ethics, and gender to the Internet. Students can participate in a variety of internships as well as in on-campus student media—The Santa Clara newspaper, The Redwood yearbook, and KSCU radio. Internship Participation: The department provides credit to students participating in the internship program after fulfilling a number of requirements. Prerequisites for formal credit include a minimum grade point average, sophomore status, and permission of the student's academic advisor and the Department Internship Coordinator. Students must work a minimum number of hours for credit and attend regular class meetings. Typically students work 20 hours a week for the duration of the 10-week quarter. Company Requirements: We require that participating companies offer interns duties that include substantive responsibilities in order to develop a student's career skills. Some clerical duties are expected, but internships must go beyond general office work. Host companies must have a designated supervisor able to evaluate the student's performance at the end of the academic quarter. Companies should provide any training for specialized or technical tasks. Compensation, though encouraged, is not required and doesn't effect eligibility for course credit. Compensation can be in the form of either an hourly wage or a stipend. Scheduling: Most students try to arrange their start and end dates around the quarter calendar but it's not required for credit. Summer hours per week may exceed the average 20 hours, since many students are not taking regular course loads. Hours may also vary during the week due to exams, vacation breaks, and registration periods. Finding An Internship: The Internship Coordinator can help a student identify a challenging and educational internship. The department maintains lists of employers and local alumni that have offered positions in the recent past plus listings of current opportunities. Students should contact the employer directly by e-mail, phone, or fax unless otherwise requested. Typically employers provide a one page description of their position including expected skills and duties, start and end dates, compensation (if any), contact information, and background on the company. Students are encouraged to begin the search in their area two to three months in advance of their internship.

The department also will screen candidates in advance if requested by the employer particularly if a specific skill set is required.

POPULAR PROGRAMS

COMMUNICATION ARTS

Department chair: Stephen Lee
Number of full-time faculty: 20
Focus/emphasis: As a comprehensive program, the communication major offers theoretical and applied courses in human communication and mass media and in the four major modes of expression—oral, written, visual, and digital. Every communication student completes both production (hands-on) and theory courses and graduates with research and expressive skills. Students participate in community-based learning through the Arrupe Center at several stages in the curriculum. In addition, each student completes a senior thesis or capstone course. Qualified students may join the Santa Clara chapter of the national Communication Honor Society.

Students Should Also Know

We want to create a community of faculty, staff, and students who combine reason with compassion—who reason compassionately and passionately; a community of people who love their neighbor with their heads and their hearts; a community whose knowledge and commitment lead them to change the world. The program seeks to help students explore what it means to create quality communication with a concern for the common good or "communication with a conscience." The program helps students develop the knowledge, skills, attitude, and commitment necessary to influence corporations or other industries so that the needs of audiences are better served. Consequently, the primary purpose of the department is to educate students who will take on leadership roles characterized by competence and conscience in communication professions. To better serve the students, the department is committed to developing a community of faculty, staff, and students who pursue research, scholarly, and professional activities and share their talents in service with the university, profession, and outside community. To do this, the department places great value on the education of the whole person: the mind, the voice, the heart.

SAVANNAH COLLEGE OF ART AND DESIGN

PO Box 3146, Savannah, GA 31402-3146
Phone: 912-525-5100 **E-mail:** admission@scad.edu
Website: www.scad.edu

Campus Life
Environment: City. **Calendar:** Quarter.

Students and Faculty
(All Undergraduate Programs)
Enrollment: 6,062. **Student Body:** 52% female, 48% male, 84% out-of-state, 4% international (77 countries represented). African American 5%, Asian 2%, Caucasian 45%, Hispanic 4%. Student/faculty ratio: 18:1. 366 full-time faculty, 78% hold PhDs. 98% faculty teach undergrads.

Admissions
(All Undergraduate Programs)
Freshman Admissions Requirements: Test(s) required: SAT or ACT. SAT Math (25/75 percentile): 480/580. SAT Verbal (25/75 percentile): 490/600. Projected SAT Writing (25/75 percentile): 550/650. Regular notification: Ongoing.

Costs and Financial Aid
(All Undergraduate Programs)
Annual tuition $22,950. Room & board $9,595. Average book expense $1,500.
Financial Aid Statistics: % freshmen/undergrads who receive any aid: 54/45. % freshmen/undergrads who receive need-based scholarship or grant aid: 15/15. % freshmen/undergrads who receive need-based self-help aid: 45/45. Priority financial aid filing deadline: 2/15. Financial aid notification on or about: 4/1.

TV/Film/Digital Media Studies Programs
Number of undergraduates in these programs: 1,668
Degrees conferred to these majors: BFA.
Also available at Savannah College of Art and Design: MFA, MA.
Number of full-time faculty in these programs: 64
Number of part-time faculty in these programs: 12
Equipment and facilities: State of the art industry-standard hardware and software, sound studios, Super Panther Dolly, audio recording labs, Symphony workstations, Sony high-definition camera, Movie Magic screenwriting, scheduling, and budgeting lab.

% of graduates who pursue further study within 5 years: 10
% of graduates currently employed in related field: 60
Career development services: Alumni networking opportunities; career counseling; central resource(s) for employers to browse headshots, writing samples, reels; internship listings; job fairs; job listings.

In Their Own Words
Savannah Film Festival, held annually, is a premier eight-day cultural event in beautiful historic downtown Savannah. The festival features more than 50 films selected from more than 600 entries submitted from all over the world. Categories include feature-length, short, animation, documentary, and student film. The screenings represent a variety of independent filmmakers, while an array of workshops, lectures, receptions, and special events gives the festival participants an opportunity to meet colleagues active in all areas of film production. Educational benefits for students are provided through the Savannah Film Festival's student competition as well as the festival student workshops.

POPULAR PROGRAMS

ANIMATION

Department chair: Jeremy Moorshead

Focus/emphasis: With a strong professional focus, the undergraduate program begins with the development of animation movement and visual storytelling skills. Building on that foundation, students may develop their skills in 2-D and 3-D character animation. They also have the opportunity to study stop motion and independent animation. Throughout the program, students are engaged in all aspects of animation production, from concept development and production design to the completion of a finished piece. In the graduate program, students develop a body of personal studio-based work while acquiring advanced technical skills. Theory and aesthetics courses provide the groundwork for rigorous exploration in animation production classes. Emphasis is on focused individual and collaborative investigation within the context of an industry-centered curriculum.

FILM AND TELEVISION

Department chair: Christopher Auer

Focus/emphasis: Undergraduate students follow a rigorous program combining extensive hands-on experience with the development of critical thinking and visual skills. The curriculum encourages a variety of production types, including narrative, documentary, experimental cinema, music video, television programming, feature film, and short film. At the graduate level, each student develops and refines an artistic vision that culminates in a thesis or final project. Graduate students become familiar with diverse critical approaches, develop writing skills, and refine their production skills.

INTERACTIVE DESIGN AND GAME DEVELOPMENT

Department chair: Josephine Leong

Focus/emphasis: With a strong professional focus, the undergraduate program prepares students to be creative thinkers, to learn new technologies and to take conceptual approaches to problem solving. To develop their analytical skills, undergraduate students take key courses in programming, information design, and interaction design. Topics in e-marketing and entrepreneurship are designed to expand students' horizons further. Students focusing on game design experiment with real-world development tools and techniques, using the latest technologies. Undergraduate students participate in studio classes and are encouraged to take electives in other departments to build on their design skills. In the graduate program, students explore the interactive design and game industries in more depth, honing their creative-thinking and problem-solving skills and focusing on research and development. Critiques form a significant part of the learning process.

VISUAL EFFECTS

Department chair: Craig Newman

Focus/emphasis: The undergraduate curriculum includes design, drawing, writing, and numerous courses in the humanities, allowing students to hone their critical thinking skills, creativity, personal vision, and a fundamental awareness of theory and history. Students work individually and collaboratively within a framework of cooperative activity that reflects the nature of the industry they are preparing to join. In the graduate program, students develop a body of personal studio-based work while acquiring advanced technical skills. Theory and aesthetics courses provide the groundwork for rigorous exploration in visual effects production classes. Emphasis is on focused individual and collaborative investigation within the greater context of an industry-centered curriculum.

SOUND DESIGN

Department chair: Robin Beauchamp

Focus/emphasis: The undergraduate curriculum encourages skill development in several areas and a broad exposure to sound as an expressive medium. Students engage in a variety of practices specific to sound design, including recording studio engineering, MIDI sequencing and sampling, film location sound recording, music and dialog editing for motion picture, and sound art. The graduate program is designed to provide students with a background in sound design and production to explore personal artistry as they master skills in areas of specific interest. Graduate students obtain professional experience through field and teaching internships.

BROADCAST DESIGN

Department chair: Peter Weishar (acting)

Focus/emphasis: The undergraduate program begins with solid artistic fundamentals, through a curriculum that includes design, drawing, writing, and courses in the humanities. Students then progress into acquiring and applying technical skills, and working collaboratively within a framework of activity that reflects the industry they are preparing to join. Students are encouraged to take electives in graphic design, traditional fine arts, visual effects, interactive design, animation, photography, film and television, and other areas. In the graduate program, students develop professional design management skills and pursue theoretical and methodological studies, enabling them to realize their potential as leaders in both practice and management. The program combines taught and self-directed studies, critical approaches to spatial and material culture, project management, design methodology, research, communication, and design theory.

SCHOOL OF THE MUSEUM OF FINE ARTS

230 The Fenway, Boston, MA 02115
Phone: 617-369-3626 **E-mail:** admissions@smfa.edu
Website: www.smfa.edu

Campus Life

Environment: Metropolis. **Calendar:** Semester.

Students and Faculty
(All Undergraduate Programs)

Enrollment: 677. **Student Body:** 66% female, 34% male, 58% out-of-state, 6% international (34 countries represented). African American 2%, Asian 3%, Caucasian 73%, Hispanic 5%. Student/faculty ratio: 9:1. 51 full-time faculty, 67% hold PhDs (or other terminal degrees).

Admissions
(All Undergraduate Programs)

SAT Math (25/75 percentile): 460/603. SAT Verbal (25/75 percentile): 510/650. Projected SAT Writing (25/75 percentile): 570/690. Regular notification: Rolling.

Costs and Financial Aid
(All Undergraduate Programs)

Annual tuition $23,850. Required fees $910. Average book expense $1,400.

Financial Aid Statistics: % freshmen/undergrads who receive any aid: 61/66. % freshmen/undergrads who receive need-based scholarship or grant aid: 56/63. % freshmen/undergrads who receive need-based self-help aid: 53/57. Priority financial aid filing deadline: 3/15. Financial aid filing deadline: 3/15. Financial aid notification on or about: 4/1.

TV/Film/Digital Media Studies Programs

Degrees conferred to these majors: BFA.
Also available at School of the Museum of Fine Arts: MFA, diploma.
Number of full-time faculty in these programs: 10
Number of part-time faculty in these programs: 16
Equipment and facilities: Whether hand-processing celluloid, shooting with the Bolex or 24-frame Panasonic digital camera, editing on the Steenbecks or in the Avid suite, animating images frame-by-frame, or projecting two screens side by side, students working with film will work with both traditional and cutting-edge processes. We encourage individual projects, and advanced students are encouraged to finish on to film, enabled by our Oxberry animation stand, JK optical printer, matchback capabilities in digital post, and the 16 mm

developer and contact printer. You also have the option to produce digitally in Final Cut Pro, Pro Tools, Avid, and Flash in our individual and group edit suites. From camera cranes and projectors to sensors, students working in video engage with cutting-edge production equipment, hardware, and software. Equipment includes: Cameras: Sony 3 Chip DSR-PD 150, Sony VX-2000, Panasonic 24P, Vx1000, Sony TVR-11, and Sony Mini-Disc Recorder cameras; Sennheiser, Audio Technica, and Sony Lavaliere microphones; Junior Jib and Bogen fluid head tripods; Proxima 1000 lumen, Proxima 600 lumen, Sanyo 600 lumen, Sony LPJ-20s, and inFocus-2X projectors; and 12 Final Cut Pro Systems with Super Drives, Max-MSP Stations, Lightwave 3-D digital editing systems. Our facilities include Mac and PC computer labs that are fully equipped with high-resolution color monitors; the latest version of desktop publishing and Web publishing software; scanners; laser, thermal-wax, and large-format inkjet printers; a state-of-the-art Iris printer; a Heidelberg GTO offset press; and complete equipment for any type of hand bookbinding.

Career development services: Alumni networking opportunities, career counseling, internship listings, job listings.

Famous alumni: David Lynch.

In Their Own Words

The film/animation area offers a range of courses that build critical, conceptual, and technical skills in production and postproduction in all genres and gauges, including single-screen and multiple projection. Seminar courses examine film and animation's history through contemporary thought, aesthetic and historical movements, and cultural practice. Video courses focus on the critical, conceptual, and technical skills that support the production of video installation, single-channel video, Web-based projects, and interactivity. Our seminars examine the many histories of video art as well as contemporary individual artists and collectives working with new technologies. The program hosts international visiting artists, critics, and curators to expose students to a range of viewpoints in contemporary art. The text and image

arts area teaches visual communication through graphic design, artists' books, interactive Web, and multimedia while encouraging students to develop a personal voice.

POPULAR PROGRAMS

VIDEO
Department chair: Mary Ellen Strom
Focus/emphasis: Interdisciplinary and self-directed.

FILM/ANIMATION
Department chair: Abby Child
Focus/emphasis: Interdisciplinary and self-directed.

DIGITAL
Department chair: Carl Sesto
Focus/emphasis: Interdisciplinary and self-directed.

SHAWNEE STATE UNIVERSITY

940 Second Street, Portsmouth, OH 45662
Phone: 740-351-4778 **E-mail:** to_ssu@shawnee.edu
Website: www.shawnee.edu

Campus Life
Environment: Town. **Calendar:** Quarter.

Students and Faculty
(All Undergraduate Programs)
Enrollment: 3,017. **Student Body:** 59% female, 41% male, 9% out-of-state. African American 3%, Caucasian 87%. Student/faculty ratio: 18:1. 138 full-time faculty, 54% hold PhDs. 100% faculty teach undergrads.

Admissions
(All Undergraduate Programs)
15% in top tenth, 34% in top quarter. Regular notification: Rolling.

Costs and Financial Aid
(All Undergraduate Programs)
Annual in-state tuition $4,518. Out-of-state tuition $8,406. Room & board $6,729. Required fees $612.

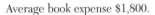

Average book expense $1,800.

Financial Aid Statistics: % freshmen/undergrads who receive need-based scholarship or grant aid: 58/65. % freshmen/undergrads who receive need-based self-help aid: 31/45. Priority financial aid filing deadline: 6/15. Financial aid notification on or about: 5/1.

TV/Film/Digital Media Studies Programs

**Number of undergraduates
  in these programs:** 111
**Number of 2005 graduates from these
  programs:** 3
Degrees conferred to these majors: BS, BFA.
**Number of full-time faculty in these
  programs:** 3
**Number of part-time faculty in these
  programs:** 2
Career development services: Career counseling, internship listings, job fairs, job listings.

POPULAR PROGRAMS

DIGITAL DESIGN AND DIGITAL IMAGING

Department chair: Matt Cram
Number of full-time faculty: 4
Number of part-time faculty: 6
Focus/emphasis: Digital design and interactive media has four tracks. The design track concentrates on print design (brochures, book covers). The imaging track focuses on image manipulation as it is applied to graphic design and digital photography. The animation track concentrates on 3-D animation as it is used for film and video. The interactive media track concentrates on interactive development for website graphics and disk media.

GAMING AND SIMULATION

Department chair: Carl Hilgarth
Number of full-time faculty: 1
Focus/emphasis: Gaming and simulation has both an engineering and fine arts focus so that students in this program learn how programming and 3-D graphics work together to produce high quality gaming and interactive simulation software.

SOUTHERN ILLINOIS UNIVERSITY–CARBONDALE

MC 4710, Carbondale, IL 62901
Phone: 618-536-4405 **E-mail:** joinsiuc@siu.edu
Website: www.siuc.edu

Campus Life
Environment: Town. **Calendar:** Semester.

Students and Faculty
(All Undergraduate Programs)
Enrollment: 21,441. **Student Body:** 45% female, 55% male, 16% out-of-state, 6% international (104 countries represented). African American 15%, Asian 2%, Caucasian 69%, Hispanic 3%. Student/faculty ratio: 17:1. 901 full-time faculty, 84% hold PhDs. 80% faculty teach undergrads.

Admissions
(All Undergraduate Programs)
Freshman Admissions Requirements: Test(s) required: SAT or ACT. 9% in top tenth, 27% in top quarter. SAT Math (25/75 percentile): 460/580. SAT Verbal (25/75 percentile): 450/590. Projected SAT Writing (25/75 percentile): 520/640. *Academic units required:* 4 English, 3 math, 3 science (3 science labs), 3 social studies, 2 academic electives. Regular application deadline: 8/22. Regular notification: Rolling.

Costs and Financial Aid
(All Undergraduate Programs)
Annual in-state tuition $5,808. Out-of-state tuition $14,520. Room & board $6,138. Required fees $1,981. Average book expense $900.
Financial Aid Statistics: % freshmen/undergrads who receive any aid: 80/78. % freshmen/undergrads who receive need-based scholarship or grant aid: 42/42. % freshmen/undergrads who receive need-based self-help aid: 50/48. Priority financial aid filing deadline: 4/1. Financial aid notification on or about: 3/15.

TV/Film/Digital Media Studies Programs
Degrees conferred to these majors: BA.
**Also available at Southern Illinois University—
  Carbondale:** MFA, MA, MS, PhD.

Equipment and facilities: The Cinema Soundstage is a film/sound recording facility where student productions are staged. It is equipped with an overhead lighting grid, sound treatment on the walls, a variety of lighting equipment, a dolly with track, and many accessories. Soundstage is part of a digital recording and mix-to-picture facility that consists of three rooms, including a control room and a mixing/editing facility.

The digital video lab in the New Media Center houses 17 Macintosh G5 computers with 20" Apple LCD monitors and a variety of peripheral devices such as DV and DVCAM video recorders, scanners, microphones, and headphones. It is also a fully functional MIDI lab with keyboards and interfaces. Software includes but is not limited to Final Cut Pro Studio, AfterEffects, Maya, Photoshop, and Flash. The lab is available outside of scheduled class times for any student working on a digital video, audio, or animation project. The New Media Center also houses an Epson 9600 Large Format color printer capable of printing to 44" widths. There is another lab with 17 20" Imac workstations dedicated to multimedia authoring, Photoshop classes, and Web design. Students working on advanced projects may make use of the high-end digital video/audio suite. In the photography lab there is a large gang darkroom with 14 Zone VI variable contrast black and white enlargers for the beginning classes in photography. Individual B/W rooms are avaiable by reservation for our students in advanced courses. The lab houses a 32" Hope/Kreonite Color Print Processor accompanied by seven individual rooms with either Chromega 4 x 5 or 5 x 7 enlargers. This is also a 10 x 10 Chromega enalrger in a private room for B/W or color work. Additionally, there is a large studio with an assortment of electronic strobe and ARRI tungsten lighting equipment. There are two digital photography workstations in the lab. One station has flatbed and film scanners as well as a MGI Solitaire 16xps Image Recorder. The other station includes an Epson 7600 large format inkjet printer as well as a smaller Epson inkjet printer for proofing and smaller output sizes.

There are also two digital Hasselblad camera systems available for use in the studio. The Digital Audio Lab consists of 14 individual 20" Imac workstations running the latest versions of Mac OS and Pro Tools. There is also a full-featured recording studio with professional grade microphones, monitors, and a sound effects library. Students can produce anything from radio commercials to multitrack musical soundtracks for video production.

Television Studio A is a 32' x 50' television production studio that features amodern lighting system installed in 1998 with dimmers controlled by a two-scene, pre-set console, including a remote focus unit, and a full lighting complement. The lighting grid is approximately 15.5' above floor level. The studio walls are lined with 120' of black curtains and 120' of hanging-sync off-white curtains. Studio A production equipment includes four NEC SP30 cameras and one Genie lift. WSIU/WUSI-TV local studio productions are split between Studios A and B as needs dictate, averaging an estimated 600 hours of actual broadcast production annually. Several WSIU/WUSI-TV productions have won regional and national awards. In addition to broadcast production, the WSIU/WUSI studios together average 18 hours of undergraduate and graduate classroom instruction each week. Television Studio B, our largest studio, is 45' x 50'. It features a lighting system similar to that in Studio A, installed in 1999, and shares the NEC SP30 cameras and Genie lift with Studio A. The studio walls are lined with 80' of black curtains and 80' of hanging-sync off-white curtains. In addition to varied broadcast productions and classroom instruction, Studio B is the home of the award-winning *River Region Evening Edition* nightly newscast.

Career development services: Career counseling; internship programs in Hollywood, New York, Chicago, and Nashville; and job listings.

Notable alumni: Chris Bury, correspondent, ABC; Gary Chapman, chairman, president, and CEO, LIN Television; Mark R. Krieschen, vice president and general manager, Chicago's WGN-AM Radio; Robert Weiss, film producer; Liz Ralston, visual effects producer.

In Their Own Words

WSIU-TV (PBS) is not a cable channel. It is a broadcast station that reaches a three-state region! Students are actively involved in most aspects of the station. Many classes are taught directly in the broadcast facilities. Students have a chance to work on many award-winning shows including a nightly student produced newscast, sports shows, and a game show, four different national award-winning entertainment programs, not to mention Division I basketball. There are two radio stations. WSIU-FM reaches a three-state region. Students gain experience in news, sports, radio production, and multiple areas of broadcast management. WIDB is a totally student-run radio station, from management to on-air talent. Digitaldawgs Records is SIUC's own recording label. Student RT Productions is a contract production unit where students work alongside faculty and staff on real client productions. SIUC offers over 200 paid positions in media production and management each semester. Many of the local stations hire SIU students. The Department of Cinema and Photography annually sponsors the CP Visiting Artists/Critics Lecture Series. Artists have included: Dean Kressman, conceptual photographic installation artist; John Paul Caponingro, digital artist, photographer/painter; and Liz Wells, media artist historian/critic.

POPULAR PROGRAMS

CINEMA STUDIES AND PRODUCTION

Department chair: Deborah Tudor

Number of full-time faculty: 15

Focus/emphasis: The cinema studies and production curriculum takes a liberal arts approach to the study of the history, criticism, and theory of cinema. Cinema studies courses address a range of topics in the areas of film analysis and film theory, film styles and genres, film authors, and the histories of documentary, experimental, and narrative film. Cinema studies prepares students for advanced academic work as well as for careers in film criticism for magazines and newspapers; in film programming for museums, festivals, and universities; and in the expanding area of film distribution. In cinema production, students may work independently or in group productions in one or more of the following modes: documentary, experimental, narrative, or animation. Courses include writing for film, animation, digital postproduction, optical printing, advanced synch sound production, digital video documentary, video art, and nonlinear editing. Students choose careers as independent filmmakers or with large organizations, producing entertainment, documentation, learning aids, and experimental statements.

FINE ART AND APPLIED PHOTOGRAPHY

Focus/emphasis: The fine art photography emphasis encourages students to realize a personal vision. Students study topics such as digital imaging, experimental photographic techniques, photographic history and theory/criticism, studio photography, advertising/illustration photography, and special topics. Experimental applications of these tools are presented in courses covering nonsilver photography and experimental darkroom and camera techniques. Studio workshops and advanced topics courses allow for individual artistic expression, as well as for investigation of special topics such as presentation and publication methods, the landscape, and environmental portraiture. The applied photography emphasis explores the fields of advertising, illustration, and publication/editorial photography while stressing original concepts.

BROADCAST NEWS

Department chair: Phylis W. Johnson

Number of full-time faculty: 21

Focus/emphasis: The rewarding aspects of a broadcast news career are in the gathering, reporting, producing, and broadcasting of information needed by members of the local, national, and world communities. Students enrolled in the broadcast news sequence take part in a concentrated program involving all facets of broadcast journalism. Courses are designed to give students opportunities for practical experience using the

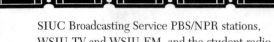

SIUC Broadcasting Service PBS/NPR stations, WSIU-TV and WSIU-FM, and the student radio station WIDB.

AUDIO PRODUCTION:

Focus/emphasis: Students in the commercial audio production area gain practical experience including on-air and production work in the radio industry, music recording, and audio production for video or multimedia. Audio production courses combine a strong design base with practical experience. Class projects are produced in a digital multitrack studio environment, and many lab exercises closely parallel industry activities in the creation of commercials and documentaries. Production students take advantage of the many opportunities available to them at WIDB Cable FM, WSIU-FM, and STUDIO A CAFE as well as at recording studios and production houses in Chicago, Nashville, New York, St. Louis, and Hollywood. Audio production also encompasses a fine arts orientation with classes in sound design, audio documentary, experimental audio, and audio theory/criticism.

TELEVISION/VIDEO PRODUCTION:

Focus/emphasis: In the Television/Video Specialization, students complete courses in one of three areas of concentration: Corporate video, video production, or writing. Students in the corporate video concentration learn to manage projects in a professional environment. The course work is practical and focuses on dealing with clients, creative problem solving, scriptwriting, studio and location production, working with graphic artists, postproduction, and future trends. Students in the video production concentration learn all aspects of program production from concept development through scripting to online editing. They may work on music videos, documentaries, narrative creative projects, or experimental video works. Courses provide a solid background in both studio and field work. Production students may also work with WSIU/WUSI-TV or with the student-produced program *River Region Evening Edition* on WSIU/WUSI-TV. Students in

the writing concentration learn the art of writing for both broadcast and nonbroadcast media. Courses provide a solid foundation in various aspects of writing including news, advertising, screenwriting, drama, and comedy.

ELECTRONIC MEDIA MARKETING AND MANAGEMENT:

Focus/emphasis: The concentration focuses on the business side of radio, television, cable, and new media. Students receive skill training in such areas as copywriting, audience research, technology, programming, promotion, sales, and sports marketing. Many students majoring in this area will choose an SIU Business School program as a minor.

SOUTHERN METHODIST UNIVERSITY

PO Box 750181, Dallas, TX 75275-0181
Phone: 214-768-3417 **E-mail:** enrol_serv@smu.edu
Website: www.smu.edu

Campus Life
Environment: Town. **Calendar:** Semester.

Students and Faculty
(All Undergraduate Programs)
Enrollment: 6,196. **Student Body:** 54% female, 46% male, 33% out-of-state, 5% international (94 countries represented). African American 5%, Asian 6%, Caucasian 75%, Hispanic 8%. Student/faculty ratio: 12:1. 603 full-time faculty, 84% hold PhDs. 89% faculty teach undergrads.

Admissions
(All Undergraduate Programs)
Freshman Admissions Requirements: Test(s) required: SAT or ACT. Average high school GPA: 3.49. 35% in top tenth, 64% in top quarter. SAT Math (25/75 percentile): 570/670. SAT Verbal (25/75 percentile): 560/660. Projected SAT Writing (25/75 percentile): 620/690. *Academic units required:* 4 English, 3 math, 3 science (2 science labs), 2 foreign language, 1 social studies, 2 history. Regular application deadline: 3/15. Regular notification: Rolling.

Costs and Financial Aid
(All Undergraduate Programs)

Annual tuition $25,400. Room & board $9,695. Required fees $3,230. Average book expense $600. **Financial Aid Statistics:** % freshmen/undergrads who receive any aid: 82/65. % freshmen/undergrads who receive need-based scholarship or grant aid: 32/34. % freshmen/undergrads who receive need-based self-help aid: 25/30. Priority financial aid filing deadline: 2/15. Financial aid notification on or about: 3/15.

TV/Film/Digital Media Studies Programs

Degrees conferred to these majors: BA.

Also available at Southern Methodist University: MFA, MA.

Equipment and facilities: The Division of Cinema-Television is located in the Umphrey Lee Center, which houses faculty offices, audio and video production areas, and media support areas. Production spaces are equipped with the latest visual technology and include basic video/audio modules; video-logging rooms; offline editing rooms; nonlinear editing labs; film-editing suites; advanced film-editing modules; storage and equipment checkout; digital audio rooms; editing labs; a seminar room; a graphics lab; viewing rooms; a television studio; and production classrooms. Two additional screening classrooms equipped for film, video, and DVD projection are located in the Greer Garson Theatre.

Other awards of note: MFA alumna Kimby Caplan's film, *Listen*, won a Student Academy Award.

Notable alumni: Cinema-Television graduates enjoy careers as directors, screenwriters, producers, media executives, and artistic directors. Their work ranges from documentaries and short and feature-length films to videos and online digital videos. Their awards include The Telly Award for Videographer, Daytime Emmys, and Academy Awards for sound mixing. SMU graduates can be found at Sony, Universal, Playtone Company, HBO, the Dallas Video Festival, the New York International Fringe Festival, and the Sundance Film Festival. Their work includes *Attraction*, *New*

Kansas, *Jimmy Neutron: Boy Genius*, *Ant Bully*, *Barney & Friends*, *Minority Report*, *Saving Private Ryan*, *Jurassic Park*, *Oz*, *King of the Hill*, and *X-Men*.

In Their Own Words

The Student Filmmakers Association (SFA) sponsored by SMU produces three films a year outside academic structure. Also, it presents an annual film festival at which student films are screened.

POPULAR PROGRAMS

CINEMA TRACK

Department chair: Rick Worland

Number of full-time faculty: 8

Focus/emphasis: The cinema track gives students experience in writing, shooting, directing, and editing film and video projects—as well as courses in the history, theory, and aesthetics of the medium. A basic video production course and two 16 mm film production courses are required. From there, advanced elective courses in screenwriting, production, and editing are offered to develop technical skills and creativity as a filmmaker.

TELEVISION TRACK

Focus/emphasis: The television track allows students to produce and edit electronic media and video projects and offers courses in the history, criticism, economics, and social effects of the contemporary mass media, including new moving image technologies. Through advanced elective courses in multimedia applications; global media systems; electronic media programming, sales, and policy; and audience research, majors are prepared for a rewarding career in the television industry.

SPELMAN COLLEGE

350 Spelman Lane, South West, Atlanta, GA 30314
Phone: 404-270-5193 **E-mail:** admiss@spelman.edu
Website: www.spelman.edu

Campus Life
Environment: Metropolis. **Calendar:** Semester.

Students and Faculty
(All Undergraduate Programs)
Enrollment: 2,229. **Student Body:** 83% out-of-state, 2% international (18 countries represented). African American 95%. Student/faculty ratio: 11:1. 169 full-time faculty, 90% hold PhDs. 100% faculty teach undergrads.

Admissions
(All Undergraduate Programs)
Freshman Admissions Requirements: Test(s) required: SAT or ACT. Average high school GPA: 3.4. 33% in top tenth, 71% in top quarter. SAT Math (25/75 percentile): 500/580. SAT Verbal (25/75 percentile): 520/560. Projected SAT Writing (25/75 percentile): 580/620. *Academic units required:* 4 English, 2 math, 2 science (1 science lab), 2 foreign language, 2 social studies. Early decision application deadline: 11/1. Regular application deadline: 2/1. Regular notification: 4/1.

Costs and Financial Aid
(All Undergraduate Programs)
Annual tuition $13,525. Room & board $8,455. Required fees $2,270. Average book expense $1,150. **Financial Aid Statistics:** % freshmen/undergrads who receive any aid: 87/87. % freshmen/undergrads who receive need-based scholarship or grant aid: 61/57. % freshmen/undergrads who receive need-based self-help aid: 82/75. Financial aid notification on or about: 2/15.

TV/Film/Digital Media Studies Programs
Number of undergraduates in these programs: 1
Degrees conferred to these majors: BA.
Number of full-time faculty in these programs: 1

Equipment and facilities: DV cameras, Apple computer cab for postproduction, TV studio, Final Cut Pro.

Career development services: Alumni networking opportunities; career counseling; central resource(s) for employers to browse headshots, writing samples, reels; internship listings; job fairs; job listings.

In Their Own Words
The independent major is designed to accommodate the interests and career goals of students with broad interdisciplinary interests that cannot be satisfied within one of the traditional Spelman College majors. Our Independent Film Major was created in 2004, with the first student graduating in May 2006; and the course of study included courses in the digital moving image salon (DMIS), studying film in the Czech Republic and at two partnering colleges in addition to courses in production, history, theory, and aesthetics at Spelman College, and participating in international production workshops. As DMIS has a special interest in the images of black women in the media, we are pleased that one of the first documentaries produced was screened at the Women of Color Film Festival in Berkeley in March 2006. The documentary looks at the recent activist activities at the college, which includes students taking on high-profile rappers and their misogynist representations of black women in music videos. Guests of DMIS include Neema Barnett, Civil Brand and the first African American woman to direct a television sitcom series; Lisa Gay Hamilton, Beah: A Black Woman Speaks and star of the television series The Practice; Pamela Jennings, assistant professor, School of Art and the Human Computer Interaction Institute, Carnegie Mellon University, digital media artist; and Niija Kuykendall, film producer, Beacon Pictures.

POPULAR PROGRAMS

DIGITAL MOVING IMAGE SALON (DMIS)
Department chair: Ayoka Chenzira

Focus/emphasis: DMIS was created in 2003 by filmmaker Ayoka Chenzira, a pioneer in Black Independent Cinema, who was invited to the college to serve as the first William and Camille Cosby Endowed Professor in the Arts. Professor Chenzira created DMIS as a mechanism through which to educate, encourage, and support women interested in film, video, and digital media production. Through DMIS, students research, develop, write, produce, direct, and edit digital video productions. In particular, stories that focus on women's culture—that being what mediates between women and society. This focus allows for a new generation of black women moving image storytellers to participate in important discussions around issues that are critical to their lives and to the lives of women locally, nationally, and internationally. The Salon's activities include a year-long course entitled "Documenting Women: Oral Narratives and Digital Media" (production and postproduction) and a critical analysis course entitled "Black Woman As Hero in American Cinema." DMIS produces the annual event Reel Women: Conversations with Black Women Who Work with the Moving Image. Women are invited to present their work in film, video, and digital media including computational storytelling. In addition, students working with DMIS and/or our independent major in film have an opportunity to work with Professor Chenzira on various digital media projects. Most recently, this has included a year-long production and postproduction workshop in Durban, South Africa that resulted in a documentary that won the ALO International Moving Image Award (www.aascu.org/alo/working/films04.htm) and attendance at various festivals.

Students Should Also Know

Spelman College is an outstanding historically black college for women that promotes academic excellence in the liberal arts and develops the intellectual, ethical, and leadership potential of its students. Spelman seeks to empower the total person who appreciates the many cultures of the world and commits to positive change. The college is in the early stages of offering a course of study for students interested in film, video, and digital media through the creation of our Digital Moving Image Salon (DMIS), as well as an independent major in film.

STANFORD UNIVERSITY

Undergraduate Admission, Bakewell Building, 355 Galvez Street, Stanford, CA 94305-3020
Phone: 650-723-2091 **E-mail:** admission@stanford.edu
Website: www.stanford.edu

Campus Life
Environment: City. **Calendar:** Quarter.

Students and Faculty
(All Undergraduate Programs)
Enrollment: 6,491. **Student Body:** 47% female, 53% male, 56% out-of-state, 6% international (68 countries represented). African American 10%, Asian 24%, Caucasian 41%, Hispanic 11%, Native American 2%. Student/faculty ratio: 6:1. 1,010 full-time faculty, 98% hold PhDs. 98% faculty teach undergrads.

Admissions
(All Undergraduate Programs)
Freshman Admissions Requirements: Test(s) required: SAT or ACT; ACT with Writing component. Average high school GPA: 3.9. 89% in top tenth, 97% in top quarter. SAT Math (25/75 percentile): 690/780. SAT Verbal (25/75 percentile): 670/770. Projected SAT Writing (25/75 percentile): 700/770. Regular application deadline: 12/15. Regular notification: 4/1.

Costs and Financial Aid
(All Undergraduate Programs)
Annual tuition $32,994. Room & board $10,367. Average book expense $1,260.
Financial Aid Statistics: % undergrads who receive any aid: 76. % freshmen/undergrads who receive need-based scholarship or grant aid: 41/45. % freshmen/undergrads who receive need-based self-help aid: 28/32. Priority financial aid filing deadline: 2/1. Financial aid notification on or about: 4/3.

TV/Film/Digital Media Studies Programs

Number of undergraduates in these programs: 25 undergraduate students

Degrees conferred to these majors: BA.

Also available at Stanford University: MFA.

Number of full-time faculty in these programs: 8

Other awards of note: Graduates of the master's program have won many honors, including Student Academy Awards, Student Emmy Awards, the Dore Schary Award, and the David Wolper Award. Faculty members in the Stanford Bachelor of Arts in Film and Media Studies major have been nominated for both Academy and Emmy awards and have had their films shown at festivals worldwide, including Sundance.

Career development services: Alumni networking opportunities, career counseling, internship listings, job fairs, job listings.

In Their Own Words

The Stanford Bachelor of Arts in Film and Media Studies major is new as of the fall of 2005. It has been off to a fast start, with guest lecturers such as film director Bennett Miller. The program benefits from the Stanford long-standing master's program in documentary film and video. Graduates of that program have won many honors, including Student Academy Awards, Student Emmy Awards, the Dore Schary Award, and the David Wolper Award. Graduates have worked at National Geographic, BBC, MSNBC, Lucasfilm, and MTV. The bachelor of arts in film and media studies provides an overall introduction to film aesthetics, national cinematic traditions, and diverse modes of production, such as narrative, documentary, and experimental films. The MFA program is designed to prepare students for professional careers in film, video, and digital media and for teaching at the university level.

POPULAR PROGRAMS

BACHELOR OF ARTS IN FILM AND MEDIA STUDIES

Department chair: Scott Bukatman

Number of full-time faculty: 3

Focus/emphasis: Provides an overall introduction to film aesthetics, national cinematic traditions, and diverse modes of production, such as narrative, documentary, and experimental films.

MFA PROGRAM IN DOCUMENTARY FILM AND VIDEO

Department chair: Kristine Samuelson

Number of full-time faculty: 2

Focus/emphasis: Designed to prepare students for professional careers in film, video, and digital media and for teaching at the university level.

Students Should Also Know

For more information, visit the Stanford website at www.stanford.edu or contact Jill Davis at jmdavis@stanford.edu or 650-725-0138.

STATE UNIVERSITY OF NEW YORK AT BINGHAMTON

PO Box 6001, Binghamton, NY 13902-6001
Phone: 607-777-2171 **E-mail:** admit@binghamton.edu
Website: www.binghamton.edu

Campus Life

Environment: Town. **Calendar:** Semester.

Students and Faculty
(All Undergraduate Programs)

Enrollment: 11,065. **Student Body:** 48% female, 52% male, 6% out-of-state, 7% international (87 countries represented). African American 5%, Asian 15%, Caucasian 50%, Hispanic 6%. Student/faculty ratio: 21:1. 537 full-time faculty, 93% hold PhDs. 90% faculty teach undergrads.

Admissions
(All Undergraduate Programs)

Freshman Admissions Requirements: Test(s) required: SAT or ACT; ACT with Writing component.

Average high school GPA: 3.7. 47% in top tenth, 87% in top quarter. SAT Math (25/75 percentile): 600/690. SAT Verbal (25/75 percentile): 560/660. Projected SAT Writing (25/75 percentile): 620/690. *Academic units required:* 4 English, 3 math, 2 science, 3 foreign language, 2 social studies. Regular notification: Rolling.

Costs and Financial Aid
(All Undergraduate Programs)

Annual in-state tuition $4,350. Out-of-state tuition $10,610. Room & board $8,150. Required fees $1,488. Average book expense $800.

Financial Aid Statistics: % freshmen/undergrads who receive any aid: 75/69. % freshmen/undergrads who receive need-based scholarship or grant aid: 38/42. % freshmen/undergrads who receive need-based self-help aid: 40/43. Priority financial aid filing deadline: 3/1. Financial aid notification on or about: 3/15.

TV/Film/Digital Media Studies Programs

Number of undergraduates in these programs: 75

Number of 2005 graduates from these programs: 40

Degrees conferred to these majors: BA.

Number of full-time faculty in these programs: 3

Number of part-time faculty in these programs: 6

Equipment and facilities: Film cameras (16-mm cameras: Bolex H16, Rex 5, Arriflex S, Arriflex 16-BL; Super 8 cameras: Nikon, Bauer, Canon, Sankyo, Minolta); generous access policies; video camcorders (mini-DV Sony TRV-8 and TRV-900, features include Firewire in/out, external mic jack, digital effects in-camera; S-VHS Panasonic AG450, Hi-8 Sony TRV-940, VHS Panasonic AG-187, AG-188, AG160); sound recorders (Nagra 1/4" reel-to-reel professional full-track recorders, Sony D-5 cassette, Marantz PMD-201 cassette, TASCAM 4-track porta-studios; microphones (Sennheiser, Sony, Shure, Audio-Technica, AKG); miscellaneous accessories (light meters: Gossen Luna Pro and Sekonic; lighting: Lowell "D", and "Tota" lights, snoots, barn-doors, filters, scrims. Other accessories include

Sony headphones, camera filters, cables, sync clapboards, tripods and body braces, tripod wheels). Check our website in the near future for updates!

Career development services: Alumni networking opportunities; career counseling; central resource(s) for employers to browse headshots, writing samples, reels; internship listings; job fairs; job listings.

In Their Own Words
Our program focuses on film and video as art forms, as distinguished from programs whose emphasis is on communication theory, broadcasting, or purely technical training. Our goal is to develop our students' understanding of the aesthetic possibilities of film and video and to provide them with the skills they need to make works of art in those media.

STATE UNIVERSITY OF NEW YORK– COLLEGE AT ONEONTA

Alumni Hall 116, State University College, Oneonta, NY 13820
Phone: 607-436-2524 **E-mail:** admissions@oneonta.edu
Website: www.oneonta.edu

Campus Life
Environment: Village. **Calendar:** Semester.

Students and Faculty
(All Undergraduate Programs)
Enrollment: 5,589. **Student Body:** 57% female, 43% male, 2% out-of-state, 1% international (19 countries represented). African American 3%, Asian 2%, Caucasian 82%, Hispanic 5%. Student/faculty ratio: 17:1. 252 full-time faculty, 78% hold PhDs. 99% faculty teach undergrads.

Admissions
(All Undergraduate Programs)
Freshman Admissions Requirements: Test(s) required: SAT or ACT. Average high school GPA: 3.4. 11% in top tenth, 48% in top quarter. SAT Math (25/75 percentile): 520/600. SAT Verbal (25/75 percentile): 510/590. Projected SAT Writing (25/75 percentile): 570/640. *Academic units required:* 4 English,

2 math, 2 science (2 science labs), 2 foreign language, 3 social studies. Regular notification: Rolling.

Costs and Financial Aid (All Undergraduate Programs)

Annual in-state tuition $4,350. Out-of-state tuition $10,610. Room & board $7,538. Required fees $1,017. Average book expense $850.

Financial Aid Statistics: % freshmen/undergrads who receive any aid: 56/57. % freshmen/undergrads who receive need-based scholarship or grant aid: 50/50. % freshmen/undergrads who receive need-based self-help aid: 43/48. Priority financial aid filing deadline: 2/15. Financial aid notification on or about: 3/1.

TV/Film/Digital Media Studies Programs

Number of undergraduates in these programs: 507

Number of 2005 graduates from these programs: 139

Degrees conferred to these majors: BA, BS.

Number of full-time faculty in these programs: 10

Number of part-time faculty in these programs: 5

Equipment and facilities: State-of-the-art computer art lab with 30 networked Macintosh computers, a projection system, a large format color printer, digital still and video cameras, scanners, and a wide variety of industry-standard software. Audio studio, fully-operational TV production complex, and a mobile production unit. Two TV studios outfitted with industrial quality cameras and Beta SP/SVHS/VHS/U-matic recording equipment. Betacam/U-matic/S-VHS-recording equipment and a Pinnacle Digital Video Effect system. Editing suites, including a media 100 digital editing unit, and several CCD camcorders.

Other awards of note: Apple Distinguished Educator, four Tellies, a Proclaim (Gabriel), a Chris, 3 FPRA's, Addy Gold, NAAEE Film and Video Award, and Best Documentary Award from the Colorado Broadcasters Association.

% of graduates who pursue further study within 5 years: 20

% of graduates currently employed in related field: 75

Career development services: Alumni networking opportunities, career counseling, internship listings, job fairs, job listings.

Famous alumni: Bill Pullman, Sal Paolantonio.

Notable alumni: Nick Lakiotes, founder, 6-point Harness studio; Dana Kuznetzkoff, producer; Frank Prinzi, cinematographer; Greg Floyd, news anchor, CBS6-Albany.

In Their Own Words

Computer art faculty members maintain strong ties with Pixar and Apple; one faculty member named Apple Distinguished Educator; internships with Disney, Pixar, major TV and radio networks, and many others; many experiential learning opportunities in productions with local service agencies.

POPULAR PROGRAMS

MASS COMMUNICATION

Department chair: Arthur Dauria

Number of full-time faculty: 7

Number of part-time faculty: 5

Focus/emphasis: The mass communication major is designed to meet the needs of students who seek careers in the fields of broadcasting, journalism, film, audio production, and video production.

COMPUTER ART

Department chair: Yolanda Sharpe

Number of full-time faculty: 3

Number of part-time faculty: 1

Focus/emphasis: Courses cover a wide range of the digital realm, and they continually evolve to incorporate the latest technological innovations as they pertain to art. The classes offered provide a thorough understanding of how the computer can be used as an art tool, and they cover topics such as raster and vector imaging, 3-D modeling and animation, digital photography, digital video, and Web and graphic design.

STATE UNIVERSITY OF NEW YORK–COLLEGE AT OSWEGO

229 Sheldon Hall, Oswego, NY 13126
Phone: 315-312-2250 **E-mail:** admiss@oswego.edu
Website: www.oswego.edu

Campus Life
Environment: Village. **Calendar:** Semester.

Students and Faculty
(All Undergraduate Programs)
Enrollment: 7,000. **Student Body:** 54% female, 46% male, 3% out-of-state. African American 4%, Asian 2%, Caucasian 89%, Hispanic 4%. Student/faculty ratio: 18:1. 317 full-time faculty, 83% hold PhDs. 93% faculty teach undergrads.

Admissions
(All Undergraduate Programs)
Freshman Admissions Requirements: Test(s) required: SAT or ACT. Average high school GPA: 3.29. 10% in top tenth, 50% in top quarter. SAT Math (25/75 percentile): 520/580. SAT Verbal (25/75 percentile): 500/580. Projected SAT Writing (25/75 percentile): 560/630. *Academic units required:* 4 English, 3 math, 3 science (2 science labs), 2 foreign language, 4 social studies. Early decision application deadline: 11/15. Regular notification: Rolling.

Costs and Financial Aid
(All Undergraduate Programs)
Annual in-state tuition $4,350. Out-of-state tuition $10,610. Room & board $8,340. Required fees $972. Average book expense $800.
Financial Aid Statistics: % freshmen/undergrads who receive need-based scholarship or grant aid: 63/61. % freshmen/undergrads who receive need-based self-help aid: 56/59. Priority financial aid filing deadline: 4/1. Financial aid notification on or about: 3/1.

TV/Film/Digital Media Studies Programs
Number of undergraduates in these programs: 350
Number of 2005 graduates from these programs: 75

Degrees conferred to these majors: BA.
Number of full-time faculty in these programs: 6
Number of part-time faculty in these programs: 7
Equipment and facilities: New full SDI digital television studios for production and news, including a Synergy 2 switcher, Final Cut Pro HD workcluster for editing using XSAN fiber networking; HDV and SDI ENG/EFP packages for students. Twenty-four workstations and the Center for Communication and Information Technology with latest Adobe/Macromedia software for Web development.
ATAS Faculty Seminar participants: 3

% of graduates who pursue further study within 5 years: 15
% of graduates currently employed in related field: 50
Career development services: Alumni networking opportunities, career counseling, internship listings, job fairs, job listings. We have an internal network of alumni who register job openings with us.
Famous alumni: Al Roker, Linda Cohen, Ken Auletta, Steve Levy, Kendis Gibson.
Notable alumni: Louis Borelli, CEO, NEP Supershooters; Sharon Newman, news producer, NBC; Steve LaBlang, senior vice president for FX network; Lauren Grey, comedy specials producer, HBO; Bill Shine, vice president, Fox News; Carl Hausman, author; Kathy Quinn, CBS primetime sales; Brian McAloon, director, the *Late Late Show with Craig Ferguson*. There are dozens more who are very successful.

In Their Own Words
We have tremendous internships at all major networks and production houses, including Late Night with Conan O'Brien, Today Show, Late Show with David Letterman, *ESPN, MTV, CNN, NBC Olympics, and Al Roker Productions. This fall Steve Levy from ESPN, Ben Bradlee from* The Washington Post, *and Ken Auletta, media critic for the* New Yorker, *were among our guest speakers. We also run a special two-week program in Hollywood where students get to talk with top producers, directors, and writers.*

POPULAR PROGRAMS

BROADCASTING AND MASS COMMUNICATION
Department chair: Fritz Messere
Number of full-time faculty: 6
Number of part-time faculty: 7
Focus/emphasis: Broadcasting and electronic mass media production, management, and writing.

PUBLIC RELATIONS
Department chair: Fritz Messere
Number of full-time faculty: 3
Focus/emphasis: Public relations management and writing.

JOURNALISM
Department chair: Fritz Messere
Number of full-time faculty: 4
Number of part-time faculty: 2
Focus/emphasis: Community journalism.

GRAPHIC ARTS
Department chair: Helen Zakin
Number of full-time faculty: 4
Number of part-time faculty: 2
Focus/emphasis: Electronic graphic arts.

Students Should Also Know
The school is starting a New Media program that will meld skills in graphic arts.

STATE UNIVERSITY OF NEW YORK– FREDONIA

178 Central Avenue, Fredonia, NY 14063
Phone: 716-673-3251 **E-mail:** admissions.office@fredonia.edu
Website: www.fredonia.edu

Campus Life
Environment: Village. **Calendar:** Semester.

Students and Faculty (All Undergraduate Programs)
Enrollment: 5,043. **Student Body:** 58% female, 42% male, 2% out-of-state. African American 2%, Asian 2%, Caucasian 85%, Hispanic 3%. Student/faculty ratio: 20:1. 253 full-time faculty, 87% hold PhDs. 100% faculty teach undergrads.

Admissions (All Undergraduate Programs)
Freshman Admissions Requirements: Test(s) required: SAT or ACT. Average high school GPA: 3.43. 15% in top tenth, 45% in top quarter. SAT Math (25/75 percentile): 520/600. SAT Verbal (25/75 percentile): 520/600. Projected SAT Writing (25/75 percentile): 580/650. *Academic units required:* 4 English, 3 math, 3 science, 3 foreign language, 4 social studies. Early decision application deadline: 11/1. Regular notification: Rolling.

Costs and Financial Aid (All Undergraduate Programs)
Annual in-state tuition $4,350. Out-of-state tuition $10,610. Room & board $7,420. Required fees $1,091. Average book expense $620.
Financial Aid Statistics: % freshmen/undergrads who receive any aid: 80/85. % freshmen/undergrads who receive need-based scholarship or grant aid: 55/57. % freshmen/undergrads who receive need-based self-help aid: 54/59. Priority financial aid filing deadline: 1/31. Financial aid filing deadline: 5/15. Financial aid notification on or about: 3/10.

TV/Film/Digital Media Studies Programs
Number of undergraduates in these programs: 130
Number of 2005 graduates from these programs: 28
Degrees conferred to these majors: BS.
Number of full-time faculty in these programs: 6
Number of part-time faculty in these programs: 4
Equipment and facilities: There are 10 DV field cameras and three pedestal-mounted studio cameras. Other production gear includes lighting kits, microphones and booms, and a dolly with tracks and jib arm. Facilities include one TV studio, one soundstage with a light grid, four nonlinear editing suites with 24-hour access, and 20 computers in a proctored computer lab with nonlinear video-edit-

ing software. There are four audio studios for recording voice and music.

% of graduates who pursue further study within 5 years: 5

% of graduates currently employed in related field: 90

Career development services: Alumni networking opportunities, career counseling, internship listings, job fairs, job listings.

Famous alumni: Brian Fronz.

Notable alumni: Eric Thom, promotion director, KUOW radio, Seattle; Jim Ranney, news director, WEBR radio, Buffalo; Winter Zemans, assistant production coordinator, *Grey's Anatomy*; Vic Baker, executive producer, WIVB TV, Buffalo; Mary Beth Wrobel, weather reporter, WIVB TV, Buffalo; Joana Pasceri, anchor/reporter, WKBW TV, Buffalo; Rob McIntyre, sound engineer/designer, Oracle Sound, Los Angeles; Goldie Jones, postproduction engineer, Pyramid Productions, Seattle; Rebecca Gibney, associate producer WXXI TV, Rochester; Ronnie Miller, program producer, The Travel Channel.

In Their Own Words

Students take advantage of a strong internship program. Students can also participate at WNYF, the student-run TV station.

POPULAR PROGRAMS

MUSIC EDUCATION

Department chair: Karl Boelter

Number of full-time faculty: 41

Number of part-time faculty: 49

Focus/emphasis: The program has always been Fredonia's primary degree program. One facet of the program sets Fredonia apart from many similar schools—music education majors receive a one-hour private studio lesson in their primary performance medium for six or seven semesters, plus weekly master classes with the other members of their studio, all culminating in the required performance of a graduation recital.

Private instruction is available, pending studio space, in secondary instruments. Music education majors receive four semesters of instruction in conducting; instruction in the performance and pedagogy of woodwinds, brass, strings, and percussion; and instruction in music education foundations and methods from music education specialist faculty. Students are involved in hands-on teaching each year, culminating in semester-long student teaching. Music education graduates are fully qualified to enter the workforce and pursue satisfying careers as music teachers.

TV DIGITAL FILM

Department chair: Ted Schwalbe

Number of full-time faculty: 10

Number of part-time faculty: 4

Focus/emphasis: Television has been and continues to be the instant informer, effective teacher, primary persuader, and great entertainer for our society. It has greatly influenced our society in a variety of ways. The video aspect has also influenced our society and is developing rapidly, having already moved from film to videotape to DVD. This major allows students to learn background theory while developing conceptual and technological skills used in the production of programs both inside the studio and on location. There are many opportunities for hands-on learning with courses in multicamera, field and postproduction, and digital applications. With the completion of the major, students participate in a video drama or documentary production capstone project.

GRAPHIC DESIGN

Department chair: Elizabeth Lee

Number of full-time faculty: 12

Number of part-time faculty: 11

Focus/emphasis: Focuses on the effective presentation of ideas and information by means of type and image, whether in traditional print media or in interactive digital formats. Graphic designers are communicators who produce visual messages to interest, inform, and persuade. They make order out of chaos; they are researchers and analysts as well as artists. The graphic design curriculum emphasizes preparation for professional practice in an increasingly complex world. Design students learn to integrate aesthetics and communication with the social, behavioral, and natural sciences. They study conceptual and process development, typography, design history, professional practices, and communication theory. Students apply their learning by developing solutions such as publications, identity systems, posters, packaging, and signage. Many students gain further experience through internships. The graphic design program is a student chapter of American Institute for Graphic Arts (AIGA).

PUBLIC RELATIONS

Department chair: Ted Schwalbe
Number of full-time faculty: 10
Number of part-time faculty: 4
Focus/emphasis: Teaches students how individuals and organizations can establish, maintain, and strengthen relationships between organizations and the public they serve. The curriculum focuses on the theoretical and professional skills necessary to effectively communicate and mediate the goals of an organization and those of the organization's public. The emphasis on ethics, campaign design, management, and the production of messages for the targeted public prepares students to serve as communication advocates in a variety of professional and civic settings.

THEATER ARTS

Department chair: James Ivey
Number of full-time faculty: 9
Number of part-time faculty: 2
Focus/emphasis: Provides training for professional, community, and academic theaters within the framework of the liberal arts education. The Department of Theater and Dance offers bachelor of arts and bachelor of fine arts degrees. The bachelor of arts degree is a general theater studies program. The bachelor of fine arts degree program is limited to those students who demon-

strate excellence or the potential for excellence in performance and/or production and design. It is designed for those students who enter the university with a firm idea of their professional goals.

STEPHENS COLLEGE

1200 East Broadway, Box 2121, Columbia, MO 65215
Phone: 573-876-7207 **E-mail:** apply@wc.stephens.edu
Website: www.stephens.edu

Campus Life
Environment: City. **Calendar:** Semester.

Students and Faculty
(All Undergraduate Programs)
Enrollment: 826. **Student Body:** 96% female, 4% male, 55% out-of-state. African American 7%, Asian 1%, Caucasian 75%, Hispanic 2%. Student/faculty ratio: 12:1. 41 full-time faculty, 51% hold PhDs. 100% faculty teach undergrads.

Admissions
(All Undergraduate Programs)
Average high school GPA: 3.5. 19% in top tenth, 59% in top quarter. SAT Math (25/75 percentile): 480/580. SAT Verbal (25/75 percentile): 540/610. Projected SAT Writing (25/75 percentile): 600/660. Regular notification: Rolling.

Costs and Financial Aid
(All Undergraduate Programs)
Annual tuition $20,500. Room & board $7,975. Average book expense $1,000.
Financial Aid Statistics: % freshmen/undergrads who receive any aid: 98/83. % freshmen/undergrads who receive need-based scholarship or grant aid: 64/54. % freshmen/undergrads who receive need-based self-help aid: 62/58. Priority financial aid filing deadline: 3/15. Financial aid notification on or about: 3/1.

TV/Film/Digital Media Studies Programs
Number of undergraduates
in these programs: 22

Number of 2005 graduates from these programs: 7

Degrees conferred to these majors: BS.

Number of full-time faculty in these programs: 3

Number of part-time faculty in these programs: 5

Equipment and facilities: Patricia Barry Television Studio, G5 Mac lab with Final Cut Pro, digital film and camera equipment.

% of graduates currently employed in related field: 80

Career development services: Alumni networking opportunities, career counseling, faculty connections with those in the industry, internship listings, job fairs, job listings.

Famous alumni: Annie Potts, Paula Zahn.

Notable alumni: Kristin Atwell, documentary filmmaker; Ken LaZebnik, Hollywood screenwriter, *Touched by an Angel*; Wendy Anderson, Austin Film Society author/TV executive; Lyah LeFlore, Tower Productions; Kayla McCormick Phillip LaZebnik, screenwriter, *Pocahontas*, *Prince of Egypt*.

In Their Own Words

Sponsor and participant in Columbia's (MO) True-False Film Festival; internships with the Missouri film office. Students have interned at Primetime Live, Today Show, Hollywood Arts Council. Summer Film Institute lecturer Judith Guest, author/screenwriter, Ordinary People, through Citizen Jane Women in Film Lecture Series; see part-time faculty section of website for other lecturers/instructors. Digital Film Program Advisory Board includes Rob LaZebnik, television screenwriter, The Simpsons, Less Than Perfect, The Ellen Show; Dawn Wells, CEO, Spud Film Institute in Driggs, Idaho, Stephens alumna and actress, Gilligan's Island; Amy Lippman, cocreator and executive producer, Party of Five; Jonathon Mostow, director, Terminator 3, U-571, and Breakdown; Alex Rockwell, vice president, Henson Productions, executive producer, Bear in the Big Blue House;

Nell Scovell, creator and executive producer, Sabrina the Teenage Witch, writer/producer of other sitcoms; Jon Collier, coexecutive producer, King of the Hill, producer, The Simpsons.

POPULAR PROGRAMS

BS IN MASS MEDIA—ELECTRONIC MEDIA PRODUCTION

Department chair: Ken LaZebnik

Number of full-time faculty: 4

Focus/emphasis: Prepares students for careers in television, on and off screen, or radio, from voice training to audio production. Courses include television programming and digital video/TV production. Students complete required internships that immediately immerse them in future careers at locations such as AOL Time Warner, MTV Studios, INCA Productions in London, or TakeTwo Productions in Kansas City. Visit www.stephens.edu/admission/programs/massmedia for more information.

DIGITAL FILMMAKING

Number of full-time faculty: 3

Number of part-time faculty: 5

Focus/emphasis: According to the college, Stephens is the only women's college in America with a producing digital film major. From pre- to postproduction, students work with other students in teams to create professional quality narrative and documentary films within a curriculum that emphasizes hands-on work with the latest in digital cameras and editing hardware and software. By senior year, students will have chosen to concentrate their work in one of four areas: narrative filmmaking, documentary filmmaking, commercial filmmaking, or corporate filmmaking. By capitalizing on the strengths of Stephens's renowned theater and mass media programs in the School of the Performing Arts, students learn the skills needed to become a successful director, writer, producer, or editor. Visit www.stephens.edu/admission/programs/digital-film/ for more information.

SUMMER FILM INSTITUTE

Number of full-time faculty: 2

Focus/emphasis: SFI is an intensive two-week, hands-on institute that centers around the production of an hour-long TV drama plot. Students join the film crew under the guidance of working Hollywood professionals. Hollywood screenwriter Ken LaZebnik (also dean of our school), Hollywood producer R. J. Visciglia, *ER*'s assistant director Princess O'Mahoney, and actor James Eckhouse are part of the professional crew. SFI takes place on the Stephens campus in Columbia, MO, July 17 to 30, 2006. Visit www.stephens.edu/academics/programs/massmedia/sfi/ for more information.

APPLE AUTHORIZED TRAINING CENTER

Number of full-time faculty: 1

Focus/emphasis: Stephens is the first and only Apple Authorized Training Center in the Midwest. All classes are taught by Apple-certified Final Cut Pro trainers. Visit www2.stephens.edu/massmedia/Apple%20Center.htm for more information.

COLUMBIA ACCESS TELEVISION

Focus/emphasis: Stephens' Patricia Barry Television Studios also are home to the City of Columbia's public access channel, Columbia Access Television. Students have hands-on experience through this arrangement.

SCREENWRITING WOMEN IN FILM SHORT SCRIPT COMPETITION

Focus/emphasis: This newly introduced screenwriting competition engages high school and college women in innovative educational screenwriting judged by Hollywood professionals and artists.

Students Should Also Know

Stephens's programs in film and TV are open only to women. Stephens is the second-oldest women's college in the country.

STETSON UNIVERSITY

421 North Woodland Boulevard, Unit 8378, DeLand, FL 32723
Phone: 386-822-7100 **E-mail:** admissions@stetson.edu
Website: www.stetson.edu

Campus Life

Environment: Town. **Calendar:** Semester.

Students and Faculty (All Undergraduate Programs)

Enrollment: 2,181. **Student Body:** 58% female, 42% male, 20% out-of-state, 3% international (41 countries represented). African American 4%, Asian 2%, Caucasian 83%, Hispanic 6%. Student/faculty ratio: 11:1. 231 full-time faculty, 91% hold PhDs. 98% faculty teach undergrads.

Admissions (All Undergraduate Programs)

Freshman Admissions Requirements: Test(s) required: SAT or ACT. Average high school GPA: 3.69. 27% in top tenth, 57% in top quarter. SAT Math (25/75 percentile): 510/610. SAT Verbal (25/75 percentile): 520/620. Projected SAT Writing (25/75 percentile): 580/660. *Academic units required:* 4 English, 3 math, 3 science, 2 foreign language, 2 social studies. Early decision application deadline: 11/1. Regular notification: Rolling.

Costs and Financial Aid (All Undergraduate Programs)

Annual tuition $23,910. Room & board $7,275. Required fees $1,455. Average book expense $800. **Financial Aid Statistics:** % freshmen/undergrads who receive any aid: 99/94. % freshmen/undergrads who receive need-based scholarship or grant aid: 57/57. % freshmen/undergrads who receive need-based self-help aid: 37/41. Financial aid filing deadline: 3/15. Financial aid notification on or about: 4/15.

TV/Film/Digital Media Studies Programs

Number of undergraduates in these programs: 25

Number of 2005 graduates from these programs: 6

Degrees conferred to these majors: BA.

Number of full-time faculty in these
   programs: 3
Number of part-time faculty in these
   programs: 1

% of graduates who pursue further study within 5
years: 20
% of graduates currently employed in related
field: 70
Career development services: Alumni networking
   opportunities, career counseling, e-mail distribution
   lists of auditions, job fairs, and other opportunities.
Famous alumni: Ret Turner, Michael Yeargan, Ted
   Cassidy.
Notable alumni: Ramon Delgado, playwright; Louis
   Phillips, playwright; Ray Hyde, actor; Heidi
   Howard, director; Hannamiller, director of entertainment, *Arabian Nights.*

In Their Own Words
*A Bachelor of Arts in Theater Arts program,
with low faculty/student ratio and lots of practical experience for students. The longest-running
theater production of any kind—professional,
educational, community—in Florida (since 1906).
Campus often used as a location for such films
as The Waterboy, From Earth to the Moon, and
Ghost Story.*

POPULAR PROGRAMS

THEATER ARTS
   Department chair: Ken McCoy
   Number of full-time faculty: 3
   Number of part-time faculty: 1
   Focus/emphasis: Bachelor of arts in theater arts.

SUFFOLK UNIVERSITY
8 Ashburton Place, Boston, MA 02108
Phone: 617-573-8460 **E-mail:** admission@suffolk.edu
Website: www.suffolk.edu

Campus Life
Environment: Metropolis. **Calendar:** Semester.

Students and Faculty
   (All Undergraduate Programs)
Enrollment: 4,595. **Student Body:** 59% female,
41% male, 24% out-of-state, 9% international (100
countries represented). African American 3%, Asian
7%, Caucasian 62%, Hispanic 4%. Student/faculty
ratio: 12:1. 352 full-time faculty, 91% hold PhDs. 90%
faculty teach undergrads.

Admissions
   (All Undergraduate Programs)
Freshman Admissions Requirements: Test(s)
required: SAT or ACT. Average high school GPA: 3.0.
10% in top tenth, 25% in top quarter. SAT Math
(25/75 percentile): 460/560. SAT Verbal (25/75 percentile): 460/570. Projected SAT Writing (25/75 percentile): 530/620. *Academic units required:* 4 English,
3 math, 2 science (1 science lab), 2 foreign language,
1 history, 4 academic electives. Regular application
deadline: 8/15. Regular notification: Rolling.

Costs and Financial Aid
   (All Undergraduate Programs)
Annual tuition $22,610. Room & board $12,756.
Average book expense $1,000.
Financial Aid Statistics: % freshmen/undergrads
who receive any aid: 63/65. % freshmen/undergrads
who receive need-based scholarship or grant aid:
47/47. % freshmen/undergrads who receive need-
based self-help aid: 55/52. Priority financial aid filing
deadline: 3/1. Financial aid filing deadline: 4/1.
Financial aid notification on or about: 3/1.

TV/Film/Digital Media Studies Programs
**Number of undergraduates
   in these programs:** 145
**Number of 2005 graduates from these
   programs:** 11

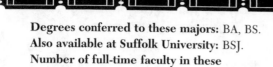

Degrees conferred to these majors: BA, BS.
Also available at Suffolk University: BSJ.
Number of full-time faculty in these programs: 4
Number of part-time faculty in these programs: 3
Equipment and facilities: Six Avid editing systems, state-of-the-art digital cameras, portable sound and listening, TV studio.
Other awards of note: Two Fulbright scholars.

% of graduates who pursue further study within 5 years: 10
% of graduates who pursue further study within 5 years: 15
Career development services: Alumni networking opportunities, career counseling, internship listings, job fairs, job listings, mock interviews.
Famous alumni: Dan Jaehnig, Fox 25, Boston, 3-time Emmy winner.

In Their Own Words

Internships available at CBS, NBS, ABC, and Fox affiliates in Boston; media internships at Boston Garden, Fenway Park, Gillette Stadium, and with numerous media enterprises in the greater Boston area.

POPULAR PROGRAMS

MEDIA STUDIES
Department chair: Robert Rosenthal
Number of full-time faculty: 4
Number of part-time faculty: 3
Focus/emphasis: Blending hands-on, practical training with writing, producing, and critical approaches to today's mass media, it gives students a broad perspective of the ways in which media interact with contemporary society.

FILM STUDIES
Department chair: Robert Rosenthal
Number of full-time faculty: 4
Number of part-time faculty: 3
Focus/emphasis: The concentration in film studies provides essential background, knowledge, and critical skills for the evaluation of film as part of modern culture.

Students Should Also Know
These programs are part of the Communications and Journalism Department at Suffolk University.

SYRACUSE UNIVERSITY
100 Crouse-Hinds Hall, Office of Admissions, Syracuse, NY 13244-2130
Phone: 315-443-3611 **E-mail:** orange@syr.edu
Website: www.syr.edu

Campus Life
Environment: City. **Calendar:** Semester.

Students and Faculty
(All Undergraduate Programs)
Enrollment: 11,441. **Student Body:** 56% female, 44% male, 56% out-of-state, 3% international (65 countries represented). African American 6%, Asian 6%, Caucasian 69%, Hispanic 5%. Student/faculty ratio: 12:1. 865 full-time faculty, 88% hold PhDs. 95% faculty teach undergrads.

Admissions
(All Undergraduate Programs)
Freshman Admissions Requirements: Test(s) required: SAT or ACT; ACT with Writing component. Average high school GPA: 3.6. 44% in top tenth, 80% in top quarter. SAT Math (25/75 percentile): 570/670. SAT Verbal (25/75 percentile): 570/650. Projected SAT Writing (25/75 percentile): 620/690. *Academic units required:* 4 English, 4 math, 4 science, 3 foreign language, 4 social studies. Early decision application deadline: 11/15. Regular application deadline: 1/1. Regular notification: 3/15.

Costs and Financial Aid
(All Undergraduate Programs)
Annual tuition $28,820. Room & board $10,604. Required fees $1,150. Average book expense $1,234. **Financial Aid Statistics:** % freshmen/undergrads who receive any aid: 76/76. % freshmen/undergrads

who receive need-based scholarship or grant aid: 54/52. % freshmen/undergrads who receive need-based self-help aid: 51/50. Priority financial aid filing deadline: 2/1. Financial aid filing deadline: 2/1. Financial aid notification on or about: 4/1.

TV/Film/Digital Media Studies Programs

Number of undergraduates in these programs: 853

Number of 2005 graduates from these programs: 198

Degrees conferred to these majors: BA, BS.

Also available at Syracuse University: MA, MS.

Number of full-time faculty in these programs: 42

Number of part-time faculty in these programs: 14

Equipment and facilities: The S. I. Newhouse Communications Center's two buildings are known on campus as Newhouse I and Newhouse II. Both buildings have faculty offices and classrooms capable of supporting Web, PowerPoint, and multimedia presentations. Newhouse I contains most of the school's administrative offices; computerized newswriting and editing laboratories with research tools such as SPSS and Lexis-Nexis; graphics and multimedia laboratories with CD and DVD burners; and an advertising/public relations campaigns laboratory. There is a large professional photography studio equipped with laboratories for electronic imaging, digital color printing, and conventional film processing and darkrooms for black-and-white and color printing. Newhouse II contains two professionally equipped television studios with a master control room and an extensive field-equipment facility that monitors the use of dozens of digital video camera systems (DV, DVCAM, DVC-pro formats), lights, microphones, and other production accessories. postproduction facilities include linear video editing suites, nonlinear editing suites (Avid and Final Cut Pro), three digital sound studios equipped with Pro Tools digital audio workstations (5.1 surround) and 24-track state-of-the-art digital consoles, an extensive sound effects and music collection, Photoshop and AfterEffects graphic systems, and an encoder and server for video streaming on the Web. There is a multiroom complex for teaching broadcast journalism that contains a newsroom and writing laboratories equipped with Electronic News Production System (ENPS), a radio production lab where students edit digital news stories using Adobe Audition, a studio devoted to learning live reporting, and screening and viewing rooms. In addition, students are involved extensively in the university's Orange Television Network. Newhouse III is a new building that will house a convergence laboratory that will allow print and broadcast students to work together, an executive education suite, offices for communications student organizations, an auditorium, a cafeteria, and a student lounge.

Other awards of note: Students in our Broadcast Journalism program regularly enter and win awards in the Hearst Competition.

% of graduates currently employed in related field: 93

Career development services: Alumni networking opportunities; career counseling, internship listings, job fairs, job hunt seminars, job listings, 3,500+ Alumni networking database.

Famous alumni: Marv Albert, Barry Baker, Edward Bleier, Angela Bundrant, Bob Costas, Fred Dressler, Eric Frankel, Brian Frons, Ed Goren, Robert Halmi, Steven Herson, Irma Kalish, Larry Kramer, Steve Kroft, Robert Light, Arthur Liu, Paula Walker Madison, Tony Malara, Jim Morris, Jack Myers, Robert Myron, Lowell Paxton, Philip Quartararo, Lakshmi Singh, Dick Stockton, John Sykes, Mark Tinker, Mike Tirico, John Wildhack, Howard Woolley.

Notable alumni: Eric Bress, director, *Final Destination II*, *Butterfly Effect*, *Frozen*; Eric Abrams and Matt Berry, writers, *Crocodile Dundee*; Robert Anderson, Discovery Networks; Chris Andrews, ICM, Los Angeles; John Beck and Ron Hart, executive producers, *According to Jim*; Bill Bonnell, NBC Sports; Joan Adler, HMA Digital; Dennis Denniger, ESPN New Media; John Fisher, *Young and the Restless*; Tom Fontana, *OZ*, *St. Elsewhere*; Jay Francis, *The Simpsons*; Justin Freiman, Court TV, Beej Gefsky Original Films; Tanya Giles, vice president, research and planning, TVLand; Chris Godsick, vice president, New Line Cinema; Sharon Goodman, Disney Radio; Jon

Greene, writer, *Law and Order: Special Victims Unit*; Peter Guber, Sony; Gary Hahn, Time Warner; Peter Hyams, director; Jack Helmuth, SNL, HBO; Gary Kanofsky, CNBC; Steve Kent, Sony International; Meg LeFauve, producer, Jodie Foster's Egg Productions, currently independent; Mitch Messinger, Columbia/Tri-Star; Harlan Neugeboren, Time Warner; Michael Nilon, ICM; Felicia Patinkin, NBC; Alvin Perlmutter, president, Alvin H. Perlmutter Inc.; Ron Stitt, ABC/Disney; Jim Shearer, MTV-2 VJ; Gary Shapiro, USA Films; Robert Shuman, CTW; Eric Stangel, head writer, *Late Show with David Letterman*; Lew Strauss, CNN; Mark Tinker, *St. Elsewhere*, *NYPD Blue*; Jacqueline Wilson, Nickelodeon; George Verschoor, *MTV's Real World*; Chris Viscardi and Will McRobb, *Pete and Pete*, *Snow Day*; David Zeplowitz, syndicated cigar radio show; Danny Zuker, executive producer, *Don't Shoot Me*, *Oliver Beane*.

POPULAR PROGRAMS

TELEVISION-RADIO-FILM

Department chair: Michael Schoonmaker
Number of full-time faculty: 16
Number of part-time faculty: 9
Focus/emphasis: Prepares future leaders in the television, radio, film, and interactive media industries. The major consists of a minimum of 12 courses: seven core requirements and five electives. Core courses introduce students to issues, practices, and concepts fundamental to an understanding of television-radio-film environments. An extensive array of elective courses provides students the opportunity to tailor their programs of study to their unique learning objectives. Alumni have gone on to pursue a wide variety of careers as producers, writers, directors, designers, agents, editors, executives, attorneys, and media educators.

BROADCAST JOURNALISM

Department chair: Dona Hayes
Number of full-time faculty: 11
Number of part-time faculty: 5
Focus/emphasis: Students learn writing, information gathering and reporting, formatting, editing, anchoring, and producing for radio and television news. Students also study critical issues (including ethical dilemmas) faced in today's complex communications environment. Hands-on experience is emphasized in the broadcast journalism curriculum. Majors are encouraged to take advantage of university-sponsored internships at broadcast stations (both local and network) across the country. Additionally, students have the opportunity to do extracurricular work at campus radio stations and at the student-operated closed-circuit television station.

GRAPHIC ARTS

Department Chair: Anthony Golden
Number of full-time faculty: 8
Focus/emphasis: Designed for students interested in visual communications in newspapers, magazines, and other media. Emphasis is placed on computer production techniques, communications writing, and communications law and ethics. Career opportunities exist in almost every sector of the communications industries, from advertising to journalism to video and Web interface design.

PHOTOGRAPHY

Department Chair: Anthony Golden
Number of full-time faculty: 7
Focus/emphasis: The photography program offers two professionally-oriented sequences: illustration photography and photojournalism. In both sequences, emphasis is placed on digital and conventional production techniques. The program also gives students a background in graphics arts, communications writing, and communications law and ethics. Graduates work with advertising agencies, newspapers, magazines, and photographic studios.

TAYLOR UNIVERSITY

236 West Reade Avenue, Upland, IN 46989-1001
Phone: 765-998-5134 **E-mail:** admissions_u@tayloru.edu
Website: www.taylor.edu

Campus Life
Environment: Rural. **Calendar:** 4-1-4.

Students and Faculty
(All Undergraduate Programs)
Enrollment: 1,829. **Student Body:** 55% female, 45% male, 67% out-of-state. Student/faculty ratio 14:1. 128 full-time faculty, 73% hold PhDs. 100% faculty teach undergrads.

Admissions
(All Undergraduate Programs)
Freshman Admissions Requirements: Test(s) required: SAT or ACT. Average high school GPA: 3.75. 37% in top tenth, 68% in top quarter. SAT Math (25/75 percentile): 550/660. SAT Verbal (25/75 percentile): 530/660. Projected SAT Writing (25/75 percentile): 590/690. *Academic units required:* 4 English, 3 math, 3 science (3 science lab), 2 social studies, 3 academic electives. Regular notification: Rolling.

Costs and Financial Aid
(All Undergraduate Programs)
Annual tuition $20,520. Room & board $5,630. Required fees $226. Average book expense $800. **Financial Aid Statistics:** % freshmen/undergrads who receive any aid: 83/89. % freshmen/undergrads who receive need-based scholarship or grant aid: 55/52. % freshmen/undergrads who receive need-based self-help aid: 51/50. Financial aid filing deadline: 3/10. Financial aid notification on or about: 3/1.

TV/Film/Digital Media Studies Programs
Number of undergraduates in these programs: 100
Number of 2005 graduates from these programs: 25
Degrees conferred to these majors: BA, BS.
Number of full-time faculty in these programs: 5
Number of part-time faculty in these programs: 2

Equipment and facilities: FM radio station; JVC HD100u (5) for field use; Ikegami HC 400W (4) studio cameras; Sony DSRPD170 DVCam Cameras (3); Lowel; Desisti field light kits (8); TV studio 30' x 40', Macintosh G5s (dual 1.7 processor) (4) equipped with Final Cut Pro, Soundtrack, Motion, Livetype, DVD Studio Pro, Adobe's Creative Suite; (2) PC Digital Audio Workstations with Adobe Auditorium; (24) Macintosh lab; (4) HHB Minidisc recorders; (15) enlarger stations; film prep room; photo studio with professional lighting, copy stands, and background.

ATAS Faculty Seminar participants: 1
Other awards of note: Heartland Film Festival Winner, 2005.
Career development services: Alumni networking opportunities; career counseling; central resource(s) for employers to browse headshots, writing samples, reels, etc.; internship listings; job fairs; job listings; electronic portfolios.

In Their Own Words
Taylor has recently made substantial investments in high-definition equipment. The school hosts the annual Trojan Film Fest. Art building opened in 2003. Film students spend a semester in LA.

POPULAR PROGRAMS

COMMUNICATION ARTS, NEW MEDIA, MEDIA PRODUCTION
Department chair: Dr. Jessica Rousselow-Winquist
Number of full-time faculty: 5
Number of part-time faculty: 2
Focus/emphasis: A broad overview of production methods with many upper division hands-on courses and a core of courses in communication theory and practice.

VISUAL ARTS, NEW MEDIA, GRAPHIC DESIGN
Department chair: Dr. Rachel Smith
Number of full-time faculty: 5

COMMUNICATION ARTS, NEW MEDIA, FILM STUDIES

Department chair: Dr. Jessica Rousselow-Winquist

Number of full-time faculty: 5

Number of part-time faculty: 2

Focus/emphasis: Media production with an emphasis on narrative and documentary film production. Students spend a semester in Los Angeles.

VISUAL ARTS, NEW MEDIA, INTERACTIVE AND MOTION IMAGERY

Department chair: Dr. Rachel Smith

Number of full-time faculty: 5

COMMUNICATION ARTS, NEW MEDIA, MEDIA WRITING

Department chair: Dr. Jessica Rousselow-Winquist

Number of full-time faculty: 5

Number of part-time faculty: 2

Focus/emphasis: Curriculum is tailored to student interests in print/Web newswriting or magazine/PR feature writing. Also includes broadcast and interactive writing.

VISUAL ARTS, NEW MEDIA, PHOTOGRAPHY

Department chair: Dr. Rachel Smith

Number of full-time faculty: 5

Focus/emphasis: Explores darkroom and digital art forms.

COMMUNICATION, NEW MEDIA, PUBLIC RELATIONS

Department chair: Dr. Jessica Rousselow-Winquist

Number of full-time faculty: 5

Number of part-time faculty: 2

Focus/emphasis: Broad exposure to Web, writing, layout, photography, and communication theory with upper division courses specific to public relations.

VISUAL ARTS, NEW MEDIA/SYSTEMS

Number of full-time faculty: 12

Focus/emphasis: Takes advantage of Taylor's nationally known computer science department.

COMMUNICATION ARTS, NEW MEDIA/SYSTEMS

Number of full-time faculty: 12

Number of part-time faculty: 2

Focus/emphasis: Takes advantage of Taylor's nationally known computer science department.

Students Should Also Know

Students shoot in high definition even in introductory courses.

TCU
(TEXAS CHRISTIAN UNIVERSITY)

Office of Admissions, TCU Box 297013, Fort Worth, TX 76129

Phone: 817-257-7490 **E-mail:** frogmail@tcu.edu

Website: www.tcu.edu

Campus Life

Environment: Metropolis. **Calendar:** Semester.

Students and Faculty
(All Undergraduate Programs)

Enrollment: 7,056. **Student Body:** 61% female, 39% male, 20% out-of-state, 4% international (75 countries represented). African American 5%, Asian 2%, Caucasian 78%, Hispanic 6%. Student/faculty ratio: 14:1. 465 full-time faculty, 90% hold PhDs. 97% faculty teach undergrads.

Admissions
(All Undergraduate Programs)

Freshman Admissions Requirements: Test(s) required: SAT or ACT. 28% in top tenth, 61% in top quarter. SAT Math (25/75 percentile): 540/640. SAT Verbal (25/75 percentile): 520/630. Projected SAT Writing (25/75 percentile): 580/670. *Academic units required:* 4 English, 3 math, 3 science, 2 foreign language, 3 social studies, 2 academic electives. Regular application deadline: 2/15. Regular notification: 4/1.

Costs and Financial Aid
(All Undergraduate Programs)

Annual tuition $22,980. Room & board $7,520. Average book expense $810.

Financial Aid Statistics: % freshmen/undergrads who receive any aid: 78/71. % freshmen/undergrads

who receive need-based scholarship or grant aid: 34/37. % freshmen/undergrads who receive need-based self-help aid: 30/34. Priority financial aid filing deadline: 5/1. Financial aid filing deadline: 5/1. Financial aid notification on or about: 3/1.

TV/Film/Digital Media Studies Programs

Number of undergraduates in these programs: 325

Number of 2005 graduates from these programs: 86

Degrees conferred to these majors: BA, BS.

Number of full-time faculty in these programs: 8

Number of part-time faculty in these programs: 2

Equipment and facilities: 12 Avid DV Systems, three Avid Media Composer 9000, two Avid Express media composers, two full digital TV studios/soundstages, Foley room, dolly with jib arm, 30" Cam Mate jib arm, three Beta/SP field cameras, DV camera for studio and field use. Full compliment of lighting and grip equipment, including HMI's, full compliment of field audio equipment, 40" five camera sports production truck, video and DVD library with 14,000 titles.

ATAS interns: 1

Other awards of note: Faculty have won two Daytime Emmy Awards, 10 Telly Awards, four Communicator Awards, ADDYs, and multiple Videographer Awards.

Career development services: Faculty contacts within the business.

In Their Own Words

We send interns to Hollywood and New York on a regular basis to shows and places such as Curb Your Enthusiasm, Will & Grace, Emeril Live, Days of Our Lives, As the World Turns, The Tonight Show with Jay Leno, The Late Show with David Letterman, Another World, Guiding Light, The Young and the Restless, ESPN, ABC Sports—Monday Night Football, Super Bowl, Indy 500, Rhino Films, The Jerry Springer Show, J. Todd Harris Productions, Orly Adelson Productions, Abandon Pictures, Sony/Columbia Tri-Star, The Chase, Anywhere But Here, Paulie, Dancer Texas, The Alamo, A Little Inside, Lifetime/HBO, PBS Cliburn Documentary (Peabody Award Winner), Olga, Peter Rosen Productions, Passions, General Hospital, Dreamworks, Half & Half, NBC Network News, MSNBC, WFAA, KXAS, KTVT, KTCK-AM, KRLD-AM, WBAP-AM, Barney and Friends, Big Bad Wolf Productions, Mad River Post, Fox Business Affairs, Fox Sports Network, Dallas Mavericks Productions, Dallas Cowboys Radio Network, AAC Productions, Dallas Morning News, NBC Page Program, Atomic Casting, The MTV Awards, The Dodgers (Footloose, Music Man, Into the Woods), and The Bachelor. Our last two student soap operas were purchased by Burly Bear Entertainment, which was owned by Lorne Michaels at the time.

TEMPLE UNIVERSITY

1801 North Broad Street, Philadelphia, PA 19122-6096
Phone: 215-204-7200 **E-mail:** tuadm@temple.edu
Website: www.temple.edu

Campus Life
Environment: Metropolis. **Calendar:** Semester.

Students and Faculty
(All Undergraduate Programs)
Enrollment: 24,194. **Student Body:** 57% female, 43% male, 25% out-of-state, 3% international (123 countries represented). African American 19%, Asian 9%, Caucasian 57%, Hispanic 3%, Other 8%. Student/faculty ratio: 17:1. 1,225 full-time faculty, 77% hold PhDs.

Admissions
(All Undergraduate Programs)
Freshman Admissions Requirements: Test(s) required: SAT or ACT with Writing component. Average high school GPA: 3.29. 19% in top tenth, 51% in top quarter. SAT Math (25/75 percentile): 500/600. SAT Verbal (25/75 percentile): 500/600. Projected SAT Writing (25/75 percentile): 560/650.

ACT composite (25/75 percentile): 20/24. *Academic units required:* 4 English, 3 math, 2 science (1 science lab), 2 foreign language, 2 social studies, 1 history, 1 academic elective. Regular application deadline: 4/1. Regular notification: Rolling.

Costs and Financial Aid (All Undergraduate Programs)

Annual in-state tuition $9,140. Out-of-state tuition $16,736. Room & board $7,798. Required fees $500. Average book expense $800.

Financial Aid Statistics: % freshmen/undergrads who receive any aid: 72/71. % freshmen/undergrads who receive need-based scholarship or grant aid: 72/71. % freshmen/undergrads who receive need-based self-help aid: 61/62. Priority financial aid filing deadline: 3/1. Financial aid notification on or about: 2/15.

TV/Film/Digital Media Studies Programs

Number of undergraduates in these programs: 1,452

Degrees conferred to these majors: BA.

Also available at Temple University: MA and PhD in mass media and communications; MFA in film and media arts.

Number of full-time faculty in these programs: 25

Equipment and facilities: Three television/film studios; Avid High Definition and Final Cut Pro HD nonlinear film/video-editing systems; hypermedia laboratories for computer controlled and computer generated media; high-definition camcorders; and 24-hour access to graduate editing suites in HD, DV, DVCam, Betacam-SP, and digital nonlinear with extensive effects and computer graphics capabilities. Philadelphia-area production houses provide professional high-definition, Betacam-SP, DVCam and D2 transfer facilities and digital intermediates. Film facilities include a 16 mm processing laboratory; a 16/35 synchronous multitrack recording studio; multitrack digital sound; animation stands; optical printer; Aaton A-Minima Super 16 mm, Aaton XTR Super 16 mm, Arriflex SRII, Eclair, and CP-16 cameras; 24P and HDTV cameras, and state-of-the-art audio and grip equipment including Steadicams.

The School of Communications and Theater is housed in buildings designed for teaching, research, and production. The Theater Department, located in Tomlinson Hall, features two theaters and rehearsal rooms, and costume and scene shops. The Department of Strategic and Organizational Communication is housed in Weiss Hall. The primary location of the school is Annenberg Hall, which houses the departments of film and media arts; broadcasting, telecommunications, and mass media; journalism; and advertising.

Television and film production areas (studios and editing, graphics, and film labs) occupy the first floor. Located on the lower level are extensive video- and film-editing areas, a 75-seat multimedia screening room, photographic labs, and a modern graphics laboratory with Macintosh computers and laser printers. The third floor includes computerized news writing and editing rooms, and classrooms. The Joe First Media Center, SCT's newest addition, is located on the first floor, linking Annenberg and Tomlinson Halls. The center is a communications and media hub for the school and includes a cyber-café, a multimedia information center, and a venue for displaying student work and film screenings. The Student Center provides 35 mm screening facilities. The Tech Center provides nearly 600 computer workstations, including labs dedicated to graphics, sound, and high-definition film/video editing, available to students 24 hours a day.

Notable alumni: David Jacobson, writer/director, *Down in the Valley*, Dahmer; Lawrence McConkey, steadicam operator, *Kill Bill*, *Vanilla Sky*, *3 Kings*, *Goodfellas*; Keith Fulton and Louis Pepe, *Lost in La Mancha*, *Brothers of the Head*; Ross Katz, producer, *Lost in Translation*, *In the Bedroom*, *Marie Antoinette*; Lise Yasui, documentary filmmaker, *Family Gathering*, *The American Experience*, *The Gate of Heavenly Peace*; Derek Guiley, writer, *Chasing Liberty*; Chris Manley, director of photography, *Prison Break* TV series; Long Cheng, editor, *House of Flying Daggers*.

In Their Own Words

The FMA Internship Program provides students with a bridge across the precarious gap between studying media arts as a student and working in media arts fields as a professional, by providing hands-on opportunities in the craft, creative voice, and entertainment businesses. In addition to local internships, Temple's Film and Media Arts Department offers FMA juniors and seniors an internship program each summer in Los Angeles. This experience provides the opportunity to explore career ideas, make contacts, and develop job hunting strategies to get ahead in today's competitive job market. The School of Communications and Theater offers a program in London, focusing on British theater and media with an international faculty. The Temple University Japan (TUJ) study abroad program offers undergraduates the opportunity to study in Tokyo for a semester, summer, or full academic year alongside bilingual Japanese and other international students. Film and other communications courses are offered at TUJ on a regular basis.

The Diamond Screen Film Festival is an annual event that showcases the most creative and outstanding student work at Temple, in documentary, narrative, experimental, and animation. The NextFrame film festival features animation, experimental, documentary, and narrative work. The festival offers low entry fees and few restrictions. Unlike a traditional festival, the NextFrame award-winning films embark on a year-long international tour. The chosen films screen in dozens of cities throughout the United States and around the globe. The new media interdisciplinary concentration (NMIC) is an optional specialization for undergraduate students in the School of Communications and Theater.

POPULAR PROGRAMS

BROADCASTING, TELECOMMUNICATIONS, AND MASS MEDIA (BTMM)

Department chair: Matt Lombard

Focus/emphasis: Through a mix of classroom instruction and hands-on experience, the BTMM degree candidate will be uniquely prepared with the skills and understanding needed to have a successful career in today's rapidly growing communications fields. The Department of BTMM provides an exciting undergraduate curriculum in the study of media. The department emphasizes several interrelated areas of course work including production, performance, recording industry, new medial, and organizational management and media studies. Both theory and practice are balanced and integrated into all areas of study in broadcasting, telecommunications, and mass media so as to allow students to become well-rounded communications professionals as well as knowledgeable media consumers.

FILM AND MEDIA ARTS

Department chair: Paul Swann

Focus/emphasis: The Department of Film and Media Arts offers a Bachelor of Arts program in media production and theory. The undergraduate program focuses on the development of creative and technical skills in film, video, audio, new media, and the theoretical understanding of media and culture. The program recognizes and explores the creative tension between individual expression and the social, political, and economic forces that shape the culture at large. Students are trained in developing content as well as craft, and theory as well as practice. In learning independent and commercial approaches to production and theory, graduates are prepared to develop their own independent productions and/or to assume a creative role in the motion picture and television industries.

TEXAS A&M UNIVERSITY–COMMERCE

PO Box 3011, Commerce, TX 75429
Phone: 903-886-5106 **E-mail:** admissions@tamu-commerce.edu
Website: www.tamu-commerce.edu

Campus Life
Environment: Rural. **Calendar:** Semester.

Students and Faculty
(All Undergraduate Programs)
Enrollment: 4,815. **Student Body:** 4% out-of-state, 1% international. African American 17%, Asian 1%, Caucasian 74%, Hispanic 5%, Native American 1%. Student/faculty ratio: 17:1. 283 full-time faculty. 17% faculty teach undergrads.

Admissions
(All Undergraduate Programs)
Freshman Admissions Requirements: Test(s) required: SAT or ACT. Average high school GPA: 3.35. 13% in top tenth, 26% in top quarter. SAT Math (25/75 percentile): 410/560. SAT Verbal (25/75 percentile): 410/540. Projected SAT Writing (25/75 percentile): 480/600. *Academic units required:* 4 English, 3 math, 2 science, 2 history and social studies. Regular application deadline: 8/1. Regular notification: Rolling.

Costs and Financial Aid
(All Undergraduate Programs)
Annual in-state tuition $3,224. Out-of-state tuition $9,764. Room & board $4,786. Average book expense $900.
Financial Aid Statistics: % freshmen/undergrads who receive need-based scholarship or grant aid: 56/51. % freshmen/undergrads who receive need-based self-help aid: 33/43. Priority financial aid filing deadline: 5/1. Financial aid notification on or about: 6/1.

TV/Film/Digital Media Studies Programs
Number of undergraduates in these programs: 110
Number of 2005 graduates from these programs: 20

Degrees conferred to these majors: BFA.
Number of full-time faculty in these programs: 1
Number of part-time faculty in these programs: 16-25
Equipment and facilities: Three computer labs with Mac and Windows (50 total). Everything from Photoshop to Maya, including Flash, InDesign, and Dreamweaver.

% of graduates who pursue further study within 5 years: 2
% of graduates currently employed in related field: 80
Career development services: Career counseling, job fairs, job listings. The department has its own alumni network.
Famous alumni: Chris Hill, Dick Mitchell, Michael Schwab, Ray-Mel Cornelious.
Notable alumni: Byron Reaves, Kevin Flatt, Alison Burton.

In Their Own Words
The Communication Arts Program at TAMUC is the most award-winning program of its type in the Southwest. We have earned numerous regional and national awards with the Houston Show, The 1 Show, *and* CMYK *publications.*

POPULAR PROGRAMS

NEW MEDIA
Department chair: Stan Godwin
Number of part-time faculty: 16–25
Focus/emphasis: Conceptual 3-D animation.

Students Should Also Know
For more information, please visit the website at http://tamu-commerce.edu/art.

THOMAS EDISON STATE COLLEGE

101 West State Street, Trenton, NJ 08608-1176
Phone: 888-442-8372 **E-mail:** admissions@tesc.edu
Website: www.tesc.edu

Campus Life

Environment: City. **Calendar:** Continuous.

Students and Faculty
(All Undergraduate Programs)

Enrollment: 10,904. **Student Body:** 44% female, 56% male, 45% out-of-state, 2% international. African American 12%, Asian 2%, Caucasian 67%, Hispanic 6%, Native American 1%.

Admissions
(All Undergraduate Programs)

Regular notification: Rolling.

Costs and Financial Aid
(All Undergraduate Programs)

Annual in-state tuition $3,780. Out-of-state tuition $5,400.
Financial Aid Statistics: % undergrads who receive any aid: 14.

TV/Film/Digital Media Studies Programs

**Number of undergraduates
in these programs:** 161
**Number of 2005 graduates from these
programs:** 30
Also available at Thomas Edison State College: BA in Communications, BA in Photography.
Equipment and facilities: The college offers a variety of options for earning credit toward a degree. Students can take advantage of Guided Study and online courses, which use the Internet to facilitate interactive distance learning. Students may earn credit toward a degree by demonstrating college-level knowledge learned outside the classroom through Prior Learning Assessment (PLA). In addition, it is possible for students to receive credit for professional licenses, certificates, and courses that they have taken at work or through the military.
Famous alumni: Dick Sheeran, Steven E. de Souza, Keith Benson.

POPULAR PROGRAMS

COMMUNICATIONS

Focus/emphasis: Explores the various aspects of creating, transmitting, and analyzing messages that flow among individuals, groups, organizations, and societies. Within the major area of study, students may focus on communication courses relating to oral communications and/or mass media communications, including those related to film style and genre, motion picture production, television news, television production, video communication theory, voice and diction, and voice production.

PHOTOGRAPHY

Focus/emphasis: The photography major provides an opportunity to earn credit (primarily through Prior Learning Assessment) in the areas of film production, fine arts photography, and professional photography. Students may choose from various electives, such as Film Production and Film Analysis & Criticism.

TRINITY UNIVERSITY

One Trinity Place, San Antonio, TX 78212
Phone: 210-999-7207 **E-mail:** admissions@trinity.edu
Website: www.trinity.edu

Campus Life

Environment: Metropolis. **Calendar:** Semester.

Students and Faculty
(All Undergraduate Programs)

Enrollment: 2,406. **Student Body:** 52% female, 48% male, 35% out-of-state, 5% international (30 countries represented). African American 2%, Asian 6%, Caucasian 70%, Hispanic 11%. Student/faculty ratio: 10:1. 228 full-time faculty, 99% hold PhDs. 100% faculty teach undergrads.

Admissions
(All Undergraduate Programs)

Freshman Admissions Requirements: Test(s) required: SAT or ACT. Average high school GPA: 3.5.

51% in top tenth, 81% in top quarter. SAT Math (25/75 percentile): 620/690. SAT Verbal (25/75 percentile): 600/690. Projected SAT Writing (25/75 percentile): 650/720. *Academic units required:* 4 English, 3 math, 3 science (2 science labs), 2 foreign language, 3 social studies, 1 academic elective. Early decision application deadline: 11/1. Regular notification: 4/1.

Costs and Financial Aid
(All Undergraduate Programs)
Annual tuition $19,806. Room & board $7,805. Required fees $774. Average book expense $620. **Financial Aid Statistics:** % freshmen/undergrads who receive any aid: 85/74. % freshmen/undergrads who receive need-based scholarship or grant aid: 41/39. % freshmen/undergrads who receive need-based self-help aid: 31/33. Priority financial aid filing deadline: 2/1. Financial aid filing deadline: 4/1. Financial aid notification on or about: 4/1.

TV/Film/Digital Media Studies Programs
Degrees conferred to these majors: BA.
Number of full-time faculty in these programs: 8
Equipment and facilities: The Sid W. Richardson Communications Center houses faculty-directed media operations: KRTU, a 24-hour jazz and alternative music and news FM radio station operated by an all-student management team and staff; a newsroom serving journalism courses and the radio station; a master control center with a fully-equipped television studio serving television production courses and the TigerTV station, a student-staffed campus cable television operation; and a fiber optic remote television production unit staffed by a student production team that telecasts special events to San Antonio. The center is maintained and supervised by a full-time operations manager.
Notable alumni: Maritza Nuñez (1998) was the station manager of TigerTV her senior year and worked as a production intern at KMOL-TV, the NBC affiliate in San Antonio. She was hired immediately after graduation as a production assistant on various news and public affairs programs. She is now the producer at KMOL for the 10 P.M. newscast, the most heavily viewed time slot in local news

programming. Amy McGee (1992) is president and CEO of City Pulse Communications, a public relations, advertising, and marketing firm in Houston that has a special focus on using the Internet and e-mail. "Trinity helped launch my career in many ways," says McGee. "There were a lot of people who helped me get the right experience and to make the right connections. At the top of that list is my advisor in communication. Without her, I very likely would not own my own public relations agency today."

In Their Own Words
Extensive opportunities for hands-on experience on campus—even during the first semester—in radio, television, newspapers, the yearbook, and digital editing. Professional staff and facilities, including an 8,900-watt broadcast radio station, a closed-circuit cable television station, and state-of-the-art digital workstations. Interdisciplinary minors in communication management and new media, preparing students for a wide range of professions. Communication students can take advantage of numerous professional internships in San Antonio as well as opportunities for competitive national internships at magazines, broadcasting outlets, public relations agencies, advertising agencies, and government and corporate institutions. Students have had internships at National Geographic, Good Housekeeping, MTV, Fox News, *ABC's* Nightline, Fleishman-Hillard, Ketchum, Bromley Communications, *the Smithsonian Institution, U.S. Chamber of Commerce, San Antonio Spurs, and USAA insurance company. As a result of their classwork and internships, communication students are getting their work published or aired in local, regional, and national venues. They also are winning national research, writing, and production competitions.*

POPULAR PROGRAMS

COMMUNICATIONS

Department chair: William Christ

Focus/emphasis: The curriculum allows for considerable flexibility, reflecting the communications revolution that is rapidly creating new challenges and opportunities. The curriculum is divided into three interrelated areas common to media and media-related systems: Media studies: history and theories of social and mass communication; public policy related to communication systems; structure, organization, technology, ethics, criticism, and social and aesthetic functions of communication institutions and media. Media messages: writing and production skills as well as other procedures related to audio, print, video, and interactive multimedia message making. Media management: planning, research, management, and legal regulation in contemporary communication media and media-related organizations. These fundamental areas, combined with a strong interdisciplinary liberal arts and sciences background, should enhance lifelong learning and the ability to adapt to change while preparing students for an entry-level specialty in areas such as broadcast, print, or electronic journalism, public relations, advertising, and production of audio/radio, television/video, and multimedia/Internet messages.

UNIVERSITY OF AKRON

277 E. Buchtel Avenue, Akron, OH 44325-2001
Phone: 330-972-7077 **E-mail:** admissions@uakron.edu
Website: www.uakron.edu

Campus Life
Environment: City. **Calendar:** Semester.

Students and Faculty
(All Undergraduate Programs)
Enrollment: 16,288. **Student Body:** 52% female, 48% male, 2% out-of-state. African American 15%, Asian 2%, Caucasian 78%. Student/faculty ratio: 18:1.

701 full-time faculty, 85% hold PhDs. 84% faculty teach undergrads.

Admissions
(All Undergraduate Programs)
Freshman Admissions Requirements: Test(s) required: SAT or ACT. Average high school GPA: 3.0. 12% in top tenth, 18% in top quarter. SAT Math (25/75 percentile): 440/590. SAT Verbal (25/75 percentile): 440/570. Projected SAT Writing (25/75 percentile): 510/620. Regular application deadline: 8/1. Regular notification: Rolling within two weeks of application receipt.

Costs and Financial Aid
(All Undergraduate Programs)
Annual in-state tuition $6,810. Out-of-state tuition $15,534. Room & board $7,208. Required fees $1,148. Average book expense $900.

Financial Aid Statistics: % freshmen/undergrads who receive any aid: 80/85. % freshmen/undergrads who receive need-based scholarship or grant aid: 33/34. % freshmen/undergrads who receive need-based self-help aid: 56/55. Priority financial aid filing deadline: 2/1. Financial aid notification on or about: 4/15.

TV/Film/Digital Media Studies Programs
Number of undergraduates in these programs: 185

Number of 2005 graduates from these programs: 50

Degrees conferred to these majors: BA.

Also available at University of Akron: MA.

Number of full-time faculty in these programs: 6

Number of part-time faculty in these programs: 15

Equipment and facilities: TV studio, LanShare.

% of graduates who pursue further study within 5 years: 10

% of graduates currently employed in related field: 50

Career development services: Career counseling, internship listings, job fairs, job listings.

Notable alumni: Curt King, vice president, promotions and production, NBC.

In Their Own Words

Approximately 20 interns each semester; interns at NBC in LA and MTV News in NY; student productions won Telly awards and regional Emmys; work has been broadcast in Akron area (17th largest market) and on PBS 45/49.

POPULAR PROGRAMS

RADIO/TV

Department chair: Dudley Turner
Number of full-time faculty: 4
Number of part-time faculty: 5
Focus/emphasis: Progamming, operations, and production.

MEDIA PRODUCTION

Department chair: Dudley Turner
Number of full-time faculty: 1
Number of part-time faculty: 2
Focus/emphasis: Single-camera production.

NEWS

Department chair: Dudley Turner
Number of full-time faculty: 2
Number of part-time faculty: 6
Focus/emphasis: Print, broadcast, and new media news.

UNIVERSITY OF BRITISH COLUMBIA

Room 2016, 1874 East Mall, Vancouver, BC V6T 1Z1 Canada
Phone: 604-822-3014 **E-mail:** international.reception@ubc.ca
Website: www.welcome.ubc.ca

Campus Life

Environment: Metropolis. **Calendar:** Semester.

Students and Faculty
(All Undergraduate Programs)

Enrollment: 29,911. **Student Body:** 56% female, 44% male. Student/faculty ratio: 15:1.

Admissions
(All Undergraduate Programs)

Freshman Admissions Requirements: Test(s) required: SAT (from Summer Session 2007). Average high school GPA: varies by program (most generally require the equivalent of a B+ or A-). Academic units required: graduation from an academic or college-prep program, 4 English (not ESL), 3 math (to the junior level), 4+ senior-level academic subjects. Regular application deadline: 2/28. Regular notification: Rolling.

Costs and Financial Aid
(All Undergraduate Programs)

In-province tuition CA\$4,174–\$5,009. Out-of-province tuition CA\$4,174–\$5,009. International tuition CA\$17,577–\$21,093. Room & board CA\$6,650. Required fees \$600. Average book expense CA\$1,100.

TV/Film/Digital Media Studies Programs

Number of 2005 graduates from these programs: 33
Degrees conferred to these majors: BA, BFA.
Also available at University of British Columbia: Diploma, MFA, MA.
Number of full-time faculty in these programs: 12
Career development services: Alumni networking opportunities, career counseling, internship listings, job fairs, job listings.

In Their Own Words

Film Program adjunct professor John Zaritsky, Oscar and Gemini Award winner.

Students Should Also Know

UBC offers high-quality programs in film studies and film production at both undergraduate and graduate levels. The Department of Theatre, Film, and Creative Writing offers a four-year undergraduate film studies major leading to a bachelor of arts degree and a four-year program leading to a bachelor of fine arts in film production. Two-year graduate programs lead to master of arts and master of fine arts degrees. The number of available places is strictly limited: Application and submission of supporting materials is required. Preference will be given to students with strong evidence of creative ability. The time commitment required in film production is not the typical workload-to-credit relationship one finds with other university courses. There is a great deal of time outside of class, which involves cooperating with other film students as a productive and reliable member of a team. The program is based on learning by experience, so students are expected to develop their skills and confidence by working on their own and on other students' film projects. The Department of Art History, Visual Art, and Theory offers four-year programs leading to bachelor of arts and bachelor of fine arts degrees in which students may specialize in digital art, multimedia, and critical study of cyber-culture.

UNIVERSITY OF CALIFORNIA– BERKELEY

Office of Undergraduate Admissions, 110 Sproul Hall #5800, Berkeley, CA 94720-5800
Phone: 510-642-3175 **E-mail:** ouars@uclink.berkeley.edu
Website: www.berkeley.edu

Campus Life
Environment: Metropolis. **Calendar:** Semester.

Students and Faculty
(All Undergraduate Programs)
Enrollment: 23,447. **Student Body:** 10% out-of-state, 3% international. African American 4%, Asian 41%, Caucasian 31%, Hispanic 11%. Student/faculty ratio: 15:1. 1,496 full-time faculty, 99% hold PhDs. 100% faculty teach undergrads.

Admissions
(All Undergraduate Programs)
Freshman Admissions Requirements: Test(s) required: SAT or ACT; SAT Subject Tests; ACT with Writing component. Average high school GPA: 3.9. 98% in top tenth, 100% in top quarter. SAT Math (25/75 percentile): 630/740. SAT Verbal (25/75 percentile): 590/710. Projected SAT Writing (25/75 percentile): 640/730. *Academic units required:* 4 English,

3 math, 2 science (2 science labs), 2 foreign language, 2 social studies, 2 history, 1 academic elective, 1 visual or performing arts. Regular application deadline: 11/30. Regular notification: Posted on website by 3/31.

Costs and Financial Aid
(All Undergraduate Programs)
Out-of-state tuition $18,710. Required fees $6,512. **Financial Aid Statistics:** % freshmen/undergrads who receive need-based scholarship or grant aid: 50/49. % freshmen/undergrads who receive need-based self-help aid: 39/38. Priority financial aid filing deadline: 3/2. Financial aid filing deadline: 3/2. Financial aid notification on or about: 4/15.

TV/Film/Digital Media Studies Programs
Degrees conferred to these majors: BA.
Also available at University of California— Berkeley: MFA, MA.
Number of full-time faculty in these programs: 20
Number of part-time faculty in these programs: 11

In Their Own Words
The Film Studies Program is especially fortunate to be affiliated with the Pacific Film Archive, an internationally-known cinematheque that screens films six nights a week and often brings filmmakers to campus. Although film production is not a focus of this program, some hands-on production is possible. Students may also take advantage of internship opportunities at the Pacific Film Archive, with the journal Film Quarterly, *and with local film and video production companies. Many students go on to graduate school in film or the humanities, others enter law school or business administration, and others find work in media. All acquire a high level of visual literacy and analytical and writing skills. The Berkeley Film Seminar of UC Berkeley provides a forum for faculty and graduate students in the Bay Area to present new research on, and to debate theoretical, historical, and methodological questions related to the study of*

the moving image. The Media Resources Center (MRC) is the UC Berkeley Library's primary collection of materials in electronic nonprint (audio and visual) formats. These formats include videocassettes, DVDs, and laser discs; compact audio discs; audiocassettes; slides; and interactive multimedia materials. The MRC collection is intended to support the broad range of study and research interests on campus. There are particularly strong holdings in humanities and social sciences materials, as well as a broad range of general interest materials in the fields of science and technology.

POPULAR PROGRAMS

MASS COMMUNICATIONS

Department chair: Thomas Goldstein

Focus/emphasis: Faculty comes from a variety of disciplines, bringing the perspectives and methods of their fields to bear on the analysis of the mass media. Our emphasis in this major is analytical and historical; we are largely concerned with developing in students the ability to assess the roles and impact of the major mass media on American life, rather than with developing specific media production skills. In our four core courses, students learn the history, values, and structure of mass communication in the United States and abroad. Students learn to analyze the effects of electronic and print media, to consider the impact of the media on public policy, as well as the impact of public policy on the media. In addition to our core courses, students must take an approved methods course in the social sciences and a number of approved major electives offered in other disciplines on campus—anthropology, sociology, political science, linguistics, and journalism, to name a few. The major itself also offers several elective courses and an honors thesis course (MC H195).

FILM STUDIES

Department chair: Michael Mascuch

Focus/emphasis: This rich and diverse program engages with all forms of moving-image culture, exploring the most popular media forms of the last century (film and still photography) and the most exciting new media form of the new century (digital media). It teaches students to think historically, theoretically, and analytically about a wide range of images within the broad context of humanistic studies. Production opportunities in digital media are available to students who have demonstrated excellence in theory, history, and analysis.

UNIVERSITY OF CALIFORNIA– IRVINE

Office of Admissions & Relations with Schools, 204 Administration Building, Irvine, CA 92697-1075
Phone: 949-824-6703 **E-mail:** admissions@uci.edu
Website: www.uci.edu

Campus Life
Environment: City. **Calendar:** Quarter.

Students and Faculty
(All Undergraduate Programs)
Enrollment: 19,930. **Student Body:** 51% female, 49% male, 3% out-of-state, 2% international (102 countries represented). African American 2%, Asian 49%, Caucasian 26%, Hispanic 12%. Student/faculty ratio 19:1. 992 full-time faculty, 98% hold PhDs. 100% faculty teach undergrads.

Admissions
(All Undergraduate Programs)
Freshman Admissions Requirements: Test(s) required: SAT and SAT Subject Tests or ACT; ACT with Writing component. Average high school GPA: 3.72. 96% in top tenth, 100% in top quarter. SAT Math (25/75 percentile): 570/680. SAT Verbal (25/75 percentile): 540/630. Projected SAT Writing (25/75 percentile): 600/670. *Academic units required:* 4 English, 3 math, 2 science (2 science lab), 2 foreign

language, 2 history, 1 academic elective, 1 visual or performing arts. Regular notification: 3/31.

Costs and Financial Aid (All Undergraduate Programs)

Annual in-state tuition $6,633. Out-of-state tuition $25,359. Room & board $9,875. Required fees $629. Average book expense $1,593.

Financial Aid Statistics: % freshmen/undergrads who receive need-based scholarship or grant aid: 40/42. % freshmen/undergrads who receive need-based self-help aid: 36/37. Financial aid filing deadline: 3/2. Financial aid notification on or about: 4/1.

TV/Film/Digital Media Studies Programs

Degrees conferred to these majors: BA.
Number of full-time faculty in these programs: 22
Career development services: The UCI Career Center provides services to students and alumni including career counseling; job listings, a career library, and workshops on resume preparation, job search, and interview techniques.

In Their Own Words

Film and media studies students can complete professional internships in the fields of film or television production, distribution, writing, and related areas for elective course credit. They also have the opportunity to spend their junior year in France studying at the Inter-University Center for Film and Critical Studies in Paris, through the university's Education Abroad Program. Information is available both in the Film and Media Studies Office and the Education Abroad Program Office.

POPULAR PROGRAMS

FILM AND MEDIA STUDIES

Focus/emphasis: This program trains students to read and understand the audiovisual languages of modern media and new technologies and to analyze images from socioeconomic, political, aesthetic, and historical perspectives. The Department of Film and Media Studies familiarizes students with the history, theory, and art of cinema and other media. The program provides its majors with a thorough appreciation of the modern media's roles in contemporary society. Film and Media Studies, in cooperation with other units at UCI, regularly invites scholars, directors, producers, and screenwriters to campus to share their work and perspectives with students.

UNIVERSITY OF CALIFORNIA– LOS ANGELES

405 Hilgard Avenue, Box 951436, Los Angeles, CA 90095-1436
Phone: 310-825-3101 **E-mail:** ugadm@saonet.ucla.edu
Website: www.ucla.edu

Campus Life

Environment: Metropolis. **Calendar:** Quarter.

Students and Faculty (All Undergraduate Programs)

Enrollment: 24,811. **Student Body:** 56% female, 44% male, 5% out-of-state, 4% international (132 countries represented). African American 3%, Asian 38%, Caucasian 34%, Hispanic 15%. Student/faculty ratio: 18:1. 1,859 full-time faculty, 98% hold PhDs. 100% faculty teach undergrads.

Admissions (All Undergraduate Programs)

Freshman Admissions Requirements: Test(s) required: SAT or ACT; SAT Subject Tests; ACT with Writing component. Average high school GPA: 4.13. 97% in top tenth, 100% in top quarter. SAT Math (25/75 percentile): 600/720. SAT Verbal (25/75 percentile): 570/690. Projected SAT Writing (25/75 percentile): 620/720. *Academic units required:* 4 English, 3 math, 2 science (2 science labs), 2 foreign language, 2 history, 1 academic elective, 1 visual or performing arts. Regular application deadline: 11/30. Regular notification: Rolling.

Costs and Financial Aid
(All Undergraduate Programs)

Annual in-state fees $6,141. Out-of-state tuition $23,961. Room & board $11,928. Required fees $363. Average book expense $1,485.

Financial Aid Statistics: % freshmen/undergrads who receive need-based scholarship or grant aid: 48/51. % freshmen/undergrads who receive need-based self-help aid: 34/41. Financial aid notification on or about: 3/15.

TV/Film/Digital Media Studies Programs

Number of undergraduates in these programs: 66 (undergraduate)/265 (graduate).

Number of 2005 graduates from these programs: 26 (undergraduate)/78 (graduate).

Degrees conferred to these majors: BA.

Also available at University of California—Los Angeles: MFA, MA, PhD.

Number of full-time faculty in these programs: 25

Number of part-time faculty in these programs: 73

Equipment and facilities: Three fully-equipped professional studio-level shooting soundstages; two fully equipped 4-camera digital TV shooting stages with control booths, lighting grids, and storage; makeup room, camera prep room, prop room with props, production office, production flats, and storage; full orchestra-sized scoring and recording stage; one theater-sized Pro Tools rerecording stage; ADR/mix room; two multiformatted video and audio transfer and dubbing rooms. Twenty-one animation desks with rotating disks; 28 computer workstations (Mac & PC); Maya, AfterEffects, Final Cut Pro, Photoshop, Animo, and others; two 16 mm animation cranes for shooting traditional animation to film; two 16 mm animation cameras for use in the production of stop motion animation; three video lunchboxes with camera stands for the shooting of pencil tests. The postproduction Department supports the use of 43 editing rooms and suites, some rooms with multiple systems; eight 16/35 mm flatbed editing machines; 48 Apple computers with Final Cut Pro; two Apple computers with Avid Adrenaline Media composer; 16 Apple computers with Pro Tools software and Digidesign hardware for editing audio, creation, and mixing. James Bridges Theater, with 278 seats, handicapped access areas, and box office facility. 16 mm picture, 16 mm sound composite-optical, magnetic; 35/70 mm picture, 35 mm (safety or nitrate), 1.18, 1.33 silent, 1.33 TV, 1.37, 1.66, 1.75, 1.85, 2.39 (anamorphic), 2.60 (anamorphic), 16–30 frames per second, 70 mm: .85, 2.20, 2.39, 24, or 30 frames per second. 70 mm: composite magnetic 6-track (discrete, Dolby "A" or "SR") DTS 6 or 8 channel. Panasonic PT-D7600U DLP based, 6000 Lumens, HD (DVI in) 1/2" VHS Hi-Fi (NTSC, PAL-M, PAL-N, and SECAM), 3/4" Beta Cam SP DVD, NTSC or PAL, Stereo, mini-DV and Laserdisc. Cameras: Panavision 35 mm, Arriflex 16 mm and Super 16 mm; various Sony and Panasonic digital cameras in a variety of formats. Fostex and Nagra. Variety of lighting instruments ranging from 200 watts up to 2,000 watts for location work. The two production soundstages and a third instructional stage are equipped with a full complement of Mole Richardson Fresnel lighting instruments of 2,000, 5,000, and 10,000 watts for use during production on the stages.

ATAS College TV Awards recipients: 3

ATAS Faculty Seminar participants: 4

Career development services: Alumni networking opportunities, career counseling, internship listings, job listings.

Famous alumni: Directors: Allison Anders (*Gas Food Lodging, Mi Vida Loca*), Mike B. Anderson (*The Simpsons*), Daniel Attias (*The Sopranos, Six Feet Under*), Carlos Avila (*Price of Glory, Foto-Novelas*), Paul Bartel (*Eating Raoul, Scenes from the Class Struggle in Beverly Hills*), Harve Bennett (*Star Trek II, IV, V; Mod Squad*), Bruce Bilson (*Get Smart, The Odd Couple*), Charles Burnett (*To Sleep with Anger, The Annihilation of Fish*), Patricia Cardoso (*Real Women Have Curves, The Water Carrier of Cucunuba*), Francis Ford Coppola (*Godfather Trilogy, Apocalypse Now*), Alex Cox (*Repoman, Sid and Nancy*), Julie Dash (*Daughters* of the Dust, The Rosa Parks Story), Laura Gabbert (Sunset Story), Catherine Hardwicke (Thirteen, Lords of Dogtown), Charles Herman-Wurmfeld (Legally Blonde 2: Red, White & Blonde; Kissing Jessica Stein), Todd Holland (Malcolm in the Middle, The Larry Sanders Show), Louis J. Horvitz (multiple Academy Award and Emmy Award-winning shows), Neal Jiminez (The River's Edge, The Waterdance), David Koepp (Secret Window, Stir of Echoes), Bob Lally (The Jeffersons, Silver Spoons), Justin Lin (Better Luck Tomorrow, Annapolis), Ramon Menendez (Stand and Deliver, Money for Nothing), Niels Mueller (The Assassination of Richard Nixon), Gregory Nava (American Family, Selena, Frida, Bordertown), Victor Nunez (Ulee's Gold, Ruby in Paradise), Alexander Payne (About Schmidt, Sideways), Gina Prince-Bythewood (Love and Basketball, The Bernie Mac Show), Rob Reiner (A Few Good Men, When Harry Met Sally), Tim Robbins (Dead Man Walking, Cradle Will Rock), Bobby Roth (Manhood, Jack the Dog), Ray Sandrich (Mary Tyler Moore Show, The Cosby Show), Paul Schrader (Auto Focus, Affliction), Tom Shadyac (Bruce Almighty; Liar, Liar), Chuck Sheetz (Recess: School's Out; What's New, Scooby-Doo?), Brad Silberling (City of Angels, Lemony Snicket's: A Series of Unfortunate Events), Penelope Spheeris (Wayne's World, The Little Rascals), Gore Verbinski (Pirates of the Caribbean, The Weatherman), Kurt Voss (Down and Out with the Dolls, Sugar Town). Producers: Thomas Bliss (The Hurricane, Air Force One), Constance Burge (Ed, Charmed), Moctesuma Esparza (Gods and Generals, The Milagro Beanfield War), William Frederick Fray (Independence Day, The Patriot), Felicia D. Henderson (Soul Food, The Fresh Prince of Bel-Air), Richard Lewis (Backdraft, Eulogy), Jeff Margolis (multiple Academy Awards, Primetime Emmy Awards), Frank Marshall (The Bourne Supremacy, Seabiscuit), Mike Medavoy (All the King's Men, Basic), Sarah Pillsbury (Desperately Seeking Susan, How to Make an American Quilt), John Rando (Urinetown, Dance of the Vampires), Gene Reynolds (M*A*S*H, Lou Grant), Fred Roos (Godfather Trilogy, Apocalypse Now), Richard Sakai (As Good as It Gets, Jerry Maguire), Jason

Schafer (Queer as Folk, Totally Sexy Loser), Steven Stabler (Albino Alligator, Dumb & Dumber), Darren Star (Kitchen Confidential, Sex and the City), David Valdes (Unforgiven, The Green Mile), Aron Warner (Shrek, Antz), Eden Wurmfeld (Kissing Jessica Stein, Sunset Story).

Notable alumni: Cinematographers: Stephen H. Burum, ASC (Mission to Mars, Mission Impossible, The Untouchables), Chris Chomyn (Lockdown, Phantasm III and IV, Sea of Dreams), Joan Churchill (Biggie and Tupac, Kurt & Courtney), Dean Cundey, ASC (Jurassic Park, Back to the Future I, II, III, Apollo 13), Elliot Davis (Thirteen, White Oleander, Lords of Dogtown), Tom Richmond (Monster, Stand and Deliver, The Singing Detective), Tom Denove (Ally McBeal, Hollywood Boulevard, Star Trek: The Next Generation). Editors: Craig D. Kitson (8 Mile, In Her Shoes), Nancy Richardson (Selena, Thirteen, Lords of Dogtown), Pietro Scalia (Memoirs of a Geisha, The Great Raid, Black Hawk Down, Gladiator), Jefffrey M. Wishengrad (The Singing Detective, Waking the Dead), Mark Yardas (Wonder Boys, Red Dragon). Art directors, visual effects, costume/production designers: Curtis Beech (Mission Impossible 3, Idiocracy), Doug Chiang (Star Wars I, II, III; Death Becomes Her), Scott Farrar (The Chronicles of Narnia: The Lion, the Witch and the Wardrobe; Minority Report; Star Wars: The Phantom Menace), Catherine Hardwicke (Laurel Canyon, Vanilla Sky), Deborah Nadoolman Landis (Blues Brothers, Trading Places), Hoyt Yeatman (Mighty Joe Young, Kangaroo Jack, The Abyss, Armageddon). Executives/agents: Warren Cowan, Geoffrey D. Gilmore (Sundance Film Festival), Claudia Lewis (Searchlight), Vanessa Morrison (20th Century Fox), Mike Ovitz, John Ptak (CAA), Thomas Schumacher (Walt Disney), Paul Schwartzman, Stacey Snider (Universal Pictures). Writers: Shane Black (Kiss, Kiss, Bang, Bang; Lethal Weapon I & II; Last Action Hero), Jeffrey Boam (Indiana Jones & the Last Crusade, Lethal Weapon 3), Patrick Cirillo (Tears of the Sun, Dangerous Heart), Lewis Colick (Ladder 49, October Sky), Sacha Gervasi (The Terminal, The Hypnotist), Dan Gordon (Wyatt Earp, The

Hurricane), Pamela Gray (*A Walk on the Moon, Music of the Heart*), Nicholas Griffin (*Matchstick Men*), Dean Hargrove (*Perry Mason, Columbo*), Collin Higgins (*Harold and Maude, 9 to 5*), Randall Jahnson (*The Doors, The Mask of Zorro*), Gloria Katz (*American Graffiti, Indiana Jones and the Temple of Doom*), David Koepp (*Spider-Man, Mission Impossible*), Scott Kosar (*The Amityville Horror, Machinist, Texas Chainsaw Massacre*), Josefina Lopez (*Real Woman Have Curves*), Michael Miner (*Robocop*), Niels Mueller (*Tadpol, The Assassination of Richard Nixon*), Ed Neumeier (*Starship Troopers, Robocop Trilogy*), Alexander Payne (*Sideways, About Schmidt, Election*), Gregory Poirier (*Rosewood, Tomcats*), Robert Roy Pool (*Outbreak, Armageddon*), F. J. Pratt (*Frasier, Less Than Perfect*), Richard Price (*The Color of Money, Mad Dog and Glory*), Daniel Pyne (*The Manchurian Candidate, Sum of All Fears*), Paris Qualles (*The Tuskegee Airmen,* The *Rosa Parks Story*), Billy Ray (*Flight Plan, Suspect Zero, Shattered Glass*), Marco Williams (*Two Towns of Jasper*), Scott Rosenberg (*Gone in 60 Seconds, High Fidelity*), Eric Roth (*The Insider, Forrest Gump*), Paul Schrader (*Raging Bull, Taxi Driver*), Ed Solomon (*Men in Black, The In-Laws*), Dana Stevens (*City of Angels, For the Love of the Game*), Kathy Stumpe (*Cheers, Everybody Loves Raymond*), Eric Wald (*View from the Top*), David S. Ward (*The Sting, Sleepless in Seattle*), Audrey Wells (*Shall We Dance?, Under the Tuscan Sun, The Truth About Cats & Dogs*), Mike Werb and Michael Colleary (*Face/Off, The Mask*), Marianne Wibberley (*National Treasure, Charlie's Angels: Full Throttle*), Gregory Widen (*The Highlander, Backdraft*).

POPULAR PROGRAMS

CONCENTRATIONS WITHIN FILM/TV BA:

Focus/emphasis: Two-year, upper-division program for students who have completed two years of general college studies. The program provides an education in the history and theory of these art forms and basic learning experiences in production within the context of a liberal arts education.

In the first year, students are introduced to all major aspects of film, television, and digital media study. In the second year, each student completes a senior concentration chosen from film production, television production (narrative or documentary), screenwriting, animation, digital media, or critical studies. Students must also complete at least one professional internship during their senior years.

FILM PRODUCTION

Department chair: Tom Denove
Number of full-time faculty: 4
Number of part-time faculty: 7
Focus/emphasis: A deep exploration into the theory and practice of film production.

SCREENWRITING

Department chair: Richard Walter
Number of full-time faculty: 2
Number of part-time faculty: 13
Focus/emphasis: Trains writers for professional success in mainstream, commercial Hollywood film and also independent production, as well as television sitcom, one-hour drama, and long form.

ANIMATION

Department chair: Dan McLaughlin
Number of full-time faculty: 2
Number of part-time faculty: 6
Focus/emphasis: Each student makes an animated film before graduation.

TELEVISION PRODUCTION

Department chair: Marina Goldovskaya
Number of full-time faculty: 4
Number of part-time faculty: 9
Focus/emphasis: A deep exploration of the theory and practice of television production (narrative and documentary).

DIGITAL MEDIA

Department chair: Fabian Wagmister
Number of full-time faculty: 3
Number of part-time faculty: 16
Focus/emphasis: Theoretical and practical

exploration of digital media. Basic concepts and software of virtual production environments and digital postproduction.

CRITICAL STUDIES

Department chair: Janet Bergstrom
Number of full-time faculty: 4
Number of part-time faculty: 12
Focus/emphasis: Critical study of moving image art forms and contemporary and classical film theory.

Students Should Also Know

Students are admitted during their junior years only.

UNIVERSITY OF CALIFORNIA– RIVERSIDE

1120 Hinderaker Hall, Riverside, CA 92521
Phone: 951-827-3411 **E-mail:** discover@ucr.edu
Website: www.ucr.edu

Campus Life

Environment: City. **Calendar:** Quarter.

Students and Faculty
(All Undergraduate Programs)

Enrollment: 14,555. **Student Body:** 53% female, 47% male, 2% international (68 countries represented). African American 7%, Asian 42%, Caucasian 19%, Hispanic 24%. Student/faculty ratio: 18:1. 709 full-time faculty, 98% hold PhDs. 100% faculty teach undergrads.

Admissions
(All Undergraduate Programs)

Freshman Admissions Requirements: Test(s) required: SAT or ACT; SAT Subject Tests; ACT with Writing component. Average high school GPA: 3.48. 94% in top tenth, 100% in top quarter. SAT Math (25/75 percentile): 490/630. SAT Verbal (25/75 percentile): 460/570. Projected SAT Writing (25/75 percentile): 530/620. *Academic units required:* 4 English, 3 math, 2 science (2 science labs), 2 foreign language, 2 history, 1 academic elective, 1 visual or performing arts. Regular application deadline: 11/30. Regular notification: Rolling.

Costs and Financial Aid
(All Undergraduate Programs)

Out-of-state tuition $17,820. Room & board $10,200. Required fees $7,250. Average book expense $1,650. **Financial Aid Statistics:** % freshmen/undergrads who receive any aid: 80/72. % freshmen/undergrads who receive need-based scholarship or grant aid: 55/53. % freshmen/undergrads who receive need-based self-help aid: 50/47. Priority financial aid filing deadline: 3/2. Financial aid filing deadline: 3/2. Financial aid notification on or about: 3/1.

TV/Film/Digital Media Studies Programs

Number of undergraduates in these programs: 140
Number of 2005 graduates from these programs: 24
Degrees conferred to these majors: BA.
Number of part-time faculty in these programs: 50
Equipment and facilities: TV studio and links to the UC-TV system, internships in Hollywood, and Final Cut Pro facilities.
Career development services: Alumni networking opportunities, career counseling, internship listings.

In Their Own Words

Our faculty have made screen texts that have been archived in major institutions and have written Hollywood films and TV. They have also written major books about the screen.

POPULAR PROGRAMS

FILM AND VISUAL CULTURE

Department chair: Toby Miller
Number of part-time faculty: 50
Focus/emphasis: Combines learning the theory, history, and analysis of media texts with production experience.

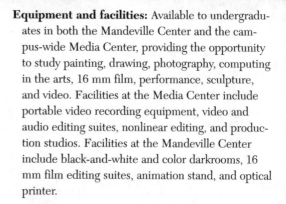

UNIVERSITY OF CALIFORNIA– SAN DIEGO

9500 Gilman Drive, 0021, La Jolla, CA 92093-0021
Phone: 858-534-4831 **E-mail:** admissionsinfo@ucsd.edu
Website: www.ucsd.edu

Campus Life
Environment: Metropolis. **Calendar:** Quarter.

Students and Faculty
(All Undergraduate Programs)
Enrollment: 20,339. **Student Body:** 52% female, 48% male, 2% out-of-state, 3% international (70 countries represented). African American 1%, Asian 38%, Caucasian 34%, Hispanic 10%. Student/faculty ratio: 19:1. 953 full-time faculty, 98% hold PhDs.

Admissions
(All Undergraduate Programs)
Freshman Admissions Requirements: Test(s) required: SAT or ACT. SAT Subjects Tests. Average high school GPA: 3.94. 99% in top tenth, 100% in top quarter. SAT Math (25/75 percentile): 600/710. SAT Verbal (25/75 percentile): 550/660. Projected SAT Writing (25/75 percentile): 600/690. *Academic units required:* 4 English, 3 math, 2 science labs, 2 foreign language, 2 history, 1 academic elective, 1 visual or performing arts. Regular application deadline: 11/30. Regular notification: Rolling.

Costs and Financial Aid
(All Undergraduate Programs)
Annual in-state fees $6,141. Out-of-state tuition $23,961. Room & board $9,421. Required fees $540. Average book expense $1,436.
Financial Aid Statistics: % freshmen/undergrads who receive any aid: 87/84. % freshmen/undergrads who receive need-based scholarship or grant aid: 51/46. % freshmen/undergrads who receive need-based self-help aid: 46/42. Priority financial aid filing deadline: 3/2. Financial aid filing deadline: 6/1. Financial aid notification on or about: 3/15.

TV/Film/Digital Media Studies Programs
Degrees conferred to these majors: BA.
Also available at University of California—San Diego: MA.

Equipment and facilities: Available to undergraduates in both the Mandeville Center and the campus-wide Media Center, providing the opportunity to study painting, drawing, photography, computing in the arts, 16 mm film, performance, sculpture, and video. Facilities at the Media Center include portable video recording equipment, video and audio editing suites, nonlinear editing, and production studios. Facilities at the Mandeville Center include black-and-white and color darkrooms, 16 mm film editing suites, animation stand, and optical printer.

In Their Own Words
The University of California's Institute for Research in the Arts (UCIRA) supports UC artists dedicated to innovative approaches to form and content in the performing, media, and visual arts. Our goal is to support imaginative projects that transcend boundaries or that fall outside the present confines of arts practice. We have a special interest in projects that are collaborative in nature and that benefit two or more UC campuses. A program of the UC Office of the President, UCIRA, is committed to diversity in all its forms The UCIRA provides grants to arts faculty and students for projects with the potential for significant artistic and cultural impact. We support projects that are innovative, experimental, and risky in their approach to form and/or content. These may include exhibitions, performances, symposia, outreach efforts, and projects that are multidisciplinary in approach. As artistic endeavors of the highest professional caliber, UCIRA projects frequently reach audiences outside the university and involve artists and scholars from around the world. As the only state-wide organization representing the arts on the nine campuses of the UC system, UCIRA also provides information and advocacy for university-based arts education and research.

POPULAR PROGRAMS

MEDIA STUDIES

Department chair: Steve Fagin

Focus/emphasis: Designed for students who want to become creative videomakers, filmmakers, photographers, and computer artists, encouraging media hybrid. The curriculum combines hands-on experience of making art with practical and theoretical criticism; provides historical, social, and aesthetic backgrounds for the understanding of modern media; and emphasizes creativity, versatility, and intelligence over technical specializations. It should allow students to go on to more specialized graduate programs in the media arts; to seek careers in film, television, computing, or photography; or to develop as independent artists. All media majors should see the departmental advisor on entrance into UCSD.

UNIVERSITY OF CALIFORNIA– SANTA BARBARA

Office of Admissions, 1210 Cheadle Hall,
Santa Barbara, CA 93106-2014
Phone: 805-893-2881 **E-mail:** appinfo@sa.ucsb.edu
Website: www.ucsb.edu

Campus Life
Environment: City. **Calendar:** Quarter.

Students and Faculty
(All Undergraduate Programs)
Enrollment: 18,114. **Student Body:** 55% female, 45% male, 5% out-of-state, 1% international (112 countries represented). African American 3%, Asian 16%, Caucasian 52%, Hispanic 17%. Student/faculty ratio 17:1. 903 full-time faculty.

Admissions
(All Undergraduate Programs)
Freshman Admissions Requirements: Test(s) required: SAT and SAT Subject Tests. Average high school GPA: 3.76. 95% in top tenth, 100% in top quarter. SAT Math (25/75 percentile): 550/660. SAT Verbal (25/75 percentile): 250/640. Projected SAT Writing (25/75 percentile): 310/680. *Academic units required:* 4 English, 3 math, 2 science (2 science lab), 2 foreign language, 2 social studies, 2 history, 2 academic electives. Regular application deadline: 11/30. Regular notification: 3/15.

Costs and Financial Aid
(All Undergraduate Programs)
Out-of-state tuition $23,961. Room & board $10,958. Required fees $811. Average book expense $1,435. **Financial Aid Statistics:** % freshmen/undergrads who receive any aid: 64/58. % freshmen/undergrads who receive need-based scholarship or grant aid: 39/38. % freshmen/undergrads who receive need-based self-help aid: 35/37. Priority financial aid filing deadline: 3/2. Financial aid filing deadline: 5/31. Financial aid notification on or about: 3/15.

TV/Film/Digital Media Studies Programs
Number of undergraduates in these programs: 473 (grads), 8 (undergrads).
Number of 2005 graduates from these programs: 125.
Degrees conferred to these majors: BA.
Number of full-time faculty in these programs: 12
Number of part-time faculty in these programs: 7

% of graduates who pursue further study within 5 years: 8
% of graduates currently employed in related field: 45
Career development services: Alumni networking opportunities; career counseling; central resource(s) for employers to browse headshots, writing samples, reels, etc.; internship listings; job fairs; job listings.
Famous alumni: Scott Frank, Don Hertfeldt, Brad Silberling, Jeff Nathanson, Morgan J. Freeman, Andrea Sperling, Toni Graphia.

In Their Own Words
With a 30-year history, the UCSB Film Department has continued to nurture creative

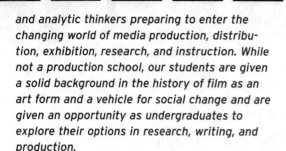

and analytic thinkers preparing to enter the changing world of media production, distribution, exhibition, research, and instruction. While not a production school, our students are given a solid background in the history of film as an art form and a vehicle for social change and are given an opportunity as undergraduates to explore their options in research, writing, and production.

POPULAR PROGRAMS

FILM AND MEDIA STUDIES
Department chair: Anna Everett
Number of full-time faculty: 1
Number of part-time faculty: 1
Focus/emphasis: Devoted to the study of film as a multicultural phenomenon and a humanistic discipline, the primary emphasis is on film history, film theory, and film analysis. The Department of Film Studies, while large enough to cover a broad range of fields, is still small enough to provide the personal atmosphere that can nurture individual interests and abilities.
Famous Alumni: Allison Anders, Peter Bloom, Edward Branigan, Lisa Parks, Constance Penley, Bhaskar Sarkar, Cristina Venegas, Janet Walker, Chuck Wolfe.
Notable Alumni: Anna Brusutti, Cynthia Felando, Paul Portuges.

UNIVERSITY OF CALIFORNIA– SANTA CRUZ

Office of Admissions, Cook House, 1156 High Street, Santa Cruz, CA 95064
Phone: 831-459-4008 **E-mail:** admissions@ucsc.edu
Website: http://admissions.ucsc.edu

Campus Life
Environment: Town. **Calendar:** Quarter.

Students and Faculty
(All Undergraduate Programs)
Enrollment: 13,588. **Student Body:** 54% female, 46% male, 4% out-of-state. African American 3%, Asian 19%, Caucasian 52%, Hispanic 15%. Student/faculty ratio: 19:1. 537 full-time faculty, 98% hold PhDs. 100% faculty teach undergrads.

Admissions
(All Undergraduate Programs)
Freshman Admissions Requirements: Test(s) required: SAT or ACT; SAT and SAT Subject Tests or ACT; ACT with Writing component. Average high school GPA: 3.51. 90% in top tenth, 100% in top quarter. SAT Math (25/75 percentile): 530/640. SAT Verbal (25/75 percentile): 520/630. Projected SAT Writing (25/75 percentile): 580/670. *Academic units required:* 4 English, 3 math, 2 science (2 science labs), 2 foreign language, 1 social studies, 1 history, 1 academic elective, 1 visual or performing arts. Regular application deadline: 11/30. Regular notification: Rolling.

Costs and Financial Aid
(All Undergraduate Programs)
Out-of-state tuition $17,304. Room & board $11,571. Required fees $7,603. Average book expense $1,332. **Financial Aid Statistics:** % undergrads who receive any aid: 60. % freshmen/undergrads who receive need-based scholarship or grant aid: 46/43. % freshmen/undergrads who receive need-based self-help aid: 45/42. Priority financial aid filing deadline: 3/2. Financial aid filing deadline: 3/2. Financial aid notification on or about: 4/1.

TV/Film/Digital Media Studies Programs
Degrees conferred to these majors: BA.
Career development services: Alumni networking opportunities, career counseling, internship listings, job fairs, job listings.
Notable alumni: Stephen Mirrione, Academy Award-winning editor of *Traffic*.

POPULAR PROGRAMS

FILM AND DIGITAL MEDIA
Department chair: Chip Lord

UNIVERSITY OF CENTRAL ARKANSAS

201 Donaghey Avenue, Conway, AR 72035
Phone: 501-450-3128 **E-mail:** admissions@uca.edu
Website: www.uca.edu

Campus Life
Environment: Rural. **Calendar:** Semester.

Students and Faculty
(All Undergraduate Programs)
Enrollment: 11,375. **Student Body:** 60% female, 40% male, 5% out-of-state, 2% international (55 countries represented). African American 16%, Asian 2%, Caucasian 74%, Hispanic 1%. Student/faculty ratio: 19:1. 478 full-time faculty, 64% hold PhDs. 100% faculty teach undergrads.

Admissions
(All Undergraduate Programs)
Freshman Admissions Requirements: Test(s) required: SAT or ACT. Average high school GPA: 3.28. 21% in top tenth, 44% in top quarter. SAT Math (25/75 percentile): 470/595. SAT Verbal (25/75 percentile): 430/575. Average ACT: 23. Regular notification: Rolling.

Costs and Financial Aid
(All Undergraduate Programs)
Annual in-state tuition $4,500. Out-of-state tuition $9,000. Room & board $4,320. Required fees $1,164. Average book expense $1,200.
Financial Aid Statistics: Priority financial aid filing deadline: 2/15. Financial aid notification on or about: 5/4.

TV/Film/Digital Media Studies Programs
Number of undergraduates in these programs: 300

Number of 2005 graduates from these programs: 40
Degrees conferred to these majors: BA, BS.
Also available at University of Central Arkansas: MFA.
Number of full-time faculty in these programs: 10
Number of part-time faculty in these programs: 8
Equipment and facilities: Television studio, local cable channel, instructional studio, multimedia lab, audio recording suite, editing suites, equipment check-outs.
Career development services: Career counseling, job fairs, internships.
Famous alumni: James Bridges, Beth Brickell.

In Their Own Words
Recent participants in UCA's Visiting Artists Series include Michael Moore, David Gordon Green, Michael Chabon, Rick Cleveland, Kevin Wilmott, and Ben Meade.

POPULAR PROGRAMS

BA/BS JOURNALISM
Department chair: Joseph Anderson
Focus/emphasis: Broadcast journalism, online journalism, and print journalism.

BA/BS DIGITAL FILMMAKING
Department chair: Joseph Anderson
Focus/emphasis: Narrative filmmaking and content creation for new technologies.

DIGITAL FILMMAKING (MFA ONLY)
Graduate program director: Bruce Hutchinson (BruceH@uca.edu)
Focus/emphasis: Independent filmmaking, narrative filmmaking, and content creation for new technologies.

UNIVERSITY OF CENTRAL FLORIDA

PO Box 160111, Orlando, FL 32816-0111
Phone: 407-823-3000 **E-mail:** admission@mail.ucf.edu
Website: www.ucf.edu

Campus Life
Environment: City. **Calendar:** Semester.

Students and Faculty
(All Undergraduate Programs)
Enrollment: 37,568. **Student Body:** 55% female, 45% male, 5% out-of-state, 1% international (126 countries represented). African American 9%, Asian 5%, Caucasian 68%, Hispanic 13%. Student/faculty ratio: 27:1. 1,192 full-time faculty, 79% hold PhDs. 100% faculty teach undergrads.

Admissions
(All Undergraduate Programs)
Freshman Admissions Requirements: Test(s) required: SAT or ACT; ACT with Writing component. Average high school GPA: 3.5. 35% in top tenth, 75% in top quarter. SAT Math (25/75 percentile): 530/620. SAT Verbal (25/75 percentile): 520/610. Projected SAT Writing (25/75 percentile): 580/660. *Academic units required:* 4 English, 3 math, 3 science (2 science labs), 2 foreign language, 3 social studies, 4 academic electives. Regular application deadline: 5/1. Regular notification: Rolling.

Costs and Financial Aid
(All Undergraduate Programs)
Annual in-state tuition $3,141. Out-of-state tuition $16,273. Room & board $7,600. Required fees $198. Average book expense $828.
Financial Aid Statistics: % freshmen/undergrads who receive any aid: 97/79. % freshmen/undergrads who receive need-based scholarship or grant aid: 18/19. % freshmen/undergrads who receive need-based self-help aid: 14/21. Priority financial aid filing deadline: 3/1. Financial aid filing deadline: 6/30. Financial aid notification on or about: 3/15.

TV/Film/Digital Media Studies Programs
Degrees conferred to these majors: BA, BFA.
Also available at University of Central Florida: Various minors, MA, MFA, MS.
Number of full-time faculty in these programs: 26
Equipment and facilities: The RTV studio and production facilities opened in 1999 as a centerpiece of the new $14-million-dollar-plus Communication Building. The facility was equipped with state-of-the-art analog and digital technology through a combination of public and private funding. A unique partnership with Panasonic Broadcast Systems along with a major donation from the Harris Corporation facilitated the outfitting of the facility. Financial contributions from Darden Restaurants, WOFL-TV, WFTV-TV, Cox Radio, and WESH-TV were also critical. The facility is staffed by two full-time engineers, an equipment checkout supervisor, and a faculty manager. The radio-television production facilities consist of a 3,200-square foot studio with a 20' x 20' hard cyc for chroma key, an 18' lighting grid, and three studio cameras equipped with TelePrompTers. The television control room is designed with tiered seating for up to 20 students for observing productions or receiving instruction. A Grass Valley 2200 digital production switcher, Sony DME 3000 2-channel DVE, and Inscriber character generator provide students with the tools for professional studio productions. Master control is equipped with three Panasonic AJ-D640 DVCPro videotape decks, a Panasonic AJ-D950 DVCPro50 deck, and a Sony PVW 2800 BetaSP deck for rerecording and playback of programs. Television audio control is equipped with an Audioarts Engineering 20-channel stereo console, two CD players, as well as a minidisc deck, a cassette deck, and a DAT recorder. Students have access to 13 mini-DV (Panasonic AGEZ1U) and 10 DVCPro (Panasonic AJD-215) camcorders for field acquisition along with a wide variety of microphones and lighting equipment. Video postproduction can be done in either a linear or nonlinear editing environment. Six linear edit bays (three for "cuts only" and 3 for "A-B roll") are equipped for

editing from either mini-DV or DVCPro while mastering to DVCPro. A Total of 18 nonlinear edit stations are available (17 Media 100 and one Avid Xpress) on the Mac platform. Sixteen of these stations are equipped with additional software for multimedia/web production. Audio production/postproduction is accomplished in five analog production rooms and one digital room. All audio production rooms utilize Pro Tools for editing. The digital production room is equipped with a Yamaha 02R 24-channel digital mixing console, a Mackie HUI, a Roland digital piano (FP-1) with MIDI interface, and a media form CD-R burner. All audio production rooms have CD, minidisc, cassette, and DAT capability. The Radio-Television Division also has the use of a 21' custom designed remote production van equipped to handle up to five cameras in a live-to-tape multicamera field recording. A presentation classroom adjacent to the production facilities provides video playback on either a 36" video monitor or large screen projection with surround sound. This teaching classroom is also equipped with video and audio editing equipment for demonstration purposes.

The Film Division offers camera, lighting, audio, soundstage and other related gear needed by students to make their short films, including 12 Final Cut Pro edit suites. Should students wish to shoot Super 16 mm or 35 mm films, they may take advantage of special rates generously offered by Panavision Orlando. Film budgets are covered by students, who also own their finished works.

Famous alumni: The five filmmakers who created *The Blair Witch Project* are graduates of UCF Film.

In Their Own Words

Internship opportunities abound in the Orlando area, so our career-bound students can work in advertising, public relations, newspapers, radio and television stations, and many other businesses to further their understandings in the communication business. These great opportunities, coupled with the more formal classes, prepare our students to be among the best prepared. We also have student organizations that provide opportunities to be further connected with industry. Our many successful graduates illustrate the strengths of our students and our programs.

POPULAR PROGRAMS

RADIO-TELEVISON
Department chair: George Bagley
Number of full-time faculty: 6
Focus/emphasis: A radio-television degree from the Nicholson School of Communication will give you the knowledge and hands-on experience you'll need to land your dream job in television or radio. Our brand new facility offers state-of-the-art equipment for training in both the analog and digital domains. You may choose from three academic tracks, which include classes in writing and production, as well as mass communication history, regulation, management, and media effects. Radio-Television students also manage and staff WNSC, a 24/7 radio station broadcast over closed-circuit campus cable on Channel 21 and online at htttp://wnsc.ucf.edu. Here, students gain constant hands-on experience with radio equipment, learn digital audio editing, and come to understand what is involved in managing a fully operational radio station, all while providing informational and entertaining content to their fellow UCF students and the world.

SCHOOL OF FILM & DIGITAL MEDIA (SFDM)
Department chair: Terry Frederick
Focus/emphasis: The SFDM is part of UCF's College of Arts & Humanities. The school is divided into three programs: the Film Division, the Digital Media Division, and FIEA (the Florida Interactive Entertainment Academy). The Film and Digital Media Divisions offer both undergraduate and graduate programs. FIEA focuses on video game design and offers an MS degree in Interactive Entertainment. Please see below for division descriptions.

FILM DIVISION

Division head: Steve Schlow

Focus/emphasis: This division offers degrees in three areas of study: production, cinema studies, and world cinema. The production and world cinema tracks are limited access; a total of about 30 students are admitted each year into those tracks. Cinema studies is an open major. The production BFA track provides students with a grounding in the history, theory, and aesthetics of film while developing their individual skills, styles, and voices as entrepreneurial cinematic storytellers. The program involves the student in the technical, economic, and artistic processes of film and encourages creative exploration of the medium and its potential. Students take courses in directing, editing, screenwriting, and production and actively seek the support and guidance of the many film industry professionals located in the Orlando area. (UCF FILM also offers a limited-access MFA program that is geared toward micro-budget feature-length digital filmmaking. About five students are accepted each year to this three-year program.)

The BA in cinema studies offers courses in film theory, history, and criticism. The emphasis is on the aesthetics, styles, and forms of film. The first two years of the program provide students with a general background and introduction. In the second two years, the program concentrates on the analysis of specific film practices such as editing, color, sound, staging, cinematography, narrative form, and theoretical and historical perspectives. The BA in world cinema focuses on the documentary; this includes the traditional genre of reportage as well as a broader view of documentary as a way of seeing—a technique of experiencing, interrogating, and reflecting on the world through cinema. The principal concern is storytelling that allows communities to use film, video, and digital media in innovative and creative ways that articulate the community's voice. The program is concerned not only with the intellectual, artistic, and technological, but also with the civic implications of filmmaking.

For further information, visit www.ucffilm.com.

DIGITAL MEDIA DIVISION

Division head: Clint Bowers

Focus/emphasis: The Digital Media Division offers two tracks of study: a BA in visual language and a BA in Internet and interactive systems. Visual Language provides students with the multi-disciplinary skills required by designers, technical animators, and game programmers. Visual language is a limited-access program (due to the need to evaluate a student's artistic ability before entering the major). Visual language students concentrate on how to tell imaginative and engaging stories that communicate by using the moving image, animation, and cinematic visual effects. Internet and interactive systems students concentrate on design in multiple media, teambuilding, and project management. Students can learn tools related to visual design, digital image manipulation, multimedia system design, web design and development, scripting, video editing and manipulation, 3-D modeling, and project management. (The Digital Media Division also offers an MA in visual language and interactive media for students with an undergraduate degree in a media-related creative or technical field such as art, film, animation, theater, music, digital media, computer science, English, or education in the arts. Thesis projects are geared toward advancing the field in Digital Media though research, production methodologies, and interpretation of the visual language.)

For further information, visit www.dm.ucf.edu.

FIEA (MS ONLY)

Division head: Ben Noel

Focus/emphasis: The Florida Interactive Entertainment Academy (FIEA) is a graduate video game design school offering an accredited an MS interactive entertainment. It offers a team-based, industry-focused education in a world-class facility in downtown Orlando (soon to be home to the entire School of Film & Digital Media). Areas of study include game design, development, art, programming, and production. FIEA faculty have spent dozens of years in working in some of the most recognizable gaming studios—Microsoft,

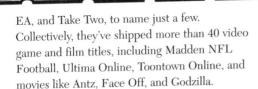

EA, and Take Two, to name just a few. Collectively, they've shipped more than 40 video game and film titles, including Madden NFL Football, Ultima Online, Toontown Online, and movies like Antz, Face Off, and Godzilla.

UNIVERSITY OF CENTRAL OKLAHOMA

100 North University Drive, Edmond, OK 73034
Phone: 405-974-2338 **E-mail:** admituco@ucok.edu
Website: www.ucok.edu

Campus Life
Environment: Metropolis. **Calendar:** Semester.

Students and Faculty
(All Undergraduate Programs)
Enrollment: 14,625. **Student Body:** 59% female, 41% male, 4% out-of-state, 7% international (73 countries represented). African American 9%, Asian 3%, Caucasian 67%, Hispanic 3%, Native American 6%. Student/faculty ratio 21:1. 411 full-time faculty, 73% hold PhDs. 95% faculty teach undergrads.

Admissions
(All Undergraduate Programs)
Freshman Admissions Requirements: Test(s) required: SAT or ACT. Average high school GPA: 3.17. 13% in top tenth, 24% in top quarter. *Academic units required:* 4 English, 3 math, 2 science (2 science lab), 1 social studies, 2 history, 3 academic electives. Regular notification: Rolling.

Costs and Financial Aid
(All Undergraduate Programs)
Annual in-state tuition $2,811. Out-of-state tuition $7,821. Room & board $4,476. Required fees $807. Average book expense $1,000.
Financial Aid Statistics: % freshmen/undergrads who receive any aid: 62/54. % freshmen/undergrads who receive need-based scholarship or grant aid: 33/28. % freshmen/undergrads who receive need-based self help aid: 30/27. Priority financial aid filing deadline: 5/15. Financial aid notification on or about: 4/15.

TV/Film/Digital Media Studies Programs
Number of students in these programs: 592
Number of 2005 graduates from these programs: 127
Degrees conferred to these majors: BA.
Number of full-time faculty in these programs: 22
Number of part-time faculty in these programs: 25
Equipment and facilities: We have a 25-station-broadcast computer newsroom, a 24-hour cable TV channel serving the local community with five daily newscasts each week, and a student run radio station, primarily Web. We have an 18-station Mac lab for writing, a 20-station Mac lab for photography, and a 15-station open lab for students. We have several Avid editing stations and a still photography studio. In addition, we just received a $150,000 grant to help with the digital conversion of our broadcast studio—matching the $150,000 we have in the bank. This won't quite get us there, but it'll get the major phases underway.

In Their Own Words
Our students intern at all local TV stations, many radio stations, the Daily Oklahoman, area newspapers, and public relations agencies and hospitals throughout the metro area. We primarily offer tuition waiver scholarships through the university. We are a working class university, with a majority of students working more than 20 hours a week. We have 820 majors; this includes 184 in broadcast, 94 in journalism, 146 in PR, 67 in photography, and 91 in advertising.

POPULAR PROGRAMS

BROADCASTING
Department chair: Dr. Terry Clark
Focus/emphasis: We're known in the state as the program that teaches writing and demands internships with a basis of hands-on learning, experience, and good teaching.

UNIVERSITY OF CINCINNATI

PO Box 210091, Cincinnati, OH 45221-0091
Phone: 513-556-1100 **E-mail:** admissions@uc.edu
Website: www.uc.edu

Campus Life
Environment: Metropolis. **Calendar:** Quarter.

Students and Faculty
(All Undergraduate Programs)
Enrollment: 18,993. **Student Body:** 49% female, 51% male, 8% out-of-state, 4% international (124 countries represented). African American 13%, Asian 3%, Caucasian 74%, Hispanic 1%. Student/faculty ratio: 15:1. 1,151 full-time faculty, 72% hold PhDs. 40% faculty teach undergrads.

Admissions
(All Undergraduate Programs)
Freshman Admissions Requirements: Test(s) required: SAT or ACT. Average high school GPA: 3.33. 16% in top tenth, 37% in top quarter. SAT Math (25/75 percentile): 470/610. SAT Verbal (25/75 percentile): 470/600. Projected SAT Writing (25/75 percentile): 540/650. *Academic units required:* 4 English, 3 math, 2 science, 2 foreign language, 2 social studies, 2 academic electives. Regular application deadline: 9/1. Regular notification: Rolling.

Costs and Financial Aid
(All Undergraduate Programs)
Annual in-state tuition $7,458. Out-of-state tuition $21,210. Room & board $7,890. Required fees $1,425. Average book expense $1,140.
Financial Aid Statistics: % freshmen/undergrads who receive need-based scholarship or grant aid: 43/33. % freshmen/undergrads who receive need-based self-help aid: 60/47. Financial aid notification on or about: 3/15.

TV/Film/Digital Media Studies Programs
Number of undergraduates in these programs: 240
Number of 2005 graduates from these programs: 38
Degrees conferred to these majors: BFA.

Number of full-time faculty in these programs: 7
Number of part-time faculty in these programs: 4
Equipment and facilities: Television studio, Eng/EFP equipment, digital postproduction stations in video and audio, multimedia lab, writing lab, newsroom, audio studio, audio postproduction labs, virtual studio, radio station (Internet), cable TV station, extensive portable video production equipment: lights, microphones, cameras.
Other awards of note: Caucus Foundation Outstanding Film Award, Regional Emmy Awards, Radio Mercury Award, NBS Regional and National Awards, NAPTE Scholarship Award, NATAS Scholarship Awards.

% of graduates who pursue film study with 5 years: 10
% of graduates currently employed in related field: 80
Career development services: Alumni networking opportunities, career counseling, internship listings, job fairs, job listings, joint effort with the OAB.
Famous alumni: Earl Hamner, Dan Guntzelman.
Notable alumni: Tom Bruehl, senior vice president, video operations, Paramount Productions, Hollywood, CA; Kimberly Monning, anchor, WB 64, Cincinnati, OH; Susan Brannigan, account director, Showtime, Chicago, IL; Tom Sandman, creative service director, Warm 98, Cincinnati, OH; David Ashbrook, production manager, Fox 19, Cincinnati, OH; Emily Wen, director, KING-TV, Seattle, WA; Nancy Harmeyer, bureau chief, Central America, Fox Network, Miami, FL; Tanja O'Rourke, anchor, WCPO, Channel 9, Cincinnati, OH; Cary Harlow, global training officer, P&G, Cincinnati, OH; Patrick Thomasson, general sales manager, KPWR-Power 106, Burbank, CA; Lisa Ripley-Becker, producer, 20th Century Fox Television, Studio City, CA.

In Their Own Words
There are extensive internship opportunities locally, regionally, and nationally with CNN, Paramount Productions, CBS Studio Center,

DMG Sound Delux, Procter & Gamble, and Soap Opera Productions, and overseas in Munich, Germany, at the IRT. Host of Annual Fredric W. Ziv Awards Banquet, support of Industry Advisory Panel.

POPULAR PROGRAMS

ELECTRONIC MEDIA DIVISION
Department chair: Manfred K. Wolfram, PhD
Number of full-time faculty: 7
Number of part-time faculty: 4
Focus/emphasis: Extensive exposure to audio/video/multimedia production and post-production experiences as well as electronic journalism.

Students Should Also Know
In addition to the available classroom and laboratory experiences, the program offers opportunities to work for a radio (Bearcast) and/or television (UCast-TV) station operated within the program. Many internship opportunities exist locally as well as nationally. The program enjoys strong local industry support and celebrates an annual banquet underwritten and attended by media professional from across the United States. The Electronic Media Division also offers the Munich Summer Curriculum (MSC) academy in Munich, Germany, an intensive, discipline-specific program, designed for the above average student.

UNIVERSITY OF COLORADO AT DENVER AND HEALTH SCIENCES CENTER
PO Box 173364, Campus Box 167, Denver, CO 80217
Phone: 303-556-2704 **E-mail:** admissions@cudenver.edu
Website: www.cudenver.edu

Campus Life
Environment: Metropolis. **Calendar:** Semester.

Students and Faculty
(All Undergraduate Programs)
Enrollment: 7,780. **Student Body:** 55% female, 45% male, 4% out-of-state, 2% international (522 countries represented). African American 4%, Asian 10%, Caucasian 64%, Hispanic 11%, Native American 1%. Student/faculty ratio: 15:1. 579 full-time faculty, 82% hold PhDs. 60% faculty teach undergrads.

Admissions
(All Undergraduate Programs)
Freshman Admissions Requirements: Test(s) required: SAT or ACT. Average high school GPA: 3.27. 13% in top tenth, 37% in top quarter. SAT Math (25/75 percentile): 490/600. SAT Verbal (25/75 percentile): 490/590. Projected SAT Writing (25/75 percentile): 550/640. *Academic units required:* 4 English, 3 math, 3 science, 2 foreign language, 2 social studies, 1 history, 1 academic elective.

Costs and Financial Aid
(All Undergraduate Programs)
Annual in-state tuition $4,224. Out-of-state tuition $15,394. Required fees $797.
Financial Aid Statistics: % freshmen/undergrads who receive need-based scholarship or grant aid: 33/31. % freshmen/undergrads who receive need-based self-help aid: 23/37. Priority financial aid filing deadline: 4/1. Financial aid notification on or about: 5/1.

TV/Film/Digital Media Studies Programs
Number of undergraduates in these programs: 185
Number of 2005 graduates from these programs: 46
Degrees conferred to these majors: BA, BFA.
Number of full-time faculty in these programs: 6
Number of part-time faculty in these programs: 12
Equipment and facilities: Up-to-date inventory of film, video, sound, lighting, and digital editing equipment. The multimedia emphasis in the BFA program through the Department of Visual Arts utilizes three multimedia computer labs. The digital

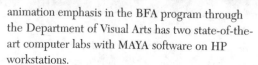

animation emphasis in the BFA program through the Department of Visual Arts has two state-of-the-art computer labs with MAYA software on HP workstations.

Career development services: Alumni networking opportunities, career counseling, internship listings, job fairs, job listings. All listed services are provided through the campus Career Center.

In Their Own Words

These programs all offer hands-on production experience housed in a broad-based university and arts education.

POPULAR PROGRAMS

FILM AND VIDEO PRODUCTION IN THEATER/FILM

Department chair: Daniel Koetting
Number of full-time faculty: 2
Number of part-time faculty: 8
Focus/emphasis: The BFA four-year curriculum that builds on the studio program, a foundation of experiential course work in the narrative arts of film and theater. The program is complemented by advanced course work and skill-based training in the arts and crafts of writing and directing. The BA degree offers concentrations in writing and directing, cinematography and videography, and postproduction. Topics are woven together by faculty from a variety of performance and production disciplines to include introductions to acting, directing, dramatic and cinematic literature, camera equipment and techniques, production design, criticism, and dramatic style.

MULTIMEDIA EMPHASIS

Department chair: Joann Brennan
Number of full-time faculty: 2
Number of part-time faculty: 3
Focus/emphasis: Concerned with the history, conceptual process, artistic design, usability theory, criticism, and legal aspects of the design of electronic media and includes a fine arts foundation in drawing, 2-D and 3-D design, color theory, and art history. The focus of the emphasis is on theory and criticism of design and art using digital tools.

DIGITAL ANIMATION EMPHASIS IN BFA PROGRAM

Department chair: Joann Brennan
Number of full-time faculty: 2
Number of part-time faculty: 1
Focus/emphasis: Offers instruction in the theory, practice, and application of digital 3-D media with a fine arts foundation in drawing, painting, photography, and sculpture.

UNIVERSITY OF DAYTON

300 College Park, Dayton, OH 45469-1300
Phone: 937-229-4411 **E-mail:** admission@udayton.edu
Website: www.udayton.edu

Campus Life

Environment: City. **Calendar:** Semester.

Students and Faculty
(All Undergraduate Programs)

Enrollment: 7,270. **Student Body:** 49% female, 51% male, 33% out-of-state. African American 4%, Asian 1%, Caucasian 83%, Hispanic 2%. Student/faculty ratio: 14:1. 446 full-time faculty, 93% hold PhDs. 82% faculty teach undergrads.

Admissions
(All Undergraduate Programs)

Freshman Admissions Requirements: Test(s) required: SAT or ACT. 24% in top tenth, 50% in top quarter. SAT Math (25/75 percentile): 540/650. SAT Verbal (25/75 percentile): 520/620. Projected SAT Writing (25/75 percentile): 580/660. *Academic units required:* 2 foreign language. Regular notification: Rolling.

Costs and Financial Aid
(All Undergraduate Programs)

Annual tuition $23,000. Room & board $7,190. Required fees $970. Average book expense $800. **Financial Aid Statistics:** % freshmen/undergrads who receive any aid: 93/90. % freshmen/undergrads who receive need-based scholarship or grant aid: 59/58. % freshmen/undergrads who receive need-based self-help aid: 55/55. Priority financial aid filing deadline: 3/31. Financial aid notification on or about: 3/31.

TV/Film/Digital Media Studies Programs

Number of undergraduates in these programs: 99

Number of 2005 graduates from these programs: 24

Degrees conferred to these majors: BA.

Number of full-time faculty in these programs: 4

Number of part-time faculty in these programs: 4

Equipment and facilities: We are slowly transitioning our studio and field production capabilities to digital formats. In the near future, we need a major upgrading in our graphics capabilities, both in the control room and for digital editing. In the longterm, the school will need to upgrade both studio and field production to high-definition formats. This will include, but will not be limited to, high-definition field and studio cameras, record decks and servers, and editing software.

Other awards of note: Regional Emmy Award for the Fall 2000 student production entitled *Silent Fall*.

% of graduates currently employed in related field: 90

Career development services: Alumni networking opportunities; career counseling; central resource(s) for employers to browse headshots, writing samples, reels; for-credit internship listings.

Famous alumni: Dan Patrick.

Notable alumni: Paula Cwickli, director, NBC daytime programs; Garry McGuire, president and COO of Williams Communications; Jeff Wagner, public affairs director, Flour-Fernald/DOD.

In Their Own Words

Despite our limited facilities, we've had very good success in the past few years in placing our graduating students (about 90 percent). Our students have been placed in a number of news organizations, as well as video production facilities, primarily in the Midwest. We have solid internship programs with several businesses and organizations and expect those to expand and continue.

POPULAR PROGRAMS

ELECTRONIC MEDIA

Department chair: Donald D. Yoder, PhD

Number of full-time faculty: 4

Number of part-time faculty: 4

Focus/emphasis: Provides students with course work and experience in both the traditional and newer media and in emerging communication technologies. Students also study the social, economic, and international dimensions of electronic media.

UNIVERSITY OF DENVER

University Hall, Room 110, 2197 South University Boulevard, Denver, CO 80208

Phone: 303-871-2036 **E-mail:** admission@du.edu

Website: www.du.edu/admission

Campus Life

Environment: Metropolis. **Calendar:** Quarter.

Students and Faculty
(All Undergraduate Programs)

Enrollment: 4,813. **Student Body:** 55% female, 45% male, 50% out-of-state, 4% international (87 countries represented). African American 3%, Asian 5%, Caucasian 81%, Hispanic 7%. Student/faculty ratio: 11:1. 484 full-time faculty, 92% hold PhDs. 92% faculty teach undergrads.

Admissions
(All Undergraduate Programs)

Freshman Admissions Requirements: Test(s) required: SAT or ACT. Average high school GPA: 3.57. 36% in top tenth, 69% in top quarter. SAT Math (25/75 percentile): 530/640. SAT Verbal (25/75 percentile): 530/630. Projected SAT Writing (25/75 percentile): 590/670. Regular application deadline: 1/15. Regular notification: 3/15.

Costs and Financial Aid
(All Undergraduate Programs)

Annual tuition $29,628. Room & board $8,351. Required fees $474.

Financial Aid Statistics: % freshmen/undergrads who receive any aid: 81/76. % freshmen/undergrads who receive need-based scholarship or grant aid: 44/42. % freshmen/undergrads who receive need-based self-help aid: 40/39. Priority financial aid filing deadline: 3/1. Financial aid filing deadline: 3/1. Financial aid notification on or about: 3/15.

TV/Film/Digital Media Studies Programs

Number of undergraduates in these programs: 107

Number of 2005 graduates from these programs: 27

Degrees conferred to these majors: BA.

Also available at University of Denver: MA.

Number of full-time faculty in these programs: 6

Number of part-time faculty in these programs: 4

Equipment and facilities: The school teaches on the latest operating systems of both Macs and PCs. All design classes are taught on Mac. Most production courses are taught on PCs. The nonlinear video-editing systems are Mac (Media 100). One 15-station Windows XP classroom in Sturm Hall; ine 24/7 10-station Windows XP lab in Sturm Hall; one 15-station Mac classroom and one 12-station Mac lab in the Shwayder Art Building; one 15-station Windows XP lab in mass communications; four Media 100 nonlinear editing suites and two Final Cut Pro/DVD suites in the mass communications video production studio; one MIDI lab with a dual XP capture/control station, MIDI keyboard controllers for software synthesis, and Mackie 16-channel mixer in Sturm; one video lab with Mac, SVHS, and DV in Sturm. Each lab is equipped with scanners, CD burners, video and audio capture, digital cameras, and high-speed Internet access (10-100 Mb). The school currently run the latest versions and updates of 3-D modeling/animation/multimedia: Maya, LightWave, Ray Dream, Flash Audio Production: SoundForge, Acid Pro, Sonar, Ableton Live, Absynth, Reaktor; Max/MSP Video/Motion Graphics Development: AfterEffects, Premiere, Media100, Final Cut Pro, Vegas, Quicktime, MediaCleaner, DVD Architect, DVD Studio; VJ Production: Arkaos, Resolume; Image Production: Photoshop, Illustrator, Fireworks, Freehand; Web development: Dreamweaver, Flash, ColdFusion, and ASP.

Career development services: Alumni networking opportunities, career counseling, internship listings, job listings.

In Their Own Words

DMOC pairs University of Denver students in need of professional digital media development and design experience with Colorado nonprofit organizations. DMOC is designed to provide instrumental support for those organizations that wish to develop, establish, maintain, and expand a digital presence via any type of digital media, including multimedia presentations, videos, web development, audio production, branding, or community networking tools. By combining the expertise of a small DMOC staff with the budding talent, energy, and commitment of undergraduate and graduate students enrolled in digital media-related programs at the University of Denver, the Digital Media Outreach Center plans to quickly reshape the NPO digital landscape in Colorado. DMOC provides media planning, design, development, administration, education, and ongoing support for clients. DMOC gives students and faculty opportunities to apply and extend curriculum-based learning to community-based projects. This approach also involves our students in socially redeeming digital projects that, we hope, will encourage them to consider technology careers in the nonprofit sector and provide them with the desire to remain civically engaged throughout their professional lives.

POPULAR PROGRAMS

DIGITAL MEDIA STUDIES

Department chair: Jeff Rutenbeck
Number of full-time faculty: 6
Number of part-time faculty: 4

Focus/emphasis: Fosters the work of innovative students interested in using digital methods and forms to creatively explore, and critically comment on, the digital conditions rapidly altering every aspect of our reality. DMS provides cross-disciplinary support for the study and practice of digital media with courses in art and design; 3-D; animation; video and audio; interactive media; games; HCI design; Web and network development; flash remoting; and seminars and lectures exploring the critical, philosophical, legal, political, and cultural dimensions of digital media. Our program combines a rigorous foundational curriculum with a flexible set of electives and opportunities for directed research and production. DMS further supports students through a diverse network of internship and community outreach situations throughout the Denver area.

UNIVERSITY OF DUBUQUE

2000 University Avenue, Dubuque, IA 52001-5050
Phone: 319-589-3200 **E-mail:** admssns@dbq.edu
Website: www.dbq.edu

Campus Life

Environment: Village. **Calendar:** Semester.

Students and Faculty
(All Undergraduate Programs)

Enrollment: 1,101. **Student Body:** 36% female, 64% male, 57% out-of-state. African American 10%, Asian 1%, Caucasian 78%, Hispanic 4%, Native American 3%. Student/faculty ratio: 14:1. 70 full-time faculty, 74% hold PhDs. 100% faculty teach undergrads.

Admissions
(All Undergraduate Programs)

Freshman Admissions Requirements: Test(s) required: SAT or ACT. Average high school GPA: 3.0. 7% in top tenth, 21% in top quarter. SAT Math (25/75 percentile): 410/560. SAT Verbal (25/75 percentile): 400/540. Projected SAT Writing (25/75 percentile): 470/600. *Academic units required:* 4 English, 3 math, 3 science, 3 social studies, 3 academic electives. Regular notification: Rolling.

Costs and Financial Aid
(All Undergraduate Programs)

Annual tuition $16,660. Room & board $5,700. Required fees $185. Average book expense $850. **Financial Aid Statistics:** % freshmen/undergrads who receive any aid: 85/85. % freshmen/undergrads who receive need-based scholarship or grant aid: 85/87. % freshmen/undergrads who receive need-based self-help aid: 82/83. Priority financial aid filing deadline: 4/1. Financial aid notification on or about: 3/1.

TV/Film/Digital Media Studies Programs

Number of undergraduates in these programs: 100
Number of 2005 graduates from these programs: 20
Degrees conferred to these majors: BA.
Number of full-time faculty in these programs: 7
Equipment and facilities: Three production labs and one postproduction lab. Classes are limited to the number of workstations.
Other awards of note: University of Dubuque students consistently win awards through the local chapter of the National Tecky Awards program.

% of graduates currently employed in related field: 95
Career development services: Alumni networking opportunities, career counseling, internship listings, job fairs, job listings.

In Their Own Words
Students work for national and international companies.

POPULAR PROGRAMS

COMPUTER GRAPHICS/INTERACTIVE MEDIA
Department chair: Alan Garfield
Number of full-time faculty: 7

Focus/emphasis: Computer animation and website development.

UNIVERSITY OF FLORIDA

201 Criser Hall, Box 114000, Gainesville, FL 32611-4000
Phone: 352-392-1365 **E-mail:** ourwebrequests@registrar.ufl.edu
Website: www.ufl.edu

Campus Life
Environment: City. **Calendar:** Semester.

Students and Faculty
(All Undergraduate Programs)
Enrollment: 33,094. **Student Body:** 53% female, 47% male, 4% out-of-state. African American 9%, Asian 7%, Caucasian 72%, Hispanic 12%. Student/faculty ratio: 23:1. 1,622 full-time faculty, 90% hold PhDs.

Admissions
(All Undergraduate Programs)
Freshman Admissions Requirements: Test(s) required: SAT or ACT; ACT with Writing component. Average high school GPA: 3.9. 85% in top tenth, 90% in top quarter. SAT Math (25/75 percentile): 590/690. SAT Verbal (25/75 percentile): 570/670. Projected SAT Writing (25/75 percentile): 620/700. *Academic units required:* 4 English, 3 math, 3 science (2 science labs), 2 foreign language, 3 social studies. Early decision application deadline: 10/1. Regular application deadline: 1/17.

Costs and Financial Aid
(All Undergraduate Programs)
Annual in-state tuition $3,094. Out-of-state tuition $17,222. Room & board $6,260. Average book expense $930.
Financial Aid Statistics: % freshmen/undergrads who receive any aid: 97/84. % freshmen/undergrads who receive need-based scholarship or grant aid: 21/24. % freshmen/undergrads who receive need-based self-help aid: 18/25. Priority financial aid filing deadline: 3/15. Financial aid notification on or about: 4/1.

TV/Film/Digital Media Studies Programs
Degrees conferred to these majors: BA.
Equipment and facilities: Weimer Hall is considered one of the finest educational journalism buildings in the nation. The school moved into the $6.3 million building in 1980 and added the $3.1 million Alvin G. Flanagan Telecommunication Wing in 1990. In addition to 20 classrooms and laboratories, the 125,000-square-foot Weimer Hall houses four working newsrooms, four radio stations, two television stations, a 110-seat library, research facilities, a 250-seat auditorium, and 11 satellite ground stations. As an acknowledged leader in communication technology, the college has put forth a set of computer requirements requiring that each student have access to a personal computer. In support, the college provides some 400 networked computers equipped with the latest computer hardware and software packages. Well-equipped laboratories and classrooms also provide experience with professional-quality equipment, including television and radio production hardware, reporting and editing terminals, digital still cameras, and computerized graphics equipment. The computer laboratories, including three state-of-the-art desktop publishing labs, connect the college's newsrooms and offices to the rest of the campus and the Internet. Interactive Media Lab Development of the Interactive Media Lab began in the summer of 1994. The college bought eight then-state-of-the-art 486-class networked computers to open the lab. Development, innovation, and computer upgrades have continued. The lab now has its own T1 connection to the Internet, as well as more powerful computers, television monitors, and wire services from the Associated Press, Reuters, *New York Times* News Service, and Scripps Howard News Service. Radio & TV students can gain practical experience working at the college's four radio stations (WRUF-AM, WRUF-FM, WUFT-FM, and WJUF-FM) and two television stations (WLUF-LP and WUFT-TV). The college also uses satellite ground stations to link Weimer Hall to PBS, NPR, CBS, NBC, Reuters, the Associated Press, *New York Times* News Service, and ABC. The Allen H. Neuharth Journalism Library is a departmental library located

on the first floor of Weimer Hall serving the students, faculty, and staff in the College of Journalism and Communications. The library supports the instructional and research programs of the college, and materials held in the library are generally chosen in support of the curriculum. Computer workstations are available for access to the extensive databases and other resources supplied by the George A. Smathers Libraries and to the Internet. The purpose of the Documentary Institute is to create a worldwide center of excellence for the production of television documentary, to provide state-of-the-art instruction in the production of documentary, and to serve as a clearinghouse for issues dealing with the production and teaching of documentary film.

POPULAR PROGRAMS

TELECOMMUNICATIONS

Focus/emphasis: According to the school, this is one of the country's premier programs in electronic mass media. As a result, there are a large number of applicants for admission. The program is highly selective, and the academic standards of the courses are rigorous. It is tough to get into the department, and once in, the course work is challenging, time consuming, and interesting! The school is accredited by the Accrediting Council on Education in Journalism and Mass Communications (ACEJMC). This means that every six years the program prepares an exhaustive report on facilities, faculty, students, and curriculum and invite a team from ACEJMC to visit our campus and evaluate our educational program. According to the school, of the 400-plus radio-TV programs in the United States, only 80-some are accredited. "We are proud of our accreditation; it means that we have been measured against a rigorous national standard and judged to be among the best. It also means that you will get an excellent education in electronic mass media. We limit our department enrollment to 408 juniors and seniors." About 30 MA and four PhD students also study telecommunication. Our teaching staff includes 20 faculty members;

four of these also have professional responsibilities at the university's radio or television stations, and another four make up The Documentary Institute. Affiliated with the college and located in the same building are six broadcast stations. These include two commercial stations, WRUF-AM and WRUF-FM, and four noncommercial stations, WUFT-FM/WJUF-FM, WLUF-LP, and WUFT-TV. WUFT-FM also transmits a Radio Reading Service for the blind on a subcarrier, and WUFT-TV's news department feeds local news inserts to the Gainesville cable system for insertion into CNN Headline News. The radio and television stations are professional operations that serve North Central Florida, but they utilize students in virtually all operational capacities, thereby affording students the opportunity to get valuable station experience.

DIGITAL AND ART SCIENCES

Department chair: Trisha Suggs

Focus/emphasis: The Digital Arts and Sciences (DAS) Program is an interdisciplinary program focusing on digital media in the 21st century; it prepares students for the highly demanding digital industry. The program focuses on education as a participatory experience, whereby students learn aesthetic, technical, and production skills in a hands-on environment. Students in the DAS program work individually and on teams to create digital media projects that explore art and technology as a unified subject.

UNIVERSITY OF GEORGIA

Terrell Hall, Athens, GA 30602
Phone: 706-542-8776 **E-mail:** adm-info@uga.edu
Website: www.uga.edu

Campus Life
Environment: City. **Calendar:** Semester.

Students and Faculty
(All Undergraduate Programs)
Enrollment: 24,791. **Student Body:** 57% female, 43% male, 12% out-of-state. African American 5%,

Asian 5%, Caucasian 86%, Hispanic 2%. Student/faculty ratio: 18:1. 1,691 full-time faculty, 93% hold PhDs. 79% faculty teach undergrads.

Admissions
(All Undergraduate Programs)

Freshman Admissions Requirements: Test(s) required: SAT or ACT; ACT with Writing component. Average high school GPA: 3.74. 52% in top tenth, 84% in top quarter. SAT Math (25/75 percentile): 570/670. SAT Verbal (25/75 percentile): 560/660. Projected SAT Writing (25/75 percentile): 620/690. *Academic units required:* 4 English, 4 math, 3 science (2 science labs), 2 foreign language, 3 social studies. Regular application deadline: 1/15. Regular notification: 2/15.

Costs and Financial Aid
(All Undergraduate Programs)

Annual in-state tuition $3,648. Out-of-state tuition $15,864.

Financial Aid Statistics: % freshmen/undergrads who receive any aid: 27/25. % freshmen/undergrads who receive need-based scholarship or grant aid: 26/21. % freshmen/undergrads who receive need-based self-help aid: 13/17. Priority financial aid filing deadline: 3/1. Financial aid notification on or about: 5/15.

TV/Film/Digital Media Studies Programs

Number of undergraduates in these programs: 347

Number of 2005 graduates from these programs: 137

Also available at University of Georgia: ABJ (BA in Journalism and Mass Communication).

Number of full-time faculty in these programs: 18

Number of part-time faculty in these programs: 1

Equipment and facilities: The department has three audio production studios, two color-equipped television studios, complete packages of portable color television cameras, video recorders, and six editing room suites. In addition, broadcast news majors learn their skills in a fully operational computerized broadcast newsroom complete with satellite and broadcast monitors, Associated Press, and Reuters news wires, custom scripting and rundown software, police and fire scanner, two phone lines, and full Internet computer access from all eight workstations.

Career development services: Alumni networking opportunities, career counseling, internship listings, job fairs, job listings. Full-time career services director works with students individually and develops professional programs and outreach, including a popular e-mail career message series. Director also collaborates with the UGA Career Center on services for our majors.

Famous alumni: Deborah Roberts; Deborah Potter, ABC; Deborah Norville, *Inside Edition*; Randy Travis, WAGA-TV; Julie Moran, *Entertainment Tonight*; Chip Caray, baseball play-by-play broadcaster, *WTBS/Turner South*; Condace Pressley, WSB radio; John Holliman.

In Their Own Words

The Department of Telecommunications offers students both conceptual and practical education in the electronic media. The department boasts an outstanding faculty ranked at the top of the profession with a wide range of academic and professional contacts in radio, television, cable, and emerging technologies. In addition to their classroom work, students have the opportunity to produce programs for the university's cable system. Grady College is also home to the George Foster Peabody Awards, which offers students a chance to be involved in many phases of this prestigious program recognizing excellence in broadcasting. The college also cosponsors an annual Robert Osborne Classic Film Festival.

POPULAR PROGRAMS

TELECOMMUNICATION ARTS

Department chair: Joe Dominick, Professor of Telecommunications

Number of full-time faculty: 13

Focus/emphasis: Designed to train students in production, electronic media studies, management, and broadcast news emphases. The major provides students with professional courses of study in both the theory and practice of electronic media.

BROADCAST NEWS

Number of full-time faculty: 5

Focus/emphasis: The Broadcast News Program is designed to train students in the skills necessary for on-air opportunities in gathering, analyzing, and delivering the news in radio and television. The major provides students with professional courses of study in both the theory and practice of broadcast journalism.

Students Should Also Know

Admission to Telecommunication Arts and Broadcast News, as well as Grady's five other undergraduate majors, is by application, when UGA students reach 45 hours and meet other key criteria found at www.grady.uga.edu under the Undergraduate link. Telecommunication Arts and Broadcast News are high-demand majors at UGA. Selection is based on academic criteria (an average of grades in selected core courses and a score on a written statement of interest). For information about UGA and Grady admissions, prospective students are encouraged to visit www.grady.uga.edu.

UNIVERSITY OF IDAHO

UI Admissions Office, PO Box 444264, Moscow, ID 83844-4264
Phone: 208-885-6326 **E-mail:** admappl@uidaho.edu
Website: www.uidaho.edu

Campus Life

Environment: Town. **Calendar:** Semester.

Students and Faculty
(All Undergraduate Programs)

Enrollment: 9,047. **Student Body:** 45% female, 55% male, 22% out-of-state, 2% international. Asian 2%, Caucasian 85%, Hispanic 4%, Native American 1%. Student/faculty ratio: 20:1. 545 full-time faculty, 80% hold PhDs. 70% faculty teach undergrads.

Admissions
(All Undergraduate Programs)

Freshman Admissions Requirements: Test(s) required: SAT and SAT Subject Tests. Average high school GPA: 3.4. 20% in top tenth, 47% in top quarter. SAT Math (25/75 percentile): 500/620. SAT Verbal (25/75 percentile): 490/610. Projected SAT Writing (25/75 percentile): 550/660. *Academic units required:* 4 English, 3 math, 3 science (1 science lab), 1 foreign language, 3 social studies, 2 academic electives. Regular notification: Rolling.

Costs and Financial Aid
(All Undergraduate Programs)

Annual in-state tuition $4,200. Out-of-state tuition $9,600. Room & board $5,034. Required fees $3,632. Average book expense $1,286.

Financial Aid Statistics: % freshmen/undergrads who receive need-based scholarship or grant aid: 37/43. % freshmen/undergrads who receive need-based self-help aid: 43/51. Priority financial aid filing deadline: 2/15. Financial aid notification on or about: 3/23.

TV/Film/Digital Media Studies Programs

Number of undergraduates in these programs: 100

Number of 2005 graduates from these programs: 75

Degrees conferred to these majors: BA, BS.

Number of full-time faculty in these programs: 2

Number of part-time faculty in these programs: 4

Equipment and facilities: 12 digital media edit bays; three digital audio workstations; KUOI-FM student radio station; KRFA-FM public radio station; KUID-TV television studio; digital ENG/EFP video/audio production equipment.

Other awards of note: Students routinely win awards in student competitions held by Idaho Press Club, regional chapters of The Society of Professional Journalists, and earn scholarships from media organizations.

% of graduates who pursue further study within 5 years: 5

% of graduates currently employed in related field: 50

Career development services: Alumni networking opportunities, career counseling, internship listings, job fairs, job listings.

Famous alumni: Michael Kirk, Otis Livingston, Russ Leatherman.

Notable alumni: Many alums working successfully in the field as news reporters, sports reporters, news producers, writers, and editors.

In Their Own Words

Students in Radio-TV-Digital Media and Broadcast Journalism intern at radio and television stations, video/audio production companies, and production departments in companies; produce daily radio newscasts and weekly television programs; host an annual student digital media festival called Moscow Kino; and work at on-campus video and audio service departments.

POPULAR PROGRAMS

RADIO-TV-DIGITAL MEDIA

Department chair: Kenton Bird
Number of full-time faculty: 2
Number of part-time faculty: 4
Focus/emphasis: Faculty members bring substantial experience as media professionals to the classroom. We take a hands-on approach, and we expect our students to get plenty of real-world training in our state-of-the-art digital facilities as they complete their degrees. Each year, our top advertising students team up to produce a multimedia advertising campaign as part of a national competition. Many journalism majors work for the award-winning campus newspaper, the *Argonaut*. Other students work as DJs or news reporters for KUOI-FM, UI's student-operated radio station. Students also get the opportunity to produce television programs for UITV and to work on projects for Idaho Public Television, PBS, and Northwest Public Radio. Senior television production students showcase their work at an annual Digital Media Festival. In public rela-

tions courses, students design PR campaigns for local clients. Our students earn credit for their work as interns, and many spend their summers in newsrooms, at advertising or public relations agencies, or on television production crews.

Students Should Also Know

The University of Idaho School of Journalism and Mass Media (JAMM) combines hands-on professional programs with a liberal arts approach to the study of the mass media. It offers bachelor's degrees in journalism, radio-TV-digital media production, advertising, and public relations. The curriculum is based on a premise that journalists, broadcasters, public relations professionals, and advertising executives should be broadly educated. Accordingly, students must take at least 80 of the 128 credits needed for graduation outside the school.

UNIVERSITY OF ILLINOIS AT URBANA-CHAMPAIGN

901 West Illinois Street, Urbana, IL 61801
Phone: 217-333-0302 **E-mail:** ugradadmissions@uiuc.edu
Website: www.uiuc.edu

Campus Life

Environment: City. **Calendar:** Semester.

Students and Faculty
(All Undergraduate Programs)

Enrollment: 30,909. **Student Body:** 47% female, 53% male, 11% out-of-state, 5% international (111 countries represented). African American 7%, Asian 13%, Caucasian 68%, Hispanic 6%. Student/faculty ratio: 14:1. 2,271 full-time faculty, 87% hold PhDs. 77% faculty teach undergrads.

Admissions
(All Undergraduate Programs)

Freshman Admissions Requirements: Test(s) required: SAT or ACT. 48% in top tenth, 86% in top quarter. SAT Math (25/75 percentile): 620/730. SAT Verbal (25/75 percentile): 560/670. Projected SAT Writing (25/75 percentile): 610/700. *Academic units* *required:* 4 English, 3 math, 2 science (2 science labs), 2 foreign language, 2 social studies, 2 academic electives. Regular application deadline: 1/2. Regular notification: Rolling.

Costs and Financial Aid (All Undergraduate Programs)

Annual in-state tuition $7,708. Out-of-state tuition $21,794. Room & board $7,176. Required fees $2,174. Average book expense $1,000.

Financial Aid Statistics: % freshmen/undergrads who receive any aid: 65/60. % freshmen/undergrads who receive need-based scholarship or grant aid: 38/38. % freshmen/undergrads who receive need-based self-help aid: 34/38. Priority financial aid filing deadline: 3/15. Financial aid notification on or about: 3/15.

TV/Film/Digital Media Studies Programs

Number of undergraduates in these programs: 222

Number of 2005 graduates from these programs: 72

Degrees conferred to these majors: BA, BS.

Also available at University of Illinois at Urbana-Champaign: MA, MS, DFA.

Number of full-time faculty in these programs: 21

Number of part-time faculty in these programs: 6

Equipment and facilities: ENG Field Units: six Sony DSR-300L DVCAM camcorders, five Sony DSR-250 DVCAM camcorders. ENG editing: two Sony linear edit bays (DSR-60 DVCAM player, DSR-1800 DVCAM edit recorder, RM-450 edit controller), 17 Avid Xpress Pro HD V5.2 nonlinear editing systems. Audio production: Arrakis 500SCT-8M, two Arrakis 150SCT-6M consoles, Adobe Audition 1.5 nonlinear audio editing software, Software Audio Workshop (SAW), 6.4 nonlinear audio editing software, Digilink on-air radio software. Studio production: EZNews (Integrated news production and automation system software), two Sony DXC-300A 3-chip cameras, Sony BCS-3200C television production switcher with Chromakey Chryon Lyric character generator, Arrakis 500SCT-

8M audio console. The Theater Department prepares students for careers in television and film through acting and directing. They gain experiences in this area at The Krannert Center for the Performing Arts. The center features four indoor theaters with a total audience capacity of nearly 4,000. It is most famous for the excellent acoustics of its concert hall, the Foellinger Great Hall, designed by renowned acoustician Cyril Harris. Other venues include the multipurpose Tryon Festival Theater, the Colwell Playhouse, and the intimate Studio Theater. An outdoor amphitheater provides a unique site for student productions and a music festival held each summer. Two decades ahead of its time, Krannert Center was designed for complete wheelchair accessibility. Infrared hearing amplification systems have been added to all four indoor theaters.

ATAS College TV Awards recipients: 4

% of graduates currently employed in related field: 80

Career development services: Alumni networking opportunities, career counseling, internship listings, job fairs, job listings.

Famous alumni: John Chancellor, Hal Bruno, Dennis Swanson, Roger Ebert, Bill Geist, Rick Kaplan, Ang Lee, Alan Ruck, Lynne Thigpen.

Notable alumni: Steve Osunsami, correspondent, ABC News; Sandra Hughes, correspondent, CBS News; Ash-Har Quraishi, bureau chief, CNN, Islamabad, Pakistan; Elaine Quijano, correspondent, CNN; Drew Griffin, investigative correspondent, CNN; Ryan Baker, sports anchor, WMAQ-TV, Chicago; Eric Horng, correspondent, ABC News; Philip Krupp, executive vice president, Braun Entertainment Group, Inc.; Ross Cavitt, reporter, WSB-TV, Atlanta; Judy Hsu, anchor, WLS-TV, Chicago; Kyung Lah, correspondent, CNN; Anne Woodward, director of technical operations, CNN International; Demetria Kalodimos, anchor, WSMV-TV, Nashville; Sophia Tsiliyanni, anchor, Alpha Television, Athens, Greece; Robert Johnson, founder and CEO, Black Entertainment; Laura Bauer, costume designer, Broadway, television, and films (including films by Woody Allen); Mark

Brokaw, director, both on and off Broadway, and winner of the Obie Award for his direction of Paula Vogel's *How I Learned to Drive*; Michael Colgrass, composer and writer, received an Emmy Award in 1982 for a PBS documentary *Soundings: The Music of Michael Colgrass*; Robert Falls, artistic director, the Goodman Theater, Tony Award-winning director for *Death of a Salesman* in 1999; Michael Filerman, recently produced *Tea at Five* on Broadway, starring Kate Mulgrew as Katharine Hepburn, television background includes developing and executive producing the long-running series *Knots Landing*, *Falcon Crest*, and *Dallas*; Dominic Fumusa, actor on and off Broaway, in such productions as *Wait Until Dark* with Marisa Tomei, many soap-opera credits, currently a regular on *The Sopranos*; Adam Graham, actor, singer; Richard Greenberg, CEO, R. Greenberg & Associates, a graphic design firm, famous for visual effects consultation on Hollywood films; Robert Greenblatt, head of his own production company, Greenblatt/Janollari Studios, produced such TV series as *The Hughley's*, *Melrose Place*, *The X-Files*; A. C. Hickox, freelance lighting designer in New York, senior theatrical designer, Domingo Gonzalez Design, an architectural lighting design firm; Mary Elizabeth Masterantonio, actress, significant supporting roles in *Scarface* (1983), *The Color of Money* (1986, earned her an Academy Award nomination for Best Supporting Actress), *The Abyss* (1989); Jerome B. Orbach (deceased), renowned TV and film actor who started on Broadway, best known for his roles in the film *Dirty Dancing* and TV shows *The Law and Harry McGraw* and *Beauty and the Beast*, played Lennie Briscoe on *Law & Order*; Peter Palmer, actor, *Lil Abner* (1956), *Edward Scissorhands* (1990), cinematographer, *Hellgate* (1989), at least 50 years in show business; Barbara Robertson, film and television credits include *David Lynch's Straight Story* (1999), *Soul Survivors* (2001), *Will of Their Own* (NBC), *Early Edition*, *The Untouchables*, *In the Best Interests of the Children*, and *A Mother's Courage* (Disney); Fred Rubin, leading writer/producer for TV series including *Night Court*, *Diff'rent Strokes*, and

Family Matters; Donald L. Bitzer, Robert Willson, and the late H. Gene Slottow received a Technical Achievement Emmy for their invention of the plasma display monitor—forerunner of the modern flat panel television screen; Christopher C. Landreth won the 2005 Academy Award for Best Animated Short Film *Ryan*, his second Oscar nomination.

In Their Own Words

The Department of Journalism at the University of Illinois at Urbana-Champaign has earned a national reputation as a world-class program with a long-standing commitment to providing students with a complete journalism education. For more than 75 years, the College of Communications program has been teaching people how to become fair, balanced, ethical journalists, and it is consistently ranked among the top 10 journalism programs in the country. The college is also the birthplace of public broadcasting and the alma mater of Pulitzer Prize winners and Emmy Award winners. Among the faculty members are two Pulitzer Prize winners and successful journalists who practice what they teach. UI journalism students receive internships at major news organizations and often move into full-time employment with those same organizations, serving in decision-making and leadership roles in a variety of journalism careers.

POPULAR PROGRAMS

THEATER

Department chair: Robert Graves
Number of full-time faculty: 15
Number of part-time faculty: 4
Focus/emphasis: Prepares students for careers in theater, film, television, commercials, directing, stage, lighting, costume industries, etc. Students' classrooms are the stage and studio. Most classes, rehearsals, workshops, and productions are housed in the Krannert Center for the Performing Arts, one of the finest and most active theater complexes in the nation. Krannert Center

attracts dozens of internationally renowned artists each year, and Department of Theater students regularly work with them on productions and workshops. One of the medium rehearsal spaces is completely equipped as a television studio for classroom projects and for the teaching of acting for the camera and television lighting. It is equipped with three color cameras, two monitors, switchers, mixing control boards, and television lighting equipment.

BROADCAST JOURNALISM

Department chair: Walt Harrington
Number of full-time faculty: 6
Number of part-time faculty: 2
Focus/emphasis: Prepares students for varied and long-term careers as journalists for newspapers, magazines, radio, television, and online media, with the primary aim of training students as public affairs journalists. The Journalism Department seeks to prepare broadly educated professionals who will assume decision-making and leadership roles.

Students Should Also Know

The University of Illinois has active programs in graphic design in the College of Fine and Applied Arts and graphic engineering in the College of Engineering, but they are not degree programs, so we are not able to count individual students who enroll or graduate in them. Many hundreds of students take classes in these areas every year and obtain internships and jobs with companies every year. Additionally, many of our English, journalism, political science, sociology, psychology, and engineering majors enter careers in TV, film, and digital media every year.

UNIVERSITY OF MASSACHUSETTS– LOWELL

Office of Undergrad Admissions, 883 Broadway Street Room 110, Lowell, MA 01854-5104
Phone: 978-934-3931 **E-mail:** admissions@uml.edu
Website: www.uml.edu

Campus Life
Environment: City. **Calendar:** Semester.

Students and Faculty
(All Undergraduate Programs)
Enrollment:. **Student Body:** 12% out-of-state. Student/faculty ratio: 15:1. 383 full-time faculty. 90% faculty teach undergrads.

Admissions
(All Undergraduate Programs)
Freshman Admissions Requirements: Test(s) required: SAT or ACT. Average high school GPA: 3.14. 13% in top tenth, 39% in top quarter. *Academic units required:* 4 English, 3 math, 3 science (2 science labs), 2 foreign language, 2 social studies, 2 academic electives. Regular notification: Rolling.

Costs and Financial Aid
(All Undergraduate Programs)
Annual in-state tuition $1,454. Out-of-state tuition $8,567. Room & board $6,311. Required fees $6,712. Average book expense $600.
Financial Aid Statistics: % freshmen/undergrads who receive any aid: 94/92. % freshmen/undergrads who receive need-based scholarship or grant aid: 44/42. % freshmen/undergrads who receive need-based self-help aid: 38/42. Priority financial aid filing deadline: 3/1. Financial aid notification on or about: 3/25.

TV/Film/Digital Media Studies Programs
Number of undergraduates in these programs: 389 (undgraduate), 2 (graduate).
Number of 2005 graduates from these programs: 25
Degrees conferred to these majors: BFA.
Also available at University of Massachusetts— Lowell: BM, MM.

Number of full-time faculty in these programs: 3

Number of part-time faculty in these programs: 4

Equipment and facilities: 6 recording control rooms, state-of-the-art recording studio, critical listening studio.

Other awards of note: TEC award for Outstanding Recording School/Program.

% of graduates who pursue further study within 5 years: 10

% of graduates currently employed in related field: 85

Career development services: Alumni networking opportunities, career counseling, internship listings, job fairs, job listings.

In Their Own Words

Internships required. The Sound Recording Technology (SRT) Program at the University of Massachusetts–Lowell is one of the few programs in the United States that offers this course of study and provides the motivated student with the practical and theoretical background needed for success in the industry. We have faculty that are well-trained educators and active industry professionals, drawn from the wealth of high-technology, broadcasting, recording, and production talent in the greater Boston area.

POPULAR PROGRAMS

FINE ARTS-GRAPHIC DESIGN

Department chair: Dr. James Coates

Focus/emphasis: This program is designed for students who seek knowledge of the basic art processes and an opportunity to develop specialized skills in an area of concentration within the fine arts or graphic design degree areas.

SOUND RECORDING TECHNOLOGY

Department chair: Dr. William Moylan

Focus/emphasis: Students enroll in certain specific courses for their specialization in the sophomore year; retention in the program requires an application to the program coordinator prior to the junior year. This program is designed to provide graduates with in-depth knowledge of current and experimental audio technologies, sound recording technology, production practice, and research practices and techniques. Graduates of the program will be well qualified to assume significant technological and artistic responsibilities in the audio-related industries. These industries are well represented in our region and have a strong presence throughout the world.

UNIVERSITY OF MIAMI

Office of Admission, PO Box 248025, Coral Gables, FL 33124-4616
Phone: 305-284-4323 **E-mail:** admissions@miami.edu
Website: www.miami.edu

Campus Life
Environment: Town. **Calendar:** Semester.

Students and Faculty
(All Undergraduate Programs)
Enrollment: 9,741. **Student Body:** 59% female, 41% male, 45% out-of-state, 6% international. African American 9%, Asian 6%, Caucasian 52%, Hispanic 24%. Student/faculty ratio: 13:1. 877 full-time faculty, 87% hold PhDs.

Admissions
(All Undergraduate Programs)
Freshman Admissions Requirements: Test(s) required: SAT or ACT. Average high school GPA: 4.04. 62% in top tenth, 88% in top quarter. SAT Math (25/75 percentile): 590/680. SAT Verbal (25/75 percentile): 570/670. Projected SAT Writing (25/75 percentile): 620/700. Early decision application deadline: 11/1. Regular application deadline: 2/1. Regular notification: 4/15.

Costs and Financial Aid
(All Undergraduate Programs)
Annual tuition $29,020. Room & board $8,906. Required fees $483. Average book expense $830.

Financial Aid Statistics: % freshmen/undergrads who receive need-based scholarship or grant aid: 55/52. % freshmen/undergrads who receive need-based self-help aid: 41/43. Priority financial aid filing deadline: 2/15. Financial aid notification on or about: 3/15.

TV/Film/Digital Media Studies Programs

Degrees conferred to these majors: BA.

Equipment and facilities: The School of Communication provides a wide range of facilities and related equipment to students, including broadcast and film studios, photography and computer laboratories, a reading room, a cinema, a radio station, and a cable TV channel. The school currently owns Mac-based Avid nonlinear editing systems. Three of them are broadcast-quality PCI bus Media Composers (MC 1000) with the film option, and the fourth is a NewsCutter. The NewsCutter is housed in LC 150-B and is used by Broadcast Journalism students. In addition, the school has six Avid Xpress DV PC-based workstations and four Avid Xpress Mac-based workstations for motion picture students. The School of Communication also has two fully equipped television studios and control rooms that are used for producing UMTV programs, as well as teaching video production and broadcast journalism courses. Studio B is 30' by 30' and includes the AP News Center with 16 computers and two servers. It is equipped with three CCD Sony cameras. The control room includes a Ross switcher, a Chyron CG, four U-MATIC recorders, a Beta SP recorder/player, and an Air Trak audio board. The control room includes a Ross switcher, a Chyron CG, three U-MATIC recorders, a Beta SP recorder/player, an Air Trak audio board, and eight Shure wireless microphones. Located next to the cable studios, the School of Communication's soundstage is a 40' X 40' space fully equipped with grip and lighting equipment for motion picture production. The grip equipment includes a fully loaded taco cart, dedicated dolly, and jib arm. This soundstage is used by undergraduates and graduates for film projects and also as a teaching space for cinematography courses. The School of Communication's computer facilities, the Macintosh labs in Frances L. Wolfson 3032 and 3033, and the PC labs in Frances L. Wolfson 3034 and 3035, are open for use to communication students or students taking communication courses when no classes are being taught. These labs are designed to mirror one another as closely as possible in software applications. UMTV is the University of Miami's cable television channel, owned and operated by the School of Communication. It is carried on AT&T Broadband and can be seen throughout the university on channel 40 as well as the surrounding Coral Gables community on channel 96. The cable channel provides local programming throughout the fall and spring semesters. A large part of this programming is student produced.

In Their Own Words

The School of Communication's internship program enables students to seek communication-related positions for academic credit or not in the South Florida area during the academic year. It is also possible for students to intern in their hometown during the summer. This program is designed to provide students with quality career-related work experience prior to graduation. They can arrange the work hours to accommodate their academic schedule. One of the advantages of attending the University of Miami School of Communication is the city itself. South Florida offers a wealth of internship opportunities in journalism, motion pictures, broadcasting, public relations, advertising, and other industries.

POPULAR PROGRAMS

BROADCASTING

Department chair: Paul Driscoll

Focus/emphasis: Students study all aspects of television, radio, and cable operations toward a career working as producers, directors, etc. Sample courses taken by students include broadcast and cable programming, social control of broadcast and cable media, and broadcast sales. Students consistently win Emmys and first place awards in national broadcasting competitions. Both a major and a minor are offered in broadcasting. After completing core broadcasting courses, students elect additional courses in the specialized areas of broadcasting, cable, and telecommunication. Students specializing in broadcasting are prepared for professional careers in broadcast and cable production and operations. All broadcasting students are encouraged to become involved in UMTV, the campus cable television channel that has a potenial viewership of 600,000 cable subcribers, or the student-run radio station, WVUM-FM, a 1.3 kilowatt station serving South Florida.

BROADCAST JOURNALISM

Department chair: Paul Driscoll

Focus/emphasis: Students work in the media as a writer, reporter, or news anchor. Sample courses taken by students include news reporting and writing, electronic media production, and social control of broadcast and cable media. Students consistently win Emmys and first place awards in national broadcasting competitions, including the Society of Professional Journalists. A major is offered in broadcast journalism. After completing core broadcasting courses, students elect additional courses in the specialized area of broadcast journalism. Broadcast journalism emphasizes writing skills and requires that students take course work in a combination of political science, history, or economics. Students are prepared for professional careers in broadcast news and allied fields. All broadcast journalism students are encouraged to become involved in UMTV, the campus cable television channel that has a viewership of 600,000 cable subcribers, or the student-run radio station, WVUM-FM, a 1.3 kilowatt station serving South Florida.

MOTION PICTURE

Department chair: Paul N. Lazarus, III

Focus/emphasis: Offers a complete program for majors, including writing, production, the business of film, and film studies. Students graduating from the program have not only studied motion picture theory, but have also had the opportunity to learn how to script a film or television program,

produce that program (lighting, sound, set design, photography, and editing), and how to promote and market a film or television production. Sample courses offered in the program include history of motion pictures, legal aspects of motion pictures, electronic media production and editing, and scriptwriting. Student films have been accepted by Sundance and film festivals in New York, London, and throughout the world. A major is offered in motion pictures. Minors are offered in motion pictures and motion picture film studies. Motion picture majors may elect to specialize in one of four areas: production, screenwriting, business, or film studies. Production and screenwriting specialties allow students to concentrate in narrative film, documentary, animation, or experimental filmmaking. Most production courses utilize a 16 mm motion picture format. Film studies examines the history, theory, and criticism of film, while the business specialization concentrates on financing, distribution, and related aspects of the industry.

VIDEO/FILM

Department chair: Paul N. Lazarus, III

Focus/emphasis: Emphasizes production and includes courses in both motion picture and video production. Special facilities in the motion picture program include Bill Cosford Cinema, a site for the showing of first-run and alternative films; Avid nonlinear editing suites; and digital production and postproduction tools. The Canes Film Festival showcasing UM undergraduate and graduate films is held every year on campus with additional screenings in Los Angeles. Special programs include the summer Film Program in Prague, Czech Republic; the summer Film Program in England and Ireland; and an annual trip to Los Angeles that offers an opportunity to meet with film and television professionals.

VISUAL COMMUNICATION

Department chair: Lelen Bourgoignie-Robert

Focus/emphasis: Emphasizes the convergence of digital media, combining photography, print design, web design, new media, and video into a program that enhances the power of visual story-telling. Sample courses in the major include photography, multimedia, Web design, and electronic media production. Alumni of the program include award-winning journalists with *Time Magazine*, Agence France Presse, AP, and leading newspapers and websites. Students are required to take a mixture of theory and skills courses. After completing the core visual communication courses, students elect an additional seven courses in the specialized areas of photography, design, Web/new media, and video.

UNIVERSITY OF MINNESOTA–TWIN CITIES

240 Williamson Hall, 231 Pillsbury Drive Southeast, Minneapolis, MN
55455-0213
Phone: 612-625-2008
Website: www.umn.edu

Campus Life
Environment: Metropolis. **Calendar:** Semester.

Students and Faculty
(All Undergraduate Programs)
Enrollment: 28,957. **Student Body:** 53% female, 47% male, 26% out-of-state, 2% international. African American 5%, Asian 9%, Caucasian 79%, Hispanic 2%. Student/faculty ratio: 15:1. 1,680 full-time faculty, 69% hold PhDs.

Admissions
(All Undergraduate Programs)
Freshman Admissions Requirements: Test(s) required: SAT or ACT; ACT with Writing component. 34% in top tenth, 74% in top quarter. SAT Math (25/75 percentile): 570/690. SAT Verbal (25/75 percentile): 540/660. Projected SAT Writing (25/75 percentile): 600/690. *Academic units required:* 4 English, 3 math, 3 science, 2 foreign language, 3 social studies, 1 history.

Costs and Financial Aid
(All Undergraduate Programs)
Annual in-state tuition $6,590.88. Out-of-state tuition $17,326.08. Average book expense $900.
Financial Aid Statistics: % freshmen/undergrads who receive need-based scholarship or grant aid: 36/35. % freshmen/undergrads who receive need-based self-help aid: 42/43.

TV/Film/Digital Media Studies Programs
Number of undergraduates in these programs: 600
Degrees conferred to these majors: BA.
Number of full-time faculty in these programs: 12
Number of part-time faculty in these programs: 4

In Their Own Words
The study of human communication has been valuable to our students, and they have gone on to a variety of career opportunities after graduation. The ability to communicate clearly and persuasively is highly valued by employers in many fields. Many BA graduates in communication studies have found work in the business world (sales, management, human resources), social services, education, and government (information specialists, speechwriters, training and development), along with many of the newer information sector careers, including public information specialists, electronic media writing and production, marketing, advertising, and public relations. Our graduates have found communication studies a useful foundation for professional studies in law, medicine, journalism, and business. Local business and social service organizations offer a variety of internship opportunities for students to apply course concepts to issues in actual communication situations. The Career and Community Learning Center (135 Johnston Hall) coordinates a variety of internships that communication studies students may be interested in (612-624-7577). The undergraduate advising office (278 Ford Hall) also receives internship announcements that are posted on the bulletin boards outside the office.

Students are encouraged to begin studying career options and making job search plans early in their junior year. The CLA Communications and Media Student Advising Community also has pages with relevant event information and scholarship, job, and internship information that you may find useful.

POPULAR PROGRAMS

COMMUNICATION STUDIES

Department chair: Ronald Walter Greene
Number of full-time faculty: 12
Number of part-time faculty: 4
Focus/emphasis: This program pursues a wide range of interests including the criticism of public discourse, interpersonal communication, language and gender, small group communication, discourse analysis, intercultural communication, mass media studies, feminist and African American rhetoric, communication theory, and rhetorical theory. We offer courses focusing on social scientific approaches to communication that deal with human interaction in a variety of contexts, spanning interpersonal, group, and intercultural settings. Our faculty members have interests in topics such as communication in personal relationships, message formation, and processing in group decision making, language usage, conflict situations, persuasive campaigns, and intercultural communication settings. Our courses in rhetoric and public address treat speech and communication as a humanistic/critical study. As such, rhetoric conceives discourse as a process of establishing, maintaining, negotiating, and opposing social truths. Courses in this area emphasize argumentation and persuasion, rhetorical theory and criticism, American public address, the rhetoric of diverse groups and cultures, and the study of ethics in public communication. Our studies in electronic media focus on historical, structural, cultural, and critical aspects of domestic, foreign, and international electronic media. Interest areas of our media faculty include historical development of media, media programming, and audience impacts, critical/ethical evaluation of radio, TV, and a variety of new electronic media.

UNIVERSITY OF MISSOURI– COLUMBIA

230 Jesse Hall, Columbia, MO 65211
Phone: 573-882-7786 **E-mail:** MU4U@missouri.edu
Website: www.missouri.edu

Campus Life
Environment: City. **Calendar:** Semester.

Students and Faculty
(All Undergraduate Programs)
Enrollment: 21,046. **Student Body:** 52% female, 48% male, 19% out-of-state, 1% international (119 countries represented). African American 6%, Asian 3%, Caucasian 85%, Hispanic 2%. Student/faculty ratio: 18:1. 1,066 full-time faculty, 91% hold PhDs. 100% faculty teach undergrads.

Admissions
(All Undergraduate Programs)
Freshman Admissions Requirements: Test(s) required: SAT or ACT. 27% in top tenth, 57% in top quarter. SAT Math (25/75 percentile): 540/650. SAT Verbal (25/75 percentile): 540/660. Projected SAT Writing (25/75 percentile): 600/690. *Academic units required:* 4 English, 4 math, 3 science (1 science lab), 2 foreign language, 3 social studies, 1 fine arts. Regular notification: Rolling.

Costs and Financial Aid
(All Undergraduate Programs)
Annual in-state tuition $6,960. Out-of-state tuition $16,085. Room & board $6,540. Required fees $898. Average book expense $920.
Financial Aid Statistics: % freshmen/undergrads who receive any aid: 62/57. % freshmen/undergrads who receive need-based scholarship or grant aid: 39/36. % freshmen/undergrads who receive need-based self-help aid: 35/35. Priority financial aid filing

deadline: 3/1. Financial aid notification on or about: 4/1.

TV/Film/Digital Media Studies Programs
Degrees conferred to these majors: BA.
Number of full-time faculty in these programs: 86
Career development services: Career counseling, internship listings, job listings.
Famous alumni: Elizabeth Vargas (1984), broadcast journalism, co-anchor, *ABC World News Tonight*; Chuck Roberts (1971), broadcast journalism, anchor, CNN Headline News; Major Garrett, (1984), broadcast journalism, field reporter, Fox News.

In Their Own Words

The Missouri School of Journalism has awarded its Missouri Honor Medal for Distinguished Service in Journalism since 1930. Medalists are selected by the faculty of the school on the basis of lifetime or superior achievement, for distinguished service performed in lines of journalistic endeavor such as shall be selected each year for consideration. The annual awards shall not be restricted necessarily to any particular forms of journalistic service, nor will there be, necessarily, any designated number voted annually by the school. The award, or Medal of Honor, in each instance shall consist of a bronze medal, uniform in size, of appropriate design, and suitably inscribed with the recipient's name. Awards shall be made only to those people who, on invitation, are present in person to receive them, or in the case of newspapers, periodicals, radio and television stations, or other organizational entities, when such are represented in person by an official representative.

Students Should Also Know

Welcome to Mizzou, as the University of Missouri is widely known, where Walter Williams started the world's first school of journalism in 1908. Williams, first dean of the school, believed that journalism education should be professionalized and provided at a university. Today, many in the profession of journalism rank the Missouri School of Journalism not only as the first in the world, but also the best. In survey after survey, Missouri finishes at the top when broadcast and advertising executives and editors are asked, "What school does the best job of preparing students for work at your company?" We're proud of that success, which depends on much more than mere reputation. Each year, Missouri students win national contests—some even in competition with working professionals—that demonstrate conclusively just how much they have learned. Each year, our alumni win major national and international competitions, further illustrating the value of a Missouri journalism degree. Many have won Pulitzer Prizes, the news profession's highest honor; Silver Anvils, the top prize for public relations professionals; and similar awards. Indeed, our alumni can be found in newsrooms and corporate boardrooms of media companies and advertising and public relations agencies around the globe. From the beginning, Williams envisioned a school of journalism that would positively influence the quality of journalism and advertising worldwide. Williams made certain that the lessons of Missouri Journalism reached worldwide by training journalists from China and bringing a World Press Congress to Missouri. He also wrote *The Journalist's Creed*, a statement of journalism and advertising professionalism cherished as the most important pronouncement of its kind. It adorns the walls of the National Press Club in Washington in bronze. But perhaps Williams's greatest achievement was his establishment of the school around an all-important principle: The best way to learn about journalism and advertising is to practice them.

UNIVERSITY OF MONTANA

Lommasson Center 103, Missoula, MT 59812
Phone: 406-243-6266 **E-mail:** admiss@umontana.edu
Website: www.umt.edu

Campus Life
Environment: City. **Calendar:** Semester.

Students and Faculty
(All Undergraduate Programs)
Enrollment: 11,302. **Student Body:** 53% female, 47% male, 27% out-of-state, 1% international (60 countries represented). Asian 1%, Caucasian 83%, Hispanic 1%, Native American 4%. Student/faculty ratio: 19:1. 547 full-time faculty, 80% hold PhDs. 99% faculty teach undergrads.

Admissions
(All Undergraduate Programs)
Freshman Admissions Requirements: Test(s) required: SAT or ACT. Average high school GPA: 3.24. 17% in top tenth, 41% in top quarter. SAT Math (25/75 percentile): 486/578. SAT Verbal (25/75 percentile): 508/585. *Academic units required:* 4 English; 3 math; 2 science (2 science labs); 3 social studies; 2 history; 2 academic electives; 2 foreign language, computer science, visual or performing arts, or vocational education. Regular notification: Rolling.

Costs and Financial Aid
(All Undergraduate Programs)
Annual in-state tuition $3,653. Out-of-state tuition $12,642. Room & board $5,646. Required fees $1,233. Average book expense $800.
Financial Aid Statistics: % freshmen/undergrads who receive any aid: 56/58. % freshmen/undergrads who receive need-based scholarship or grant aid: 38/42. % freshmen/undergrads who receive need-based self-help aid: 50/53. Priority financial aid filing deadline: 2/15. Financial aid notification on or about: 4/1.

TV/Film/Digital Media Studies Programs
Number of undergraduates in these programs: 175 (undergraduate)/16 (graduate)

Number of 2005 graduates from these programs: 44 (undergraduate)/5 (graduate)
Degrees conferred to these majors: BA.
Also available at The University of Montana: MFA.
Number of full-time faculty in these programs: 8
Number of part-time faculty in these programs: 7
Equipment and facilities: Television studio (statewide broadcasts, PBS) and student FM radio station, with all applicable equipment, used for extensive experiential instruction (production, direction, digital editing of news, documentaries, features). Media arts production studio; digital video cameras; lighting kits; five computer labs with 80 stations with the latest software for editing, composition, and animation.
Other awards of note: AEJMC Most Promising Professor Award to Denise Dowling.

% of graduates who pursue further study within 5 years: 10
% of graduates currently employed in related field: 60
Career development services: Alumni networking opportunities, career counseling, internship listings, job fairs, job listings.
Notable alumni: Don Oliver, national correspondent, NBC News; Shane Bishop, Emmy Award-winning producer, *Dateline NBC*; Jack Cloherty, Emmy Award-winning producer, *Dateline NBC*; Meg Oliver, correspondent, CBS News; Hilary Hutcheson, anchor, KPTV, Portland, OR; David Sirak, WPTV-TV news operations, Orlando FL; Terry Meyers, executive producer, WNBC-TV.

In Their Own Words
Five-time regional Emmy Award winners for Student Documentary Unit and other student-produced programs. Swept TV category for Society of Professional Journalists Northwest Chapter last two years. Numerous scholarships from BEA, NATAS-NW, NPPA, and others. Media arts students have own postproduction computer/software. Students are working in

varied areas–advertising, business, education, film/video production, and political organizations. *Alumni connections to Hollywood and film industry via Palmer West (produced* Requiem for a Dream*) and Gerald Molen (produced* Schindler's List, Jurassic Park*). Access to International Wildlife Film Festival and Big Sky Documentary Film Festival.*

POPULAR PROGRAMS

BROADCAST JOURNALISM (RADIO-TV)
Department chair: Ray Ekness
Number of full-time faculty: 3
Number of part-time faculty: 5
Focus/emphasis: Skills in reporting, writing, producing, photojournalism, and digital editing for radio and television through classroom instruction and experiential learning/field experience.

RADIO-TV/BROADCAST PRODUCTION
Department chair: Ray Ekness
Number of full-time faculty: 3
Number of part-time faculty: 5
Focus/emphasis: Intensive laboratory experience in producing and directing news, documentaries, and other programs, in addition to learning the basics of television photojournalism and digital editing.

DIGITAL ART/DESIGN
Department chair: Michael Murphy
Number of full-time faculty: 2
Focus/emphasis: The creation of works of digital art, design, and animation.

VIDEO PRODUCTION
Department chair: Michael Murphy
Number of full-time faculty: 3
Number of part-time faculty: 2
Focus/emphasis: The creation of narrative works of digital video, including fiction, documentary, experimental, and commercial work.

DIGITAL MOVIEMAKING
Department chair: Michael Murphy
Number of full-time faculty: 4
Number of part-time faculty: 1
Focus/emphasis: The training of writers and directors in the creation of digital movies.

Students Should Also Know
Students also have the opportunity to work with UM's athletics production facilities/equipment: FB stadium Griz Vision, state-of-the-art message center/screen (largest in I-AA, was brought in from Times Square in NYC), features game statistics, player profiles, digital replays, and shots of the crowd; Dahlberg Arena (basketball) big-screen live coverage of game action, crowd shots.

UNIVERSITY OF NEBRASKA– LINCOLN
1410 Q Street, Lincoln, NE 68588-0256
Phone: 402-472-2023 **E-mail:** admissions@unl.edu
Website: www.unl.edu

Campus Life
Environment: City. **Calendar:** Semester.

Students and Faculty
(All Undergraduate Programs)
Enrollment: 17,037. **Student Body:** 47% female, 53% male, 20% out-of-state, 3% international (112 countries represented). African American 2%, Asian 3%, Caucasian 85%, Hispanic 3%. Student/faculty ratio: 19:1. 1,048 full-time faculty, 94% hold PhDs.

Admissions
(All Undergraduate Programs)
Freshman Admissions Requirements: Test(s) required: SAT or ACT. 27% in top tenth, 54% in top quarter. SAT Math (25/75 percentile): 540/670. SAT Verbal (25/75 percentile): 530/660. Projected SAT Writing (25/75 percentile): 590/690. *Academic units required:* 4 English, 4 math, 3 science (1 science lab), 2 foreign language, 3 social studies. Regular application deadline: 5/1. Regular notification: Rolling.

Costs and Financial Aid
(All Undergraduate Programs)

Annual in-state tuition $4,530. Out-of-state tuition $13,440. Room & board $5,861. Required fees $1,068. Average book expense $920.

Financial Aid Statistics: % freshmen/undergrads who receive any aid: 42/44. % freshmen/undergrads who receive need-based scholarship or grant aid: 37/36. % freshmen/undergrads who receive need-based self-help aid: 33/38. Financial aid notification on or about: 4/15.

TV/Film/Digital Media Studies Programs

Number of undergraduates in these programs: 66

Number of 2005 graduates from these programs: 13

Degrees conferred to these majors: BA.

Number of full-time faculty in these programs: 9

Equipment and facilities: Television studio.

Career development services: Career counseling, central resource(s) for employers to browse headshots, writing samples, reels, internship listings, job fairs, job listings.

In Their Own Words

UNL is recognized nationally for its quality programs produced for Nebraska, regional, and national audiences.

POPULAR PROGRAMS

FILM STUDIES

Department chair: Wheeler Winston

Number of full-time faculty: 9

Focus/emphasis: This program is designed for students who wish to ultimately work in academic film studies and also for students who wish to understand film better as an art form, as part of popular culture, and as a major medium of communication.

FILM AND NEW MEDIA

Department chair: Paul Steger

Number of full-time faculty: 3

Number of part-time faculty: 2

Focus/emphasis: Film and digital video production and postproduction, screenwriting, new media design, digital media content, film special effects, virtual reality, website design, and computer animation.

BROADCAST JOURNALISM (RADIO-TV)

Department chair: Jerry Renaud

Number of full-time faculty: 5

Number of part-time faculty: 2

Focus/emphasis: Hands-on skill development in reporting, writing, producing, photojournalism, and digital editing.

UNIVERSITY OF NORTH CAROLINA AT CHAPEL HILL

Office of Undergraduate Admissions, Jackson Hall
Campus Box #2200, Chapel Hill, NC 27599-2200
Phone: 919-966-3621 **E-mail:** uadm@email.unc.edu
Website: www.unc.edu

Campus Life

Environment: Town. **Calendar:** Semester.

Students and Faculty
(All Undergraduate Programs)

Enrollment: 16,278. **Student Body:** 58% female, 42% male, 17% out-of-state, 1% international (107 countries represented). African American 11%, Asian 6%, Caucasian 74%, Hispanic 3%. Student/faculty ratio: 14:1. 1,382 full-time faculty, 90% hold doctorate/first professional degrees.

Admissions
(All Undergraduate Programs)

Freshman Admissions Requirements: Test(s) required: SAT or ACT; ACT with Writing component. Average high school GPA: 4.33. 74% in top tenth, 95% in top quarter. SAT Math (25/75 percentile):

610/700. SAT Verbal (25/75 percentile): 600/690. Projected SAT Writing (25/75 percentile): 650/720. *Academic units required:* 4 English, 3 math, 3 science (1 science lab), 2 foreign language (of same language), 2 social studies (1 U.S. history), 2 academic electives. Regular application deadline: 1/15. Regular notification: 1/31.

Costs and Financial Aid (All Undergraduate Programs)

Annual in-state tuition $3,205. Out-of-state tuition $17,003. Room & board $6,516. Required fees $1,408. Average book expense $900.

Financial Aid Statistics: % freshmen/undergrads who receive any aid: 65/58. % freshmen/undergrads who receive need-based scholarship or grant aid: 34/33. % freshmen/undergrads who receive need-based self-help aid: 15/19. Priority financial aid filing deadline: 3/1. Financial aid notification on or about: 3/15.

TV/Film/Digital Media Studies Programs

Number of undergraduates in these programs: 432

Number of 2005 graduates from these programs: 122

Degrees conferred to these majors: BA.

Number of full-time faculty in these programs: 12

Number of part-time faculty in these programs: 1

Equipment and facilities: We have a television studio, a convergence lab that serves as the newsroom for *Carolina Week* and *Carolina Connection*, 22 audio editing suites with Adobe Audition, 22 video-editing suites with Media 110s or Pinnacle, nine Canon XL1s, and 20 Opturas as digital field equipment. Swain Hall houses the core of the production facilities for the Department of Communication Studies, consisting of several large broadcast and recording studios, a hard-disk audio recording studio, equipment room, a primary instructional non-linear computer lab, and satellite nonlinear editing suites. The large broadcast and recording studios serve as rehearsal spaces, instructional spaces, and video and film studios. A nonlinear audio editing studio, featuring a 24-track 8-buss Mackie board with surround sound capabilities, operates as a control room for one of these studio spaces. Additionally, this studio contains a chroma-key set and sound isolation baffles. The equipment room, which serves both the faculty and students, inventories assets such as Sony PD-170 mini-DV cameras, Canon Xl-1s mini-DV cameras, field recorders, DATs, Bolex 16 mm cameras, Arri 16 mm cameras, Sony TRV-950 cameras, Sony HVR-Z1E HDV cameras, Mathews dolly with tracks, Mole-Richardson and Lowell light kits, and a large selection of microphones and accessories. The second floor of the production facility houses 14 G5 Apple workstations designed for NTSC video editing, web authoring and interactivity, animation, compositing, and audio production. Each station features a Sony DSR-20 (DSR-25) DVCAM deck and Sony NTSC monitor. In addition, HDV decks (Sony HVR-M10U) and cameras (Sony HVR-Z1E) are currently being integrated into the program in the HDV initiative. Final Cut Pro HD Studio, Flash Pro, Dreamweaver, PhotoShop, and AfterEffects are among the software packages used for instruction and media authoring. Furthermore, through our UNC community, students have access to several streaming media servers, student television, WXYC radio, and Podcast aggregation.

Other awards of note: In the past three years, our students have won two second place awards and a first in the Student Newscast Emmy competition for ATAS Foundation College Television Award Winners. Francesca Talenti (faculty), honorable mention at Sundance Film Festival, 2002; Gorham Kindem (faculty), Grand Festival Award at Berkeley Video & Film Festival, 2005; Sean Overbeeke (undergraduate), Priddy Bros. Triumph Award at 2005 Angelus Awards (largest student film festival in the world).

% of graduates currently employed in related field: 50

Career development services: Alumni networking opportunities, career counseling, internship listings, job fairs, job listings. There is a Career Services Director within the program. He helps students find internships and full-time jobs, and also works with alumni interested in switching jobs.

Famous alumni: Stuart Scott, Rick Dees, Michael Piller, Woody Durham, Rick Fox, William Irvin Morton, Peyton Reed, Scott Williams, Brad Doherty, Billy Crudup, Jeb Stewart, Eric Montross, Sam Perkins

Notable alumni: Ken Lowe, founder of Home & Garden Network; Fred Shropshire, anchor and reporter, WGN, Chicago; Melissa Sowry, field producer, ABC, Chicago; Brigida Mack, WSOC, Charlotte; Tim Nelson, WTVD, Durham.

In Their Own Words

Our students do internships in major markets across the country and have had internships at CNN, ESPN, and NBC (three interned with the Winter Olympics in Torino). Guest lecturers have included Lesley Stahl of CBS, Sam Donaldson of ABC, Larry King, Carol Lin of CNN, and Anne Garrels of NPR, just to name a few. Richard Griffiths of CNN comes each spring to recruit students and work with them on resume tapes. As part of our Summer Hollywood Internship Program, students intern with various production companies. As part of our London Summer Internship Program, students participate in internships with BBC and other media companies. We also host the Yearly Screen Arts Film and Media Series.

POPULAR PROGRAMS

MEDIA STUDIES AND PRODUCTION

Department chair: Dr. Dennis Mumby
Number of full-time faculty: 8
Focus/emphasis: As part of the larger Communication Studies department, Media Studies and Production is concerned with the historical, theoretical, and cultural contexts within which audio, video, film, new media, and popular culture are produced and experienced. We address these concerns by considering aesthetics and interpretation, media production and reception, and power and everyday life. Scholars in this area of the department focus on various international, national, and community media organiza-

tions, institutions, and interests, and on the purposes and impact of those operating at the forefront of technological innovations associated with global, national, and local communication and information networks. Besides coming to a theoretical understanding of media, the department also offers students at the undergraduate level the instruction and resources to create audio/visual productions in a wide variety of forms: narrative, documentary, experimental, animation/motion graphics, interactive/new media, and audio production. The department offers strong initiatives and is coupled with a Hollywood Internship program, the London Internship Program, and a minor in stage and screenwriting. In its production component, the department has among its goals: 1) The development of individual talent and the ability for the student to work in collaboration with others within a diverse and vibrant community; 2) the providing of as high a production standard possible, thereby allowing students the ability to create portfolios that will enable them to go on to graduate-level work in this realm or to begin employment in the professional world of audiovisual production; 3) the continuing development of internship programs, thereby helping the student gain a sense of integration in the global community. Master's and PhD students primarily deepen their theoretical understanding of media in this department but are encouraged to integrate production work into their thesis project if appropriate.

ELECTRONIC COMMUNICATION

Department chair: Dr. Charlie Tuggle
Number of full-time faculty: 4
Number of part-time faculty: 1
Focus/emphasis: To train television and radio news producers and reporters. We also train some students to be on-air talent. The mission statement of *Carolina Week*, which is the anchor of our program: "We are a supplementary news source for viewers in our area. As such, we will cover less hard/breaking news than a typical news operation might. We will be professional in all of

our dealings with the public and will do our best to be 'capital J' journalists. We will not shy away from 'bad' news, but we will seek out stories of courage, perseverance, and kindness. We will bring to light the good news, so we can celebrate, and the bad news, so we can work together to correct the problems we encounter. We will always treat others with dignity and respect."

UNIVERSITY OF NORTH CAROLINA– GREENSBORO

123 Mossman Building, Greensboro, NC 27402-6170
Phone: 336-334-5243 **E-mail:** admissions@uncg.edu
Website: www.uncg.edu

Campus Life
Environment: City. **Calendar:** Semester.

Students and Faculty
(All Undergraduate Programs)
Enrollment: 12,172. **Student Body:** 68% female, 32% male, 7% out-of-state. African American 20%, Asian 3%, Caucasian 70%, Hispanic 2%. Student/faculty ratio: 16:1. 771 full-time faculty, 81% hold PhDs. 100% faculty teach undergrads.

Admissions
(All Undergraduate Programs)
Freshman Admissions Requirements: Test(s) required: SAT or ACT; ACT with Writing component. Average high school GPA: 3.48. 14% in top tenth, 45% in top quarter. SAT Math (25/75 percentile): 470/580. SAT Verbal (25/75 percentile): 470/580. Projected SAT Writing (25/75 percentile): 540/630. *Academic units required:* 4 English, 3 math, 3 science (1 science lab), 2 foreign language, 1 social studies, 1 history, 1 academic elective. Regular application deadline: 8/1. Regular notification: Rolling.

Costs and Financial Aid
(All Undergraduate Programs)
Annual in-state tuition $4,056. Out-of-state tuition $25,992. Room & board $5,000. Required fees $2,838. Average book expense $1,314.

Financial Aid Statistics: % freshmen/undergrads who receive need-based scholarship or grant aid: 30/31. % freshmen/undergrads who receive need-based self-help aid: 39/42. Priority financial aid filing deadline: 3/1. Financial aid notification on or about: 4/1.

TV/Film/Digital Media Studies Programs
Number of undergraduates in these programs: 225
Number of 2005 graduates from these programs: 32
Degrees conferred to these majors: BA.
Also available at University of North Carolina— Greensboro: MFA.
Number of full-time faculty in these programs: 13
Number of part-time faculty in these programs: 6
Equipment and facilities: Television studio with 4 digital cameras, TelePrompTer, character generator; 16 mm Bolex and Arriflex sync sound cameras; Final Cut Pro editing labs; range of DV cameras; audio and lighting equipment.
Career development services: Career counseling, internship listings, job fairs. Department handles utilization of alumni for career advice and assistance.
Notable alumni: Jeff Clarke, president, KQED, San Francisco; Emily Spivey, writer, *Saturday Night Live*.

POPULAR PROGRAMS

FILM AND VIDEO PRODUCTION CONCENTRATION
Department chair: Dr. John Lee Jellicorse
Focus/emphasis: Designed for students pursuing careers in film and/or television production.

NEWS AND DOCUMENTARY CONCENTRATION
Focus/emphasis: Designed for students pursuing careers in broadcast journalism as on-air talent or writers/producers. Also designed for documentarians.

MEDIA WRITING CONCENTRATION

Focus/emphasis: Designed for students pursuing careers in fiction writing for film and/or television.

FILM AND TELEVISION STUDIES CONCENTRATION

Focus/emphasis: Designed for students considering postgraduate work in media studies, film criticism, or law school.

MEDIA MANAGEMENT CONCENTRATION

Focus/emphasis: Designed for students considering careers in radio, television, or motion picture management.

UNIVERSITY OF NORTH CAROLINA– PEMBROKE

One University Drive, PO Box 1510, Pembroke, NC 28372
Phone: 910-521-6262 **E-mail:** admissions@papa.uncp.edu
Website: www.uncp.edu

Campus Life

Environment: Rural. **Calendar:** Semester.

Students and Faculty
(All Undergraduate Programs)

Enrollment: 4,454. **Student Body:** 63% female, 37% male, 5% out-of-state. African American 24%, Asian 2%, Caucasian 47%, Hispanic 3%, Native American 22%. Student/faculty ratio: 16:1. 238 full-time faculty, 69% hold PhDs. 99% faculty teach undergrads.

Admissions
(All Undergraduate Programs)

Freshman Admissions Requirements: Test(s) required: SAT or ACT; ACT with Writing component. Average high school GPA: 3.05. 9% in top tenth, 30% in top quarter. SAT Math (25/75 percentile): 430/520. SAT Verbal (25/75 percentile): 420/510. Projected SAT Writing (25/75 percentile): 490/570. *Academic units required:* 4 English, 3 math, 3 science (1 science lab), 2 foreign language, 1 social studies, 1 history. Regular notification: Rolling.

Costs and Financial Aid
(All Undergraduate Programs)

Annual in-state tuition $3,809. Out-of-state tuition $13,187. Room & board $5,517. Average book expense $1,000.

Financial Aid Statistics: % freshmen/undergrads who receive any aid: 75/72. % freshmen/undergrads who receive need-based scholarship or grant aid: 61/58. % freshmen/undergrads who receive need-based self-help aid: 56/57. Priority financial aid filing deadline: 3/15. Financial aid notification on or about: 4/15.

TV/Film/Digital Media Studies Programs

Number of undergraduates in these programs: 70
Number of 2005 graduates from these programs: 12
Degrees conferred to these majors: BS.
Number of full-time faculty in these programs: 3
Number of part-time faculty in these programs: 3
Equipment and facilities: Chevy van for remote broadcasts (3-camera switching); television studio for live and taped shows; cable channel in the surrounding community; Macintosh lab for computer animation, digital image manipulation, video postproduction, etc.
ATAS Faculty Seminar participants: 1
Career development services: Career counseling, etiquette workshops, internship listings, interviewing workshops, job fairs, resume workshops.
Notable alumni: Newy Scruggs, sports anchor, Dallas.

In Their Own Words

One internship is required for graduation, and a second internship is elective. Students participate in a cable TV station and Internet radio station for credit, work-study, or volunteer work. We get out of the studio using our TV van to cablecast live basketball, wrestling, volleyball, and football (as of Fall 2007), as well as community events such as the Christmas parade. We offer a minor in media integration jointly with the art and music departments. The major is a

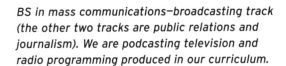

BS in mass communications–broadcasting track (the other two tracks are public relations and journalism). We are podcasting television and radio programming produced in our curriculum.

POPULAR PROGRAMS

BROADCASTING TRACK IN MASS COMMUNICATIONS
Department chair: Dr. Jamie Litty
Number of full-time faculty: 2
Number of part-time faculty: 1
Focus/emphasis: Covers both radio and TV concerns in lecture courses. Covers TV/video in production courses (and audio-for-video).

BROADCASTING MINOR
Department chair: Dr. Jamie Litty
Number of full-time faculty: 2
Number of part-time faculty: 1
Focus/emphasis: Covers both radio and TV concerns in lecture courses. Covers TV/video in production courses (and audio-for-video).

MEDIA INTEGRATION MINOR
Department chair: Interdisciplinary
Number of full-time faculty: 2
Number of part-time faculty: 2
Focus/emphasis: Convergence of digital art, video, music.

Students Should Also Know
Students can tailor their course projects to their personal interests. Some students make movies, for example, rather than pursuing only the stereotypical broadcasting genres, such as news.

UNIVERSITY OF NORTH CAROLINA– WILMINGTON

601 South College Road, Wilmington, NC 28403-5904
Phone: 910-962-3243 **E-mail:** admissions@uncw.edu
Website: www.uncw.edu

Campus Life
Environment: City. **Calendar:** Semester.

Students and Faculty
(All Undergraduate Programs)
Enrollment: 10,249. **Student Body:** 58% female, 42% male, 13% out-of-state. African American 5%, Asian 2%, Caucasian 89%, Hispanic 2%. Student/faculty ratio: 18:1. 491 full-time faculty, 87% hold PhDs. 100% faculty teach undergrads.

Admissions
(All Undergraduate Programs)
Freshman Admissions Requirements: Test(s) required: SAT or ACT; ACT with Writing component. Average high school GPA: 3.62. 21% in top tenth, 60% in top quarter. SAT Math (25/75 percentile): 540/610. SAT Verbal (25/75 percentile): 520/600. Projected SAT Writing (25/75 percentile): 580/650. *Academic units required:* 4 English, 3 math, 3 science (1 science lab), 2 foreign language, 2 social studies, 1 history, 5 academic electives. Regular application deadline: 2/1. Regular notification: 4/1.

Costs and Financial Aid
(All Undergraduate Programs)
Annual in-state tuition $1,928. Out-of-state tuition $11,863. Room & board $6,412. Required fees $1,767. Average book expense $1,000.
Financial Aid Statistics: % freshmen/undergrads who receive any aid: 54/58. % freshmen/undergrads who receive need-based scholarship or grant aid: 24/30. % freshmen/undergrads who receive need-based self-help aid: 24/31. Financial aid notification on or about: 4/1.

TV/Film/Digital Media Studies Programs
Number of undergraduates in these programs: 258
Number of 2005 graduates from these programs: 55

Degrees conferred to these majors: BA.

Number of full-time faculty in these programs: 6

Number of part-time faculty in these programs: 7

Equipment and facilities: Film studies has a growing arsenal of video and film equipment. The department uses Final Cut Pro and Adobe AfterEffects in the editing lab. Production courses are designed to familiarize students with equipment and all phases of production. The department boasts a new computer lab with 25 G5 Macs, and a production space; it also has smart classrooms, which handle all media forms. In addition, a new auditorium is being renovated for film studies use as classroom space and for film screenings. It will feature digital, 16 mm projection, and a 35 mm change-over system. A new 350-seat state-of-the art theater is being completed on campus; this will also be used for film studies classes and screenings.

Career development services: UNC—Wilmington has a proactive, high-energy Career Services division that provides students with one-on-one help, with everything from resume writing to finding a job. There is an expanding alumni network with graduates in the film business from Los Angeles to New York. The Film Studies Department also works closely with EUE Screen Gems, the production home to hundreds of independent films and television programs. Students intern, serve as extras, and occasionally actually get hired to be a part of a major motion picture set. The contacts made there and in the dozens of ancillary agencies provide students with the much-needed network to transition into the film business. There are also opportunities for students with the many production facilities in Wilmington, and opportunities to work with faculty on films and documentaries, which builds students' reel portfolio. The department has also initiated an internship program in Los Angeles, with another such program to begin in New York City in the summer of 2007.

In Their Own Words

The Film Studies Department prepares students to participate in a world increasingly shaped by moving pictures. Through courses that offer a foundation for understanding cinema—and its relation to culture, history, technology, and aesthetics—film studies teaches students to create and analyze moving images, to produce research, and to make art. The primary mission of the Department of Film Studies is to provide excellent undergraduate teaching in the study of cinema and the practice of making motion pictures. The department advances the production and scholarly understanding of motion pictures by employing experienced, talented film scholars and filmmakers and through activities in support of faculty and student scholarship, research, and creative work. The department is founded on the principle that the study of cinema and the artistic production of motion pictures complement each other, and all film studies majors perform substantial work in both areas. In critical studies courses, students learn the history, aesthetics, business, and social significance of film and filmmaking. Film production courses teach students to make their own fiction and nonfiction works, under the guidance of professional filmmakers. Courses in the Film Studies Department serve the university's liberal arts mission and develop skills and knowledge that students can apply to a variety of professions within and outside the film industry and to graduate study in film production, cinema studies, and other fields. Students in the program develop knowledge and skills in filmmaking and cinema studies, critical thinking, persuasive and creative writing, research and analysis, business and budgeting, visual design, computer use, and oral presentation.

POPULAR PROGRAMS

FILM STUDIES
Department chair: Dr. Lou Buttino
Number of full-time faculty: 6
Number of part-time faculty: 7
Focus/emphasis: Students learn to see film as an artistic medium, a cultural expression, a rhetorical device, a technical production, and a commercial enterprise. The major develops students' analytical, research, and writing skills, as well as their creative and technical abilities. Drawing on the expertise of department faculty, filmmaking professionals, and scholars and filmmakers in other departments in the College of Arts and Sciences and the Cameron School of Business, the Film Studies Department offers a variety of courses in the art, history, production, and business of film. Courses in the film studies major teach students to meet the following learning objectives: to communicate story, mood, character, and ideas cinematically; to understand the preproduction, production, and postproduction filmmaking process by conceiving, planning, writing, scheduling, budgeting, shooting, and editing motion pictures; to have a basic knowledge of how motion pictures are marketed, promoted, and distributed; to develop research and writing skills to compose cogent, persuasive, and valid essays about film; to have a broad knowledge of film styles, genres, and various national cinemas; to analyze closely the formal aspects of film, including narrative, cinematography, sound, script, genre, performance, editing, and other stylistic components; to understand the history of film, film criticism, film theory, and the relationship between film style and the modes of film production; to develop knowledge and skills applicable to work in the film industry and related fields and to graduate study in filmmaking and cinema studies.

Students Should Also Know
The department runs various film series, such as Cinema Nouveau (which deals with French cinema), and brings in other international films and documentaries. The department also runs a weekly MovieMakers and Film Scholars Series that showcases local and national filmmakers who talk to students and the public about their work and about the film industry. Featured presenters have included Academy Award-winner Jim Taylor (*Sideways*), Sundance winner Ira Sachs, and film actor Pat Hingle (*Batman*, *Splendor in the Grass*).

UNIVERSITY OF NORTH TEXAS
PO Box 311277, Denton, TX 76203-1277
Phone: 940-565-2681 **E-mail:** undergrad@unt.edu
Website: www.unt.edu

Campus Life
Environment: City. **Calendar:** Semester.

Students and Faculty
(All Undergraduate Programs)
Enrollment: 32,047. **Student Body:** 57% female, 43% male, 37% out-of-state, 4.5% international (137 countries represented). African American 12%, Asian 4%, Caucasian 67%, Hispanic 11%. Student/faculty ratio: 19:1. 936 full-time faculty. 83% faculty teach undergrads.

Admissions
(All Undergraduate Programs)
Freshman Admissions Requirements: Test(s) required: SAT or ACT. 19% in top tenth, 49% in top quarter. SAT Math (25/75 percentile): 500/610. SAT Verbal (25/75 percentile): 500/600. Projected SAT Writing (25/75 percentile): 560/650. *Academic units required:* 4 English, 3 math, 3 science, 2 foreign language, 2 social studies, 2 history. Regular application deadline: 8/19. Regular notification: Rolling.

Costs and Financial Aid
(All Undergraduate Programs)
Annual in-state tuition $2,107. Out-of-state tuition $16,232. Room & board $5,190.
Financial Aid Statistics: % freshmen/undergrads who receive any aid: 62/66. % freshmen/undergrads who receive need-based scholarship or grant aid: 36/37. % freshmen/undergrads who receive need-based self-help aid: 36/39. Priority financial aid filing deadline: 6/1. Financial aid notification on or about: 4/1.

TV/Film/Digital Media Studies Programs

Number of undergraduates
in these programs: 1,002

Number of 2005 graduates from these
programs: 140

Degrees conferred to these majors: BA.

Also available at University of North Texas:
MFA, MA, MS.

Number of full-time faculty in these
programs: 14

Number of part-time faculty in these
programs: 10

Equipment and facilities: New digital cameras
(field and studio), upgraded digital nonlinear editing stations, new film cameras for shooting for digital output.

Other awards of note: First place Feature
Screenplay in Great American Film Fest, first place
Documentary in Austin Film Festival, first place
Experimental in Sol Ross Film Festival, second
place Short Films in Great American Film Fest,
first place Documentary in University Film and
Video Association, Leah Bell named Emerging
Young Filmmaker by Kodak.

**% of graduates who pursue further study within 5
years:** 10

**% of graduates currently employed in related
field:** 55

Famous alumni: Phyllis George; Scott Murphy,
writer, *Angel*, Miramax Films; Matt Hirsch, production executive for studios; Michael Phillips, first
assistant director, *Prison Break*.

In Their Own Words

*Many students have won awards this past year
for screenplays, narrative film, experimental
film, and documentary films, as well as radio
news and TV news and shows.*

POPULAR PROGRAMS

RADIO, TELEVISION, FILM

Department chair: Dr. Alan Albarran
Number of full-time faculty: 14
Number of part-time faculty: 8

UNIVERSITY OF OKLAHOMA

1000 Asp Avenue, Norman, OK 73019-4076
Phone: 405-325-2252 **E-mail:** admrec@ou.edu
Website: www.ou.edu

Campus Life

Environment: City. **Calendar:** Semester.

Students and Faculty
(All Undergraduate Programs)

Enrollment: 20,967. **Student Body:** 51% female,
49% male, 23% out-of-state, 2% international (98
countries represented). African American 5%, Asian
5%, Caucasian 76%, Hispanic 4%, Native American
7%. Student/faculty ratio: 22:1. 1,276 full-time faculty,
84% hold PhDs.

Admissions
(All Undergraduate Programs)

Freshman Admissions Requirements: Test(s)
required: SAT or ACT. Average high school GPA:
3.63. 37% in top tenth, 72% in top quarter. *Academic
units required:* 4 English, 3 math, 2 science (2 science
labs), 2 social studies, 1 history, 3 academic electives.
Regular application deadline: 4/1. Regular notification: Rolling.

Costs and Financial Aid
(All Undergraduate Programs)

Annual in-state tuition $2,862. Out-of-state tuition
$10,755. Room & board $6,361. Required fees
$1,546. Average book expense $1,067.

Financial Aid Statistics: % freshmen/undergrads
who receive any aid: 75/74. % freshmen/undergrads
who receive need-based scholarship or grant aid:
11/17. % freshmen/undergrads who receive need-
based self-help aid: 39/38. Priority financial aid filing
deadline: 3/1. Financial aid notification on or about:
3/15.

TV/Film/Digital Media Studies Programs

Number of students in these programs: 301

Number of 2005 graduates from these
programs: 59

Number of part-time faculty in these
programs: 35

Degrees conferred to these majors: BA.
Number of full-time faculty in these programs: 26
Equipment and facilities: Edith Kinney Gaylord Library specializes in materials covering areas of interest to the five sequences of the college: Advertising, broadcasting, and electronic media, journalism, professional writing, and public relations. The College of Journalism and Mass Communication Macintosh computer labs are open to students enrolled in JMC courses approximately 70 hours each week, offering a wide array of software applications, including MS Office, Adobe PhotoShop, Illustrator, InDesign, GoLive and Acrobat Professional, Macromedia DreamWeaver, Flash and FreeHand, Final Cut Pro HD, SPSS, Final Draft, Roxio Toast/Easy CD Creator, and more. Only students currently enrolled in JMC broadcast classes may use the editing facilities, studio, or field equipment. Reservations for field gear may be made in master control. Reservations for editing time may be made on the sign-up sheets at the edit bays, audio production rooms, or Avid room. A signed equipment liability policy and agreement must be on file before a student can take out field equipment or use the production facilities. The Gaylord College of Journalism and Mass Communication has progressed into the digital age of photojournalism. Courses are taught in a state-of-the-art computer lab. Students produce assignments on film and scan negatives or on digital cameras. Students refine the images on the computer and submit them for evaluation. For more information on the computer lab schedule, please refer to the computer lab section of the JMC website. The FVS program has a multipurpose library that has six computer editing stations, more than 3,500 DVDs and videos, 700 books, and 300 screenplays in the library collection. There are also eight high-quality digital cameras, as well as audio equipment and three editing stations available to students for their academic and recreational film projects.

In Their Own Words

JMC Broadcasting and Electronic Media: Students are strongly encouraged to supple-ment traditional classroom experience with on-the-job training. The location of the college on the edge of a major metropolitan market in Oklahoma City will provide you with outstanding professional opportunities while you earn your degree. Such experience may come in the form of full-time or part-time positions with professional communication organizations and departments. Opportunities on campus range from reporting, editing, advertising sales, and print production to broadcast announcing and production. Students may seek volunteer and/or paid positions on The Oklahoma Daily newspaper; The WIRE, a music station broadcast on Cox Cable Channel 4; National Public Radio station KGOU; or the telecommunications center located within Copeland Hall, which produces live and pre-recorded programs for Norman cable television. Another work experience option is the college's internship program. Experience gained through the internship program may take the form of paid or unpaid positions. Students may arrange their own internships or choose one of the many positions offered through the college. Students who rely solely on course work as preparation for entry into the professional world are missing a valuable opportunity to expand their professional preparation and development through the completion of an internship. You may apply for internship credit if the eligibility requirements are met. Please note that credit internships are not for everyone. Internships are supervised, on-the-job learning experiences designed for highly motivated and able students who have demonstrated the best overall preparation for professional success. The credit internships also require the completion of academic work while the internship is in progress. You may elect not to seek academic credit for internships and may choose to regard the work experience itself as valuable real-life experience that adds to your preparation for first-time employment.

Film and Video Studies: This program offers numerous internships for credit in Hollywood,

New York, London, New Zealand, Greece, and many other locations, covering everything from feature filmmaking to documentary filmmaking to film archive work and film criticism and journalism. Students have, for instance, done internships on Lord of the Rings, Harry Potter, and other features, as well as television shows such as 24 and Judging Amy. The program also encourages overseas study with official semester or year-long programs in 67 nations including New Zealand, England, and France. A variety of film scholars and filmmakers are brought to campus to meet with students including in recent years scholars such as Tim Corrigan, David Bordwell, and John Belton, and filmmakers such as James Garner, Ed Harris, and Michael Moore, along with award-winning filmmakers coming from South Africa, New Zealand, Greece, England, France, and many other nations. Student films are submitted to a variety of festivals, including– each year–to the Clermont International Short Film Festival in France.

Students have won awards at major festivals including Sundance and Tribeca in New York, and go on to get good jobs in Oklahoma, Hollywood, New York, and around the world. Students greatly appreciate the great professors, the strong relationships among the students, and the good advising. They also speak of the courses as being fun and in-depth, including such topics as Iranian cinema, the horror film, film noir, TV comedy, violence and American cinema, Japanese cinema, and children's cinema. Students appreciate the study abroad opportunities, the visiting professors, and what film theory and history can teach them, even if they want to become filmmakers and not film historians. The FVS office is also the national home office for The Society For Cinema and Media Studies, the world's largest film studies organization.

POPULAR PROGRAMS

BROADCAST AND ELECTRONIC MEDIA (IN THE GAYLORD COLLEGE OF JOURNALISM AND MASS COMMUNICATION)
Focus/emphasis: For further information, visit www.jmc.ou.edu.

FILM AND VIDEO STUDIES PROGRAM (IN THE COLLEGE OF ARTS & SCIENCES)
Number of full-time faculty: 4
Number of part-time or associate faculty: 35
Focus/emphasis: The FVS Program specializes in film and media studies and requires courses such as film history, film theory, writing about film, and senior capstone. The program also offers production in the guerrilla cinema course, screenwriting, and acting for the camera.

For further information, visit www.ou.edu/fvs.

UNIVERSITY OF SOUTH ALABAMA
182 Administration Building, Mobile, AL 36688-0002
Phone: 334-460-6141 **E-mail:** admiss@jaguar1.usouthal.edu
Website: www.usouthal.edu

Campus Life
Calendar: Semester.

Students and Faculty
(All Undergraduate Programs)
Enrollment: 9,957. **Student Body:** 60% female, 40% male, 14% out-of-state, 5% international (102 countries represented). African American 18%, Asian 3%, Caucasian 68%, Hispanic 1%.

Admissions
(All Undergraduate Programs)
Freshman Admissions Requirements: Test(s) required: SAT or ACT. Average high school GPA: 3.07. SAT Math (25/75 percentile): 468/570. SAT Verbal (25/75 percentile): 460/605. Regular application deadline: 9/10. Regular notification: Rolling.

Costs and Financial Aid
(All Undergraduate Programs)
Annual in-state tuition $3,810. Out-of-state tuition $7,620. Room & board $4,428. Required fees $692.

Average book expense $1,000.

Financial Aid Statistics: % freshmen/undergrads who receive any aid: 70/70. % freshmen/undergrads who receive need-based scholarship or grant aid: 29/33. % freshmen/undergrads who receive need-based self-help aid: 32/41. Financial aid notification on or about: 5/15.

TV/Film/Digital Media Studies Programs

Number of undergraduates in these programs: 63

Number of 2005 graduates from these programs: 15

Degrees conferred to these majors: BA.

Also available at University of South Alabama: MA.

Number of full-time faculty in these programs: 3

Number of part-time faculty in these programs: 3

Equipment and facilities: Fully equipped television studio with DVCam recorders, mini-DV and DVC Pro cameras, Avid and Final Cut Pro nonlinear editing, Arri and Lowel light kits, Arriflex and Bolex 16 mm motion picture cameras, Eyemo Q 35 mm motion picture camera, 16 mm Moviola flatbed film editor, animation stand.

Career development services: Career counseling, job fairs, job listings.

UNIVERSITY OF SOUTH CAROLINA–COLUMBIA

Office of Undergraduate Admissions, University of South Carolina, Columbia, SC 29208
Phone: 803-777-7700 **E-mail:** admissions@sc.edu
Website: www.sc.edu

Campus Life
Environment: City. **Calendar:** Semester.

Students and Faculty
(All Undergraduate Programs)
Enrollment: 17,781. **Student Body:** 54% female, 46% male, 12% out-of-state, 1% international. African American 14%, Asian 3%, Caucasian 71%, Hispanic 2%. Student/faculty ratio: 19:1. 1,166 full-time faculty, 86% hold PhDs. 72% faculty teach undergrads.

Admissions
(All Undergraduate Programs)
Freshman Admissions Requirements: Test(s) required: SAT or ACT. Average high school GPA: 3.8. 26% in top tenth, 60% in top quarter. SAT Math (25/75 percentile): 540/640. SAT Verbal (25/75 percentile): 520/630. Projected SAT Writing (25/75 percentile): 580/670. *Academic units required:* 4 English, 3 math, 3 science (3 science labs), 2 foreign language, 2 social studies, 1 history, 4 academic electives, 1 physical education or ROTC. Regular application deadline: 12/1. Regular notification: Rolling.

Costs and Financial Aid
(All Undergraduate Programs)
Annual in-state tuition $6,914. Out-of-state tuition $18,556. Room & board $6,083. Required fees $400. Average book expense $785.

Financial Aid Statistics: % freshmen/undergrads who receive any aid: 95/83. % freshmen/undergrads who receive need-based scholarship or grant aid: 0/26. % freshmen/undergrads who receive need-based self-help aid: 0/41. Priority financial aid filing deadline: 4/1. Financial aid notification on or about: 4/1.

TV/Film/Digital Media Studies Programs
Degrees conferred to these majors: BA.

Equipment and facilities: The program hosts its fifth symposium on the preservation, study, and use of "orphan films." Orphans 5 focuses on neglected media artifacts related to science, industry, and education. These categories are broadly conceived, with presentations on industrial filmmaking, the role of cinematography in the history of science, moving images of industries, classroom movies, uses of media for an array of educational ends (political campaigns, news, training), formats developed for nontheatrical films, nature documentaries, the history of technology, and scientific and technological developments in film and media preservation. The Orphan Film Symposium brings together an eclectic mix of moving image archivists, cinema and media scholars, preservation experts, curators, and filmmakers who work with orphaned material. Speakers lead three days and four nights of presentations, screenings, and discussion, but all registrants are encouraged to participate in the discussion.

POPULAR PROGRAMS

FILM STUDIES

Department chair: Susan Courtney
Number of full-time faculty: 5
Focus/emphasis: Interdisciplinary program in the College of Liberal Arts devoted to the study of film from various humanistic perspectives. Courses in the program may apply to the college's fine arts and cognate requirements, as well as to a minor and a major.

UNIVERSITY OF SOUTH FLORIDA

4202 East Fowler Avenue, SVC-1036, Tampa, FL 33620-9951
Phone: 877-USF-BULL **E-mail:** admissions@admin.usf.edu
Website: www.usf.edu

Campus Life

Environment: Metropolis. **Calendar:** Semester.

Students and Faculty
(All Undergraduate Programs)

Enrollment: 32,898. **Student Body:** 59% female, 41% male, 4% out-of-state, 3% international (132 countries represented). African American 13%, Asian 6%, Caucasian 65%, Hispanic 11%. Student/faculty ratio: 18:1. 1,262 full-time faculty. 85% faculty teach undergrads.

Admissions
(All Undergraduate Programs)

Freshman Admissions Requirements: Test(s) required: SAT or ACT; ACT with Writing component. Average high school GPA: 3.54. 23% in top tenth, 59% in top quarter. SAT Math (25/75 percentile): 520/610. SAT Verbal (25/75 percentile): 510/600.

Projected SAT Writing (25/75 percentile): 570/650. *Academic units required:* 4 English, 3 math, 3 science (2 science labs), 2 foreign language, 3 social studies, 3 academic electives. Regular application deadline: 4/15. Regular notification: Rolling.

Costs and Financial Aid
(All Undergraduate Programs)

Annual in-state tuition $3,310. Out-of-state tuition $16,076. Room & board $6,900. Required fees $74. Average book expense $800.

Financial Aid Statistics: % freshmen/undergrads who receive any aid: 60/50. % freshmen/undergrads who receive need-based scholarship or grant aid: 22/26. % freshmen/undergrads who receive need-based self-help aid: 12/19. Priority financial aid filing deadline: 3/1. Financial aid notification on or about: 3/15.

TV/Film/Digital Media Studies Programs

Number of undergraduates in these programs: 200
Number of 2005 graduates from these programs: 90
Degrees conferred to these majors: BA.
Number of full-time faculty in these programs: 18
Number of part-time faculty in these programs: 20
Equipment and facilities: Telecommunications students at USF use a modern facility that includes two fully-equipped television studios as well as digital video electronic field production cameras and 12 Macintosh-based digital video nonlinear editing stations using Media 100 software with titling and effects. In addition, Betacam SP field production and editing equipment is used for producing advanced television magazine programs (30-minute shows). Seven computer laboratories support the television facilities. In all, more than 100 computers are available to support student projects.
Career development services: Career counseling, internship listings, job fairs, job listings.

POPULAR PROGRAMS

TELECOMMUNICATIONS PRODUCTION
Sequence advisor: Kenneth C. Killebrew
Number of full-time faculty: 5
Number of part-time faculty: 2
Focus/emphasis: News or entertainment production

TELECOMMUNICATIONS NEWS
Number of full-time faculty: 5
Number of part-time faculty: 2
Focus/emphasis: News reporting, anchoring, and producing.

UNIVERSITY OF SOUTHERN CALIFORNIA

Admissions Office: Student Administrative Services, 700 Childs Way, Los Angeles, CA 90089-0911
Phone: 213-740-1111 **E-mail:** admitusc@usc.edu
Website: www.usc.edu

Campus Life
Environment: Metropolis. **Calendar:** Semester.

Students and Faculty
(All Undergraduate Programs)
Enrollment: 16,428. **Student Body:** 51% female, 49% male, 37% out-of-state, 8% international (153 countries represented). African American 6%, Asian 21%, Caucasian 48%, Hispanic 13%. Student/faculty ratio: 10:1. 1,495 full-time faculty, 89% hold PhDs. 75% faculty teach undergrads.

Admissions
(All Undergraduate Programs)
Freshman Admissions Requirements: Test(s) required: SAT or ACT; ACT with Writing component. 85% in top tenth, 95% in top quarter. SAT Math (25/75 percentile): 650/730. SAT Verbal (25/75 percentile): 620/710. Projected SAT Writing (25/75 percentile): 660/730. *Academic units required:* 4 English, 3 math, 2 science (2 science labs), 2 foreign language,

2 social studies, 3 academic electives. Regular application deadline: 1/10. Regular notification: 4/1.

Costs and Financial Aid
(All Undergraduate Programs)
Annual tuition $31,458. Room & board $9,610. Required fees $550. Average book expense $750. **Financial Aid Statistics:** % freshmen/undergrads who receive any aid: 67/63. % freshmen/undergrads who receive need-based scholarship or grant aid: 39/41. % freshmen/undergrads who receive need-based self-help aid: 43/45. Priority financial aid filing deadline: 1/20. Financial aid notification on or about: 3/15.

TV/Film/Digital Media Studies Programs
Number of undergraduates in these programs: 728
Number of 2005 graduates from these programs: 270
Degrees conferred to these majors: BA, BFA.
Number of full-time faculty in these programs: 64
Number of part-time faculty in these programs: 120
Equipment and facilities: Production equipment for student checkout: two Sony F900H/3 (HD Cameras), 17 Sony DSR-PD170 DVCAM camcorders, 50 Sony DSR-PD150 DVCam camcorders, 100 Sony DSR-PD100 DVCam camcorders, 30 Sony DSR-PDX10 DVCam camcorders, 11 Sony TRV-900 DV camcorders, nine Sony VX-1000 DV camcorders, eight Sony DSR-500 DVCam cameras, five Sony Betacam BVW-D600 cameras, 40 boom kits (with mics), 27 Mole Richardson lighting kits, 20 Lowell Kits (DP light, Omni Light, Pro Light, with chimera), 90 16 mm Arriflex Camera Kits, nine 16 mm Arriflex SR2 Camera Kits, three 16 mm Aaton Camera Kits (two are S16), 100 lighting kits, two Chapman Super PeeWee Dollys, four Doorway Dollys, 300 Century Stands. Production facilities: Visual effects lab, Final Cut Pro high-definition editing systems, dual processor G5 Macintosh Computers (Avid, Maya, Boujou, Shake, AfterEffects, Photoshop), Sony HDW-F500, HDCam, VTR, Sony high-definition video monitor,

Vicon 3-D Motion Capture System, Kurosawa Stage (2,250 square feet), Kubrick Stage (2,250 square feet), Lloyd Stage (3,600 square feet), Carson Stage-3,600 square feet. Spielberg scoring stage: Euphonix System, five digital console with 82 channels, 24 channels of input from Pro Tools, HD Tascam MX 2424 hard disc recorder, and DA-98 digital tape recorders. Studio holds up to 40 musicians. Interactive media division facilities: Alucid Custom Usability Lab, separate observation room and subject rooms; hi-res dome-enclosed video-monitoring system, integrated audio monitoring and intercom system, PC/Console/Wireless device capture capabilities, hi-res VGA to video converter, Sony VAIO control, PC running UsabilityWare 4.0, User Research Software. Zemeckis Media Lab: 270+ degree (5+4+5) surround projection, 14 NEC ceiling-mounted projectors, AMX multi input video/audio routing touch panel system, 5.1 Surround Sound with Mackie speakers.

Other awards of note: In addition to winning two Oscars (*The Face of Lincoln*, Best Two-Reel Short 1955; *The Resurrection of Bronco Billy*, Best Live-Action Short 1970), students at the School of Cinema-Television consistently place well in competitions around the nation and the globe. Recent results: Sundance Film Festival 2006, *In Between Days*, Special Jury Prize for Independent Vision, Dramatic Jury; *TV Junkie*, Special Jury Prize, Documentary Jury; *The Wraith of Cobble Hill*, Jury Prize in Short Filmmaking, Shorts Jury; Slamdance *Guerilla* Gamemaker Competition 2006; *Cloud*, Student Philosophy Award (Artistic Achievement), DC Independent Film Festival 2005; *The Elephant's Egg*, Best Student Film Award, ZoieFest 2005; *Love Sick & Love Sick 2*, Best Student Animation, USA Film Festival/Dallas, Short Film & Video Competition 2005; *West Bank Story*, Student Award Worldfest, Houston 2005; *Antebody*, Special Jury Award, NYC Home Film Festival 2005; *Induction*, Honorable Mention, Best Actor, Tahoe/Reno International Film Festival 2005; *Antebody*, Best Student Film Los Angeles International Film Festival 2005; *Tahara*, Best Female Director, Orinda Film Festival 2005; *Five*

Stages of Grief, Best College Short Angelus Awards Student Film Festival 2005; *Shelter*, Finalist Kamea, Finalist Heartland Film Festival 2005; *A Kiss on the Nose*, Crystal Heart Award Winner Queens International Film Festival, 2005; *The Futurist*, Queens Spirit Award, Best Student Filmmaker WorldFest, Lexington, TX 2005; *Antebody*, Platinum Award Berkeley Film Festival 2005; *Induction*, Grand Festival Award, Student Film; *Golden Knight*, Malta International Film Festival, Malta 2005; *Five Stages of Grief*, Silver Knight Award.

Career development services: Alumni networking opportunities; career counseling; central resource(s) for employers to browse headshots, writing samples, reels; internship listings; job listings. Each spring, just prior to graduation, the school organizes "First Pitch," an expo that enables seniors (and students from the MFA program) to present their scripts to some 50 representatives from leading agencies, management firms, producers, and studios.

Famous alumni: John August, John Carpenter, Al Gough, James Ivory, Randal Kleiser, George Lucas, Andrew Marlowe, Bill Mechanic, Miles Millar, John Milius, Walter Murch, Shonda Rhimes, Jay Roach, Stacey Sher, Bryan Singer, John Singleton, John Wells, Robert Zemeckis, Laura Ziskin.

Notable alumni: Producers: Bryan Burk (*Lost*), Barry Hennessey (*The Amazing Race*), Jon Landau (*Titanic*, *Solaris*), Damon Lee (*Undercover Brother*), Kevin McCollum (*Rent*, *Avenue Q*), Ed Saxon (*Adaptation*, *Silence of the Lambs*), Steve Turner (*The Gilmore Girls*, *Deadwood*). Writer/Producers: Jeff Davis (*Criminal Minds*), Javier Grillo-Marxuach (*Lost*), Evan Katz (*24*), Jack Orman (*ER*), Todd Slavkin (*Smallville*), Matthew Weiner (*The Sopranos*). Directors and writer-directors: Jay Roach (*Meet the Parents*, *Austin Powers*), Stephen Sommers (*The Mummy*, *Van Helsing*), Robert Zemeckis (*Forrest Gump*, *Castaway*), Randy Zisk (*Monk*). Writers: Robert Guza Jr. (*General Hospital*), Karey Kirkpatrick (*Chicken Run*), Ross Lamanna (*Rush Hour*), David Weiss (*Shrek 2*). Cinematographers: Chris Baffa (*Nip/Tuck*, *Running with Scissors*), Sandra

Chandler (*Eyes of Tammy Faye*), Robert Elswit (*Boogie Nights, Syriana*), Richard Fannin (*Felicity*), Woody Omens (*Coming to America, Boomerang*). Editors: Tim Atzinger (*Survivor*), Lee Haxall (*Arrested Development*), Paul Nielsen (*The Amazing Race*), Edith Weil (*NYPD Blue*). Production designers: Greg Fonseca (*Gladiator*). Sound editors and rerecording mixers: Erik Aadahl (*I, Robot*), Richard L. Anderson (*Raiders of the Lost Ark*), Doug Hemphill (*Walk the Line, The Insider*), Gary Rydstrom (*Saving Private Ryan, Finding Nemo*). Animators: Valerie Mih (*A Bug's Life, Toy Story II*), Toni Nugnes (*South Park*). Composers: John Ottman (*The Usual Suspects; Kiss Kiss, Bang Bang*), Basil Poledouris (*The Hunt for Red October*). Visual effects: Richard Edlund (*Alien, Star Wars*), Michael McAlister (*Indiana Jones and the Temple of Doom*), Lewis Siegel (*The Matrix*, technical director). Documentary filmmakers: Jeanne Begley (*A&E Biographies*), Jeff Blitz (*Spellbound*), Sandra Chandler (*Living Dolls*), Alec Lorimore (*IMAX: Everest*). Executives (film/television/interactive): Polly Cohen (senior vice president of theatrical production, Warner Bros.), Bob Osher (chief operating officer, Columbia Pictures Motion Picture Group), Michelle Raimo (senior vice president, production, Paramount). Agents: Charlie Ferraro (United Talent Agency), Gregory McKnight (William Morris Agency), Elizabeth Swofford (Creative Artists Agency). Scholars/authors: Mary Kearney (University of Texas, Austin), Hilary Nerone (University of Vermont), Abé Markus Nornes (University of Michigan), Mark Williams (Dartmouth College). Critics: Scott Foundas (*Variety*, www.Indiewire.com), Holly Willis (*RES Magazine*).

In Their Own Words

The Office of Student-Industry Relations was established in 1992 specifically to aid the transition of students from their academic to professional pursuits. Among its primary tasks are to provide career counseling services to students beginning in their freshman year and extending into the first year or so after they graduate; to assist students and recent graduates to obtain internships with agencies, studios, networks, and other organizations; and to assist students to enter their film and animation projects in some 125 national and international competitions each year. Trojan Vision is USC's student-operated television station. Broadcasting from the Robert Zemeckis Center for Digital Arts 24/7, Trojan Vision programming includes news, sports, talk shows, documentary specials, student films, and more. Trojan Vision provides its staff with a hands-on learning experience in all areas of television, as well as the opportunity to have student work seen across the city and beyond. Nationally-known guest lecturers: John August, Ken Burns, Robert Downey Jr., William Friedkin, Bing Gordon, Tom Hanks, Ray Harryhausen, Anne Kopelson, Arnold Kopelson, Eugene Levy, George Lucas, William H. Macy, Michael Moore, Oliver Platt, Sidney Poitier, Gary Rydstrom, Steven Spielberg, Agnes Varda, Lina Wertmuller, Robert Zemeckis. Nationally-known instructors: Leonard Maltin (critic), Tomlinson Holman (inventor of the THX sound system), Mark Jonathan Harris (three-time Academy Award-winning documentary filmmaker), Jeremy Kagen (Emmy Award-winning director/writer/producer), Marsha Kinder (cultural theorist), David James (expert in Asian and avant garde cinema).

POPULAR PROGRAMS

DIVISION OF FILM AND TELEVISION PRODUCTION

Department chair: Michael Taylor
Number of full-time faculty: 29
Number of part-time faculty: 71
Focus/emphasis: Designed to develop specialized skills on a foundation of general knowledge. All aspects of cinematic storytelling are covered, from writing and producing to directing, editing, sound design, cinematography, and editing. In addition to focusing on a specific aspect of the production process, students can choose an emphasis on documentary production or electronic media, as well as narrative film.

DIVISION OF CRITICAL STUDIES

Department chair: Tara McPherson
Number of full-time faculty: 14
Number of part-time faculty: 5
Focus/emphasis: Examines mass media, popular culture, and the social, political, economic, and aesthetic influences of film, television, and digital media. Students are encouraged to formulate thoughtful responses to the material and to pursue independent research topics.

DIVISION OF WRITING FOR SCREEN & TELEVISION

Department chair: Howard Rodman
Number of full-time faculty: 13
Number of part-time faculty: 39
Focus/emphasis: Enables students specializing in writing to work closely with a mentor, pitch their best work to industry professionals, and produce a portfolio of feature screenplays and television scripts.

DIVISION OF INTERACTIVE MEDIA

Department chair: Scott Fisher
Number of full-time faculty: 8
Number of part-time faculty: 5
Focus/emphasis: Combines a broad liberal arts background with a specialization in game design and development, interactive/mobile media, and traditional media production skills.

Students Should Also Know

In addition to superb faculty and resources, the greatest strength of the USC School of Cinema-Television is the underlying philosophy that the best education comes from creating an environment where theory and practice are in constant interaction. To this end, we have structured our programs so that all students, regardless of their specific major, are required to take classes from the full spectrum of the school's offerings. Through this process, writers take courses in directing and work one-on-one with actors to understand better how the words on the page actually sound and play. Directors take courses in the history of film, television, and interactive media so they can gain the perspective that they are standing on the shoulders of those who passed before them. Critical studies majors get behind the camera and in the edit-

ing suites to bring their own productions to life, so their hands-on knowledge of the creative process can be reflected in their scholarly understanding of it. As our alumni roster reflects, this philosophy clearly prepares students to pursue their ambitions and dreams in the realm of entertainment. Perhaps more significantly, it instills in them the sense of discipline, teamwork, imagination, and persistence that enables their contributions to our society to go well beyond their specific fields.

UNIVERSITY OF SOUTHERN MISSISSIPPI

118 College Drive #5166, Hattiesburg, MS 39406
Phone: 601-266-5000 **E-mail:** admissions@usm.edu
Website: www.usm.edu

Campus Life
Environment: Village. **Calendar:** Semester.

Students and Faculty
(All Undergraduate Programs)
Enrollment: 12,468. **Student Body:** 61% female, 39% male, 10% out-of-state. African American 28%, Asian 1%, Caucasian 67%, Hispanic 1%. Student/faculty ratio: 18:1. 708 full-time faculty, 80% hold PhDs. 95% faculty teach undergrads.

Admissions
(All Undergraduate Programs)
Freshman Admissions Requirements: Test(s) required: SAT or ACT. Average high school GPA: 3.07. 19% in top tenth, 47% in top quarter. SAT Math (25/75 percentile): 480/565. SAT Verbal (25/75 percentile): 460/575. *Academic units required:* 4 English, 3 math, 3 science (3 science labs), 1 social studies, 2 history, 2 academic electives, computer applications. Regular notification: Rolling.

Costs and Financial Aid
(All Undergraduate Programs)
Annual in-state tuition $4,312. Out-of-state tuition $9,742. Room & board $5,800. Required fees $30. Average book expense $800.

Financial Aid Statistics: % freshmen/undergrads who receive need-based scholarship or grant aid: 41/44. % freshmen/undergrads who receive need-based self-help aid: 49/53. Priority financial aid filing deadline: 3/15. Financial aid notification on or about: 4/1.

TV/Film/Digital Media Studies Programs

Number of undergraduates in these programs: 190

Number of 2005 graduates from these programs: 42

Degrees conferred to these majors: BA, BS.

Number of full-time faculty in these programs: 5

Number of part-time faculty in these programs: 3

Equipment and facilities: Film: two Aaton 16 mm camera packages, three Arri BL, 16 mm camera packages, two CP, 16 16 mm camera packages, five Bolex 16 mm cameras, three Canon Scoopic 16 mm cameras, one 16 mm Animation Stand Canon GL1 Digital Video Camera, three Nagra audio recorders with various mics and accessories, five location lighting kits, various mole richardson lighting instruments, Western-Style Doorway Dolly, two Steenbeck 16 mm flatbed editing suites, two Final Cut Pro digital editing suites, one Pro Tools Audio Suite Screening/Classroom with 16 mm, DVD, DV, SVHS, VHS projection capability Television: Grass Valley 110 switcher 3, three Sony DXC-D30 video cameras, Sony MXPS390 audio mixer Inscriber VMP character generator 2, two Sony UVW 1800 Beta-SP recorders, Sony UVW 1600 Beta-SP player, approximately 1,500 feet of Triax camera cable on-board, approximately 250 feet of multicore camera cable on-board, RTS intercom system, Studio Technologies IFB system 2, two cellular phones on-board Ku Band Satellite Uplink Vehicle, 2.4 meter Vertex antenna/single path providing transmit and receive in opposite polarities, RC-8097B RCI dish positioning system, RC-8097GPS RCI global positioning receiver, satellite uplink/downlink equipment, analog Ku equipments, two Xicom Technologies XTRD 400K TWT amplifiers, Xicom Variable Phase Combiner 2, two Miteq VM100-R NTSC video modulators 2, two Miteq UVE-9696-125K Ku upconverters, Miteq RSU-S redundant switchover, Standard MT830BR satellite remote receiver package, Tektronix 1705A spectrum monitor, Tektronix 1710J video waveform monitor, digital Ku equipment. Currently nonredundant Wegener DVT-2001 MPEG-2 encoder, Wegener Unity 4000 integrated receiver/decoder, Wegener KUTLT test loop translator, SSP-10 Pico satellite signal processor.

ATAS College TV Awards recipients: 1

ATAS interns: 1

ATAS Faculty Seminar participants: 1

Other awards of note: Student films produced at USM have won numerous awards, including ACE Award for Editing, CINE Eagle(s)

% of graduates currently employed in related field: 60

Career development services: Alumni networking opportunities, career counseling, internship listings, job fairs, job listings. Staff and faculty in the school work closely with students seeking internships and entry-level jobs.

Famous alumni: Natalie Allen, MSNBC anchor; Kathleen Koch, CNN reporter; Chuck Scarborough, WNBC news anchor.

Notable alumni: John Duffy, A.C.E. Hollywood editor with 25 years of credits on major television and film projects; Keith Potter, D.G.A. assistant director with numerous feature credits; Patik-Ian Polk, writer/director of two features: *PUNKS* and *Noah's Arc*, executive produced *Noah's Arc* as a TV series; Nina Parikh, deputy director, The Mississippi Film Office Monte Kraus, owner, Krauscape Films, full-service production company for commercial/industrial film; Ted Chandler, owner, ChandlerImage, motion graphics for film and television; Don Warren, freelance cinematographer, clients include NASA; Rory King, freelance cinematographer with numerous independent feature credits; Diego Velasco, director/cinematographer; Claudia Velasco, producer for Cox Communication; Mark Shilstone, crew member, *Trading Spaces*; Caroline Eselin, costumer/costume designer credits include *Monster's*

Ball, *The Badge*, and *Sueno*; Sam Watson, freelance sound recordist/mixer with numerous feature and documentary credits; Shaun Tarkington, unit production manager with numerous television credits; Jim Allen, *Miss Power*; Kurt Brautigam, *Miss Power*; Don Carson, Godwin Group; Dan Barton, WDAM reporter; Karamaddox Hoffpauir, WDAM sports anchor; Nick Ortego, WDAM reporter; Jessica Watkins, WDAM, associate producer; John Sobolewski, WLOX production/ editor; Scott Ford, WLOX technical director; Mathew Hutchinson, WLOX ENG/Graphics/Font.

In Their Own Words

The School of Mass Communication and Journalism has maintained a close relationship with the university's broadcasting and media production unit for over 20 years. This relationship allows MCJ students to become involved in the day-to-day production activities of WUSM-FM, television production (both studio and field), mobile uplink, and EFP activities and the operation of the Daktronic Video Scoreboard. We have an excellent relationship with the Mississippi Film Office. As a result, our students know about internship and employment opportunities with film productions that come to Mississippi. Our students have interned or been hired on numerous feature films, television programs, and documentaries, including O' Brother Where Art Thou; Sister Island; The Blues documentary series, and Trading Spaces. We also have a very strong and active advisory board made up of working professionals. Mr. Stuart Margolin, who has extensive credits as an actor, writer, and director (Rockford Files), helps demystify the motion picture and television business by sharing his experience. Nina Parikh, deputy director of the Mississippi Film Office, makes regular presentations to film students. Monte Kraus, owner of Krauscape Films, has helped several students by offering internships or by offering technical assistance on their film projects. Jim Allen, director of media services for Mississippi Power Company, has offered technical support to the film program and has hired numerous stu-dents as temporary production assistants. The advisory board, as a whole, is instrumental in keeping the film and broadcast media programs relevant by assisting the faculty and staff of the program in futures planning, new technology, and current trends in the industry.

POPULAR PROGRAMS

BROADCAST JOURNALISM
Department chair: Marilyn Ellzey
Number of full-time faculty: 2
Number of part-time faculty: 1
Focus/emphasis: Television news (producing, editing, reporting).

FILM
Department chair: Dixon McDowell
Number of full-time faculty: 2
Focus/emphasis: Filmmaking.

BROADCAST PRODUCTION
Department chair: Dennis Webster
Number of full-time faculty: 1
Number of part-time faculty: 1
Focus/emphasis: Television production (editing, shooting, postproduction).

UNIVERSITY OF TAMPA

401 West Kennedy Boulevard, Tampa, FL 33606-1490
Phone: 813-253-6211 **E-mail:** admissions@ut.edu
Website: www.ut.edu

Campus Life
Environment: Metropolis. **Calendar:** Semester.

Students and Faculty
(All Undergraduate Programs)
Enrollment: 5,202. **Student Body:** 62% female, 38% male, 54% out-of-state, 5% international (101 countries represented). African American 6%, Asian 2%, Caucasian 64%, Hispanic 9%. Student/faculty

ratio: 15:1. 208 full-time faculty, 90% hold PhDs. 100% faculty teach undergrads.

Admissions
(All Undergraduate Programs)
Freshman Admissions Requirements: Test(s) required: SAT or ACT. Average high school GPA: 3.25. 20% in top tenth, 50% in top quarter. SAT Math (25/75 percentile): 500/500. SAT Verbal (25/75 percentile): 490/580. Projected SAT Writing (25/75 percentile): 550/630. *Academic units required:* 4 English, 3 math, 3 science (2 science labs), 2 foreign language, 3 social studies, 3 academic electives. Regular notification: Rolling.

Costs and Financial Aid
(All Undergraduate Programs)
Annual tuition $17,906. Room & board $6,936. Required fees $942. Average book expense $870. **Financial Aid Statistics:** % freshmen/undergrads who receive any aid: 87/88. % freshmen/undergrads who receive need-based scholarship or grant aid: 53/5. % freshmen/undergrads who receive need-based self-help aid: 43/45. Financial aid notification on or about: 2/1.

TV/Film/Digital Media Studies Programs
Number of undergraduates in these programs: 400
Degrees conferred to these majors: BA.
Equipment and facilities: We have DV, 24p as well as 16 mm; students learn to cut both traditionally on flatbeds as well as on the latest Mac G5s; we have four digital labs (including graphic and interactive media design and two levels of postproduction); in '07 we'll be adding one more media lab, a media writing lab and four new screening/class rooms; we have a soundstage and an on-campus, public access television studio; we have a student run on-campus radio station.
Career development services: Alumni networking opportunities, career counseling, internship listings, job fairs, job listings.

In Their Own Words
We are a liberal arts program that blends theory and application. All of our students take both critical studies as well as production classes. We offer within our one department traditional as well as digital cinema production, TV Studio and New Media courses, and a wide array of media writing classes. Our department hosts the Tampa International Film Festival, which annually attracts films as well as filmmakers from around the globe.

POPULAR PROGRAMS

COMMUNICATION
Department chair: Dr. Gregg Bachman
Focus/emphasis: Broad, liberal arts curriculum requiring students to choose courses from the following areas: Culture and society, visual aesthetics, media writing, and production. Courses emphasize human values, appropriate uses of communication media, historical perspectives, and critical thinking.

FILM AND MEDIA ARTS
Focus/emphasis: Combines critical studies with production experiences, providing students with a foundation of theory and application. Blending "story" with "technology," students study critical perspectives and practice implementing techniques in traditional (16 mm) as well as emerging (digital) formats. Courses cover classic narrative, documentary, and experimental forms.

ELECTRONIC MEDIA ARTS AND TECHNOLOGY
Focus/emphasis: Interdisciplinary program, including courses offered in art, communication, information and technology management, music, and writing. The program emphasizes designing and producing for interactivity and Web-based products for both commercial and artistic intent. It reflects the convergence between these areas in academic scholarship, aesthetic exploration, and technical applications.

ADVERTISING AND PUBLIC RELATIONS
Focus/emphasis: The major is designed to prepare students for professional and academic opportunities in strategic communication.

Students Should Also Know

All of these majors are administered through the Department of Communication. All communication students are free to take courses from all of the programs.

UNIVERSITY OF TEXAS AT AUSTIN

PO Box 8058, Austin, TX 78713-8058
Phone: 512-475-7440
Website: www.utexas.edu

Campus Life
Environment: Metropolis. **Calendar:** Semester.

Students and Faculty
(All Undergraduate Programs)
Enrollment: 35,734. **Student Body:** 52% female, 48% male, 5% out-of-state, 3% international (121 countries represented). African American 4%, Asian 17%, Caucasian 58%, Hispanic 16%. Student/faculty ratio: 18:1. 2,482 full-time faculty. 100% faculty teach undergrads.

Admissions
(All Undergraduate Programs)
Freshman Admissions Requirements: Test(s) required: SAT or ACT; ACT with Writing component. 68% in top tenth, 92% in top quarter. SAT Math (25/75 percentile): 570/690. SAT Verbal (25/75 percentile): 540/670. Projected SAT Writing (25/75 percentile): 600/700. *Academic units required:* 4 English, 3 math, 2 science, 2 foreign language, 3 social studies, 2 academic electives. Regular application deadline: 2/1. Regular notification: Rolling.

Costs and Financial Aid
(All Undergraduate Programs)
Annual in-state tuition $6,972. Out-of-state tuition $16,310. Room & board $7,638. Average book expense $800.
Financial Aid Statistics: % freshmen/undergrads who receive any aid: 77/74. % freshmen/undergrads who receive need-based scholarship or grant aid: 57/47. % freshmen/undergrads who receive need-based self-help aid: 56/51. Priority financial aid filing deadline: 4/1. Financial aid notification on or about: 3/15.

TV/Film/Digital Media Studies Programs
Number of undergraduates in these programs: 950 (undergraduate), 160 (graduate).
Degrees conferred to these majors: BS.
Also available at The University of Texas at Austin: MFA, MA, PhD.
Number of full-time faculty in these programs: 28
Number of part-time faculty in these programs: 15
Equipment and facilities: Studios, digital labs, cameras, internships, extensive field equipment.
Other awards of note: Faculty: Peabodys, National Writers Guild, Emmys, Kodak Awards; Academy Award nominations; Students: Student Academy Award, Kodak Awards, Cannes Awards.

% of graduates currently employed in related field: 50
Career development services: Alumni networking opportunities, career counseling, internship listings, job fairs, job listings. We have a student-run organization that facilitates finding crew and cast and helps with festival entries.
Famous alumni: Robert Rodriguez, Matthew McConaughy.
Notable alumni: Rob Walker, columnist, the *New York Times*; Jordan Levin, former head of Warner Bros.

In Their Own Words
We've produced several students who have won prizes at Cannes and national festivals. Internships are available, both locally and around the country. We offer a semester in LA program that includes an internship as well. Most faculty have had work aired on national television, and faculty have won Peabody Awards as well as fellowships from the Rockefeller and Guggenheim Foundations. Our master class brings in lecturers such as Mike

Judge, Richard Linklaer, Ray Harryhausen, Chuck Norris, and Mark Cuban. We also have a film institute affiliated with a commercial production company, Burnt Orange, that produces low-budget theatrical films. Many students work on these productions alongside professionals.

Students Should Also Know
The program includes production as well as studies courses. Students get a well-rounded education in media practice and theory.

UNIVERSITY OF TEXAS AT DALLAS
PO Box 830688, HH 10, Richardson, TX 75083-0688
Phone: 972-883-2270 **E-mail:** interest@utdallas.edu
Website: www.utdallas.edu

Campus Life
Environment: Metropolis. **Calendar:** Semester.

Students and Faculty
(All Undergraduate Programs)
Enrollment: 9,353. **Student Body:** 46% female, 54% male, 3% out-of-state, 5% international (130 countries represented). African American 7%, Asian 20%, Caucasian 58%, Hispanic 10%. Student/faculty ratio: 20:1. 457 full-time faculty, 92% hold PhDs. 83% faculty teach undergrads.

Admissions
(All Undergraduate Programs)
Freshman Admissions Requirements: Test(s) required: SAT or ACT; ACT with Writing component. Average high school GPA: 3.56. 41% in top tenth, 74% in top quarter. SAT Math (25/75 percentile): 580/700. SAT Verbal (25/75 percentile): 540/670. Projected SAT Writing (25/75 percentile): 600/700. *Academic units required:* 4 English, 4 math, 3 science (3 science labs), 2 foreign language, 3 social studies, 1 academic elective. Regular application deadline: 7/1. Regular notification: Rolling.

Costs and Financial Aid
(All Undergraduate Programs)
Annual in-state tuition $6,831. Out-of-state tuition $15,111. Room & board $6,412. Average book expense $1,200.
Financial Aid Statistics: % freshmen/undergrads who receive any aid: 83/65. % freshmen/undergrads who receive need-based scholarship or grant aid: 23/30. % freshmen/undergrads who receive need-based self-help aid: 30/36. Priority financial aid filing deadline: 4/12. Financial aid notification on or about: 4/15.

TV/Film/Digital Media Studies Programs
Number of undergraduates in these programs: 406
Number of 2005 graduates from these programs: 28
Degrees conferred to these majors: BA.
Also available at The University of Texas at Dallas: MFA, MA.
Number of full-time faculty in these programs: 15
Number of part-time faculty in these programs: 10
Equipment and facilities: Motion capture laboratory (MOCAP), Institute for Interactive Arts and Engineering.
Career development services: Alumni networking opportunities, career counseling, internship listings, job fairs, job listings.

In Their Own Words
This program provides students with the opportunity to learn about interactive advancements in communication, entertainment, education, training, and scientific and medical applications. The Institute for Interactive Arts and Engineering provides a research venue in motion-capture, interactive 3-D narratives, game development, and animatronic robotics.

POPULAR PROGRAMS

BACHELOR OF ARTS AND TECHNOLOGY

Department chair: Dr. Thomas Linehan
Number of full-time faculty: 15
Number of part-time faculty: 10
Focus/emphasis: Studying and fostering the interaction of art and technology with specific emphasis on the interplay of visual art, music, video, and narrative with the new media that have emerged from the convergence of computing and media technologies.

MFA IN ARTS AND TECHNOLOGY

Focus/emphasis: An interdisciplinary program that focuses on the creation, application, and implications of technologically sophisticated interactive communication with emphasis on the creation and application of computer-based arts and narrative.

MASTER OF ARTS IN ART AND TECHNOLOGY

Focus/emphasis: An interdisciplinary program that focuses on the creation, application, and implications of technologically sophisticated interactive communication with emphasis on the fusion of creative with critical thinking and theory with practice.

UNIVERSITY OF TULSA

600 South College Avenue, Tulsa, OK 74104
Phone: 918-631-2307 **E-mail:** admission@utulsa.edu
Website: www.utulsa.edu

Campus Life

Environment: Metropolis. **Calendar:** Semester.

Students and Faculty
(All Undergraduate Programs)

Enrollment: 2,749. **Student Body:** 50% female, 50% male, 34% out-of-state, 8% international (61 countries represented). African American 7%, Asian 2%, Caucasian 66%, Hispanic 4%, Native American 5%. Student/faculty ratio: 11:1. 306 full-time faculty, 96% hold PhDs. 100% faculty teach undergrads.

Admissions
(All Undergraduate Programs)

Freshman Admissions Requirements: Test(s) required: SAT or ACT. Average high school GPA: 3.7. 63% in top tenth, 81% in top quarter. SAT Math (25/75 percentile): 550/710. SAT Verbal (25/75 percentile): 540/700. Projected SAT Writing (25/75 percentile): 600/720. Regular notification: Rolling.

Costs and Financial Aid
(All Undergraduate Programs)

Annual tuition $20,658. Room & board $7,052. Required fees $80. Average book expense $1,200. **Financial Aid Statistics:** % freshmen/undergrads who receive any aid: 95/86. % freshmen/undergrads who receive need-based scholarship or grant aid: 23/28. % freshmen/undergrads who receive need-based self-help aid: 44/43. Priority financial aid filing deadline: 4/1. Financial aid notification on or about: 3/1.

TV/Film/Digital Media Studies Programs

Number of undergraduates in these programs: 28
Number of 2005 graduates from these programs: 9
Degrees conferred to these majors: BA.
Number of full-time faculty in these programs: 5
Number of part-time faculty in these programs: 2
Equipment and facilities: New film production lab, film scoring lab, other editing labs, television studio.

% of graduates who pursue further study within 5 years: 20
Career development services: Alumni networking opportunities, career counseling, internship listings, job fairs, job listings.

In Their Own Words

Study abroad at the University of Leicester, England; internships with corporations and videographers; national guest lecturers/instructors include Tim Blake Nelson and Sonny Kompanek.

POPULAR PROGRAMS

FILM STUDIES

Department chair: Joseph Kestner
Number of full-time faculty: 3
Focus/emphasis: Includes film history, criticism, and production (BA).

GRAPHIC ART

Department chair: Teresa Valero
Number of full-time faculty: 2
Number of full-time faculty: 1
Focus/emphasis: This program teaches graphic skills and knowledge and prepares students for a career either as a professional or commercial artist (BFA or BA).

FILM SCORING

Department chair: Joseph Rivers
Number of full-time faculty: 1
Focus/emphasis: This minor program teaches musical scoring techniques for film.

Students Should Also Know

Students can also study television production as part of our Communication Program (BA).

UNIVERSITY OF UTAH

201 South 1460 East, Room 250 S, Salt Lake City, UT 84112
Phone: 801-581-7281 **E-mail:** admissions@sa.utah.edu
Website: www.utah.edu

Campus Life

Environment: City. **Calendar:** Semester.

Students and Faculty
(All Undergraduate Programs)

Enrollment: 21,695. **Student Body:** 44% female, 56% male, 15% out-of-state, 2% international (108 countries represented). Asian 5%, Caucasian 82%, Hispanic 4%. Student/faculty ratio: 15:1. 1,175 full-time faculty, 86% hold PhDs. 64% faculty teach undergrads.

Admissions
(All Undergraduate Programs)

Freshman Admissions Requirements: Test(s) required: SAT or ACT; SAT and SAT Subject Tests or ACT. Average high school GPA: 3.51. 27% in top tenth, 51% in top quarter. SAT Math (25/75 percentile): 500/630. SAT Verbal (25/75 percentile): 495/630. *Academic units required:* 4 English, 2 math, 3 science (1 science lab), 2 foreign language, 1 history, 4 academic electives. Regular application deadline: 4/1. Regular notification: Rolling, within two weeks of file completion.

Costs and Financial Aid
(All Undergraduate Programs)

Annual in-state tuition $3,672. Out-of-state tuition $12,860. Room & board $5,422. Required fees $670. Average book expense $1,100.

Financial Aid Statistics: % freshmen/undergrads who receive any aid: 31/41. % freshmen/undergrads who receive need-based scholarship or grant aid: 22/29. % freshmen/undergrads who receive need-based self-help aid: 20/29. Priority financial aid filing deadline: 3/15. Financial aid notification on or about: 4/15.

TV/Film/Digital Media Studies Programs

Number of undergraduates in these programs: 230
Number of 2005 graduates from these programs: 94
Degrees conferred to these majors: BA.
Also available at University of Utah: MFA.
Number of full-time faculty in these programs: 4
Number of part-time faculty in these programs: 4

UNIVERSITY OF VERMONT

Admissions Office, 194 South Prospect Street,
Burlington, VT 05401-3596
Phone: 802-656-3370 **E-mail:** admissions@uvm.edu
Website: www.uvm.edu

Campus Life
Environment: City. **Calendar:** Semester.

Students and Faculty
(All Undergraduate Programs)
Enrollment: 8,784. **Student Body:** 55% female,
45% male, 63% out-of-state. African American 1%,
Asian 2%, Caucasian 93%, Hispanic 2%. Student/faculty ratio: 15:1. 560 full-time faculty, 87% hold PhDs.
84% faculty teach undergrads.

Admissions
(All Undergraduate Programs)
Freshman Admissions Requirements: Test(s)
required: SAT or ACT; ACT with Writing component.
21% in top tenth, 55% in top quarter. SAT Math
(25/75 percentile): 540/630. SAT Verbal (25/75 percentile): 530/630. Projected SAT Writing (25/75 percentile): 590/670. *Academic units required:* 4 English,
3 math, 2 science (1 science lab), 2 foreign language,
3 social studies. Regular application deadline: 1/15.
Regular notification: 3/31.

Costs and Financial Aid
(All Undergraduate Programs)
Annual in-state tuition $9,452. Out-of-state tuition
$23,638. Room & board $7,332. Required fees
$1,296. Average book expense $865.
Financial Aid Statistics: % freshmen/undergrads
who receive any aid: 78/75. % freshmen/undergrads
who receive need-based scholarship or grant aid:
49/51. % freshmen/undergrads who receive need-based self-help aid: 46/48. Priority financial aid filing
deadline: 2/10. Financial aid notification on or about:
3/15.

TV/Film/Digital Media Studies Programs
**Number of undergraduates
in these programs:** 41
Degrees conferred to these majors: BA.

**Number of full-time faculty in these
programs:** 6
**Number of part-time faculty in these
programs:** 1

In Their Own Words
*This is the first year of our program, and we
already have 41 majors.*

POPULAR PROGRAMS

FILM AND TELEVISION STUDIES
Department chair: Todd McGowan
Number of full-time faculty: 6
Number of part-time faculty: 1
Focus/emphasis: Theory, analysis, and history of
film and television.

UNIVERSITY OF VIRGINIA

Office of Admission, PO Box 400160, Charlottesville, VA 22904
Phone: 434-982-3200 **E-mail:** undergradadmission@virginia.edu
Website: www.virginia.edu

Campus Life
Environment: City. **Calendar:** Semester.

Students and Faculty
(All Undergraduate Programs)
Enrollment: 13,387. **Student Body:** 54% female,
46% male, 28% out-of-state, 4% international (119
countries represented). African American 9%, Asian
11%, Caucasian 66%, Hispanic 4%. Student/faculty
ratio: 15:1. 1,193 full-time faculty, 90% hold PhDs.

Admissions
(All Undergraduate Programs)
Freshman Admissions Requirements: Test(s)
required: SAT or ACT; ACT with Writing component.
Average high school GPA: 4.04. 86% in top tenth,
97% in top quarter. SAT Math (25/75 percentile):
620/720. SAT Verbal (25/75 percentile): 600/710.
Projected SAT Writing (25/75 percentile): 650/730.
Academic units required: 4 English, 4 math, 2 sci-

ence, 2 foreign language, 4 social studies. Early decision application deadline: 11/1. Regular application
deadline: 1/2. Regular notification: 4/1.

Costs and Financial Aid
(All Undergraduate Programs)

Annual in-state tuition $7,845. Out-of-state tuition
$25,945. Room & board $6,389. Required fees
$1,768. Average book expense $1,000.

Financial Aid Statistics: % freshmen/undergrads who
receive any aid: 53/46. % freshmen/undergrads who
receive need-based scholarship or grant aid: 21/19. %
freshmen/undergrads who receive need-based self-help
aid: 14/17. Priority financial aid filing deadline: 3/1.
Financial aid notification on or about: 4/5.

TV/Film/Digital Media Studies Programs

**Number of undergraduates
in these programs:** 35

**Number of 2005 graduates from these
programs:** 22

Degrees conferred to these majors: BA.

**Number of full-time faculty in these
programs:** 5

**Number of part-time faculty in these
programs:** 3

**% of graduates who pursue further study within 5
years:** 20–25

**% of graduates currently employed in related
field:** 80

Career development services: Alumni networking
opportunities, career counseling, internship listings,
job fairs, job listings.

In Their Own Words

*The Media Studies Program maintains alumni
and professional networks made up of highly
placed media professionals who provide exclusive mentoring to only our majors. We also
maintain an ever-growing internship database
that is available only to our majors. Media studies majors may also do internships for course
credit. Our majors have interned at organizations that include:* NBC Nightly News, Time
Magazine, Rolling Stone Magazine, ABC
Nightline, *and* The Daily Show with Jon Stewart.

*Our graduates are working at companies that
include: MTV, Fox News, Miramax Pictures,* The
News Hour with Jim Lehrer, NBC Nightly News,
Good Housekeeping *magazine. Recent graduates have been admitted to USC Film School.*

UNIVERSITY OF WEST FLORIDA

11000 University Parkway, Pensacola, FL 32514-5750
Phone: 850-474-2230 **E-mail:** admissions@uwf.edu
Website: http://uwf.edu

Campus Life

Environment: City. **Calendar:** Semester.

Students and Faculty
(All Undergraduate Programs)

Enrollment: 9,655. **Student Body:** 60% female,
40% male, 13% out-of-state. African American 10%,
Asian 4%, Caucasian 77%, Hispanic 5%, Native
American 1%. Student/faculty ratio: 19:1. 308 full-
time faculty, 85% hold PhDs.

Admissions
(All Undergraduate Programs)

Freshman Admissions Requirements: Test(s)
required: SAT or ACT. Average high school GPA:
3.62. 40% in top tenth, 84% in top quarter. SAT Math
(25/75 percentile): 490/600. SAT Verbal (25/75 percentile): 500/600. Projected SAT Writing (25/75 percentile): 560/650. *Academic units required:* 4 English,
3 math, 3 science (2 science labs), 2 foreign language,
3 social studies, 4 academic electives. Regular application deadline: 6/30. Regular notification: Rolling.

Costs and Financial Aid
(All Undergraduate Programs)

Annual in-state tuition $2,147. Out-of-state tuition
$14,654. Room & board $6,600. Required fees
$1,051. Average book and supplies expense $1,000.

TV/Film/Digital Media Studies Programs

**Number of undergraduates
in these programs:** 107

Number of 2005 graduates from these

programs: 55

Degrees conferred to these majors: BA, BS, BFA.

Number of full-time faculty in these programs: 2

Number of part-time faculty in these programs: 3

Equipment and facilities: Digital equipment, switchers, audio boards, DVE's, studio and field cameras, and contemporary nonlinear editing systems incorporating animation software.

ATAS interns: 1

% of graduates who pursue further study within 5 years: 35

% of graduates currently employed in related field: 60

Career development services: Alumni networking opportunities, career counseling, internship listings, job fairs, job listings.

Notable alumni: Schams Elwazer, CNN Beirut producer; Xanthe Tilden, CNN International, produces and hosts fashion program.

In Their Own Words

We have placed UWF students with MTV, CNN, CNN International, and local ABC, CBS, Fox, and NBC affiliates.

POPULAR PROGRAMS

COMMUNICATION ARTS

Department Chair: Dr. Bruce Swain

Number of full-time faculty: 1

Number of part-time faculty: 1

The communication arts department has five areas of specialization: advertising, journalism, organizational communication, public relations, and telecommunication and film. This last area has a variety of offerings, including: (1) Basic Television Studio Production: Intensive hands-on instruction in live television studio production; (2) Electronic Field Production: Intensive hands-on instruction in nonstudio television production (EFP); (3) Nautilus News: Emphasis on student production and airing of live weekly newscasts; (4) Advanced Television Production: Instruction in all television production except news; (5) Filmmaking: Intensive hands-on instruction in filmmaking; (6) History of Film I & II: Instruction in the history and evolution of the film industry; (7) Film Practicum: Concentration on a single filmmaking project; (8) Modern Filmmaking Techniques: Instruction in modern and contemporary filmmaking production techniques; (9) Media Ethics: Examination of the ethical considerations of the broadcast industry; (10) Constitution of the Press: Examination of media law.

UNIVERSITY OF WEST GEORGIA

1601 Maple Street, Carrollton, GA 30118

Phone: 678-839-4000 **E-mail:** admiss@westga.edu

Website: www.westga.edu

Campus Life

Environment: City. **Calendar:** Semester.

Students and Faculty
(All Undergraduate Programs)

Enrollment: 8,346. **Student Body:** 60% female, 40% male, 3% out-of-state, 1% international (66 countries represented). African American 23%, Asian 1%, Caucasian 71%, Hispanic 2%. Student/faculty ratio 19:1. 383 full-time faculty, 78% hold PhDs. 90% faculty teach undergrads.

Admissions
(All Undergraduate Programs)

Freshman Admissions Requirements: Test(s) required: SAT or ACT; ACT with Writing component. Average high school GPA: 3.04. SAT Math (25/75 percentile): 460/550. SAT Verbal (25/75 percentile): 470/560. Projected SAT Writing (25/75 percentile): 540/620. *Academic units required:* 4 English, 4 math, 3 science (2 science lab), 2 foreign language, 1 social studies, 2 history. Regular application deadline: 7/1. Regular notification: Rolling.

Costs and Financial Aid
(All Undergraduate Programs)
Annual in-state tuition $2,438. Out-of-state tuition $9,754. Room & board $5,568. Required fees $832. Average book expense $900.

Financial Aid Statistics: % freshmen/undergrads who receive any aid: 66/78. % freshmen/undergrads who receive need-based scholarship or grant aid: 51/39. % freshmen/undergrads who receive need-based self help aid: 44/43. Priority financial aid filing deadline: 4/1. Financial aid notification on or about: 3/1.

TV/Film/Digital Media Studies Programs
Number of undergraduates in these programs: 115

Number of 2005 graduates from these programs: 38

Degrees conferred to these majors: BA.

Number of full-time faculty in these programs: 3

Number of part-time faculty in these programs: 1

Equipment and facilities: Television studio; ENG/EFP equipment, nonlinear editing suites, computer labs, access to on-campus Georgia Public Broadcasting FM station.

% of graduates currently employed in related field: 70

Career development services: Career counseling, internship listings, job fairs, job listings.

Notable alumni: Sam Crenshaw, sports anchor, Atlanta; Tyler Sieswecda, news anchor, Austin, TX; Jeff Styles, radio talk show host, Chatanooga, TN.

In Their Own Words
Internships at major Atlanta area firms: CNN, Georgia Public Broadcasting; Commercial TV stations; NATAE internships.

POPULAR PROGRAMS

MASS COMMUNICATIONS
Department chair: Dr. David Goff

Number of full-time faculty: Dr. Brad Yates

Number of part-time faculty: Ms. Connie Williams

Focus/emphasis: Video production, journalism, public relations.

Students Should Also Know
Radio and television production facilities are approaching 100 percent digital status; program operates on 24/7 cable access channel serving the university and community.

UNIVERSITY OF WISCONSIN– LA CROSSE
1725 State Street, LaCrosse, WI 54601-3742
Phone: 608-785-8939 **E-mail:** admissions@uwlax.edu
Website: www.uwlax.edu

Campus Life
Calendar: Semester.

Students and Faculty
(All Undergraduate Programs)
Enrollment: 8,814. **Student Body:** 59% female, 41% male, 18% out-of-state. Asian 3%, Caucasian 93%, Hispanic 1%. Student/faculty ratio: 21:1. 339 full-time faculty, 79% hold PhDs. 100% faculty teach undergrads.

Admissions
(All Undergraduate Programs)
Freshman Admissions Requirements: Test(s) required: SAT or ACT. 30% in top tenth, 80% in top quarter. SAT Math (25/75 percentile): 520/660. SAT Verbal (25/75 percentile): 500/610. Projected SAT Writing (25/75 percentile): 560/660. *Academic units required:* 4 English, 3 math, 3 science (2 science

labs), 3 social studies, 4 academic electives. Regular notification: Rolling.

Costs and Financial Aid
(All Undergraduate Programs)

Annual in-state tuition $5,590. Minnesota residents tuition $6,040. Out-of-state tuition $13,000. Room & board $5,020. Average book expense $300.

Financial Aid Statistics: % freshmen/undergrads who receive any aid: 65/72. % freshmen/undergrads who receive need-based scholarship or grant aid: 26/28. % freshmen/undergrads who receive need-based self-help aid: 48/52. Priority financial aid filing deadline: 3/15. Financial aid notification on or about: 3/10.

TV/Film/Digital Media Studies Programs

Degrees conferred to these majors: BA, BS.

Equipment and facilities: The program is housed in a $9.9 million recently remodeled building. We have digital ENG/EFP cameras, nonlinear Mac & PC edit bays, and NewsKing, state-of-the-art newsroom software.

Career development services: Alumni networking opportunities, career counseling, internship listings, job fairs, job listings.

In Their Own Words

The students have excellent internship possibilities. La Crosse has four TV stations that employ many of our students part-time. Since this is an entry-level market, graduating students are hired immediately at a local station.

UNIVERSITY OF WISCONSIN– GREEN BAY

2420 Nicolet Drive, Green Bay, WI 53411-7001
Phone: 920-465-2111 **E-mail:** uwgb@uwgb.edu
Website: www.uwgb.edu

Campus Life

Environment: City. **Calendar:** Semester.

Students and Faculty
(All Undergraduate Programs)

Enrollment: 5,321. **Student Body:** 66% female, 34% male, 5% out-of-state. Asian 3%, Caucasian 91%, Hispanic 1%, Native American 1%. Student/faculty ratio: 23:1. 179 full-time faculty, 88% hold PhDs. 99% faculty teach undergrads.

Admissions
(All Undergraduate Programs)

Freshman Admissions Requirements: Test(s) required: SAT or ACT. Average high school GPA: 3.34. SAT Math (25/75 percentile): 520/610. SAT Verbal (25/75 percentile): 478/558. *Academic units required:* 4 English, 3 math, 3 science (1 science lab), 3 social studies, 4 academic electives. Regular notification: Rolling.

Costs and Financial Aid
(All Undergraduate Programs)

Annual in-state tuition $4,500. Out-of-state tuition $14,600. Room & board $4,300. Required fees $1,148. Average book expense $700.

Financial Aid Statistics: % freshmen/undergrads who receive any aid: 52/51. % freshmen/undergrads who receive need-based scholarship or grant aid: 33/31. % freshmen/undergrads who receive need-based self-help aid: 36/40. Priority financial aid filing deadline: 4/15. Financial aid notification on or about: 11/1.

TV/Film/Digital Media Studies Programs

Number of undergraduates in these programs: 51
Number of 2005 graduates from these programs: 29

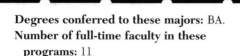

Degrees conferred to these majors: BA.
Number of full-time faculty in these
   programs: 11
Number of part-time faculty in these
   programs: 5
Equipment and facilities: Campus television studio
   produces programming for residence life.
   Wisconsin Public Radio and Wisconsin Public
   Television have studios on campus.

% of graduates who pursue further study within 5
   years: 30
% of graduates currently employed in related
   field: 75
Career development services: Alumni networking
   opportunities, career counseling, internship listings,
   job fairs, job listings.

In Their Own Words
*Students have access to many excellent
internship opportunities in the Green Bay
region.*

POPULAR PROGRAMS

ELECTRONIC MEDIA
Department chair: Tim Meyer
Focus/emphasis: Production techniques, writing,
   editing, advertising and sales, market and audience research, and new media and their impact
   on society and culture.

PHOTOGRAPHY
Department chair: Sarah Detweiler
Focus/emphasis: Photography as a problem-solving process, mastery of tools and materials, integration of theoretical concepts and practical experience.

UNIVERSITY OF WISCONSIN–
MADISON

Armory & Gymnasium, 716 Langdon Street, Madison, WI 53706-1481
Phone: 608-262-3961 E-mail: onwisconsin@admissions.wisc.edu
Website: www.wisc.edu

Campus Life
Environment: City. Calendar: Semester.

Students and Faculty
(All Undergraduate Programs)
Enrollment: 28,458. Student Body: 54% female,
46% male, 30% out-of-state, 3% international (110
countries represented). African American 3%, Asian
5%, Caucasian 83%, Hispanic 3%. Student/faculty
ratio: 13:1. 2,365 full-time faculty, 92% hold PhDs.

Admissions
(All Undergraduate Programs)
Freshman Admissions Requirements: Test(s)
required: SAT or ACT; ACT with Writing component.
Average high school GPA: 3.66. 56% in top tenth,
91% in top quarter. SAT Math (25/75 percentile):
600/700. SAT Verbal (25/75 percentile): 560/670.
Projected SAT Writing (25/75 percentile): 620/700.
Academic units required: 4 English, 3 math, 3 science, 2 foreign language, 3 social studies, 2 academic
electives. Regular application deadline: 2/1. Regular
notification: Rolling.

Costs and Financial Aid
(All Undergraduate Programs)
Annual in-state tuition $6,284. Out-of-state tuition
$20,284. Room & board $6,500. Required fees $333.
Average book expense $860.
Financial Aid Statistics: % freshmen/undergrads
who receive need-based scholarship or grant aid:
10/17. % freshmen/undergrads who receive need-
based self-help aid: 23/34. Financial aid notification
on or about: 4/1.

TV/Film/Digital Media Studies Programs
Degrees conferred to these majors: BA, BS.
Equipment and facilities: Center for
   Communication Research.

Other awards of note: Christopher Neal Heinlein Memorial Scholarships are available to communication arts majors who will be continuing students in the fall of 2006. Qualified undergraduate majors may nominate themselves or may be nominated by a member of the communication arts faculty or staff. Students who come from urban areas of the East Coast will be given preference. The Charline M. Wackman Awards are available to communication arts majors who will be continuing students in the fall of 2006. Qualified undergraduate majors may nominate themselves or be nominated by a member of the communication arts faculty or staff. Only "bona fide residents of the State of Wisconsin" are eligible.

Notable alumni: Kelly Kahl (BS, 1989) is an executive vice president of program planning and scheduling at CBS. Kahl oversees all scheduling of prime-time series, specials, television movies, and mini-series for both CBS and UPN. Kahl played an instrumental role in making CBS the top choice for Thursday nights, breaking NBC's decades-long stronghold, by shifting the network's popular shows *Survivor* and *CSI: Crime Scene Investigation* and adding the hit show *Without a Trace* to that slot. Kahl has also been responsible for high ratings of other CBS time slots, creatively scheduling shows such as *JAG*, *Everybody Loves Raymond*, and *The King of Queens*. Cori Abraham (Finkelstein) (1994), after working in television development at Comedy Central, VH1, and FX, is now the director of development and programming at Bravo in LA.

In Their Own Words

The University of Wisconsin–Madison Cinematheque is a coalition of academic departments and student film groups dedicated to showcasing films that would otherwise never reach Madison screens. The Kevin M. Anderson Memorial Film Mentorship provides a currently enrolled undergraduate student from the University of Wisconsin–Madison with the opportunity to spend one summer in Los Angeles, working with a mentor for a film production company. The student will have direct exposure to all aspects of film production, net-working opportunities, and will be given a stipend.

POPULAR PROGRAMS

COMMUNICATION SCIENCE AND RHETORICAL STUDIES

Department chair: Vance Kepley

Focus/emphasis: This program of study emphasizes the understanding of communication events and human interaction in their psychological, social, and philosophical aspects. Students in this area focus on communication in interpersonal settings, in groups and organization, in oratory and public address, and in the mass media, with attention to scientific methods as well as critical analysis. Students will be expected to master qualitative and quantitative research skills, conceptual and analytical thinking, and effective oral and written communication.

RADIO-TELEVISION-FILM

Department chair: Vance Kepley

Focus/emphasis: This concentration provides an opportunity to study the history, theory, criticism, cultural uses, and production practices of radio, television, and film. While there is no production major, students are required to take a video production course to gain a concrete understanding of the possibilities of this medium. Critical analysis as well as creative and scholarly expression are emphasized.

Students Should Also Know

The University of Wisconsin—Madison was one of the first universities to establish a program in communication, and its Communication Arts Department has taken a leading role in the development of the discipline throughout its history. The department offers a variety of courses focusing on the principal media and modes of human communication. Our goal is to help students deepen their appreciation of the communication process and increase their communication skills. Whether a course deals with film, electronic media, rhetoric, or interpersonal communication, it is

designed to encourage students to enhance and develop their own capacities for critical appraisal, reflection, and expression and to expand their capacities for participation in the communication-driven social and civic life of the 21st century.

UNIVERSITY OF WISCONSIN–OSHKOSH

Dempsey Hall 135, 800 Algoma Boulevard, Oshkosh, WI 54901
Phone: 920-424-0202 **E-mail:** oshadmuw@uwosh.edu
Website: www.uwosh.edu

Campus Life
Environment: Village. **Calendar:** Semester.

Students and Faculty
(All Undergraduate Programs)
Enrollment: 9,740. **Student Body:** 60% female, 40% male, 2% out-of-state. Asian 3%, Caucasian 91%, Hispanic 1%. Student/faculty ratio: 20:1. 381 full-time faculty, 85% hold PhDs. 99% faculty teach undergrads.

Admissions
(All Undergraduate Programs)
Freshman Admissions Requirements: Test(s) required: ACT. Average high school GPA: 3.29. 11% in top tenth, 38% in top quarter. *Academic units required:* 4 English, 3 math, 3 science (3 science labs), 3 social studies, 1 history, 4 academic electives. Regular application deadline: 8/1. Regular notification: Rolling.

Costs and Financial Aid
(All Undergraduate Programs)
Annual in-state tuition $4,981. Out-of-state tuition $15,207. Room & board $4,884. Average book expense $800.
Financial Aid Statistics: % freshmen/undergrads who receive need-based scholarship or grant aid: 56/48. % freshmen/undergrads who receive need-based self-help aid: 56/48. Priority financial aid filing deadline: 3/15. Financial aid notification on or about: 4/1.

TV/Film/Digital Media Studies Programs
Degrees conferred to these majors: BA, BS.
Number of full-time faculty in these programs: 8
Number of part-time faculty in these programs: 4
Equipment and facilities: Two multicamera TV studios with Sony DXC D30 WS, widescreen, cameras and 12 input audio arts production board; Grass Valley 200-2 switcher and DPM 700 DVE generator; Inscriber CG/Supreme graphics and character generator; Master Control with Marshall LCD video monitors and Wohler audio monitors; seven Betacam SP camcorders for field production; one Sony VX2000 mini-DV camcorder; multicamera remote product facility for live sports remotes; Titan TV chanel 66 master control with Leightronics TCD/IP automated controller, 360 Systems Image Server 2000, Betacam SP, mini-DV, and DVD playback-provides programming capabilities 24 hours a day; Miranda multiformat virtual monitor wall display system for production control room. Titan TV Center, located in the Arts & Communication West building, is where students write, produce, direct, and edit weekly television shows and various class-related projects. The Titan TV Center features two multicamera studios, six edit suites with varying features, office, and newsroom facilities, a facility where students may reserve and check out audio, video, and film field equipment, and Master Control—the nerve center of the UW Oshkosh cable channel, Titan TV. Unlike many other communications programs, the Radio/TV/Film Program at UW—Oshkosh encourages students to begin gaining experience in all aspects of TV production as early as freshman year. One Sony MSW 900 camcorder (IMX format); 1 Aaton XTR+ 16 mm film camera (used on the feature film *Leaving Las Vegas* and the TV series *Homicide*); Sony Betacam SP video camcorders; three CP16 sync sound film cameras; six Bolex 16 mm film cameras; Oxberry 16 mm animation stand; Cameleon camera dolly; three Audio Technica 48-volt phantom powered long shotgun microphones (used on the TV series *24*); three Audio Technica 48-volt phantom powered short shotgun microphones

(used on the TV series *24*); one Sennheiser 12-volt T powered long shotgun microphone; one Sennheiser 12-volt T powered short shotgun microphone; three Nagra Ares-BB+ flash card recorders; three Nagra reel-to-reel audio recorders (two Nagra3 and one Nagra4); Arri, LTM, and Lowel light kits; six C-stand kits-equipped with a single scrim, a double scrim, a flag, and a silk; the deluxe kit also includes a wooden cukaloris, a celo cukaloris, fingers, and dots; Foamcor reflectors mounted with Rosco gold, silver, and blue reflection material; multiple lens filter kits, equipped with ND filters, polarizers, color correction filters, low contrast filters, #25 red filters for black and white photography, and black pro-mist filters. One Avid Adrenaline nonlinear digital editing suite using IMX format; one MAYA5.0 animation workstation; one Avid Express nonlinear digital editing suite; three Pinnacle nonlinear editing suites utilizing Adobe Premiere software; one Final Cut Pro nonlinear editing suite equipped with mini-DV format; two Betacam SP cuts only editors; three 3/4 Umatic cuts only editors.

Other awards of note: One of the strengths of the program is that film and television are fully integrated. Through producing weekly television shows, students learn the importance of meeting deadlines. Through producing motion picture shorts, students learn quality control while developing sample reel material. Recently, the school has built stronger bridges on campus with the Theater and Music programs. As a result, advanced film production students have the opportunity to work with actors and production designers from theater and composers and sound designers from music. Over the past dozen years, many film productions and scripts have won national awards, including 21 Grand Prizes in the National Broadcasting Society competition. On the basis of these projects, film and scriptwriting students have been able to gain entry into some of the best graduate film schools in the nation, including New York University, the American Film Institute, Chapman University, Loyola Marymount University in Los Angeles, California Institute of the Arts, and Florida State University.

POPULAR PROGRAMS

JOURNALISM

Department chair: Dr. James Tsao
Number of full-time faculty: 8
Number of part-time faculty: 4
Focus/emphasis: We offer emphases in news-editorial and advertising-public relations, in addition to a newly established focus on visual journalism. In the news-editorial emphasis, students are prepared to take entry-level positions on daily and weekly newspapers and magazines. In the advertising-public relations emphasis, students are prepared to take entry-level positions with media, agencies, and related organizations. The visual journalism focus enables students to learn both press and commercial photographic skills before entering into the entry-level positions in the visual industry. Education on new communication technology and journalism diversity has been integrated into different courses across the emphases.

RADIO/TV/FILM

Department chair: Douglas Heil
Number of full-time faculty: 9
Focus/emphasis: The radio/TV/film major requires students to sample courses in each of the three areas of radio, television/video, and film production. After completing prerequisite courses, students may choose to concentrate in a specific discipline, such as radio station management, film/television directing, screenwriting, or broadcast news. The requirements for radio/TV/film majors and minors and course descriptions can be found through the links at the radio/TV/film home page and at the UW Oshkosh course descriptions page. The faculty and staff of radio/TV/film have built their program around a primary goal to inspire students into elevating our culture through the creation of thoughtful, responsible communication. To accomplish this goal, radio/TV/film educates its students in the following ways: Mastering professional skills and procedures, unleashing creativity in the service of a point of view, and developing an analytical approach to media communications.

UNIVERSITY OF WISCONSIN– STEVENS POINT

Student Services Center, Stevens Point, WI 54481
Phone: 715-346-2441 **E-mail:** admiss@uwsp.edu
Website: www.uwsp.edu

Campus Life
Environment: Town. **Calendar:** Semester.

Students and Faculty
(All Undergraduate Programs)
Enrollment: 8,328. **Student Body:** 54% female, 46% male, 6% out-of-state, 1% international (28 countries represented). African American 1%, Asian 2%, Caucasian 93%, Hispanic 1%. Student/faculty ratio: 21:1. 357 full-time faculty, 87% hold PhDs or other terminal degrees. 100% faculty teach undergrads.

Admissions
(All Undergraduate Programs)
Freshman Admissions Requirements: Test(s) required: SAT or ACT. Average high school GPA: 3.4. 14% in top tenth, 42% in top quarter. SAT Math (25/75 percentile): 438/605. SAT Verbal (25/75 percentile): 465/575. *Academic units required:* 4 English, 3 math, 3 science, 3 social studies, 4 academic electives. Regular application deadline: Rolling. Regular notification: Rolling.

Costs and Financial Aid
(All Undergraduate Programs)
Annual in-state tuition $4,277. Out-of-state tuition $14,324. Room & board $4,322. Required fees $785. Average book expense $450.
Financial Aid Statistics: % freshmen/undergrads who receive any aid: 79/79. % freshmen/undergrads who receive need-based scholarship or grant aid: 22/26. % freshmen/undergrads who receive need-based self-help aid: 44/46. Priority financial aid filing deadline: 3/15. Financial aid filing deadline: 6/15. Financial aid notification on or about: 5/1.

TV/Film/Digital Media Studies Programs
Degrees conferred to these majors: BA.
Equipment and facilities: WWSP-FM with a radius of over 60 miles, 90 FM broacasts in stereo and

hosts the world's largest trivia contest. *The Pointer*, the student-run university newspaper, offers involvement in reporting, advertising, photography, and all other facets of production. Student television conducts regularly scheduled programming on public access cable.

POPULAR PROGRAMS

COMMUNICATIONS
Number of full-time faculty: 17
Focus/emphasis: The Division of Communication offers a single comprehensive communication major and minor. Working with a faculty advisor, you can prepare for a wide range of communication careers in broadcasting, journalism, public relations, management, training, sales, and human services, as well as receive personal enrichment in the humanities and liberal arts. You must complete all course work required for the major or minor and are also expected to acquire strong oral and written communication competencies. The division encourages everyone to participate in one or more of the student organizations and in the internship program. These enhance job opportunities upon graduation by providing practical communication experience.

WEB AND DIGITAL MEDIA DEVELOPMENT

COMMUNICATION WITH MEDIA STUDIES EMPHASIS

UNIVERSITY OF WISCONSIN– SUPERIOR

Belknap & Catlin, PO Box 2000, Superior, WI 54880-4500
Phone: 715-394-8230 **E-mail:** admissions@uwsuper.edu
Website: www.uwsuper.edu

Campus Life
Environment: City. **Calendar:** Semester.

Students and Faculty
(All Undergraduate Programs)
Enrollment: 2,583. **Student Body:** 60% female, 40% male, 42% out-of-state, 5% international (32 countries represented). Asian 1%, Caucasian 88%, Native American 3%. Student/faculty ratio: 18:1. 118 full-time faculty, 72% hold PhDs. 100% faculty teach undergrads.

Admissions
(All Undergraduate Programs)
Freshman Admissions Requirements: Test(s) required: SAT or ACT. 14% in top tenth, 44% in top quarter. SAT Math (25/75 percentile): 500/625. SAT Verbal (25/75 percentile): 485/605. *Academic units required:* 4 English, 3 math, 3 science, 3 social studies, 4 academic electives. Regular notification: Rolling.

Costs and Financial Aid
(All Undergraduate Programs)
Annual in-state tuition $4,547.70. Out-of-state tuition $14,321.70.
Financial Aid Statistics: % freshmen/undergrads who receive any aid: 72/73. % freshmen/undergrads who receive need-based scholarship or grant aid: 22/34. % freshmen/undergrads who receive need-based self-help aid: 41/52. Priority financial aid filing deadline: 4/15. Financial aid notification on or about: 3/15.

TV/Film/Digital Media Studies Programs
Number of undergraduates in these programs: 50
Number of 2005 graduates from these programs: 15
Degrees conferred to these majors: BS.
Also available at University of Wisconsin-Superior: MS.
Number of full-time faculty in these programs: 2
Equipment and facilities: Four Windows-based nonlinear edit suites featuring the Adobe Creative Suite Production Studio; 12 complete sets of remote production equipment including lighting, sound and grip equipment, covering the DVC Pro,

mini-DV, Digital 8 and Hi-8 video formats; real-time television studio, including studio space with grid lighting, 3 cameras, 32-channel audio board, Grass Valley 100 switcher, and DVC Pro videotape recorders.

% of graduates who pursue further study within 5 years: 20
% of graduates currently employed in related field: 75
Career development services: Career counseling, job fairs.

POPULAR PROGRAMS

VIDEO PRODUCTION
Department chair: Martha Einerson
Number of full-time faculty: 2
Focus/emphasis: Prepare students for careers in single camera and studio-based video production.

URSINUS COLLEGE
Ursinus College, Admissions Office, Collegeville, PA 19426
Phone: 610-409-3200 **E-mail:** admissions@ursinus.edu
Website: www.ursinus.edu

Campus Life
Environment: Metropolis. **Calendar:** Semester.

Students and Faculty
(All Undergraduate Programs)
Enrollment: 1,555. **Student Body:** 52% female, 48% male, 39% out-of-state, 1% international. African American 7%, Asian 4%, Caucasian 77%, Hispanic 3%. Student/faculty ratio: 12:1. 115 full-time faculty, 93% hold PhDs. 100% faculty teach undergrads.

Admissions
(All Undergraduate Programs)
Average high school GPA: 3.5. 41% in top tenth, 65% in top quarter. SAT Math (25/75 percentile): 560/670. SAT Verbal (25/75 percentile): 550/660. Projected SAT Writing (25/75 percentile): 610/690. *Academic*

units required: 4 English, 3 math, 1 science (1 science lab), 2 foreign language, 1 social studies, 5 academic electives. Early decision application deadline: 1/15. Regular application deadline: 2/15. Regular notification: 4/15.

Costs and Financial Aid (All Undergraduate Programs)

Annual tuition $33,200. Room & board $7,600. Average book expense $600.

Financial Aid Statistics: % freshmen/undergrads who receive any aid: 78/83. % freshmen/undergrads who receive need-based scholarship or grant aid: 78/83. % freshmen/undergrads who receive need-based self-help aid: 78/83. Priority financial aid filing deadline: 2/15. Financial aid filing deadline: 2/15. Financial aid notification on or about: 4/1.

TV/Film/Digital Media Studies Programs

Number of undergraduates in these programs: 74

Number of 2005 graduates from these programs: 28

Degrees conferred to these majors: BA.

Number of full-time faculty in these programs: 7

Number of part-time faculty in these programs: 2

Equipment and facilities: State-of the-art new media lab, including 20 dual-processor PowerMac G5s with 20" cinema displays, XServe G5, Adobe Creative Suite CS 2, Macromedia Studio 8, Final Cut Studio (FCP HD, DVD Studio Pro 4, Motion 2) AfterEffects. Television production studio with three digital studio cameras, lighting grid and mixer, TelePrompTer, SEG (switcher), CG (character generator), mini-DV VCR, DVD, S-VHS VCR. Linear and nonlinear editing suites for broadcast journalism.

% of graduates who pursue further study within 5 years: 25

% of graduates currently employed in related field: 50

Career development services: Alumni networking opportunities; career counseling; central resource(s)

for employers to browse headshots, writing samples, reels; internship listings; job fairs; job listings.

In Their Own Words

UCTV student-run local origination cable channel, WVOU online student-run campus radio station, Grizzly student-run newspaper, internships at various TV Stations in Center City, Philadelphia along with several production companies, advertising agencies, marketing and PR firms, some internships in NYC, notably production assistantships at ABC's Good Morning America.

POPULAR PROGRAMS

Department chair: Lynne Edwards

Number of full-time faculty: 7

Number of part-time faculty: 2

Focus/emphasis: The Media and Communication Studies Department offers an interdisciplinary course of study in which students examine the aesthetic, cultural, economic, legal, political, and ethical implications of communication in society. Based in the liberal arts and drawing on social scientific and humanistic traditions, our program focuses on the creation, structure, criticism, and impact of messages. This course of study aims to increase awareness of the centrality of communication to identity, social order, and democratic processes.

Students Should Also Know

Ursinus is one of the very few liberal arts colleges to offer a degree program in undergraduate television, film, and digital media studies.

VALDOSTA STATE UNIVERSITY

1500 North Patterson Street, Valdosta, GA 31698
Phone: 229-333-5791 **E-mail:** admissions@valdosta.edu
Website: www.valdosta.edu

Campus Life
Environment: City. **Calendar:** Semester.

Students and Faculty
(All Undergraduate Programs)
Enrollment: 9,015. **Student Body:** 59% female, 41% male, 4% out-of-state. African American 22%, Asian 1%, Caucasian 73%, Hispanic 2%. Student/faculty ratio: 20:1. 435 full-time faculty, 78% hold PhDs. 93% faculty teach undergrads.

Admissions
(All Undergraduate Programs)
Freshman Admissions Requirements: Test(s) required: SAT or ACT. Average high school GPA: 3.03. SAT Math (25/75 percentile): 470/570. SAT Verbal (25/75 percentile): 480/560. Projected SAT Writing (25/75 percentile): 540/620. *Academic units required:* 4 English, 4 math, 3 science (2 science labs), 2 foreign language, 3 social studies. Regular application deadline: 7/1. Regular notification: Rolling.

Costs and Financial Aid
(All Undergraduate Programs)
Annual in-state tuition $2,438. Out-of-state tuition $9,754. Room & board $5,524. Required fees $840. Average book expense $1,000.
Financial Aid Statistics: % freshmen/undergrads who receive any aid: 92/82. % freshmen/undergrads who receive need-based scholarship or grant aid: 51/48. % freshmen/undergrads who receive need-based self-help aid: 46/52. Priority financial aid filing deadline: 5/1. Financial aid notification on or about: 5/15.

TV/Film/Digital Media Studies Programs
Number of undergraduates in these programs: 280
Number of 2005 graduates from these programs: 51

Degrees conferred to these majors: BFA.
Number of full-time faculty in these programs: 8
Equipment and facilities: DVC-Pro Field Equipment, Avid Editors, TV station, radio station, two TV studios, remote production truck.
ATAS Faculty Seminar participants: 3
Other awards of note: Fulbright, two RTNDF fellowships, one RIAS fellowship, one SASAKAWA fellowship

% of graduates who pursue further study within 5 years: 5
% of graduates currently employed in related field: 70
Career development services: Career counseling, central resource(s) for employers to browse headshots, writing samples, reels, internship listings, job fairs, job listings.

In Their Own Words
Students have won nine national awards in the past two years.

POPULAR PROGRAMS

MASS MEDIA
Department chair: Dr. Frank Barnas
Number of full-time faculty: 8
Focus/emphasis: Bachelor of fine arts in mass media with emphases in audio, video, international documentary production, and broadcast journalism.

Students Should Also Know
Please visit www.valdosta.edu/comarts/bfamdia.html.

WALDORF COLLEGE

106 South Sixth Street, Forest City, IA 50436
Phone: 641-585-8112 **E-mail:** admissions@waldorf.edu
Website: www.waldorf.edu

Campus Life
Environment: Rural. **Calendar:** Semester.

Students and Faculty
(All Undergraduate Programs)
Enrollment: 573. **Student Body:** 53% female, 47% male, 6% international. African American 4%, Caucasian 99%. Student/faculty ratio: 15:1. 64 full-time faculty, 25% hold PhDs. 100% faculty teach undergrads.

Admissions
(All Undergraduate Programs)
Freshman Admissions Requirements: Test(s) required: SAT or ACT. Regular notification: Rolling.

Costs and Financial Aid
(All Undergraduate Programs)
Annual tuition $14,599. Room & board $5,670. Required fees $662. Average book expense $350. **Financial Aid Statistics:** % freshmen/undergrads who receive need-based scholarship or grant aid: 79/81. % freshmen/undergrads who receive need-based self-help aid: 68/73. Priority financial aid filing deadline: 3/4. Financial aid notification on or about: 3/4.

TV/Film/Digital Media Studies Programs
Number of undergraduates in these programs: 45
Number of 2005 graduates from these programs: 12
Degrees conferred to these majors: BA.
Number of full-time faculty in these programs: 2
Equipment and facilities: Wal-TV features three Sony BetaCams, professional lighting and sound, TelePrompTers, and an anchor desk. Multimedia labs feature 13 Macintosh G5s with 21-inch flat screen monitors and powerful server. Software includes Adobe CS package; Mac's iSync, iCal, iChat, iMovie, iTunes, iPhoto, and iDVD; Macromedia Dreamweaver; Microsoft Word, Excel, PowerPoint; and Internet access. Radio station features Scott Studio system, Pro Tools DigiDesign, and a marti unit. All full-time communication majors are provided with a laptop computer.

% of graduates currently employed in related field: 20
Career development services: Career counseling, internship listings, job fairs, job listings.
Notable alumni: Cory Crawford, East Coast representative for Safari Productions; Philip Shtoll, owner of Norman Street, a postproduction company in Santa Monica, CA; Lawrence (Eljay) Sinniah, executive director of Cahayasuara Communications Center in Kuala Lumpur, Malaysia; Liz Sorensen (Barker), website content director for Winnebago Industries.

In Their Own Words
We require two internships as part of our program and have students intern at Access Hollywood; Fox Sports in Boston; KROC in Rochester, MN; Disney World College Program in Orlando, FL; WHO-TV in Des Moines, IA; and Iowa Public Television.

POPULAR PROGRAMS

COMMUNICATIONS, TV EMPHASIS
Department chair: David Damm
Number of full-time faculty: 2
Number of part-time faculty: 2
Focus/emphasis: postproduction and broadcast television.

Students Should Also Know
In addition to our outstanding equipment, we feature hands-on teaching, opportunities in media from day one on campus, faculty with professional experience, a 100 percent placement rate the past two years and 97 percent for the past 10 years, and the required two internships.

WARTBURG COLLEGE

100 Wartburg Boulevard, PO Box 1003, Waverly, IA 50677-0903
Phone: 319-352-8264 **E-mail:** admissions@wartburg.edu
Website: www.wartburg.edu

Campus Life
Environment: Village.

Students and Faculty
(All Undergraduate Programs)
Enrollment: 1,768. **Student Body:** 53% female, 47% male, 23% out-of-state, 5% international (37 countries represented). African American 3%, Asian 1%, Caucasian 85%, Hispanic 1%. Student/faculty ratio: 12:1. 106 full-time faculty, 80% hold PhDs. 100% faculty teach undergrads.

Admissions
(All Undergraduate Programs)
Freshman Admissions Requirements: Test(s) required: SAT or ACT. Average high school GPA: 3.5. 31% in top tenth, 61% in top quarter. SAT Math (25/75 percentile): 500/650. SAT Verbal (25/75 percentile): 500/600. Projected SAT Writing (25/75 percentile): 560/650. Regular notification: Rolling.

Costs and Financial Aid
(All Undergraduate Programs)
Annual tuition $20,500. Room & board $5,765. Required fees $630. Average book expense $800. **Financial Aid Statistics:** % freshmen/undergrads who receive any aid: 90/85. % freshmen/undergrads who receive need-based scholarship or grant aid: 77/78. % freshmen/undergrads who receive need-based self-help aid: 64/68. Priority financial aid filing deadline: 3/1. Financial aid notification on or about: 3/21.

TV/Film/Digital Media Studies Programs
Number of undergraduates in these programs: 190
Number of 2005 graduates from these programs: 53
Degrees conferred to these majors: BA.
Number of full-time faculty in these programs: 3

Number of part-time faculty in these programs: 1

Equipment and facilities: The students' classroom theory is enhanced with the use and practical application of the hardware and software typically encountered in the television and digital media work environment. The digital ENG/EFP camcorders and support equipment are equivalent in form and function to those used by professionals in the industry. Students learn proper care and operation of field equipment from a technical aspect while learning the artistic elements of video/audio composition and lighting techniques to record source material for production of documentary programs, packages for inclusion in news and entertainment programs, and elements for spot announcements of promotional, commercial, and public service nature. The equipment is also used for live productions of convocations, sports events, and other campus events. Weekly programs and special event coverage is produced in a fully functional, student managed television production facility. A network computer system is used to create program rundowns and compose scripts. The video switcher, tape machines, graphics system, audio mixer, and studio cameras are representative of the equipment that students will encounter in the workplace. Students learn the nature and value of interactions of studio camera operators, floor director, anchors, TelePrompTer operator, production director, audio operator, producer, video tape operator, and graphics operator. Productions can be intense, which provides the insight to function under pressure and knowledge of how best to recover when things go wrong. Selected programs are then repurposed for podcasting from the television website.

Other awards of note: Northwest Broadcast News Association Awards to Wartburg TV in the Best Newscast category four times since 2000 and two first-place awards for Best Documentary during the same timeframe. WTV also has recently won awards for sports reporting and sports play-by-play. Iowa Broadcast News Association awards: four best newscast awards since 2000, as well as three overall excellence awards, and one for best sportscast, in addition to many individual student honors for news and sports reporting. Society for Collegiate Journalists: In national competition, WTV typically takes home half of the TV awards presented, including first place last year for best commercial/PSA and best news story. The WTV student staff was recognized in the most recent feature done by the national *Broadcasting and Cable* magazine as one of the ones to watch.

% of graduates who pursue further study within 5 years: 7

% of graduates currently employed in related field: 25

Career development services: Alumni networking opportunities, career counseling, internship listings, job fairs, job listings.

Notable alumni: In 2002, Eric Hanson, KCCI-TV in Des Moines, Iowa, and photojournalist Jeff Christian received a regional Emmy award for one of their feature stories. Hanson has also earned awards from the Iowa Broadcast News Association, the Associate Press, and the Wisconsin Broadcast News Association. In 2003, Hanson and Christian won the national Edward R. Murrow Award. The award from the Radio-Television News Directors Association honors outstanding achievements in electronic journalism. Out of the 2,770 entries, only 49 news organizations were honored with the award. Hanson also won a regional Murrow Award in 2005 for his writing.

In Their Own Words

More than 250 alumni continue involvement with Wartburg communications through membership in the Society for Collegiate Journalists as well as assisting students to acquire internships and professional positions. Field experiences and internships are provided by numerous radio and television stations. Wartburg also hosts the Iowa Broadcasters Association Summer Broadcasting Workshop. Each summer students learn about television, radio, and the business of broadcasting. They do live broadcasts on Wartburg radio 89.1, KWAR-FM, and Wartburg Television/WTV8 and use Wartburg's state-of-the-art digital equipment and facilities. The summer workshop also includes tours of professional radio and TV facilities, meetings with area media professionals, and activities to help students develop the skills needed to get ahead in this exciting profession.

POPULAR PROGRAMS

ELECTRONIC MEDIA

Department chair: Dr. William Withers

WASHINGTON STATE UNIVERSITY

PO Box 641067, Pullman, WA 99164-1067
Phone: 509-335-5586 **E-mail:** admiss2@wsu.edu
Website: www.wsu.edu

Campus Life

Environment: Town. **Calendar:** Semester.

Students and Faculty
(All Undergraduate Programs)

Enrollment: 19,585. **Student Body:** 52% female, 48% male, 11% out-of-state, 5% international (91 countries represented). African American 2%, Asian 5%, Caucasian 72%, Hispanic 4%, Native American 1%. Student/faculty ratio: 15:1. 1,057 full-time faculty, 89% hold PhDs. 85% faculty teach undergrads.

Admissions
(All Undergraduate Programs)

Freshman Admissions Requirements: Test(s) required: SAT or ACT; ACT with Writing component. Average high school GPA: 3.45. 37% in top tenth, 57% in top quarter. SAT Math (25/75 percentile): 510/610. SAT Verbal (25/75 percentile): 490/600. Projected SAT Writing (25/75 percentile): 550/650. *Academic units required:* 4 English, 3 math, 2 science (1 science lab), 2 foreign language (American Sign Language or a Native American language accepted), 2 social studies, 1 history, 1 academic elective. Regular notification: Rolling.

Costs and Financial Aid
(All Undergraduate Programs)

Annual in-state tuition $5,432. Out-of-state tuition $15,072. Room & board $6,592. Required fees $933. Average book expense $912.

Financial Aid Statistics: % freshmen/undergrads who receive any aid: 77/74. % freshmen/undergrads who receive need-based scholarship or grant aid: 26/34. % freshmen/undergrads who receive need-based self-help aid: 37/46. Priority financial aid filing deadline: 3/1. Financial aid notification on or about: 4/15.

TV/Film/Digital Media Studies Programs

Number of undergraduates in these programs: 742

Number of full-time faculty in these programs: 35

Number of part-time faculty in these programs: 4 (plus faculty from diverse disciplines who contribute to multidisciplinary programs).

Equipment and facilities: 175-seat auditorium with walls that open to reveal a digital TV studio; Cable 8 news studio; communication children's media research lab; computer facilities; digital recording studio for music students; director's booth and four edit suites for broadcast journalism students; electronic piano and computer instruction lab; library digital services/collections and media material reserves.

% of graduates currently employed in related field: 60–100% (varies by program)

Career development services: Alumni networking opportunities, career counseling, internship listings in all fields, required internships in some fields, placement assistance, job fairs, job listings.

In Their Own Words

Washington State University named its communication school after alumnus Edward R. Murrow, the network newscaster who set the standard for broadcast journalists. The university's academic programs in the realms of television, film, and digital media uphold the Murrow tradition and stand among the nation's finest.

Broadcasting students consistently win awards and receive wide recognition from industry professionals. They learn by doing and graduate ready to take their places behind the scenes or in front of the camera or microphone. Broadcasting graduates are employed at top stations and networks with exciting careers in news, program development, station operations, and more. Advertising students often win national competitions and have been featured in the New York Times *and* USA Today. *Advertising graduates work at top firms in the country's best markets. Agricultural communications students, who enjoy both the resources of the Murrow School and those of one of the nation's finest agriculture programs, have won national awards and fellowships. One hundred percent of agricultural communication graduates enter careers in communications, agricultural communications, or public relations. Digital technology and culture students learn to think critically and integrate ideas from different disciplines; this prepares them well for graduate school and professional careers. Film studies students gain human insights that are important for leadership in all professions. Many graduates pursue careers in television, photography, and advertising.*

POPULAR PROGRAMS

DTC PROGRAM

Department chair: George E. Kennedy (program is located in the Department of English; Patricia Freitag Ericsson is the program coordinator)

Number of full-time faculty: 3

Number of part-time faculty: Because this program spans many disciplines, dozens of faculty teach courses required for the major.

Focus/emphasis: This interdisciplinary program draws from more than 10 departments and emphasizes an understanding of the interaction between humans and machines. Some students see the major as their route to a career designing Web pages, video games, and Wiki sites. Students choose from three concentrations: hyper-/multi-media rhetoric and composition, electronic research and knowledge management, or language, technology, and society. Students select many of their own courses; these range from anthropology to information technology to poetry writing.

AGRICULTURAL COMMUNICATIONS PROGRAM

Department chair: Dr. William Pan (program is located in the Department of Crop and Soil Sciences)
Number of full-time faculty: 1
Focus/emphasis: The program provides a broad education in agriculture, combined with courses (advertising, broadcasting, journalism, and public relations) offered through the Edward R. Murrow School of Communication. Students may tailor the program to their individual interests. Required internships in related industries enable students to apply classroom knowledge as they explore career choices.

DIGITAL MEDIA PROGRAM

Department chair: Carol Ivory (program is located in the Department of Fine Arts)
Number of full-time faculty: 3
Number of part-time faculty: 1
Focus/emphasis: Students enrolled in digital media at Washington State University explore a range of digital processes including Web art, digital video, and digital imaging. The degree allows students to bridge traditional and digital processes and explore other media, particularly printmaking and photography, in conjunction with the computer. The role of digital media in culture is consistently addressed; students explore such themes as the Web, a contemporary curiosity cabinet, and the role of truth in the digital age.

COMMUNICATION PROGRAM

Department chair: Erica Austin (interim director of the Edward R. Murrow School of Communication)
Focus/emphasis: The Edward R. Murrow School of Communication offers course sequences in

advertising and broadcasting, among other fields. Advertising students receive a solid grounding in communication theory and the liberal arts, then put their knowledge to use in preparing media plans, writing advertising strategy and copy, and planning and executing complete campaigns. The broadcasting sequence offers emphases in production, news, and management. In the production track, students receive studio and field training in both audio and video production and gain hands-on experience with the school's state-of-the-art equipment. Broadcast news students are exposed to both radio and television news reporting. They generate nightly television cablecasts, which they anchor, shoot, edit, and produce.

FILM STUDIES PROGRAM

Department chair: Birgitta Ingemanson (program coordinator; this multidisciplinary program is offered through the College of Liberal Arts)
Focus/emphasis: Students earning a minor in film studies explore how cinema both reflects and influences the facts, ideas, and activities of a given society and how to discern the cinematic and narrative features that are used in cinematography and the ways culture can influence them. The study of film encourages critical thinking, respect for cultural diversity, and detailed knowledge of film as a text of facts and ideas.

WEBER STATE UNIVERSITY

1137 University Circle, Ogden, UT 84408-1137
Phone: 801-626-6744 **E-mail:** admissions@weber.edu
Website: www.weber.edu

Campus Life
Environment: Village. **Calendar:** Semester.

Students and Faculty (All Undergraduate Programs)
Enrollment: 17,688. **Student Body:** 50% female, 50% male, 5% out-of-state. Asian 2%, Caucasian 60%, Hispanic 3%. Student/faculty ratio: 22:1. 465

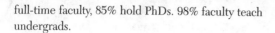

full-time faculty, 85% hold PhDs. 98% faculty teach undergrads.

Admissions
(All Undergraduate Programs)
Average high school GPA: 3.34. 63% in top quarter. Regular application deadline: 8/22. Regular notification: Rolling.

Costs and Financial Aid
(All Undergraduate Programs)
Annual in-state tuition $2,547. Out-of-state tuition $9,008. Room & board $6,500. Required fees $591. Average book expense $900.
Financial Aid Statistics: % freshmen/undergrads who receive any aid: 84/87. % freshmen/undergrads who receive need-based scholarship or grant aid: 24/32. % freshmen/undergrads who receive need-based self-help aid: 17/25. Priority financial aid filing deadline: 3/1. Financial aid notification on or about: 3/15.

TV/Film/Digital Media Studies Programs
Number of undergraduates in these programs: 45
Number of 2005 graduates from these programs: 10
Degrees conferred to these majors: BA, BS.
Number of full-time faculty in these programs: 3
Equipment and facilities: Television studio and control room, eight digital editors, six digital ENG cameras.

% of graduates currently employed in related field: 90%
Career development services: Career counseling, internship listings, job fairs, job listings.
Notable alumni: Staci McKay, news producer; Sean Milner, video director; Andrew Tyler, video director; Stacey Cragun, news producer, April Marsh, video production house; Sean Anderton, videographer; Aaron Gee, chief videographer; Randy Kendall, videographer; Jeremy Brunner, sports producer; J Bates, sports producer; Andrew Jackson, sports magazine editor; Marty Carpenter, sports

anchor; Ira Cronin, sports anchor; Megan Jones, sports anchor; Tamara Davies, news producer; Angie Burton, freelance rodeo anchor; Clark Wilson, independent video producer; Todd Kohler, commercial producer; Chad Jemmett, news producer; Ian Auger, news producer.

In Their Own Words
The National Broadcasting Society has named our student newscast, Weber State News, *the best newscast in the region six years running. This year our newscasts swept the best newscast category. We also took first, second, and third places in the news reporting and feature reporting categories. An annual video we produce for the arts and humanities convocation has won numerous awards, including national finalist and grand prize winner. We place interns at all the Salt Lake City stations.*

POPULAR PROGRAMS

TELEVISION NEWS PRODUCTION
Department chair: Dr. Randy Scott
Number of full-time faculty: 3
Focus/emphasis: Preparing future news reporters, producers, videographers, editors, and managers.

RADIO PRODUCTION
Number of full-time faculty: 3
Focus/emphasis: Preparing students for jobs in radio on-the-air, and in management, sales, and production.

VIDEO PRODUCTION
Number of full-time faculty: 3
Focus/emphasis: Preparing students for commercial, corporate, and educational video production.

ENTERTAINMENT
Number of full-time faculty: 3
Focus/emphasis: Preparing students for entry level jobs in the entertainment (television/film) industry.

WESTERN ILLINOIS UNIVERSITY

One University Circle, 115 Sherman Hall, Macomb, IL 61455-1390
Phone: 309-298-3157 **E-mail:** wiuadm@wiu.edu
Website: www.wiu.edu

Campus Life
Environment: Village. **Calendar:** Semester.

Students and Faculty
(All Undergraduate Programs)
Enrollment: 13,400. **Student Body:** 50.7% female, 49.3% male, 6% out-of-state, 2% international (50 countries represented). African American 6.3%, Asian 1.3%, Caucasian 81%, Hispanic 3.4%. Student/faculty ratio: 17:1. 649 full-time faculty, 71% hold PhDs. 95% faculty teach undergrads.

Admissions
(All Undergraduate Programs)
Freshman Admissions Requirements: Test(s) required: SAT or ACT. Average high school GPA: 2.90. 5% in top tenth, 22% in top quarter. Regular notification: Within 24–48 hours after receiving application.

Costs and Financial Aid
(All Undergraduate Programs)
Annual in-state tuition $5,439. Out-of-state tuition $8,158. Room & board $6,445. Required fees $1,931. **Financial Aid Statistics:** % freshmen/undergrads who receive any aid: 76/75. % freshmen/undergrads who receive need-based scholarship or grant aid: 35/38. % freshmen/undergrads who receive need-based self-help aid: 47/49. Priority financial aid filing deadline: 2/1. Financial aid notification on or about: 4–6 weeks after filing.

TV/Film/Digital Media Studies Programs
Number of undergraduates in these programs: 212
Number of 2005 graduates from these programs: 38
Degrees conferred to these majors: BA.
Number of full-time faculty in these programs: 7
Equipment and facilities: Live sports truck, digital television studio, digital master control, broadcast radio station, nonlinear digital editing suites, animation, online journalism.
Other awards of note: Illinois Broadcasters Association, Illinois News Broadcasters Association.

% of graduates who pursue further study within 5 years: 10
% of graduates currently employed in related field: 70
Career development services: Alumni networking opportunities; central resource(s) for employers to browse headshots, writing samples, reels; job fairs; job listings.
Famous alumni: Brian Cox, Mike Scifres.
Notable alumni: Tim Abshire, director of TV commercials; Robert Gould, ATAS; William Bund, ABC.

In Their Own Words
Internship program, hands-on program, digital broadcasting, quality equipment in television and radio.

POPULAR PROGRAMS

BROADCASTING
Department chair: Dr. Sharon Evans
Number of full-time faculty: 7
Focus/emphasis: Students in the broadcasting program study digital audio and video production techniques, including nonlinear editing, post-production, animation/graphics, and sports. WIUS-FM and WWIR-TV give students the opportunity to put into practice learned skills. They also examine the impact of history, law, and programming on broadcasting, cable, and satellite operations. Graduates of the program enter various careers in television, radio, cable, satellite, and postproduction operations, including directing, producing, reporting, on-air talent programming, sales, advertising, sports, and postproduction.

WESTERN KENTUCKY UNIVERSITY

Potter Hall 117, 1906 College Heights Boulevard, Bowling Green, KY 42101-1020

Phone: 270-745-2551 **E-mail:** admission@wku.edu
Website: www.wku.edu

Campus Life

Environment: Town. **Calendar:** Semester.

Students and Faculty
(All Undergraduate Programs)

Enrollment: 15,341. **Student Body:** 58% female, 42% male, 17% out-of-state, 1% international (55 countries represented). African American 9%, Caucasian 86%. Student/faculty ratio 19:1. 694 full-time faculty, 74% hold PhDs. 93% faculty teach undergrads.

Admissions
(All Undergraduate Programs)

Freshman Admissions Requirements: Test(s) required: SAT or ACT. Average high school GPA: 3.0. 15% in top tenth, 36% in top quarter. SAT Math (25/75 percentile): 440/560. SAT Verbal (25/75 percentile): 450/550. Projected SAT Writing (25/75 percentile): 520/610. *Academic units required:* 4 English; 3 math; 3 science (1 science lab); 2 foreign language; 3 social studies, 1 health and physical education, history, or performing arts. Regular application deadline: 8/1.

Costs and Financial Aid
(All Undergraduate Programs)

Annual in-state tuition $5,316. Out-of-state tuition $12,732. Room & board $4,876. Average book expense $800.

Financial Aid Statistics: % freshmen/undergrads who receive any aid: 53/54. % freshmen/undergrads who receive need-based scholarship or grant aid: 35/35. % freshmen/undergrads who receive need-based self-help aid: 33/38. Priority financial aid filing deadline: 4/1. Financial aid notification on or about: 3/1.

TV/Film/Digital Media Studies Programs

Degrees conferred to these majors: BA.

Other awards of note: The School of Journalism & Broadcasting finished 3rd overall in the 46th Hearst Intercollegiate Journalism Awards Program. Photojournalism students finished first overall in the Hearst photojournalism competition, with the highest accumulated school points from two out of the three photo competitions. This is the 15th time in 17 years for WKU to win the overall P.J. competition. Christian Hansen took 5th place, and Jenica Miller tied for 11th place in the Picture Story/Series Competition. In the Photojournalism Sports & News Competition, William Deshazer won 2nd place, and Nathan Morgan won a 17th-place tie. Allen Bryant placed 5th, and Christian Hansen placed 6th in the Portrait/Personality & Feature Competition. William Deshazer and Allen Bryant qualified for the 2006 National Championship Finals in Photojournalism. Broadcasting students placed 6th overall in the Broadcast News division. Brenna Gallegos won 5th place in Radio News and qualified for the 2006 National Championship Finals. Katie Burcham placed 19th in Radio News. Cory Paul won 1st place in the Spot News Writing competition and qualified for the 2006 National Writing Championship. The Hearst Journalism Awards Program is presented annually under the auspices of the Association of Schools of Journalism and Mass Communication (ASJMC) with full funding by the William Randolph Hearst Foundation. The program's mission is to encourage and support excellence in journalism and journalism education in America's colleges and universities.

Career development services: Internship listings.

In Their Own Words

All students are encouraged strongly to obtain internships, primarily during the summer, because they provide invaluable professional experience. The majority of students have one or more internships before graduation. Almost all students seeking internships in their respective fields are able to obtain employment. Only advertising, broadcasting, and PR students may take internships for credit in their majors. There are many internships available to all students. Students should check with the program coordinator and department books for current internship opportunities.

POPULAR PROGRAMS

MASS COMMUNICATIONS

Program coordinator: Jo-Anne Ryan (interim)

Focus/emphasis: The major in mass communication offers students the opportunity to acquire a broad, flexible, interdisciplinary liberal arts education that is aimed at a comprehensive understanding of the dynamics of mass communication in society. For this reason, the major is unique in the School of Journalism and Broadcasting, in that it is not a specialized professional program. The mass communication major emphasizes critical thinking about the role of mass media in society. Graduates seek a wide variety of careers and post-graduate work. The major (reference number 725) requires 36 semester hours and leads to a bachelor of arts degree. A minor or second major from outside the School of Journalism and Broadcasting is required. The major is made up of 18 hours of required courses and 18 hours of elective courses chosen in consultation with the student's departmental advisor, within designated areas.

BROADCASTING

Department chair: Stephen White

Focus/emphasis: The broadcasting curriculum offers classroom and practical experience in radio, television, and film production; broadcast news; station management; sales; and on-air performance. The major prepares students for direct entry into the television, cable, radio, commercial, and noncommercial production industries. Students entering the major in broadcasting may choose from three sequences for their study emphasis as listed below: Broadcast news sequence, television production sequence, radio and television operations sequence.

NEWS/EDITORIAL

Program coordinator: Gordon D. McKerral

Focus/emphasis: The major in News/editorial journalism requires 39 semester hours in the School of Journalism & Broadcasting. Specific objectives are to: Prepare students for professional careers in newspaper journalism; instill in students a high degree of professionalism, which consists principally of practical competence and ethical understanding; and enhance students' understanding of the role of the press in a democratic society.

PHOTOJOURNALISM

Program coordinator: James Kenney

Focus/emphasis: The major in photojournalism requires 39 semester hours in the School of Journalism & Broadcasting. Specific objectives are to: Develop the artistic, technical and personal qualities of those who pursue a professional career in photojournalism; develop a background for understanding the role of photojournalism in shaping and reflecting contemporary society; and provide instruction in photographic theory, principles and practice for the student in any area of scholarly pursuit where such knowledge is needed to improve understanding and abilities. Students declaring a major in photojournalism may select from two unique curriculum tracks: photojournalism track or new media publishing track.

Students Should Also Know

The school embraces the concept that broad-based liberal arts curriculum is essential for a well-rounded understanding of society. It upholds the ideal that the American press system should be free, independent, and responsible. Through its course work and extracurricular activities, the school and its faculty encourage students to be critical thinkers and competent communicators, to be aware of ethical values and historical perspectives, and to gain insight into the functions and responsibilities of contemporary communications institutions. A high priority is the encouragement of students to be able to adapt, both intellectually and creatively, to the realities and challenges of an increasingly diverse and complex information society. Students are encouraged to seek practical experience through work on student publications and broadcasting outlets, other campus publications, local media, and internships at newspapers, magazines, advertising firms, radio and television stations, businesses, public relations agencies, and other institutions. Students may gain experience by working on the *College Heights Herald*, the campus newspaper; WWHR, a licensed noncommercial FM station managed and staffed by students; the student advertising and public relations agency ImageWest; and the student TV newscast *Newschannel12*. Qualified students may gain additional experience on campus through staff work at the National Public Radio station, WKYU-FM, or crew employment at the Public Broadcasting System member station, WKYU-TV24.

WILKES UNIVERSITY

84 West South Street, Wilkes-Barre, PA 18766
Phone: 570-408-4400 **E-mail:** admissions@wilkes.edu
Website: www.wilkes.edu

Campus Life
Environment: City. **Calendar:** Semester.

Students and Faculty
(All Undergraduate Programs)
Enrollment: 2,147. **Student Body:** 53% female, 47% male, 19% out-of-state. African American 2%, Asian 2%, Caucasian 91%, Hispanic 2%. Student/faculty ratio: 15:1. 131 full-time faculty, 87% hold PhDs. 100% faculty teach undergrads.

Admissions
(All Undergraduate Programs)
Freshman Admissions Requirements: Test(s) required: SAT or ACT. 20% in top tenth, 48% in top quarter. SAT Math (25/75 percentile): 480/600. SAT Verbal (25/75 percentile): 480/580. Projected SAT Writing (25/75 percentile): 540/630. *Academic units required:* 2 introduction to computing. Regular notification: Rolling.

Costs and Financial Aid
(All Undergraduate Programs)
Annual tuition $20,592. Room & board $9,240. Required fees $1,054. Average book expense $1,050. **Financial Aid Statistics:** % freshmen/undergrads who receive any aid: 93/91. % freshmen/undergrads who receive need-based scholarship or grant aid: 86/81. % freshmen/undergrads who receive need-based self-help aid: 83/77. Priority financial aid filing deadline: 3/1. Financial aid notification on or about: 3/1.

TV/Film/Digital Media Studies Programs
Number of undergraduates in these programs: 6
Degrees conferred to these majors: BA.
Career development services: Alumni networking opportunities, career counseling, internship listings, job fairs, job listings.

POPULAR PROGRAMS

INTEGRATED MEDIA
Department chair: Eric Ruggiero

YALE UNIVERSITY

PO Box 208234, New Haven, CT 06520-8234
Phone: 203-432-9300 **E-mail:** undergraduate.admissions@yale.edu
Website: www.yale.edu/

Campus Life
Environment: City. **Calendar:** Semester.

Students and Faculty
(All Undergraduate Programs)
Enrollment: 5,319. **Student Body:** 49.5% female, 50.5% male, 92% out-of-state, 9% international (108 countries represented). African American 8%, Asian 14%, Caucasian 51%, Hispanic 7%. Student/faculty ratio: 6:1.

Admissions
(All Undergraduate Programs)

Freshman Admissions Requirements: Test(s) required: SAT and SAT Subject Tests or ACT; ACT with Writing component. 95% in top tenth, 4% in top quarter. SAT Math (25/75 percentile): 700/790. SAT Verbal (25/75 percentile): 700/790. Projected SAT Writing (25/75 percentile): 720/780. Regular application deadline: 12/31. Regular notification: 4/1.

Costs and Financial Aid
(All Undergraduate Programs)

Annual tuition $21,575.

Financial Aid Statistics: % freshmen/undergrads who receive need-based scholarship or grant aid: 42/41. % freshmen/undergrads who receive need-based self-help aid: 44/42. Priority financial aid filing deadline: 3/1. Financial aid filing deadline: 3/1. Financial aid notification on or about: 4/1.

TV/Film/Digital Media Studies Programs

Degrees conferred to these majors: BA, BS.
Also available at Yale University: PhD.
Equipment and facilities: The Yale Film Study Center is the home for a growing collection of film titles in various formats, as well as scripts, books, and other reference material. They have more than 2,000 16 mm prints; 3,300 titles on DVD; 600 titles on laser disc; and 4,300 titles on VHS. The Whitney Humanities Center was inaugurated in 1981 as an interdisciplinary institution built on Yale's long-standing commitment to the humanities; it was designed to enable and enhance research, thinking, and scholarly exchange in all fields of the humanities and throughout the university. The center seeks to support and strengthen the activities of faculty and graduate students in the humanities and neighboring fields by creating a sense of intellectual community that transcends departmental boundaries and by fostering collegial dialogue, informed debate, and the pursuit of new fields of inquiry. The center's programs include symposia, lectures, faculty seminars, and working groups. Some of these bring distinguished visitors to the university; others are primarily designed free and informal exchange of ideas among faculty and advanced graduate students on topics of more than disciplinary interest. At the core of the center is a set of fellows, drawn from the several departments of the humanities and from other fields.

POPULAR PROGRAMS

FILM STUDIES

Department chair: Dudley Andrew and Charles Musser
Number of full-time faculty: 22 (45 faculty total are associated with the program)
Focus/emphasis: Film studies is an interdisciplinary program that focuses on the history, theory, and criticism of cinema and other moving image media. Undergraduates can major in film studies while graduate students can pursue a film studies PhD in conjunction with another department. Courses examine cinema's role as a unique art form that now spans three centuries and the contributions of moving image media as practices of enduring cultural and social significance. The program draws on courses from a number of disciplines and departments, including American studies, anthropology, art, comparative literature, English, French, German, history, history of art, Italian, Slavic, sociology, and theater studies. As an interdisciplinary program, film studies offers students latitude in defining their course of study within the framework established by the Film Studies Committee. With this freedom comes the responsibility of devoting careful thought to planning a coherent and well-focused program. Because of the special demands of film studies and the diversity of its offerings, potential majors are encouraged to consult with the director of undergraduate studies early in their academic careers. With the help of the director of undergraduate studies in film studies, each student defines an area of concentration making up six courses. The six courses should form a coherent program in which the study of film is integrated with a particular discipline (history of art, literature, philosophy, the social sciences) or area of investigation (film theory, production, race and

gender, photography, national or regional cultures and their cinemas). The focus of the concentration may also be a given historical or theoretical problem drawn from two areas, such as German expressionism in film and in art or narrative theory in film and in the novel. Students choosing a production-related concentration must take at least seven critical studies courses in the major (four in addition to the prerequisite and required courses).

GLOSSARY

GLOSSARY

above the line. For budget, all production costs related to story and script, including those of employing the producers, director, and cast. For industry professionals, all individuals involved in the creative process of a production.

Academy of Motion Picture Arts & Sciences. Organization made up of motion picture industry professionals; recognizes excellence in motion pictures through the annual Academy Awards®.

Academy of Television Arts & Sciences. Organization composed of television industry professionals; recognizes excellence in television through the annual primetime Emmy® Awards.

alternative programming. Television programming that is outside the confines of conventional primetime, half-hour comedy (sitcom), hour drama, daytime, or late night programming. The term is used to describe shows that are unscripted and usually nonfiction-based; it is inclusive of *reality* programming. A network's Alternative Programming Department also oversees the development of variety and music/concert specials such as the Academy Awards, Emmy Awards, Grammy Awards, MTV Music Awards, and Christmas or other holiday-themed special programs.

American Broadcasting Company, The. Commonly referred to as ABC. *Variety*'s term: "the alphabet network." Part of the Walt Disney Company.

animation. Process of creating static figures that appear to move. Cell animation figures, background, and so forth are created on individual cells and photographed to make it appear as if they move (*Lion King*). Computer animation entails the same process as above, but figures and background are created on computers (*Finding Nemo*). Other processes of animation include stop-motion (*Wallace & Gromit in the Case of the Were-Rabbit*) and claymation (which itself is a form of stop-motion animation). In these processes, figures are moved and filmed incrementally to create a sense of movement. In television, children's programming is composed primarily of animation, but animation moved to primetime with such shows as *The Flintstones, Rocky & Bullwinkle*, and *The Simpsons*. Primetime animated series and characters have generally pushed the behavioral and language limits of traditional television (Comedy Central's *South Park*). *Television Academy Peer Group:* Animation checker, animation computer programmer, animation modeler, animation sculptor, animation technical director, animator, background artist/stylist, camera operator, character designer, director, animation voice director, executive producer, film-tape editor, ink and paint supervisor, layout artist, producer.

arc. See **character arc, story arc**.

art director/set director. Individual responsible for the work of designing sets for television and films. Set decorators create the décor in collaboration with the production designer or art director. *Television Academy Peer Group:* Production designer, art director, set decorator, scenic designer.

attach a star/"attached". Securing the interest or commitment of an actor to a project for the purpose of attracting the interest of a network; may also apply to director or writer of high caliber or to special effects. "Attaching" is usually done with the hope of enhancing the project as a package, but it may involve a star who wants a producer credit and a share in the profits; this decreases profit participation for the producer.

back end. A financial term used to describe profits taken after a series or film has recouped its production and marketing costs or after it has sold into domestic and international syndication. Sometimes talent (including stars) are given more on the back end to compensate for a lower up-front salary. The flip side is front end, for which salary or up-front perks make up the primary financial compensation for participation in a project.

beat sheet. An abbreviated outline of a story, or a blueprint for a script, with brief descriptions of each scene, usually broken down into acts.

below the line. For budget, all production costs other than story and script, producers, director, and cast. For industry professionals, all individuals involved in the technical process of a production.

biopic: *Variety*-coined term; biographical film or original television movie.

blind commitment. Refers to a deal made by network or studio with a producer, a writer, or an actor to develop new projects following the success of a current project. This is done primarily to reward a successful producer, writer, or actor, or to maintain exclusivity on his or her talent to ensure the future success of the network or studio.

branding. Advertising term; the creation of a specific identity for an item or a service. Used extensively by broadcast or cable to attempt to create an identity for its programming. For example, Lifetime's brand is women's programming; FX's brand is adult male, cutting-edge programming.

breakout/breakout hit. A television show or film that distinguishes itself from the competition either by ratings, box office, or public interest (not necessarily in large numbers). Sometimes used to describe an actor who distinguishes himself or herself from other actors in a season of television.

broadcast. In television and radio, the distribution system in which programming is delivered over the airwaves to viewers who are not charged for the service.

broadcast network/network TV. ABC, CBS, FBC (Fox), NBC, CW; "parent" company and major programming supplier that provides programming in all-day parts to a group of television stations that are broadcast locally in markets across the United States. These stations air this programming using broadcast airwaves. Stations can be either owned and operated by the parent company (O&Os) or owned by another company and financially affiliated with it (affiliates). Broadcast networks are usually the most desirable place to develop and produce original programming because the broadcast reaches the largest audiences; note, however, that this position has changed substantially with the continued growth of cable.

Broadcast Standards and Practices. Network department that reviews scripts and finished products to ensure that legal and broadcast (FCC) standards are upheld. Sex, violence, and offensive language are the primary issues.

Business Affairs. In studio or network, the department usually composed of attorneys who negotiate deals on behalf of the studio or network for writers, producers, directors, actors, and others working with creative and production departments. They are conversant with guild and craft contracts and precedents of the industry.

buyer. A television network or cable network, program syndicator or station group, film studio, or production or financial entity that has the capability to fund, in whole or part, production of a television show or motion picture, and thereby possesses complete or partial creative control over the project and product.

cable/cable network. In television, the distribution system in which programming is delivered by cable to subscribers, who typically pay a monthly fee to one of many regionally-based cable companies. Options include basic cable (multiple channels offered to subscribers at a fairly low cost) and premium or pay channels (which require a fee in addition to basic cable fees).

cast-contingent. When a buyer makes a commitment to finance and produce a project based on specific casting (see **attach a star**). All cable and television network movies are now cast-contingent. This may also take place when a pilot for a series is picked up for production, cast-contingent on finding a lead actor or actress whom the network and producer agree upon.

casting director. The person responsible for casting (identifying actors, setting up auditions, readings, and making deals) a motion picture or television show. He or she manages everything related to casting actors/voices, from auditions to making offers to agents. *Television Academy Peer Group:* Casting executive, casting director, casting associate, assistant, and coordinator.

character. Individual part or role in script played by an actor.

character arc. Generally refers to how a character changes or grows emotionally or in some other specified manner throughout a story. For example, Carmela Soprano began the series as a spirited but unquestioning wife of mafia don Tony Soprano, and over several seasons, became a woman struggling with her own identity, religious conviction, and marriage. This is a key element in the structure of a script.

character-driven. Project, story, script, or screenplay that relies on the strength of the main character or a group of characters whose decisions and actions drive the plot forward, rather than relying on the story concept or artificial plotting to sustain the narrative. Also used to describe films or television shows with smaller stories, less plot, and few special effects.

children's programming. Programming designed to appeal to children. Cable channels such as Saturday Morning Cartoons, Nickelodeon, Cartoon Network, and the Disney Channel program almost entirely for children. *Television Academy Peer Group:* Executive, producer, writer, director, or performer in children's television or new media programming.

chopsocky. Another industry term first coined by *Variety*; this refers to a martial arts film form perfected by Hong Kong stars and directors such as Jackie Chan and Wang Kar Wei.

cinematography/cinematographer. Cinematography is the art and technique of making motion pictures using a camera, or capturing moving image/visuals using a camera. The cinematographer is the person in charge of cameras and visual look of a motion picture or television program; also known as director of photography. *Television Academy Peer Group:* Cinematographer, director of photography, film camera operator, camera crew, provider of camera equipment or supplies.

Columbia Broadcasting System, The. Commonly referred to as CBS. *Variety*'s term: "the eye network." Merged with Paramount in 2004 by Viacom.

commercial. Short film or video designed by advertisers to promote a product or service that is inserted between original or syndicated programming. Can also refer to entertainment that appeals to a large segment of the population or something that makes money. *Television Academy Peer Group:* Includes individuals from advertising agencies, commercial production and postproduction, and performers in national commercials.

concept. A general idea that conveys a specific philosophy, theme, or tone without detail; used as a selling tool to capture the attention and interest of the buyer, then used in selling the show or film to the audience. (For example, "A rising young star brings his best friends along for the ride," *Entourage*, HBO; "Two friends crash weddings to pick up girls," *Wedding Crashers*.)

costume design and supervision. Person who designs the costumes or the look of the wardrobe for a project. Designing can entail original costumes executed from design or purchased. The wardrobe supervisor is the on-set person who sees that the designer's look is carried out for all cast members and extras. *Television Academy Peer Group:* Costume designer, costume supervisor, costume set person, head tailor, workroom supervisor, or head of independent costume manufacturing facilities.

The CW. The CBS–Warner Television Network. Network resulting from the 2006 merger of weblets UPN (owned by CBS Corporation) and the WB (owned by Warner Brothers Entertainment).

daytime programming. Morning, afternoon, and early evening shows; includes morning news, local news, syndicated talk shows such as soap operas, *The Oprah Winfrey Show*, and *Dr. Phil*. *Television Academy Peer Group:* Includes associate director, associate producer, contestant coordinator, director, performer, producer, production executive, talent executive, television executive, writer.

deficit financing. In television, the difference between the network license fee and what the project (series or movie) actually costs. If a MOW (movie of the week) license fee is $3.2 million and the budget for the MOW is $4.5 million, then the amount the producer must deficit-finance is $1.3 million.

demographics ("demos"). Data on the television viewing audience that are collected and broken down by categories including age and gender. These data are then converted into numbers representing ratings and households, total audience, and audience share. The department that coordinates and interprets data and testing is the Research Department.

development. The processes of bringing ideas from inception to the finished script and/or production go-ahead. Sometimes extends through the production phase and into postproduction.

director. The person responsible for all visual components of a film or television show; the ultimate authority on the set during filming. *Television Academy Peer Group:* Director, director's team—unit production manager, first director, second assistant director, associate director (video), stage manager (video), script supervisor (film and/or video), choreographer.

docudrama. A film or television dramatization based on fact that combines documentary and fiction elements. Different designations such as "a true story," "based on," or "inspired by" denote the extent to which the program is based on fact.

draft. A completed script with each version (first, second, third, and subsequent drafts, polish, production, and rewrite) included to represent the development process.

drama. In television, usually a one-hour series with dramatic content. In feature films, a movie with a major dramatic throughline.

dramatic hook. In traditional dramatic structure, the inciting event that engages the viewers and pulls them into the plot and story.

dramatic premise. What the story is about and on what it is based. Similar to concept but with more description. For example, the dramatic premise of *The Brady Bunch* might read as follows: "A widowed man with three sons meets a single mom with three daughters, and they combine to become a family."

dramedy. A genre-crossing drama and comedy that originated in the mid to late 1980s with shows like ABC's *Moonlighting* and *The Wonder Years*. ABC's *Boston Legal* is a dramedy set in the legal world.

edge/edgy. A particular dark tone or feel to a series or feature film that usually involves trendsetting visual style, irony, dark or black humor, and violence. For example, FX's *Nip/Tuck* depicts successful plastic surgeons whose friendship is tested by medical ethics, sex, and their God-like powers as surgeons. Surgeries are filmed such that they present a visual edge to the show as well.

editor. Person responsible for assembling the video or film in logical fashion. *Television Academy Peer Group:* Picture editor, assistant editor, postproduction supervisor, postproduction facilities personnel.

electronic production. Video, live camera production (news, late-night, variety). *Television Academy Peer Group:* Lighting director/lighting designer/director of photography (video); electronic cameraperson; engineer; technical director; technical operations/new operations personnel; video control person; videotape editor; videotape operator.

element. An essential piece of a project that contributes to obtaining a development deal or production order from the studio or network for a project or script. Also, an actor, a writer, a producer, or a director who, once attached, moves the project forward to green light or production.

ensemble cast/ensemble show. A series, movie of the week, or feature film in which there is no single lead character; rather, a group of characters who are of equal importance are responsible for moving the plot forward. Examples in television include ABC's *Desperate Housewives*, Fox's *The O.C.*, HBO's *Rome, Entourage*.

event/event programming. A program that stands out by the nature of its subject matter or casting, wherein a single element or combination of elements makes the programming easily promotable and recognizable to the mass audience. Programming usually airs during sweeps periods. The final episode of *Survivor*, in which the winner is chosen, takes place during sweeps. Also, as in "specials and events," televised events such as the Olympics, the Super Bowl, Academy Awards®, Emmys®, and so forth.

fantasy/fantasy-horror. Series and movie genre in which suspense and the supernatural can figure in storytelling. In television, this was popularized by the success of *Buffy the Vampire Slayer, The X Files,* and *Supernatural*. The Sci-Fi Channel shows primarily fantasy-horror.

Federal Communications Commission (FCC). An independent U.S. government agency established by the Communications Act of 1934; reports directly to Congress. The FCC is charged with overseeing the regulation of all interstate and international communications by radio, television, wire, satellite, and cable in the fifty states, the District of Columbia, and all U.S. possessions. Based in Washington, DC.

Financial Interest and Syndication Rules (Fin-Syn Rules). Implemented by the FCC in 1970, and they were solidified by the Justice Department in 1977. The Fin-Syn Rules, as they came to be called, forbade vertical integration (control of production, distribution, and exhibition) by the broadcast television networks. This removed their long-term monetary rights in programming and restricted the networks' participation in syndication, thereby eliminating the financial incentives for networks to be program producers and giving independent producers and production companies a larger slice of the programming back end. These rules were relaxed in 1991 and eliminated in 1995, once again opening the way for network participation in series ownership.

first look/first-look deal. In motion pictures or television, when a studio (or network) strikes a deal with a producer, director, writer, or talent who may have some status and track record, it provides certain perks (including an office and overhead) in exchange for a first look at any new projects developed (prior to any showing of those projects elsewhere).

Fox Broadcasting Network. The fourth network, and the first to challenge the big three broadcasters (ABC, CBS, NBC). Part of News Corporation.

franchise. Traditional series episodes in which a story is concluded in each episode. An example is the popular series *Law & Order*. In this type of series, the situation, place, and set of relationships involved ultimately bring the characters together and give them motivation to stay together from week to week. The hospital at which all characters work or are patients is the franchise in *ER*. CBS's *CSI* explores crimes from the points of view of forensics experts (crime scene investigators).

front end. A financial term used for compensation that takes the form of salaries and up-front perks. The flip side is back end, which consists of profits taken after production and marketing costs have been recouped. Front end compensation does not require the talent to assume risk, but it also may not ultimately generate profits as great as those found on the back end.

genre. A type of storytelling or filmmaking that is distinguished by similarities in narrative, characterization, setting, theme, tone, and film technique. Genres include mystery, police procedural, science fiction, horror-fantasy, thriller, children's, soap opera, and action adventure. For example, TNT's *The Closer* is a mystery/police procedural; USA's *The Dead Zone* is a horror-fantasy thriller. Fox's *The O.C.* is a primetime soap opera.

hammock. Programming strategy in which a new or struggling show is placed between two currently popular shows on the schedule.

hook. A story element, a theme, or an approach to a show that makes the sales pitch irresistible to the buyer. For example, in the UPN's *America's Next Top Model*, the hook is clearly stated in the title.

in-house production. As the Financial Interest and Syndication Rules were relaxed in 1991, the broadcast networks developed their own in-house production companies (ABC Productions, CBS Productions, NBC Studios). This enabled them to produce and own their own shows; they then aired these on their own broadcast and cable networks, and in some cases sold them to others. Now it is accepted practice for networks to produce programming for themselves. See **vertical integration**.

interactive media. Includes the Internet and World Wide Web, video games and interactive media, CD-ROM and other forms of multimedia, and the intersection between motion pictures and television. *Television Academy Peer Group:* Producer, director, or senior designer or technician involved in the creation of interactive content or services.

"jump the shark". Phrase coined in 1997; according to jumptheshark.com, it is used to describe a defining moment at which a favorite television show has reached its peak and can only subsequently decline; also describes the moment of decline for any pop culture reference. The phrase, used during the late 1980s (according to the website), refers to the actual moment in the ABC series *Happy Days* when the character Fonzie went water skiing and literally jumped the shark.

limited series. Program known to have a specified number of episodes going into production, with limited opportunity to go beyond that prescribed number. Hybrid of series and miniseries. TNT had success with the limited series *The Grid* and will try the format again with *The Company*.

logline/TV Guide logline. Coined from the one-line sentences used in the publication *TV Guide* to describe a movie, a television show, or an episode succinctly. In the sale or pitching of a project, it is a single sentence that best presents the hook and will attract viewers. It should quickly convey the situation, tone, and sense of where the story will go.

makeup artist/hairstylist. In film and television, a makeup artist is responsible for actors' makeup; the hairstylist is responsible for actors' hair. *Television Academy Peer Group:* Makeup artists, hairstylists, any individual who designs, supervises, sculpts, or manufactures makeup or hairstyling products but who does not apply it.

mid-season/mid-season replacement. In program scheduling, to launch a new program at any time other than in the fall (the start of the traditional television season) or during the summer; usually in the spring, some time between January and March. When fall pilots to series pickups are announced each May, a certain number of pilots are likely to be given mid-season commitments to go to series the following spring as back-ups for new series that may fail to become established in the fall.

miniseries. Long-form narrative drama designed to be broadcast in a limited number of parts; not really a series but mostly appearing in serial form. At one time a staple of broadcast networks, but now found principally on cable networks. Examples include TNT's *Into the West*, Lifetime's *Human Trafficking*, or the Sci-Fi Channel's *The Triangle*.

MOW/movie of the week. See **original TV movie**.

multiplatform. As relates to television, the use of broadcast, cable content, and advertising on the Internet and in wireless interactive media platforms and devices (e.g., podcasting).

music. Typically created or acquired for the background of film or television or composed for performance in film or television. *Television Academy Peer Group:* Composer, music director, conductor, credited writer of lyrics or special material, arranger or orchestrator, musician, programmer, composer assistant.

narrative. Coherent telling of plot or story, usually from a single point of view. Contemporary dramas and comedies often play with straightforward narrative. *Lost* is an example of a drama that reorders traditional narrative in a one-hour series.

National Broadcasting Company, The. Commonly referred to as NBC. *Variety's* term: "the peacock network." Part of General Electric (GE).

network-approved/network approval. The basis on which many creative decisions are made; as a network supplies the distribution outlet and funding for a project, it participates or controls the decision-making of a project, thus compelling a producer to look to it for approval on creative decisions. The network may have approval on the selection of writer, director, line producer, cast, and during production, it may have a say in the hiring of the key personnel for filming, such as the director of photography and the composer. For motion pictures, the studios hold the approval power.

niche-programming. Television programming or channels that target particular demographics or interests such as the History Channel or Lifetime.

nonfiction. Documentary; reality programming.

one line/one-liner. Similar to the logline; one line that encompasses the general theme or story of project. An example for *Malcolm in the Middle* might read as follows: "Academically brilliant kid struggles with his smart-kid image and his eccentric family"; an example for *The Shield* might read thus: "A corrupt cop is often an effective police officer."

on the bubble. Series or programs that have adequate ratings but are not consistent winners in their time slots. As a result, networks often remain uncertain as to their future. Determining factors include the demographics to which they appeal and the advertiser interest in the show. For example, Fox's critically acclaimed comedy *Arrested Development* was on the bubble since its first airing.

original TV movie. Original made-for-television movie (this contrasts with a feature film aired on television); also known as movie of the week, MOW, TV movie, telepic, telefilm, made-for. As recently as 1995, the original TV movie was a staple of every network's schedule; however, now, due to loss of viewer interest, broadcast networks make few original TV movies. Cable entities, however, are still producing MOWs as part of their overall programming. Examples include CBS's *Jesse Stone: Night Passage*, Showtime's *Our Fathers*, and HBO's *Warm Springs*.

outline. The story for a series episode, original TV movie, miniseries, or motion picture laid out in short form with some detail, including plot, character, and tone; for television movies or series, often broken down into acts with a dramatic hook that carries the story from one act to the next (not to mention through commercials and remote control syndrome).

package. The combination of several desirable elements of production or script deal, put together and sold as the basis of a project. This includes producers, writers, directors, and actors or star talent, usually represented by the same agency, managers, or attorneys.

performer. Actor, singer, dancer, and voice-over artist.

pick-up. See **series pick-up**, **mid-season**.

pilot/series pilot. Prototype and usually the first episode of a series; lays out the story and characters, describes the origin of character relationships and franchise, and often displays the most effective elements of the show. Also, the execution of a pilot script that has been developed and given a production go-ahead.

pitch. The presentation of the basic idea or brief outline of a program or feature film, told as persuasively as possible to a buyer with the intent to sell. Usually presented verbally, sometimes on paper.

plot. Particular events in the story that propel the action forward; the plotting of a series of actions or beats in a feature film, television movie, or series.

presentation. Abbreviated, produced pilot created as a result of growing production costs.

primetime. The time of day or day part in which the greatest number of viewers are watching television; EST/PST 8:00 P.M.–11:00 P.M., CST/MT 7:00 P.M.–10:00 P.M.

producer. The person who manages the finances, creation, and presentation of a series or motion picture. The producer is often involved in hiring the talent and making creative decisions.

production executives. Studio, or production company executives who oversee production. *Television Academy Peer Group:* Individual holding a major executive position in telecommunications production company.

production order. The go-ahead given to a project to go to film or to go into production; also, *green light*. In series development, script and production orders may be broken down into smaller increments, with a full season consisting of 22 episodes, a half season 13 episodes, and short orders ranging from 4 to 8 episodes. A production order for an initial 13 episodes can be followed by an order for the back 9 to total 22 episodes. Cable networks tend to pick up series orders for 13 episodes.

production representatives. Studio or production company representatives who provide related services. *Television Academy Peer Group:* Individual holding a major executive position providing legal, financial, business, and career management services to artists or to production, distribution, broadcasting, or telecommunications companies or unions. Also, agent, manager, attorney, and business affairs executive.

prototype. An original episode designed to serve as a model for others. A pilot is usually the first episode/show with an introduction to story, characters, and their relationships; a prototype is often designed to be the "seventh show" of the season and is meant to demonstrate how episodes will lay out.

public relations. The art and science of building a relationship between a person, product, or service and the public or an audience. *Television Academy Peer Group:* Individual involved in the publicity of telecommunications programs in the areas of photography or promotions.

put pilot. Term for series pilot guaranteed a production order because it's created by a successful writer/executive producer such as David E. Kelly or Peter Tolan. In such cases, the creator is assumed to be able to deliver.

reality shows. Nonfiction primetime programming based on real people in various settings. Three types of reality programming exist: the game show/competition (e.g., *The Apprentice, Survivor, Fear Factor*); the documentary/docudrama (e.g., *Queer Eye for the Straight Guy, Extreme Makeover, Real World*); and variety/talent show (e.g., *American Idol, Dancing with the Stars*). Generally less expensive to produce than primetime hour drama or half-hour comedy series forms; a significant proportion of primetime schedule is devoted to reality programming.

Research Department. The group that coordinates and interprets demographics.

revisions. Script changes for film or TV based on notes or production requirements; generally implemented in part on a variety of colored paper to be integrated into the original script or distributed in a whole draft.

sci-fi. Abbreviated term for the science fiction genre; used in television and features. An example is *Star Wars* and its sequels and prequels in features. The Sci-Fi Channel schedules heavily with sci-fi and fantasy-horror and features series such as *Stargate SG1* and *Stargate Atlantis*.

script commitment/blind script commitment. A commitment by a network or studio to a producer or writer to a deal for a new but still unspecified script or project; this is subject to the buyer's approval, usually based on previous successes or other factors. It sometimes extends to a series commitment for titan series producers such as David E. Kelly, John Wells, and Dick Wolf, following the success of a show. In feature films, it may extend to a three-picture deal or greater, dependent upon the success of the original movie.

script deal. The first and initial stage of script development, at which point the buyer has agreed to develop a project and invests financially by striking a deal to hire a specific writer.

season. The time during which a network's ratings and shares are measured and compared with those of the competition. The television season usually starts in fall (mid-September) and runs through May sweeps; however, FBC, The WB, and UPN sometimes premiere their series in late August to get a jump on ABC, CBS, and NBC. Seasons for series also have selling seasons (the end of June through November is the selling season for the following fall) and pilot seasons (the time during which networks develop scripts for new shows and make decisions on pilots to be produced in the spring). Networks usually announce their series commitments for fall in May. Anything bought after the traditional fall buying period becomes a mid-season show and debuts, generally speaking, between October and May.

serialization. A dramatic program in which stories and characters are threaded throughout an entire season of a series, and any episode relies upon the previous episode for continuity of story. The term was used traditionally to describe early novels published serially, and soap operas, which are the quintessential serial form. Examples include *The O.C.* and *24*. By contrast, *Law & Order* and *CSI* are traditional franchise series with stand-alone episodes.

series pick-up. The official notice of commitment from the network, premium channel, or cable channel that a developed and produced pilot for a series will go into production as a series for a specified number of episodes, or that an already established series or series currently on the air will be back on the network's schedule the following season. Most pick-ups are given in May for the upcoming fall season, while others, picked up for the mid-season, are given the nod at the same time or later in the year.

sitcom (situation comedy). A half-hour comedy program with recurring characters that derives its franchise from comic characters in comedic situations (Fox's *Malcolm in the Middle,* The WB's *Reba*). Fox broke the half-hour sitcom rule by developing the hour-long comedy *Ally McBeal.*

sound. Individuals responsible for sound recording on the set and sound mixing in postproduction. *Television Academy Peer Group:* Audio recordist, audio consultant, boom operator, sound mixer, production sound mixer, front of house mixer, rerecording mixer, research and development head, scoring mixer, sound department head, sound engineer, Foley mixer, music mixer production, audio assistant.

sound editors. Editors who put sound elements together in postproduction. *Television Academy Peer Group:* Sound editor/sound effects editor, dialogue editor, music editor, Foley artist.

spec script. Script written on speculation; not commissioned by a studio or production company. In television, writers sometimes write a spec script to prove their versatility or to break out of a creative rut. For example, Marc Cherry wrote *Desperate Housewives* to prove he could write a one-hour drama. Greg Garcia wrote *My Name Is Earl* to prove to network executives that the story was viable.

spin-off. A series that is developed based on another (usually successful) series, with the new series usually based on a popular character or set of characters from the original. For example, *Law & Order,* currently the longest-running show on the air, has spins-offs such as *Law & Order: Special Victims Unit, Law & Order: Criminal Intent,* and *Law & Order: Conviction.* Ditto for CBS's *CSI* (*CSI: Miami, CSI: New York*).

step outline/outline. Scene-by-scene breakdown of plot/story; sometimes required prior to going to the first draft of the script, or when reworking the script. Similar to treatment, or expanded version of **treatment**; the two are sometimes used interchangeably. Same as **outline**.

story arc. A series that extends a story through several episodes to maintain viewer interest, as is the case in *Alias*, *Gilmore Girls*, and *Everwood*. Often the arc is threaded throughout a season and comes to a climax during May sweeps. Fox's *24* has the ultimate story arc and moves incrementally hour by hour through the 24 hours of a day over an entire season, ending after the 24th hour.

stunt casting. Often occurs during sweeps seasons; a well-known actor/celebrity will appear in a single or multiple episodes of a series. NBC's *Will & Grace* has used stunt casting with Glenn Close, Matt Damon, Michael Douglas, Jennifer Lopez, and Madonna.

stunts. The extreme physical action too dangerous for the actor to perform. *Television Academy Peer Group:* Stunt coordinator, stunt double, stunt player (nondescript, character role, utility), fight or aerial coordinator, stunt safety, safety stunt driver.

sweeps. One of several times during the year when advertising rates for a network's upcoming quarter are set; rates are based upon the A. C. Nielsen company measurement of the ratings and share of television programming. The networks pull out their strongest commercial projects for the purpose of attracting a maximum number of viewers and ultimately of attaining the highest ratings so that they may set higher prices for advertising. Traditionally, there are four sweeps periods: September, November, February, and May.

syndication. Original programming, whether dramatic or nonfiction, created to sell to station groups rather than to networks. Most daytime talk shows based on personalities are syndicated, and many game shows are syndicated. Examples include *The Oprah Winfrey Show, Dr. Phil, Wheel of Fortune,* and *Jeopardy*. A network series goes into syndication when it reaches 100 episodes; that is, the minimum number required to sell in a block to stations groups, which run the series in a stripped format five to seven evenings per week. (Stations need a large number of shows to maintain a nightly presence.) A series often becomes profitable (usually after approximately four years) for a studio only after it is sold into syndication. In the past, the key to studio profitability and survival on an expensive series rested on the ability to sell the show into syndication at a high price.

synopsis. Used in script analysis/coverage report or literary analysis/coverage report, a portion of the report summarizing the story of script or book in beat-by-beat form, including description of the main characters, plot and action, and sometimes tone.

tent pole. In television programming strategy, the most popular show airing on a given evening. Examples include *ER*, which has been the tent pole of NBC's Thursday night for years, and *Everybody Loves Raymond*, which was the tent pole for CBS on Monday nights. Networks will often schedule a new show either preceding or following a tent pole show to help establish the show with the audience.

throughline. The ultimate objective of the main character(s).

title design and special visual effects. Design and creation of titles and graphics. *Television Academy Peer Group:* Title designer, graphic artist, special visual effects.

treatment. Written material in short form, and the basis for a script or screenplay; includes the full exploration of a story, including character, plot, subplots, setting, theme, and tone. See also **outline** and **step outline**.

true crime. A dramatic genre mostly used in original TV movies. These movies for television highlight a story based on fact, with a crime as the focus of the central plot. Popularized by lurid tabloid-type news headlines.

UPN. United Paramount Network. Weblet (part of CBS Corporation) that merged with the WB to form the CW (The CBS-Warner Television Network) in 2006.

vertical integration. Process of one media company acquiring another media company elsewhere in the production process in order to produce and distribute content and product. Following the elimination of the Financial Interest and Syndication Rules (Fin-Syn Rules) in 1995, large media corporations came together to form conglomerates, such as Walt Disney Studios buying Capital Cities/ABC; Viacom buying CBS; and more recently, General Electric acquiring NBC. In many of these cases, the corporate parent has eliminated entire divisions or existing portions of companies due to duplication of divisions and departments throughout. Staff and costs were reduced in the process.

The WB. Weblet (part of Warner Brothers Entertainment/Time Warner); merged with UPN to form the CW (The CBS-Warner Television Network) in 2006. *Variety* calls the WB "the frog network" for its original mascot, the Tennessee Frog.

Web/Net. A television network with a full primetime, seven-day schedule; namely: ABC, CBS, FBC (Fox), NBC, and the CW (fall 2006).

Weblet/Netlet. The newer established networks that do not have a full primetime, seven-day schedule; namely, UPN and the WB.

writer. Person who writes original material for television, film, or media or adapts source material into a script. Writers receiving on-air credit "written by," "teleplay by," "story editor," "executive story consultant," or "created by" for daytime or primetime programs.

APPENDIX

APPENDIX: RELATED DEPARTMENTS

You will find great variation in how institutions organize areas of academic study in general—and, in particular, how they organize the study of television, film, and digital media. Don't be scared off by the variety! After all, variety is the spice of life. Note that related programs are typically designated under the auspices of television, theater, computer science, computer engineering, film, visual and media arts, or visual and performing arts. You may contact schools directly if you have specific inquiries. To help you further navigate the sea of choices, we've devised the following partial list of different names for departments that generally cover television, film, and digital media. *Bon voyage!*

audiovisual communications technologies. Practical study of existing and emerging technologies for print, broadcast, and interactive media.

broadcasting. Practical and theoretical study of radio and television communication.

cinema and media culture. Emphasis on cinema and its place in social, historical, and cultural audiovisual forms of communication.

cinema and television arts. Study of history, concepts, theory, and practices of cinema (film, motion pictures) and television; emphasis on practical knowledge and creative skills.

communication arts. Practical and theoretical study of communication science, history, theory, criticism, cultural uses, and production practices in radio, television, film, and rhetoric.

communication design. Study of the structure, processes, aesthetics, functions, and effects and creation of media communications with the goal of acquiring knowledge and skills in a broad array of highly integrated design applications.

communications. Study of all forms of communication (exchange of information, messages, or data) including verbal, written, and person-to-person, or via television, radio, film (media), and theater. Study of television, film, theater, advertising, public relations, and public address may be under communications or rhetoric.

communication science and rhetorical studies. Study of speech, speech making and writing, public address, and mass media.

communication studies, theater, and art. Practical as well as theoretical studies of communications, theater, and art.

communication and theater. Practical as well as theoretical studies of communications and theater.

computer art/digital imaging arts. Creative and artistic expression using computers; may include graphic arts, computer-generated animation, and visual effects.

digital media arts and technology. Study of the creation, production, and research of present and emerging digital media.

digital media studies. Theoretical and practical study of emerging media; interdisciplinary studies through schools of art and art history, communication, and engineering and computer science.

entertainment studies. Theory, trends, and practices in entertainment; covers traditional television, film, and music industries as well as entertainment-related fields such as tourism, sports, gaming, merchandising and retail stores, and new media.

film and animation. Practical as well as theoretical study of live action and animated film.

film and digital media. Study of theoretical and practical filmmaking and use of new technology; digital media can be an interdisciplinary program through the art, English, music, and computer science departments.

film studies. Study of the history, aesthetics, and criticism of film and of film and video production.

information and media science. Study of the role of information, media, communications, and information technologies in the lives of individuals and in society; and of the creation, management, distribution, storage, display, and use of information through media and technology.

interactive media production and design. Study of production and design of interactive forms, such as website design, interactive CD-ROMs and kiosks, and computer-based training. Interactive multimedia is the study of basic skills in all the component media in multimedia production environments, including visual design, audio, programming, writing, animation, photography, and video.

journalism. Theory and practice of gathering, processing, and delivering news for print and electronic (radio, television, and Internet) media with the goal of preparing individuals to be professional journalists, news editors, and news managers. Instruction in news writing and editing, reporting, photojournalism, layout and graphic design, journalism law and policy, professional standards and ethics research methods, and journalism history and criticism.

journalism and technical communication. Studies in computer-mediated communication, news-editorial journalism, public relations, specialized and technical journalism, television news, and video communication.

journalism/telecommunications. Practical and theoretical study of reporting, writing for the media (print, television, Internet), and cultural and legal practices; prepares students to apply communication knowledge and skills professionally.

mass communication/media studies. Analysis and criticism of media institutions and media texts, how people experience and understand media content, and the role of media in producing and transforming culture.

mass media. All industrial forms of mass communication combined (radio, television, film, Internet).

media arts/media arts and technology. Program that works on the science/technology side with emergent media; computer science; engineering; electronic music; digital art research, practice, production, and theory. Designed to explore new art forms and invent new expressive media. (This is typically a graduate-level program.)

media arts and design/media arts and sciences. Theoretical and practical study of graphic design, multimedia, and animation techniques as well as computers and software applications. May include interdisciplinary studies (journalism, telecommunications, information studies, and media) of current practices in the history, criticism, and theory of media arts.

new media. Usually refers to relatively recent mass media based on information technology; that is, the Internet, World Wide Web, video games, interactive media, CD-ROM, and other forms of multimedia from the 1990s forward.

public relations. Study of the art and science of establishing favorable relations among audiences, producers, talent, and networks/studios.

radio-TV. Theories, methods, and techniques used to plan, produce, and distribute audio and video programming and messages; emphasizes current theory, practice, research, and skill development through the fundamentals of history, cultural influence, production, and storytelling concepts.

radio-TV-film. Theories, methods, and techniques used to plan, produce, and distribute audio, video, and film programming and messages; emphasizes current theory, practice, research, and skill development through the fundamentals of history, cultural influence, production, and storytelling concepts.

speech-communications/speech and communication. Theoretical and practical studies of communication, including public communication (broadcasting), organizational communication, human communication, and rhetorical communication.

telecommunications. Practical and theoretical study of media dispersed by electronic transmission via cable, computer, radio, satellite, telegraph, telephone, or television.

visual and media arts. Program emphasis on visual expression and media as powerful art forms affecting human thought, emotion, and behavior.

visual and performance arts. Department designation that groups visual arts such as television, film, studio art, and digital media with traditional performing arts such as music, dance, and acting.

INDEX

A

B

C

D

E

F

G

W

Y

THE INFINITE POWER OF STORY

FILM · SCREENWRITING · ANIMATION · RECORDING ARTS · TELEVISION

STORY

CURIOSITY · DIVERSITY · CREATIVITY · COMMUNITY · COLLABORATION · TRANSFORMATION · GLOBAL

ACCESS VIDEO INTERVIEWS WITH THE PIONEERS OF TELEVISION - ONLINE!

The Academy of Television Arts & Sciences Foundation's *Archive of American Television* has made many of its hundreds of exclusive interviews available on Google Video. These long-form oral history interviews provide in-depth looks at the history of television and the individuals behind it.

"We're happy to join with the Foundation to preserve the rich history of television by showcasing the individuals who pioneered the medium."
- *Susan Wojcicki, Vice President of Product Management for Google Video*

Interviews available online include:

Alan Alda	Andy Griffith	Joyce Randolph
James Arness	Robert Guillaume	Frances Reid
Joseph Barbera	Larry Hagman	Carl Reiner
Bob Barker	Florence Henderson	Gene Reynolds
Ed Bradley	Don Hewitt	Fred Rogers
Steven Bochco	Kim Hunter	Jay Sandrich
James Burrows	Quincy Jones	Sherwood Schwartz
Sid Caesar	Don Knotts	William Shatner
Stephen J. Cannell	Angela Lansbury	Buffalo Bob Smith
Diahann Carroll	Norman Lear	Leonard Stern
Julia Child	Jim Lehrer	George Takei
Dick Clark	Bob Mackie	Grant Tinker
Richard Crenna	Robert MacNeil	Ted Turner
Ossie Davis	Delbert Mann	Dick Van Dyke
Phyllis Diller	Jim McKay	Dennis Weaver
Phil Donahue	Ed McMahon	Joseph Wershba
Barbara Eden	Ricardo Montalban	Betty White
Elma Farnsworth	Rita Moreno	Jonathan Winters
Michael J. Fox	Bob Newhart	Dick Wolf
John Frankenheimer	Agnes Nixon	David Wolper
James Garner	Carroll O'Connor	
Curt Gowdy	Fess Parker	

Google Video BETA

Visit **www.emmys.tv/foundation/archive** to find out more or check out the Archive's blog for the latest information about online access and links to the newest interviews at **tvinterviewsarchive.blogspot.com**

ACADEMY OF TELEVISION ARTS & SCIENCES FOUNDATION

Archive of American Television • 5220 Lankershim Blvd. • N. Hollywood, CA 91601 • 818-509-2260

Study in A State-of-the-Art Studio

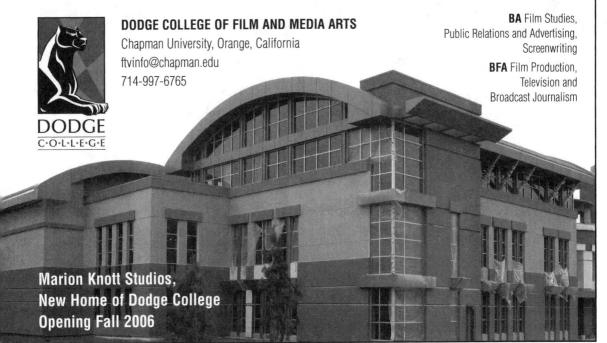

Not just a media arts student. I'm a poet. A writer. A storyteller. My roommate's helping me shoot this scene just like I helped him with his last art installation. Later tonight, we're both giving this drummer down the hall a hand with his new CD. It's amazing. We're all different artists from different places with different ideas but we're all driven to get to the same place. We want to be creative for a living. And Columbia is making it happen.

create... change

19 majors • Faculty who've been there and done it • Nationally renowned programs in television and filmmaking • A student body that redefines diversity

www.colum.edu

Columbia COLLEGE CHICAGO
INNOVATION IN THE VISUAL, PERFORMING, MEDIA AND COMMUNICATION ARTS

600 S. Michigan Avenue, Chicago, IL 60605 ph. (312) 344-7130

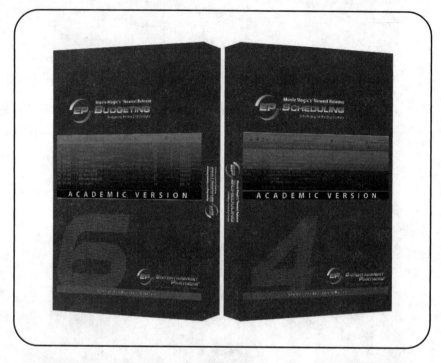

ACADEMY OF TELEVISION ARTS & SCIENCES FOUNDATION

Unparalleled opportunities for students pursuing careers in the television industry

ollege Television Awards

national competition for original film, video and digital works produced by college udents; cash prizes are awarded and winners receive industry recognition

ummer Internship Program

ver 30 "hands-on" television industry internships rated among the nation's top 10 ternship programs by Princeton Review

rchive of American Television

ver 500 exclusive interviews with the very people who shaped and created levision. Visit Google video at http://video.google.com and search for Archive of nerican Television

red Rogers Memorial Scholarship

0,000 scholarships to two worthy individuals ho wish to pursue careers in Children's edia upon graduation. To see if you are igible to apply for this scholarship please sit www.emmys.tv\foundation and click on e Fred Rogers icon.

learn more about the levision Academy undation and all the pportunities available, ease visit ww.emmys.tv/foundation call 818.754.2800

ACADEMY OF TELEVISION
ARTS & SCIENCES
FOUNDATION

ACADEMY OF TELEVISION ARTS & SCIENCES FOUNDATION
and
JOURNEYS BELOW THE LINE
present

"Journeys Below the Line" is a groundbreaking, behind-the-scenes series of DVDs highlighting the variety of exciting careers in television production -- a unique educational tool that informs and inspires.

ACADEMY OF TELEVISION ARTS & SCIENCES FOUNDATION

DVD I: "24" The Editing Process
DVD II: ER The PropMasters
         available Summer 2006
DVD III: Lost: The Cinematography Team
         available Late 2006

For more information, please visit
www.emmys.tv/foundation.